COMPLETE POETIC WORKS

Robbie Moffat

For Frankie,

'I'll Love You In The Morning ...

C000165407

Palm Tree Publishing

PALM TREE PUBLISHING
Wilmington, Delaware 19801, USA
Iver Grove, Iver SL0 0LB, UK

© Robbie Moffat 1974-2022

Simultaneous published in
United Kingdom and USA

NOVEMBER 2022

Typeset: Verdana 7pt

ISBN-10: 0 907282822
ISBN-13: 9780907282822

PREFACE

When I first started writing poetry I didn't know what I was doing or what I wanted to say. I had read poetry at school, been taught to dissect it, and reflect on it in exams. However, I had also been brought up on Robert Burns. At my primary school poetry was center stage in our weekly teachings, a picture of Burns was on the wall not the Queen or the Pope. I was also center stage when the poetry adjudicator for the national poetry reciting competition came to my class to hear me read aloud a poem about a trout. I was nine years old.

Masefield, Browning, Tennyson, Kipling, Stevenson, Yeats and of course Burns – that was my introduction to poetry. The Highwayman, Cargoes, Innisfree, To a Mouse, Tam O'Shanter, I learned them by heart. At secondary school, poetry was Shakespeare, Owen, Betjeman and Auden. Less enjoyable to read but more thought provoking. Outside school it was a different influence, poetry as song – Bob Dylan, Lennon and McCartney, Paul Simon, Donovan Leitch, combined with the folk songs I learned in the youth hostels and pubs in the Highlands.

This was the basis for my own kind of poetry when I started in earnest at the age of nineteen. I had a vague idea that it should rhyme and scan, that there should be some kind of structure. The ballad form was inherent in me as a west coast Scot though I was aware of iambic pentameter, trochaic etc. as I had passed my English Higher (Scottish A-level). That aside I had not tried to put down my own ideas though I had been keeping diaries from the time I left school aged seventeen. The diaries were more about what I did and who I met rather than what I thought.

My earliest poems continued in the same kind of external observation until I wrote Froggies when I was India. Here was something new for me, not the form, but the content. Thereafter I began tapping into who I was rather than just my daily experiences. As I progressed through my twenties, I mixed it up as life provided romance, travels, marriage, poverty, happiness or discontent. I moved around a lot in those early adult years, took employment when I had to while experimenting with my poetry style. Simultaneously I was writing novels but I could not find a publisher – it was frustrating but I never let the novel writing interfere with my poetry. They were two separate worlds.

This first phase of my poetry, the Young Man, ended in 1983 when I was admitted to Newcastle University to study English Language and Literature. My poetry changed from the moment I began The Undergraduate, the diary of an English student. Much of my new poetry came from reading as part of my studies. Although I had written five novels by this time, at university I read only one novel, which perhaps was not a smart move as I may have found out where I had been going wrong with my prose. Hindsight of course.

This second phase of my poetry, the Middle Aged Man, lasted eleven years. First and foremost during this time poetry was my first love despite writing another four novels and staging seven plays. As well as *The Undergraduate*, the works included the *Universal Being* and the three *Wanderer* sagas but by 1994 I'd had enough and the poetry tapered to a trickle. I got into screenwriting and directing films. However, I made a pact with myself that I would return to poetry when I was sixty.

While composing my film work I wrote a few verses and songs that amounted to very little. Then a few weeks before my sixtieth birthday I started composing poetry again. This was to be my third stage, the Old Man. And this is where I leave it now. I am burnt out by poetry, it hurts, and I intend to abandon it for good.

I love poetry, it has been with me for almost fifty years but I do not want to continue to torture myself. It is a pitiful admission, but there it is, I am done. The final poem in this book sums that feeling up. Perhaps some time in the future I will have remorse and reconsider, but for the time being, this book is the summation of my poetic endeavors, I can do no more.

Robbie Moffat
24th October 2022
Iver

NINETEEN
[Spring 1974]

Dreaming by the Tyne, thinking of what life is –
If I applied myself, what a genius I could be.
I'm really rather clever, though it isn't plain to see –
My guiding dream is to be accepted by society.

Fighting for an army just isn't for my likes –
Sailing with the navy? I can't stomach the sea.
Thoughts of flying high, don't fill me with joy –
For now it's bus conducting and saving to break free.

A1 SOUTH
[11th Aug 1974, A1, Gateshead]

Maggie and me going over the sea
To see what we can see.
We're standing here with all our gear
Waiting, and waiting and waiting in fear
In case we can't get a lift our of here –
Who knows, we might be here a year
Before we make it abroad.

DOVER
[12th Aug 1974, Dover]

Waiting on the Dover quay –
Passport in hand,
Francs from the bank –
Just waiting, waiting, waiting.

STUCK
[15th Aug 1974, France]

The sky is blue, the grass is green,
The air is clear, the water is fresh;
But what a shitty place to be dropped,
And left.

BARCELONA (fragments)
[17th Aug 1974, Barcelona]

We have reached Barcelona,
And now we venture forth …
To hitch our way to Madrid
To end this tortured road.

The room is great, it has white walls,
The floor is tiled and easy on the soles.
The beds are soft, with pin-stripped tops
And Maggie's happy, laughing at it all.

LERIDA
[18th Aug 1974, Lerida, Spain]

Maggie says she's losing weight,

I think she's just joking –
Her lily legs resemble
The plucked skin of a chicken.

Rain, rain, go from Spain,
Go back to England once again.

NO MORE FEARS
[19th Aug 1974, Madrid]

Phones to my ears, the music
Bringing me to tears –
My sentiments are running high,
My doubts are lost in blue skies;

Here worries don't exist,
Happiness is not a myth,
Everything is working out –
I have no more fears.

FRANCO
[19th Aug 1974, Madrid]

Franco's got a bad leg,
Cancer or something they say.
Who should be believed though?
The Church? The Doctors? The Army?
How long will he live?
Tomorrow? Next year? A decade?
We'll all find out when he's dead –
And fascist Spain is saved.

MAGGIE
[19th Aug 1974, Madrid]

Maggie has taken some prunes
To help with her digestion –
I guess we'll know soon enough
If they've aided, helped or hindered
Her constipation.

A RAINY DAY IN MADRID (fragments)
[20th Aug 1974, Madrid]

Back a hundred years as the power fails –
The darkness splits into a thousand sectioned shadows
By candlelight.

Madrid is – the Prada,
Piatza de Roma
The Calle de Goya,
The Banco de Espana,
And the Metro
Under the centro.

We lived by the autopista,
A life of leisure and ease,

With friends Inaki and Joahna –
Some Premmies from Arturo Soria.

The rain poured, and poured –
The washing got wetter and wetter.

(ii)
Britain seems a long way north –
Scotland, Glasgow, Shawlands Cross.
The rain brings back many thoughts
Of times in youth I had forgotten;

Those days when summer came and went
And winter passed on to Lent;
I'd cock a snoot, have no cares
If outside it was fine or fair.

The rain for me cleansed the streets,
I'd pad and paddle, sodden footed;
My mother, worried for my health
Would try to coop me up indoors.

She'd say 'You'll catch your death by cold!'
I'd not agree, and speak out boldly –
An action that oft brought regret
When I got a clout on the head.

Back then, all I had to pass the time
Was the burgh clock's distant chimes;
I'd watch the raindrops earthwards fall
Into puddles, pools and holes –

The steamed up windows, my only fun
Drawing pictures with my thumb -
All other things seemed unimportant
To the make-belief of an infant.

The rain stops, my memories fade
I return from my childhood daze –
The sun begins to split the clouds
To shower rays on my reflections.

For now I'm free to go outside
With no fear of a mother's chide;
I choose in Madrid to stay indoors
And dwell upon my fading innocence.

GERALD R FORD
[21st Aug 1974, Madrid]

Gerald R Ford made a statement today,
And it wasn't about the weather –
In fact it concerned the new vice – pres,
The ex-major of New York – Rockafeller.

Nelson, you see, is really quite pleased
At being appointed over Barry Goldwater;

He was full of big smiles, a mouth full of cheese –
But I doubt if things will get better.

For Nixon by now, we know all about,
His friends Erlichmann, Haldeman and Dean,
And history will say, without shadow of doubt
That they were dirty, crooked and mean.

But all of them now have bitten the dust
With the exception of Spiro Agnew –
He's been forced to resign amidst public mistrust
Over the back tax bill he's accrued.

President Ford has the task of his life
To get callous America straightened –
Let's pray it's the end of what we've lived thru
Since Kennedy was murdered in Dallas.

TOMORROW IBIZA
[23rd Aug 1974, El Saler, Spain]

Tomorrow we sail to Ibiza –
That golden isle of sun;
Perhaps we'll think it's worth it
For all the miles we've come.

I TRAVEL NOT IN INCHES
[24th Aug 1974, Valencia Ferry, Spain]

One foot on the ventilator,
One foot on the wall,
One eye straining at the door,
The other closed.

My cabin mates scurry to and fro,
I lie here, calm and cold –
Perhaps they should be told
That in my mind, I travel

Not in inches, or by hashish,
But to an inner land, a distant star
No amount of cash can get you to.

My star is reached by thought,
Thought alone, this far land
I am trying to know, to reach
my journey's end.

FORMENTERA
[26th Aug 1974, Formentera, Balaeric Isles]

The beach last night, it was okay.
I could have hoped for better –
But now I don't care – the weather
Has turned wet. It rains, it shines,
It rains, it shines – I think we wait
For winter. Who knows? Who cares?

8

I do not for this island Formentera.

ROUNDED UP BY THE FASCISTS
[27th Aug 1974, Formentera, Balaeric Isles]

Formentera – we must leave
For the police say so. Rounded up,
Passports taken from the hippies.
To sleep on the beach is not
The Franco way – they've let us
Know so.

To Ibiza we must now go –
To find a place to sleep -
Herded on to the ferry –
at gun point, we shuffle like cattle
on to the crowed deck -
the spirit of Europe's youth
made to revisit Auschwitz.

IBIZA
[27th Aug 1974, Ibiza, Balaeric Isles]

Ibiza is a shitty place,
I really am pissed off –
But I must keep a smiling face
For Love and Peace, man.

MAN OVERBOARD
[30th Aug 1974, Ibiza-Barcelona Ferry, Western Med]

A man fell overboard,
As the ship sailed on –
The alarm was raised,
The ship blew its horn

We searched for an hour
Or two, then much more –
Still we saw nothing,
We gave up all hope.

Suddenly – someone pointed
Far into the dark –
The searchlights played the water,
We'd found him at last.

But it still wasn't over –
The ship couldn't stop.
We cruised for ten minutes
Well past the poor chap.

A boat was finally lowered,
It retraced our wake –
We all hoped, some prayed
That he would be saved.

We waited, and waited

For the boat to return –
And then it was sighted,
The light on its stern.

When out of the darkness
five figures appeared –
four were the boatmen,
the fifth we all cheered.

As everyone inwardly
Let out a sigh –
Amazed that the man
Stepped aboard still alive.

FRANCE 1974 (fragments)
[31st Aug 1974, Cerbere]

Out of Spain, and the rain –
Into France, and *bon chance*.

[1st Sept 1974, Toulouse]

I went for some food
To fill myself up,
And what did I do?
I broke a china cup.

The lift I had hitched in a sports car
Of all things, with this man who
Was a flier. He drove into a ditch
Which bent his springs, that gave
Him a bloody flat tyre.

[1st Sept 1974, Ussel Sur S...]

A man bought me a meal last night,
And boy, it sure was alright –
I took some beautiful bites –
Every bite a delight – when I slept
I went out like a light.

[3rd Sept 1974, Thiers]

Yesterday, we took the train
From Ussel to Clermont
Because of all the rain –
Hitching was just not on.

Instead of buying tickets,
We rode the train for free.
The ticket collector came,
We jumped and ran away.

GENEVA HOSTEL
[3rd Sept 1974, Geneva]

I'm sitting on the hostel stairs

In the beautiful town of Geneva,
Chatting away to two young birds
About nothing much as yet.

Now, they are talking to me about mint
And the patch that they going to grow,
About work permits, and things like that,
And of course, *Catch 22*.

ALMOST KNOCKED DOWN
[4th Sept 1974, Lorrach, Germany]

I crossed over the frontier, and into a town
Where so many Germans, wore serious frowns;
The roads they were busy, and I being a clown
Eager to cross over was almost knocked down.

MUNICH (song)
[5th Sept 1974, Munich]

At last I come to Munich –
That town of song and beer,
Perhaps if I remain for long
I'll also know good cheer.

It is a place I know so well,
It holds to me quite dear –
The last time I came here
Was pre-Olympic year.

MUNICH IN THE RAIN
[6th Sept 1974, Munich]

Sitting in a nice, clean restaurant,
Drinking coffee, eating chocolate,
Listening to soothing music
Making with the conversation,
Thinking about some distant nation.
It's Munich in the rain.

It plips, it plops upon the roads,
Shoppers passing, very drenched,
Umbrellas flying in the wind,
Wet hair sticking to their necks –
The town seems quite and very dead.
It's Munich in the rain.

It has no end, the hours pass,
The light it fades, there is no lapse –
In every pool, the water rises,
Workers weave and dodge the splashes
Made by other workers dashing.
It's Munich in the rain.

It drips from every leaf and twig,
Raindrops carried with the breeze
Into gutters, down the drains

11

Into the S-bahn gurgling sewers,
Lost to our overworld of light.
It's Munich in the rain.

It eases off, the wind now dropped,
Strollers smile, begin to chatter,
Gaze above, view the sky,
The clouds part, the sun breaks through –
At last, the day reveals its truth.
It's Munich in the sun.

BACH
[7th Sept 1974, Herrsching, near Munich]

Bach plays softly in my ears,
And I begin to lightly doze,
The echoes of the many strings
Carry me off to a distant land.

The rising lark winging high,
The trees and meadows speeding by,
The hills and valleys over which I fly
To rest, and lounge here, now.

Relaxed, though tired as I am,
I lie here thoughtful, relaxed, and calm
As innocent as a suckling lamb
Without the stirrings of the ram.

Time, it passes – I notice little
So deeply lost in my own thought;
I'm happy here with what I've got –
Though Bach, I've found Bavaria.

THE NUN WITH A FAG AND A MONK
[8th Sept 1974, Andechs, Bavaria]

The saintly nun with graceful air
Ambles with a monk – but not in prayer;
She holds not in her hand her beads,
But disgracefully what we call – the weed.

The halo that surrounds her head
Comes not from the life she's led –
It is in fact some man-made stuff,
Not holy smoke on which she puffs.

The fag she holds to her lips,
In contrast to the cross she grips -
In joy removed, then slightly raised,
She gives the cigarette her praise.

I SLEPT IN A HAYSTACK
[10th Sept 1974, Mittendorf, Austria]

I was picked up by a girl,
And invited to stay the night.

Then I found out –
I'd have to pay ten Marks.
I slept in a haystack.

LIKE A SCOTTISH DAY
[10th Sept 1974, Mittendorf, Austria]

The rain drives down again,
I huddle against the wall
Of a little log cabin.
It's not unlike a Scottish day,
The mist rolling down
To flood the valley below.

BULGARIAN-TURKISH FRONTIER
[12th Sept 1974, Turkey]

They asked me for Dollars –
I said I had none.
The asked me for Francs –
I said I had some.
They asked me for Marks
I refused then to pay.
They asked me for Pounds –
And that saved the day.

ANKARA
[13th Sept 1974, Ankara, Turkey]

I walked five K into Ankara,
Far up Cankaka Hill –
I was asked by a stranger
If things were difficult.

I didn't say all that much –
Then we took a car.
Now I have a weekend room
In villa-side Ankara.

THE CHILDREN'S CRIES ECHO
[16th Sept 1974, Ankara, Turkey]

The trees sway in the wind.
Then I notice the lack of birds.
The children's cries echo,
I see only in the distance, clouds.

The sun radiates its warmth.
I see a man watering his lawn.
The people pass quickly by –
I see that I watch all alone.

CHESS AND CLUES
[17th Sept 1974, Ankara, Turkey]

I sit here with the chessboard in front of me,
The game won. Upstairs I hear the voices

Of the neighbours and cops, and an American
Recounting his story of the break-in.
I hear them probing about searching for clues
As to the identity of the intruder.

RAMADAN
[18th Sept 1974, Ankara, Turkey]

It is the eve of my departure
After my long Ankara stay.
It coincides with the start
Of the fasting through the day.

From early in the morning
Until the sun has fled away –
The Muslims who are faithful
Eat by candlelight after prayer.

THE FRENCH CANADIAN
[24th Sept 1974, Ankara, Turkey]

His name is Jacques, he lives at the back
Of a hotel in Ankara.
We talk about dope, about our hopes
And the days we still have to come.

FLAG DRAPED COFFIN
[25th Sept 1974, Bus to Erzarum, Turkey]

On a bus to Erzarum,
Through the window, a passing car
With open boot –
A flag draped coffin
Sticking out the back.
Is there much ceremony
Over the dead these days?

IRANIAN FLY
[27th Sept 1974, Maku-Tabriz, Iran]

He's a happy little fly, this fly.
He crawls on my hand full of life –
He feeds on my blood with great pride –
He rubs his wings in delight –
And I try to squash him on sight –
He succeeds just in time to take flight –
He's a smart little fly, this guy.

HASHISH (fragments)
[3rd Oct 1974, Herat, Afghanistan]

My creativeness is dissipated,
My body drained, and my thoughts.
The culprit –
the abominable hashish plant.

Climb every mountain

Cross every wall
Ride every camel
Beware every fall.

KABUL
[5th Oct 1974, Kabul, Afghanistan]

The flies are buzzing around my head –
I'm lying here playing dead –
Staring upwards, my thoughts astray,
Light bulb swinging, its cord well frayed.

The calling birds are chirping out –
Aggressive dogs in barking bouts –
A woodman chopping – his echoes bouncing
Back and forth between the mountains.

HIMALAYAS
[17th Oct 1974, Manali, Himarchal Predesh, India]

The bus winds its weary way slowly to the top,
The engine whining all the time as if it's going to stop;
The passengers grip their seats in fear of pending doom,
The driver steering round the bend with none or little room.

Until at last we reach the crest and gasps give way to sighs,
The view I've travelled far to see is now before my eyes –
The peak is its centre piece, its minions scattered round,
The roof of the world – Mount Everest – lies cloudy bound.

MANALI TO KULU
[13th Nov 1974, Simla, India]

From Manali to Kulu,
We pass the mountains by.
Onward to Mandi
And darkness plays its hand.
The road disappears –
The headlights form the path,
We career round bends,
The driver in command;
Trucks scrapping past -
It's no time for a laugh.

THE DEALER
[1st Dec 1974, Delhi, India]

Delhi, the city of dope and hope
When you're gambling with your money.
Delhi, the city of folk and scope
If you're looking to make some money.
For money makes the living easy,
Gives you a style that's free and breezy;
An air of confidence gained with rupees,
With an appearance that is rather freaky,
You are as straight as the next man –
Just a bit sneakier.

15

MARIJUANA IN CALCUTTA
[28th Dec 1974, Calcutta, India]

Smoking on down the river,
Passing people on the shore.
Smoking on, winding ever –
Scrapping bottom at the fords.

Puffing hard, moving upstream,
Grass is green, head feels more.
Easing off, to drop the anchor,
At last I've docked, reached the shore.

SHARING WITH PIGEONS
[4th Jan 1975, Puri, Orissa, India]

Cigarette ends lie on the table
Scatted amongst the mounds of ash,
Candle wax and spent matches.
The light dances in the breeze
In tune to the pounding waves,
The ceaseless clicking-buzzing
Of the insect world.

My book lies open at page 327,
My mosquito cream lies at arm's length,
And my chillum still feels warm.
My room mates, four in number,
Belay their presence with feathered
droppings.

HOTEL ROOM IN INDIA
[10th Jan 1974, Madras, India]

Just another typical hotel room –
Bare light blue walls, and
The inevitable five speed fan,
A paint splattered mirror,
Six plastic, two broken, wall hangers,
And an energy saving 40w bulb.

Two wooden thin mattressed beds,
check covered, plus a metal legged
Paint chipped three-by-two pink clothed table,
resting on a well swept smooth surfaced
Grey concrete floor – makes it just
another typical hotel room in India.

CLOCK
[10th Jan 1974, Madras, India]

At midnight, pointing northwards,
Heart beat steady, with a white face
And hands clasped together as in prayer –
They slowly part, to present us with
The beginning of another day.

A COW BATHES IN THE OCEAN
[15 Jan 1975, Pondicherry, India]

Lonely palm trees,
Empty-netted fishermen,
White topped waves
And bobbing sail boats.

Fly infested sand,
Horizon forming clouds,
Long striding man,
And in she goes again.

HARIJAN
[15th Jan 1975, Pondicherry, India]

Harijan woman, praying to the son of God,
Jesus Christ.
Harijan woman, religion means so much
In your lower class.
Devotion to an idea, to a super being
Has left you in the depths of the world.

Lift up your head,
For even I find it easy to be taken in
By the surroundings.
Painted statuettes, and stain glass windows,
And just for a fleeting moment,
I too, believe in it all.

MOSQUITOES
[17th Jan 1975, Pondicherry, India]

Mosquito net billowing in the draft to form a door.
A droning heard, increasing to high-pitched scream
Within inches of my head. And then ...
My paranoia begins that makes each hour
Of the night an endless age without sleep or rest.
Each hour becomes a fear of death itself -
Until by dawn, my enemies depart, each one a winner
 in the game that rules their lives;
The game – survival.

A FAR OFF SIGH
[26th Jan 1975, Madurai, Tamil Nadu, India]

I find looks matter not in this far off land.
To groom oneself is, I am afraid, a pointless task.
Admiration is a far off thing that reaps no fruit;
A passing glance, a flirty smile –
And always in the end, a far off sigh.

LETTER FROM HOME
[26th Jan 1975, Madurai, Tamil Nadu, India]

Half a letter is better

17

than one, or none;
For if none, you have nothing,
But if one, you get one,
But you never get one again,
As the last one
Left me with nothing to say
In the next one.

THE GOOD SHIP SRI LANKA
[9th Feb 1975, Colombo]

In the good old days of the king,
Her maiden name was Ceylon –
But when she had her complete refit
Sri Lanka was how she became known.

Rocking gently afloat in the ocean,
She stands the chance of running aground –
For she's steered by Capt Bandiaranaike
Who flies the red flag over the bow.

She calls into Havana quite often,
Each time the cargo the same –
But the hold is a bit on the small side
And she must take on visits elsewhere.

Peking offers most for the Sri Lanka
And her hold is really quite full –
A rough sail northwards to Russia,
And leave Valdi low on her fuel.

Back in her home port of Colombo,
Wheat, rice, and sugar shared out –
There seems to be an overall shortage
Though the crew look to be doing alright.

DEAD BANANA FOR THE COWS
[25th Mar 1975, Tiruchirappali, India]

As the train begins to slow –
A sticky hand lets it go;
It hits the track all arms and legs
To lie prostrate in a manner
Unbecoming to the dead.

From a nearby filed, heads are raised –
Blacks, browns, whites, greys,
Some with horns, and some with stripes,
Their rolling tongues revealing thoughts
Over which they'd fight.

FIRST TIME FLYING
[21st Birthday, 25th Mar 1975, Jaffna-Colombo train, Sri Lanka]

The sea forming into layers of skin –
Wrinkled, pitted,
Flashing, dying,

Rising, flowing,
Pulsating, living,
A thousand streams and rivers going nowhere
Foaming, falling,
Forming, folding layers,
Of oceanic skin.

SWEAT
[14th Apr 1975, Madras, India]

Sweat dripping from my forehead,
Streams and torrents rushing down,
Until at last they reach my neck
And trickle down my spine.

MONSOON RAIN
[14th Apr 1975, Madras, India]

And the rain never ceases
Flash and smash
And the heavens give a warning of
A broken peace with the Gods.

But their anger never lasts
And in the end
They shed a tear to cleanse the wrongs of
A world that's in their hearts.

UNFURL THE DAWN
[10th May 1975, Hydrabad, India]

As the cockerel sounds reveille,
Nature hoists her flag –
Background greys, subdued rays
Cascading forth in spectrum
To unfurl the dawn.

THE FROGGIES
[10th May 1975, Hyrdrabad, India]

All my friends are little froggies
Who live in a pond,
And each little froggy
Lives in a world of his own,
Each has a green leaf
Which he calls as a home,
In a pond where each froggy
Is bored to the bone.

Each froggy can swim
But not as well as he leafs,
And when he goes out
It's to a friend's leaf,
For his friends live close by
And there's no need to swim,
So each little froggy hops
From leaf rim – to leaf rim.

What goes under the pond
Is a mystery to them,
For they never go diving
And in the end never learn;
What happens beneath them
Is of little concern,
To them all that matters
Are their friends and themselves.

So none of the froggies
Care much for the pond,
Apart from the part
They're particularly on –
But they don't know that either,
Because they don't swim,
So due to this failing
Their knowledge is thin.

If the froggies went swimming
And dived down real deep,
And left the security
Of all their green keeps,
To see if just briefly
They really could cope,
Then all they'd be risking
Are their watery hopes.

There are many more froggies
And leaves in the pond,
In parts that have been heard of
And parts that have not –
So if each froggy has time
To come up to scratch,
The pond could become more
Than just a green patch.

PRESENT DAY
[16th May 1975, Allahbad, India]

Tomorrow is an endless waste
Of shifting blue-moon sands
Surrounding the thirsty man
Who cannot drink
From the worn well
Termed present day.

OH INDIA
[16th May 1975, Allahbad, India]

Oh India, oh India –
I'd love to call you my own,
So why do you all always ask me
Where do I come from?

Oh India, oh India –
I like you as my home,

Yet sometimes I really wish
You'd leave me well alone.

Oh India, oh India –
I want the love you've shown,
But I fear the heartbreak's come
And now this bird has flown.

Oh India, oh India –
Parts of me still remain,
But when I return some future day
It won't be quite the same.

JOHN LENNON'S AMSTERDAM
[16th May 1975, Allahbad, India]

For me John Lennon's Amsterdam was different,
I didn't spend all my time in bed,
I didn't have a Yoko who could listen
To all the things I had to leave unsaid.

The tulips there were far from being pretty,
They really looked as though they all were dead,
I found the cafes were full of too much acid
Which had withered far too many tulip heads.

The diamonds no longer had their sparkle,
It's glass beads the public were being fed,
The jewellers there were all small-time chemists
Whose stones turned many living into dead.

The dykes of self-restraint had been blown,
The kids were hanging on by a thread –
The wards were full of many flipped-out heroes
Who were the only ones in Amsterdam in bed.

BY THE GANGES
[18th May 1975, Benares, India]

The steps leading down to the river
Radiate more than a gentle warmth
As dusk designs its fall.

Three snowy geese
Crack the incense air
Of tolling bells and near to distant voices.

Small boats rock
In the wave of pleasure cruising vessels
Avoiding shaven-headed swimming pilgrims.

By the water's edge
The last smouldering of emberd fires,
Each pyre, a loved one lost.

The laments unceasing,
The mourners wait patiently to torch

21

Another funeral pile.

Darkness comes! One small spark,
Heat and light
Reclaiming man to endless night.

NINE MONTHS of PENNING
[22nd May 1975, Benares, India]

This page is all that's left to end
Nine months of pennings, and yet
Not enough to catch the endless meaning
That lies within my mind.

For only time will free the mental tongue
To offer the words
for every context
In the right degree.

THE WALLS AROUND ME
[22nd May 1975, Benares, India]

The walls around me have no shape –
My memories keep me from my sleep;

Reaching out – I find one left,
A striking match preludes its death.

The room becomes a shady show -
The match goes out, the ciggy glows.

STONED ON HASHISH
[17th June 1975, Peshawar, Pakistan]

My mind is bottled up like glue;
I've had too much – I think that's true;
My thoughts are sticking to my skull,
My tongue feels useless, dry and numb.

But what's the use of using both,
I needn't think, or talk, or croak;
For all is here to look and watch –
The rising sun, a babbling brook.

MIDSUMMER'S DAY, KABUL
[20th June 1975, Kabul, Afghanistan]

Midsummer's day, and what a way to spend it –
Eating alone, speaking in tones that reflect it.
Lying around, listening to sounds to forget it.
Smoking a joint, reading of Quant, enjoying it.
Drinking mint tea, scratching at fleas, regretting it –
Till soon, the moon replaces, the sun's bright face
And brings on Midsummer's night.

CARRY ON GIRL
For Zindra Zita Skesteris

[4th July 1975, Macou, Iran]

So carry on girl,
And travel the world
But make sure you find a true friend.

You may travel the world
To all of its ends
But you might never find a true friend.

So open your heart
And let your love free
Look out for that true friend.

SHE SLAMMED THE DOOR
[15th July 1975, Aaathal, Switzerland]

She slammed the door,
And that was that –
But a few hours later
It really hit me that
More and more
That slammed door
Had cracked the frame
Of my pictured life.
It left me nothing,
Just completely numb,
Just an empty nothing,
Just a nothing,
Just nothing,
Nothing.

LOSS OF A BEST FRIEND
[23rd July 1975, Edinburgh]

The Royal Mile, and I smile – I'm back again.
Nothing's changed - ain't that strange.

The music's sweet o'er by Arthur's Seat,
Life's rearranged – two of everything;
Gold wedding rings, the hope of little feet,
Him working hard; sending Christmas
Cards to her kin.

Tuesday's washing day –
Nightly telly plays make life sadder,
While his guitar lies idle, no longer
Vital to stop his decay into
mediocrity.

BUNNY
For G
[26th July 1975, Glasgow]

Blue-jersey woman with green dreaming eyes,
Chocolate brown hair, milky cream thighs,
Silver tipped lashes, long strawberry nails,

Black stockinette legs, and a fully puffed tail.

WHY DON'T WE KNOW IT (song)
[4th Aug 1975, Edinburgh]

Why don't we know it,
Why don't we show it,
Why do we hold it to ourselves?

What are our feelings,
What are our reasons,
What are we hiding from ourselves?

Where are we going,
What are we seeking,
What are we finding out about ourselves?

Who are we fighting,
Who are we kidding,
Who are we really but ourselves?

Why don't we know it,
Why don't we show it,
Why don't we be just ourselves?

THE SCIVIES LAMENT (fragment)
[5th August 1975, Edinburgh]

I wash the dishes
From seven till three –
I scrub the pots,
I make the tea.

THE FALL
[14th Aug 1975, Queen's Rd, Newcastle-upon-Tyne]

The fall being early
It was time to sweep
The autumn leaves
Into a pile.
As the rain descended
Upon the bronzed stack
With blackened tears
And fading smile,
In harking frosty nights
Of frozen sleep,
Of warm less stars
And hostile owls.

For summer green had gone,
And ice-cream cones
Gave sway to hot broth soups
For steaming colds,
As time ticked by
A little faster every day,
A little slower,
As the evenings

Long and lengthening,
Stretched on to winter.

TWENTY ONE
[1st Sept 1975, 10 Chester Cresc, Newcastle]

Twenty one, and still a lad
Whose knowledge mounts to nothing less
Than nothingness.

At twenty five, more a man,
Perhaps my knowledge will mount to nothing less
Than nothingness.

At forty – that's getting on,
My knowledge will mount to nothing less
Than nothingness.

The day I die, a child once more
My knowledge with be nothing less
Than worthless.

FLIES
[1st Sept 1975, 10 Chester Cresc, Newcastle]

Flies leading a fuzzy summer life,
Hopping and buzzing,
Humming and flying,
And getting around to laying eggs,
And eating at sores,
And walking on floors,
And dog shit,
And dustbins,
And everything that smells.

But heat is a problem
For these little pests,
It singes their wings,
It scotches their legs,
It freezes their bodies
And kills them stone dead;
In the darkness of winter
They meet a cold end,
To lie prostrate at windows,
Cocooned – in cobwebs.

SHOE GIRL
[1st Sept 1975, Chester Cresc, Newcastle]

Toe nails so large and red,
And on each foot a little ball
Of flabby skin, and worn out corns
From constant use of shapeless shoes
And flashy boots that impressed the vicar
As he is on the outlook for a wife.

PAY DAY

25

[5th Sept 1975, Chester Cresc, Newcastle]

Friday, pay day, some I dare say
Feel it means much more than
Just a day to have a few pints,
A dance, a winch, a quick bite
On a bag of chips before the night
Sets in and the evening's gone.

For it's the weekend, no work tomorrow
Morn, and guaranteed a good time
With no going home as early as usual
On last orders … for finding ourselves
Out on the street swaying slightly,
Yet still on our feet, looking for a party,
But with little hope unless a friend
Is on the know.

And she's disappeared, the entertainment
Stops – there is nothing left to -
But stride it out on the homeward walk
And think what might have been.

PEOPLE LIKE YOU
For Carol
[12th Sept 1975, Newcastle]

People like you are changing all the time.
You now accept the dangerous marijuana,.
You talk of liberation at the front;
You sip Martinis, yet seem never to be drunk;
You drop the pill in case you might get fucked;
You lead a nice life – one day you'll hit a rut;
People like you are changing all the time.

CONTENTED 21 YEAR OLD ON TYNESIDE
[12th Sept 1975, Newcastle]

Why change? A time old question.
I'm happy as I am,
Sitting every evening
My young wife at my arm.

I've got a colour TV,
A kid in a pram,
A dog that still needs weaning,
And a cat I canna stand.

My job is really steady,
No threat of laying off,
I reckon when I'm sixty
That's time enough to stop.

Meanwhile, the day's tick by,
One night's like the next –
I'm really looking forward
To taking my wife to bed.

THE FASCIST
[13th Sept 1975, Newcastle]

I'm not a revolutionary;
Today there are no revolutions.
I'm not a reactionary –
There are no real causes.
There is -
no government to overthrow;
no army to fight;
no suppression;
no intimidation;
no poverty;
no racial disharmony.
This is the UK –
Not farthest Africa.

FORLORN
[13th Sept 1975, Chester Crec, Newcastle)

I feel it coming on –
The urge to be forlorn
And hopelessly lost and obscure
So that no one understands a word,
Not one word of what I say.

For if they did –
They'd say I'm wrong
Or mad, or lock me up
For being different from what
They think I really am.

So what I think, I think,
And only now and then
Do other people learn
Of what I'm thinking.

Only then is it someone special,
Someone who will understand
Not what I say,
But what I am.

SEEING IT MY WAY
[14th Sept 1975, Newcastle]

They said 'Try to see it my way',
But I know I've tried that too.
I've tried to see it their way
And found it's not what's in my head.

I see their point, I understand
But still I think I have better plans
To live my life the way I see
That I should.

YOU KNOW WHAT I THINK

For Ollie
[14th Sept 1975, Newcastle]

Woman, full of understanding,
You've lived abroad
And still you're only twenty.
You say you're always free,
You want to head out East
And see old India – I think that's ….
Well, you know what I think.

You spend your time with men
And you have no lady friends,
You have a little flat, so
It's not so hard to get away
To be alone. I think that's ….
Well, you know what I think.

You like to get around,
And keep your eyes up,
You always smile and wear the clothes
which haven't yet come into style,
you feel your international;
I think that's ….
Well, you know what I think.

THE ART OF LOVE
[15th Sept 1975, Newcastle]

The art comes from being apart,
Keeping from falling over heels
And ending on your knees
So that the music no longer plays
At the same speed
As your poor old heart.

LETTER TO MY MOTHER
[15th Sept 1975, Newcastle]

It's like a maze, a garden full of images,
The mind works fast, but the head just drags
Its weary weight across the page.

Perhaps, someday, in times to come
I'll just sit down, put up my feet, and close my eyes
And think before I fall asleep
Everything I wish to say.

And bang! When my piece is said,
I'll have a long tape of all my thoughts
Ready just to stamp and post
And sent to you.

BLIND CONVERSATION
[16th Sept – 20th Oct 1975, Newcastle]

I feel words say little and not enough.

I imagine the flickering of an eyelid
Can convey a truer, fuller meaning
Of what I should have said
But for which I couldn't find the words.

An eye for an eye -
And yet the quickest briefest insight
Can split the heart asunder
And pale the stoutest fellow
To a mediocre fool.

In this kaleidoscopic world,
Inside a maze of optic mind,
Beyond the sight of all the blind –
Words don't say it all.

THE NIGHT TIME BUZZ
[7th Oct 1975, Newcastle]

The night time buzz
Of humming lights and fridges,
Of clicking clocks and hinges
Creaking in the draught.
The mellowed moans
Of melting fires,
Of circling hawks,
Of chiming churches,
The watery hush
Of dockland tugs and foggy horns
Of rumbling cars
over mumbling manholes
Carrying through the dark.

THE SPIDER OF LOVE
[12th Oct 1975, Newcastle]

I try and I try again,
Perhaps another time -
The sorrow is just a passing
Phase of consciousness.

It will pass tomorrow,
Or the next day,
Providing not much thought is spent
in useless channelled trains
Of pointless reminiscence.

I will try again
And hang my past.

TIME TO GO
[12th Oct 1975, Newcastle]

I'll see you to the door –
It's time to go,
Though the music's still playing,
And the dope is still lying

Somewhere between
On the floor.

INTERNMENT
[20th Oct 1975, Newcastle]

Would you be a friend
To a friend who breaks the law?
To help himself,
When the deal he's getting is raw,
And more than just
A petty useless squabble -

While an anonymous somebody,
In an obscure and grubby
Paper strewn office in some
Hitherto anonymous government lobby
Goes on a power trip -

And brands your friend
A red, or fascist pig,
And locks him up!

Would it be just another friend
Forgotten, and a friend abandoned?
Would you be a friend to a friend
who speaks out, breaks the law?

THE FOLLY OF SHEEPFIELD FAYRE
for Maureen Scoffield (Reuss)
[27th Oct 1975, Newcastle]

Roll up, roll up, and join the queue
all these people come to view,
a right old bunch of rags and sods,
and brooms and mops along with slops,
and hose and rake and spade and plough,
and hammers, sickles, by the thou',
and pots and kettles black and new,
and round and worn and caked in stew;
a hundred different kind of pan,
a big one, small one, nowt that grand,
but enough to fill the village square,
the day of the Sheepfield Fayre.

Now, Sheepfield without a doubt,
the smallest, quietest, shyest,
least heard about hamlet,
in medieval Yorkshire times;
if numbering more than fifty souls,
half must have been with sheep in folds,
yet still by some peculiar twist,
this place was chosen from a list,
with pin it's guessed, must have been,
mistakes were frequent, so it seems,
tho' Sheepfield be small that day,
it certainly would not for the Fayre.

The word it spread, as it were known
that this would be the greatest showing
of all that's Yorkshire's proud and boast,
in things of iron, brass and lead,
with prizes for the brightest, best
to strongest, smallest, simplest, least
squashed flat, blown out, to thickest pressed,
as long as made with metal base,
and open to all the Yorkshire race,
no matter what the entry be,
it stands the stoutest hope with rest,
with prizes minor in degrees,
but winner takes the handsome stake
of ten thousand gold guineas.

Now, the man who stood to gain the most
from this wager, as it's host -
was none other than the Duke of York,
the fayre had been his brainwave thought,
as lacking backing from the people,
was turning now to every scruple,
to scrape together half a kingdom,
and capture Lancaster's wide dominion,
and have it all to himself,
as King of England's war torn lands,
made as such by squabbling barons,
fighting for power to take command.

But, the Duke was not a Midas,
he couldn't fund a battle crisis,
against a castle defying allegiance,
that required deploying a siege plan,
and incurred a long purse wait,
of months of meat filled soldiers' plates,
or keeping them drunk on ale and wine,
to stop their grumbling starving minds,
from turning from the siege at hand,
to thoughts of pillaging the land,
and giving up their sieging duty,
to go instead to hunt for booty,
for if he couldn't provide their pay,
he wouldn't maintain their loyalty.

Then he had his stroke of genius,
while being caressed by his mistress,
and up he shot to leave her speechless,
and quickly fastened up his breeches,
and galloped madly through the night,
until the filtering of daylight,
brought him finally to his castle,
the drawbridge lowered with a rattle,
and over the cobbled yard he pounded,
calling his page to gather the knighted,
and to the great hall they collected,
the Duke foaming in wild delight,
while the herald called for order,

31

so silence all the lords and knights.

The noise abated in the great hall,
till not a word was heard to fall,
till not an eye was seen to wander,
as the knights began to wonder,
if the Duke had seen the anguish,
and felt the knights growing anger,
and heard of towns burning down,
in the fight for England's crown,
with not a hand of Yorkshire raised,
by the Duke to win the realm.
Was this why he called his lords?
Was this why they gripped their swords?
Was this why their hearts beat quickly?
Were they waiting – to go to war?

Meanwhile locked up in her chamber,
brooding with her tending maidens,
sat the Duchess scheming vengeance,
for her husband's faithless actions,
with his saucy vixen mistress,
a mindless creature devil sent,
to trap the Duke with her body,
by her ways with foreign love,
learnt to her by gypsy tinkers,
in the heat of summer passion,
dwelt upon in long cold winters,
by the lords with foolish hearts,
like the Duke – another suitor,
to the knowledge of her arts.

But women now were second place,
as the Duke prepared his speech,
all thoughts of love had drained away,
stolen the colour from his cheeks,
and replaced it, with a fierceness,
that his knights knew as false,
that his knights knew as madness,
their master's most enduring fault;
at best of times a weak-kneed coward,
incompetent in love and war,
who left a lot to be desired,
by his ladies and his lords -
who by his flighty make-shift nature,
should never have been the Duke of York.

Yet that foul tale's another thing,
and covers deeds of treacherous tricks,
and every knight knew the stories,
of the Duke's rise by blood so gory,
that even babes had met an end,
houses burnt, and witches condemned,
devils seen in every honest farmer,
unable to raise the taxes demanded -
these heretics perishing in the flames,
fueled by accusations false made;

innocent souls speaking out boldly,
soon found themselves thrown in dungeons;
for such was the justice in the Duke's court,
the poor man paid for the rich man's sport.

The Duke spoke up to his lords,
his knights, retainers, in the great hall,
"I have not called you thus to war" -
great disappointment filled them all.
"I have some want to raise some cash,
and then we may have our war!
I shall arrange to have a fayre,
then with the takings, Yorkshire arm.
But first we must make it known,
to all that dwell in this fair realm,
that prizes wait for those who bring,
the Duke of York their finest things,
of metal made, and iron ware,
and bring it to the Sheepfield Fayre!"

And once the word was out to all,
for news flies quick by the crow ...
and soon it spread from hills to coast,
and o'er the dales, and on to moors;
and bells that rang first in praise,
with iron ring at evening prayers,
were quieter now, and being hauled,
thru deep streams and waterfalls,
on rusty chains, by trusty horse;
thru driving sleet, wind gale force;
ne'er had the county seen such rashness,
ne'er had the county bred such madness,
to reach in time, the only care,
to make in time the Sheepfield Fayre.

And yet the hunt had just begun,
beneath all stairs, among all junk;
ne'er a spider's web untouched,
ne'er dusty cupboards left unlocked,
in ranking, raking, mucky stanks,
searching every nook and crack,
no needle left in one corn stack,
no cranny missed, no store unsacked,
no stone unturned, no treasure missed,
no mislaid rainy savings spared,
all minds in greedy hunt at work,
in frenzy stripped all secrets bare,
in hope of finding something rare,
to win a prize at Sheepfield Fayre.

The thought of gold had spread its wings,
to cover neighbour, friends, and kin,
and signs of joy, and happy times,
were soon replaced with money minds;
and for two weeks it didn't stop,
they shut the pubs, closed the shops,
to hunt for metal base and likes,

to hell with jack, he's be alright,
his tin, his lead, his iron bed,
his door knob, hinges, lock and keys,
no, not one scrap was left to chance,
to stray of find its wanton way,
into the hands of thieves or friends,
who ever they may be.

Soon, horses' special treaded clops,
came to sound, a clipped like trot,
with shoes, and nails, and sometimes horse,
vanishing, without as much as a nod,
or wink, from man or fellow beast,
no sign of metal to be seen!
Yet, farmers milking cows were safe,
tho' urns, and churns, not quite the same,
disappeared along with kettles,
and pans of roast, mince and special,
hot-pot pie and Yorkshire pud,
all the best in home-made food,
all to find their own way there,
to make their appearance at the fayre.

With fights and brawls about the streets,
and in the ginnels about tin sheets,
and copper plate, and owt that'd make,
the winning of the Duke's gold stake;
while unknown to all, there was a lad,
not quite so daft, or quite so mad,
who had a bit of this and that -
out of copper, tin, iron, and lead,
and soon with patience had it made,
he packed his bags, and ring, with care,
to cross the moors to Sheepfield Fayre.

And so the day finally came -
and came, and came, and came the freemen,
came the farmers, grocers, lawmen,
blacksmiths, tailors, cobblers, marksmen,
coopers, saddlers, millers, churchmen,
beggars, thieves, gypsies, badmen,
with all the lost metal things,
missing pots, and pans, and urns,
and shoes, and nails, and hitching rails,
and door knobs, hinges, bent up screws,
piping, roofing, all soon due,
to be assembled at the fayre,
and judged by Duke, the devil's heir,
whom even monks cursed in prayer.

Each entry first was written down,
and each was grouped by design,
and whether under horse or pot,
or tin, or iron, or lead, or what,
the entries mounted up and up;
the Duke sat warmly with his cup
of wine, and meat, and pretty wench,

wringing hands, and quoting French,
completely wrecked, and jabbering nonsense,
playing checkers with his coffers,
laughing, screaming, crying, dancing,
hoping, praying, begging, helpless,
kneeling, singing out his thank yous,
to the Lord for his new found richness.

For the Duke, whose prize was sought,
gave the crowd but little thought,
his need of metal for his war,
outweighed the virtue of a lord;
for though he's traveled far to south,
and been yon o'er to other side,
and seen one here, and this one there,
he nowt as much as seen a hair,
of metal good, and true, and clear
as Yorkshire's best there at the fayre;
all got a place among the lot,
with one condition in the plot -
that the losers forfeited all,
to the Duke for his war.

The crowd on hearing such cruel news,
cursed the Duke for his deceivement,
for up till then, none dared guess,
the fayre was meant to rob and cheat them
of their precious metal goods,
their tools of work, their livelihood;
the farmers with their grandest ploughs,
and shearers with their finest knives,
and blacksmiths with their blackest anvils,
the alarmed army of angry wives,
whose pots and pans as old as time,
would soon be arms, melted down,
by the Duke's men standing strong,
preventing entries from being withdrawn.

The best of each was finally selected,
and on display before the crowd -
each bit, itself a masterpiece
of Yorkshire craft and sweet technique,
of all the things that help to make,
the metal work of them so great;
the stoutest nail, the finest sword,
the sharpest blade, to smallest lock,
they ranged from alum on to zinc,
and missing nothing, bar kitchen sink;
but nowt at all was near to winning,
'cept the ring that lad had made,
a bit of copper, iron, tin and lead,
greater in beauty than all the rest.

The moment came, the trumpets sounded,
the fanfare scaled to royal heights,
the judges nod, they have decided,
the Duke appears in all his might;

35

the gathered thousands standing there,
assembled for the Sheepfield Fayre,
jeer, and drown the Duke's weak voice,
he calls for silence, with little joy;
and trying again to quell the mob,
orders his archers to loose some shots,
o'er their heads, and at their feet,
till silence reigns, and Duke can speak
- but not a word parts his lips,
the judges shuffle in their seats.

They hand their verdict to the Duke,
who doesn't really want to look,
at who the judges name as winner,
for deep down the Duke's a sinner,
who does not want to turn the key
to unlock the chest with the gold guineas.
"Let us pray" the Duke calls out,
taking a stance that does him proud,
looking the thousands in the eye,
but not at once, time drags by,
the baited breaths, hearts loudly beating,
the buzzing of a fly heard briefly,
rising, waiting, waiting there, hovering,
as the Duke kneels down in offering.

"Dear Lord above, give us guidance,
show us light, do not blind us,
keep us on a path that's pure,
keep us rich, and poor man, poor."
And while the Duke says his prayers,
from among the rabble at the fayre,
a drunken peasant, swaying widely,
pushes forward through the crowd,
blaspheming, swearing, bottle swigging,
almost at the point of singing, shouts
"He's wasting time, the swine!"
that was the last from him they heard,
the Duke's men dragged him by his feet,
and quickly pulped him into mince meat.

Because the old drunk thought,
the Duke was having second thoughts,
about his plan to share his coffers,
when he didn't want to do the coughing.
The assembled crowd forward swayed,
the Duke squirmed, backed away,
a deep mumble, became a rumble
as the crowd began to tumble -
The Duke, scared, and chicken white,
his ruffled feathers falling out,
looks for horse, but long since gone,
with shoes, and nails, and bridle on,
and sword, and shield, and armour bright,
and metal chest with coffers inside.

Plucked and ready for the broiling,

the crowd's fury, hot and boiling -
advancing quickly, roaring for blood,
the Duke now lost, no longer lord.
Gone his chest! Tears on his cheeks,
for all was missing, bar the key,
which dangled deftly round his neck,
on a chain inside his vest.
But lo!, he had no time for woe,
the Duke escaped with just his clothes,
ten thousand pieces, one by one,
meant a golden piece for everyone,
from o'er dale, or from far farms,
who trekked their way to the fayre.

And to this day, the story's told,
to the children, by the old,
of how the Duke of Yorkshire's crown
went for a price he ne'er lived down,
and how fair Yorkshire melted down,
all that metal, and built a town,
as many stayed, gave up their land,
and went about constructing a plan,
to design factories on the spot,
where Duke's archers lobbed their shots.
They set to fencing in the fields,
and began upon a different yield,
to produce the finest stainless steal,
since evermore, stamped 'Sheffield'.

ART
[4th Nov 1975, Larkspur Terr, Newcastle]

Art? Now that's a subject
Wide and vast,
Pointless, fruitless,
Classed as wasteful
By the tactless, thoughtless
Senseless individuals
Of artless minds
And stone cold hearts.

WALLFLOWER
[9th Nov 1975, Newcastle]

They all think they're great here –
Living in style,
Hitting the straight parties,
Getting the odd smile,
Knowing a few people,
Thinking it's enough
To get themselves by with
But not out the rut.

AMNESTY DAY
[11th Nov 1975, Newcastle]

Amnesty Day –

37

It's about front lines,
And trenches deep
And full of mud –
Where soldiers died,
Where few survived
To pick red poppies.

The sad red poppies,
Still blooming after fifty seven years,
With the world still fighting
To shed it's warped fears –
Right and Left still killing
To erase the other's ideas.

While the soldiers remember,
With scarred eyes,
Crippled sighs,
Tortured cries,
And march,
To shed their last tears
For the senseless agony,
Of wasted lives,
Of wasted lives.

ASCOT GOLD CUP CHASE
[14th Nov 1975, Newcastle]

The Black and White whiskey Gold Cup Chase,
And how many Ascot gentlemen
Are already one over the eight
On yet another great outing of hats,
Bobbing heads, and mounted mares;
As Easby Abbey, the odds on favourite
Flashing by – a cert – the nagging doubts
Of taking a tumble forgotten
As she takes the last fence
And romps home by a clear length
To the cheers of 'Well done, girl!'
By her backers at the post.

KEEP CITIES POLLUTED
[14th Nov 1975, Newcastle]

Big city liver,
The rest, just won't forgive you
For being brought up
Where they never had the chance
To sample and feel
The city's inbred arrogance
For them, the country bums
And small town weeds.

But big city liver,
Don't you worry one hit,
The pigs aren't worth it,
They know nothing of your ways –
They breathe through their noses,

And complain about the air.
But what do they know?
Let them all go back
To their small time snares.

WHY ARE WE DIFFERENT?
[4th Dec 1975, Newcastle]

Why are we all different?
I sometimes feel ashamed
To think that I might think faster
Than my closest friend.

She's supposed to understand me,
But really never does ...
I'm frightened to admit it
In case it causes hurt.

I MIGHT HAVE GOT IT WRONG
[4th Dec 1975, Newcastle]

Who's right? I guess it isn't me,
No by heck, it isn't me.
For what on earth can I be sure of
When today, I know it, and tomorrow
I've forgotten it, yet in between,
I might have got it wrong.

A STAGE SHE'S GOING THROUGH
[8th Dec 1975, Newcastle]

She goes on and on,
Nagging all the time –
It drives me mad,
She's pushing me with her voice
To the edge of sanity.
She feels she's being had
As a fool. What can I do
But treat this present hell as a stage
She's going through out of love
For me.

PROFOUND WORDS
[21st Dec 1975, Newcastle]

For once I've found some truth –
No more lies to hide behind,
No more twisted minds in battle
Hell-bent in gaining superiority.

Being myself, untied and loose to find
A way of being great with myself –
Free to choose the options without force
From sources pure in life.

Saying yes and no -
without the doubt of being wrong

reaching deep within myself
to give advice and keep the peace;
help the helpless help themselves;
feed starving minds with profound words.

UPS AND DOWNS
[24th Dec 1975, Newcastle]

The ups and downs, ins and outs
Though our minds, lost in words,
Trying hard to cope with life.

Who trusts who? I don't know –
I guess I feel my way until the trust
Eventually shows itself to me by
What you say and do to make me understand
Your inner self as well as you do.

I CAN'T FIND THE BEACH
[24th Dec 1975, Newcastle]

I'm feeling high and dry,
Though my feet are on the bottom
And the waves are winding past my ears;
For sure I'm not drowning,
I'm swimming,
But I can't find the beach.

WE ALL HAVE DOUBTS
[9th Jan 1976, Newcastle]

We all have doubts.
I expect each of us has felt
That moment when the world
Has seemed a place that has no point
Of being in existence but to infinitely
Serve the cause of birth and death.

WHISPERING WINDS
[3rd Feb 1976, Newcastle]

Whistling, whispering winds,
Wynd through the weary winter months;
Till spring appears in showers
And dreamy snowdrops shyly sheltered
'neath the crooked., twisted boughs
And budding apple blossom branches –
Half in shifting shadow or luke warm sun,
The clouds meander quietly by ...
The silence broken by a blackbird's cry.

LACK OF HEART
[9th Feb 1976, Newcastle]

Thought to brain,
Conscience holding back,
Frustrating all my senses,

Restricting me to facts.
I can't imagine, or
Invent my own space.

Space to earth,
Gravity pulling hard,
Like the white stallions
Tethered in my head –
Reined by experience
And a lack of heart.

LOVE
[3rd Mar 1976, Stell Green, Northumberland]

Love is ….
What need I say that hasn't found its way
On to the lips of all past and present lovers
Who have trod the road of passion.

But love forever changes,
Hearts stay golden, the harvest ripens
Until the winter comes and the snows begin
To freeze a love that rarely stays.

ANNIE
[8th Mar 1976, Newcastle]

Annie, you've drained my soul
And my hope has gone
And left me empty,
But much at peace.

Our ties are broken,
Our strings have finally fouled,
And yet, our parting words
Were on the soft side
Of our senseless speech.

I feel the need to say more,
But I think it's best
To leave things as they stand –
Tomorrow may hold a different look
From the day that's gone.

MISGIVINGS
[20th Mar 1976, Larkspur Terr, Newcastle]

Not a happy day would pass
Without containing an unhappy hour.
Not an inch be gained with out a fight
About our stupid self-centred, narrow
Pig-headed beliefs.

No room for change,
No sun to make the buds bloom forth
To show their hidden colours.
No concrete legs of understanding

41

To give support to our towering problems.

No compromise to our needs or wants,
But cries of selfishness to chill the ears.
No basis, no reality.
No contentment, no fantasy.
No present, no future, just past.

No hope, no faith,
No trust, no love, just hate.

AT THE CROSSROADS
For Chrissie Brown
[21st March 1976, Newcastle]

Such a long and ponderous time,
How the years fly by,
How the memory takes a jolt
When confronted by a friend
Who's just blown in.

And still the ease with which
The words flow off –
No sticky 'How are you?',
But something warm and touching,
Tender beyond the smallest flicker.

How I'd missed the presence
Of a stretching past –
Not a new and freshly found acquaintance,
But a friend who's had her changes
Close to mine.

How the world seems a different place –
Not as transient, and ever changing
As life might suggest –
That people pass, stop awhile,
And wander on.

Every path that leads away has a crossroads.
There lies the choice –
The smooth surfaced track of conformity,
or to take off on the rough and tumble
bandit ridden road.

How the years fly by –
And the rough and tumble road
Finds friends waiting at the crossroads.

SINGER IN A BAND
[23rd Mar 1976, Newcastle]

Singer with a band, a merry life?
Riding round the towns,
In and out the bars,
Just to make a few bob.

Knocking back the jars,
Entertaining hard to please punters
Who think they know a star
When the see one.

On the road again,
Sleeping in the van for a few hours,
Crowding over a coffee
As the night turns to dawn.

Back behind the wheel,
Rain driving down,
Wipers waving through the spray
Of heavy laden trucks.

LIGHT
[26th Mar 1976?, Newcastle]

Rays of changing scenes,
transcending all the pasts,
Bringing forth a view,
haloed in a sheen, as to last,
but fading on to new
and brighter flashing paths.
Time winds its hand around
its fleeting shafts,
To cause a change.

POPULAR
[3rd Apr 1976, Newcastle]

One day you are nothing,
Then it all clicks with all
the dudes around you,
that your company, somehow
really gives them kicks.

How long will it last?
A couple of hours?
A number of days?
Several weeks?

Or will it be back
To the old type of life,
the ordinary every-day bum,
who shares in the laughs,
has fun for awhile.

Your company once vibrant,
Exciting, unstyled –
Becomes to the dudes
Like a disinterested smile –
Something returned with a frown.

THE BOSS
[5th Apr 1976, Newcastle]

He doesn't care about his minions,
He hasn't time for their opinions,
He treats them all as if they're shit,
Or worthless useless bits –
Of maladjusted and illiterate scum
Who work for him – the boss;
A jumped up, two faced, cunt and bastard,
No good bum.

THE WINO
[8th April 1976, Larkspur Terr, Newcastle]

Hurtling down the street in rags,
Shoed in plastic lace-less flats,
looking wretched, smelling foul,
pitted dirt on his lapels,
hair beneath a grease stained hat,
fingers picking at a scab,
grey-coat coated thick with spew,
shirt beneath like matted glue,
trousers rotting with his piss,
bottle out to touch his lips.

RONNIE
[2nd May 1976, Newcastle]

Two children, and ten years later
With still no sign
Of being a bitter life hater.
Only the smile of a beautiful lady,
Capturing the heart
Of her much younger playmate.

POETS DREAM
[9th June 1976, Newcastle]

Poets dream of a better life,
Of lovers flocking to their side
In hope of some laughs and smiles
To balance up their minds
Of tumbled, broken, hard-luck times.

Lovers wait for their poets
To make the sun shine,
Make life fun and understandable.
They give their love -
while poets dream of a better life
And not of them.

THE HUMAN JUNGLE
[12th July 1976, Larksput Terr, Newcastle]

The human jungle zoo,
full of lifeless zombies,
wailing forth obscenities
and foul niceties.

THE ART GALLERY
[12th July 1976, Larkspur Terr, Newcastle]

Peeking over rounded shoulders,
under elbows, up bronze noses,
looking for the hidden meanings
to these statues grotesque poses.

STONED ON A CIGARETTE
[Aug 1976, Larkspur Terr, Newcastle]

Getting stoned on a cigarette
is an effective short term high,
though not for those chain puffers
always crashing out the ash.

For the man who is modest,
who keeps his intake down,
the pleasure of an odd tab
is a special form of high.

HULL
[11th Aug 1976, Hull-Rotterdam Ferry]

Here to find ourselves alone
Aboard a ship –
Here to find ourselves once more
In life, adrift.

ROMA
[19th Aug 1976, Brindisi, Italy]

Roma, a city in ruins –
Incomplete on many levels.
Roma, built on empires –
Now a mound of crumbling earth.
Roma, the tourist's nectar –
Rip-off merchant's ten-a-penny.
Roma, the Christian's Mecca,
For those who kiss the ring.

TWA FLIGHT MEAL
[29th Aug 1976, Athens-Cairo flight]

A cold meal of turkey, fish, cheese on bread,
One mushroom, a tomato, an olive, and
a sprinkle of parsley, followed by coffee -

Orange juice served before -
Coca-cola served after to wash it down.
A piece of cherry cake to round it off.

LUXOR
[2nd Sept 1976, Luxor, Egypt]

The journey to Luxor a trip and a ride,
That took me one day from Cairo by train.

I arrived at the heart of the Pharaoh's domain
That since Amun's time has crumbled, decayed;
The memories of Karnak, the pillars, the lake –
Thebes and the heights its dynasty once scaled.

THE VALLEY OF THE DEAD
[? Sept 1976, Luxor, Egypt]

Sun peeking over the horizon,
And extendable Marks and Sparks umbrella
Along for the shade.

A wooden boat with inboard motor
Ferrying me across the Nile.

Eight miles to the Valley of the Dead,
Primeval villages like disused cannons
To the left and right.

Near the Valley entrance, stopping, listening,
The barren rock, surrounding semi-desert
Devoid of vegetation – the air still,
Nothingness.

No birds, no breeze,
Nothing – only silence.

A complete emptiness;
A world of non-existent life, the dead
Shadowless, whisper-less reaching out
To touch the fingertips of the living.

The silence disturbing – the burning sun,
Heavy breathing, lungs in gasps for air,
Reminding the living, of life.

ON THE NILE
[9th Sept 1976, Aswan Dam, Egypt]

Lying on the roof of a flat-topped paddle steamer
With the sun an hour to set.
The Arabs wait patiently to eat –
One idly chops salad for the daily end to Ramadan,
While penny-whistle music heats the humid air.
Irritated chatter fills the pauses between
The banging noise of the cattle loading –
Heavy footsteps weigh the gangway;
With a last minute toot,
Tyres screech on the hot sand, produce passengers.

Over to the east in contrast to the dying sun –
The silver of the rising full moon;
The water calm, a tickling wind
Stretches out its rippled surface skin
As the battered smoke-stack issues forth
Its chronic scarring black to the ancient chug
Of an empire worn Perkins engine,

The ferry drags its wooden slated paddle
Through the thick Nile mud.

UPPER NILE
[23rd Sept 1976, south of Kosti, Sudan]

The brown and sombre Nile;
Its smile now gone,
Its weeds floating thick –
Its hyacinths,
Scabbing at the shore.

UP THE NILE
[2nd Oct 1976, The Sudd, Sudan]

We were paddling on a boat
Up the river Nile,
On the bank the trees grew,
Tall and straight, and wild.

We chugged on through the jungle,
A thousand miles in length –
Steaming out of rain storms,
Steering round long bends.

EVERYONE'S COMPLETELY SMASHED
[24th Oct 1976, Kappoeta, Sahel, Sudan]

From Khartoum, up to Kathmandu,
From Kabul, down to Kinshasa –
Everyone is blowing grass,
Everyone is wrecked on hash,
Everyone's completely smashed
On ganja, bang and charis.

DEATH OF SUMMER
[3rd Nov 1976, Lokichogio, Turkana, Kenya]

Let me take you in my hand
Through the fields of slaughter –
Past the years of uncut grass
Down the path of slumber –
Onwards to the days of breath
Beyond a given number –
To seek a meeting with your death,
A slow and crippling murder –
At the jaws of Winter's cur,
Cruel, deceiving Autumn.

Until your life is squeezed and crushed,
Your green a conquered black –
until your gentle, soft caress
is stilled by Autumn's bark –
until the point your light of day
is cut by Winter's dark –
until at last your breath is cold,
your body white, your stare is stark.

OUT OF THE DESERT
[26th Nov 1976, Kitale, Kenya]

Stepping from the innocent wilderness
Into the concrete jungle of sophisticated,
Wheeling dealing down-town Kitale.

Just tripping on nightclubs, bars, and loose women;
Spade-type suits on henchman type dudes –
Fast talking, moving, jiving people,
Zipping, zooning, zapping evil.

Hitting the beers, crashing the ash,
Splashing the cash, living real flash
- just amazing.

Stepping from the bush into the concrete jungle
Of downtown Kitale.

THE HITCH HIKER
[10th Jan 1977, Livingstone, Zambia]

There was young hiker
Who was sick to the teeth,
So he hitched across Europe
To the Indian truth –
He searched for a guru
But instead found himself,
Then returned to the concrete
Contended, but with little else.

He went back to his habits
Of dope, beer and bed;
Signed on the dole -
Felt it was good for his health,
Met a young woman
Who gave him sheer hell,
Until having enough –
He trucked off, sick once again.

The desire for change
In the African vein,
Gave him malaria
But straightened his aims;
He saw the new sunrise
As a dream he'd slept through;
Finally, he realised
What it was he should do.

He went back to the concrete,
The jungle, the race –
Cut at his hair,
Shaved at his face,
Held down a job,
Married his hell –
Then steeped in the boredom

Withdrew into his shell.

But then came an explosion
And wrecked him again,
When he started to think
'Christ where will this end?
I'm heading for nowhere,
Got to get off my ass!'
So he abandoned his wife,
His three kids, packed up his bags.

'But where will I go?'
he asked of himself –
'India's no mystery,
and Africa's the past.'
He looked to the sky –
'I'll reach for the stars!
I'll future the cosmos,
Find galactic highs!'

While down on the earth
His children played on,
His wife cried in sorrow,
For her husband was gone –
As two men in white coats
Led him away,
To a straight-jacket life
And a world of grey.

BLACK SUNRISE
[27th Jan 1977, Johannesburg, South Africa]

So Soweto finally broke the chains of bondage,
my bonnie yappies.
its made you think that blacks aren't happy
being slaves.
and soon you better watch out for those
militant kaffirs;
for once Zimbabwe's free, your slaves are next to be
the new world braves.

LYING POETS
[7th March 1977, Johannesburg, South Africa]

The words issue forth like tumbling waterfalls,
As alliteration allures addictively in every situation.
Yet all the phrases uttered in despair
Are hardly compensated by the semantics aired
By the university educated bard – who's never
Experienced life as hard, and tough, and shitty
Beyond real words – who's never hit rock bottom,
Or been disturbed beyond the frivolous nice sounding
lines made neat, and trim, and pretty one hundred
times rewritten until the message dies – and all that's left
are metered rhymes and stanzas of premeditated lies.

DOWN AND OUT

49

[7th Mar 1977, Johannesburg, South Africa]

Down and out without a cent –
Temptation is trying to make me bent.
I'm trying hard to play it straight –
Hell knows when I'll get that break
To take me back on the road –
To happiness and freedom.

TUT-TUT IN THE VALLEY OF THE KINGS
[April 1977, Johannesburg, South Africa]

(I) The Tomb

Sixty discovered, six open
To the eroding steps of visitors.

Biban el Muluk, Tutankamun's the smallest.
Dug deep into the bedrock,
Downwards carved a hundred feet.
Downward steps – passing faded
Coloured wall-crafted hieroglyphics;
The dark enclosing – finally opening
Into the burial chamber, the sarcophagus
That housed the Pharaoh and his wealth
Before the robbers came and stripped
The tomb of its priceless treasures.

To take to Cairo, Paris, London.
New York, Tokyo – around the world
Several times and back.

The tomb now bare – the stone sarcophagus
Empty – the Pharaoh snatched to decompose,
Consumed by jet lag.

(ii) The God Of Afterlife Ignored

Osiris shed a tear for another lost one.

Curse that Carter – and cursed he was,
Fooling himself he acted for posterity.
The bandwagon-haggling over artefacts,
While selfishly unconcerned about the spiritual –
Unlike Osiris.

The cultured always fool themselves.
They are no better than the looters
Of the millenniums, the robbers spurned by greed,
Jabbing horses sides like Spaniards –
Eyes turned green by gold – the heart left
Untouched – their spirits cheaply bartered.

(iii) The Left Overs

In the chamber the Pharaoh's biography remains.

Endless rows of figures on the walls –
A lifetime's work by the artists of Karnak.
I wonder at their devotion for their king,
Each artist unaware that their descendants
Would reflect and wonder at their work.

They, by time worn acclaim, are successful;
They, the artists are immortal -
Not just Anubis, Apis and Aten.

GET OFF MY BACK (song)
[20th Apr 1977, Johannesburg, South Africa]

Get off my back!
I can't stand your laugh.
Get off my back!
Before I knock you, Jack!

I can't pay my rent,
I would pay every cent,
I'm out of work,
I'm out of luck.

If I could I'd leave,
So don't act smart!
'Cause if you do,
I'll knock you, Jack!

Get off my back!
Before I knock you, Jack!

ITS JUST NOT LIKE HOME
[23rd April 1977, Newcastle, England]

Goodbye Johannesburg, South Africa,
Hello, Europe, England – I'm back.
Nice to see you all again.

Would you like to sip my African wine?
It's none of your shitty stuff.
But gee, it's nice to be back.

How's things? Snow, colds, unemployment?
Inflation and no hash? Deary me!
It's still nice to be back – Africa was fine -
But it's just not home.

SEVEN SOULS ADRIFT
[Spring 1977, Newcastle]

Wrecked and slung adrift,
aboard a raft, seven souls apart,
in search of the mainland.

The pessimist is moaning that
things are bad, tomorrow will be worse,
floating on is prolonging his end.

51

The egocentric enjoying the adventure
is settled in the best part of the raft
as he tucks into the rations.

The optimist knows tomorrow will be better,
he's not afraid, things are not so bad,
everything will work out.

The observer notes the happenings
of the others in his logbook, plus
the behaviour of the sea and the winds.

The altruist wants nothing for himself,
he assists the others in their suffering,
gives them everything he has.

The stoic not believing in anything,
to him death or rescue is the same -
fate will steer their course..

To the child it is all a dream,
the nightmare will be explained tomorrow
and a shoreline will appear.

Seeking the horizon, he stares ahead
but everywhere is blue sea,
the waves the only scars.

SATURDAY NIGHT
[21st May 1977, Newcastle]

Saturday night highlight –
Going to the pub and getting drunk,
Involved in the gossip
Of who slept with who last night.

Yet it all seems normal,
The talks polite, the introductions formal,
With occasional hints of boredom,
Overshadowing the party still to come.

Outside – a cloudy night -
Ringing footsteps find the right house,
Give a knock, someone opens up
To let us in.

The music is blaring, party-goers
Standing, leaning, dancing, moving –
Smiles all around –
It's nice to see the usual faces.

Have you got a drink?
I never got round to bringing a bottle.
I like the music –
Fancy letting go and having a jig?
You're moving well – how come

You haven't been around for ages?
Been away somewhere?
Still working in the city, maybe?

Really out of touch ....
I lost out on that encounter –
Approaching others, but the phrases
Are wearing thin.

Got a light?
Hell, it's really getting late –
The women leaving, the guys
Drinking on the dog-end dregs.

I guess it's home, nothing left
To make a stay worthwhile;
Anyone I know? Nope ...
No one living down my way.

Heading up the road, black cats
Staring from high walls –
Front door key – Saturday night
And going home to bed, alone.

ROSIE
[29th May 1977, Newcastle]

Rosie, Novocastrian Liverpudlian,
Stare intent, smile forgiving,
Wanting nothing else
But to give yourself
And keep on giving.

THREE WAY AFFAIR
[4th Jun 1977, Newcastle]

Really dig this chick,
But my best friend's in the way.
Every time we look,
His shadow lurks, as if to say –

'Please I am a nice guy,
Please don't hurt me in this way,
I met her first.
So let me have this break –

I'm sure she's going to love me,
If you give me time to make
Her understand my love.
Please do it for my sake.'

How can I tell him?
Should I tell him straight?
Should I really let the chick
Know the situation -

How we've come entangled

In a three way love affair –
Where we lovers are kept apart
By my best friend's stare.

AFTER THE QUEEN'S JUBILEE (song)
[8th June 1977, Newcastle]

I got kind of drunk last night,
Ended up standing out in the crowd.
I usually blend in with the scene,
But last night I freaked out
And ended up using foul language,
Gyrating my body quite obscenely.

Everybody laughed, or looked the other way,
Some played along, I was doing the entertaining
Being a one man cavalcade,
Being a one man cavalcade.

Earlier, everything had gone right,
Then I met this chick who told me
I knew nothing – I just didn't understand,
So I said 'To hell! Screw you!'

I went on the booze, became degrading,
Knocked holes in egos, screamed at the band –
Everyone thought I was another punk rocker,
Some even thought I was a New Wave shocker,

Then I met another drunk –
She was also doing some screaming,
I swayed in her direction,
And we found ourselves competing.

I got kind of drunk last night,
Ended up standing out in the crowd.

DYING FOR A CAUSE
[12th June 1977, Newcastle]

As a realist viewing the world,
He didn't understand,
The subtleties of nature
And its wandering roving hand –
He didn't have intuition,
He didn't have much at all,
He didn't know the proverb –
Pride before a fall.

And down and down he tumbled,
Hurting all the way,
The realist lost to nature,
Nature had its say –
He developed inhibitions,
He dwelt on foolish dreams,
He believed in foolish ideas
And idiotic schemes.

As realist, now idealist
On the absurdities of life,
A semi-politician
Who sanctified all strife –
He now had intuition,
He had it all to give –
Yet foolishly he'd forgotten
Why it was he lived.

NOT QUITE A FEMINIST
For Caroline
[21st Aug 1977, Newcastle]

A woman in search of the mystic,
Bar what she's already found
To be non-existent.

A woman who love to live,
And is loved for living
By the ones who have nothing to give.

A woman surrounded by the weak,
The boys, the little crying babies,
The mediocre and the meek.

A woman who wants a man,
To hack down the weeds
And face her with her garden.

A woman with a need -
That none can fill
While her heart bleeds.

WE PICTURED OURSELVES
For Diana
[30th Aug 1977, Newcastle]

We pictured ourselves in a beautiful garden
Where only the ones who saw beauty in nettles
Saw beauty they could handle.

Too many stings have smitten our gardeners.
They shy, turning to their roses –
To the beauty of delicate petals they fatally damage.

Yet we know differently; how not to be stung.
Those wonderful nettles – caress them gently,
Let their acids - not burn.

It's said they smother the roses.
Ah, those poor roses! Need we feel their pain?
Fertile upon the finest soil.

If the roses cannot fight should they survive?
Why must the nettles be uprooted,
Cast aside, and left to die?

Are we not compassionate gardeners?
Let us brush aside our dock leaves,
And leave the roses to the weak at heart.

LEAVING NEWCASTLE
[9th Sep 1977, Newcastle]

Granville, our days are almost over,
I turn to Stockton in despair,
Yet London lingers in my thoughts,
My heart, belongs there.

I'm tossed between three homes –
One is old, one is new, and one
Is where I want to be –
Time will make it clear.

IN MAN'S IMAGINATION
[October 1977, Newcastle-upon-Tyne]

In man's imagination,
the face of cubed Picasso,
a jar of ripe tomatoes,
two shoulders side by side sleeping on,
lying bare in life's aquarium,
a unicorn or bird at dawn.

THE ROAD TO WHERE?
[1st Dec 1977, Newcastle]

Fucked up again,
Is it expression or pain
That brings the tears pouring down.
Screwed in the head ,
The body's a mess,
Feeling that life's a pointless end.
Strange.
Where to begin on the road –
The road?
The road to where?

WHY DO WOMEN TAKE MY BODY
[28th Dec 1977, Newcastle]

Why do women take my body
And squeeze the life that's left,
Suck on the juice of living
Till I lie here soaked in sweat;
They're not content to listen,
Or be mastered by the tongue –
They'd rather be roughly ridden
Than have their praises sung.

They crave for my attention –
My smile, my wit, my guile,
Behind their coy expressions,

Their passion's running wild;
They lie against my shoulder
And cry of love affairs,
I turn gently to caress them
In their apparent tear'd despair.

And more they cry for loving,
And more and more and more –
My smile. my wit forgotten,
It's lust they're craving for;
That's why they take my body
And squeeze the life that's left,
Suck on the juice of living
Till I lie there soaked in sweat.

CAROL
[25th Jan 1978, Newcastle]

She's tearing up my mind
By being so hard –
Yet she doesn't know
What she's doing at times.

Her mind is fixed
In one track –
And her confusion
Brings a blank.

THE BUS DEPOT CANTEEN
[March 1978, Wheatsheaf, Sunderland]

She fished out a tea-bag from a metal biscuit box,
and threw it into a brown ringed-stained mug.
She poured stewed water over the top,
till the tea-bag surfaced in a splutter and cough.
Then drenched in long-life sickly milk,
she shovelled in sugar to thicken it further,
and sliding the gruel over the splatter marked counter,
she said – 'Five pence a mug, luv. Hope that you like it.'

MAKING CONNECTIONS
[30th Apr 1978, Port of Spain, Trinidad]

The usual waiting ……
Travelling is usually waiting,
For the next bus, or boat,
Or even plane if you're not broke.

Waiting for that next ride,
To move you on to something new.

Then waiting once again,
For the next bus, or boat,
Or even plane – once you're bored.

When the new has passed to old,
And the penalty of boredom,

Is to wait anew.

GUYANA (song)
[5th May 1978, Georgetown, Guyana]

We don't have no soap for our hair,
We don't have no salt for our peanuts,
We don't have no milk for our children,
Heh, tell me what's wrong with Guyana?

We don't have no glass for our windows,
We don't have no bowls for our toilets,
We don't have no books for our libraries,
Heh, tell me what's wrong with Guyana?

We don't have no jobs for our Indians,
We don't have no smile for our Negroes,
We don't have nothing for our Amerindians,
Heh, tell me what's wrong with Guyana?

LIFE'S HARD ON THE ROAD
[6th May 1978, New Nickerie, Surinam]

Life's hard on the road –
The pennies jingling,
The notes jaded, crumpled, torn;
A back pocket as a wallet
In a pair of jeans,
Faded, creased and worn.

THE BANKS OF THE OYAPOCK
[15th May 1978, Saint George, Guyana-Brazil]

By the banks of the Oyapock,
The Amazon growth – matted and wild,
The Indians undiscovered by white men,
Cast their nets for the fish in the night.

By the banks of the Oyapock,
The dug-out canoes – graceful and still,
The Indians, figures outlined in the moonlight,
Haul their nets for the fish in the night.
By the banks of the Oyapock,
The silvery glint – thrashing and tied,
The Indians, white teeth gleaming in knowledge,
That their nets provide for the tribe.

THE THREE LEGIONARIES
[May 1978, St George, French Guiana]

We Legionnaires propping up the bar
No desert sands for us
No Arabs with which to war
For the days of camels are over
The raids in the night are dead
By the strength of a bottle of vino
We'll crawl back to our beds tonight.

We Legionnaires arriving in our boat
We are the finest soldiers
Who ever went afloat
Though the days of camels are over
The raids in the night are dead
We're here to protect our Guyana
For France has need of her yet.

STEERING BY THE STARS
[May 1978, Northern Brazil]

Oh, Orion when I'm dying
Will you cleanse my soul?
Oh, Sirius bright and twinkling
Will you light the road?
Oh, twins of fiery nature
Will you let me go?
To rest up in the heavens
Amidst your sparkle and your glow?

Oh, Centaurus will you hasten
When I'm dying slow?
Oh, Scorpio will you tarry
In dealing the final blow?
Oh, Great Bear will you harken
At the nature of my hope?
To rest up in the heavens
Midst your sparkle and your glow

Oh, I'm tired of steering blindly
By Orion's bow
Oh, I'm weary of the darkness
Sirius's light nightly shows
Oh, I'm longing for the brightness
Of the furthest sparkling pole
To rest up in the heavens
Midst the sparkle and the glow.

PLAIN SAILING
[28 May 1978, Securiju, Brazil]

Give me rough sea, the gathering cloud,
The wind, the wail of the scavenging gull;
The sail full sheet, the waves breaking aft,
The cracking of timber, the sway of the mast.

OLD MAN ATLANTIC
[30th May 1978, North Brazil]

The beautiful sea, his waved greying top,
Combed by the breeze, uncurling his knots,
Bleached by the sun, his last golden locks,
Swept back from his brow by the bow.

AMAZONAS
[1st Jun 1978, River Amazon, Brazil]

Sweet waters of the Amazonas,
The Rio Negro makes you smooth,
And darks your brown –
While by your shores the rubber trickles,
The crocodiles slither,
The toucans hang your jungle
With myriad sound.

Sweet waters of the Amazonas,
Mankind intends to cleanse his wrongs,
And pollute you black –
While by your shore the oil trickles,
The chemicals slither,
The factories slake your jungle
With concrete slag.

I'M BRAZILIAN
[May 1978, Tranamazonas, Brazil]

Take away my drink,
I don't need it,
Take away my dope
I won't want it.
All I ask of you
Is a gentle kiss or two
But don't leave me
When I'm having my siesta.
Don't let me forget
that I'm Brazilian!

THE GIRL FROM IPANEMA
[22nd Jun 1978, Rio de Janeiro, Brazil]

Where was that girl?
I looked on Ipanema;
But all I saw ….
Was hazy Corcovado,
With Christ, outstretched arms
Looking too.

COCA LEAVES
[15th Jul 1978, Cochabamba, Bolivia]

Leaves of broken green and acrid taste,
Ground by an eager jaw on ragged teeth,
Sucked by numbed out tongue in vain relief.
Did Christ take the cross for cocaine's sins?

Black cat on the prowl, doing the rounds,
Razors out his lines in double vision,
Counts one, two, and three in mild derision.
Did Christ take the cross for cocaine's sins.

SOUTH AMERICAN GUNSHOTS
[18th July 1978, La Paz, Bolivia]

Politics of the heart,
Emotion of a sort,
Expressed in an action
Of violence,
Against the negation of words.

As the young cry.
Freedom of thought.
Freedom's what they want,
Not chains,
Not a dictator's bonding laws.

Rise up in anger,
Destroy all the fear,
Tear down the national flag.
It's slavery
Not justice that you have.

Burn down the palace
Drag out the minions.
Hang every single one
On lamp posts.
Finish them all off.

For you need change.
To bury the loss
Of those years of dark,
Of youth wasted,
Your fathers humbled.

The shadow of tyrants.
You shall remove them,
So your old men
Can straighten
Heightened by your youth.

You shall succeed.
Teach your children
To know the value
Of freedom,
And open speech.

For you all know,
That in a lifetime,
One revolution is enough.

CONDOR
[19th Jul 1978, La Paz, Bolivia]

Wingless condor in a windless day,
Carrying wishful messages of peace
Across the desert plains,
Passing through the door of sun,
Diving down to Titicaca's shore,
Where once the Spaniards came
In quest of gold.

BUENOS DIAS
[27th Jul 1978, Aguas Calientes, Peru]

Buenos dias, dear Diegos,
buenos tardes, mulhers,
buenos noches, senhora,
puedo tener cafe?
Si, si, un momento,
espere, por favor,
voy mirar ahora
pero creo no hay.

VANITY
[4th Aug 1978, Lima, Peru]

Its vanity, that's all,
the mirror tells the tale,
self-importance and the rest,
in a silvery image of one's self.

The lies that sleep fixes,
the conscience withholds judgement,
the sole jury, the only witness
in the search for one's soul.

I am God, all alone
to find the spirit in my heart,
the buried burning anger
within my shimmering eyes.

I am deep in self love,
I forget who I am,
if I begin to cry,
it is vanity, that's all.

FIESTA
[29th Jul 1978, Chalhuanca, Peru]

Trumpet and horn,
While drumming along,
While natives in bowlers,
Dance in circles together,
Keeping time with a bottle
That's keeling them over –
As they sway down the street,
The fiesta continues
Far into the night.

COLOMBIAN COPS AIN'T SO BAD
[10th Aug 1978, Guayaquil, Ecuador]

It was a heavy situation,
Cloak and daggered,
Whips at the ready,
Cops soon on hand to drag us
Down to the station
And beat us up.

But it turned into a joke
Of Keystone humour –
Good natured captain
Lounging behind a large wooden desk
In off-hand manner,
Letting us depart with a waving finger,
And a word in our ears
About behaving ourselves.

We, all smiles and chuckles,
Relieved at our freedom,
Went skipping into the sun filled day;
Praising justice,
Extolling liberty,
Thankful at our skill
To tell bold lies,
Agreeing they should have locked us up
Just the same.

QUITO
[13th Aug 1978, Quito, Ecuador]

Quito was quiet in the still of the night,
the flycatchers winged silently
catching insects in flight.

MARIJUANA
[15th Aug 1978, Pasto, Columbia]

Its starts. The grass begins to grow,
blow in clouds to shroud my head,
to dream away in bed.
Tomorrow's but an ounce away,
to fill my head with fancy thoughts.

BELIEVING TO RECEIVE
[20th Aug 1978, Botata, Columbia]

God, when I am broke
and five thousand miles from home,
and no-one wants to help
or spare some cash to help me on,
when the hunger's taking root
and the pains are growing in length
and the cries of deep frustration
stem from self concern.

The gift of one banana
or meagre loaf of bread,
or single piece of meat
from a plate with little left,
sums up the word of 'giving',
the meaning 'to receive' -
the experience of hunger
has taught me to believe.

63

SUICIDE ACT
[22nd Aug 1978, Turbo, Colombia]

Stuck between the going on,
And the point of no return.
Held up, broke and hungry,
With little hope of moving on.

I have no chance of catching
The shadows in the night,
Exchanging hope for despair
I've lost all my rights.

For I'm nothing without my courage,
My will to combat life.
I care nothing for my freedom,
I've given up the fight.

Tomorrow will bring nothing,
Tonight I die alone.
Tonight I take my own life,
For which I shall not mourn.

So do not pity suicide,
It glorifies the act;
Forget I died of hunger
And be nourished by that fact.

LIVING ON CREDIT
[27th Aug 1978, Port Obaldia, Darien, Panama]

Living on credit,
never receiving a debit,
never seeing a one dollar bill.
Living O'Reilly,
at the expense of old Barclays,
with cheques far from a till.

OLD MAN ON A PARK BENCH
[28th Aug 1978, Port Obaldia, Panama]

Blow blossom, blow wind
Through the trees of the mind.
Blow helpless, blow gently,
Scatter leaves on my past.

Hush quickly, hush quietly,
The autumn returned –
Coat softly, coat velvet,
The pains of gone love.

For the wind howls swiftly
Over crab-crinkled boughs,
Gathering the seasons,
While beginning to plough

The past into future,

The past's scattered leaves,
Helplessly blown
In an attempt to deceive

The old man's own memory
Of what was before.
A clarity of reason
That sensibility has bourn -

To make the old man
Remember an age
Of romance, emotions
Of passionate rage –

That since then has gone
And left him to gaze
At Springs falling blossom,
Rather sadly replaced -

By hazes of old age
In its last final blaze,
The slumber of waiting,
A solitary wait,

For the wind to come rushing,
To silence the birds,
Hushing a stillness,
A murmur of words –

Blowing blossom, blowing wind
Through the trees of the mind.
Hushing quickly, hushing quietly,
The thoughts of old time.

YOUNG CAPTAIN COSMOS
[7th Sep 1978, Taboga Isle, Gulf of Panama]

I supposed him an old sea-dog
Hit by hard times –
But he turned into a captain,
Harbour locked by design.

He was the youngest afloat
The Pacific sea-board,
But time was fast gaining
On his barnacled boat.

Oh young Captain Cosmos,
Just wasted away –
He'd deserted the wind,
And traded the waves.

His sails needed mending,
The anchor a new chain,
The hull wanted painting,
His deck was salt-stained.

But he lay on his bunk,
Rolling the waves –
In the safety of harbour
In a Pacific coast bay.

I watched on as first mate
As my captain declined,
And I felt growing anger
In the seas of my mind.

I unslung my hammock,
And we then parted ways,
I shipped out of harbour
Of that Pacific coast bay.

I gazed back at the Princess,
The captain's doomed ship,
And watched to my horror
As she began to side-slip.

I saw young Captain Cosmos
Erect at the bow,
As the Princess keeled over
And finally went down.

I supposed him an old sea-dog
Hit by hard tides –
But he turned into a captain
Harbour locked for all time.

BELIEFS
[12ᵗʰ Sep 1978, Panama City]

When the pages of one's life,
Blow out the window,
Bourn by a storm that's raging –

The feeling that the heart
Stops ticking -
And the damage to the mind they're leaving

Is not relieved by forgetting
- a loss -
That's not regained by recollecting.

SCANDAL MONGERING
[14ᵗʰ Sep 1978, Panama City]

May I stop to curse the dawn
Of evil thoughts and abject wrongs,
Raised against her noble head.

For me, she is the one I love
And no one in the depth of anger
Shall wrought lies in sweet revenge.

For I am the protector of my maiden's honour,

For in my bosom rests my
Maiden's heart.

CREATIVITY
[15th Sep 1978, Taboga, Panama]

Night draws in – and the artist lost in ink,
Little knowing where the next stroke
Will lead his thought.

His imagination, once so immersed in reality
Now quickly altered to flounder momentarily
In the dark.

The light and vision of his work,
Lost beneath a wave of endless new frightening
Possibilities.

SELF INDULGENCE
[17th Sep 1978, Panama City]

The erect penis, and the steady hand,
Teasing, squeezing, stroking,
Extracting warming juices,
With a fragrance mutely floating,
Across the barrier of man.

With the rising, inner wanting,
Tempered with a sexual longing,
Frustrating ever haunting,
For the release of nature's giving
That symbolises man.

For without woman's coupled body,
Deemed as instrumental normal,
He turns an inner dwelling,
To a sin that's only mortal
That typifies all men.

PARTING
[18th Sep 1978, Panama]

When the love flows over and out,
And down beyond the edges,
To the limits of restraint.

When the longing for desire departs,
And loses all momentum
Beneath the pain.

When rejection of well meant intention,
Is spurned and hurled backwards
As abuse.

Then it's time to burn the bridges of approach,
And retreat in hasty action of divorce,
Before the massacre ensues.

THE AFRICAN GIRL
For Carol
[28th Sep 1978, Newcastle]

From the mountains of Morocco,
she came garnished in sea shells,
with a smile to stir the waves
on to the pounding English shore.

To the bleak moors of Northumberland,
She went to be tarnished by the cold winds,
Made bitter by an east-chill
So typical of home.

And there banished in a northern field,
She cried – her tears evoking
a song bird to softly lullaby
her Moorish sighs.

THE SYSTEM
[26th Oct 1978, Newcastle]

Existing, more than just,
Living with a lust for life,
Greater than the forces out to hinder and restrain,
The progress of the questing mind –

Going beyond the boundaries of conditioning,
Forced upon the individual by a benefactor
Who guides divergent thought
Into the funnel of opportunity –

That channels all the minor tracks
Back upon themselves,
To converge as abstract ways
On the beaten path -

And life quite simply nut-shelled as –
A house, a job, a car.

LOVE HUMANISES
[2nd Nov 1978, Newcastle]

Love straddles the body
And empties the thoughts
Of all other idle curiosities
Regarding life.

Love encompasses the being
Like a shrouding mist,
And envelops in its veil
A cloak of secrecy.

Love embellishes the heart
With gentle tears,
For tender reminiscences

Of lovers in the past.

Love humanises the soul
In enlightenment,
And opens up the void
To show compassion.

THE GIRL IN THE PONCHO
[9th Nov 1978, Newcastle]

You breezed into my life about noon,
And asked if you could without being prude,
Take my dog for a walk.

I was as busy as hell writing my book,
And you upset my rhythm with your sweet euphemism
'I'll be coming back in awhile'.

I tried sensibly to ignore your return –
But your innocent style and childish smile,
Had me head over heels wrapped in love.

LENNY
[26th Nov 1978, Akenside Terrace, Newcastle]

She rang my door bell,
Then asked me shyly
If I could remember who she was.

I had been expecting her,
But showed great surprise
As I let her in.

With the log fire ablaze,
The candle illuminating her face,
How could I not fall in love.

GREY TITS
[30th Nov 1978, Newcastle]

Settling in for winter
Midst falling snow,
And withering garden poppies.

Idly watching grey tits
Steal discarded tit-bits
From the wheelbarrow.

Stroking my agile dog,
Eager in her instinct
To be off in hot pursuit.

READING IN CHEAP ACCOMMODATION
[12th Dec 1978, Akenside Terr, Newcastle]

With the grey light,
unique in its setting,

in the dawns and winter days
of festive England.

Reading from a book
'neath the opaque rays
of dull and cheap
bought light-bulb hours –

destroys the vision
of a childhood's brilliance,
and decays the twenty-twenty
of a young man's life.

PARAGUAYAN MORMONS
[19th Dec 1978, Newcastle]

Oh we are two wide-eyed Mormons,
Spreading out the word,
Who dance and sing and like to think
It's in the name of God –

But really all we're doing
Is running form ourselves,
Convinced we know the answers
From within our empty selves.

Oh we'd love to go to Rio
And try the rumba thing,
We'd love to visit Chile
For the wine we cannot drink –

We'd cry to see old Lima,
Of the drugs we've heard so much –
But we're hooked up in religion
As saviours of the Church.

Oh we'd love to break our morals,
And go back to being slaves,
In a world full of sorrows
And of people filling graves –

But we haven't got the courage,
We no longer feel that brave,
We are blind to all the changes
Because we are afraid.

So we go on with our conversations,
With humour and with plum,
We endeavour to spread wisdom
On you and everyone –

We try to make it easy,
But it isn't always fun,
Though we hope you understand,
We're trying to harm no one.

LONELY CHRISTMAS

[23rd Dec 1978, Newcastle]

It's almost Christmas and there's no snow;
Tradition lets us down again.
The radio stations of the world
Are jingling bells and interviewing
Thoughtful people passing helpful words
Of love to the lonely.

It sounds sad –
Yet Christmas underneath it all
Is a sad time of realisation at where
And with whom, one stands alone
Or on the fringes of care –
As others go off home to be
With Ma and Pa.

What would many say if they knew
That your Christmas dinner was
A half pound of sausages
And a boiled parsnip?

No one's so unfortunate –
But Christmas highlights the alienation
Of living on one's own.
It hides the truth 'neath the tinsel
And the gifts beneath the tree.

TIME TICKS BY
[27th Dec 1978, Akenside Terr, Newcasle]

With Christmas gone,
And all the wrapping paper
Crinkled in the dustbins
To await collection –
Time moves on to the New Year.

Yet, we must wait,
Each ticking second,
From the Christmas let-down
To the drinks of Hogmanay.

The last hours of the year,
Edging forwards,
With a week of quick remembrance
Of the fifty-one before.

The final waiting days
Of another festive season,
That work pervades
And money leaves an empty pocket.

As we all wait for New Year,
As time ticks,
We hang the past,
And raise our hopes.

NEW YEAR 1979
[2nd Jan 1979, Newcastle]

Another anno,
Another carnival over,
And the seriousness of life
Waiting with a hangover
In the heavy morn.

WEST COAST LIFE
[4th May 1979, Seattle, Washingston State]

LA, Frisco, Portland, Washington,
A West Coast hike from Sun State,
Through Oregon –
Green trees, black roads,
Blue skies over mountains high,
Pacific waves and silver fish,
And shells in the sand.
Seattle, Spokane, Olympic, Rainer –
Washington State,
Without its beauty -
Red lights, walk signs,
Squirrels dancing there,
Campus girls with golden hair
And bluebells 'neath the trees.

U of W meets 15th at 45th,
College types -
Lying in the grass to think,
Dreaming on white clouds,
On coffee cups and raindrops,
Everything of student work
That makes for simple life.

While at 16th and 52nd,
A writer –
Smokes a reefer every hour,
Sees only blank walls,
Dying plants and cheap bulbs,
Living with his type-machine,
Alone and unaware.

JAKE'S CORNER
[15th May 1979, Beaver Creek, Yukon, Canada]

It's beautiful here. Tranquil and picturesque.
The small hotel and gas station,
With its free ice-cream for every customer.
The road to Atlin winding down to the frozen lake.
The sun still high, the breeze cool and icy.
The mountains glazed in snow – the Alaskan
Highway long and stretching and deserted.

Out in the bush, always, the cry of birds,
Singing their spring songs, helping the sun
along in its battle against the ice.

Soon the trees will be breaking into leaf,
The flowers into blossom, and the grass into seed.

THE AMERICAN TRAVELLER
[21st May 1979, Seattle, Washington State]

Back in Seattle, looking to settle,
Mellow out and search for a job.
Or instead head for Frisco,
Or across to Dakota –
To a friend out in Fargo
Who'll be busy all summer
Playing music and spaced out on pot.

Or what about Palm Beach,
To lie in the noon heat,
And bake out on cocaine and snort.
Or the bubble of New York,
To hussle the back street,
To get pissed and run with the dogs.

Or the jazz of New Orleans,
Walking to blue-beat,
Wher lamp-posts prop up the broads.
Or freeway-land LA,
Jacked up on bad speed,
To be choked and gagged on the smog.

As the rain in Seattle,
Fallls real, and falls gentle –
Summer slips by green and wet.
For to remain in Seattle,
Is the question to settle,
Before melancholy makes me inert.

OLD MAN PHILIP
[28th May 1979, Seattle, Washington State]

Old man Philip
Rolled the brush along –
With painting cares
That greyed his hair
But never aged his spirit.

IT
[1st June 1979, Seattle, Washington State]

Women plan it,
Men don't understand it,
In between that difference,
Lies the lie.

Hearts rule it,
Heads ruin it,
And bodies make it speak
Before it dies.

Children take it,
Aged break it,
Rulers turn its power
Into war.

Hate beats it,
Greed defeats it,
Time rots its apple
To the core.

Fools deride it,
Pride blinds it,
Rejection when its given
Kills the soul.

The wise take it,
The smart make it,
It fills their all
With its gold.

ALASKA
[5th June 1979, Seattle, Washington State]

Alaska's snowy hoary wastes
That beckoned gold-diggers, then oil sheiks
Was long before I drove and lost my nerve
On the road into the deepest north
Of Arctic fox and permafrost –

Now go-go girls dance and sing,
Paid in kind by the rugged rich
Who slave their guts welding line,
Canning fish, or trapping fur –
Out their minds in drunken stupor,
Fleeced by robbing pimps, rip-off tykes
Who've forced Alaskans to sell up -
Make way for the rotting future.

VAGRANT OF THE WORLD
[10th June 1979, Seattle, Washington State]

The broken steps of Macchu Picchu,
I climbed not long ago –
The raging falls of Livingstone
To which I barred my soul –
The holy waters of Benares
Where I lost my hope –
The majestic powers of the Taj
Said words I never spoke.

The drifting sands by Pharaohs tombs
Withheld a timeless power –
The Herat fort Iskander built
Detracted and devoured –
The bleakness of the Roman Wall
Awed and it inspired –
The slender columns on Athens's hills

Set history's torch on fire.

Six minarets of Islam's might
Held my Byzantium in a spell –
The Rio Christ outstretched arms
In grace before, I knelt –
The Golden Temple of the Sikhs
Dwarfed my beggar man –
While Siddartha's fragile boa tree
Gave shade on my content.

The bottomless pit of Kimberley
Threw diamonds from its depths –
The obelisk of Hatshepsut
Needled hieroglyphic death –
The treasure house of Paris art
Drew a smile that paralysed –
The artefacts of Inca gold
Blinded my weakened eyes.

The Colosseum of Caesar times
Echoed roaring lions –
The neat white crosses of Verdun
Recalled fields of iron –
The Lucknow fort of blood red brick
Relived an Empire's trial –
The missing nose of Giza's sphinx
Napoleon's marching files.

The visions bought by travelling far
subverts modern standards –
The foreign culture of abroad
Oft as left me branded –
The bridges crossed into these worlds
Here I have reflected–
The pictures of a vagrant life
Is all I have intended.

IRELAND
[13th June 1979, Seattle, Washington State]

For centuries the battles have raged,
Irish hands have been blood-stained,;
In cypress shadows the children have been raised
In endless wakes, the morning broken
By Fenian blasts or Loyalist shots –
The covenant of the Lord – broken.

THURSDAY NIGHT POKER
[29th June 1979, Fairbanks, Alaska]

Who's in for poker?
If so, bring some beer …
We're going to have a party.
The game's at my place tonight –
I'm lining up the shots of tequila,
So get your asses moving

And come on over.

You name it, we'll play it –
From High Chicago
To Follow the Whore –
Or Mexican Sweat –
Or Five Card Draw with Jacks
Or better to open to win –
Seven Card Stud, or whatever.
Just bring some beer.

THE GALS OF ALASKA (song)
[5th July 1979, Fairbanks, Alaska]

It is the time to loosen my tongue
And let out a howl, then ease to a hum,
Set free my heart with a wilderness song
Straight like a trail that bumps right along –

Oh the gals of Alaska, so sweet and so pure,
They'll take a man's heart and he'll never be cured.

I'll tell of my days in Fairbanksian bars,
My nights with those gals under the Northern stars,
A bottle in hand, and the Lights as my guide
Making love by the pipeline over Quarter Mile side

Oh the gals of Alaska, so sweet and so pure,
They'll take a man's heart and he'll never be cured.

THE CANNERY BLUES
[25th July 1979, Seward, Alaska]

Who wouldn't gets the cannery blues
When a toke of marijuana,
Or a lunch-time beer obliterates,
And wipes away the slime
Of another fourteen hour day
Bent over the silver salmon
That finds its way onto the tables
Of families living high on life.

Back in the cannery,
Slimmers slit the lumps of flesh,
Rip the guts and innards,
Inspect, and score and scale
The King of Fish –
Until it disappears as a silver slush
Along a chute headed for the canner
And a half-pound home of metal,
Destined to be shelved at a store,
And bought by some housewife
For some outrageous retail price.

BACK TO LIVING
[21st Aug 1979, Anchorage, Alaska]

I can hardly believe the work is over
And I can get back to life.
Twenty nine days of slog at the cannery
And I need a rest.
It reminds me of quitting the oil rigs –
The same physical exhausted feeling,
The constant desire to sleep,
The vacuum left by having spare time
After a period in which very minute
Was accounted for.

MOUNT MARATHON
[23rd Aug 1979, Seward, Alaska]

Resurrection Bay stretched exquisitely south
to meet the Pacific Ocean. The piercing mountains
hemmed in the dark blue arm of sea dotted
with tiny sailing boats and a large lumber ship
trailing timber, heading for port.

Gouged out cums and ragged crags knifing
north from razor cut arêtes – hollowed and sheltered
timeless snows and glaciers from the Arctic sun.

Conifers of spruce and firs halted the eye
from tracing the ice down gullies and canyons
to the very sea. A warm southern wind made
hardly a ripple of white to disturb the calm.

THE BEACHCOMBER
[28th Aug 1979, Kodiak Island, Alaska]

Howling gales are all too common,
Splintered boats to deepest fathom,
Drift ashore locked in flotsam,
Beach combed up, lost in flames
To the reaper of the waves,
Sitting with his star-struck gaze.

Lost to all the world over,
Wind swept souls perdu at sea,
Gusty fires sweep the heart-ache,
Steal the voice and lonely hope,
Replaced by a mighty blankness,
Tighter than the wettest rope.

Forgotten lives are time immortal,
Saddened figures – we know them all,
Raging storms we learn to live with,
Feel the pulse of nature's war,
Thrown at the broken shoreline,
At the man who knows no love.

GOING TO HAWAII
[5th Sept 1979, Fairbanks, Alaska]

Paradise, being what it is –

I'm expecting to eat a lot of fruit,
Stroll a lot of beach,
And catch up on a lot of sleep.

LEAVING ALASKA
[6th Sept 1979, Anchorage, Alaska]

Some call it Oil-Capital of America,
Others - Last of the Wild Frontier,
Where pipelines are in confrontation
With the natives hunting seals.

Tourists fondly recall the snow peaks,
A number can name all the bars –
And most can't forget the long evenings
Or the night sky without any stars.

For Alaska is Alaska, and no less
A state once founded on gold –
Where a man is a man in his own right
And an old man at twenty years old.

I came to Alaska in Seventy Nine,
I arrived unshaven and broke –
I worked fifteen hours a day on average
And left with a wallet of notes.

THE LOWER FORTY-EIGHT
[8th Sept 1979, Anchorage, Alaska]

Alaska, I ask you –
What are you going to do?
Wrapped in wool
By government rules,
They are slowly fleecing you.

THE LIFE OF A BUM
[21st Sept 1979, Lydgate State Park, Kauai, Hawaii]

Flying high on full sail,
Just breezing along –
With my girl overseas,
And a reason to sing,
A reason for whiskey,
A reason for rum,
An object for living
The life of a bum.

PAINTING A PICTURE
[22nd Sept 1979, Lydgate, Kauai, Hawaii]

When a coca-cola can
Without its quaffed brew,
Becomes a ready cup
For a coco split in two –
The turquoise of the ocean
Prints an artist's view,

That roots the painter's easel
And halts his brushing hues.

For his eye in subtle magic
Transcends the tropic hues,
That belie a postcard's softness
To crush and harshly bruise –
As in person on the shoreline
The artist dabs anew,
The kaleidoscopic ocean
Ripens wholesome, fresh reviewed.

LOVELY HAWAIIAN MAIDENS (song)
[25th Sept, Lydgate, Kauai, Hawaii]

Captain Cook blundered
As God ripped asunder –
His blood dripped red on the shore.
The Owyhee'ns turned savage,
Devoured and savaged,
A man their maidens adored.

Then later the whalers,
Four-year mast sailors –
Their lust so patiently stored;
Would watch as the maidens,
Naked and swimming,
Climbed ready and giving, aboard.

And now it's no different
In Oahu's light districts
Or Waikiki Beach dance-floors;
If the pockets play jingle,
And the eye holds a twinkle,
The maidens will love you as yore.

THE HUNTERS
[28th Sept 1979, Kokee, Kauai, Hawaii]

Green in its shadow, bright in its sky,
The mynah birds cry to the winds –
Storms pass through as whistling words
As strangers tarry in the towering woods
offering shelter and shade to wild creatures.

These visitors, armed and round bellied
Who come to take all that they want –
Depart with their trophies, spoil and gain,
Unknowing leaving their souls behind -
Lost in a wood of far greater deception.

THE SECOND OF OCTOBER
[2nd Oct 1979, Kokee, Kauai, Hawaii]

Today is a day of non-thought
Spent lingering in the sunshine
Being close to nature and to life -

Feeling not a heartbeat,
Nor a stirring of the soul
That usually stirs the mind.

For today is a time lock,
Tied in tangled vines
And captured now forever –

Stored as a keepsake
To ponder over slowly
As a time sublime.

Today is a day of all days
That listens to the silence
That seals this final line.

ON SKID ROW
[14th Oct 1979, San Francisco, California]

Being broke sometimes ain't no fun.
The feeling of deprivation -
brought on by a hungry and a knotted stomach
is further intensified by being destitute
in a hostile city.

The streets of San Francisco are paved
With many such men down on their luck,
Crippled by work, and maimed by a society
That is at a loss to help them.

In other finer cities, the citizens turn
Their heads the other way on seeing a bum
Collecting ciggy-butts, or wine-eyed slumped.

In Frisco it is hard to turn one's head
Without eyeing a worse case of hardship –
The lonely figure with the shakes –
The bum talking to himself.

These bums are no different from their
Counterparts in Bombay or Calcutta –
Living their lives by hand-outs, sorting through
The garbage that others see fit to discard.

Only their dis-figurations make them less
Obvious a case for making them social outcasts -
Yet on closer look, many dockside winos
Or park grass-dwellers are mental-home rejects,
Disability pensioners, one-time petty crooks
Who couldn't make a living by petty crime.

Few are there by choice – circumstance
Has led them down a road of degradation,
Left them jobless, homeless, spouse-less
And utterly useless to the general community.
In Dickens's London, through the eyes of a child,

80

The same world existed as now in San Francisco
Where I find myself on Skid Row.

CANNERY ROW VISITED
[15th Oct 1979, Monterey, California]

A cold wind blew along Cannery Row,
The workers looked haggard and old;
Eighteen long hours they hungered their lives,
Lay bare their muscles for gold –
That gleamed in the eye of the bartender's wife
And the girl next-door - a whore,
The work-shy who only worked at night -
Thieving everyone on Cannery Row.

MONTEREY BAY
[17th Oct 1979, Pacific Grove, California]

Silent flies the gull,
Soundless swims the cod –
But roaring breaks the ocean,
Foaming, churning surf.

NO HOLLYWOOD BUNGALOW
[30th Oct 1979, Hollywood, Los Angeles]

Those LA nights –
Hollywood striving, fighting –
My heart pounding, frightened
Not for myself, but for the future
Beneath Sunset's famous lights.

The running never stops –
Only the looking back
Takes longer to forget.

HOLLYWOOD
[4th Nov 1979, San Diego, California]

Strung on the thread
That wove the coat of fame -
Success wore a dress –
Spun from the cloth
Of another's distress
And cloak of pain.

IMPERIAL VALLEY
[9th Nov 1979, Mayan Hotel, El Centro, Calif]

Home in the valley,
A bed down by the tracks,
In a beat-up old motel
Besides a lettuce patch –

Where gypsies camp or tarry,
Where vagrants soil their hands,
Where winter blows in workers

81

Who migrate from other lands

DISENCHANTMENT
[11th Nov 1979, El Centro, California]

How come, as every day passes
I feel the need I must be somewhere else?
How come as each moment ceases,
I sense I must return from where I went.

THE COUNTRY CLUB (ON ACID)
[18th Nov 1979, Holtville, California]

The singer-pianist Nancy was a professional,
The manager was just another crook –
The clientele were rich Vegas people
Who used a bottle as I use a pen.

The bar staff and waiters were -
Starched minds squeezed into white coats;
The Country Club was Sinatra and Martin,
The acid didn't help – they threw us out.

DESPAIR
[23rd Nov 1979, Holtville, California]

I have lost touch with the high life,
I have sunk to the depths of despair,
I am crushed internally, I cry in pain,
I detest that I have to dirty my hands.

I soil my clothes and play second best
To individuals who should be my pupils,
I am delving into introspective terms,
My total dissatisfaction with present life.

My love for living has shrivelled -
Lies buried in a woodworm riddled casket
Far beneath the earth that soils
The lowest labourer's hands.

I have been driven by the devil
To the furthest edge of torture,
Racking hate for all members
Of my fellow man.

I have reached the muddy bed
Of a lake of fear,
That stirs the mind to act
In twisted outlook.

I am torn between two ponies
Sent east and west for distraction.
I am dying every second,
Every pain filled moment.

I have lost my freedom,

I am nothing, I am gone,
I am dead in my head -
I remain incarcerated,

Chained in this dungeon
I have nailed myself in.
Southern California -
It may be my grave.

THE FARMER'S DEMISE
[23rd Nov 1979, Holtville, California]

Pain is no sorrow
In the fields of the morrow,
Where cotton runs high
And white as pure snow –
Where the furrows run dead-eye,
And the burrows hold vermin,
And the wind howls treetops
To an old preacher's sermon
In a rickety torn barnyard,
The corners in cobwebs,
Harbouring young field mice
And a one-eyed old owl,
That sits on an oak beam
Hushed by the Lord's words
That carries the law
Across the wide country miles –
That rings in the hollows
'The Farmer has died'.

ARIZONA FARMERS
[26th Nov 1979, Holtville, California]

Arizona farmers are cantankerous, old
Twisted, gruff voiced, ill mannered,
Totally unreasonable, cripple-minded,
Damn pig-head sons of bitches, that ever
Walked - no – crawled this earth!

COTTON PICKING
[26th Nov 1979, Holtville, California]

If ever there was a more boring job
Than cotton picking – you name it.
Cotton picking may sound like an occupation
That reaps of humour and bad jokes
About racism and callous slave masters.
It is not so. The humour is non existent,
The racism exists – Mexican, not Black –
The white slaver is now an Arizona farmer.

THE PICKER'S LINE
[26th Nov 1979, Holtville, California]

The Arizona farmer's whip
Lashed the air about to hit

ROBBIE MOFFAT

A poor lost Mex losing ground,
Falling behind the pickers line –
The pickers line, the pickers line,
Picking cotton all the time;
Picking fat white snowy balls,
Picking, picking, until he falls.

And thus the farmer drives his slaves,
Picking cotton every day;
From dawn to dusk the Mexies toil,
Tilling deep the cotton soil –
Picking cotton all the time,
As pickers on the pickers line;
The pickers line, the pickers line,
Picking cotton all the time.

THE DUNES OF GLAMIS
[4th Dec 1979, Holtville, California]

Thirty days beneath the broiler,
Windswept nights, huddling closer,
Wastes of sea taking over;
Beached upon the dunes of Glamis,
Riding on a four-wheeled camel,
Slinging beers in buggy travel.

9,394th DAY OF MY LIFE
[12th Dec 1979, Holtville, California]

Today was the 3,633rd day of the decade,
The 20th last day of the Seventies,
And the 9,394th day of my life.

THE DESERT WORKER
[13th Dec 1979, Holtville, California]

Winsome grows the winter harvest,
Green and yet unripe to pick;
Dry the eyes the dust has reddened,
Hoarse the throat the wind has whipped;
Fierce the sun has blazed the forehead,
Hot the sweat has coolly dripped;
Hard the back has bent in labour,
Toiling on the desert strip.

Evening fades the end day shadows,
Red and black the mountain sky;
Quietly ate the hands that mastered,
Quieter still the hands that sighed;
Quietly lay the hands together,
Silent prayer on which to die;
Still-like lay the rake so life-like,
By the hoe that gently cried.

Windward blew the winter's harvest,
Seeded and o'er ripe to pick;
Wet the eyes the tears had deadened,

Prayer-less was the tongue equipped;
Piercing pain had creased the forehead,
Cold the icy mountains ripped,
At the back bent down in sorrow,
Toiling on the desert strip.

A POSTCARD
[19th Dec 1979, Holtville, California]

Where is this land where the river runs bold,
Where the arbres catch sunlight in fiery glow?
Where the mosses lie red 'neath shimmering gold
Of cascading leaves descending like snow –
To garnish like ribbons, tie up as bows
A bower of seclusion in quiet undergrowth?

DO WHAT YOU CAN
[23rd Dec 1979, Holtville, California]

Do what you can
While you can.
Ask what you can
Before you can't.

BACK ON THE ROAD
[Christmas Eve 1979, Mexicali, Baja, Mexico]

Back on the road that winds down on south,
Back to a life of waiting for time –
Waiting for time to frizzle away –
Waiting to pass it down Mexico way.

TEQUILA FOR CHRISTMAS DINNER
[26th Dec 1979, San Quentin, Baja, Mexico]

Ensenda lies behind me –
The residue of my stomach with it
Why did we start on that glass flagon of tequila
With the coiled snake lying at the bottom?
I had hitched to Aguas Calientes -
It was Christmas. The Yaqui Indian bar-tender
Born in New York, raised in California,
Was straight out of the book of life.
Saint Simon he called himself –
Jesus never had no disciples like him;
Tequila for Christmas dinner –
The last thing I remember was the snake's head
Looking at me from the flagon –
A car in a ditch - a fist fight - with Mexicans
Trying to help us – a thunderstorm,
Before waking up in a hotel room in Ensenda.

THE RAINBOWS OF ROCK PURDAH
For Lee (and Heiko)
[1st Jan 1980, Mazatlan, Mexico]

Washed in the waves of recaptured love,

Gently relaxed by the murmur of words
Whispered and aired in passionate sides,
Floatingly said in idle soft hours.

Patroned by gentry and beauty forlorn,
Fringed by low artists midst psychic reform,
Searching the rainbows of rocky purdah,
Seeking immortal the seaside bazaar.

Laid on the shores for amorous designs,
Caressed by the surf on lazy moon nights,
Filtering the gaze of starry-eyed want,
Sharing the peace of the palmed waterfront.

A SMALL MEXICAN VILLAGE
[3rd Jan 1980, Mazatlan - Puerto Villarta Road, Mexico]

To be dropped in a small Mexican village,
Is one of the delights of travelling, but
One of the nightmares of hitch-hiking.

Something to savour and dislike,
Cherish and abhor, it requires little compulsion
To move on, but also fosters a compulsive
Desire to remain on the road out of fear
Of permanent abandonment in a quaintness
That suggests a forlorn acceptance of life.

A dream and a nightmare, it is best solved
Sitting by the roadside, watching labouring peasants,
Sleepy shopkeepers, lounging locals out of work,
whilst warily keeping an eye on the stretching
highway offering a choice of leaving or remaining,
on the whim of a thrown thumb.

SO BE IT THE DOGS
[3rd Jan 1980, La Cumbre, Mexico]

When the sun goes down,
So does the tequila.
When the rivers run dry,
So do the teardrops.
When the music stops,
So ends the heartache.
If something must die,
So be it the dogs.

THREE LINES
[3rd Jan 1980, Manzanillo, Mexico]

It takes free verse
To string three lines
To make a rhyme.

LO PRIMERO VERSO (Muy Malo)
[4th Jan 1980, Guadalajara, Mexico]

En al mercado a la lado
De la calle Mexico
Hay una casa para el peon
Quien no haber una lugar
Ni una casa pero la via
No conoce iqual a los campos
El partir hace un rato
Para la vida barata
En un pueblo de Mexico.

HOW NOT TO COMPOSE A POEM
[8th Jan 1980, Mexico City]

To understand more fully, the different kinds of rhyme,
A general little rule should be utmost in the mind,
It requires little knowledge beyond a simple line
To comprehend the meaning the words knot and bind.

If you take the word *creation*, it means nothing on its own,
But add a word like *freedom*, then a phrase begins to roll;
A phrase that starts as nothing but a thought of rough design,
Completed, starts to sound as poetry of a kind.

Creation of *freedom* we try for all the time,
And there we have a sentence brought to life divine,
So next we need a phrase that will fit into the rhyme,
So add *imagination*, creation undermined.

Creation of *freedom* is creation undermined,
Investigated deeply by a prying artful clown,
Out to prove by values, *imagined* metal crimes
Existing within the walls of the structured prisoned mind.

PAMELA
[12th Jan 1980, Isla de Mujeres, Mexico]

A small Kiki bird
With an eye for the bottle
We emptied together
Then made love by the water
On a long Mexican night.

PUNTA GORDA
[30th Jan 1980, Punta Gorda, Belize]

Trapped at the end of the world,
A jungle waste, the last of the colonies
Clinging like a dead man to a sinking ship.
Trapped in a tropical hinterland
Not fit to grow bananas,
A steaming forest of nothing.
Marooned by a river -
Waiting for a ship.

JUNGLE TREK
[1st Feb 1980, Cuyamelma, Honduras]

One day in Guatemala and we took to
The jungle and crossed into Honduras.

It was quite a way and one for a novel.
Banana trains and jungle treks are usually
Only restricted to movies.

I have taken other jungle trails before,
But none so enjoyable as the journey
We undertook into the heart of nowhere.

TRAVELLING WITH A GERMAN
[12th Feb 1980, Managua, Nicaragua]

In volcanic eruption
The problems poured forth,
Fiery and hot and flaming –
To consume all my forest,
To cover in ash - my unripe bananas
and coco-hung palms;
That I had pictured as perfect,
That had formed my sublime,
Before her smoke had enveloped
My quiet peaceful mind.

NICARAGUA
[12th Feb 1980, Managua, Nicaragua]

Nicaragua is a land of volcanoes and lakes,
Rolling hills and green sweet fields –
A land of pleasant smiles and peasant dreams,
Of almond blossom and red flame trees.

ELKE
[15th Feb 1980, San Juan del Sur, Nicaragua]

We are alone now – we rest quietly
In a small fishing village on the Pacific
Coast, and we have just passed a warm
breezy day, sipping coffee, ravishing
innumerable cones of soft ice-cream.

Each of us dreams of another world
Unknown to the other. We maintain
A company with one another as though
We have known each other fifty years.

We rarely speak. Occasionally we exchange
Warm smiles – we are lost to one another
By the circumstances in which we find
Ourselves in a strange affair of love.

UNEASY SLEEP
[16th Feb 1980, San Juan del Sur, Nicaragua]

Uneasy sleep steals my dreams,
As uneasy rests the coming dawn –

Hard on its heels, the hungry storm.

The nightmare in a fit, seizes my throat,
Strangles my life, destroys my hopes
Of clear blue sky tomorrow.

WAR
[16th Feb 1980, San Juan del Sur, Nicaragua]

Morning, coming morning,
Only in a dream,
Fastened by steel bolts
Riveting the seams
Of all the plans being moulded,
Of all those welded beams
That support the central structure
Of fabricated schemes.

Dawning, slowly dawning,
Emerging from a sleep,
Rolling, thundering steel stock,
Rumbling death machines –
Made from all these mouldings,
All these welded beams,
To fissure and to rupture
Regardless of the means.

Morning, bright red morning,
No longer just a dream,
With streaks of jagged lightning
Muffled, strangled screams –
Choked by spitting mouldings,
Crushed by welded beams,
all buried under rubble
To end further schemes.

SAN JOSE
[18th Feb 1980, San Jose, Coast Rica]

This is not the place for a lonely man.
I have had it with Latin America,
The romance is over. Each day has become
A pointless journey through a land
Lost to me.

LONELY MAN IN THE TROPICS
[18th Feb 1980, San Jose, Costa Rica]

Another day gone and where was it lost
Between the bus journey, and an empty
Coke glass, that stared back with a coldness,
Its icebergs in cubes, while the sun melted
Ice-creams with a long sticky look that
Defrosted my face, crinkled my brow –
A red-faced white-man in a tropical land.

AFTER THE REVOLUTION

[19th Feb 1980, Managua, Nicaragua]

Back in the land of smoking volcanoes,
Black market excesses
Amidst the continuing process
Of alphabetization -
Now the dictator is gone.

An illiterate nation
In revolutionary phases,
In propaganda phrases,
With great effort erases
The dictator's debases
As the volcanoes smoke on.

A NATION OF FOOLS (song)
[20th Feb 1980, Managua, Nicaragua]

As a nation of fools,
No longer rulers of the waves,
We think nothing of our pomp
And nothing of our ways.

God save the British!
Let them dig their graves!

We go blindly in our thinking
And deaf like poor slaves
To the values of our peers
And the ideas of today.

God save the British!
It's too late to make the change!

EL SALVADOR
[22nd Feb 1980, San Salvador, El Salvador]

There are people everywhere,
And not all are rich.

On the contrary, there is much poverty here.
A revolution is just around the corner,
I can feel it in the atmosphere.

It is a hostile environment –
We evoke cold receptions and stand-off
Behaviour from the citizens of this city.

But what I see, I like, despite the tanks
And the children with no shoes.

BROKE IN MEXICO
[28th Feb 1980, Oaxaca, Mexico]

On the road in Mexico,
Tired, hungry and broke,
No money for a coke,

No pesos for a smoke,
Only dust to make me choke
The long grueling miles.

On the High Sierras in a truck
That's broken down –
No shade is no joke,
No water, and no hope,
Only sun and heat stroke
The long grueling day.

In the cold mountains of the night
In the starry dark –
No poncho as a cloak,
No wife as my whore.

NEW ORLEANS
[3rd Mar 1980, New Orleans, Louisiana]

And the lazy river rolled on by
The home of Jazz –
While a tap dancer on the levee,
Tap-tapped his heart out.

SUNDAY IN BATON ROUGE
[9th Mar 1980, Baton Rouge, Louisiana]

Sunday is a day of rest,
Meant to satisfy the clans
That flock to worship at the feet
Of silk-robbed priests intent on sending
The yawning throng of ties and bonnets
To the edge of sleep.

It is a Spring morning -
Bounded by the scriptures,
The God-blessed good-soul folks
Sprout like flowers
From their window-box churches.

CRUMBS ON THE FLOOR
[1st April 1980, 1700 Dollie Madison Blvd, McLean, Virginia]

Coffee and toast reveal so much
About a lifestyle of breakfasts,
And lunches, and late evening snacks,
With pretty, lonely girls who've come
To talk their blues away, and perform
a repertoire of perversion –
before smoothing out their skirts,
combing back their hair,
drinking the dregs of their cup,
and crunching the toast crumbs
on the floor, as they amble to the door,
and leave.

LIFE ACROSS THE OCEAN (fragment)

[2nd Apr 1980, DMB, McLean, Virginia]

To the misogynist man,
Or miscreants of other lands,
Life across the ocean
To the distant glistening sands –
Is a sea of pale-blue calmness,
Of cloudless perfect want,
Containing every dream
Of heavenly thought.

Thus carried on this notion,
Sets forth this sadist man,
To voyage the unknown vastness
To attack and savage hearts –
As a barbarian, cold and sanguine,
Like a pirate stealing plunder,
He vents his treacherous hatred
'neath a thick veneer of wonder.

IN A HAUNTED HOUSE
[4th Apr 1980, DMB, McLean, Virginia]

In a haunted house off the highway,
Creaking floorboards, crunching driveway
Sends the lonely tenant crazy
Listening to the shutters bang.

Doorknobs rattle, ne'er a hand
But his, cold-sweat shaking bones
For forty years a recluse –
Locked up in his own jail.

Rarely seen but as a shadow,
Flirting past the curtained windows –
Already of the other world,
His lips satanic black.

GLOOM, DARK GLOOM
[9th Apr 1980, DMB, McLean, Virginia]

Gloom, dark gloom, blow from me,
Sweep the shadows of a love
Into a forgotten room,
And not my lounge.

Ladies, fair-blooming in Spring,
Strike at me in torment,
Throw fits of anguish,
Enough to end my life.

CLASSLESS
[9th Apr 1980, DMB, McLean, Virginia]

So they think I'm an uncouth adult,
Born an adolescent,
Who talks like a foul-mouthed parrot

In their den of enchantment.

Please refrain from laughing, dear people,
The joke is not on me –
Although I have an accent,
All my thoughts are pure.

What of those other poor fools out there?
Noses to the wind –
Avoiding the smell of the garbage
They're up to their necks right in.

AT SEA IN D.C
[9th App 1980, DMB, McLean, Virginia]

Lost in a wave of colossal dimensions,
Hung on a breaker of misapprehensions,
Tottering on the edge of illusions,
Crushed by the force of utter confusion.

CATHY
[16th Apr 1980, DMB, McLean, Virgina]

There was a lady named Cathy,
Who I met over coffee,
Then took to my chambers
To caress her soft body;
Love had is way –
Oh, you poor sad babe.

DAFFODILS THRU LILACS
[20th Apr 1980, DMB, McLean, Virginia]

I met her when the daffodils
Were first in bloom;
Our relationship went right through -
The cherry blossom,
The primroses,
And the lilacs.

THE SEED
[20th Apr 1980, DMB, McLean, Virginia]

A squirrel out in Spring-time forage,
Dodged a car and crawled a hedgerow,
Crossed a field and forged a ditch,
Swam a stream and found a niche
Beneath a wizened budding oak,
Protruding roots brown-leaf cloaked,
That hid a hollow secret store
On which the squirrel clawed in chore.

A fox stalked quietly through the woods,
The birds perched mute in the trees –
Observant of the hungry reynard,
Scornful, full of their own fears -
On the scent the fox now followed

That led him from his peaceful den
Towards the kill he sadly wanted
To feed is green-eyed discontent.

The hounds, they rallied to the horn
That crossed the field that Spring-time morn,
That forged the ditch, swam the stream,
That found the fox beneath the oak,
Its jaws locked-hard around the squirrel,
Grey, but streaked a red day-glow –
While on the earth lay the store
From which one day an oak would grow.

THE PROMISE
[26th Apr 1980, DMB, McLean, Virginia]

Ah, Miss Laura Cann, my flower,
Unfold your fragile petals
And allow this honey bee
To plunder and to rape
Your heaven-given pollen
And honey-scented residue;
In turn I'll make you fertile
And pledge my love to you.

ANOTHER TAKES THE STAGE
[26th Apr 1980, DMB, McLean, Virginia]

Another young lady takes the stage,
And lays open her desires to the rake;
Break not her heart, my sweet fellow -
As tender as the petals open,
Cruelly does the blossom fade.

NO MORE LONELY ROADS
[May Day 1980, DMB, McLean, Virginia]

Thrown, no, tossed my cares,
Cast aside the doubts, the heartless tears,
The childish thoughts and selfish introspection –
And instead grasp I, the naked flame.

Abandoned, no, discarded
The lonely man's illusion of happiness,
The solitary soul and island dreamer –
For instead touch I, the blood red rose.

Forgotten, no, erased,
The sceptic views the ignorant holds,
The conceited fool, the ways of old –
To instead brave I, love's fragile kiss.

For thrown, abandoned and forgotten
Seem the nights I slept alone
On the road and pass to heaven –
That instead cross I, and her I hold.

THE SISTER LIGHTHOUSES
[5th May 1980, DMB, McLean, Virginia]

On one side of the might ocean,
Two lost souls held hands,
Gazing far across the barren sea
To glimpse their thoughts in dreams.

They stood bound hand in hand,
Inseparable as the mist from heather,
Gasping at the fear that bit
Their cheeks with salty blows.

They pondered in their isolation
All that mattered most,
They heaved great sighs of love
That they grew close to understand.

They felt the new life coming
And dared not look behind,
They dared not move their wet toes
Washed white by the tide.

They were frozen in their terror,
And stone-struck in their awe,
They remained forever on the shoreline
Beacons in a fog.

They cheered a mariner home-bound,
They tear'd one fond farewell,
They stood sentinel 'neath the cliffs
Witnessing the swell.

WET DOWNTOWN
[18th May 1980, Washington DC]

The police, in siren-wails
That cut the ocean's howl,
And the driving of the sleet –
Tore the glassy surface
Of the deserted blacked-out street
With their screeching tyres.

SCARRED BY VIOLENCE
[20th May 1980, DMB, Mclean, Virginia]

A pretty face scarred by violence,
Tempestuous love, brutally branded
By the vicious arcing hand
Of a man's cruel command.

IDEAL HOME OF A NOMAD
[22nd May 1980, McLean, Virginia]

Just a little place on a hill,
A stile across a fence,
A horseshoe at the door,

The roses framing hedges,
A dog upon the lawn,
The parlour full of servants;
And a lady of fabric -
To furnish my earthly wants.

OLD VIRGINIA
For Terry Paine
[30th May 1980, Bull Run, Virginia]

The old Virginia pine grew tall,
Near shady dell and trickling creek,
That bleached the bones of Johnny Red –
A bullet and a century gone,
Remembered only in a song
The dogwood natives learn at birth.

A cardinal flamed the forest dark
And streaked the hickory hollow quiet,
Sunlight crashed upon the pine,
A bluejay sang its morning song,
Like the Yankee soldiers heard
The day they shot old Johnny Boy.

Yet who can find that lonesome pine
Or Johnny's bones bleached so white?
A bullet and memory hidden,
Forgotten bar a whistling song –
About the lost old southern nights
Of peace before the Union dawn.

FROG (an illustrated collection)
[22nd Jun – 25th Jul 1980, 2 Victoria Sq, Newcastle]
(Not reproduced here)

THE MILKING BOY
[22nd June 1980, Newcastle]

Summer rain and English weather,
Slow, and gently closing in,
On a dawn of soft, light yellows
Resting on the hedgerow sprigs;
Crossing swiftly through the meadows,
Green and ripe in the rain –
As the cows lay 'neath the shelter
Of a spreading, towering plane.

Slowly wound the walkers' pathway,
Broken and betrayed by mounds,
Tractor wheels and muddy boot-steps
Traced all life upon the ground,
Brown and mangled in with pebbles,
Soil, and grass, and daisy rings,
Vetch, and clover thrown in daring,
Tempting bees and other things.

Down the pathway walked the young boy,

Whistling on a humble tune;
Cloth cap resting on his blonde hair,
Shoulders haunched, his arms limp still,
He ambled on down the pathway
Hidden by the tall hedgerows,
Toes-tapping on the pebbled highway,
The only road he'd ever known.

The whistling ceased like a songbird
Made to think upon its vow –
As he leaped the five-bar field gate
And began to call the beasts,
Whistling now like a herdsman
With great loving for the land;
Whistling with a country frankness
That the world could understand.

LIFE AS A DREAM
[27th June 1980, Newcastle]

Some see life as a dream,
In that others pay the price
For all the little niceties
That coat the cake in ice.

They cannot see the labour
And the toil to struggle free
Of their subtle inner-wanting
In one giant pot-pourri.

While one soul shelves the shekels,
The other amply spends
All the saved up pennies
The other scrapes to lend.

And so in some great sulk,
I dwell on my affairs –
Financially and private,
A partner takes her share.

NO MORE LONELY ROADS TWO
[27th June 1980, Newcastle]

No more lonely roads to travel –
Jungles, deserts – it little matters,
Life has grabbed me by the legs,
And shackled me with all its weight –
Lead balls and ankle chains,
Woes and pain, the tears and strain
by which responsibility, it appears,
Has been my only worthwhile gain.

ARTISTIC WRANGLES
[1st July 1980, Newcastle]

Caught in a tangle of artist rights wrangles,
Brought on by confusion from every angle,

Initially caused by the change in a plan –
The change being better than the original design
Of having three artists, scribble and draw
For the privilege of embellishing a poet's words;
When all that needs done is one artist to dab,
And the poet to comment to avoid the drab –
Instead of having headaches, and petty squabbles
That develop enemies – overnight - over baubles.

CAUGHT IN A ROOM
[3rd July 1980, Newcastle]

Caught in a room
With the window open wide,
Affording a gaze
Across the wild countryside,
To the far-away mountains,
While I am trapped inside.

WHY ARE YOU ALL IN CAGES (fragment)
[28th July 1980, Newcastle]

I have never been caged –
I sleep where tiredness overtakes me,
I eat where providence leaves me.
I know the stars better than any mystic
Who pretends to deceive with his charts
and horoscopes.

I'm not one to live by astrological reckoning,
We live in an age of science, not ignorance;
Superstition adds only senseless confusion
To a world already rotten with deceit.

So tell me another, brothers, I shall not listen
To stories woven on lies and excuses.
My eyes do not deceive me –
You are one and all, trapped in cages.

THE THIRTY THREE YEAR OLD HIPPY
[4th Aug 1980, Newcastle]

He was just another flower Hippy,
Lost within an age of reason,
At a time when peace wilted
Beneath contempt and treason.

For over green and pleasant hills,
Glanced his gaze in higher thought,
While underneath his sandalled feet
Marched his enemies to war.

He let his soul and spirit fly,
Free transcendence in his look;
But all around in abject chains,
Masters led their slaves to work.

He cast aside his outer garments
And bared his chest to all the world
That honesty had taught him how –
That instead – they drained of love.

For who cared then to spend the time
To listen to a Hippy's words –
That a heathen world rejected
By sacrificing God's own son.

ME AND THE ROAD
[4th Aug 1980, Newcastle]

I have no greater desire in this world
Than to travel the four corners and seven seas
To take me to the boundaries of understanding.

For without the freedom of time and place,
And the knowledge that restrictions of movement
Are non-existent – then I am a traveller programmed
By nationality, a tourist controlled by visas,
And a tramp restrained by the fact I'm broke.

THE ARTIST AND HIS WORK
[1.25pm, 4th Aug 1980, Newcastle]

Before the artist drew a line,
He had somehow to pay the bills –
So knowing that the rent was due,
He dropped his brush, laced his shoes.

Off we went up the street,
Immersed in bright, pastel colours,
Until he reached a building site,
Punched his card, joined his brothers.

He wheeled a barrow up a plank –
All day long he carted bricks,
Hauled the cement from the mixer,
Clocked the hours, bit his lip.

At dusk, and time to travel home,
He shuffled weary legged and weak,
Knowing that the rent was paid –
The following day he'd work for food.

But underneath, he gnawed to work
On his art and not his keep –
For every night he raised his brush,
Tired and worn, he fell asleep.

BACKWOODSMAN BLUES (song)
[7th Aug 1980, Newcastle]

In a land, I know not of -
A lonesome man, and his dog
Listened to the driving rain –

Descending on their ill-lit place,
A log-hewed timber home of peace,
Lost in a wood of tall pine trees.

The drumming on the porch outside,
Imbibed him freely to recite –
A lilting love-song melody;
Released upon the dark rough walls,
Hummed to a portrait on the tall-boy,
A handsome face, age has destroyed.

The rain like time's own sweet blood,
Caught the woodsman in a flood,
Recalling sweet surrender moments -
Of his life his ballads told of –
Songs not yet quite fully sung,
Of life not yet completely run.

The fire spat, threw some light
Upon his hound stretched outright,
Close by his masters feet –
Inches from his Fender lead,
Plugged into his ten-watt amp,
The woodsman picked on his guitar.

I've been a woodsman all my life
I've preferred blues to having a wife.
And if you think me wrong ... Oh yeah?
Then don't listen to my blues songs.
I'm a backwoodsman .... Yeah ....
I'm a backwoodsman .....
With a howling dog ....
And this this is my song.

IT'S A MATTER OF LATITUDE
[3pm, 9th Aug 1980, Newcastle]

As it happens, I was born
Faraway to the north –
And when I finally left home,
I went south to sun and warmth.

I lazed about by hotel pools
And mingled with the idle rich,
Petty, silly in their whims,
I spent their money, getting kicks.

A mirage - my town of birth
Cloaked in a mountain mist,
Lost its lure to champagne corks
And lines of easy chicks.

For living in the sunny south,
Was like living with the devil –
While returning to the icy north
Was beyond my latitude level.

CROSSROADS
[21st Aug 1980, Newcastle]

Crossroads again, and what choice now?
The ways divergent beyond the far hill-brow.
The winding broken road, the twisted fence
I lean thoughtfully on, in lull.

CALLED FROM EVE IN THE GARDEN
[28th Aug 1980, Newcastle]

On an evening, on a pale mild night,
The telephone commenced singing,
With its insistent constant rhythm
That drowned out all the birds.

I left the garden and my cocktail,
And the maiden waiting there
With a look of earnest longing,
That I return forthwith to talk of love.

I strode swiftly, beckoned quickly
By the ringing pending misery
That I knew must be the reason
For being disturbed on such a night.

For I lived lonely in the country,
And knew no one who would want to
Disturb my peaceful love nest,
Lest I perchance return the deed in kind.

So I glanced back at the garden,
And saw the sweet-faced maiden,
Waiting with a patience
That not all men have as theirs to pass.

And I plucked at the receiver
Like some ill-tempered no-believer,
That the person on the far-end
Was someone else, and not my wife.

CONSTRUCTING WORLDS
[11.20pm, 5th Sept 1980, Newcastle]

The builder packed away his tools
And laid aside his white hard-hat,
Unslung his coat from a nail,
Closed the door, and that was that.

The day had gone to grey with rain,
The trees they dripped, sagged draped-wet;
The builder dry and soothed by work,
Homeward went in casual pace.

And home he reached, to settle down
To an evening of reflective thought,
Of what the day had offered him,

And what of life the day had taught.

And quiet the evening faded on,
Soft fell the novel from his hand –
The builder lulled into a world
Constructed by another man.

SAD POET, UNHAPPY PUBLISHER
[10pm, 10th Sept 1980, Newcastle]

I published a man's poems the other day
Though the contents brought on despair,
And gloomy depressive long thoughts
That the poet had written in misery –
Telling us why he was a poet, not a man
Who went about the world without a pen,
Nor armed himself with a smile
And a wit that won all to his cheerful side.

So why did I publish the poet, you ask?
I would like to know this myself –
For all his stanzas dwelt on heartache,
And mended none of life's cruel flaws
That he pointed at; that he amplified so large
As to make everything bare and empty;
It wrenched from me, a happy man,
Moral tears, from both sad eyes.

THE BAND WHO CAME TO DINNER
[10.15pm, 10th Sept 1980, Newcastle]

We had a band who practiced in our basement,
Who came and went, sometimes stayed for dinner;
A male band who went about their business,
A magic band everybody agreed were winners.

Then one day - close to the end of summer,
A girl appeared, all charm and glitter –
She, it was announced, was the new lead singer,
And everyone agreed she was a stunner.

Then in an instance, as if a wand was waved,
The magic band no longer played together –
The lead guitarist ran off with the glitter,
And the band no longer came to dinner.

PICKING GRAPES AND BAILING STRAW (song)
[5.47pm, 16th Sept 1980, Newcastle]

The day I gave up work, I laughed –
The money jingled as I jumped.
I made my way into a bar
To spend my celebration, drunk.

I'd grafted on the open fields,
Picking grapes and bailing straw;
The produce of the land lay stored,

The farmer paid my time by law.

All the while I laboured there,
Three months of sweat, knuckled bone,
I thought on my time passing by,
The water flowing o'er unturned stones.

I thought of the girls I missed –
Their sweet bodies, their tender lips,
Their homely gossip by the hearth
Whilst fired by their fingertips.

I pondered on the missing treats
That coaxed a man to spend his change;
The courteous passing in a street
Of a face that was not strange.

I was just a fresh-faced lad
Living far from home to work –
A foreigner in another realm,
Earning riches from ploughing dirt.

And now back home, instead of pain,
My time abroad was not a waste –
The memory of those labour fields
Are happy as the memory fades.

TWENTY SIX LETTERS in SEVEN WORDS
[9.45pm, 3rd Oct 1980, Newcastle]

When gazed above,
Sixty jumpers fly quick

HOMELESS
[5th Oct 1980, Newcastle]

On the run is a family man,
Woman and kid, bags in hand
Walking the streets in search of a home,
Wandering like beggars with nowhere to go.

Asking for change on meeting a friend,
Looking for cash that someone can lend,
To fill the mouths of the starving kin
That the family man has led to ruin.

Knocking on doors in utter despair,
To see if someone can spare a room,
Or a floor, or corner out of the way,
As long as its somewhere they can stay.

The council man had offered them beds,
Kipping in with the down and the helpless –
A hostel where thieves and tramps had shelter,
But where they never receive any further help.

It was better he thought to stick together,

The bandage of love that had brought them hither,
Was more precious than any refuge from rain
Given in exchange for heartbreak and pain.

So they wander the streets, still together,
United in their love for one another –
Though already they've spent a night in the cold,
They'd rather die than let go of each other.

LOOKING FROM THE OUTSIDE
[9.02pm, 6th Oct 1980, 10 Akenside Terr, Newcastle]

Cold and hungry gazed the tramp,
Haggard mouthed and blood-shot eyed
On a man who read a book
By the warmth of his hearth-side.

Envy flashed across his troubles,
Memories of his life of old,
Before the decay and the rot,
Ate his love and stole his heart.

But pity also lingered there
For the man that life passed by,
Trapped beside his open book,
Old and grey beside the fire.

For had that man another life,
He would not thus be sitting so –
He would be travelling with the tramp
Turning now to walk the road.

MARRIAGE
[9pm, 12th Oct 1980, Newcastle]

The ring upon his finger shone with light,
Illuminating the future, bright and clear;
While his wife held his hand in happy faith –
Secure in joy, and tears.

OCTOBER 13TH IN ENGLAND
[6.05pm, 13th Oct 1980, 87 Byker Terr, Walker, Newcastle]

Autumn's almost gone now,
Yet broad green leaves still hang
From drooping boughs.

Thistles not long dead
Stand brown un-barbed
Upon the pastured ground.

Lapwings catch their meals,
Before flocking on a few more miles
To lakeside perches.

Bees at the end of plenty –
Cool and thoughtful

On the verge of barren days.

Grey and black, bleak views
Carry the eye across the wasteland
To reconcile the mind for winter.

THE WALKER FISHMAN
[6.30pm, 13th October 1980, Walker, Newcastle]

There is a fishmonger with a shop
In a place called Walker, England,
Who feeds the working folk
With a fresh and smiling look,
That agrees with all their comments,
But disagrees with all their social views.

He's a conservative at heart, he admits it,
For after all, he is a businessman
Who takes the money from the locals
With a fresh and smiling look
That accepts their hard luck stories,
Yet refuses credit, as it's against his rules.

He is a pleasant man, that is true;
He buys his fish fresh from the docks
And opens his shop at seven for the locals
With a fresh and smiling look
That sympathises with their ills,
But knows that's why the hospitals are full.

Just the same, he is a good man –
He talks to the children and old folk,
And finds time to chat to the locals
With a fresh and smiling look
That keeps the customers happy,
And keeps the orders full on his books.

One cannot complain about this man;
He is English and a citizen,
Placed amongst the shipyard folks
With his fresh and smiling look –
He is the ideal corner-shop chappy
Who with his fish has the locals hooked.

THE GATESHEAD JEW
[1.05pm, 14th Oct 1980, Walker, Newcastle]

BANG! BANG! "Hello, are you there?"
A scrawny voice shouted out
As Laura pulled the door ajar -
A little man jumped with fright.

"Hello? Are you the tenant of this house?
I've come to see about the rent.
I think we haven't met as yet.
I think it's time to talk. Right?"

"I'm not the tenant" Laura said,
"I'll get my husband to speak to you.
Robert! Can you come right now?
It's one of those Gateshead Jews."

"Yes, can I help you?" I asked the Jew,
"Yes" he said "I want the rent …"
"I'm sorry, mate, I've no cash today.
Can you come back next Friday?"

"I'll get the law on your back!"
He threatened me with vile spite,
"One more word" I said to him
"I'll pull your beard, squash your hat."

The little Jew squealed in fear
And ran pell-mell from our door –
We lived there all of three months more
And only heard from him by post.

SLEEPING UNDER NEWSPAPERS ON A PARK BENCH
[12.32am, 15th Oct 1980, Walker, Newcastle]

Turn another page towards the future,
And what transpires?
Another word towards an ending,
Another line towards a sentence
Laid upon me by a judge –
The God Creator, up in heaven.

Turn another page towards the future,
And what comes next?
Another leaf towards my autumn,
Another black print day of horror,
Pressed upon me by the Devil,
Counting me amongst the fallen.

Turn another page, I dare not,
And what occurs?
Another page turns itself –
Another day of written torture,
Forced upon me by my failings –
This bench my bed, my sheets sodden.

FAME
[11pm, 30th Oct 1980, Walker, Newcastle]

Before he had the world – a pearl
Safely held within his palm,
A shining sphere of precious love
That yielded all its dazzling charm.
And then the fame came.

Then as he grew to be known
And share his solitude of calm,
He lost the inner-wanting peace
That always lulled away the harm.

But the fame stayed.

The present that the fame now stole
Took the pearl without a qualm,
Substituted a fist of gold
That broke his once perfect calm.
And the fame went.

And with it went no sad regret –
Anew the pearl he quietly palmed,
He returned to peace and inner love;
His ethos simple – Fame be damned!
And then the fame came back.

FROM EAST TO WEST
[11pm, 18th Nov 1980, Walker, Newcastle]

When I get to America
I'm going to buy a car
And drive across the continent
From east to west, and back.
I'll set out on a journey
That few will ever make,
I shall travel on forever,
Leave memories in my wake.

The dream that inward burns
Isn't mine alone -
I've known countless others
Less able, far more prone
To fits of homesick languor,
Depressive pining thoughts,
To home's alluring comforts
Easy times once brought.

For me, well, I'm different,
I like the life of skies –
The peaceful inner warmth
Revealed on every rise
That I wander as an innocent
Of lingering inner-doubt;
The past one step behind
My road stretching out.

But when I get to New York,
I'm trading in my boots
For the automated comfort
Of a pedal underfoot –
A car, perhaps an old one,
I'm going to take a car
And drive across the continent
From east to west, and back.

PERFECT LOVE
[11.15pm, 18th Nov 1980, Walker, Newcastle]

When love is perfect

And untouchable,
And neither sad nor tearful,
Nor unapproachable,
Then love is perfect.

For what without love
Can life be?
As neither likeable, nor gay,
Nor permeable,
Then love is dead.

Love makes the snowflakes dance,
While hate makes the heart freeze.

THE WILD HEBRIDES
[11.30pm, 18th Nov 1980, Walker, Newcastle]

Sitting by the lakeside,
Idly passing memories
From the ripples of pictures
Created by the tide,
And ocean carried seaweeds
Washed along the loch,
The Scottish fishers sail on
Hauling crayfish pots.

The purple long since gone,
Lingers in the sand,
each tiny speck of past
counting time while tightly clasped
to the bosom, and the heart,
tuned into the gulls
plunging on the waves
with reckless cries.

Where ploughs the crofter
Now that winter's come?
The grey wind borne clouds
About the waters turn –
To maul and howl in tempest
The black swirling sea,
By the Highland shores
Of the wild Hebrides.

28TH NOVEMBER 1980
[10.40pm, 28th Nov 1980, Walker, Newcastle]

The snow came down to paralyse
The thoroughfares and walkways;
With knee-high drifts and overhangs,
All life moved precarious.

INSPIRATION
[11.02pm, 28th Nov 1980, Walker, Newcastle]

All inspiration has gone;
All causes have died,

And only the wind washes memories
Once washed by the tides
That roared, and brought change -
Adventure and freedom,
Lust, and excitement –
That inspired when over.

CREATION
[11.12pm, 28th Nov 1980, Walker, Newcastle]

When the mountains were dragged
From the bowels of the earth;
And the oceans were melted
From the rocks nature cleft;
And the skies were coloured
From the blood of God's themselves –
Man was little more than
four billion years ... behind.

THE BLIZZARD
[4pm, 6th Dec 1980, Walker, Newcastle]

Snow again coats all the earth,
The stubble corn on winter fields,
the dying fern on barren heath –
lost beneath white icy sheet.

The trucks labour on the roads,
The salt and grit turned to mush,
The heavy, grinding axles groan,
Chewing slush and throwing mud.

Trains halt snowbound on the moors -
While far at sea a tempest roars
To drive all ships upon the rocks,
To wreck upon the blizzard'd shore.

And there the farmer, no better placed,
Cloistered by the winter snows –
Sits cut-off in his granite croft,
Perched upon sleet-beaten slopes.

I'M GLAD TO GO (song)
[13th Dec 1980, Heathrow, London]

I'm leaving Walker now,
Leaving England now, yeah.
I'll work here no more,
I guess I've had enough.

I'm on a bus for Heathrow,
To catch a plane to San Fran,
To land in the sunshine.
I'm sure glad to go.

Surfing on the waves, yeah,
Driving by the shoreline –

109

Living like a man should,
I'm sure glad to go.

NICARAGUA (song)
[11pm, 13th Dec 1980, Heathrow, London]

Watching the old volcano smoke,
Shadowing the small sailing boats.
Licking on an ice-cream cone,
Sipping a Nicaraguan coke –
The clouds drifting over the slopes
As the locals sat telling jokes.

Still the tall volcano smoked.
I reached the rise to travel on.
Chewing on my thoughts to go,
I left the scene for the road;
The sun setting on the sailing boats,
And those Nicaraguan folks.

SIX THOUSAND THOUGHTS OF EXILE
[14th? Dec 1980, England-California]

Six thousand thoughts of exile,
Across six thousand miles,
Across the Arctic heartland
To the other side of life.

Beyond six thousand memories,
During six travelling years,
Six thousand east or west,
It's six thousand just the same.

Goodbye England, little kingdom,
Goodbye six thousand ways –
Welcome to the U.S,
Six thousand miles away.

Six thousand thoughts of exile,
Across six thousand miles –
Across the Arctic heartland
To the other side of life.

SAN FRANCISCO BAY
[21st Dec 1980, 14619 Darius Way, San Leandro, Calif]

I came to my newest dream
As a stranger to the scene –
Coastal breaks upon blonde shores
Girt by a cold sea-board.

THE SINGING DRUG-PUSHER (song)
[1.56pm, 21st Dec 1980, San Leandro, California]

Drugs again. Well, damn
I wouldn't ever tell the landlord
Or the devil. What's my latest plan?

Who's my latest girl?
I've got drugs, man ...
I don't have to say a thing.

Time flies. That's right,
I share it every day with the Parking
Man and my lover. What's my craze?
What drugs I rate.
I've got life, mate ...
I don't have to sing.

THE WEEKEND TRAIL (song)
[5.33pm, 22nd Dec 1980, San Leandro, California]

On the weekend adventure trail
Of alcohol and drugs –
Rolling on the highway straights,
Driving through the night.

High on the weekend road
Of kicks and rubber –
Gliding through the bright lights,
Reflections in my mirror.

Travelling those weekend lines
Of cocaine and life –
Coasting on the evening black,
Driving through the night.

LAST CHRISTMAS EVE
1.54pm, 24th Dec 1980, San Leandro, California]

Looking back on last year,
Last Christmas Eve,
I remember facing Mexico
On a dark dusty street.

The chicken wire towered over,
Over Christmas Eve,
I remember watching prostitutes,
Sell love on the cheap.

'Felix Navidad' boomed the guard,
guarding Christmas Eve,
as I marched into Mexico
to take a girl for sleep.

'Twenty dollars' she whispered,
whispering Christmas Eve,
as I left behind America
to fulfil my needs.

Looking back on last year,
Last Christmas Eve,
I left behind Jesus,
To sow wild Christmas seed.

111

JACK LONDON'S TOWN
[2.56pm, 24th Dec 1980, San Leandro, California]

I drove past Jack London's bar today,
There were nine at least.
I almost pulled in at the Nanuk,
But there was a heavy traffic squeeze.
Well, that's Oakland for you folks –
The Tribune and the Temple.
The docks, the tracks, Piedmont Hill
Where your dollar bills won't wrinkle.

I drove past Jack London's bar again –
It was ten o'clock at least.
I almost killed a drunken honkey,
One of a hundred on First Street.

So I took a right on a red,
And a right on 12th going east,
Until I hit the Nimitz Freeway.
Goodbye Oakland! Jack London's town.

Well, that's Oakland for you folks –
The Tribune and the Temple.
The docks, the tracks, Piedmont Hill
Where your dollar bills won't wrinkle.

GREEN IS ME
[10pm, 27th Dec 1980, San Leandro, California]

Blue is the crudest form to take,
It streaks, it burns, its searing pain
In many forms – from steel to sea,
From eyes to mind, blue's not me.

Red is passion at its height,
It floods, it bloods all love's veins –
Romantic Latins, Commies, rebels;
From peace to war – red proves fatal.

Green is the peasant's hue,
It's fields, it's leaves, it's cooling rain;
Shades of fences, windows, doors,
Green is me – nature's core.

GOD IS AMERICA
[7.49pm, 29th Dec 1980, San Leandro, California]

California – haze and onshore mist;
San Francisco Bay – from the bridge
America looks beautiful, rises tall
Over the world as a whole.

The Leninist from Kurdistan –
He believes like the Afghan man
That Russia rules, that America bullies
The lesser nations in third world lands.

But today – let me tell you,
From the San Francisco Bay Bridge,
America looks beautiful, rises tall
To frighten and to awe.

WALTER KRONKITE
[10.16pm, 29th Dec 1980, San Leandro, California]

When Walter failed to show tonight,
As gagging clay bound his morale,
The news from the desk in tote
Featured deadline dropping notes
That dredged the depths, but stole the show.

ANOTHER DAY AS WORKING CLASS
[11.30pm, 2nd Jan 1981, San Leandro, California]

Another day as working class,
A common labour man –
Sixteen tons and no reward
Except another verbal beating
From a fag - the boss
Who's never shovelled shit
Except from his mouth
Into my trench, this hell.

Who cares for my soul
As condemned working scum –
A hundred dollars towards my debts,
Fifty bucks to live on,
To stave off crippled, tired bones,
Muscles bruised and torn –
Every year an older man
In a rented cold tap abode.

There is no priest to save me,
No art to free my heart,
No love to grow and flourish,
No secret, hidden spark
To fire my broken spirit,
To flame my wildest aims –
I'm just a working navvie,
You'll never know my name.

ROAD TO HEAVEN (song)
[12th Jan 1981, San Leandro, California]

As I was walking the road to heaven
I saw the end –
As I was walking the road to heaven
I saw no friend –
I saw no name
But hers.

I TRIED TO PASS THE MESSAGE ON (song)
[14th Jan 1981, San Leandro, California]

I tried to pass the message on
Before you tried to cry.
I thought it'd be an easy thing
Before I said goodbye.

I've got to move along
The only road I know.
You never got the best of times
That's why I had to go.

As I travelled on that night
The night I made you cry,
I left our love a broken thing,
A broken hearted sigh.

The rain swept the lonely road
The road I've always known;
I'm back upon endless track,
The track I know as home.

PRAYER
[8.20pm, 14th Jan 1981, San Leandro, California]

Not another word will pass
Beyond these silent lips –
Not another phrase be heard
That is not His.

THE TWO DOGS
[18th Jan 1981, San Leandro, California]

Boris was a poor man's dog,
And Bart a homeless hound,
Whose wagging tongue belied his thirst,
His tail – his mellow mind.

Though Bart, a simple wandering soul,
Suffered many moral blows,
He never scorned a trusted friend;
For what was life alone?

'Tell me, tell me' he seemed to yap
to Boris, young and dumb –
a clumsy German Shepherd mutt,
his heart – his saving love.

But Boris couldn't bark to Bart,
He was barely nine months old –
Instead he shook his sheepish head
To answer yes or no.

And thus the bosom buddies played
With stick, or stone, or bone –
They shared the pleasures given them
Along the doggie road.

114

THE WATER IN THE BAY (song)
[12.50am, 21st Jan 1981, San Leandro, California]

And the water on the bay lapped gently,
And the fog with the tide rolled in,
And the boat on the waves sailed over
And under the last harbour bridge.

And the bird in the sky soared higher
And the land faded off from view –
And I guess that's the end of the story
As the sun sank, and evening grew.

OAKLAND DOCKS
[4.50pm, 28th Jan 1981, San Leandro, California]

The evening – black and lonely
The patroller walked his rounds;
He clocked the passing hours
And logged the boring night.

Dim lights glazed the darkness,
The waters slapped the docks,
A labouring diesel shunted stock
Along the harbour lines.

No shore-men showed their faces
Beneath the shore land lights;
No human form emerged
To dim or shadow time.

The watchman sipped his coffee
To pry his blackened eyes –
He cursed his job in hardware,
His second forty hours.

And forty times he nodded
Between each hourly round –
A guard in west dock Oakland,
Asleep each dockland night.

THE DRUNK
[14th Feb 1981, San Leandro, California]

Yesterday is a lost day,
The day before a blur –
Three days ago forgotten,
And four a misty murk
No denser than the fifth day,
The sixth completely blank –
In tote a week of nothing,
A week of being drunk.

THE BOXER
[14th Feb 1981, Joaquin Av, San Leandro, Calif.]

Another day, another dime,

115

Another ring, another night,
Another time, another life,
Another thing, another fight.

HILL-BILLY LIVING
[8.05pm, 14th Feb 1981, San Leandro, California]

Life on the hill, on a dead-end street,
Ended a two month lull
Of hill-billy living.

Sleeping like dogs on a carpet,
Close to the earthquakes
And cosmic vibrations.

Who said that the free spirit died
The day pot arrived
And God departed.

The world careers on downhill –
Saturn, then Luna Drive,
And on into space.

GYPSY LOVING LAURA
[10pm, St Valentine's Day, San Leandro, Calif.]

What's happened to Laura?
What's become for her?
Her beauty, her eyes of moonlight,
Their silver beams of love?

He loved her softer than satin,
He adored her sweeter than musk,
He cared for her more than Jesus
Cared for the creatures and birds.

He carried her bundles of flowers
Through the corn and rains –
He chased the rising lark skywards
On the path to lover's gate.

She loved him like no other,
She drained her heart for him,
She lay with him all summer,
Fanned by the summer winds.

The gypsies warned of heartache
By the fires of their circled nights;
They whispered of shooting horses
And of lovers taking flight.

And like the skylark soaring
In song and rising free,
The singing ceased, and silence
Followed in its lee.

And in the falling darkness,

Suddenly, he was gone –
With him went her spirit
Her heart, her flesh, her blood.

And left behind was Laura –
A sad and cure-less soul,
Who let her good looks fade -
Who finally let life go.

That's what became of Laura –
That's what became of her.
Her beauty, her eyes of moonlight
Stolen by a gypsy boy.

OVERDOSED ROCK STAR (song)
[9.15pm, 17th Feb 1981, San Leandro, Calif.]

His career was almost over,
So he took an overdose;
They found him lying in his car
In a comatose.

While the world played his records,
He was buried 'neath the news -
His girl found another,
As the faithless always do.

His band went acoustic,
And finally fell apart –
The genius of his music
Joined forgotten art.

THE WELDER'S TORCH
[11.55pm, 20th Feb 1981, San Leandro, Calif.]

The welder's torch lit the night
And burnt a hue of steel,
That flashed up on to the clouds
As blue electric beams.

The tungsten power arced though
The workshop of the world –
A lava burst of magma welds
And a line of molten seams.

FRESNO
[7.40pm, 24th Feb 1981, Fresno, California]

Working thirteen hours without a break.
Each day another.
Awake. Work. Eat. Sleep.
Fresno, California.
Who cares.

THE HIGH SIERRAS
[7.30pm, 27th Feb 1981, Fresno, California]

Across the Central Valley
The High Sierras rose,
As the winter snow descended
Half a mile or more
To cover every high ridge
And Ponderosa pine,
While every creek froze solid
Beneath the silver ice.

Frostbitten in a hollow,
A climber fought the night –
Delirious, and dying
He dreamt of city life
That spread across the valley
Towards the golden coast
Of towering palms and blondes –
A world he knew, now lost.

By morning all was pristine,
The High Sierras stood
Breathtaking on the skyline
Beneath the heaven's flood
That outlined every high ridge
And Ponderosa pine
As life began to trickle
Down the mountainside.

It wound across the valley
Towards the golden shore,
It entered rolling waters
By palms and bathing blondes;
It spread upon the ocean
The spirit of a man,
Freed upon the thawing
Of the High Sierra lands.

TO FIND HER ROBBIE, SO
[9.50pm, 1st Mar 1981, Fresno, California]

What would Highland Mary say
If she found her Robbie o,
Dancing with the serving maid
In the parlour naked so?

Would she not cry aloud
For her wretched Robbie o,
Drunken, footloose with the proud
Young Laura, white and virgin so?

For would it not break her heart
For to watch her Robbie o,
Stroke the red hair in the dark
Of lovely Laura laying so?

And would she not finally die
To hear her Robbie whisper o,
That he loved without lie

118

Young Laura he had taken, so?

And would they not bury her,
The wife of wretched Robbie o,
If we could not stop the hurt,
To see the maid with Robbie, so?

MILLIONAIRES IN DEBT (song)
[5.50pm, 8th Mar 1981, San Leandro, Calif.]

They pay for their cars,
They pay for their yachts,
They pay for their mansions,
They pay for their jets,
They pay for their art,
They pay for their friends,
That's six reasons why
There are millionaires in debt.

They spend on their business,
They spend on their wives,
They spend on their drugs,
And they spend all their life –
Spend to stem boredom,
Spend to hold back time,
Spend until they die
Without a single dime.

They buy for their comfort,
They buy for their blondes,
They buy for the future,
And buy government bonds –
Buy social status,
Buy climbing stock,
Buy cheap religion,
And buy cheap gods.

They sell all their faith,
They sell all their pride,
They sell all their morals
For a million dollar ride;
They sell short their children,
Sell short themselves,
Sell short their riches
In millionaire style.

So there goes the money,
There goes the cash,
And there goes the capital
Before the final crash –
And there goes the mansion,
And there goes the jet,
And there go the friends
Of a millionaire in debt.

MY WIFE AND MY TYPEWRITER
[9.25pm, 10th Mar 1981, San Leandro, Calif.]

When my wife began to type, she asked
'What do I do at the end of a line?
How do I get the margins straight?
Where do I put our address and the date?
How do I indent the paragraphs?
How do I make a capital F?
And where do I find the number 1?
What do I do when the bell has rung?
And if I happen to make a mistake,
What corrections can I make?'

Well, you can imagine the peace I got,
And the strain on my temper the questions
Brought every time that damn bell rang,
Every minute she continued to bang,
And thump, and hammer my poor typewriter.
Who said ladies fingers were lighter?
I'll tell you now, all poets and authors,
Playwrights and fellows of our professional collar –
Never be so silly or so innocently nice
To let your wife use your electric device.

BALLAD OF THE BLACK ISLE
[10ᵗʰ-11ᵗʰ Mar 1981, San Leandro, Calif.]

When the plague broke out
On the southern seas,
Of the ninety-two men,
They buried four a day.

Their skins blistered yellow
Beneath the frying sun
As scurvy killed the crew,
And the rats seaward plunged.

Then, on the port horizon,
Land broke the voyage,
A wisp of smoke escaping
From a black volcanic void.

While green threw the ocean
Upon its mangrove shore,
Upon the island smoldering
Beneath black lava rocks.

White horses dragged the shingle,
Dark mermaids combed the sands,
Pink conches sounded over
Pink coco-nutted palms.

Beige sky mirrored heaven
In a wispy cirrus mime,
Shrouding the volcano
As the molten tempest climbed

And thundered out of Hades –

Unleashed its storm,
Burnt the steaming forest
With its back ash rainfall.

And soon the roaring magma
Ran to the sea –
Till the island lay barren
Beneath black lava scree.

As the crew watched in horror
The destruction of the isle,
The scurvied souls prepared
To spend their final hours.

And towards an end they headed
Beneath the southern stars,
Until the black isle faded
And the white seagulls cried.

REAFFIRMATION OF LOVE
[12.17am, 14th Mar 1981, San Leandro, Calif.]

When lazy words crossed my lips,
I meant no harm to you –
Your simple love was all you gave,
All you wished was my love too;
But all I had was cheap reply,
A thing I never meant to do.

An offered pledge of servitude,
Of death, if need be known,
Should not be treated with a laugh,
Not treated lightly like a stone
Tossed thoughtlessly towards a lake
To watch the ripples turn to shore.

Far better that a flickering flame
Burns with all its fire,
Than have a man dowse its light
Or sate its glowing ember pyre;
For like the rose that blooms a day,
Love is sweet, should be admired.

Yet still my heart, my head deceives,
For you – my only girl!
With whirling eyes and swirling smile,
With crimson cheeks and hair a twirl,
I could not think of anyone
To give me more of love's sweet thrill.

THE PAST STILL BURNS TOO STRONG
[12.35am, 19th Mar 1981, San Leandro, Calif.]

Ne'er have the shores of England seemed so far.
Ne'er have the pains of languor been so strong.
Though oceans separate two nations and the past;
Though people's different ways keep each apart.

121

Ne'er have the hills of England seems so lost.
Ne'er have the thoughts of fiends been so dad.
Though language bonds two nations so alike;
Though continents create such wide divide.

Ne'er have the rains of England seemed to missed.
Ne'er have the aches of lovers been so stirred.
Though freedom grants the two with equal rights;
Though day shines there; while here is night.

Ne'er has the lure of England seemed so true.
Ne'er has the call of England been so clear.
Though Liberty resounds with song so loud;
Ne'er shall I turn again from England now.

EL SALVADOR IS NOT THE PROBLEM
[11.10pm, 22nd Mar 1981, San Leandro, Calif.]

While others bear the cross of Salvador,
Or decry the Polish labour crisis –
I gaze around me at the tramps and winos
Destitute upon the Bay city streets.

Beneath the Stars and Stripes,
Beneath the democratic lights,
Beneath the granted rights,
Beneath the surface of American life –

Please don't tell me about Calcutta,
I've seen the poverty for myself;
I've seen the bodies face down in the garbage;
I've seen the flies, the fleas, the lice,
Eat the sores and take Indian life for granted.

Such memories fade as time passes on –
They only come as demons in the night,
As mystic remains - horrors retreating
Into the subconscious of the mind.

Now I spend my time in America,
Where dreams exist for all to grasp;
Where bridges span the gap of class,
Progress speaks its own refrain
'Another day, another dollar -
some get bigger, some get smaller'.

Who really shares their wealth
With those who struggle on the street?
With their ragged clothes, shoeless hobos
Drunk and living with the trash
That represents our own foul waste –
A down-town district, deserted, desolate,
Inhabited by bums and derelicts.

Give a man some wealth, he forgets his brother;
Give a man some pride, he rides another;

Give a man truth, he turns and shudders.

Had you been born the son of a child molester?
Or the daughter of a cruel and twisted parent?
Would you be a social dreg, a parasite,
A twisted broken human fragment -
Living by handouts and dying from neglect.

A blindness to poverty exists –
For the moon is made of cheese and lemon fizz?
How can anyone really believe in this?

The President in a pathetic political fix,
Cites thirty-two pages of help-wanted ads.
His point? The nation has no desire to work.

Winos and tramps all around us,
And the plight of El Salvador scares the youth.
The mighty Republic of Fifty Unions,
Frightened by the consequences of Salvador.

Please don't try to tell me about socialism,
And how it will destroy the morals of the world.
Look around you, friends,
the person at your elbow –

The answer is not the defence of the Panama Canal.
The answer is not in total Cuban withdrawal.
The answer is your own sweet American self.
And your own bitter American selfishness.

WEST GRAND AND SAN PABLO (song)
[7.38pm, 24th Mar 1981, San Leaondro, Calif.]

A black spare-changed upon the side-walk,
The streets the ladies strolled or lounged,
Each lamppost offering refuge to someone
In the dark ghetto district of down-town.

The girls whistled out in hope of custom
To the honkies idly waiting at the lights,
While around the corner in an alley,
A mugger dragged a lady out of sight.

A baby screamed out form an attic window
As a hustler sold a kid a stolen watch,
And from the noise of the wailing cop-car,
Another grocer store had just been robbed.

A young girl gave into a rapist
After pleading at the point of a gun –
While a gang of high-school dropouts
Set fire to a disused house for fun.

A shoeless wino riffled in a trash can,
Just before another knifed him for his loot,
As a man beat his unfaithful lover,

While a junkie fixed his last poisoned shoot.

In all it was quite a summer's evening,
Nigh before the sunset finally came,
And brought the streaming red of evening
As blood filled very down-town drain.

MARCH OF TIME
[10.25pm, 29th Mar 1981, San Leandro, Calif.]

Weary Time wobbled on along the cobbled way,
Feeble hand on the shaft of his sickle blade;
White beard trampled by this trembling step,
He marched one step ahead of Death.

Loud tolled the tintinnabulation,
Shaken by the weight of Time's forced passing,
Pushed on by the lifeless breath,
Released from Death in fits of frothing.

Wretched wailing welled the ailing life,
Death solved that which Time passed by;
Step for step they marched together,
Arresting not for man, nor child.

APRIL IN CALIFORNIA
[2.30pm, 4th Apr 1981, San Leandro, Calif.]

What could be better in April
Than to sit, watch the hummingbirds
Dart beneath the blossom trees
Ablaze with springtime colour.

Or listen to the tickling breeze
Playing in the Chinese chimes,
Blowing gently on the petals
Of the pansies and snapdragons.

As I, sit by the lettuce patch
Whittling away the hours,
Under the shade of maple leaves
And a towering eucalyptus.

I study an ancient bonzi tree,
Sheltered by a redwood giant,
On such a sunny April's day
Under a Californian sky.

THE HIDDEN GLEN
[10.50pm, 5th Apr 1981, San Leandro, Calif.]

What is real in Highland lands
Of heathen fields and windswept mountains,
Peopled by such hardy peasants,
Driven on, and wind blast hardened,
By the harshness of their future
Dwelling in their wild domain –

124

Made braw by the soaring heather
Lashed and hewn by the rain.

Craggy were the rocks and faces
Of that hidden Scottish glen –
Across the moors, beyond the loch-side
- Misted by the swirling wet,
Hazed and fogged a million mornings,
Black and dead a million nights,
Never seen and never crossed,
by cottage light, nor crofter dykes.

Who passed such lonely hostile life
Beneath that roof. Who dwelt there?
A question that gave no answer
As the mist shroud-wound the air,
And brought with it an evil shiver
That made me cower deep inside,
To wrap my tweeds about my body
And leave that haunted mountainside.

BANKRUPT SWINDLER
[10.48pm, 11th Apr 1981, San Leandro, Calif.]

It started with a dodgy check,
And wages docked for income tax –
And other little simple things
That didn't seem to matter much.

The next he knew a letter came
Calling for an unpaid debt,
And then ten others on the mat,
Signaled that the rot had set.

His creditors came to take their goods
While their lawyers sued for more –
The sheriff locked the factory gates,
The workers sacked, went home.

Some said he'd do five straight years,
Some thought he'd go Scot-free –
But some saw a roaring jet
Carry him to sun and sea.

They were right, strange enough,
He went to hot Belize –
To swim in surf in coral bliss
And laze 'neath coco trees.

A WANDERER
[8.10pm, 12th Apr 1981, San Leandro, Calif.]

The question loomed out the sky
Like a spate of rolling cloud
Heading for the rain-thirst slopes,
To rescue and revive –
Every small blade of grass

Sun-battered to the ground.

Two eyes blazed upon my own
Like a vision of a God
Staring down in bloody want,
In need of a sacrifice –
As I counted out the cattle
Grazing on the land.

I cast my eyes to the hills
Like a wanderer on the move,
Roaming endless distant ways
In search of paradise –
As every thought I ever had
Answered in reply.

The question faded from the sky,
The burning died in his eyes
To whistle high above the rise
Of cattle grazing fields –
As I left the farmer there
Asking where go I.

NAPOLEON'S SOLDIER

[10.50pm, 19th Apr 1981, San Leandro, Calif.]

Versed in wisdom, not in sense,
Immersed in knowledge but not its love,
You traveled high the weathered trail
Through thickets thorned and barbed –
You carried countless inner doubts
That set your jawline hard.

Hard against the cold wind,
Cruel upon the snow
That buffeted your great-coat
As you struggled onwards home –
Broken like the army
The Emperor called his own.

Marching on to Moscow
And scattered in retreat,
While all France trembled naked
In the wake of raped defeat –
Why did you leave bright Paris
For Napoleon's sad elite.

Why forsake your lover
To fight for glory's sake,
I'll never understand the foils of war,
It only leads to wakes –
that women tend, and cry at
For men's proud mistakes.

Marching on to Moscow
To be scattered in burnt fields,
You left behind a trail of blood,

126

The Russians at your heels –
You left behind the one you loved
To die for your ideals.

HE WORKED TEN HOURS EVERY DAY
[9.35pm, 21st Apr 1981, San Leandro, Calif.]

He worked ten hours every day,
And hour there, an hour back,
By bus he traveled in the morn,
By train he left to journey home.

His wife waited for her man,
And kissed him warmly like she should,
His son asked if he could help
Fix his bicycle if he could.

The clock ticked on in gentle sighs
As he struggled with the bike –
His hunger pains grew very loud
While his wife took a shower.

While his hands were smeared in oil,
His son sat and quietly read –
His wife clean, and prettied up,
Felt tired, and went to bed.

He laboured on with the bike,
Instead of caring for himself,
And finally when he nodded off,
He hadn't eaten, hadn't showered.

Thus cheated of his leisure time,
He worked his life for his wife
And his son - who hated him
For never spending time with them.

JAPANESE GARDEN
[9.27pm, 27th Apr 1981, San Leandro, Calif.]

The Japanese garden
By the turtle lake
Beneath the awning maple
And mugo pine –

The juniper arrows
Raining on azalea heads –
There should be no flowers
In a proper bonzi bed.

CHINATOWN
[10.05pm, 10th May 1981, San Leandro, Calif.]

Sitting by the gates of Chinatown
Having a burger and shake,
In a sardine-box type café
Across from a sushi place –

While the tourists click away merrily
The taxi's roar through the gates,
As the sightseers crowd the side-walks
In the shove for gifts and keepsakes

That glitter in every store window
The colour of emerald jade –
Fans and frogs of fertility
Sending flushes to every awed face –

Trapped by the paintings of tigers,
By cymbles and tinkling chimes,
Climbing with the chittering chatter
Into the lit lanterns of Chinatown.

DEATH OF A YOUTH
[24th May 1981, San Leandro, Calif.]

When life is taken from the young,
It's sadder than a man of age,
Or graceful lady passing,
Who had time to pick a plot.

There is no peace, no solitude,
No preparation for this end –
It comes, the panic on its heels,
No prayers to let the dust descend.

There is no hope of quelling grief
While fault and blame bloods all minds –
There is no way of turning back
The clock before the fateful hour.

There is no more, no cold return
From tombstone etched in churchyard plot –
Greying, like those left to live,
To grieve the young so early lost.

Yet who knows why the grief is so?
Perhaps we know, but will not say –
Youth rushes at us all ablaze;
It comes, flames, and then it fades.

FREEWAY ACCIDENT
[12.25am, 29th May 1981, San Leandro, Calif.]

He was only twenty seven,
Manhood sparked in his eyes –
He blazed a trail through dreamland
Before being paralyzed.

The wheels for legs slowly spin
Along the corridors of white –
Everything is flying castles,
Pink butterflies and soaring kites.

Before the star-bursts fade off,
Become a grey lasting zone,
Slowly darkening each last second
Until all light – is gone.

ONLY THE BEST WILL DO
[12.54am, 29th May 1981, San Leandro, Calif.]

Soldiering on, Duke Wellington
At the battle of Waterloo,
Between a fit and a temper
Called his bugler to.

He said in an order of 'Bugler!
Be damned if you don't play true.
Signal the Royal Scot Greys
To charge Napoleon's Blues.'

No sooner the order carried,
The bugler bursting his gut –
For King! And Country! And Glory!
Made the Scots Grey horses charge.

They sliced through the terrified French,
Who fled from the hooves of the Greys,
Losing their coveted standard –
That Ensign Ewart snatched away

And carried to cheers and rejoicing
To the camp of the Iron Duke –
Who turned aside to his bugler
With a satisfied military look.

JUNE MAY COME TOMORROW
[5.35pm, 30th May 1981, San Leandro, Calif.]

This month a day but gone,
Pre-fades in sight of coming June,
Rides out my cantering thoughts
Cantering over the urban gloom
Of spending life in idle waste,
Paying rent and sundry bills,
That neither rid, nor further help,
Not cure the soul, to leave it still.

Will June be the answer then -
Tomorrow come as my rescue
Straddling every broken fence
Hemming in the city ruins
Of crumbling nerves and tired limbs,
Fettered to the urban tether?
Thank God that May has almost gone –
Bring on the summer weather.

FAREWELL SWEET POETS
(written on completion of another notebook)
[31st May 1981, San Leandro, Calif.]

One year of poems fill this book,
Through many thoughts and passing moods,
Sketched by peaceful flowing brooks
Or penned behind black masks and hoods.

Yet, here we are, at the end
And who shall say I did not try
To capture dreams and real intent
That time has gladly passed on by.

For who can count the inspired hours
My pen has flashed across the page,
Or dragged its ink in useless power
While inside my soul has raged.

But now, my work is nigh complete,
The words alone now will speak,
I'll leave this stage in slow retreat –
Farewell, sweet poets, farewell in peace.

BEFORE THE RAINBOW COMES
[31st May 1981, San Leandro, Calif.]

America's given me stage-life,
Performing my work to crowds
Who gather like rumbling clouds
Before clapping with loud shouts
In a thunderous shower of applause.

HOT PRAIRIE SUMMER
[20th Jun 1981, San Leandro, Calif.]

The chords of wood stood by the road,
By fields of corn hemmed in by woods.
A crane passed over in looping swoops.

A sleep-eyed mouse shook the sheaves,
A cool draught seeped around its nest
So steeped in heat, no breeze could dowse.

THE VALLEY OF BIG SUR
10.47pm, 28th June1981, San Leandro, Calif.]

Sentinel stood the pinnacle, the buttress and the peak,
Over all the forest – oak and giant redwood,
Shadowing the sur, the river gouged and stripped,
Leaving yellow gleaming pools with silver trout.

Foreboding o'er the treetops, an eagle swooped,
Magnificent, majestic, across the valley floor,
Chasing the wind sent up from the shoreline,
The ocean flowered in polka-dotted blossoms.

Ruefully passed a miner, his donkey and his load,
Along the eucalyptus, birch and aspen path –
Following the lust the wilderness denied him

By washing the golden flakes beyond his grasp.

Blinding sped the water, the cataracts and falls,
Surging off the basalt cliffs and canyon rocks,
Sweeping jewel-bright leaping trout into eddies
On which the eagle swooped as the miner watched.

Sad he turned, to search another raging creek -
Hazy fell the forest of oak and giant redwood;
Dark closed the sur on the river streaked with gold;
Misty grew the pinnacle, the buttress and the peak.

MURDER ON THE CATHEDRAL STAIRS
[10.27pm, 29th Jun 1981, San Leandro, Calif.]

Hollow sounding steps rung the night –
A woman high-heeled, heavy-thighed,
Quickly passed beneath the courtyard lights,
Near which a shadow lurked, tense and quiet.

The mist of Montmartre swirled about,
Her low-hem dress, her naked ankles, white,
Frozen in a cold sweat from sudden fear,
As behind the lurking shadow – neared.

Hurriedly her footsteps clawed stone stairs.
Too late! The shadow met her there!
Too young, the *fille de joie* lay there –
Severed bowels, red against her ankles bare.

THE WAY WE INTEND
[11.37pm, 29th Jun 1981, San Leandro, Calif.]

It's crazy how these things begin,
And how they never seem to end –
But go on – time on endless time,
Not the way we intend.

PUTTING THE BOSS STRAIGHT
[30th June ? 1981, San Leandro, Calif.]

Lazy, that's how I feel today.
Digging holes ain't my cup of tea.
For you tell me, amigo,
Have you spent the summer working
And sweating without payment?

Hell, no! You prissy little mother-fucker,
I sure ain't going to work for no bum!
Work? Screw it, man! Love!
Love is what I need, brother.

You give me your money,
And I'll give you my love.
Lazy, Christ no!
I'm just smart to know
I ain't working for fun.

IN DEBT TO THE TUNE OF YOUR LIFE
[9.17pm, 11th July 1981, San Leandro, Calif.]

I've tried to be tolerant of my debtors,
Of creditors, I've rarely had one –
And if I have somehow been negligent,
It was accident, not malicious intent.

It was because of my debtors lies,
My debtors deceits and crimes.
I have with all honesty,
Tired to pay my debts, at all times.

I am angry with all my debtors,
I have my gun loaded and primed –
While my creditors are looking for me,
I'm gonna mow my debtors down.

THE POET LEFT IN ME
[10.15pm, 16th Jul 1981, San Leandro, Calif.]

If the poet always has his wealth in poverty,
Is not his spirit then in debt?
Is not his hope a fragile longing
Of wasted words, idle talk, regret?

If a poet always quotes the truth aloud,
Is not his voice then in chains?
Is not his wisdom shackled by his honesty,
On which all lies, are truths just the same?

If a poet always speaks for the people,
Is not his thought then enslaved?
Is not his ego locked in essence,
On which all men are bound depraved?

If a poet always is and never was,
He's not the judge we see him as.
He's not the jury set to try us.
Then that poet is the poet left in me.

THE RAINBOW ROAD
[10.55pm, 21st Jul 1981, San Leandro, Calif.]

I once knew the world as a lonely place,
A place where man took his own stand,
A stand that separated him from others,
So that everyone knew each, apart.

These were old times, young wandering days,
Days spend upon the carefree road,
A road quiet, a way long -
That stretched towards the rainbow's glow.

I suppose now, that I was blind then,
Blind but young, and free and sold,

132

Sold to an idea of pots of gold
At the end of the rainbow road.

HEROES
[7.30pm, 26th Jul 1981, San Leandro, Calif.]

Heroes come in forms sublime,
Divine, yet surely fragile seeds
Borne by the storms of war,
Planted by the ploughs of peace.

Visions fall on those, so few
Selected from the seas of corn,
The grasses wild upon the plains,
The cradle of the voice unborn.

Too soon the cause has risen clear,
To run, to shun the final call –
A hidden hand pushed forth,
The hero stands, erect to all.

Stories told, in time unfold,
Of deeds, of inspiration cloned –
And statues tower in the parks,
Where victories raised, saw heroes fall.

JULY 29TH 1981
(for Laura's Thirtieth Birthday)
[8.45pm, 28th Jul 1981, San Leandro, Calif.]

On a summer's morn in English fashion,
The grey dawn will be long in brightening –
Silent, yet waiting for the city sleep
To turn the bells and drums which beat
To sound the coming of the carriages,
Carrying the Prince and his sweet Princess.

Yet for Laura, in distant California,
Such a morn of smoggy summer heat,
Takes the tenderness caught in her room
To mean that dawn has brought too soon
The passing of youthful age –
And the rising of a fuller shining moon.

NEVER TO BE FORGOTTEN
WILL COME MY SWEETHEART'S DAY
[00.00am, 29th Jul 1981, San Leandro, Calif.]

Never to be forgotten will come my sweetheart's day,
As dawn in England brings two million forth
To view and cheer for Charles, Prince of Wales,
Surrendering sweet love to his royal bride.

Which corner of the earth will not take note,
To trumpets ringing on the beat of drums,
To pipers singing in the lift of London's bells
That draw on people to hold their breath.

133

Yet, within my soul burns freedoms fire!
As violence, riots, starvation are forgotten,
While Ulster sickness ravishes Liverpool and Leeds,
And Glasgow nears the edge of open revolution.

The storm looms imminent in fascist Britain,
While I imprisoned, interred on hunger strike –
It started as a cause for equal rights,
Not rebellion, as the law has called my crime.

Meanwhile my love is far across the hills,
Across the wildest moors in hidden Irish heaths;
Awakening to the whistle of a hopping blackbird
On the garden fence, close by her window.

Grey clouds will rise from out the black North Sea,
As dawn presents her with a birthday gift –
Her thirty years of life run below the bridge
On which I imprisoned, must let the water flow.

The soldiers with their bullets, the police their shields,
I alone, call and cry these words for her.
Our love as a thing – cannot be broken,
Like the revolution that flowers and grows.

Never shall be forgotten my sweetheart's day,
I shall wait on God, to be set free –
A thousand years of English class oppression,
Shall be appeased, the day my sweetheart rejoins me.

SITTING AT A CAB STAND
[3rd Aug 1981, 13st & Mission, Hayward, Calif.]

When you're sitting at a cab stand
And waiting for a fare,
You watch all the action
Outside the bars and transit bays –
The to and fro of people
Beneath the falling night,
The drunks, the late-tired shoppers,
The aged, and wide-eyed types –
The old, and not so healthy
Who can't afford to ride.

TURN OF FATE
[10pm, 4th Aug 1981, Hayward Bart, Calif.]

Its strange how life takes so many turns
That is somehow incongruent with fate.
How many times have you barely wondered
That each step wasted could have been a hundred.

SIMPLE LIFE
[10.05pm, 4th Aug 1981, Hayward, Calif.]

How others' lives seem to simple;

134

So full of dull, and weathered living;
So bliss with boring, sameness days,
The same old thing, day in day out.

THE DICE PLAYER
[11.25pm, 10th Aug 1981, Hayward, Calif.]

When you can't make money,
Then you have to take a rest;
You might as well forget
The fortune in your head.

Who knows, perhaps tomorrow,
Or the next at least,
When you can't make money
What's the point of losing sleep.

When the day goes too quickly
And things are left undone –
What's the use of being angry
In the glowing, setting sun?

Who knows, perhaps tomorrow,
The anguish will not burn
As hot and deep and troubled
As today's frustration churned.

When the night fails to linger
And dawn begins to light,
You may feel the spirit
Rebirth in your life.

Who knows, perhaps by evening
The dice will have rolled –
With your fortune ready made
And your world turned to gold.

THE GET-AWAY
[10th Aug 1981, East Bay, Calif.]

On a rare cloudy night in California,
Near midnight on a chilly August evening,
On the outskirts of a large spreading city,
By the shores of San Francisco Bay –

A sleeping taxi-driver, in a dream
Set in a windswept Safeway parking lot,
Was suddenly awakened by a shot.
The 7-11 across the way was being robbed.

The gunman sped away in an '80's Chevy,
Burning rubber like some high-school kid,
In panic, doing wheelies on the side-walk,
Made his get-away with a last escaping skid.

THE IRISH
[19th Aug 1981, Hayward, Calif.]

135

Why does the Irish issue burn sweet tongues
With bitter words and stinging taste,
With acrid fire and acid pain
While Irish palates stay unstained?

Where I came from midst the working class,
Irish men wore handkerchiefs for hats,
Irish eyes were blank, and cheeks bright red,
And alcohol reeked from their every breath.

That's not to say they were low men,
For ne'er was one to hold a grudge –
And ne'er was found a broken soul
Who could not belly-ache a laugh.

Yet scourging every Irish tongue
Were tales of legend and of myth,
Mingled with a touch of truth,
Stretched beyond all common sense.

And who could doubt Irish love
Woven from the fear of God –
That honest women never gave
Till after wedding in a church.

Yet, please believe, I have no beef,
I've shared sweet nights with Irish girls;
I've drunk till dawn with Irish men
And had no foes, but many friends.

VETERANS CAB
[8.13pm, 21st Aug 1981, East Bay, Calif.]

Another night on the road –
Though rather different from the past;
Riding out in working life,
Driving round for Veterans Cab.

THE TRAVELER
[24th-26th Aug 1981, East Bay, Calif.]

I've spent a year in California,
But its not the only place I've been –
I was twenty-one in India,
And traveled Europe at seventeen.

I passed some time in Brazil,
And Kenya, not so long ago –
I crossed the Andes to Bolivia,
To rock-n-roll on the radio.

Now I'm flying out for Bangkok,
And India a second time around –
Can't say when I'll be returning;
Traveling is a fate blown life.

LET SWEET PEACE ABIDE
[1.47am, 27th Aug 1981, East Bay, Calif.]

Its always nice to let things slide,
To let things blindly, smoothly ride –
To lay all things off to the side,
And amply let sweet peace abide.

IN A FARAWAY LAND
[2nd-3rd Sep 1981, Hayward-San L, Calif.]

Clear be the day and blue the dawn
Before the gathering coming storm,
The unleashing of child, still unborn,
Coming, coming, until dawn's long gone.

Clammy the heat of the tropical noon
Before the thundering clamour rolls –
The storm, storm imminent looms,
Heralding, heralding a roaring typhoon.

Heavy the lashing and dark the simoom
Tearing palms from century old roots –
The rain, rain drumming tin roofs,
Bringing, bringing the wet monsoons.

Cool be the night and huge the moon
Through the door of the lighted room –
Crying, crying, carries a voice,
Born, born from a native's womb.

Clear be the day and blue the dawn,
The childbirth room beginning to warm –
The palms, palms whistling hum,
As gathering, gathering the storm it comes.

PARADISE
[6pm, 7th Sep 1981, San Leandro, Calif.]

Other worlds wait far beyond the seas,
Fired with long tanned, naked legs
And breasts heaving in the waves –
On a golden beach in Paradise.

UNFULFILLED ATTAINMENT
[6.02pm, 7th Sept 1981, San Leandro, Calif.]

How many years must the spirit wait
To catch the glory of the times;
Why must the soul bend its knee
To filter out the evil in the light?

No answer waits the unsure mind,
No treasure yields to the wanton heart;
Blank is the empty demon's love
Raging on, and on, through life.

THE MONOLITH ISLE
[14th-15th Sept 1981, Hayward, Calif.]

Every day I tire of city life
I cry for the lost still hours,
I spent by the healing black waters
That circled the Monolith Isle.

I long for the endless peace found
Down by the pebbles and stone –
Circling the ghosts and the spirits
Cast by the mist on that shore.

For there I discovered silence
Skimming the black lake swell,
Gently cutting the white tops
While stars as raindrops fell.

Till I ground ashore on the agate
That clung to the Monolith Isle,
I tied my skiff and unclothed -
And ascended in primitive bounds

To a cave I know on the summit,
Where naked and utterly alone –
I listened as the echoes recited
The beat at my deep heart's core.

And curled like an unborn baby
In the chill of the cavern womb,
I grasped the lost millenniums
And the cave as a sacred tomb.

And still as I tramp the city
I hear the inner, clear cries
Of the spirits leashed in the darkness
In the depths of the Monolith Isle.

MY TWENTY-THREE FIRST-COUSINS
[23rd Sept 1981, Hayward, Calif.]

Of my twenty-three first-cousins, Allen's now in jail,
Brian got released last week, certified sane –
And Cathy is a prostitute, barely in her teens,
And there's cousin Ian Barrie who's confessed as being gay.

There's George, a shipyard worker, always out of work,
And cousin Alec Hoban, who's never heard the word,
And there's little Annie Jean, now a convent nun,
And her brother Jamie John, a lying, cheating bum.

There's Marjory, a spinster, with a colic rubber heart,
And Margaret, a singer in the Sunday Mass church choir –
And Hughie lost to reason, wandering the world,
And cousin Robert Aitken who grows his own pot.

There's Carol born at Christmas, angelic, pure and dumb,

There's Davie, a gambler, a rogue, a thief, a pimp –
And lovely sweet young Gillian who drops them all the time,
And her sister Esther Bauld whose love produced a child.

There's Joan, a factory seamstress that suicide almost
claimed,
And cousin Jimmy Moffat that religion has reprieved;
And Hilary, the rebel, spouting high on L.S.D,
And Laura, slimming down on purple pills and cheese.

There's Robin, fallen woman who's been married seven times,
And there's cousin Isabel, an old fashioned girl,
And finally, there's Albert, who just this week was born –
I guess when added up, that's twenty-three in all.

24TH SEPTEMBER
[24th Sept 1981, Hayward, Calif.]

On the 24th September, the rain began –
'Earlier than usual' said the tramp.
'I guess I'll be looking for somewhere warm
to hole up before long'.

And he was right as the leaves fell
And bare the skyline stood –
As rain dropped, and wind blew
In every neighbourhood.

And the floods came, and deluge followed,
And homeless fled the rising tide –
While on the higher land, water carried
The soil off in endless mudslides –

That never lent not let hinder
The never stopping rain that came –
Dropping like pennies falling
From a Las Vegas slot machine.

Soon stripped, the covers of the sky
Lay bare the naked stars in bed –
And instantly the waters fell
As rising dawn like cockerel broke

The tramp awake from his sound sleep;
Oblivious to the passing flood –
In idleness of yawning breath,
He arose from the sea of mud.

THE TWENTY TWO TRIALS OF A TRAVELER
[29th Sept- 6th Oct 1981, San L – Hayward, Calif.]

He has lived the life of a wanderer,
and much has he conquered and borne,
he's lived with the twenty-two troubles
in order to learn and to know

That though weakened & ravished by hunger

139

and covered in rivers of veins,
he'd take only his rationed measure
and wander on cheerful and sane -

And refrain from drinking cold water
though gagged by tropical thirst,
restrained by shame and aversion
to discover the happiness sought.

Avowed, austere, and ascetic,
occasionally plundered by cold,
he'd never walk without reason
beyond what the scriptures controlled.

He'd suffer from heat on his body,
he'd suffer from summer's hot winds,
but he'd never lament discomfort
nor wipe the sweat from his limbs.

And suffering from insects and gad-flies,
he'd not chase the creature flood,
he'd tolerate all living beings
though they fed on his flesh and blood.

With his clothes torn, he'd go naked,
it mattered not to him ...
complaint was for poor weaklings
whose robes were spun from whims.

And born a man of our essence,
with women a natural desire,
he'd prefer to perform his duties
than search for the ego in I.

Thus different from those about him
he'd acquire no chattels nor goods,
unattached to house or house-holders,
he'd sleep wherever he could.

In a burial place or roofless house
or below a tree he would sit,
alone, without moving, and fearless,
he would study encircled by birds.

And having found good lodgings,
he would never tarry long,
the nature of penance and inner-self
would make him travel on.

Thus house-less and poor, the wanderer
from town to village did roam,
Passionless, perfect, and sinless,
he'd wander on tireless, alone.

And if a layman somehow abused him,
he'd grow neither angry, nor cruel,
he'd take torment with silence

140

and keep his soul a jewel.

And when beaten, he was not angry,
he'd vent no vengeful thoughts,
with calm resign and patience,
he'd revise what wisdom taught.

And in the quandary for perfection,
he'd debate to beg, or starve,
for all, or some, or nothing,
he'd hold out his bowl and ask.

And when denial produced hunger,
in the grip of deep desire,
in the wake of gathering sadness,
he'd still produce a laugh.

And when ill, he'd take no treatment,
he'd sojourn on alone ...
to find the firm and fast,
and the future for his soul.

And naked, rough, and sun-burnt
hurt by grass, by wind ...
he would not search for new clothes
to cloak his dust-stained skin.

For to carry such filth on his body
until expiration on death,
while not lamenting discomfort,
was noble and true to the path.

Which led him to harbour no cravings,
nor have resent for pleasant things,
for not being dainty and sorry,
he took what life might bring.

And such remembered past actions,
as a product of ignorance and youth,
To understand was the answer -
the way of reaching the truth.

Turned from the lust of the senses,
he lived with huge restraint,
he practiced religious austerities
until his path was clear.

He thought of the future coming,
the exulted state received,
he journeyed from village to village
until this was achieved.

And this is the life of the wanderer!
The ascetic who travels alone!
Who bears the twenty-two trials
the length of the heavenly road!

IN THE MENDICINO MOUNTAINS
[13th-14th Oct 1981, Hayward, Calif.]

In a smoky little cabin in the mountains
Where the girl of my dreams had taken me –
I discovered while watching leaves fall,
The love that was blind to me.

To doubts I'd had about the word forever,
To which my lover whispered answers with her touch;
In the dark as naked flames danced to music,
I clearly saw life, and death, and love.

In reflection, in that solitude and calmness,
True love showered and showed itself to me;
In the silence between the drumming raindrops –
Eternity bound my true love to me.

IN GEORGE'S NAME
[14th Oct 1981, East Bay, Calif.]

If only George had known
That his face would fly above
The aspirational wanting
Of a nation on the burn –
That everything he stood for
Would be written on the back,
In green, and blessed by God,
And signed as ONE.

And in the city of his name,
Huddle fascist heads –
Scheming arbitration
With Egyptians and the Lebs;
As green-backs reach the ceiling
Of the U.S. Fed Reserve,
Stamped – DESTINATION BEIRUT,
SPEND ON ARMS AND LEAD.

And above Jerusalem's wailing
From the tallest minaret,
The muezzin's cries befalling
On subdued Arab heads –
Suppressed and bent to order
While planning sweet revenge,
On walls daubed with slogans
And machine-gun epithets.

And no wonder George is angry –
He's being used to kill,
All P.L.O. fanatics
And to pay for Muslim girls,
Brought by Yiddish soldiers
Occupying the Strip –
To the clapping of the world
And a blitz of dollar bills.

IF JOHN LENNON HAD BEEN A WOMAN
[16th Oct 1981, East Bay, Calif.]

If John Lennon had been a woman
Where would she be now,
And if he had been a woman,
Would Sadat have been shot down?

And what about Abe Lincoln,
Pursuer of equal rights –
And poor Mahatma Gandhi,
A spirit in the night.

They could have all been women
With love in their souls,
To guide with mother kindness
Till all were aged and old.

Yet if only sad John Lennon
Had been less dreamer like,
And Anwar Sadat hadn't let
Bodies float on down the Nile;

And if Lincoln hadn't sent
A nation into war –
And Gandhi hadn't put
The Muslims to the wall.

If only they'd been women!
With gentle, subtle minds,
To rule with love and conscience,
In peace with all mankind

If only man were woman ...
And woman, only love.

BETWEEN THE SHEETS
[11am, 17th Oct 1981, San Leandro, Calif.]

White in spring,
Brown in summer,
Golden in autumn,
Me and my lover.

THE CONTINUATION
[11.40pm, 20th Oct 1981, East Bay, Calif.]

And hot the brown heath rose in flames
Around the dying sunflower stem,
And hot the fire-dust stung the eyes
As weeping screamed the flower near death –
As black wings beat the blackened air
As war the country swept.

And after, when the war was dead
And skeletons silhouetted every field –
Cool the rain wet the earth

And swollen soil hid the unmarked graves;
As steamy dew turned to misty haze
And life emerged as a sunflower's face.

EARLY MORNING IN EAST BAY
[1.35am, 21st Oct 1981, East Bay, Calif.]

Cloudy fog and dampened streets,
Trundling freight and rolling stock –
Deserted cafes and side-walks.

Glaring lights and hanging palms,
Lifeless cars and smile-less tramps,
Traffic signs and billboards.

Stop lines and cop sounds,
Long waits and bus brakes,
High-heels and gays.

Radio waves and darkened stairs,
Mean towers and lofty stars,
All through the night.

DRIVEN TO MAKING EXCUSES (song)
[1am, 27th Nov 1981, East Bay, Calif.]

Mr C.H.P man –
Why're you giving me a ticket?
I was only doing ninety
Like a million other idiots.

Mr. County Sheriff –
I ain't been heavy drinkin,
I only had twelve beers
And your talking prison!

Mr. City Cop –
I never ran that red,
You blinked and missed the amber,
I ran through pink instead.

Mr. District Judge –
I'm telling you the truth,
That for every bad offense
I've a plausible excuse.

DOWN BY THE BAY
[27th Nov 1981, East Bay, Calif.]

Around the Bay today
There's too many towns to name;
Five million people living
Life crazy, and insane.

There's Berkeley – loony haven
For the brilliant and the dregs;
Full of cosmic happenings

On the street and inside heads.

There's phony Palo Alto
And its love of social class
While the leaves on the street
Are as thick as piles of trash.

There's lovely west-side Oakland
Next to Alameda borough,
Where the Fleet dries its ships
By the quaint wooden houses.

There's geriatric San Leandro
Where the whites are full of fight;
Where the cops return the black folks
To Oakland every night.

HONG KONG
[1.50pm, 18th Dec 1981, Hong Kong]

The visitor to Hong Kong notices
That the air smells like day-old egg sandwiches.
It is a combination of motor vehicles,
Frying rice and piles of garbage
Spiced by the oil-streaked harbour
Carried by the sea-breezes.

A journey by cable-car to the top
Of Victoria Peak is only a respite
From the choking atmosphere,
That makes the head reel, the stomach wretch,
The legs wobble as if coping with the tremor
Of an endless earthquake.

But better to suffer the streets
Than the warren, crowded tenements
With their black void of daylight
In box-size rooms serving whole families,
The rationing of water between set hours
Making most human functions a chore.

These inconveniences do not make living
inexpensive in a city where a hotel room
costs fifteen dollars a night -
A meal in a crummy dive more than
A spotless restaurant in San Francisco.

Hong Kong is riding on a wave of prosperity
That almost makes the cost of living bearable,
The overcrowding acceptable, and the smell
Of day-old egg sandwiches almost unnoticeable.

BANGKOK
[22nd Dec 1981, Bangkok, Thailand]

Sampans and coco-palms,
Bamboo and banana fronds –

145

All along the waterfront
Of the Bangkok canals ….

CHRISTMAS DAY IN THAILAND
[Christmas Day 1981, Sukothai, Thailand]

Christmas Day in Sukothai –
Wats and ancient stupas,
Buddhas reaching for the sky,
Their heads like rising steeples.

Casting needle shadows down
Upon the pink pond-lilies –
Sailing in a pool of green
Of calm, serene, sweet beauty.

Blocking out all Christian thought
Of Saint Nicolas and Jesus –
Jingling bells and powder-snow,
Parceled gifts, and candy.

All so far away and lost,
Neither missed nor wanted –
Christmas just another day
Where Buddhas brood, undaunted.

HEAD IN THE CLOUDS
[1st Jan 1982, Bangkok, Thailand]

Anyone who's been to Hong Kong or Bangkok
Will know what I'm talking about –
They're gas chambers of smog and pollution
That strangle and choke, day and night.

It's no surprise the eyes start weeping
And the nostrils cake opium black –
And the throat begins to rasp like a file
Grinding down a laryngitis attack.

It's wise to get out of such cities
And give your lungs a rest –
Clear the throat with a whiskey
On a flight to somewhere else.

SONG FOR BANGLADESH (song)
3rd Jan 1982, Dacca, Bangladesh]

Did George ever really come here?
Did Mr.Raman really lead the crowds?
Between the floods and the famine –
Oh Bangladesh. Oh, my!

Bangladesh, ah yes!
Bangladesh, aa chaa!
Bangladesh, oh man!
Bangladesh, oh my!

BRAHMAPUTRA
[10th Jan 1982, Sylhet, Bangladesh]

The Himalayan snows lay faraway
Beyond the shimmering solitude.
From hence the Brahmaputra rose,
A thousand miles it washed lost Tibet.
Until, it turned and rained Assam
Of all its rain that ran like blood,
Red with silt, and weighed with mud,
All carried westwards, high in flood.

And when it reached the Bengal plain
And broke its banks while turning south,
The waters spread, carried miles
To form a hundred rivers and a thousand isles.
While joyous farmers, hungry from the drought,
Cried and sung their joy into the night;
The Brahmaputra, smooth like glass,
Threw the moon into a splintered mirror of light.

And in the small hours of the dawn,
The sacred Ganges waters merged;
Swelled by tears that pilgrims wept –
The rivers joined, and onwards swept
As the monsoon storms blew in
To cloud the distant delta flow –
The Brahmaputra, once so proud,
Gave out beyond the Bengal shore.

MONASTERY OF GHOOM
[Jan 1982, Darjeeling, India]

Sweet mountain rising over all,
Cypress wound, the mist it falls
As cloud upon the foothill ridge
Where perched - the tribal flags
Unfurled, meet the creeping wall of fog
That falls on the monastery at Ghoom.

IN THE GUTTER IN CALCUTTA
[Late Jan – 17th Feb 1982, Calcutta & Madras, India]

Down in the gutter in Calcutta
With the waste, the sewage, and trash,
I am smoking a chillum, and watching
From behind my opium haze -
The commotion of rickshaws and taxis,
Trams and buses jam packed –
While sitting on a bench in a chai shop
And throwing piasa in a beggar's plate.

It's a long way down, a Calcutta gutter –
I've fallen in with ruin, and drugs;
I can count three lepers as comrades
And two French dopers as chums;
There's a girl I've declared my love to,

Who refuses to listen to me –
She scorns, and curses my position
At the bottom of the social tree.

My enemies seem like the whole world,
Guilty and pitiless free –
A seething mass of faceless souls
Afloat in a shipwrecked sea,
Filled with waste, and with garbage
And the vomit of a thousand years –
I'm just an opium addict …
Drowning in opium tears.

MALARIA
[31st Jan 1982, Puri, Orissa, India]

Mosquitoes of India!
Killing me with stinging, gnawing bites.
In fever I am hemp-roped in bed
For four days, three nights?

I am delirious … the shutters are closed,
The punkah looms still.
The waves are pounding on the shoreline,
A black crow sings –

Oh the wonder of the sunrise!
I am carried to the Indian Ocean -
Bathed in the soothing brine.
The fever leaves me, and I cry.

HUNTERS OF THE SEA
[7th Feb 1982, Puri, Orissa, India]

Out beyond the warm, shore sands -
Where sit the village wives and mothers,
As hungry as the burnt-back men -
The hunters of the deep blue waters
Thrash out against the sharks
Whilst reaping in their casting nets –
A basketful of bone-backed fish
And a turtle, to sustain their faith.

No man lets his children starve,
If out beyond the shore he knows,
Swims a beast his neighbour craves,
And eats because there are no fish;
For like the hunter who finds no fowl,
Turns he then to larger game;
Likewise the fishermen are forced
To bring their turtle back to shore.

To the fisher of the Eastern seas,
The turtle is not sacred, not returned -
And there, upon the golden sands,
Midst wives and naked children,
They let the turtle's red-blood flow

148

And trickle down into the waves,
As the sky becomes a crimson glow,
And evening falls upon the shore.

The turtle fills a score of hands,
That drip their way to each dark hut,
Lit only by quiet, naked flames
As through the night as hunger died,
The dogs lick out the turtle shell.
Three days later, bleached and wormed,
Two girls scrape the shell with bone,
Ocean washed – then carried home.

While the hunters, with nets untangled
for the depths set their sails -
Flexed sore muscles, torn by toil,
Burnt-backed, hungry, leave the shore.

DEEP IN THE TROPICS
[9th Feb 1982, Puri, Orissa, India]

Laziness is conducive on a sunny day
As the white sands stretch,
And the palms hang limp in the heat.

Idleness is not a foolish dally
Among the white, cool waves,
Or beneath the cloudless sky.

Laughing is not a rich man's domain
Under the leaning shade,
And a spreading banyan.

Leisure is not a noon-day sleep
Upon a hemp-rope bed,
While a fan slowly turns.

Inactivity is a way of life,
Lethargy is human nature
In the tropical south.

SHORES OF ORISSA
[12th Feb 1982, Puri, Orissa, India]

Quietly come the shadows of evening
On the wake of the day.
As the fishing boats beached in the sand.
Ashore went the warriors and heroes
To the fires of the night,
Soon ablaze with the catch.

Asleep fell the feasters and drinkers
Close to the break of the tide.
The lapping counted out time
As full, rose the moon in blister
To hush the night murmurs
Before the rebirth of day.

Ferociously the dawn woke crimson
To colour the fishermen's limbs
Fighting the in-bound surf –
And soon, mere dots on the skyline,
Tiny specks of brown sail,
The fishermen laboured till night.

IDLE EVENING
[1035pm, 13th Feb 1982, Puri, Orissa, India]

And evening of little doing and doing little,
Letting the seconds trickle and the hours whittle,
As the days tumble and the months rumble,
And the years slip by in tens.

A night of thinking little and little thinking,
Letting the thoughts slither and ideas slide,
As the candle dims and the shadows claim
The world on either side.

THE LAND OF OM-NA-ONG
[13th Feb 1982, Puri, India]

Sitting under the mango tree
Awaiting the fruit to fall –
Is how the fairies collect their wealth
In the woods of Om-Na-Ong.

OLD MADRAS
[17th Feb 1982, Madras, India]

Mobs of bare-footed beggars
Littering the cow-dung streets,
Crowded with vendors and merchants
Talking business over tea and sweets.

Discussing the latest in shipping,
The price of tobacco or wheat,
The state of the country in general,
The abuse of government seats.

The excessive lining of pockets,
Leaving the poor little to eat,
But little morsels of gossip,
Trampled under uncaring feet.

A community striving for progress
In a rumble and tropical beat,
Kept alive by the suckling of babies
On milk from naked teats –

Once fired by the hands of lovers,
Faithless and ready to cheat,
Or abandon their armies of children
Thrown out to compete –

For food and worldly attention,
Who as beggars, learn to greet
Life with a shrug of acceptance
And *hello* as meaning *baksheesh*.

Home as a roadside mattress
A couple of cardboard sheets,
In the open, or under a tree
On one of a hundred streets.

THE MADRAS CAFÉ
[4.50pm, 20th Feb 1982, Madras, India]

In a city famed for its cuisine,
And noted for *dossa* and *bakala*;
Between the savouries and sweet things,
The *bajis* and *gulabjamons* –
There is *pongle*, *poori* and *semia*,
Noodles in a variety of sauce –
And the famous *massala dossa*,
Madras's own special love.

At the heart of the culinary wonders,
Is Shree Krisna's enormous Lunch Home –
Where an order of oothappam
Is like ordering spaghetti in Rome;
Where coffee's the price of a phone call,
And as good as you get in Rio;
Where the service is swift and pleasant,
And the bill a few rupees all told.

I doubt they know what they're missing
In the cafes of Paris and Rome,
In London, or New York, or Moscow,
Or Berlin, Buenos Aires, and Tokyo.
For Shree Krisna's, the venerable Lunch Home
Is above, and beyond their know –
Oh hail, Shree Krisna's Lunch Home!
I café in Madras where I go.

And thus, having lavished my praises
On this oasis of gastronomical power,
And thus having emptied my cravings
For the endless dishes I've devoured;
I shall rise from my idle longing
And prepare for my daily show
At the Shree Krisna Lunch Home -
The café in Madras that I know.

A LOT OF EFFING NOTHING
[5.10pm, 20nd Feb 1982, Madras, India]

Free flowing thought flying furtively
With foreign fancies and familiar feelings.
Fighting furiously to flourish forth
And fill fresh fantasies of fame,
Fortune and future, in finely

151

Fixed, formulated fiction flying
Fatalistically from fact to false
Fits of frustration, faulting few,
Yet fatiguingly forcing flimsy faith
In fate to the fore.

ARJUNA'S PENANCE
[11.20pm, 24th Feb 1982, Mahabalipuram, Tamil Nadu, India]

Arjuna was a warrior prince
Who summoned Lord Siva to grant him a wish -
That his foes be destroyed,
And he released from his penance.

THE ASOKA (THE PARK)
[25th-26th Feb 1982, Mamallapuram, TN, India]

The jasmine blossom open there
Incensed with love, the night-air stirred,
Rippled by the sea-wave pound,
Mumbled on by drunken mirth,
As stars broke bright and hazy through
The cypress standing by the palm –
What better arbour was there made
For lovers and the bliss of kiss.

The stories of a universe –
Sands as endless as all life,
Sprung to form, fired the night
Like flaming parakeets in flight;
As falling stars streamed the dark
To carry jungle callings far –
Far into the longing hearts
Of dreamers caught in want of love.

And deep within the floral park,
The scents of content, issued forth
To grant a heavenly grove of jewels,
A paradise of isolated mood –
A place where lovers' only food,
Was love, and love a constant woo –
Where jasmine blossom wildly grew,
And love was all that lovers knew.

SAGUNTHALA
[11.20pm, 7th Mar 1982, Pondicherry, India]

The Lady of the Forest one day appeared
To the hunter lost in fear;
Gripping tight his unslung bow,
He could not let an arrow go –
Such beauty, he had never seen;
She stood erect – a queen.

THANDUVAM (NATARAJA)
[11pm, 12th Mar 1982, Chidambaram, TN, India]

Bharata Natyam, thus is called -
Lord Shiva, poised in awesome sight,
The Cosmic Dance to destruct all,
With Nataraja posed in flight.

EDGE OF NIGHT
[5.45pm, 13th Mar 1982, Tiruchirappalli, TN, India]

Here I am at the end of the day
Far in the Indian south –
With the reward of a shimmering evening,
And a breeze of refreshing delight.

But how does one know heaven
In the middle of paradise –
How can the blue of the night sky
Be anything but an illusionary sight.

How can this circle of palm trees
Be but the fringe of twilight –
Or more than a perimeter of blackness
Close to the edge of the night.

MATTER OF OPINION
[13th Mar 1982, Tiruchirappalli, TN, India]

Some people say I have the Devil in me,
And others that I am God himself –
I think the latter are righteous,
And the former don't see themselves.

Who can dispute the difference
Or the shade of the character unseen,
When working on being mischievous
Or preaching religious belief.

For some say I am a villain,
And others, I am a perfect saint;
So take it from me when I say –
I can't always be what you paint.

FINE MANGO TREES
[8.30pm, 17th Mar 1982, Courtallam, TN, India]

I'll tell you of a very fine town
With healing falls and spectacular views,
With bands of thieving monkeys
Living in the fine mango trees.

It is land which is rich in honey
And flowing with sweet, nectar juice,
And spiced with fennel and nutmeg,
And the oils of essence and wood.

And where, tell me, is this haven
Of radiant green and flowering forest;
In what such a land do monkeys live

153

High in the fine mango trees?

And why no talk of shady dark things,
Can there be such a perfect land
Of sylvan walks, and ripening fruits
Rarely visited by outside man?

Well, I'm not about to tell you
And risk spoiling such a perfect place;
The town where all can plainly see
The monkeys in the fine mango trees.

FATE IN PARDISE
[9.05pm, 22nd Mar 1982, Kanniyakumari (Land's End), India]

One person's paradise is another man's home
Across the globe's oceans and shores,
Coloured by the spectrum ever spinning,
Rolling out sand-dust or gold.

While others foul or sell their bodies,
We lie in the naked sun parade –
Fanning the breeze of sweet desire,
Squeezing out diamonds from rain.

While others shout out for peace and freedom,
Or sap growing power into strength;
One man's universe is another's prison,
And paradise a vision dreamt.

For all that is born and passes
Under the blaze of the galaxy stars –
One is created, and one is expended,
And we, willing or not, take part.

Where would we be without paradise
In the worlds of a thousand myths;
One man's fate is another's faith,
And fate in paradise a gift.

THE NAGERCOIL TWIT
[9.55, 24th Mar 1982, Allepey, Kerela, India]

Every beggar is a human performance
Of mime and theatrical tricks,
Laced with a touch of mockery,
Sarcasm, and biting hard wit.

But none was the equal of Natty,
The half-cocked Nagercoil twit,
Who could drool at the hint of a penny
Or break into a hysterical fit –

That broke the bounds of convention
And drew spitting and shrieking disgust
That once made a lady from Delhi
Vomit on him from a bus.

Which somehow improved his appearance,
Made him overjoyed with his filth
As he danced like a raving madman,
And clung to the legs of the rich.

Yes! Natty was hero of some kind,
In the swamps of the nondescript,
He drew stares for his pathetic condition
And more than the occasional kick –

That sent him into the gutter,
Where he rolled and laughed in the stink –
For even hell was a heaven
To Natty, the Nagercoil twit.

AS THE LIGHT CONTINUED TO BURN
[3.05pm, 2nd Apr 1982, Mysore, India]

How bright the light shone in the window!
And how the eye carried over miles.
Yet dark within were the words expounded
And whispered to unravel time.

And like gold, the palace reflected,
And crimson the mimosa tree flowered.
Yet sad were the thoughts interrupted
And ceded to the piercing sunlight.

And how the jade hills beckoned,
And the sky enveloped the world.
And how the dark of the skyline room
Absorbed the heat of the afternoon.

And sweet blew the breeze to embellish,
The air afire with temple-scent woods.
Yet unmellow the whispers continued
To unruffle the infinite smooth.

Till a hawk in the sky hovering higher,
Ended time in a downward plunge.
And the talk in the dark subsided
As the candle continued to burn.

THE COLONY
[9th – 10th Apr 1982, Goa, India]

Fishing boats raced to be first on the ocean,
And sparrows hopped the roofs of red-tile,
And men in white shirts and ladies in blouses,
Bused and walked the streets of the town.

Clouds that were grey, shifted and lightened,
And the breeze in hints unfurled the flags,
And children in temper would settle for ices,
As friendly policemen joked loudly and laughed.

White limousines sped to rich destinations,
And poor tired workers headed for home,
And the sun in the west set on the ocean,
As the restaurants threw open their doors.

Life in the colony was endlessly changeless,
Where everything new became repeatedly old,
Where the sun in the east rose out of jungle
That only the towers of the churches broke.

Then one day in-marched the invaders,
Proclaiming the colony under a new flag,
And the men in white shirts and ladies in blouses,
Bent to the force of the invader's new laws.

Till no-one remembered the names of old rulers,
And the poor tired workers headed for home,
And the clouds above, shifting and passing,
Where everything new became repeatedly old.

ARABIAN SEA
[11th Apr 1982, Arabian Sea, Daman, India]

The aquamarine hue of the tortoise-shell water,
Broke from the bow in a stream of white slake,
As a black-headed gull trailing the stern wake,
Befriended a tanker till the land disappeared.

The sky above was a picturesque brightness
Of milky-cream beauty tossed on the breeze –
The world – now a saucer of endless ocean,
And the name of that water – the Arabian Sea.

BOMBAY
[14th-15th Apr 1982, Bombay, India]

There is nothing much to speak of
But vendors and rinky-dink stalls,
Obscured by the rude general public
Viewing the overcrowded side-walks -

Hugging the wide central roadways –
The choked arteries of the city's guts,
Kept blocked by red twin-decker buses,
And by yellow-topped taxi cars.

As the trains in the station depart,
Or screamingly halt, and unload
A seething mass of pain-faced foes,
Rushing to join the jostling hordes.

Like all of Bombay's ten million souls
Careering on their personal courses,
Up the steps of the Post Office stairs,
All arms and legs in a beaded-brow pant.

Or along the road past the Indian Times,

156

Where the chatter of presses drown the chants
Of mourners, bearing a fallen-one's pall
Through the streets till the procession is lost –

In the snarls of temper, the whiplash of steel,
Of human reactions to the machines on wheels,
Vehicles reeking of cheap gasoline fumes,
The pollution as thick as whipped double-cream.

The cream as sour as the government's schemes,
The city as decadent as a westerner's dream –
Of drugs, sex, where everything is legal,
Where money rules, and killing comes easy –

Where crime employs a tenth of the people,
And pigeon shit is an unavoidable evil,
That adheres to walls, statues and vehicles,
And drops like rain in the monsoon season.

A man without shit is a man without reason
To complain about Bombay's indifferent treatment
Of stranger, of friend, of tourist or fool,
Trapped in the melee of the city's dark mood.

KATHMANDU
[10pm, 24th Apr 1982, Kathmandu, Nepal]

The so and so birds, in the such and such trees,
Swaying with the blossom, carried by the breeze,
Caught in the short grass, covering the fields,
Stretching like patchwork.

LORD FARTINGSON
[25th Apr 1982, Katmandu, Nepal]

Lord Fartingson was a bully, and a rogue
Who captained the house team-side –
While ruling with a cane on the inside,
He whipped and stung the boys to the quick.

THE SYMBOLS OF KATHMANDU
[27th Apr – 4th May 1982, Kathmandu, Nepal]

Snow Buddhas lined the high ridge path,
Descending at a waterfall,
Towards the ancient city walls,
Twelve hundred years evolved
From even older truths and vedas –
The Symbols of the North.

1
The Conch Shell symbolises Victory
Sounding o'er the land -
Returning armies spoiled by war,
Courageous battles fought, and won,
Never lost, and ne'er forgotten
When even playfully blown.

157

2

A Vessel denotes Mental Purity
In an abstract form -
A vase containing crystal clear water,
Or a pitcher, the sweetest oils;
So thus the mind in perfect solution
Fixes on absolute thought.

3

The Endless Knot symbolises Long Life,
Like the boughs of an oak -
The intertwined vine growing profusely
Upon the ancient and crumbling past,
Woven and strengthened, ever lengthening,
Never unravelled, nor snapped.

4

The Umbrella denotes Spiritual Supremacy,
Aloofness from life -
Celestial aspects and knowledgeable insight,
Patronised protection of truth and ideals;
Enlightened are those by history made,
Canopied beneath the umbrella's shade.

5

The Lotus weeps Spiritual Purity,
The essence of beauty -
Accepted by all who are cosmically gifted,
In search of the honey-milk pond,
A drop of sap, manifest as amber
In the palm of the hand.

6

The Banner portrays the Power of Knowledge
Held over all -
Waved at the fore of all confrontation,
Or flying as prayers, written as vows,
Or transcribed as tantras telling of mantras;
The secret of learning to be found.

7

The Wheel is the wheel of Dharma,
Truth never ending -
The soul reborn in continuous life,
Bound by the codes of ancient time;
Rewarded are those of chivalrous fame,
Released from the cycle of rebirth's pain.

8

Two alike Fish is Spiritual Wealth,
A banquet of plenty -
The spirit kept in supply of substance,
Without the cravings of hunger and greed
That lie beyond the mind, embedded
And rooted in every-day deed.

Even now, on the high ridge paths,
The snow Buddhas melt –
And though the crumbling city walls decay,
And time runs through the cracks,
The Symbols of the North prevail
As the future reads the past.

YAB YUM
[4th May 1982, Kathmandu, Nepal]

This peculiar little delight,
Once popular in Tibet,
Practised by sexual union,
Sets the soul alight.

CONDEMNED ON A FOREIGN WALL
[6th May 1982, Kathmandu, Nepal]

We may be condemned on a foreign wall,
Hated by one and all, and spat upon.
Our ideals may be treated with loathing,
Despised and trampled supremely on,
But never is a head raised, face to face
To tell us of those things, rightly wrong.

Ireland on a foreign wall is tyranny,
Oppression, human rights, blood and bigotry,
Civil war, occupation, and fascism,
Colonialism, Maze Prison and anti-Popery,
But never will a foreign clenched fist outstretched
Refuse a cheque for aid with scorn.

We may be condemned for Argentina,
Hated by one and all, and spat upon,
Our principles may be rooted in the past,
With the dogs now barking at our doors,
But to lay down our arms, and all that?
Such living in the past won't bring it back.

We know our enemies on the foreign walls,
The fronts of their houses are daubed with us,
Our actions may fill them with loathing,
Yet our armies still make them cower in fear;
But what use are foreign wall slogans,
In places where the people cannot read.

We may be condemned, but still unbeaten,
Hated by all foreigners, but never defeated,
Our culture may turn their very stomachs,
While our dominance smashes their very ego;
We may be condemned on a foreign wall,
But we are we, and the walls our people.

TEN THOUSAND DAYS
[9.30pm, 8th May 1982, Kathmandu, Nepal]

Another day older, one of ten thousand

That have passed on like clouds in the sky;
They seem short, can't all be remembered,
And have gone before the future arrives.

LEADING THE WAY
[9.50pm, 8ᵗʰ May 1982, Kathmandu, Nepal]

Pushing on, trying to reach somewhere, somehow;
Pulling along somebody who doesn't know how;
Leading the way like a goat up a mountain;
Tight roping the cliffs like a clown on a wire.

SUPPLYING A FATHER'S WANTS
[10.05pm, 8ᵗʰ May 1982, Kathmandu, Nepal]

'Give me more pot' cried the father
as the boy quivered and filled the bowl –
'Hurry up, boy, or I'll give you the slipper,
you sad wretched, rag of a child!
One more moment of wasted pleasure,
I can't stand it. Get on the go!
Hurry up, child, fire the mixture,
Your father's waiting, fill that bowl'.

PLAYTIME
[14ᵗʰ May 1982, Kathmandu, Nepal]

The thunder storm was over
And the birds were singing loud,
The sun was shining though
The floating pillow clouds –
And the children were playing
In the school playground,
And little pools and puddles
Were being splashed about.

Then unexpectedly, the bully
Splashed a girl, got her wet,
And ne'er was there such fury
As she wrang his sorry neck –
And the thunder storm came back
As the bell for classes went,
The bully lay in a puddle
As the first raindrops fell.

VULTURES
[19ᵗʰ May 1982, Kathmandu, Nepal]

In the high trees, caught in the breeze,
The vultures sat with their fearsome faces,
Hooked to the wind carrying wild seed,
Widely sown against walls, in quiet places.

Clover thrived in fields of cow pasture
Ringing the city in an emerald glow,
While the vultures, black upon the horizon,
Sat in the trees as the darkest of foes.

The breeze continued to blow on the city,
Wild grass sprouting from the cement in the walls.
The vultures remained sitting in the branches,
Watching the crumbling city walls fall.

They sat there, up in the high trees,
Bills to a wind carrying wild seed;
Getting old just like the city –
Soon a place of grasses and weed.

And still they sat there in the high trees,
For where else were they likely to go?
Until the city was a desolate wasteland,
The dust a scattering of powdered bone.

PARADISE AND HELL
[31st May 1982, somewhere over Turkey]

Paradise may be found at a rainbow's end;
After being to the ends of the earth,
Such a paradise is also a hell –
An experience never to talk of.

But having been through pleasure and pain,
Prying open oysters in search of pearls,
Seeking life's truths seeping from wells
Springing from wealth that nobody sells -

We emerge at last into the light
To continue the quest that began long ago –
With a crescendo of ringing, peeling of bells,
Slowing towards the last final knell.

There we shall leave it measuring time,
Like an old clock spring winding down –
May tall trees fall but never be felled
As we pass through paradise and hell.

THE SURRENDER OF PORT STANLEY
[14th Jun 1982, Newcastle, England]

We have just heard on the radio,
the Prime Minster announcing
that the Argentinians have surrendered,
to the British forces on the Falklands.
Everyone in our house gave a great cheer.

WHAT HAPPENED TO HIPPIES
[27th Jun – 2nd Jul 1982, 259 Shields Rd, Newcastle]

It used to be drugs, now its booze,
What happened to the hash and the acid?
That went with the clothes, like fashion –
Blue jeans with holes and arse hanging out,
Hair the length of a floor mop – and a crotch
That never got washed night to night.

No one really cared about V.D,
It was something of which to be proud.

Those dark lines from tripping till dawn,
The tiny crow's feet, wrinkled and formed
From keeping the dope smoke out of the eyes;
Or the blindness caused by dance-hall strobe lights,
Beating the life out of rock-an-roll tunes,
Blasting the ear-drums in a dance frenzied room –
A sea of hair, and ocean of bare feet,
Getting their rocks off as best they could.

Now that same guy who wouldn't work,
Who collected his dole for something to do,
That same guy who used to say 'Shove it!'
Instead of putting on a tie for job interview –
This same guy with his jeans worn through,
Now looks like the rest of the middle-age crew
'Hell, if you can't beat them, join them!'
Hippies are now off drugs, and well into booze.

THE FALL OF SIR CRESTWELL
[10.15pm, 20th Jul 1982, Newcastle]

After that fella broke into the palace,
It was scapegoats and hangings they wanted;
Nothing to do with Her Majesty at all,
It was her bodyguard Sir Crestwell they haunted

For nine years Sir Crestwell had guarded the Queen,
I wouldn't want the job for a million pounds –
And after nine years they made him resign,
After telling the world he was queer.

Everyone knows he wasn't disgraced by the break-in,
Or his prostitute friend's threats of blackmail –
It was the fact he was plainly homosexual,
A cruel admission that ended his career.

The country feels pity for mistreated Sir Crestwell,
Denounced in the Commons, stripped of his 'hood –
It stinks of creeping conservative morality,
Shall we call it - the castrated Eighties decade?

I'm sorry Sir Crestwell, and for all who are gay,
I hate the way this government disgraced you –
It will be sometime before the country forgets,
That honour bestowed, can be taken away.

THE NEIGHBOURS
[20th-21st Jul 1982, Newcastle]

Receding wanes the whining car engine,
Out in the lane, an hour past twelve.
What would prompt a good living citizen
To be abroad and about at this time?

162

Just five minutes back, I heard a loud crack
That reminded me of a starter's track-gun,
And almost inaudible, I could be mistaken,
I heard a scream, and a mention of God.

I also recall a clatter of footsteps,
In haste, and running along the side-walk –
A car-door opening, and closed in a hurry,
An engine started in a deafening roar.

Who would disturb the peace of the night hours,
All good neighbours were meant to be home?
Only prowlers and miscreant persons
Would venture out so late on the road.

EGO GOES WHERE I GOES
[20.05pm, 11th Aug 1982, Newcastle]

Everywhere I go, EGO goes too,
Talking and changing my mind.
One hour we're laughing, next crying
Over things of various kinds.

I try to forget about EGO,
Lurking and weaving about,
But time after time he saves me
From lingering boredom and doubt.

EGO has rights like I have,
I cannot command his power.
We are like a rainy day –
I am the cloud, EGO the shower.

Sometimes I tend to hate EGO,
Others, he's the best friend I have.
So, I kind of live with EGO,
And EGO lives with me, and that's that.

BARBARIANS OF THE WEST
[12pm, 19th Aug 1982, Byker Rd, Newcastle]

The arose from the mists mounted on horses,
Armed with weapons dripping in blood –
They crossed the wastes from desolate places
To arrive like the anger of a terrible storm.

Savage in battle, they ravaged the rich lands,
Their brown eyes burning all that they saw;
Felling all order with axes and terror –
Spears and swords their dispensers of law.

All before them toppled and crumbled,
The night skies blazed as the cities burnt;
Corpses lay slain and brutally quartered
As the fleeing fled the slaughtering hunt.

No folk survived the merciless carnage

That the barbarians finally invoked –
Who taking their dead over their horses,
Cleansed their weapons and turned towards home.

And into the mist that unveiled their existence,
They faded like ghosts from a terrible sleep;
Blown by cold winds to far away places,
Chased by the tales of their heinous deeds.

LIVING WITH CHANGE
[21.39pm, 25th Aug 1982, Byker Rd, Newcastle]

Autumn began with showers and wind,
Caught the folk in shirt sleeves and blouses,
Over-night, milk suddenly stopped turning,
Everyone at once had a sudden yearning
To stop time dead with the wave of a hand,
For Summer had gone, and leaves were falling.

It wasn't as bad as it was made out to be,
Not as terrible as some would make you believe,
For even if life could be one eternal summer,
There would still be complaints about the weather;
Autumn or Winter, or Spring for that matter,
There wouldn't be one without the other.

TO HELL WITH WEALTH
[10pm, 3rd Sept 1982, Byker Rd, Newcastle]

Poverty of mind is a less obvious evil
Than running around shoeless and naked,
For who's to know the desert of knowledge
Without first bleeding and surviving the cold,
The physical pain endured to keep living,
The hunger of begging, the racking of want.

For the wisest are those with nothing at all
To hinder their thoughts or enslave their souls,
For the man with money buys and keeps,
While the man with nothing shares what he seeks -
Usually little more than a happy mind,
Believing that this is all he needs.

For what use are paintings, and fancy goods
When a man talks to man about love or looks -
For looks they say form half the character,
And once formed, what does wealth matter,
The other half of man is his accrued knowledge
Used to spread humour and laughter.

It's a sad world without a smile a day,
It's silly to think that money's the answer;
Yes, more people croak crying in bed
Than in wars, on roads, from drugs, or crime.
I don't care what the history books say,
Historians die in their beds just the same.

While in fact the poor laugh all the time,
While the wealthy and learned are famous indeed
For their lengthy scowls and troublesome looks
Of frowning discomfort and unhappy moods;
The idea that knowledge begins with laughter,
Passes them by like a tramp with a blanket.

BOREDOM
[10.45pm, 3rd Sept 1982, Byker Rd, Newcastle]

Boredom comes from within, not without,
so don't blame your companions.
Boredom is a disease, like mumps or measles,
it spreads like molten lead,
it poisons every single thought
that could lead to an interesting end.

COFFEE
[11pm, 3rd Sept 1982, Newcastle]

I drink coffee like a kid eats candy,
or like a dog attacks a bone –
and like a desert in a rainstorm,
parched again, I need some more.

THE BRIDGE OF LOVE
[6.30pm, 5th Sept 1982, Byker Rd, Newcastle]

The water was polished and reflective of nature,
Nature was changing every ripple of time,
Time was passing over the weir stone,
Falling away in a blinding of white.

The arch of the bridge spanned the horizon,
The horizon was filled with cedar and pine,
The pines were dropping cones in the water,
The ripples were breaking on the bank-sides.

The reeds were catching the debris of autumn,
Autumn was sweeping down from above,
Above was no longer cloudless and sunny,
Filled with magpies, swallows and doves.

The water was grey and dark to the bottom,
The bottom was lost as night drew nigh,
The night forgiven for stealing the magic
As lovers departed with longing sighs.

THE POOR PROVIDER
[9.22am, 8th Sept 1982, Byker Rd, Newcastle]

Ever tried to feed the dog when you're broke,
Never mind the wife, the son, the daughter,
The lodger, the mother, grandfather, and grandmother
When they all sit there at the dinner table
With big eyes and enormous appetites,
And thoughts of how things could be better,

If, as provider, I went out and found a better job.
Why is it always other peoples' ambition
That drives a man on.

ADDRESS FOR THE MARRIED
For Robert Langdon and Amanda Nork
[16.15pm, 13th Sept 1982, Byker Rd, Newcastle]

Oh who has not heard of young Lochinvar,
So wrapped in love, he took on the world,
And stole a bride from the groom at the altar,
To gallop into the mists of the moors.

Will such spirit ever be forgotten
By all lovers caught by such fire –
Where death together is finer than parting,
And parting as thoughtless as quarrelling words.

What of fathers, and mothers, and kinsmen,
Companions and friends, each with their part
In keeping quiet council, and not dividing
Something love made forever to last.

Romance is like gold, and love a magic
Not conjured, but allowed to blossom and grow,
Marriage not sacred, but an incredible journey
Along the length of the rainbow road.

So here's to the bride! Here's to the groom!
Here's to the bridesmaids, ushers and all!
The fathers, the mothers, kinsmen and friends.
God bless this couple. God bless us all.

GRETNA GREEN
[13.05pm, 22nd Sept 1982, Byker Rd, Newcastle]

Gretna Green is a haven for lovers,
Close to the Wall, by the Western Sea,
Where rain sweeps in along the Solway,
Its trees as scarce as scattering leaves.

The anvils ring and the carriages clatter
Over the cobbles of the old inn-yards,
Their windows filled with elopers and couples,
Huddled together, every moment their last.

Blackbirds sing, enliven the hedgerows,
And runaways come, and the married go –
Back to the cities, or onwards to new lives
Made in homes far from the old.

The grey clouds roll and darken the moorland,
The lapwings soar or cry from the ferns,
Across the marsh are grey-stone houses,
Dry-stone walls that never quite end.

The quiet road in, leads quietly out,

The border a mile for those with a mind
To flee from parents, or the laws of religion,
To be united o'er the anvil at night.

So hasten you lovers, take to the dark,
Run to the frontiers of love and be seen
Kissing and hugging by the fires of romance,
In the windows of inns in Gretna Green.

ACTING LIKE AN ENGLISHMAN
[13.25pm, 22nd Sept 1982, Byker Rd, Newcastle]

To act like an Englishman,
Is to think of one's own superiority.
A superiority that leads to an attitude
That reveals the silly man.

SOCIAL SECURITY
[28th Sept 1982, Byker Rd, Newcastle]

We had a visit from the Social Security,
The officer was pleasant and reasonable,
Not a prying low beast so often found
In such professions.

He had a sense of humour –
And once his questions were answered
He said it would be the last home visit
for three years.

A review of our circumstances –
Three years is a long time;
But with today's unemployment,
Social Security officers are very busy men.

GYPSY HILL
[21st-23rd Sept 1982, Byker, Newcastle]

The grey slate tops to the red brick houses,
Ran like stripes to the valley floor;
The drabness dressed with smears of parkland,
Dipped and clung to the sagging, steep slopes
Traversed by lines of cobble-stone roads,
Hazed in a canopy of choking coal smoke.

Off in the distance the Civic Hall shone,
The Cathedral spire circled by cloud,
The iron-swing bridge spanning the river,
Creaked and opened like a rusty mousetrap
Set to catch the industrial output
Of machinery and steel leaving the town.

But Gypsy Hill was a place for horses,
Broken pit-ponies tethered on ropes,
Where kids with faces as round as melons,
Played hooky, and choked on roll-your-owns;
Where men on the dole took long strolls

To forget their thoughts about getting old.

SELF-PLAYING CHESS SET
for John Boyd
[15th Oct – 6th Nov 1982, Byker Rd, Newcastle]

The Pawns to the fore of the battle front,
Rolled along on wheels of steel,
Driven by a will to breach all defences,
They ploughed away with mercenary zeal,
Advanced to challenge the threatening noise
Of an army equally ready for war.

With scythes and bludgeons, the Knights attacked
And hacked a sway with irresistible force,
That drenched the air with springs and pistons,
Rivets and axles, and shafts of iron,
Sickening all hearts with fear and terror,
All valour and honour lost in the toil.

When into their midsts whirled the Bishops,
Upholding and backed by the power of God;
Guided by faith, they rushed into slaughter,
Slicing apart the massacring flood –
With scriptures and mantras, holy and tantric,
They sacrificed all in the name of their Lord.

Never was life so quickly extinguished,
As on the blades of the pole-axing Rooks,
Splattered red in the front line carnage,
They relentlessly carved till entrails steamed,
And bowels and heads lay like flowers
From horizon to horizon on the battlefield.

Headlong forth the Queens careered,
Storming and crushing the screaming hosts;
Compelled by nature and self-preservation,
They exacted a result with such heavy toll,
That mounds of dead rose like mountains,
And opposition fell like harvested corn.

The Kings stepped back, clumsy, ungainly,
Like creaking monsters of dinosaur gait,
To await defeat or take the surrender
On the final mating of the hated foe –
Victory brandished as the ultimate glory
To end the self-playing chess set show.

MY LOVER'S LIPS
[7th Nov 1982, Byker Rd, Newcastle]

My lover's lips were icy cold,
She had no heat to give –
Her passion once so hotly kept
Was now a hazy kiss.

TIME HAS A WAY

[7th Nov 1982, Byker Rd, Newcastle]

Time has a way of taking
Everything that once was plain –
Simple times and simple minds
Once had a part to play:
The sunset of another day,
The past decays.

THE CANNERY
[16th November 1982, Newcastle]

Like a river, the conveyor system carried the fish
into the throbbing interior of the cannery,
plummeted them into gigantic steel tanks
that frothed like beer. Large clanging traps
gaped open to unleash leering salmon onto
the shiny work benches dripping with blood.

Guts fell to the floor to splatter the iron legs
of the slimer troughs and slicing tables
receiving their overloads of flesh from
the circular decapitating saws.

Compressors sucked the jelly egg roe
from the mutilated bodies that bisecting blades
pushed down chutes to land with a thud
onto roller belts that led towards the can-line.
Severed fish tails flew like swallows from
ancient machines overloaded and gushing steam
upwards to the girded arches of the roof.

Water seeped from every bolt-head and rivet
vibrating loose from the never ceasing use
of such worn equipment. Strange knocks and
course friction noises, clacking valves and
creaking bearings, grating cogs and squeaking
rocker arms testifying to the senile movements
of mechanised parts. Chains that worked the
flywheels looked ready to snap.

The lethal hewing steel blades flashed like
blue-birds zipping by, buzzing on backbones,
or fins, or down the bellies with measured zeal.
Heads corkscrewed into mammoth bins,
entrails blocked the drains, and gore ran
like claret from the dockside sluices to empty
into the harbour to make the gut filled surface
the colour of a ship's underside.

THE RED WOOD
[28th November 1982, Newcastle]

The trees had been there since history began,
beneath their soaring canopy, man stood dwarfed
and time tread an endless circle.
Saplings sprouted from a thousand generations

169

of ancestral decay that enriched the forest floor
to outstrip and overshadow every living thing.

There was no conflict beneath the somber redwoods,
tranquility was the essence of their environment,
silence the nature of their contribution to life.
From their rustic course bark bases to the tip
of their highest stem, not a murmur or a creaking
of weakness emitted from the mighty trees.

Their girths out-measured all imagination, a single
span led lazy thinkers to dwell on a prehistoric past,
skywards rising like pillars for nature's own temple.
Stoically they stood rooted and permanent as
testimony to the powers of creation. Everlasting
and over stretching, to inspire and awe.

Many were the skeletons of ancient ones felled
by age; colossal trunks straddling cascading streams,
uprooted torsos saddled across gigantic boulders.
Indestructible, these timbers lay, root boles inhabited
by rodents gnawing grimly on the pulp that a century
or more could not rot. Red, their innards turned t opowder.

Maintaining the iron colouring of the forest soil
carpeted by slender needles and pear shaped cones,
sunlight streamed through the branches like light
through slats in a darkened room. Warmth radiated
into the shadows of the diffused-lit hinter parts of
the forest's nether regions where nothing stirred.

The air was dry and hung with the essence of sapped bark
and scented new growth so characteristically redwood.
Only the odd pink flowering of a rhododendron in bloom
carried the eye downwards from the umbrella of green
or trunks of umber that enclosed the wood in a beauty
of unparalleled scale and greatness of design.

WINTER FARM
[2nd – 7th Dec 1982, Byker Rd, Newcastle]

The winter fire warmed the iced hands
Of a farmer hunched on a backless chair,
Huddled in blankets of coats and garments
Once the better of wear and tear.

He sat with a face of serious expression,
Lost in the flames of imaginary thought,
Drowning in memories of previous evenings
As the farm froze in layers of frost.

The windows shook and the cold edged in
Through every crack; brittle like glass,
And glazed in hoar, the night wind murmured
At the door and on the farmer's back.

Black were the scars he mentally ploughed

170

Through the years of harrowed ground;
Fallow the pastures newly unearthed,
The seed of rebirth for the sepulchered.

Memories cascading like waterfalls remained
Like the berries on holly and rowan,
While all else shriveled, something existed
In the immediate snow, the lingering mist.

Life survives beyond the grey dawn,
Something is born during the black night:
Creation plummets like a hungry hawk,
Also glides like a graceful swan.

As windows rattle, and doors knock,
And strangers warm pasts by friendly fires:
Winter comes as a seasonal trial
Of inner resolve and mental thought.

Likewise, the farmer retreading his own past,
Hunchbacked upon his backless chair –
Likewise for him it was logic to rest
While the worries of winter were wrestled.

Sleet washed the land, mastered the sky,
Took command of the near-distant sea,
As the glowing fire warmed the hands
Of the farmer hunched with his cares.

IGNOBLE BEASTS
[14th – 16th Dec 1982, Byker Rd, Newcastle]

Ignoble beasts that turn about and stampede
At the sound of distant war.
What dismay and panic their actions dispel
As the rumbling grows louder.

Beasts that bow and shield their ears
At the whine of crashing shells.
How subdued and tame is their slavery
As the sibilant echoes pound.

Beasts that cower from the flames
At the sight of consuming fire.
What disgust and scorn their behaviour entreats
As the vanquishing army arrives.

Beasts that hide themselves in their lairs
At the sound of marching footsteps.
What shame and fear they take from life
As the trembling earth resounds.

Beasts that wet themselves in their terror
At the silence of halted footsteps.
What rape and death their cowardice brings
As the lasting screams fade out.

Beasts that give themselves to their foes
At the command of foreign officers.
What pity and hatred their meekness evokes
As the marching fire-squad comes.

Beasts that go blindfold to their fate
At the utterance of final prayers.
How quick and easy their cowardice ends
As the quavering gunshots kill.

ON RISING TOO EARLY
[18th Dec 1982, Byker Rd, Newcastle]

The first snows fell just yesterday
While I was still in bed.
The silent nature of its first descent,
Left white images as I dreamt
Of past winters spent in hammock huts
With girls in passing idleness.

All those thoughts receded, went
As I drew back the drapes –
The silken blanket of the virgin cold,
Unlocked the child within,
As the jack-frost friends of old
Re-emerged to play in the snow.

Stark, yet pretty, the trees stood bare
As I turned from the window.
The chill of winter had frozen my breath:
Rekindling the fire,
I went to the mirror in a dreamer's daze
As the sunshine outside blazed.

What true secrets the looking glass told
As I stroked my thoughts:
The sullen sag of saddened eyes
Searching for a glimmer of hope,
As I returned again to the falling snow,
And to bed to escape the cold.

LONGEST NIGHT
[22nd Dec 1982, Byker Rd, Newcastle]

It was never ending like the path
Trodden by those who travel in circles.
The darkness was its clinging virtue,
Preserved by the stars and moon dancing.

My soul was immersed in mystery
Unearthed by the planets shining down.
The silence was its keenest weapon,
Cutting through the briar of entangled life.

The stillness gripped the solid ice,
Cracking on unrest and growing louder.
The tree owls preyed upon the black

Bats flaying through the snares of woodland.

Hook-beaked crows rose like coal-smoke
Blown before the south-west gales.
The shortest day broke in a lingering fit
Lengthened by the shadows of the vales.

THE BANK HOLIDAY
[6.09pm, 29th Dec 1982, Byker Rd, Newcastle]

Never ending the road wound down
Like a serpent coiling to bask.
Sleek and shiny like a polished boot,
It ran before the wheeled mania
Of the lemmings racing to the sea.

They had sprung from the lairs
Like courting mad-march hares.
Grey and oily like the beach sands,
They viewed across the promenade,
Just like seamen fevered by the sea.

They wrestled before their castles
Like wild beasts of distant jungles.
Snorting and charging like mad rhinos,
They launched themselves on the ocean
As lifeboats attacking the sea.

Never ending the road wound back
Like a snake uncoiling to wake.
Rippled and black to smoky towns,
It returned the ants to their hills
At their end of the day at the sea.

GRAVEYARDS
[2.20pm, 13th Jan 1983, Byker Rd, Newcastle]

Graveyards are meant for the dead and mourning,
Tall, long fir, and weeping pine,
Yews that cry with a soft wind blowing,
And willows drooping with the weight of time.

Graveyards are not for the young and living,
Morning roses, bled in their prime,
For briar and bramble, encroaching and thriving,
Meet hemlock bearing in from the sides.

Monuments shall rise, and headstones shall stay,
Graveyards are there, for always.
The high walls exclude the trials of life,
The creeping motion of passing age.

The high walls enclose the future to come,
Cypress and holly forever leaved.
Graveyards appeal to the tired and lonely,
And those of us who are not afraid.

173

Graveyards are meant for the dead and mourning,
Tall, long fir, and weeping pine,
Yews that cry with a soft wind blowing,
And willows drooping with the weight of time.

DRY STONE DYKER
[3.45pm, 13th Jan 1985, Byker Rd, Newcastle]

Stones or rocks like pebbles lie
In the hands of the dry stone dyker.
Turned aside by the plough in the fields,
They lie piled like mountains to the sky.

The dyker, steady, tapping, tapping,
Echoing across the grey whin sill.
The wind against the crags, and howling,
Carries the tapping o'er the wild dale-sides.

His lonely company kept with songs,
Joins the curlew's whistling tune.
Love ballads penned for old and parted,
Chase the bloom across the scree.

Ancient poems washed from memory,
Sweep the fern and heather slopes.
Tall standing stones by Celtic circles,
Tell lichen tales of spells and druids.

All the time, tapping, tapping,
Each day goes, another looms.
Years of passing like the gurgling waters,
Trickling from a dale-side combe.

Now like ribbons across the hills,
The miles pass from lake to peak.
The fells split into walled domains,
The dyker taps, hums a tune.

AS MY SHADOW SAT BESIDE ME
[10.26p, 1st Feb 1983, Byker Rd, Newcastle]

Without beginning, like all stars stretching,
Beyond my eyes belief and comprehension,
The fateful moment came and sat beside me,
And I flinched not, dared not.

What is company without conversation?
Of which there was none …
Not even the motion of nervous chatter,
That accompanies all heart-to-heart matters.

It was as though evening had come,
And brought nought by darkness, and sadness,
When moonbeams should have outlined shadows,
Out shone all misery.

As my other self sat there beside me,

I blinked not, tried not, then barely nodded,
And my shadow comprehended, nodded,
Which was something after all.

CONVERSATION WITH A STATUE
[23rd Feb 1983, Byker Rd, Newcastle]

The other day I had a conversation in a park
with the statue of a great philosopher.
'Nice day' I said, and a leaf fell
off a tree and skidded off his head.

'You must have been a great thinker
before they moved you to this place'.
His grey eyes stared motionless,
his hand resting upon his lapel.

'Aren't you going to answer me?'
And lo, there read his epitaph –
'I passed my life in blindness,
and let my words fall on deaf ears'.

MORE DEAD WORDS THAN STARS
[6th Mar 1983, Byker Rd, Newcastle]

Between the stars that fade,
Little will be remembered.

And so written words
Become like well played records,
Old and scratched, then dated.

Yellow pages, and yellowed memories,
Distorted and rejected, discarded and neglected,
And fast forgotten.

All newer work is likewise destined
To a similar fate of mildew sentiment
On the toppling stack of nostalgia.

Many words are written,
But few are worth recalling.
Add this poem to the pile.

SADDEST CLOWN IN THE WORLD
[6th Mar 1983, Byker Rd, Newcastle]

I had a friend who was a clown,
And he had worked in a circus,
Making the audience joyous,
But what a sad man he was.

His wife had been his pride and joy,
High on a trapeze - a graceful bird,
She left him for a strongman,
he hadn't made her laugh for years.

175

He was heart-broken, depressed.
Have you ever seen the tears of a clown?
He flooded the tent, a customer complained
That he had come to laugh, not drown.

The ringmaster tried to explain
That even clowns have their bad days.
The audience were sympathetic,
But my friend's blues remained.

His sadness spread far abroad –
People came to make him laugh;
The ringmaster introduced him as
The Saddest Clown By Far!.

Overnight he was smash-hit
Success arrived and saved his soul;
His new wealth outweighed everything
But the loss of his wife.

Then one day, his wife returned,
Bruised from the beatings of her strongman's love.
She begged him to be forgiven,
She cried a flood and moved back in.

She went back to the trapeze,
And once more flew like a bird,
but my friend gave up the circus,
ran off with the ringmaster's wife.

SPRING EQUINOX
[22nd Mar 1983, Byker Rd, Newcastle]

The Spring equinox brought new snows
on old experiences.
Winter having been forgotten,
white crocus hid in the flurried fall.
The sun did not rise, slept the whole day,
and so did I.

TREASON
[22nd Mar 1983, Newcastle]

Treason seeps from pressed mouths,
Contorted and cruelly twisted.
Going over to the other side
Is like buttering bread both sides.
Once you've spread it,
You have trouble taking a bite.

Sticky fingers and spying,
They go hand in hand alright.
Treason is for the hungry –
The hungry men of power.

TWENTY NINTH BIRTHDAY
[3.45pm, 25th Mar 1983, Byker Rd, Newcastle]

Just a day older than twenty-eight.
It was hard enough accepting twenty.
Now at twenty-nine, it seems crazy
That I doubted I'd survive
Nine more years.

It used to be hard believing in tomorrow.
Winter mornings and tropical dawns,
Ten thousand gone.
Now, tomorrow comes, and likely
fifteen thousand more.

Age strikes a man like waves
Upon a rocky shore.
It beats all roughness from him,
It drains him, tames him.
Age is the only gain.

Twenty nine? There is still
A long way to the crest of the hill,
The roller coaster ride,
That slides out of the clouds,
Down into the basking sunshine.

BLANKS
[25th Mar 1983, Byker Rd, Newcastle]

More and more I leave blanks –
Then after all, blanks fill space.
Space after all is the fifth dimension
Where time knows no bounds.

MISSIONARY HERO
[7th Apr 1983, Newcastle]

I had a namesake, a relative,
No, an ancestor let's say –
He went from Scotland
With God on his lips
And arrived in Africa.

Robert Moffat, yeah,
That was his name.
The missionary hero of Kuruman.
Kuruman?
Hell, where is that place?

POETICAL POVERTY
For Michael Hamburger
[3rd May 1983, Byker Rd, Newcastle]

Poets are renowned for being poor,
Poor in wealth,
Usually poor in health from drinking.
Too many bars,
Too many late nights,

Not enough sunshine,
Not enough money.
Poets are ill-fated alright.

PASSING OF FATES
[3rd May 1983, Byker Rd, Newcastle]

Easy words to not give easy meanings
To hard expressions of fate –
The diamond cut to dazzle,
The hapless believers in fame –
The illusion that lingers like snow
Upon the mountains of faith –
The child covered in mud,
dragged through the rains.

This is the beauty of fate paraded
That the elements, weather and fade.
Those men, once strongly broad
With their pasts still to face.
The human clock counting
Till mortal heartbeats fail –
The gathering of the mists
To shroud the frail.

The quest for immortality
That God-like creatures fake.
Yet, this is it, they cannot stop
The passing of the fates.

OLD HAT
[12th May 1983, Byker Rd, Newcastle]

Instead of mouthing like a politician,
Or sprouting like a jacked-up puppet,
I think I'll turn the TV off,
The stereo up, smoke a joint,
Get down to making love
With the same old girl.

It might be old hat,
Better a hat than no hat,
Unless it's the Tory party
Who've left four million dying,
Starved for want of work.

Better a hat than no hat –
I'd rather see Cruises going up,
Than Pershings raining down,
X's aimed at my behind,
My trousers round my ankles.
But only with my wife.

IDLENESS
[4.05pm, 24th May 1983, Byker Rd, Newcastle]

Idleness is once more my preoccupation,

What better than relaxation;
What better than no mental stimulation;
None better than laziness,
None better than forgetfulness,
None better than laziness.
Idleness suits me.
Idleness is the only decent life.

ELECTION NIGHT
[10th June 1983, Newcastle]

On our side of town
We voted in Nick Brown -
'Labour! Labour! was the chant,
The Conservatives got shouted down.
The S.D.P got their asses licked.
The North! The North!
The South sold us out!
The fascists live were jobs are sold
And socialism dies!

Yes, socialism weeps tonight,
Red the eyes with fear.
Keir Hardie! In the streets they cry,
While behind closed doors committees sit
Planning Tory campaign lies.
The North! The North!
The South holds us down!
The clicking heels are stompin' o'er
MacDonald's grave tonight.

On our side of town
We're neither adverb'd or nouned.
Fuck! Fuck! was the chant -
Five more years of that!
Witch Thatcher's Gorgon smile.
The North! The North!
The South, the Iron Fist!
The secret police watching you
From within our very midst!

On our side of town
We voted Labour, not for bombs,
Not for money, not for jobs,
But for health, and welfare,
Equality, minorities, and poverty.
The North! The North!
The South, we spit on you.
We shall not forget the crimes
And take revenge on you!

And now, I better hasten
Away from this heaving room.
The whispering words echo
Commie! Nigger! Jew!
I see two men pushing through.
The North! The North!

179

The South drains us dry.
You may stifle our voices
But you'll never dowse our fire!

MOVING HOME
[16th Jul 1983, Helmsley Rd, Newcastle]

Gone are the chimneys and red brick houses,
The roads running to the valley floor
Substituted now are gardens of roses,
Drifting voices in well-to-do tones.

Lace curtains conceal hidden mementos,
Gathered and stored, but never shown –
Eyes alert, dart at the windows,
Curiosity dies, as the gossip grows.

Neighbours all smiles are shadows at home,
Flirting about in dim yellow rooms –
The cars in the street are big metal cans,
Ketchup coloured, and mustard green.

Here, pet dogs, respectable and clean,
Bark, are kept to back-lane yards,
Doves, though many, are rarely menaced,
Cats well-fed, are content to stare.

Shop-keeper service panders to station,
Snobbery is part of community pride,
Avocado, guava, chilli, and pasta –
Forget about finding any white bread.

I miss the chimneys and red-brick houses,
The roads running to the valley floor,
The views I exchanged for cultural status,
Now are nothing to write about home.

HEIGHT OF BORDER SUMMER
[10th Aug 1983, Ferniehurst Castle, Jedburgh]

The barley grew high in the midsummer heatwave,
Neat rows of soldiers, heads to the sky,
Hawks, their plumage ruffled and moulting,
Deposited feathers on thistle-down fields,
Edged in wild grass, cross-seeded and tall,
Flattened not crushed by the harvester's cull.

The barbed-wire fences covered in bramble,
Staggered, fragile and rusted, ready to crumble
Upon poppies, campanula, thriving midst nettles,
While out of a beech copse, a wood pigeon re-entered,
And between the corn stalks, a beetle hunted
Through the dust of soil turned to powder.

Firm round breast of hillocks, yellow and ocre;
Pastures falling sweetly to shallow fords;
Heat and sunlight like never imagined,

Carry the cares of the world to the skyline,
The summer heatwave in the open fields,
Haystacks as beds and stars as good omen.

THE BORDERS
[11th Aug 1983, Snoot, Hawick]

Horses, docile and playful as children,
Ran to the fences in want of petting,
While sheep taking shade by oak fringed hedges,
Looked up with black faces before bolting
Down to the edge of the round pebbled river
Crossed by a bridge looped like a serpent.

Roads wound and uncoiled over the shiel lands,
Paths wandered through pasture where tracks
Lined for breaks in walls, skirted mountains,
Fringed cliffs to criss-cross on hilltops,
Where once had stood iron-age forts,
Where ancients watched the northern sky glow.

ON THE MOORS
[12th Aug 1983, Broadmeadows, Selkirk]

Moor walking leaves the city behind,
Forgotten, the troubles of the structured,
Responsibility, society, fame and bright lights,
None of that is worth the time it devours.

Alcohol, hashish, coffee, bills,
Headaches, pains, tiredness, boredom,
Work, commuting, pollution, money.
Death! Death! While nature thrives.

Fresh air, flowers, scenery, peace,
Tall trees, sun, mountains, fields,
Streams, clouds, insects, grass.
Life! Life! While the city dies.

Telephones, buses, cars, roads,
Television, radios, stereos,
Buy, sell, hustle, kill.
Death! Death! The city rings.

Sheep, cows, rabbits, deer,
Cliffs, gorges, moors, dales,
Hawks, crows, finches, wrens.
Life! Life! While nature flies.

Downers, scroungers, clingers, nuts,
Doubters, beaters, battered, scarred,
Suiciders, homiciders, drunks, OD'ers.
Death! Death! The city brings.

Health, loose, unbonded, free,
Yet still the city weighs on me.
Time drags the weary miles along,

Beyond each hill, a city runs.

USHERS ADDRESS
For Frank Parris & Carol Aitken
[2nd Sept 1983, Helmsley Rd, Newcastle]

Who can remember a summer this hot,
The grass as high as savannah corn,
The fireweed flaming the glens and braes,
The burns dry, the earth parched dunes.
Let us drench our own slaked thirst,
And toast the bride and groom.

And even when this winter comes,
And hard packed snow hems us in,
And driving rain frays our thought,
And icy winds flay the gloom,
Let us wet our own chaffed lips,
To the lovely bride and groom.

And when the summer months return,
And people hark on last year's blaze,
And think upon such rainless days,
And we upon this afternoon.
Let us stand and raise a glass,
And praise the bride and groom.

And when love is on our very tongues,
And happiness our only thought
To find such bliss outside ourselves,
We need not search beyond this room,
Just look upon this cherished union!
This charming bride! This handsome groom!

So let us bless this blushing couple,
And strive to help them on their way,
As duty bound and honour tokened,
Twinned together like earth and moon,
To glide in love through the cosmos,
Long live the bride and groom!

AUTUMN IN SANDYFORD
[15th September 1983, Helmsley Rd, Newcastle]

And autumn was upon us without warning.
Grey pillow skies that changed and ran by;
Gusty brown-tipped leaf carried afternoons;
Dark shadow shifting laundry days;
Mild back-door ajar boiled potato evenings;
Nigh before the cold breath of winter
Descended on the grey-slate streets.

FOREST IN MY BEDROOM
[18th Sept 1983, Helmsley Rd, Newcastle]

I wake up every morning,
With daylight in my eyes,

We never draw the curtains,
We have too many plants.

It all began in March,
When we seeded in a tray;
By April we needed a ready score
Of plants in pots on tables.

By May, they'd grown so much,
We put them on the floor.
Bigger pots … more space,
And the net curtains lowered.

By June, they were three feet.
By July, four ….
By August, they were so big
They could be seen across the road.

We raised the net curtain,
And they grew even more.
August went, September came
Before the flowers showed.

Now the things are six feet tall,
Four feet wide, three plants deep.
If you walk past our house,
You can smell them in the street.

My friends are understanding –
They're all doing the same.
Backyards, rooftops, window sills.
Home grown's the game.

Grass … pot … marijuana
Ganja … bud … and weed.
I wake up every morning
With it towering over me.

It's worth the paranoia,
It's a fine illegal sight!
Nature in its finest bloom
Amidst the urban blight.

Yes, I wake up every morning
With daylight in my eyes.
The forest needs the sunshine,
In turn it gets me high.

Can't say more than that –
For that's the plan.

BALLAD OF THE CELTIC SOUL
[21st – 22nd Sept 1983, Helmsley Rd, Newcastle]

The Highlands will forever call
Me back to glen-braed bens.
The gloaming roams on peat and fern,

The heathered straths, and birks.

The cnocs and stak column tower
Me whole to lochan strands,
Beneath the dhu dark watered band,
The deepest legends lie.

The pibroch strains aye-ever skirl
Me swirling to the eils,
The invers stride the allts and streams
Of sleet seeped basalt cairns.

The clachans reek the silver birch
Me mind the kil and dun,
The clash of clans and kilted sons,
The brackened wild grass hums.

The brochs upon the ruhbas stand,
Me lashed to ard by seas,
The gales beat the crag and scree,
The butt-ben lichened shiels.

The levens shade the heather leas,
Me rest to linn and burn;
The pens and fells to sands aye-run
By granite-stane dyked walls.

The Highlands will forever call
Me heart to ken its shires,
The dirging pipes in lament fire,
Aye drone to soul me back.

ITS SUCH A LOVELY MORNING
For Brian, Jack and Jeffrey
[23rd – 24th Sept 1983, Helmsley Rd, Newcastle]

Brain, Jack and Jeffrey,
Me mates from Villa Four,
It was such a lovely morning,
We went collecting harvest store.

Jack was in a wheelchair,
And Jeffrey in one too –
And Brian filled the plastic bag
With ferns, grass, and thorns.

Jack was kind of silent,
And Jeffrey laughed a lot,
Brian did all the work
Though he thought work a bore.

They each ate a bramble,
Though Jeffrey made a face,
Jack quietly savoured his
While Brian searched for more.

We collected leaves and hogweed,

And elderberry spreads,
Though Brian thought it shameful
To pick the flower heads.

Jeffrey, sweet cute Jeffrey,
Rolled his head and smiled,
While Jack heard the birds sing
And felt the warm sunshine.

Brian trailed behind us
With the bag of leaves and grass,
And we stopped to pick willowherb,
And other withered plants.

It was such a lovely morning,
And we raced Jeff and Jack,
Their wheels spinning madly
Across the grassland park.

We waited up for Brian,
Puffed to catch with us,
His blue eyes were sparkling
And we all had a laugh.

And as we slowly ambled
Back towards the home,
A pair of large magpies,
Flew up then were gone.

It was such a joyful outing,
For Brian, Jeffrey, Jack,
Who collected in the harvest
In a black plastic bag,

We left them at the villa,
In time to have their lunch.
It was such a lovely morning,
They were such a lovely bunch.

THE CANDIDE OF A YOUNG SCOTSMAN IN ENGLAND
[19th Feb - 24th Sept 1983, Sandyford, Newcastle]

Where do I begin my story.
I'm a Scotsman, but mind you now ....
My language may leave you hanging,
Though I'll try the best I can
To make my statements plain
So that Geordie, Scouse, or Brum
May heed my every word.

Now, when I left Scotland
I was eighteen, and from Glasgow,
And though that sounds bad
That I came from 'Glesca',
As the largest sprawl in Scotland
At least you've heard of it.

185

Because if I'd been from Tignabruich,
Or Auchenshuggle, or Auchtermuckty
Or some Highland village in the wilds,
Instead of talking Glaswegian,
I'd be speaking Gaelic and swinging a kilt.
But instead of eating bens of porridge,
Or Cairngorms of haggis,
Or drinking lochs of whiskey,
And dreaming Rabbie Burns ...
I settled on being a typical Scotsman
And went to England to find work.

Nothing wrong with that is there?
In Scotland, England is a dirty word,
Its only redeeming factor is ...
An easy living and a fast buck.
So leaving Scotland by its only decent thing,
I crossed the border by National Bus,
And I heard the bagpipes droning
As I left behind my homeland mists.

Of course, when I got off the bus
I was typically tartan-pissed,
But still wide-eyed and hungry
I stopped a man 'Heh, Jimmy!'
But he turned and fled.
Some welcome I thought.
I looked around the bus station
and said 'So this is England!'
'And Newcastle? This is it!'
I'd seen more life in a Glasgow midden,
no kidding, it made me sick.

But a wee women passing by
Gazed at me and asked
'Are ye lost, pet? Can 'a help yee?'
'I can tell yee'r nae a Geordie lad.'
And I surprised took a step back,
Then grinned and blurted out to her
'I've come to Newcastle to find my Uncle Jock'
'To stay with him until I find some work.'

She kind of shook her head and said
'Well, I hope you have some luck'
'Its kinda hard round here r'eet noo'
'Ma husbands oot of wurk himself'
'He's a shipbuilder, a Walker lad'
'But since the cuts, the strike, the dole'
'The only thing afloat on the Tyne is ducks.'
'But maybe ye'll have an easier time'
Being young, an' having yer Uncle Jock.'

Uncle Jock was my mother's brother,
And about ten years younger.
I fished a piece of paper from my pocket
And showed it to the little woman.
'Jesmond?' she said in great surprise

'He's a stoo'dent then?' she asked
I answered that I didn't know
But that I thought he was about thirty-five.
'Then more than likely' she said
'Jesmond people are students until they die!'

She put me on the right bus,
That went past the University and Poly,
The school of Arts and Technology,
And in no time, the bus was full of students
Reading books and making paper aeroplanes,
Re-enacting primal scream and Shakespeare,
All bubblegum fanatics and graffiti scribblers,
Could tell that from what they were drivelling.

'You know, Daphne' one tulip was whispering,
'Your eyes are 100 watt light-bulbs against the moon.'
'Oh yeah, Steve, and you can forget tonight'
'A 9 volt battery would make you drool.'
I turned and looked at Daphne and Steve
And saw a pampas of orange hair.
'A pair of hairies' I said to myself
As Daphne burnt me with her 200 watt stares.

'Acorn Road!' the driver shouted
Flicking the lever of the bus-door WHOOOSH!
Flushing every student on to the pavement ...
And carried along in the panic and rush
I took refuge behind a lamppost,
And remained there staring at the posh surroundings
As the students disappeared into their flats
Or bedsits, or to the place at the end of the street
Which overhead read 'Willow Teas',
Which being a place for students
Meant I could only buy coffee.

'Where are you from, luv? ......'
The girl behind the counter smiled.
I told her, and immediately she frowned
And began to tell me a very long story
About a bloke from Glasgow she knew
Who once she'd fallen madly for.
'I'd let him move into my place'
'And after six months of feeding him'
'He turned round one day with a smile on his face'
'And declared he was off to India or some place!'
'I suppose it came as a shock' I said
And she answered 'No, he was kind of weird.'
And I asked 'Did he ever get to India?'
And she said 'No. He got scared'
'He got as far as Acorn Road Post Office'
'To ask for a passport form.'
'And now he lives across the street'
'Smoking up a hashish storm.'

This was the first time I'd heard that word
Used in public and branded aloud.

I looked about, but nobody was listening
They were all in their own hashish cloud.
'You looking for somewhere to stay, luv?'
'I've plenty of space at my place, if you like?'
She looked into my eyes, red and blazing
And I saw great fires of lust,
But I panicked and burst into a blush -
'No thanks, I've an Uncle I have to look up!'

She seemed disappointed, yet took it well,
I had my coffee, and a crumpet with jam
And she pointed with a wave of her hand
'You'll find your uncle's street across the tracks.'
I took that as a sign ......
That I wouldn't have to walk very far.
How wrong I was, I got lost!
I walked in circles until darkness fell,
Till the smell of fish and chips drove me wild.
I scoffed a supper, and threw the bag to a dog
Which whimpered when it found the paper empty,
But it being such a nice English dog,
It didn't even give me a parting growl.
I was tempted to take him home with me,
But I didn't have a home myself.

At last I found Uncle Jock's house,
I knocked on the door, it sounded so loud,
The echo vibrated down the whole street -
All red brick, and green doors
And white lace, and curtains
That moved, and threw bolts of light at me.
It was like being suspected of murder,
But it was only students watching for the police.
The door creaked open, a figure appeared
And slowly came forward into the light.
I smiled and spoke 'Hello, Uncle Jock'
'I wrote, I hope you got my letter alright.'
'Robbie-boy!' he gasped in great delight
'The devil has brought you into my grasp.'
'Come-in, come-in, I've got friends over'
'Bill, Tom, Pete and lovely Frances.'

And straight-way from the company I got the idea
My Uncle Jock was no nancy-dandy,
All his friends were weirdos,
Painters, poets, bums and dancers.
Frances was the local queen of aerobics
And Uncle Jock was her fancy man and lover.

That night the world exploded.
Frances made me take off all my clothes,
Then Uncle Jock said 'Here, take these'
'Two little bluies. You'll never be the same.'
He told me that it was L.S.D.,
But I thought nothing of it at the time,
I was enjoying the hash-pipe going around
When the tingling started in my brain -

Flashing lights and cosmic oscillations.
'Waves, man!' was the phrase Tom named.

I drifted off to Lally Land,
Bill said I was on 'Overload'.
I was out my head .....
But still wide awake to see the dawn.
Youth rushes at us all ablaze,
The experience of L.S.D. can make anyone strange.
But I'm not going to dwell on this.
Who has time anyway?

Uncle Jock saw me alright,
He apologised for what he'd done to me.
'If I'd known you were so naive'
'I'd have kept you strictly on beer.'
But I shrugged my shoulders and said
'I have a friend who's into solvents'
'And another really into speed'
'Finding something bad like acid'
'Is just the thing I need.'
'Don't worry, uncle ......'
'Just give me more of this L.S.D.'

Time passed quickly at my uncle's place
Until I did a thing with Frances.
It was all so innocent, I mean,
Well, I suppose it was a mistake!
Uncle Jock was more than furious,
And Frances was incredibly red-faced,
I was given two days to pack
And forced to find another place.

Frances told me 'I love you'
But stayed on with Jock just the same.
Uncle Jock buttered all her bread
And in all the right sort of ways.
Frances was strung out on Jock,
And Jock summed it up by saying
'You're very young, Robbie-boy,'
'And I wonder what your Mum would think'
'If she found out you were cheating'
'Playing around with her brother's chick.'

He was right, I felt a heel,
But he wouldn't give me a second chance,
So I went back to Willow Teas
And double-talked the girl I first met.
'Yeah, my uncle's moving away from here
I've got to move in somewhere-else.'
And would you know it, she said
'You better move into my place, then.'

Her name was Sandra, and kind of cute,
I moved in that night, and kissed her good.
Well, at least I think I did,
She smiled too sweet to lie ......

189

But my experience of women then
I could count on either hand.

And soon we were making plans.
She talked of sunny Spain,
I dreamt of far Japan.
Eventually we made a ferry trip
To exotic Rotterdam.
Don't ask me what we did in Holland,
Except I can tell I enjoyed myself;
I've told you of my first time in England,
The second time's a tale to itself.

AUTUMN IN SANDYFORD
[15th September 1983, Helmsley Rd, Newcastle]

And autumn was upon us without warning.
Grey pillow skies that changed and ran by;
Gusty brown-tipped leaf carried afternoons;
Dark shadow shifting laundry days;
Mild back-door ajar boiled potato evenings;
Nigh before the cold breath of winter
Descended on the grey-slate streets.

POETS ARE NO DIFFERENT
[8th Oct 1983, Helmsley Rd, Newcastle]

Poets are no different from workers,
Shirkers, tramps and drifters,
Lawyers, statesmen, salesmen,
Painters.

Poets are as base as winos,
Pimps, war-dogs, crooks, liars,
Brokers, killers, cops,
Scientists.

Poets are for truth and justice,
Avarice, hate, imperial causes,
Racist, right-wing, left-wing,
Rubbish.

Poets are, and poets die,
Cry, laugh, frown, fart,
Piss, wank, come,
Crap.

Poets are like you, or him,
Her, it, men, women,
Those, these, them,
And more.

[END OF EARLY WORKS]

THE UNDERGRADUATE - TERM 1
[16th Oct – 17th Dec 1983, Helmsley Rd, Newcastle]

WEEK 1

FRESHERS

I got to meet many girls, and guys and tutors.

The timetable ran like a Sunday school outing
And laughs peeled louder than distant thunder.
Belts and canes and classroom blues
Melted like troubles on hot buttered scones.
Who could have dreamed of such ivory towers
Hidden in brick-block and concrete seclusion?
Who would have reckoned to pillars of salt
Surrounded by treasures of wisdom and learning?

The knowledge there stood, steady and daunting
While above grey clouds crossed like lighting,
So swift that time had passed without warning.
A week of one's life gone forever,
Experiences new upon pathways now stretching.
Conquer before you, and burn all the bridges,
Scan the horizon for the dawn of ripe openings,
Secure the knowledge the honest palm offers –

Capitalise on education's rich coffers,
Look not back - Ego warned I.

While God damns us, but helps us –
The world despises students –
the unemployed hate us – the elite,
the sleek, the young and beautiful;
The slender, the tender, the gentle, the virgin
who know not life as twisting and hurtful,
painful and hollow, empty and shallow,
wanton and glutted, cruel and o'er shadowed.

The shimmering today, the shattered tomorrow,
The cream of our children taken and eaten,
Devoured by ambition, need and greed.
The rungs of the ladder swing in the breeze.
Grasp hold, guide our tutors with smiles,
The road to perfection before you lies.
Here is a list of the books for the journey,
A ninety week travel of history and prose.

Beware ye of Marlowe, Jonson and Shakespeare,
And Bede, and Caedmon, and Geoffrey of Monmouth,
Malory, Chaucer, Langland and Dunbar;
Better to know not, than try to know all.

For some rush to split the atom
Before the apple falls.

191

WEEK 2

THE APPLE IS BITTEN

And the next week on, the apple is bitten,
Teeth-marks scar the delicate skin ...
But penetrate not to the core of fruition.
The pip is not ready to seed.

Volpone and Faustus, and Utopia mellow,
And Wyatt and Sidney speak from the grave.
Raleigh looms like a grey apparition
While Erasmus coughs every turn of a page.

Who would have thought that medieval poets
And thinkers thought of nature as base;
Beneath the cobwebs of books they consulted,
Spoke Cicero, Horace, Ovid and Plato.

Original thought was a mighty wet blanket
Covering sex and sinning prelates –
Bestial conduct and fornicating standards,
Their course didactic, coital love-plays.

Which student of English, newly left home
Does not blush on discussing such things?
Sex is not the possession of ages
Read while thumbing history's frayed pages.

Nubile young bodies squirm in hard chairs,
Pulses quicken, engorging occurs.
The edited texts of high school days
Are not to be found in varsity texts.

Screwing and balling, lewd and telling,
Form the basis of submitted essays –
Bartholomew Fair is literature's answer
To the porn books of illiterate taste.

You can't tell me that tutors are cold,
Students not aroused by the bawd of the stage?
Decadence starts in English departments
And ends in students getting laid –

What of these virgins, the guys and dolls,
The eighteen year olds, shy and naive?
Will their time come during the first term?
Or after completion of their final year?

And what of the ones who lost it at fourteen?
Or the ones with lovers waiting at home?
Or the ones hung up because they are frigid,
Ugly, impotent, frightened or alone?

The icy cold wind of a winter's study
Can destroy the will of the freest soul.
The towers of learning may stand like castles

Or prisons where hearts are vamped to stone.

Or where hermits dwell in their library cells,
Windowless jails where no sun shines –
Where year by year mothball fumes
Yellow the treasures of human kind.

*For time is the only human dwelling
Where we can abide to count the chimes.*

WEEK 3

DARK ARTS

Suddenly dark shadows enter in study,
The Changling flirts across the page.
Beatrice dies with tragic De Flores,
A Lady MacBeth transplanted in Spain –
Her deflowerer like he of Montmartre fame,
Her father a tyrant in everything but name.
And in a whiff! They are gone –
And Marlowe rears with a breath if fired air.

'Faustus! Faustus! How vice has ruined you!
The powers of darkness ruled your soul.
Your humanist learning gave out to yearning
For knowledge beyond the infinite known.'
Such are my thoughts on *Doctor Faustus*,
A set essay piece for my drama course;
But drama is only part of the substance
That embodies the spirit of literature's bones.

At the heart lies the poetry –
Of Sidney, of Raleigh, of Spencer and Pope,
And Wyatt 'we did' in a half-hour lecture,
His expressiveness singularly worthy of note.
But I must away from all this claptrap
To talk of people instead of books –
About Sarah and Andy, Ellen and Steven,
Diana and Margaux, Ken and Jean.

The world of students, teachers and colleagues,
Friends, peers, competitors and sloggers,
Wrestling to fit into the mix –
Of working class values and upper class maxims.

Each caught in the middle and a little unsure,
whether up is the way, or down the truth –
The dichotomy of bourgeois-socialist views,
Is certainly clear for all to see;
Each individual is a burning sphere
As the world around them totters to war.

For only two days have passed since Grenada
Was invaded by droves of American marines –
And barely five days since the Americans lost
Two hundred and twenty with a Lebanese bomb.

193

The world at present is a fast changing nightmare
Where 'nuclear' is the word on everyone's lips –
And even the bomb proof burrows of wisdom
Can not be pristine at the end of all this.

WEEK 4

THEORY

The fourth week has gone, gone and gone.
And weekend of drugs has erased much.
Plato's attack on the essence of poetry
Bores to the heart of dramatic illusion.

The mimesis of form, reality, imitation –
The grandchild of God – the epic deludes;
Where truth is the light, the finest creation
Without being a mirror reflection of life.

Not Jack went up the hill with Jill;
Not Jack fell down and broke his crown –
But more a clarity of truth ...
That even simple thinks may have a root.

Yet let us turn from such serious thought,
And travel the realms of lyrics and ballads;
For even Plato said it was fair
For poetry to return from exile as song.

So what of these ballads that canter and ride
Through the gloom and terrible sleep –
Of lovers caught by cruel circumstance
And warriors lost so that mothers weep?

Oh would such laments fire the hillsides?
Oh would such grief whip up the sea?
Oh would such loss destroy the heavens,
The stars, the planets far from me?

Come listen, come sit, and hear my words
While the wind howls over crooked bent trees;
For ten long years the rain has fallen,
For ten cowed years I've been on my knees.

Oh mother! Oh father! How could you leave me!
Oh brothers, and sisters, why are you gone?
If I had known such disaster would take you,
If I had known I'd be left so alone!

The price I have paid to be a traitor –
The reward I've received for my cowardly work;
Is to be left so broken, lonely, and hated,
And hunted, and haunted by those I once loved.

For ten years now I've languished in prison;
For ten lives now I've shriveled and died.
For ten more eons I'll rot in this dungeon,

But ne'er will I shed a tear for my crime.

The war has killed my mother and father;
The struggle has taken my sister too.
My brothers are dead, slaughtered and butchered,
And freedom a word they never heard used.

Oh would such laments fire the hillsides!
Oh would such grief whip up the sea!
Oh would such loss destroy the heavens –
The stars, the planets, so far from me.

WEEK 5

READING WEEK

How different each week is from the last –
Each day a moment never to be,
As back to the grind the world shudders,
Or forward by fate it slides ill at ease.

Forward through theories in open throttle,
Down poetry lane towards Aristotle –
With even some time to brush up on Horace.

Ne'er was the luck of those caught in limbo
Thrown away like an empty milk-bottle;
Or blown away like dandelion or thistle,
To seed away in a broken egg-carton.

What better shelter in a wild world,
Than faculty halls on a wet day –
Each student a foetus unhatched and dormant
Packed in a box, and stored away.

Fed on Miller, Lewis and Spenser,
Regurgitating essays without a break –
Yet one canto of Dante ...one phrase of Houseman,
Can ease the troubles of a murky noon;
Sweating and turning, frigid and daunting
Facing the circle of tutorial groups.

One dash of *Green Knight* ...
a wave of the *Fair Queen* ...
beats a room of dirty knaves –
prancing across a Jacobean stage!

Drama, they say, is here to stay;
But give me good poetry ...
And a dictionary to paw it ...
And I'm as good as sold for the day.

And having had a week off classes,
Reading Week, yeah, to stay home and swot –
I feel as though I've been up every evening
Reading the lines between the blue dots.

The invisible markings, the allegorical meanings,
The knowledge lost that I haven't got.
Have you ever felt sick because you're missing
What you think everyone else wants a lot?

Like dancing, and singing, rocking and swinging,
Boogie, and jive, and reggae –
Punk, New Wave, Romantic and Classic –
Bright yellow ties and shocks of blue hair.

I was never into boots, muffs and bovver,
Crombies, braces, and very close shaves –
I was far-out geezer with dreadlocks,
And jeans ripped at the knees.

I was into drugs and druggies,
While others were into bikes and sleaze;
I got into sun and traveling –
While Bowie sang his brand of blues.

I was smoking hashish in India
When the Vietnam War came to an end;
I was flat on my back in Kenya
At the ripe old age of twenty two.

I went savouring the delights of Rio,
Rather than sit watching the tube.
I went to west coast America
Three days before Thatcher took rule.

I witnessed the waste in Managua city
Just after the Sandinistas took over;
I was in the plain of Kathmandu
When the Falkland War broke out.
I*'ve been to Argentina* ...
I *can see both sides.*

You would think I've had an education
But here I am back at school –
Five laps gone in a ninety lap course,
And it's getting cool in the pool.

WEEK 6

SAXON TALES

Winter's coming on and fast –
The light fades off at four o'clock.
Grey days and black, dark nights;
Sweater weather and overcoat times.

I sit through the chilly hours
Huddled over Saxon tales –
I drift with the rising moon
Lifting o'er the terraced roofs.

Then back to study's earnest pages,

Syntactic structured simple phrases –
Soon tired and bleary of all learning,
My poet's heart craves for peace.

But my mind will not slumber
Upon the thoughts of daily need;
My mind will not quietly rest
Upon the deeds of past and present.

I seek to fly on the air-waves
Of the buzzing wireless lines.
My secret thoughts of incarnation
Burning on the private kind.

My drifting notions caught and strangled
By the notes of draining life –
Incognito pass the strangers
Filing on through out the night.

Until my little duck comes waddling,
From her pond filmed in oil –
Comes to have her feathers smoothed,
Comes to have her body warmed.

For such is love and lust together,
Locked and roped, and inter-twined;
Passions risen once in anger,
Pass, and give to lover's murmurs.

Subdued talk of future longings,
Present times and lasting chimes;
The church bells ring and count the years –
CHIME! In endless chime they rhyme.

Atomic clocks TICK TOCK the hours,
Each second like cold corn seed
Dropped into a miller's quern –
Ground and powdered into flour.

Time passes all too soon,
White-washed moments caked to you –
A swimming swill of overtures,
Forgotten pains and mellow tunes.

A jukebox full of old dead songwriters;
A bookshelf sagging drab, crap titles;
A string of photographic snap-shots,
Pinned on the wall with thumb tacks.

Coffee stains ring the table;
Bong-smoke clings to the shade;
The light bulb yellow, dim and glaring
Down upon a threadbare room.

Armchair broken, ashtray chipped;
Fireplace tiles cracked and scored;
Floorboards warped and always creaking;

197

A *door ajar that never latches.*

Ceiling bowed and ever peeling;
Walls gouged and brick-work holed;
Mirror flaked, and hanging crooked
Reflects the student's poor abode.

I turn to – Tennessee Williams,
And sink to the depths of New Orleans,
Back to the Quarter and the Mississippi –
Down south where I have been.

Back to the world of sad Hart Crane;
Down to the pit of ghetto towns;
I haven't seen anything of Orleans proper
That I didn't think was a crying shame.

When I was there, broke and hungry,
I didn't see the street-car called Desire;
I was just a traveling nobody –
Who saw nothing, met no one, and starved.

New Orleans is a very cruel city,
And this is no story just for laughs;
I know the world of Stella and Stanley,
And I've met girls like Blanche de Bois.

So getting myself back to England –
And my boring, little Newcastle flat;
Six weeks have gone at university,
And that's where I'm at.

WEEK 7

STUDENT SOLITUDE

Its not often time I come to this
Midst earnest thoughts of intellect –
But come I have to lay my mind
Upon the white of vacant page;

And having started I must contend
To dwell upon some fancy terms.
Yet, dark outside the night may howl,
I know not what I must attack.

The city sleeps or slumbers down,
As ice about its houses dwell.
For now the frozen heavens reveal
The coldest face of winter's hell.

And as I sit before the fire,
Silence drops into the still –
Soundless lulls moving through
the eddy of the solitude …

Dropping.

Dropping.

Then caught, and suddenly renewed,
A car whines into the night;
The light bulb hums a merry tune,
My breathing beats a fresh simoom.

Footsteps break upon the street
To wash along the terraced waste –
Dark, and misty, with no end
Winter's grasp grips the night.

Chilly thoughts and cold ambition.
Driving on my walk through wisdom,
The rain, a hazy whizzing drizzle,
Seeking, soaking, permeating –

Better dry and wrapped in weakness,
Than wet, and dead because of greatness;
Sat still, I stay before the fire -
My strength gone like summer days.

I hear the knocking stick of sadness
Chattering during these twilight hours.
I feel the pulse of growing madness
Feeding on the grey outside.

And yet, I sit in mute repose
To think upon old English poems –
Has college life ruined desire
For women, sex and carnal knowledge?

Am I a boring fart or dolt?
A bumbling, slumbering sort of fool?
To pass a chance to taste free love
When offered by a loving girl?

Would I be right to turn my eyes
To gaze upon a Saxon tale,
When challenged by a nubile woman
Of weaving thought and coy intention?

All smiles, cute, and passing -
Quick to flash, willing to mate;
Age doesn't halt lust's fire,
And desire doesn't disappear with age.

You only want more of everything,
While everything gets further away –
This is what seven weeks of college
Does to a once plain brain.

WEEK 8

BORING BORING BORING

Rosencranz and Guilderstein died last week –

Stoppard bored right into me.
Boring, boring, and boring more –
More boring than henna'd hashish.

And worse than the phonology test
That is still burning in my ears -
The homily half of the salty *Seafarer*
Spewed up crap of a superior nature.

Listen, if you ever get the chance to read
More than nursery rhymes,
Don't spend your time on modern plays,
They're as bad as Victorian jokes.

Maybe you've never heard a Victorian limerick,
But they're worse than Irish anecdotes –
Four lines of A – B poetry …
And one line of punchy sniggers.

Not one word of honest truth –
All Pollacks, Chinks, and Negroes;
The worst of taste at every turn,
The work of senseless authors.

Forget the written lines of playwrights –
Turn you to the poets!

You see, how I've primed myself,
And wet my pen to the task;
Eight weeks have passed of college life,
And like a surgeon I prepare -

My thoughts upon some idle thread,
Of mocking jibe? Yes, I'm not content
To let days pass in mute grievance,
Or let time slip in cool abeyance.

I see each hour gain with me
Some weighty wealth of judgment
Made upon the works of living men –
Here, dead men are not my victims.

The living spread their own fine lies
As truth to cloak their own sharp plans
Masked behind a rising fame –
Until accolade makes their name.

And soon, that name is on the lips
Of critics, laymen, academics -
The printing presses churn all night,
Critiques, reviews, graces, praises!

Till library shelves sag and groan
Beneath the author's awesome fame.
A work once a hundred pages,
To one hundred thousand grows.

A simple fable simply told,
Into ten volumes quickly rages –
A small idea plainly written,
Into a great ideal is driven.

A few wet verses badly hacked,
Soon flourish into major tracts.
And without a whimper, nor a word,
The author reaps his sick reward.

His name is like a billboard sticker,
Stuck and left to fade forever.
While all the time his own esteem
Is but a broken might have been.

The booze and drugs killing him –
Patrimony, alimony, screwing him –
Bad breath, bad health, ruining him –
Poets like me, abusing him.

No man is perfect like the God
We're all supposed to be part of.
Human failing oversees –
Pathetic weakness shows in deeds.

Written words twist like snakes –
Spoken words straight-away hurt –
Wisdom splattered on a page,
On the tongue is aptly just.

Book language smooth and styled enough
From the lips may sound corrupt –
Yet still the academics turn
To pick the flesh of fiction's corpse.

And we the students of their thought,
Dissect the body, cheek by jowl.
Bowels, innards, organs, blood –
An author's merit, metre, mode –

With much dissection, dissertation,
Discussion, and interpretation;
We help dismiss, junk and trash it -
The English major's modest moral goal.

WEEK 9

LOST IN BOOKS

Last week a foggy past transcends
The inner waves of difficulty.
Syntax lines of useless form
Is function into anonymity.

Johnson's coined sarcastic wit
Eats away Tom Cane's heart –
God is always on his lips

As Johnson joins what others part.

While students lounge in Union bars
And lecture time is quietly spent
Beneath the sheets on chilly morns;
The weight of literature descends –

Like snow upon the sleeping earth
To blanket white the naked truth,
Wrapped incognito, bound in books
For eager critics to peruse.

And we poor students, lost, confused,
Struggle to withstand the bruising –
The knocks they come like hammer blows
Upon our panel work of ego.

Pounding like the autumn tides,
Arriving warm, then bitter leaving;
Daily tussle these titanic forces –
haunting us with our own moaning.

Out of breath, and short of time,
No pause, no rest, no second life –
No second sight to right first done,
No second chance to fix first wrongs.

And so we students waste our chance
To grasp the universe we guess
That hides between the yellowed sheets
We never quite find the time to read.

Youth comes upon us all ablaze,
Its fire a burning inner rage …
In search of free-thinking angles,
Away from what childhood's taught.

Perhaps we came here for the beer?
Perhaps the beer's the best thing here?
But yet, such shallow depths lead on
To fails, re-sits, and change of course.

The drop-out quota must be filled –
Thirteen percent must find the door.
Now at the end of the ninth week,
We are well on down that road.

WEEK TEN

(i) **MARTYRS**

Someone committed suicide last week,
But nobody knows her name.
The rumours fly around like moths
In flight around a naked flame.

No one denies the event,

But no one knows when or where?
The Registrar in muted nothing,
Says nothing to avoid a scare.

There's always been suicides at college,
The future will hold the same;
But it seems like a terrible waste
Of life to end this way.

Youth in a blaze and a flourish
Becomes bone in a musty grave.
Better to let youth wrinkle
Than let youth pass into decay.

Young lives should pass happily
Into old lives of contentment;
Old lives should think back
On young lives looking ahead.

The young should outlive the old,
The old should outlive young thought.
The young as bright and bold,
The old as wise and mellow.

The young should have their praises sung,
The old their tales be told -
Let's pray our dead martyr has gone
Quietly to Tir na Nog.

Do I see the cape of hero Cuchulain,
The mightiest of Ireland's warrior gods?
Feel I the sword of Bran, son of Lir?
Or beneath his Isle, the cauldron of Man?

Man – that jewel in the Celtic Sea,
Lapis lazuli, ribboned in gold ...
Sand broken horses, white and rippling
On the shores of our islands.

Three kingdoms united, one divided,
And a republic, presently stand.
Yet forgive me for dwelling on myth,
'Tis the pride of a Celtic man.

For the Celtic world is one of riches
Buried beneath the English view -
That Angle came, and Saxon conquered,
And Norman did what Dane couldn't do.

But this is avoiding our academic studies,
The travels of Spenser, and Marvell,
The works of Shakespeare and Marlowe,
Middleton, Webster and Dryden.

Like a procession of princes,
They parade before me like shadows;
Men caught in limbo ...

203

Knowing no rest, no arrival.

From the human to the immortal –
Caught, they live perpetual;
Going round in circles ...
They reach central and provincial.

Every college, school and infant –
Their influence being infinite ...
Their works collected, words recited;
There are no living poets - mightier!

No playwrights thought of so highly
That critics turn to praise their work;
These great men of testament –
Lets preserve them, for they are dead!

And if you doubt my token homage,
Go you to Westminster, now;
Stand before St. Peter's church –
Pass through the great arched doors.

And once your eyes have scaled the heights
And wondered at the work of men;
Turn you to the eastern aisle
Gently pass before the marbled shrines –

Statesmen, warriors, and knights;
Until you leave all those behind
And pay your debt to travel on
Beyond the gateway that permits -

Entry to the resting place of kings.
There, close by the poets lie,
The men whose words outlived kings,
Though wretched may their lives have been.

How splendid have their names survived,
Etched upon polished stone ...
This corner of England theirs, alone.
Martyrs for our studies.

And thus ten weeks have passed;
Ceased. Lost, forever gone.
And all I leave are thoughts,
Thoughts we all must have.

The Hippies said share your love
And God will love you back.
I'd rather dwell on that –
Than put the writing on the wall.

So whoever you be, reading this,
Recall that I am mortal –
Ninety weeks at university
Is not long at all.

End of term has caught me up,
I stand to catch the wind;
The ivory towers at my back,
The artist in me quicks.

The winter evenings fast draw in,
Each morning darker slides –
But now vacation time is here
I'll sleep till noon time bides.

Wash fatigue from tired eyes,
Late study hours have strained –
One term has gone, eight remain,
The ice-berg submerged lies.

Nine lives, a cat lives out;
Nine terms a student strives,
Cloud nine the first term passes by
Across a becalmed sky.

A magic carpet ride of joy,
A free-load trip of fun;
From here on in, the path descends
The road of graft and slog.

Now I have the chance to rest –
I'll lay my pen aside;
Await the coming of New Year
As Eight Three departs.

So till you hear from me again –
Goodbye and all my love.
Student work's a better job
Than working for a boss.

(End of The Undergraduate – Part 1)

FROST CRACKED & BROKEN
[9pm, 10th Nov 1983, Helmsley Rd, Newcastle]

Life passes too quickly,
Like the wind, a rushing,
A hushing black storm clouds,
Clouds heavy with mourning,
Tears black and rolling.

The day goes too swiftly,
Like a stream, a torrent,
A raging white flood tide,
Tide bound with woeing,
Eyes downcast and flowing.

The night is not fleeting,
Like fire's flames, a licking,
A consuming blue lightning,
Thundering with cymbals,
Sight ashen and waning.

Death comes on unseeing,
Like the land, a frozen,
A frost-cracked and broken,
Split-lipped with ploughing,
Vision doubled and going.

THE DWELLING OF KNOWLEDGE
[10.30pm, 26th Nov 1983, Helmsley Rd, Newcastle]

Enter the dwelling of knowledge,
Grasp hold of wisdom,
Release the blanket of ignorance
Smooth out all memory.
Learning must progress through death,
Life must pass by steps,
Time must be the key
To the knowledge quest.

Enter the house of learning,
Reside in the cycle of time,
Study the order of being -
The duration and length of life.
The eternal circle of wisdom
Along the infinite line,
Symbolic signs of learning -
Paths forgotten but found.

Lost wisdom on fresh knowledge
Await the questing mind -
Enter the dwelling of knowledge
And reside in the cycle of life.

CHRISTMAS EVE
[9pm, 24th Dec 1983, Helmsley Rd, Newcastle]

Drinking port, and fingering -
Girls are all the same
Dressed up without knickers
Their scent lingering.

Swilling burgundy, and kissing -
Sex inside is swelling
Pumped and willing
Girls are swooning.

On the sherry, and reeling -
Held up by women
Getting in on the killing
Christmas Eve is kissing.

ENGLISH BOXING DAY
[26th Dec 1983, Helmsley Rd, Newcastle]

Natives tell me the thing to do -
Pass around drinking spirits,
Fall about in swooning stupor

After Xmas cheese and chocolate.

Friends say 'Don't feel guilty,
Work has stopped till after New Year"
And I think 'Maybe I'm foreign
And all that they tell me is true'.

Putting that aside, such idleness
Becomes a way of life too soon -
Yet locals say "On Boxing Day
You must start the New Year way".

Somehow this English train of thought
Panders to a life of ease -
But who I am, Cointreau in hand -
To be displeased.

THE DAY AFTER BOXING DAY
[27th Dec 1983, Helmsley Rd, Newcastle]

Easy flowing words
Wind effortlessly from my pen -
Such delight in simple phrases
Is what makes men act
As though God has done them favours.

BIG DICK AND LITTLE WILLY (song)
[22nd Jan 1984, Helmsley Rd, Newcastle]

Big Dick and Little Willy
Were shipyard sort of blokes,
They both lived down the Scrogg Road,
Their bairns were schooled at Walker Road -
Both their wives had varicose veins
From the weight of worry's load.

Dick's whole life was work and club,
Played football for the local pub,
Played the darts and fruit machines,
He loved his wife - a pretty thing -
But she could not stand being broke
And married to a doled shipyard bloke.

Little Willy's life was balding -
Pension schemes had long been growing,
His canny wife seven grand-kids weaned,
Threw up her arms and justly screamed -
"For every job the bastards squeeze,
Three generations of Tyneside heaves".

In any other time but now
The shipyard work has stood them proud -
Tales of Big Dick and Little Willy
Would leave you laughing in the aisles,
But this is not a happy tale
As the shipyards on the Tyne decay.

So think you long on what I say -
Every human has his day.
Today the Tory flag is raised
Above the workers in cold hate;
Shipyard work is a dying joke
And Tyneside an unemployment sore.

They were shipyard sort of blokes -
Big Dick and Little Willy.

THE UNDERGRADUATE - TERM 2
[22nd Jan – 27th Mar 1983, Newcastle mainly]

WEEK 11

THE PILLARS OF WISDOM

Of Chaucer's verse, we must foremost review
And scan the inner meaning so employed.
Yet what is this to me? And more to you?
Now that winter snows fluff down anon.
Term time's here, and we once more enjoin
To our studies, to trap and chain our minds.
The punishment of privilege is enslavement;
It is a defeat of a kind.

Yet in truth, outside hailstones fall like pebbles
Upon a large snare drum – deep the echo
Pounds into the soul until inaudible;
The vibrations modulate until the spirit's numb.
White, and right out of the sky it comes
To fall and lie and settle close to walls,
To top high layered drifts, to blanket all
This winter.

But let me drop this scant news of weather
And move to mention other more real things
Like sex, and drugs, and fellow sin bed leather;
The latest in mid-Nineteen-Eighties kink.
Nudity, free love, abortion, clone tubing,
Mastectomy, hysterectomy, and you name it clinics;
Some people stoop while others know no limit
To it all.

Where are the joggers now that blizzards run?
Where do gardeners dig now the soil is frozen?
Where do fishermen sleep while the storm's blowing?
And which mad roofer fixes drainpipes in a freeze?
Pristine overhead snow overhangs the window,
Glacial from eaves iced with stalagmites –
Fine slender crystal javelins droop streetwards
As hard as dolomite.

And so I wander off my scholar's toils,
Away from the studies that before me lie;
The distractions in the background fade
Till only my eyes sense the words before me.

Order and structure, what of it?
Chaos in beauty is there outside my window;
Known forms transformed in an eon
That decays concrete.

This simple logic, to the academic
Has no literary value, none attached;
So far I haven't mentioned anything sick or comic
And its line forty four of my attack.
I am forestalling without much tact?
Its time to tell tales about students balling;
The more serious of you might think
That's just appalling.

So the new term's begun with Chaucer,
Syntax, Hobbes, and Rochester the Rotter.
As simple as saying 'cup and saucer'?
Linguists and grammarians always stutter
Over the diphthongs in words like 'butter' –
Over the spelling of textual vowel sounds;
That in Chaucer are flat, and in Shakespeare round.
Oh what a bother!

In other rooms and other theatres,
Criticism is expounded on strained ears;
Richards, Leavis, and fifty other theories
Bring on a puzzlement of sighs and groans.
Oh the price of textbooks for the year!
Knowledge, like they say, is not cheap.
Like farming land, the sowing is costly
Before you reap.

Here I end this short tribute to Geoffrey
And close with barely a mention of his name;
I will finish this weeks ramble
With a reminder that the studies remain.
The R.S.C are coming in five weeks,
We must prepare and read our Shakespeare
Into the dead of night - all is white,
And snow is everywhere.

WEEK 12

THE POET'S TOOLS
(a)
Prose is the medium of playwrights and authors
Of fiction – creative, historic, biographic.
But poetry is the pulse and heartbreak of lovers,
The accent and stress of all things romantic.
The ecstasy, the weeping, the relic of worship,
The epic, the ballad, the quatrain, the couplet;
Hyperbole, allegory, symbol and fable,
Fallacy, emblem and paradox statement.
Petrarchan conceit, irony and pun,
Classical epithet and moral *exemplum*;
Paradox, metaphor and personification.

Devices and styles through millenniums run,
The bards are immortal, but rhythms pound on.
Assonance, consonance - internal, imperfect,
Verses rhyme on in free stanza resonance,
Through Middle-Age humour, Humanist pre-reason,
Neo-classical correctness, and restoration lewdness;
Romantic feeling and Victorian ethics –
All find voice in poetic metrical.
Decorum of genre, colic and sanguine,
Phlegmatic, melancholy to fit temperament;
Mimetic, pragmatic, myth and legend.

Thus bile, blood, phlegm, and puke contrast
With ode, elegy, and lyric chant –
Burlesque, and mock heroic puncture,
Baroque, and Manneristic banter.
Sceptic, stoic, or epicurean;
Roman catholic, deist and Puritan;
Tribe of Ben, Metaphysical and Cavalier,
Gothic, Graveyard and modern surreal.
Theory rules in poetry schools,
Stress and foot the poet's tools –
Metre the crown, and words the jewels.

(b)
Now armed, the poet can talk of love
As couples entwine in the darkness of night;
Exchanging soft glances in light finger dancing
Waltzing the length of naked delight.
White as the skin of an English virgin,
The land lies bare in winter ice.
Red as the lips of a North Country maiden,
The berries of hawthorn and rowan stand out.
Nowhere yet is crocus shooting –
Nowhere yet is snowdrop protruding –
Nowhere yet is daffodil blooming.

Beds are warm and loving nightly,
Daily, hourly through the chill;
The sun comes up and yellow flushes
Lovers lost in willing worlds.
Gutters drip and drainpipes gurgle,
Music lifts the blackbird's song;
Rooftops shake with sliding shudder
As thawing slush turns to flood.
Nowhere yet are starlings rushing –
Nowhere yet are swallows darting –
Nowhere yet are insects swarming.

As lovers laze and grace the daylight,
Coyly reaching out to share
A passion hot, with fleeting like-minds
They feel, to lay their secrets bare.
Mirrors strung about their love rooms
Steal the real, and show the new –
Reflections cast return as shadows
As fleet foot nymphs aid their play.

Nowhere yet is light rain falling –
Nowhere yet is mild wind blowing –
Nowhere yet is snow short going.

As lovers rise and greet the sunset,
To kiss and dress, and sadly part;
Like pupae in the act of shedding,
They leave a skin of bed-clothes wry.
Daylight fades and evening enters
The solitude that darkness fills;
As lovers hold each other hard,
And then release with a kiss.
Nowhere yet are night fires burning –
Nowhere yet are couples warring –
Nowhere yet are friendships waning.

As lover waves to lover going
Deep into the void of night …
We must return to other subjects
Touching on the poetry kind.
But if you want to dwell on lovers
Turn you now to John Donne's verse –
Locked within his sunk devotion
Lingers love for womankind.
Not in Donne is emotion sated –
Not in Donne is passion bloated –
Not in Donne is love outmoded.

This I shall no longer labour,
Another week has gone for good.
The academic life, a privileged calling,
Love on a grant - a simple woo.
A *Country Wife* a play to read,
And *Custom of the Country* too;
The Winter's Tale the Willie text,
and now we've moved on to *The Tempest*.
Not in memory does knowledge lie –
Not in wisdom is truth implied –
Not in love does life survive.

WEEK 13

RELAX

Relax! Take it easy
Put your troubles on the table –
Smoke some marijuana
Have a beer!

Life isn't worth a penny
When the worries are too many
And you can't enjoy a bevy
Or a bleeze!

Feelings held in ready,
Stored up in swelling plenty –
Let them go with a renting,

211

Let them free!

The mind may be counting
Doubts, rushing from a fountain,
But let hem drown a mountain,
Let them be!

Moments come and go,
Sometimes quick, sometimes slow –
Each second as it comes,
Let it flow!

Anxiety is a waste
In this double-sided place –
For life can be two-faced,
Don't we know!

While across the western race
Where technology's a blaze –
Where edifices are raised;
Let them fall!

While the astronauts count stars,
Where Jupiter conjuncts Mars,
Beyond galactic parts –
Let them wander!

While the communists yield,
When the socialists squeal,
As the capitalists do a deal –
Let things pass!

While the workers scream
At having their wages creamed,
And the bosses buy their dreams –
Let it go!

As the short days lengthen
Towards that place in heaven
That the believers crave for –
Let it come!

For when belief is weak,
Remember faith is failing,
And is a type of jailing –
To bar against!

For open thought and open mind
Stretches back to first mankind,
Whizzing on to future time –
Let it amble!

While the storms tirade,
While the icy gales ferment,
While the Arctic waste descends
From frozen tundra!

Stand awake on such days,
So its said people say,
Even when off on holiday –
It's little wonder!

While the ships ocean toss,
While the waves oil rigs rock –
While atomic subs dry dock –
Let it sunder!

Let those tempests pass,
Drink a beer let time part,
Take some drugs with your pals
Till doped under!

Relax, take it easy,
Put your feet on the table,
And tune into the radio –
Let it blast!

WEEK 14

TRAPPED IN NEWCASTLE

The Smoke That Thunders
Tumbles the Zambezi.
The sands of Giza
grate past Cheop's;
while I dwell in Newcastle
In the One-Nine-Eighties.

Tai Shan that towers,
keeps a dragon sleeping.
The burnt soil of Crete
labyrinths a creature;
while icy fogs descend
On me in England.

The white that shimmers,
mirrors shrined Kailasa.
The hissing of Iguazu
assimilates Parana;
while the clouds beyond
Durham top-cut winter.

The purple plained Karoo
splits the Orange State.
The marshland of the Sudd
silts the Nile spate;
while the viscous Tyne
slakes my campus days.

The whale that spouts
gushes green Kauai.
The beast that howls
haunts Alaska's wilds;
while gales gut Tyneside,

213

swamp my mind.

The Angel that falls
silvers dense Guyana.
The monkey that flies
hovers o'er Sri Lanka;
while North Sea winds
slash-in on me from Russia.

The volcanoes that glow
blow in Nicaragua.
The tremors of fear,
shake up California;
while Jurassic Northumberland
crumbles coal into the sea.

The giants that slumber
guard Easter Isle,
As the university of Newcastle
keeps me study bound.
Yet, I know that someday
I'll leave this town behind.

WEEK 15

LIVING HERE UNDER HEAVEN

Behind the times, we all lag on –
we marathon to the Olympic slopes,
faster than slaloms swishing with fliers,
we career through bronzes, silvers, gold
in ice rinks – where a matador's lips
take the surrender of an ice queen's lips.

Faster than sleighs tunneling burrows
in roller coaster corkscrews –
across Yugoslavia in a sightseeing tour.
Dubrovnik or Beograd,
Sarajevo and Zagreb –
we see everything on TV.

Serb and Croat, little known Kosovos,
I've been to that land five times or more;
five times is enough for the well travelled man
for it's a rough country to bear –
who will believe me, not having suffered
the memories of the Albanian front.

It brings on the trembles,
the bad nerves, the soaked temples
dripping sweat, measured in litres,
dripping to quench the parched ground;
the thirst of the farmer
the dust of the pasture
the brown walls of the churchyards
the dry walls of the chapels
the arid-eyed statues

Madonna and Peter
Paul, Andrew and Stephen
surrounded by weepers
and the baked tongues of preachers
holding aloft gold casketed relics
poor mummified creatures
wizened and shrivelled
decaying pitted-features
yellow glazed bone
skin like old leather
shiny in parts where pilgrims fingers
have touched, for good omen -
for an old saint's blessing
for a martyr's dead message
of sainthood, of spirit
hallowed by time
by the passing of ages.

Only through living memory does reverence
pass on down the generations;
thru wide gateways of veneration
thru broad doorways to the universal
thru expansive openings to the eternal
to stop in matter, to exist in the nebulae,
beyond the celestial;
to a ruined world
a globe burnt out
a corpse upon the ride of night

whilst we the mortals, back on earth
living here under heaven –
we so not like Andromeda,
chained to sub astral diversion;
we are tellurian and terrestrial …
we are mortal and perishable.

WEEK 16

IS SPRING HERE?

Monday. *The Wakefield Cycle*,
Noah's flood washed over me.
The sheep in the cradle,
Cain crippling Abel,
And the good shepherds three.

Also, the Cavalier poets –
Carew, Suckling, Waller.
Lovelace and King Charles,
the best of Court pals,
Before all that Civil War bother.

Tuesday. A long lie –
Then syntax and Oscar,
With some thought on *Earnest*,
Lady Bracknell, and 'jest'.
A look at a poem over tea.

Wednesday. Too late –
For the Diachronic lecture
On history in speech.
So I had a quick read
Of Herrick, and felt better.

Lunchtime. Common room meeting
About a barn dance evening.
Our Lit Soc's a ramble –
Our Lang Soc's a shambles –
But students are honest, not thieving.

At Two. The Gulbenkian –
And Ruskin's *Space Invaders*.
Weird play on the future,
By the RSC's fringe tour
Of actors and players.

Seven Thirty. Lopez de Vega,
And his old Spanish play –
L*ost in a Mirror* –
I doubt it's a winner.
A rewrites in order , I say.

Thursday. Pissing ol' Gissing
And his Victorian dribbling.
A discussion on Rudkin
In a tutorial mud rubbing
Where we gave his play a ribbing.

Friday. It must be Shakespeare –
A*s you Like It*, an' *Twelve Night*.
Viola and Rosalind, and most
Of the talk in reverence
For the two women's rights.

Evening. Edward Bond –
R*ed, Black and Ignorant*.
A play with little movement,
About a nuclear charred monster,
Acted with some brilliance.

The Weekend. No rest –
For the serious student.
The ardent academic,
Conscious and polemic,
So proper and prudent.

Sunday. This poetry –
Reflects the week's parting,
Post dates a week going.
And in one final partake –
There's another week starting.

WEEK 17

TUTORIAL

What have you learned, my son,
In this week's study?
I have learned may things
Of interest and wonder!
Of tragic *Lady Astolat*
Floating down to Camelot –
Of salivating *Major Barbara*
Undershafted.

And have you come to terms
With idealism in texts?
I have read my Roland Barthes,
And on Sontag made a start.
I've been lectured on Cullers
And a number of others.
I think I know my Richards,
My Olsen, and my Leavis.

This may be so,
But what do you know???
I admit I feel uneasy
About Whimsatt and Beardsley.
Intention of expression –
Invention or impression.
The fallacy's inherent.
Or no?

No one knows for sure.
But what about Saussure?
Language has its borders,
Words have their order;
Sentences have a structure,
So meaning may puncture
Our reading governed by rules.
Chomsky was no fool!

You have been reading
Your Shakespeare on evenings?
Most certainly fulfilling,
The hectic text billing!
A *Comedy of Errors* – borrowed
from Menaechmi and Alcestis.
A *Midsummer's Night Dream*
And its Sylvan moonbeams.

And twentieth century drama?
Are you maintaining your stamina?
Most certainly engaging
In these theatrical playthings.
Yeats on Baile Strand –
Cathleen Count and ni Houlihan.
Chekov's *The Seagull*
And his *Cherry Orchard* mull.

And what do you think now

217

that seventeen weeks have passed?
I believe life is worth living -
Though poverty's a misgiving
That a student takes as payment
For the wealth of mental slaving.
My brain may be splitting
But my hands are soft and clean.

WEEK 18

ABANDONMENT

All week long I have abandoned my studies
And turned to typing my latest stage play.
Instead of in-going, my thoughts have been flowing
Through my fingers. Oh, you may think
Such trivial information should slide
Into the trash can of my past – but
Half a student's life is lived in order that
He may somehow learn to record his past.

Such trite belief may be for the ignorant,
Such sentiment be an elitist precept, but
I would rather see my world in flames
Than see my time not tethered in this way.
For one day, the student will be a man,
And face men as a man not a boy –
Though, I demobbed to the rank of student
I'm seeking benefit from such a fall.

By rising to it all, I know better –
Or perhaps I can really only guess
That first class degrees are won by courage,
Risk, and spins of bare-faced gall – provided
You bandage your neck begging for the chop.
One bright idea too many, one smart remark,
First class honours hinge on more than neat
Typed essays and good tutor grades.

And hence – my plays, my stories, my
Armfuls of novels, poems and songs –
These are my profession, my kind of trade
Of which study is half, or two thirds, and
Writing practice stems from reading –
Not from scribbling merrily on to sunrise.

A word of advice to all would be writers –
Never drain the lamp while it's burning.
Sunrises come, it's the sunsets we count;
The flame may flicker in the light bulb,
But it's the sun that blinds.

Man is out to destroy himself –
It is the better part to know one's self;
Also knowing that wee hour writing is
As productive as stirring ice with a hot knife –
Lots of steaming and hissing ...

But in the end nothing left of the ice.

If only I could practice what I expound?
Wisdom is never heeded by those in whom
it abides. The smart fool is the one who
admits to this masque of pride. Blinded
by self deceit and personal esteem,
the complete fool will miss this advice.

Remember … I am here to amuse myself
As well as to hand out woeful rhetoric;
The governing laws that make the rules
May be broken, but it's not important.
Likewise I may deviate from my studies
And ramble on into the night.

Eighteen weeks gone - it seems so long a time.

WEEK 19

Here lies Old Robbie, sex has wet his lips;
And hear, m'lad, she laid him for a quid.

THE QUIET UNIONIST

Milton wouldn't have spent his time watching television,
He would have been dreaming somewhere between hell
And heaven.
But I haven't time to dwell on poetic paradise –
My debts are mounting as my cash flow dies.
The government is draining every drop of liquid
Cash out'a poor folks' pockets.
                    I feel the torture in my guts,
The knots tied by the passing of new laws;
The wrenching sickening way each one gnaws
On socialism.
                    The ministers of out noble state –
Two in very three should be held in public probate
For leading our nation to war for profit;
For abusing state powers to line their pockets,
While poor men starve and ill men die,
And the children of our morrow, have education denied
For no reason.
                    It is slavery we're given –
The chains of class are not made in heaven;
They are forged on earth at Cabinet carve ups,
Where Defence eats the breast, and Industry sups
On the beads of sweat rung from the brows of labour.
What better fare may a fascist government savour
Than inequality.
                    We face again dark feudal days –
Four classes of men – master, merchant, beggar, slave,
Where even a begging bowl is preferable to bonded wages;
Where merchant supports master in return for favours
Granted in a trade off o'wealth, property, and power
That permits the merchant class to sow and flower
And t'send their fragile seed to public school

And long vac' escapes that flout the rules
Of common brotherhood.
                    Let us not forget
That woman is not sister to herself as yet –
Despite the pipes of peace that many wind
With songs and demonstrations against nuclear bins
And silos buried deep in mother England.
For this kingdom's raped a world of lands
To rise upon the backs of blacks and the under privileged
Fathered by cheap seduction.
                    And still we pillage –
Petty puppet states and pseudo democratic nations;
Tomorrow's despots and tyrants we instruct in education,
We teach dictators politics and diplomatic code;
Indoctrinate the overseas elite in current mode
And technique as how best to divide and rule
And institutionalise subversion.
                    We are fools –
Not blind, but open-eyed imperialistic conquerors.
Our army stands in readiness to under shaft order;
Our government stands prepared to remedy disorder.
We are neither weak not ineffectual in world affairs;
We do not grow bananas, we produce atomic ware;
We rank third in a list of two hundred ethnic nations;
In order to maintain – we crate negation
By propagating destruction.
                    We are Britons –
Most nights I try to disentangle the truth on television;
But to no avail, we lie to one another without blushing;
We are no better than the Cubans or the Russians,;
In truth we may actually be a whole lot worse.
I'm sure there are many Britons who'd shoot me first
And ask their questions later.

WEEK 20

VACATION LOOMS

Silence is most times better than loud words
Together
Between the pauses, we listen coldly
As the March rains fall.

Still, motionless, to quiver in the lee
United
The quietness presses on laden movement
Stirred by Spring's forced marching.

Students read in nooks and culverts
Undecided
The numbness eases in on outer nothing
Mulled westward by the east wind rising.

Old men hover round and round in mute obedience
Hunchbacked
Flagstones smart with flaying canes
Skating on the frost of damp cast alleys.

Tempers parade into the morning skyline
Unprotected
Thoughts formed unhindered, fade unvoiced
Unuttered sweetness left bitter on the tongue.

Speechless lulls cross awkward voids
Unguarded
Moments career along at reckless canter
Unobserved, out of wind, gone in silence.

Unstressed points made in muttered words
Unemphatic
Hours spent in idle laze or fancy
In squeaking chairs or moaning couches.

No amount of movement levers action
Unintentional
Silence settles on receptive hearers
Waiting for the echo and crescendo.

End of term brings on a tiredness
Uninvited
The weeks have passed all too quickly
Vacation is a gift so quietly granted.

(End of The Undergraduate – Term 2)

A NIGHT WITHOUT LIGHT
[27th Mar 1984, Lumb Bank, Heptonstall, Yorks]

It was one of those nights, when one
Could spend an hour describing the weather.
The city clocks unsynchronised spanned
Five tolling minutes to announce
The hour before midnight.

The grey sandstone walls of the cemetery
Stifled the mumbling traffic; the yellow
Street lights hazed and numbed the shadows;
The silhouetted cypress touched branches
With the weeping willow.

John the farm worker lay stretched out
On a grave. Overhead a Celtic cross tattooed
the darkness. What life there was he had
Crushed underfoot. Poor snowdrop, cut crocus,
Greenhouse daffodil.

THE EXPERIMENTALIST
[10.55am, 28th Mar 1984, Lumb Bank, Heptonstall, Yorks]

Mistakes are gross distortions
Authors twist to reach for the real,
Delusion in a letter form
Show the lies as barely fact.
Yet others take inhuman face,

Class division - serf and lord,
Worlds turned on worker / master
Is the novel's pride of place.

States of mind ... warped or strange,
Insight into the mental bent;
Voices silent, loudly blatant
Typed upon a rambling page -
Martian culture, ultra context,
Islands in a swimming world;
Things for granted shift like sand
When held in focus to the norm.

Plots abound to hack around
Fairy tales and common myth -
Everything is cop and robber.
Steal? Authors deny this word.
Notebooks full of jotted insight,
Lines of quotes and plagiarism -
Extracts thinly veiled to hide
The source from which they're taken.

Sentence structure played upon,
Tense in past or present form;
Questions asked in unsolved rhetoric;
Sky's the limit so they say.
All these things a writer juggles
Well before he starts to write -
Experimental prose is open
Is never fixed, and lives to die.

THE UNDERGRADUATE - TERM 3
[6th May – 15th July 1984, Newcastle]

WEEK 21

(i) THEY RUN TO THE OCEAN

Some folks have all the fun
And run to the joyous ocean
To escape work.

They return wafting wood smoke
And joke about home made wine
And dead seagulls.

They leave trails of beach sand
Before hanging heads in worried thoughts
About tomorrow.

Their fortunes wave
Keyed upon unfound aims
And unmade laughter like the sea.

(ii) BEFORE CLOSING TIME

While beyond my walls -
Neighbours play the music of our times
And clink their glasses – I must dwell
On the works of Miller, Pinter,
Becket, Taylor … while friends enjoy
The fruits of their labour, I labour on,
Imbue myself in emblematic code
That leaves me drained and sober.

While out in the lane –
Dogs bark loudly at the moon
As overhead a Boeing rumbles southwards
To who knows where – somewhere far
From here, somewhere warm,
Yet cool beneath a palm – where
Memories linger on across the calm.
It makes me think of Rio,
Where the sun is white
And the music hot.

I return to my senses –
The open text books, the unfilled essay
Pages – on Miller, Pinter, Becket,
Taylor – before turning off to dream,
And thinking …
Milton wouldn't have spent his time watching television,
He would have been dreaming somewhere between hell and
heaven.

I wish that tomorrow was today,
And yesterday a day to be relived
As my thoughts drift to real-ale revels,
And bar-room afternoons when a pint of beer
and a bag of crisps was better than a frozen
dinner from the fridge.

Still the work remains undone –
As my memory turns, churns and burns
As summer rushes in first flush
In May; and I think of days when
Blackbirds drown the party song
Of revelers going strong at dawn.

I can't continue –
A thirst has gripped my throat,
Its time to stop, grab my coat
And make a dash along the road –
The local pub is paradise for those
Who haven't time to waste the night
By driveling on past closing time.

WEEK 22

DEATH ENTERS AND EXITS

Death
Enters and exits

From the taverna.

Pass black horses
And hooded people
On the profound highway
Of the guitarra.

There's an odour of salt
And of female blood
In the balsam fevers
Of the harbour.

Death
Enters and exits,
And exits and enters
Death
From the taverna.

Through the mariposas
A sad girl walks ...
Tierra de luz
Cielo de tierra.

Through a field of olives
A white snake slides ...
Tierra de luz
Cielo de tierra.

The children look to
The far away mountains ...
Tierra de luz
Cielo de tierra.

Beneath the orange trees
Lies Lola with me ...
Ay, amor,bajo
El naranjo en flor.

Her big green eyes
And her voileta voice ...
Ay, amor, bajo
El naranjo en flor.

Her slender brown arms
And her slim bare legs ...
Ay, amor, bajo
El naranjo en flor.

The music of the birds
Swimming in our heads ...
Ay, amor, bajo
El naranjo en flor.

The wind blows the dust
Yellow from the fields ...
El viento con el polvo
Hace proras de plata.

The fields are deserts
And the orange groves dunes ...
El viento con el polvo
Hace proras de plata.

Lost in our love
in the green kiss of moon ...
El viento con el polvo
Hace proras de plata.

The constellation candles
In the arch of a swoon ...
El viento con el polvo
Hace proras de plata.

Death by the taverna
Beginning and end ...
No me imparta nada
Mas que tu querer.

Amongst the mariposa
A sad girl walks ...
No me imparta nada
Mas que tu querer.

Beneath the orange trees
Lies Lola with me ...
No me imparta nada
Mas que tu querer.

The wind blows the dust
Yellow from the fields ...
No me imparta nada
Mas que tu querer.

In the singing wind
Words are lingering ...
Death exits and enters
the taverna.

WEEK 23

Each play is not as it seems – when
you catch a glimpse behind the scenes.

THE AUDITION

How can I do what you ask?
Bend over twice, two pats on the ass,
Three kisses a scene,
And stark bare in the first act???

It's easy, luv, just give a smile,
A wave will have them beguiled.
It's a hard part to play – but
You're a winner all the way!

I'm not so sure this plot's any good.
Three rape scenes, sodomy, and gays
Running about like little boy blues!
I'm like Snow White in a den of wolves?

You're tense, it's the weather, or something.
Have you eaten today?
I've known actresses survive a week
On cheese, and sex, and speed.

I'm not into downers or that sort of thing!
I like Cola, coffee and alko-fizzed drinks.
I'm not into side-lines and fixes.
I'm not hooked or ready to sink.

Never suggested you'd have a price.
Nice girls come, but real pro's survive.
If you're going to take the part –
When do you think you could start?

I think we'd be best to forget it.
Acting's a profession, not a habit.
Sex on the stage is an amateur's ploy
To legitimise porn and finger the toys.

Darling, how can you say this???
This playwright has had ten West End hits!
You can't believe his work is porn?
He's a dignified man, rich and respected.

Money gets soiled on the merry-go-round –
It picks up dirt wherever it's found.
Writers can be the dirtiest of fellows,
And most of them are incredibly shallow!

What utter rot! You silly little bitch!
Get off my stage, I'll black you for this.
This author's been with us for twenty years.
It's me! I've had enough of your sneers!

The rudest of natures always comes out
In hacks who know nothing, and shout.
Good riddance, I say, to your poxy stage!
Find another whore for your play!

WEEK 24

THE QUARREL

She had come to me almost breakfast-less,
Eyeless and draped at the breasts in silk,
The leaves of the world like darkness to me,
The dawn like a storm out of China.

I was neither a king nor a fool
As she sat thin faced with vacant stare,

She the fruit of the forbidden tree,
Wild times and valley streams rushing still.

She watched the clock tick minute by hour,
Foul, then fair as she sat and dreamed,
The caverns through which she deeply passed,
Carried me down to a sunless sea.

Down some profound dark tunnel I followed,
A voice in me said 'If you were in love
You'd whisper three words on her withering,
Before the flowers fade and sorrow yields.'

As the neighbour's dog barked in it's sleep,
She looked like coral hacked from a reef –
Every wound having cut her sharply,
I owed her no net to catch her fall.

She cried like the wind in the maple trees
'If this is us, then who is against us!'
She'd reached the verge of the knife-edge ledge
That love had brought her blindfolded to.

Affairs like seed blow in the wind,
She ran from the battle defeated and worn,
And into the storm of the day she departed,
As I sat and watched the thunder roll.

WEEK 25

(i) AMBIGUITY

Ambiguity of the first type –
Atmosphere and style.
Pure sound and Empson
Sounds like such a lot of hype.

(ii) DREAMS OF SPAIN

Sunny Spain seems so succinctly sweet,
I'll trade these days of drizzle
For a Malaga beach.

And still the evening rain descends
To dampen droll belief
Of paradise in England.

June's juices dribble from scented roses,
Chestnut blossom black-flied falling
On empty beaches.

No one goes trimming garden hedgerows,
Mowing lawns, clipping verges
In the rain.

Bluebells bend backwards 'neath birches,
Broken barked and birked

By rows of beeches.

Avoiding gurgling gargling gutter pipes,
Pedestrians push past puddles
On into the night.

Spain looms large ... then fades
As minutes master moments made
In idle image.

Illusion inconsistent with intended ideal,
Forces false impressions to the fore
Of infirm logic.

Fair misty the fine rain falls
To polka-dot and rivulet
The chip-shop window -

Where the punters round the block in line
To murder ninety-pence newspaper nosh
Of half-cod slices.

I float to Spain ... to costa
Casual days of coppertone carousing
'Neath the acacias -

As evening empties out to twilight,
Catching shadows criss-crossed by street-lights
Ocre-orange.

Little wonder workers strike in summer,
Power to them ... they are my brothers
And my sisters.

As the rain hurls in heaving hurry,
Spain retreats ... darkness starts
In on tomorrow.

WEEK 26

STUDENT PARTY

(i)
I went to a party this week –
It was a pale shade of Oscar Wilde.
I missed the cucumber sandwiches,
But the cream cake was nice.

(ii)
I sometimes wonder where everything leads;
We starve to eat cake, while others feast;
We may get a nibble at the occasional do,
But a few crumbs of gateau washed with tea
Are customary habits few of us chew.

Once, grapes were the passion of fashion –
Succulently dangled in erotic rations.

We may get a neck at a student party;
A quick pop of juice on top of brown ale
Can make any wimp ballsy and happy.

Poor sods, that's all I can say,
Waiting all year for one of those days.
So much for caviar and oyster dishes;
Champagne may was well be a place in Spain
When nursed with cocoa and McVitie's dip.

The English way is a packet of crisps,
A skinful of bitter, a bag of chips,
Fags for the party, a couple of cans,
A toke of hash, a bop and a dance,
A quick bit of natter, and it off in a van.

WEEK 27

Some weeks are better than some days,
Some wines aren't as good as some years.

I DON'T GIVE A DAMN (song)

Oh, I don't care for nothing,
I don't care a toss –
The rain may fall in dull Whitehall
While it blazes in quiet Kos.

The girls may bare their breasts a lot,
I wouldn't turn a hair –
I've seen the nicest fellow drown
Because he turned and stared.

I've had my lack of interest
Keeping me well dowsed –
God knows what would happen
If my interest was aroused.

I thrive on doing shit-all,
It gives an easy life –
An easy life's twice as nice
As one that's rich in strife.

Maybe I care too much about
Not caring very much –
But too much care so they say
Is much too care as such.

WEEK 28

The beaches of Spain are like
Glasgow gardens.

COSTA DEL SOL

Exams over, results still to come,
I sit beneath an olive tree

Thinking ... and wondering ... and
Watching the off-blue Med lap
The toes of topless bathers.

And you may think, lucky sod
Or ... that must be the life
Or ... God I'd never go to Spain
In June when the flies are outnumbered
By English tourists!

Of course – you'd be right ...
But at least ... the sun shines
And the beer is cheap ... the chicken
And chips a hundred times superior
To Colonel Sanders.

Yet, is that enough to warrant
A two week exile in a pale shade
Of paradise?

I do not know as I watch
The pequeno fishing boats beached
on the shore, and a tall masted
Racer ... flying the tricolour
Bobbing in the cove.

I sit beneath the olive tree
As the breeze gently blows ... and
ants climb the gnarled trunk
in hunt ... as the lapping waters
to and fro.

The midday sun hovers close
Overhead ... as the jubilant cries
Of bathers awake the sleeping
Slavers ... tattooing themselves
On sun beds.

Two players join me beneath
The olive tree ... strut to and fro
Quoting lengthy lines of Lorca –
'Amigos, que peza de teatro
haceres ahorita?'

I shouldn't have disturbed them -
They are artists ... working
Whilst I am here composing poetry ...
And then I hear, and understand
They are English.

I find that boring. And two
Days later, here I am poorer by several
Thousand pesos ... but healthier
Than yesterday ... something after all
The studying of late.

The playa is the place where

Students should vacate their brains –
A little bit of salt on the mind
Washes things that beer and drugs
Can't erase.

A bit of skiing ... a bit of sailing –
Surfing, dipping, bathing ...
Takes the mind from thoughts that
Otherwise over dwell
On studying.

For the pale and pasty pigment of
Civilisation is stigmatic in all
Urban populations ... hidden by slick
City clothes ... it becomes public
On the open beaches.

While only the mind goes nude at university –
And only exams bring good the teaching.

WEEK 29
Still in Spain and it hasn't rained.

GRANADA

The beaches have gone,
I'm in the Sierras,
There's snow on the tops,
But man! It is hot
In the streets of Granada.

Music is played
In every third calle;
The water flows
From each public fountain
Straight out of the mountains.

In the ancient city
Where the Alhambra towers,
The geraniums flower,
And beer washes down
The calor of the hour.

The Arab quarter hums,
Not with drums
As in Africa they might,
But who is to say
That trumpets are normal.

The traffic tails back
Through the old parts
Of the town in the dark
That is dropping fast
On the swooping bats.

Windows gape open,
People are moaning,

Talking and groaning,
Laughing and crowing –
The vino is flowing.

The bums sit about,
Well down and out,
Smoking their dowts –
Shouting about how
'*Yo tengo hambre*'.

The chalk figure drawings,
Paintings on awnings,
Flower sellers yawning,
Street vendors lolling,
Helados men calling.

Granada at sunset –
No one in bed,
Well, no adults as yet,
The night young ahead.
This city's not dead.

WEEK 30

Days pass quicker than rush hour traffic,
Nights come on with little thought given.

END OF FIRST YEAR
(i)
War is a trauma most survive
But which few return from innocent.
But how would I know, I've not been given
Front-line death as medicine.

The only gore and guts I've eaten
Are tabloid leads and lies;
Glib-lipped words dripping blood
That the boys of Fleet Street sugar.

While in some far off foreign field
A headless corpse hosts black fly;
The Stock Exchange counts the points
Of the profit war and index yield.

In some ditch the maggots crawl
And feed upon rotten flesh –
Mass graves are being dug
And bodies mount like Berlin Walls.

In some English garden sits
A magnate shooting thieving crows;
For death is all the magnate thinks -
Between cigars, the world smokes.

(ii)
The music plays on into the stars,
The rock-a-billy boys are rocking out,

232

Blues are humming the old to sleep;
The slums are awake to the reggae beat.

Down ion the clubs the New Wave sound
Quavers and totters the underground –
As the new romantics flower the street
And die hard punks freak to meet.

There they crow all peacock combed,
These rainbow-stopping Eighties clones –
Armed with monster wave machines
To fill the gaps in teenage dreams.

I'd rather shoot the bull with them
Than cut the crap with black-tied men;
The machine-gun rat-tat can be heard afar -
I'd rather hear the rasp of an electric guitar.

(iii)
Thus a student mind preambles
Through the world that I inhabit;
Far beyond the scholar's scope -
Each day I'm here, quickly goes.

Wars may come, and slowly pass,
Friends quick made, soon grow apart;
What remains is very brief,
Time can be the fleetest thief.

But this aside, life goes on,
Dust collects where timidness hides;
The warm long summer months await
To get into vacation's slide …

Of lazy days and afternoons -
Through July till harvest looms,
And grey October days recall
Us students to the marbled halls –

Where once again the hollow ring
Shall chain us the learned texts;
And we shall dream upon such days
When childhood went, and summer fled.

(End of The Undergraduate – Term 3)

IN THE BARRIO
[30th June 1984, Nerja, Andalusia]

In the barrio, women's chatter
Rattles the red tile rooftops
Which divide the mortal world
From the clear blue sky.

In the Calles, children hide
And seek between the narrow alleys
That cut the whitewash houses

And lead to the azul sea.

In the cafes, men's laughter
Shakes the taverna olive trees
Where shadows split the day
Into the orange baked ground.

In the casas, families gather
To talk in wide doorways
Where friends tease companions
Who come and go, or stay.

EL PUNTE (THE BRIDGE)
[1st July 1984, Nerja, Andalusia]

Somewhere in Andalusia
A sky blue river
Passes beneath an ancient bridge.

By the river's edge
A sombrero'd hombre
Sits under a tall Spanish pine.

He contemplates his future
As the river flows
Underneath the arches of the bridge.

The pine needles fall
And a small chaffinch
Sings to dance his dreams along.

Then the chanson ceases!
The burnt red earth
Trembles as the pine needles drop.

The old bridge shakes
The sombrero'd hombre
Awakes as the earth rumbles.

The town bells ring
As the ancient bridge
Crumbles as the hombre watches.

The central span collapses
The sky blue river
Washes over the ancient arches.

Now, somewhere in Andalusia
A dark red river
Passes over a ruined bridge.

While by the river's edge
A sombrero'd hombre
Sits under a tall Spanish pine.

LA SIESTA EN LO CAMPO
[2nd July 1984, Nerja, Andalusia]

I had four hours to kill before
My bus arrived, to take me off
Up the high Sierra roads
Away from the hot Malaga coast.

The torrid sun of the Nerja noon
Boiled my blood, and all too soon
The beer drunk to quench my thirst
Made my eyes heavy, my spirits droop.

I left the bar, settled down
Beneath a peach tree at the edge of town -
While peasants tilled the fields,
My eyes closed, I slumbered.

I awoke to loud bird singing,
Flies humming and butterflies soaring;
Time had flown, I'd missed my bus
And a cock was crowing.

BLUE SKIES IN MALAGA
[4th July 1984, Malaga, Andalusia]

Under the palm trees of southern Spain,
Lying on a park bench in the cooling shade,
Thinking of nothing but the passing day.
Oh what joy to pass life this way.

Through the frond the sunlight falls,
Catching the scales of the carp in a pool;
The hibiscus in flower, star grass in seed -
Oh what more could a poet seek.

The breeze in the branches of the sycamore trees;
Sparrows in the boughs of the orange and peach;
Doves in the braid of the oak and palm leaves -
Oh truly, what more do I need.

THE NORTHUMBERLAND PICNIC
[29th July 1984, Helmsley Road, Newcastle]

With armfuls of wine and cucumber sandwiches
They swept through the bracken and fern waist high,
The poet with pen, the artist with paper
Led the birthday party to the top of the crags -

Where beneath the thorn trees they threw their blankets
And sprawled or lay on the sheep cropped grass,
With eyes to the sky or vast horizon
The sound of the corks broke the curlew's cry.

Beer bottles popped, and lemonade fizzled,
Indian dish savouries lay with fresh fruit,
The artist sketched the sun-weathered beauty
As the poet searched for his words in the wood.

The gents idly cricketed by the castle folly
Scaled by the ladies in their scant summer clothes,
Thereafter, the company scattered like wildfire
As wander lust spread in from the moors -

Until in all directions the high fern swallowed
Or the thick woods ate the lovers of nature
Off in search of a small nook or hollow
Where happiness begins and time stands still.

As the artist rested and played with the children,
The poet emerged from the faraway trees,
Stalking a fox, sallying over hillsides,
He encountered a lady in search of the lake.

While picnickers played ball or picked the flowers
Or cracked boiled eggs on old weathered stone,
While they leap-frogged the crags or climbed the trees
Or raced through the bracken or prickly thorn -

The poet and lady conquered three field gates,
Two stone walls and the ruins of a fort,
And descended the hill in a rush and a hurry
To come to the banks of the reedy lake pool -

Where they dived from the bough of a willow
And stole a single flower from a lily ring,
Letting it drift as they raced then floated
Back to the shade of the willow hung bank -

Where they soaked up the sun as the insects hummed
And drove them uphill to a weathered outcrop -
Where they dressed and gathered an abundance of flowers
As they returned by the moors to the picnic spot -

Where first goodbyes were just being said
With the shaking of blankets and gathering of things,
The wine long gone and the food all consumed
And the artist all done drawing the kids.

With an armful of memories, carrying the empties
They started down the rocks without looking back,
Till the knee-high fern swallowed the party
And the day of their picnic on the Rothbury Crags.

BECAUSE I LOVE YOU
[A commission, 29th July 1984, Helmsley Rd, Newcastle]

Sometimes I sit and wonder,
And stare out the window,
And think about the past,
And reflect upon our times together
Before we parted.

Sometimes I lie and worry,
And dream about the future,
And cry out in my sleep,

And wring my hands in horror
Because I am lonely.

Other times I laugh and smile,
And plan my whole life,
And arrange to do things,
And do things very well
Because I am lonely.

Other times I am very sad,
And do nothing with my days,
And do nothing with my nights,
And do nothing with myself
Because I miss you.

Other times I look for someone else,
And I find no one suitable,
And I kiss no one special,
And I love no one at all
Because I love you.

THE UNDERGRADUATE - TERM 4
[7th Oct – 21st Dec 1984, mainly Newcastle]

SECOND YEAR - REGISTRATION WEEK

Grey October days and money.
Dry winds and scurvy faces.

(i) THE END OF VACATION

Living on the fringe … is
No way to make a living;
No way, but others' way:
No way of saying things
With a hope of being listened to
Without first listening to
The establishment.

Our fathers who are not in tune;
Our fathers who bend the rules.

We are not consulted,
Yet we are next to guide
Or lead the disestablished:
We are not here nor there,
Yet we are called upon
To take up the running
To follow.

Our fathers who are not honest;
Our fathers who shit upon us.

My time should not be spent,
Nor passed in unwell words,
Nor in waste; yet always
Our eyes are met upon

By looks of propagation,
The flying imagination of
Our elders.

Our fathers who are not giving;
Our fathers who are not loving.

We struggle on in ecstasy
While we strive to pay;
We see, but we have not seen:
We hear of wondrous riches,
We touch the glittering wishes
Of those we once believed –
Our overlords.

Our fathers who give ear to slaving;
Our fathers who are not sharing.

We owe them thanks
For what they've done.
For what they did
They owe us nothing,
They own us, our lives
Our future freedom.
Our tomorrow.

Our fathers who are not saviours;
Our fathers who are dictators.

They leave us on the fringe,
To the left, and cold,
Off-centre and forgotten:
We are afloat, adrift,
And must not rock the boat
Or o'er we go pushed by
Our captains.

Our fathers who are vile fascists;
Our fathers who are our masters.

As October days turn to black,
There's nowhere now to hide one's back.

(ii) **RETURN TO THE HALLS**

As virtuous men pass mildly away,
The marbled walls of university remain.
The newly painted halls, footstep echo now
With a fresh smell hanging on the familiar.

New faces glide past almost unnoticed,
Some old faces noticeably gone forever.
Renewed customs quickly become old habits,
Cast-off habits become the fad of others.

Three cups of coffee slake every hour,
Everyone's so serious over pompous trivia.

For students are such gibbering wrecks,
It takes ten tabs to brave a lecture.

Many are untruthful, a few deceitful,
But most are spaced on flipped out egos.
No one reads books, unless caught pretending
While taking a crap in the toilet.

Others are bored, most are bored,
And a lot go around boring themselves.
Some are rich, and many well-of,
But most are as skint as a rugby man's knees.

The student life – quiet hashish smoking,
Seedy beer parties, and little book work.
Another year started, and one more after,
The academic life is geared for nerds.

(iii) GRANT TIME

Grey October days bring us our grants,
Money is a student's favourite conversation.

First Year's come here for the beer,
Second Year's the two grand a year.

As in the bars, these students ponder
How long will such money last?

(iv) BACK TO THE BOOKS

So once again we tread the trail,
Down the course of this poetry road.
To stop at the wayside, to take respite,
Is now a no-no, we're in our stride.

So bear with me another year,
And hear the tales that will befall me,
And remember, sometimes I overtly lie
To protect myself and shield my friends.

For my foes, I will not blunt the truth,
Nor numb the pain that seers my morals.
So on with the prose down the poetry road;
Let's hope you're along for the ride.

WEEK 31

Illness makes no distinction.
It nobbles everyone.

MEASLES

Laid up in bed with measles,
Windows rattling in the autumn rain.

Banned from classes –

The gold chestnut leaves
Cover the damp grass parkland
Of walking thought;
- my dreams tread paths
that lead to mountain treks
and pilgrimages to India.

I recross deserts haunted
By symphonies of German masters.
I cradle in shady hollows
Where men once dwelt alone
To rediscover laughter.

While you, or are you, we
Must take the day apart
And leave it bare;
Each breathe of conversation,
Brick by brick constructing
The prisons of our own ideas.

I fight alone with myself
And turn the battles back
To replay, and rehearse misdeeds
Undone, but done without recourse
To painful memories.

I stand upon a cliff
Conversing with my only friends –
White gleeful gulls,
Descending, skeeting on the waves
With reckless cries.

Where ploughs the crofter?
I have asked this before, but
No one answers but the wind
That whispers in my cerebral
'You have been chosen'.

I never cry for freedom,
It is none other's gift to give,
Not take in token –
It is stored safely
In my breast.

We have thought to lose that
Which we have not gained
By crook or prostitution;
We are one, and I am
A liquid without solution.

Too soon external forces pull
The wool, and censor manifestos
To the shear, before they're knit
Or woven into masterpieces
Of craft and exhibition.

I am silent, uncommitted,

Unopposed to mass opinion.
I am free in the morning,
But chained by evening –
Unbroken, yet bound.

In terror, dissolute, dismayed,
I smile on misfortune
Brought about by misadventure;
Too many travels teach the traveller
To accept all things.

For fate fades with fortune;
Found in fragmentation,
Ideals formed in theory
Seldom fuel the fires of fashion,
Or flush the face of reason.

Illness makes no distinction –
It eats us all.

WEEK 32

Art is for philistines.
Oh poor miserable beings!

(i) **LOVE HAS FLED**

You hate yourself, love has fled,
Your friends have gone. United o'er the anvil
The hammer now falls. You are no more,
Your words are hollow, harsh, and ineffective.

You are my enemy, slashed and bleeding,
You barely stumble on. Dreams pour out,
Illusions cruelly blind. You are a mirage,
Your gaze is sunken, blank, and mindless.

You are pathetic, lost, and helpless,
Pitied, void of aid. Found in light,
Drowned in misery, you are forgotten,
You are rejected, now, and always.

(ii) **WAR IS FOR TROJANS**

The grey October days turn black again;
The heavens - dark oils stains, splutter,
Bubble, burst. The thunder deafens,
And the debris of the cosmos, rains on earth.

Awash, vain little islands float
Miraculously mid the storm. People drown,
Swept overboard, till only politicians survive
And fight to take command of the oars.

Debates rage into open confrontation,
Quarrels with smaller islands. Boarding parties
Gather all gung-ho, and off the they go

To occupy a sinking piddled nowhere.

Soon enough the water's round their necks,
sees glory sunk. Vain refloating
Ne'er recovers the lost limbless sons
Of thankless mother island.

They are but heads, countless, distant
Warrior cousins, dead. Marked by waves,
Their tales are the gannet's cry,
Their spirits in the call of the whale.

When the deluge waters fall, subside,
And petty islands become large continents
Detached, divided. No woman sees herself,
No man applauds another but himself.

The music of the sea, so instrumental
On island thought, lulls. Isolationists
Revel, in false solitude, on blind reflection
In the mirrors of an untruthful past.

And I, or you ... must we wait,
And wither in the wind, or storm? Unprotected,
We bend to fate, as the deluge waters fail
To drown our hopes, just our aspirations.

War is for Trojans.
Oh poor miserable losers!

WEEK 33

A toast revives the secret drinker
From the slumber of his thirst.

(i) **BARE FOOT INTO DAWN**

Dry lips make no noise
Against the chaffed voice of winter.
Frost layers its crystalled sparkle
In the silence as dead leaves drop
On hoared slate pavements or tarmac
Worn and pot-holed by uneven expectation
Passing rough-shod into night.

Out into breath chilled hours
File the natural order of things.
Heavy laden the pristine cackle
Of the pyramidal monument arises
On slick black highways or routes
Well trod by more frequent visitors
Traveling bare-foot into dawn.

(ii) **POETS IN THE GALLERY**

What of those poets in the gallery?
See they what we strain to see ourselves?

242

Ask not! Silly questions beg indifference.
Ignorance, or dumbness, pleases pertinence.
You may seek to find the moment in my mind,
And fail. But despair not, good readers,
I am not born alone, or merely once!

I have, in confidence, an insight on
My brother poets ... Milton, Marvell,
Unsightly Pope, stoic Wordsworth,
Poor sickly Coleridge. As they weigh,
I wager, you ponder, hesitate to read on,
To view their immortal lines running
Round their verse like mad dogs
Chasing one another.

Until the light shafts through the window,
and the shapeless shadows take their
former selves, and the poetry speaks,
and we see ourselves.

(iii) **MARVELL**

Marvell's *Coy Mistress* rightly speaks of love,
Of nature's tempting nature, and labours lost;
Of sensuous fruits raped, and vivacious thought;
Of youthful innocence unrobed, and ruptured hearts;
Of sunless pleasure's burns, and fettered trap;
Of lust-spent ashes piled, till the world's dust.

(iv) **POPE**

Pope, ailing, frail, yet indulgent of courtly pleasure,
Never saw beauty more, nor prized it finer
Than those out to seduce his lady Belinda.
With wit, and charm, he second guessed, those
Who knew better – no names mentioned –
Those who bore the scandal, the intrigue,
And the infamy by which he grew famous.

(v) **COLERIDGE**

Coleridge drivels on, then saves himself
From drowning in his lime tree bower, where
Trapped he sees the universe unfold, before
The dark hand of childhood lays its hand
Upon his weak sloped shoulder.

Some men are made for great achievement,
Warriors to the full, they march regardless
Of the casualties. While other weaker men
Are of stronger mind, they seldom conquer
More than their own walled castles.

(vi) **WORDSWORTH**

Wordsworth, floating, gone on cloud,
On far out wind, and back again

To heath, and dell, and leafless walk
Midst solitude, and social isolation -
He knew not where he was, or how
He went upon the lay of words, as
They gushed, then flowed, then trickled slow,
To rest upon the bed of immortality.

A *poem may revive the well-worn writer*
From the tiredness of his poverty.

WEEK 34

(i) **CHILDHOOD**

I must confess, I never wander much
Back to my childhood, to that innocence
When mountains seemed inescapably in the heavens,
And rivers seemed to flow on forever. For
Were I to know that the muddy streams
That raged in winter, and stank in summer,
Met a mightier river which met a wild sea,
Which met an endless ocean; my own large
world would have crashed in on me, and
I would have floundered in the knowledge
That only time has now immersed me in.

I still see the dip-boughed willows wash
The floating reed dancing in the current,
The large sighing elms and brooding chestnut
Standing watchful o'er the birch and thorn
Where thrush and blackies wove their song
Of cheerful play, where owl filled the dark
With steadfast wooing, where berries hung
In red array against the white of morning,
Where brown autumnal leaves burst the still,
Punctured young illusions caught in eternal
Summer years of joy, of freedom.
                                        But yet,
There was a sense of foreboding sad decay,
Erosion of all that man achieved, or built
To glorify all nature, as the urban parks
Of beech wood grove and cypress lane, stood
Bare as roofless columns to a temple art
Of salient culture troves and gardens, cured,
Cared, preserved in timeless order for those
Who braved the broad expanse of narrow path
To penetrate nature's bounded border, where
They sought questions, brought their answers.

Yet I little doubt grave thought or mood or
Such vexations taxed my youthful mind, as
Wing flew another year, and ochre frosty hiber-
Nation, slumbered, snored, awake in time for summer.
For life was long, and winter short, and spring
First felt in February, with snowdrops found
Beneath the apple trees, and wild wall crocus
Waxed and white, long before the daffodil split

The earth to turn the shady woods the colour
Of sunshine, health, and happiness; till green
Protruded, and bluebells hung, and purple-laned

A moor land ripeness, soon violet dark and
Lost beneath a cloak of first fall snow,
preparing me for adolescence. For if I can recall
a past, a childhood full of happy memories,
full of open hands presenting me the world,
then I am born in favoured times beneath
auspicious stars, bright and full, and ever
burning till the end of human time, and far
beyond into a space we ne'er perceive, nor
ken exists. A world, a galaxy, a universe.

(ii) **MY OWN GODS**

By now, the ardent scholar, may be flaying
Arms, dismayed at this verse, its simple turn
Away from classic mode, its vivid lack
Of underlying machinery, of Gods, of Demons,
And all that lies between Heaven and Hell.
There is no single Muse, no recurrent address,
No plastic moments filled by Jove's blaspheming;
There are no Cynthias, Belindas, or Sylvias,
No Colin Clouts, Don Juans, nor Saints, nor Heroes
To usurp the glory, of each page of verse.

Yet, there is a growing murmur, a gathering call
For order. Ancestral voices strain to be heard,
While poetry lovers wait to catch a glimpse
Of the fictional deities, I, the idle vehicle
Of their genius, resist to call upon the Gods
in desperation of narrowed thought and emptiness.
But inner pressure bears on me, to force my will
Against the nature of the times, to turn me
Retrogressively through history, to copy, imitate,
And unfold my universal concept in epic ode,
Or well tried octava rima, or quatrain, in even
Meter, or some other well used mode, or style.

But I resist! Though it is fair to say that
I have learned from the fathers of our language,
From the masters of our bardic heritage –
Too few to forget, too many to list – and that
I am resolved to let the Greek Gods slumber,
To let Bacchus drug those of Roman number, until
The end of poetry. For I have my own Gods,
Turning, squabbling in my head, searching for the exit
From my chained imagination, out into the realm
Of consciousness, out into the material of existence;
Gods which are nameless, Gods which I worship.

For had Wordsworth known how many sister
Moons Jupiter supported, or Milton been shown
The Devil in the atom bomb, poetry's machinations
Would now have turned upon the myths of outer

Space. For out there are our future Gods, with
Past God names, and though I will never live
To stand upon these celestial heavens, I can dream
Of wars with Mars, and inter-marriages with Venus,
For out in the furthest seas, Neptune swims, and
Pluto darkly moves through cloud storm and star shower;
Far beyond all vision, beyond all space,
Lies the void of all that's now beyond imagination.

(iii) NO FALL FROM PARADISE

I see no end to man, no fall from paradise,
Nor rise from hell. I see only flesh as atoms
Of a cosmic energy, changing, rearranged, or altered
To fit within the vessel of time, a swirling abyss
Of solid void, ending with motion, slowing
With going, coming, flowing, but never stopping,
Halting, but never standing, never unknowing,
Never absoluteness, incomplete, nor unhealing
Of old sores, cancers, and tuberous growths.
Dead flesh to ashes, dust, wind, rain, and sun,
All former forms vanish, to shape the fresh new forms.

(iv) A PROFOUND DARK TUNNEL

Down some profound dark tunnel I led
kings and fools, the caverns through which
we deeply passed, cut them sharply.

We came to a pool, and on the water
lingered words, while beneath the surface
swam the meanings. An old man hovered
round and round the pool in mute obedience
in the speechless lull that crossed the awkward
void. He began to career along in reckless
canter, making unstressed points, muttering
words from which no vowel movement
could lever action. The silence unsettled
the receptive hearers waiting for the echo
and crescendo, the quietness pressing on
the laden antics of a man's forced marching,
paraded into the cavern skyline until
his thoughts formed unhindered,
faded unvoiced, and he plunged into
the pool.

Up some steep channel to the light
I led the kings and fools, the desert
where I left them, hot and dry.

WEEK 35

(i) OF THE QUEER FOLK

I'd rather be British than just Scottish.
I'd rather be Scottish than just a man from Glasgow.
I'd rather be a Glaswegian than just from Pollokshaws.

246

I'd rather be o' the Queer Folk than be a London boy.

(ii) **SEX IS A WARRIOR**

Sometimes the wolf in me screams out
into the realm of dark and sleepless night.

In the wild Alaskan fireweed,
he was plucking wild pansy
near her forget-me-knotted lair;
while she gathered berries by
his bower of prayer.

Too late, too soon, the sun and moon,
the flaring northern light show looms,
too soon, too soon, lovers mate
In summer caves beyond logged rooms.

On into the light dark shadows
are modeled the lovers of the present.

Other wild memories seize the mind
containing the experience of sixty countries;
tropical storms lashing beach palm,
the dry desert waste of the Bolivian mountains,
the serene landscape of coral reef grotto,
the open expanse of Chaco and pampas,
Rift Valley haze, Pacific coast mist,
volcanic chains breasted in snow,
Nicaraguan cauldrons, afire, aglow.

Wordsworth didn't speak of such places
in his lengthy *Prelude* to life and nature.

Other soft recalls – let off emotions
supporting the touch of sixty women;
tempestuous mauling of body and sheet,
the wet warming place of Venus mount,
the naked extent of jungle and fruit,
the open invite of pasture and field,
sweet valley chaff, soft down still moist,
Vesuvius and Etna in heave and cough,
Stromboli gushing fiery and hot.

Eliot didn't put his finger on *Prufrock*,
or succeed in stifling frustration with talk.

Other forget tracts lead to motive
spanning the interlude of sixty seconds;
making out on a Mexican beach,
the melon mouth lips of a Kenyan kiss,
the tender caress of a Transvaal girl,
the Indian embrace of a giving French lass;
deep rich delights, within, withal,
German or Thai, thawing or melting –
Everest stands solid and daunting.

Hughes or Heaney, Harrison or Hill,
All are well over the race of the mill.

As the tone now alters, the romantic
Returns to haunt hollow ringing
Of time marching by. Goodbye, humble
Friends, invisibly hidden 'neath
Hedgerows and archways spanning
The space of the present, of past, or
Flying on future time beyond now –
Where foes are friends, where friends first
Last, where he-she knows no thirst.

Onwards to glory, obscurity, then dust –
fueled by power, pride, penis and lust.

Sex is a warrior,
Love is a spouse.

(iii) HUMOUR IN POETRY

Humour in poetry? Good poetry has none
of these long sickly lines that forever
run to the edge of the page, and die
in puns, or in crude *breviter dicam*
of the limerick kind, that punctures
the verse, and deflates the stanza,
to flatten the whole, to metre
the features with quips and asides
that most diligent readers can't abide!

Byron hated, thus loved to jibe, till
his satirical verse branded backsides.

(iv) NOVEMBER STARS

Some he-she men eye only cars,
Yet half the makes are in the stars.

Taking me down to the nether glade grove,
to room in hand with star and sky;
I see Orion in autumn hunt, and
Cassiopeia waiting high –
the sacred Twins going to bed,
Taurus tossing Aries to the west –
the Great Bear turning as the Pleiades
trail their tresses across the Milky Way –
Mercury cupped in the three quarter moon
near Canis at bay.

WEEK 36

Melancholy has passed to apathy – so who cares a toss!
Apathy breeds where melancholy swells.

(i) IT RAINS FOREVER

It must be all this rain –
It wets the soul.
It's the wet feet –
Wet socks drip before the fire
forever all winter.
It's the lank wet hair –
chaffing the forehead on the way
to the chip shop and back.
It's the wet pants –
clinging around the ankles,
the legs rubbed spotty.
It's – everything, the dark –
the studying till three chimes
or a bulb burns out.
It's the sun that's missed –
loose slates, leaky roof,
plastic buckets filling.
It's the wet sleep –
drip, drip, the echo thuds
with a continuous ring.
It's all wet blankets –
this wet November,
this damp weather.
It's rain, so what?
In Kauai and Assam
It rains forever.

(ii) SCRUPPLE, OATH and VOWS

Milton numquam deos esse negare
neque Crane qui deum esse negat.
Pro habere superstituo mentes occupavit
posse quod di immortales omen avertant.
Pro esse deos sancte, pie venerari
tentare rebus divinis interesse,
et sperare templa deorum adire,
et non aliquem in deorum numerum referre,
est imbuere pectora religione.
Audientum animos religione perfundere,
religionem ex animus extrahere,
omnem religionem tollere, delere.

(iii) MERCURY MAR AND VENUS DOVE

*Other times, simple ballads must return
to tell of men, and maids, and grief.*

Out of the mist came young Mercury Mar,
Riding across the memories of love,
Carried he forth to the boundaries of love
And into the arms of sweet Venus Dove.

Their passionate love was swift and discrete,
Old Boy Jove ne're knew of their bliss;
Venus with Mar kissed every part,
As the music played ever so sweet.

As quick as his name he whisked her on wing
To a heaven far beyond men;
She loved her fleet foot Mercury Mar,
The lover who could make her sing.

But bad ass Jove wanted back his wife,
The lion inside him growled out.
'Stand still, you bugger, I'll darken your lights!'
But Mar sliced him up with a knife.

The couple then fled to starry lone haunts
Where eagles hovered over their bower,
Their music it faded far into the night,
Till the morning lit empty and gaunt.

No one followed their endless cold flight
Of Mercury Mar and sweet Venus Dove –
But somewhere soon sweet Venus Dove
Lost Mercury Mar in a feckless fight.

And since that time Venus has cried,
Making love to Adonis and others;
For mistress or mastered in connubial love,
Non equalled the music Mercury lyred.

Remember the moral and what was done,
Lest you forget it came from my head,
Love while you can, and recall Venus Dove,
When the music ends, the dance goes on.

(iv) **CROOKED IN OUR CHAIRS**

Pitter, patter, matter, matted, molted, bolted shut, and dead.

Evening falls again, dross winter!
It's hard to catch the drift of sunlight
in this downcast season. The cold
obeys itself, we are its prey, the living
against which it stunts its growth, and ours.

Yet, I may take such bare thought comfort
From the numbness of growing idleness
That inward-out progresses slothly indolent.
Winter catches all of us out of breath,
And leaves us slumped and crooked in our chairs.

WEEK 37

*The weeks they pass like games of chance -
We never get to deal the cards.*

(i) **THREE SONNETS**

Sometimes I feel the academic life
Weighing like a ton of bricks upon my shoulders.
It is not the books, the essay sets,
But rather something more akin to loneliness.

My peers, each in a world revolves,
Till moods become obsessions to detest;
Yet, each dark moment wrought, oft'
Brings about a spark of genius to remember.
I know no way to battle with such ill,
But isolation in my books and lecture notes,
I sense that the days slip by, and
Friends once firm become like seas in tempest,
Till, where one time I beheld an island,
Slips past the wreck of some mere acquaintance.

For while others inward gaze, I outward grin,
And find small comfort humour set before me,
While others outward view the world about,
I dream or meditate or shut things out.
For what's the point in being as my brother
When the sister in me doesn't want to play,
Or as the father of my dreams and aspirations,
The mother quells ambition when the child strays.
For like the eagle hovering over barren wild,
Or mute white swan gliding down a stream,
We cry when no one's there to listen,
Or we never find a voice with which to speak;
For I weep when all the world is laughing,
And I laugh when all about me weep.

Other times I laze and idly waste
Precious moments not to be recovered or relived.
The sun comes up, and all too soon has gone
To light some other part of Earth; while I
In northern bitter cold, bear icy gales.
With my skin in shreds, my stature wan and wry,
The bronze of summer beach is a pale regress,
The tone of mountain lake, a sag of flesh.
Once clear eyes now are blue with chill,
Sallow brow now racked and creased by fever,
Hair once a fountain head of golden tresses
To grey now turns in cull to northern winter,
While hunch backed around me travel strangers,
As somewhere else goddesses join with princes.

(ii) **A BRIEF ENCOUNTER**
for Penny

Never more ready than ever,
Never more willing than now.

Mischief ... oh, oh, oh,
My penny drops and stolen
Moments in the attic of night
Lead to coitus.

Sweet, perfumed and giving
Sighs heaved into the rafters
Where time settled quietly
On love-making.

Company and comfort,
Our whispers broke the cobwebs,
We laughed beneath the quilt,
Kissing softly.

WEEK 38

Actors are vain, poets are vague.

(i) **WE FALTER**

Again, why must we falter.
The voices in the basement carry
up through feet to settle down
to murmurs. They are of little
consequence upon the creaking timbre
that groans from age old winds
sweeping in like frantic genies,
conjuring magic, invoke, and incantation
for their supper.

Yes, again, we falter.
The voices in the basement now
heavy footsteps trampling stairs
towards the light. They are largely
discordant upon the quarry silence
that grates like desert beings
crossing naked waste and denudation
to reach oasis.

Until, they arrive upon our falter.
The voices in the basement, demons
with hoods and pitch black
about withal. They are greatly
fearsome upon the earthly tremble
that quivers like jungle wild life,
stalked, trapped, and beset
upon with clubs.

They have fed upon our falter –
We live now in the basement.

(ii) **I PREFER MY DANCER**

*Talking heads said haven is a place
Where nothing ever happens.*

I prefer my dancer to my singer,
'cause I know all my singer's songs –
and though my singer's very pretty,
I love my dancer's moves, turns and all;
and though my singer's breasts are perfect,
'tis my dancer's legs that lead me on;
though I adore the lips of my songbird,
I prefer the kiss of my graceful swan.

(iii) **BEYOND MY OWN SMALL PRISON**

Beyond my own small prison, a world evolves.

In Brazil, the Selva disappears;
In the Sudan, the Sahel succeeds
Where isolated forest once gave oasis;
Or by the Brahmaputra, a country drowns;
Or by the Hudson, debris towers
Where habitation outstrips generation.

Such trite observation may be trivial,
But accusations fly about the subjective
Modernists preach as gospel.
There are no prophets in the world,
Only he-she-men with world visions
Of their own petard.

We name them not, yet we know
Their names, their thoughts, their views
On stars and turds.
We joke, we parody, and we steal
Their visions for our own locked worlds
Of fantasy and deception.

They make us weak, make us happy,
Make us cry in sheer frustration
At their rules of dogma.
Yet, do or should we care
When time makes no thing new
Between the moon and sun.

Dawn, be it now or tomorrow,
Night, be it tonight or morrow,
These are constant.
But alas our prophets fade,
Their light a tallow candle
Dripping into fate.

Till even Plato and Aristotle
Have their sagest food devoured
Off time's plate.
For it is the means of nature
To have a sapling flourish forth,
Then age and wither.

Visions are but bricks baked
To form the structure of thoughts
That perishes with nature.
There are no repairs to be made,
Rejuvenation, imitation, repetition,
Establishes good resemblance.

We, each are prophets, but
Who shall say that we
Shall be remembered.
Beyond our own small prisons,
A world evolves, metered,

Tempered by false prophets.

WEEK 39

It is easy to forget loved-ones,
When art is greater than mankind.

(i) **MY ONLY LOVER**
for Laura

Being a student, I have neglected
Everything but books. I love Chaucer,
Shakespeare, Milton. I have forgotten
The girl who cooks, who shares my bed,
Who cries rejection. What lonely life
I have given her – long, dark nights
Of silent company, my mind in Wordsworth,
My eyes on Coleridge, my humour Pope,
My anger Eliot. I have no emotion
But my literature – long lines of words
And poignant statement, my marriage dying,
Sacrificed for poetry. If this is fate,
Then I'm deceived. If this is truth,
Then I'm misguided. Give me love, or
I shall be bitter. Give me emotion, or
I'll become unstable. Books give no solutions,
They pinpoint failings. Men of action
Win women's love. Men of isolation
Lose love to others. My studies must subside,
I have drowned existence. My illness must abate,
I have fevered cold. My passion must return
Or leave me barren. Love must reconquer
Lust's contempt abuse. Feelings must replace
Uncaring thought. Softness must recline
Harsh unkind statement. Changes must be endless,
If I'm to rescue, and salvage marriage
From the rocks of study. My love is boundless
Within pride's vessel. Down! Smash the vial
That has poisoned me. I smell the scent
Of fragrant frangipani. I remember courtship,
I remember love, I remember Laura –
My wife, my friend, my only lover.

(ii) **LAURA**

Oh Laura, I am wan to let you go.
Nymph of nature, love untold;
I cry into the wind, but never hear
An echo turn my voice to song.
Wilt is my soul, my own Persephone,
Lost to me forever – banished
To far regions, where I cannot travel,
Attended by the servants of despair.

It is I who drove you hence –
My fool-fold pride – my bow;
My sharp waste words – my arrows,

Transfixing every motion of your love.
'Tis I who iced the marriage bed
with indifference and cold sleep.
'Tis I who froze your passion
with numb vague dismissal.

I am a fop, a recreant lover
To whom romance is one with lust.
I've been blind to *fin amour*,
I've been beyond the word *forever*.
I've been harsh like frost-cracked winter,
I've been uncaring beyond remember.
I've been worse than any tempest,
Or storm that beats all to submission.

I've been cruel and thoughtless,
A thousand nights in two thousand days.
I've been moody and unsmiling,
And disapproving in a million ways.
I've been stupid to the point of hurt,
I've been selfish till the tears have flowed.
I've left you crying alone, unknowing,
While my joy has fountained on the world.

I'm ignorant, uncouth and detestable,
It's been your right to take revenge.
You've slipped from the shade of shadow,
And cast your beauty on my deformed mind.
And like Persephone, pulled into the underworld,
Whose matchless beauty was unmatched by lust,
I pine for the loss of summer -
And I repent all I did, and all I've done.

WEEK 40

Drunk! I say, what? Never!
Is this what makes students clever?

(i) PARTY TIME

Party time – whoopee! End of term,
Wine the fountain of youth.
Who cares about the weather,
'cept the conscientious and the pooped.
Clatter, Riesling, new Bordeaux –
If there is more … Pour! Pour! Pour!

(ii) TYNESIDE WRITERS WORKSHOP

Last night I met with writers –
Armstrong, Beadle, Astley, Cleary!
A lowly pub high-placed in town
Where sickly poets drown on pints.
They chatted on with Northern airs
(half of them were from elsewhere)
Their weakly words weighed with beer,
They huffed and puffed poetic smear.

255

Till brooding Armstrong, at the ear
Of gout-toed Beadle set to sneer,
Said ' We're the only poets here.
We've no peers. Up yours! Cheers.'
Beadle crooked his neck and nodded,
His rimless glasses glazed and misted,
And supping on a pint of Guinness,
He spluttered out his views on nothing.
(One might think upon his genius,
but one may dismiss such feelings,
for poets who declare their brilliance,
can not be viewed as being enlightened.)
Thus fat Beadle full of gibberish,
Blurted on, and puffed, and railed,
While Armstrong off in other regions,
Leaned across his girlfriend's breast
And said aloud 'This country's full
of Tory types, fascists, racists, sexist creeps!
See them poets across the room -
They condone this country's ruin.'
'Up the Miners!' someone shouted,
and up shot clenched fist salutes;
startled, Astley's mob looked up,
till up and up their noses flew.
They sniffed the air for impoliteness,
Riff-raff, and all their noise,
To sniff for scent of Commie sweat
from the COAL NOT DOLE pickets.
Too soon they lost this certain whiff,
Too soon they found their noses pinched,
And huddling together like little boys,
They wittered on with quite a din.
Till Cleary mentioned C.N.D,
And Astley shouted out 'Belfast, Ireland!'
For such trite slogans buy their pens -
Arts Council money pays their rent.
These grants, that Astley, Cleary seek,
Weakens further, their meager verse –
What the hell, I don't care …
I was very briefly there.
I left slim Armstrong spouting on,
With Beadle drooling on his arm,
Astley nibbling poetry crumbs,
Cleary sniffing up his bum.
The sort of act that breeds disgust,
Yet minor poets thrive on such –
For I have heard and seen enough
To know these poets and their works.
So take you heed, if you're wary,
Ne'er read Armstrong, Beadle, Astley, Cleary.
They're but a bunch of bitching poets,
The truth is out, now you know it.

(iii) **ETHIOPIA**

People are dying in Ethiopia
In drought season Tigre land.

256

It is important if we are Christian,
Muslim, Buddhist, Taoist, Maoist,
Marxist, Leninist, Hindu, Janist,
Atheist or Nihilist.

For even if you believe in nothing,
Our country is wealthy.
We can pray for someone
And there's nothing wrong with that -
Though its money that's needed.
The will to give must come first,

And once relief is given –
Will the exploitation follow?
Let us pray our kindness
Goes beyond our wealth.

(iv) **END OF TERM FOUR**

It is the end of term –
I am worn out.
Nine hundred lines of verse
Takes fair clout.
A student's life is dull and grey,
I am assured.
A hundred books a term?
A lie for sure.

Meanwhile, I read mad John Clare,
I am impressed.
I search through Percy Shelley –
What a quest!
Maybe I'll get on to Swift
Before Christmas.
Maybe I'll just give up
And take a rest.

(End of The Undergraduate – Term 4)

THE DAY YOU LIED (song)
[12.26pm, 17th January 1985, Newcastle]

You know you love me
So why do you lie?
For you now you love me,
And you cried aloud.

So why did you lie?
That was the day I died.

Well, now I'm crying too,
You shouldn't have been so hard.
You were once soft like butter
Until the day you lied.

So why did you lie,
That was the day I died.

TIME AND MONEY (song)
[12.30pm, 17th January 1985, Sandyford, Newcastle]

Nothing changes … time nor money.
We all need something, and it isn't love.
Nothing changes, … place or people
We all want something, and it isn't peace.
Nothing changes … war or science,
We all have something, it isn't good times.
Nothing changes … memory or mind,
We've got something, but it isn't worth a dime.
Nothing changes time or money.
We all need something, and it isn't love.

TOO FAR GONE (song)
[12.35pm, 17th January 1985, Sandyford, Newcastle]

Somewhere someone asks for dance,
And somewhere someone takes someone home.
But we're too far gone, too far gone.

Somewhere someone takes someone out,
And somewhere someone kisses someone all night.
But we're too far gone, too far gone.

Somewhere someone makes someone smile,
And somewhere someone loves someone right.
But we're too far gone, too far gone.

THE UNDERGRADUATE - TERM 5 -
[13th Jan - 30th Mar 1985]

PROLOGUE

THE LADY ON THE STAIRWAY
(The Barefooted Lover)

Her foot scraped the riser
As she trod her way upstairs,
She wound round the newel
And strung the baluster rail.

She quarter-turned the landing
Towards the dog-leg steps
That led to the chamber
Where her next lover slept.

Her dress brushed the stringer
And her hand the open wall
Which took her from the well
and towards the chancelled hall.

She paused by the postern
She lingered by the thresh,
Her hair about her shoulders
And her hand upon her breast.

She bit her lip and tip-toed
With a rustle of her dress,
She crossed the tiled chamber
And reached her quarry's bed.

She shod her simple jewelry,
She shod her tinsel dress,
And met her stirring lover,
The chalice of her quest.

And when she had him sleeping,
She quietly slipped away
On tip-toe very softly
Down the dog-leg stairs.

Her hand wound round the newel
She grazed the final step,
She turned the big brass lock,
Closed the door and left.

WEEK 41

THE STORM EAST WIND

O storm east wind from farthest Russia!
You, from distant Arctic, bring sleet snows
And blizzards to the shores of Africa.

Grey, and black, but quietly so,
Death you bring, and white, and cold,
The seas you whip, lash, and blow.

Great ice tracts form up, and fold,
And in a rage you carry home
The fiercest bite your anger holds.

You cut, and slice, into our bone,
And take our warmth without care,
You leave us wrack, torn, and lone.

And on an eve when light is shadow,
You whisper in the trees and travel
On to where no man might follow.

And in the summer months we revel
In the warm fan of your journey
Waft and ripe through lands untraveled.

Or on the beach in naked lay,
We feel you on our skin, our foreheads
Set to sea, our thoughts astray.

We glint to see where gulls are led
And left upon the crag cliff-tops,
Your mighty gusts rock-wave wed.

Round the citadels of Time, you hone
And shape, and leave your biting mark,
Until forums crumbling, raised, are gone

And men retreating from your stark
Wild killing blade of conquest dreams,
Are poppies in a bower of park.

For you, cruel Shivite, master mean
Of all you sweep off to the West,
You triumph, ravish, switch, and glean.

You are the force to judge, to test,
to strip, and whip, all you see,
You're rarely welcomed as a guest.

O violent muse! we seek to flee
From your freezing storm behest.

Green spring we never seek from you,
It's ice and snow you bring to us,
Our skies pale blue, cold with dew.

We often greet you with a curse,
And vanish quickly to our tasks,
Thinking of no wind as worse.

But, you are gilded with a mask
You quietly smile, then vilely seize
The smallest life in your grasp.

And when you've blackened all the leaves,
You moan in greed for further offerings,
Your wanting's like the cry of thieves.

O waste wild wind! crave no following!
We'd rather see you go than howling.

Some morns you wake with bated breath,
The sun aglow, and luke, and yellow,
Its rays a boon shed on our health.

While ages pass, and cities go,
Still you come, and on, an on,
You sigh, you blow, warm, and cold.

And time turns round towards new dawns,
You retreat, as the west wind speaks
And winter sleeps, as spring-time yawns.

And back across the sea you creak
And groan, to where it always snows,
East, to a place of mountain peaks.

Where you come from no-one knows,
We're never sad to see you go.

WEEK 42

We students have got to stick together,
Especially when we're screwing one another.

(i) **AN ENGLISH LANGUAGE GIRL**

Give me an' English language girl,
All Rrr-Pee an' fine tones.
Give me an English literature girl
To ponder over poetry and prose.

Stella met me at the discotheque,
She was strong, tall, and blonde.
She whirled me round the dance-floor
And tore off all my clothes.

She made me jive bare-footed
And bump, and grind no hold.
She jigged me over broken glass,
Bought beer 'til I was blown.

She took me home in a taxi,
She lay me on the floor,
She rolled me two fat wackies,
And made me toke two more.

She roamed about my body,
Her hands like hot steam irons.
She kissed me with a passion
I thought I wouldn't survive.

I tried to drink my coffee,
But she had me in her arms,
Her lust was like French mustard
On a pie straight out the fire!

She was all Rrr-Pee and whispers,
Not weak, nor shy, nor coy.
Stella, the student of English,
Have you ever met her, boys?.

(ii) **BYRON**

Byron knew Italian,
Though he learned his best verse
From obscure British poets
Like Trere and the rest.

His Beppo was successful,
He then turned to sketch himself,
Don Juan welled and flooded
To wash poetry's shelves.

But his headlong passions rushed
To form no moral sense,
For Byron was a cad,

Who loved to fuck and wench

(iii) **TELL ME AGAIN, JONATHAN**

Hoyle,
    hibbily,
        dribbilly,
            plop!
stinky-drip flow,
jobby-pooh slop.

Hissy,
    wissy,
        piddilly,
            whoosh!
willy-whack gush,
gargle-gaa tooosh!

Slurp,
    slithilly,
        wibbilly,
            booh!
johnny-joe grunt,
gilly-gack wooh!

Ga-gaa,
    goo-goo,
        droolly-da,
            waart!
harry-haw coo,
pissy-pa gart.

Hobbilly,
    habbilly,
        wickilly,
            wong!
billy-bah dooh,
davey-la bong!

(iv) **FOR THATCHER'S CHILDREN**

This is no age to be romantic,
Into ideal, freedom, love;
The high emotion born from ego
In the Sixties, now is done:

Self-awareness, once a virtue,
Now we find is bent to vice,
Our vision once towards the East,
Now is like a martyr burnt.

All we have is ash and char,
Remains of faith and cosmic one,
We see no phoenix rise on wing,
Star war cloud blots the sun.

We mow the eco-system down,

planted barely ten-years back,
Air, once free of nuclear dust,
Gathers grey, blacks our lungs.

Rivers clear, stocked with fish,
Near fresh to drink years ago,
Foam and froth and radiate,
As red to sea slaked they run.

Oh sad child of our time,
Hear tell of what your grand-sires did,
There was an age of honest care,
When your fathers were but young;

There was a land of dream, ideal,
With greater men, and ample work;
Idleness was a happy choice,
You chose to do for fun.

O sad children, life is cruel,
Once our land an empire was -
Though with an empire gladly gone,
The wealth remained while we clung

Tightly to our treasure troves,
Of art, of business sense, and wit;
'Till Thatcher's bulldogs gobbled up
The riches two whole centuries worked.

Perhaps we have no right to weep
For what our heroes wrongly stole,
Someday our foes shall take, return
These treasures back across wild seas -

Across far blues and universe,
This is our final Diamond Age.
Can you hear the beating drum?
Our time of glory now is done.

WEEK 43

Go to bed, me darling,
Tomorrow's come, it's late.
I never thought we'd see it through,
Me darling, go, it's late.

(I) THE STUDENT'S COMFORTER

Love is the student's redeemer
From the death of study.
It is common complaint that
English poetry dwells on death,
And after death. Yet sometimes love
Creeps in between the sheets,
But not that regularly,
Not that seriously.

A student's life is too ethereal,
Full of bookish ideal
When it comes to common sense
Or matters of the flesh,
They flounder, or thrash themselves
With Gothic novels.
Beat themselves with Reader's Digests;
Exchange and Marts;
And pop like Frankie.

For music heightens the emotions ...
The silence of the lecture halls,
The muteness of tutorial conversation,
The droll of seminars ... these drive
Students to the bars
To seek their comfort;
To look for friendship;
To rush sex first into things
To exchange names later.

If this seems how it is -
Perhaps this is what it's like.

(ii) **SEPARATED**

When you've loved someone
Like you've never loved anyone,
It's hard to say goodbye.

When you see them again,
And can't find conversation,
You remember the good times.

When you part again,
The love wells up,
The heartbreak hurts some more.

When you think of them,
The wrongs are recalled,
But you love them still.

As winter turns to Spring,
Such love remains
Forever in the wind.

(iii) **THE ONE LEFT BEHIND**

We love not what we see,
We love what we do not have;
When we walk out on someone
We lose all that is material.
It is the one left behind
Who must mend the ego.

(iv) **LIVERPOOL**

This week I went to Liverpool.

I've been to Santiago,
I've been Cairo, Dar, Joburg;
Hong Kong, Bangkok, Delhi, Dacca;
Madras, Kabul, Tehran, Ankara;
Athens, Rome, Paris, Tunis;
Port O Spain, Rio, Lima, Quito;
Panama, Managua, City Mexico;
LA, San Fran, Orleans, New York.

All those place far away -
I travel with more purpose now,
I'm not the crazy hobo that I was.
Besides, 'Pool's not that bad,
I just never thought to visit it
Though it's well marked on the map.

(e) **ODE TO KEATS**

Elysian fields in minds secrete
A lasting memory of John Keats.

O Grecian urns and nightingales!
Sweet song and ode I hear.
O heart of heart within me fails,
Soft sleep and dream it nears
To wash and swim the dead of night,
I travel on in mist;
Descending verdant slopes of leave
I stumble on in bliss;
My being off in humble flight,
What pleasures have I missed?

WEEK 44

Like storms the best stories have lulls.

(i) **THE LULL**

I am not your average student,
I am at most, ten years senior
To my peers, my fellow scholars
Who are in the main quiet free
And easy going despite the studies,
Which, when said and done, are all
They have to fill their leisure.

And I? I have just barely tiny crow's feet
Walking towards my hazel eyes -
That most times contains the devil
So I'm told - while smile lines
Leave me handsome in a happy way;
(And what better wisdom need we gain
By this, unless we know that it takes
Seven facial muscles to smile, and
Twenty three to frown with disapproval).

Therefore, as we must, I've had providence,

265

Carefree love, and felicitous emotion
In my childhood and teenage years -
Joyous years of wit and honesty
Continued in my traveling years
That crossed the breadth of one full decade;
Years of faith, defence and truth
In which I triumphed over vice
Despite the human follies I encountered
And embraced in want, in cold survival.

But now I also see the present -
The two iced years since I first
Returned from half-baked Delhi
With a wife and son, all our worldly
Goods weighing less than twenty kilos;
Since then, I've lost the root of truth
And sold my ideals in pursuit of fame
And money. And for what? ....
A student's life of part-time work,
A wife estranged, a son sixteen who's
Still too young to make it in the world,
As nightly he sleeps on a sofa in a flat
In shipyard Walker by the slips of Tyne.

Meanwhile, I who has not moved
From the comfort of our home - I have
A girlfriend who makes me feel desired;
Yet how can it be love when there is
Something that is dying still alive?
It commands years to love new lovers,
And a lifetime to unlove the old -
Yet life goes on, the sun comes up
And every day is a new beginning
That never seems to double back
Upon the past turns of fate that ill-sent
The unkind experience of disillusion.

Now of late, I newly see how
I have traveled blind along the road
These last two years. I have gone
For fame, and in the process lost
The me that was the basis of my
Strength and personality, so that now
I am an empty vessel shipping light
On a wave crest driving me
Like driftwood caught in undertow
To barren shore.

Perhaps in this, I am average,
Though in other ways, like other
Individuals, I am my own persona -
But by mulling on well off the point,
Not quite explaining why I'm different
From my fellow English undergraduates,
It seems I am making mountains out
Of inner risings I cannot view myself.

If this has been a moment of interlude
Between storms. It has filled the lull.

WEEK 45

(i) **TYRANT TYRANT**

Tyrant! Tyrant! Burning vision!
Devastating, ruining Britain!
Will immortal fame or glory
Seek you out before Time's jury?

In whose future age or eon
Will you justify your reason?
In whose memory will you rule?
By whose will formed you cruel!

And will justice, and will law
Make us will what Gorgons saw?
And will our voices cry enough!
To army boots and policemen's clubs?

Will the hammer? Will the chains?
Will the people bear your pain!
Will the cross? Will our blood?
Will our veins gush and flood!

Will your words clothe our poor?
Feed the starving, sick and more?
Will your smile heal our ails?
Will your harsh laws ever pale!

Tyrant! Tyrant! Burning vision!
We are slaves in your Britain!
Will immortal fame or glory
Seek you out before Time's jury?

(ii) **GALILEE LOVERS**

I had a friend in love in Israel
With a girl from New Zealand,
Who he'd met in the orange fields
Out in the dry slopes of Galilee.

They worked on their love with a passion
Hotter than the earth they tilled
They promised each other a nation
Of children to sail the seas.

They laboured and turned the dust
That built a country of strangers,
Lying in the burnt grass by starlight
They mumbled a heaven of words.

They stood on the banks of Jordan
Pledging an undying immortal faith
And on the Mount of Olives

267

They swore to never break.

But fate had other roads to take,
They were separated for two days;
My friend sent down to Galilee
Returned to faces weighed.

For everything that lovers know
It is not enough to guess -
She could not wear the world
And had craved for death.

They showed him her wan body -
He shed a lake of grief,
He kissed his suicide lover
And swore he'd always weep.

But time has eased his misery,
My friend now often laughs,
Yet still I see in his tragic eyes
His time with that Galilee lass.

(iii) **NEWCASTLE ENCLAVE**

Meanwhile in Newcastle,
On the northern fringe of England,
Far away from all the fascism,
We have a youth culture
Fired and burning.

You can have your Liverpool's,
Bristol's, Birmingham's and Leeds
And cold calculating London,
There's nothing there but heartbreak
For the young and hungry.

Rebels - you'll find them in Newcastle
On the frontier with Scotland -
For if you like to sing, dance,
Paint, film, write or crow,
There's plenty here who'll listen.

(iv) **THE BITE OF THE WRITER**

A writer lives in a world of his own,
He's always probing into worlds he doesn't know.
You'll find him nobbing where no other artist goes -
Whores, housewives, debs, his inky fingers roam;
Crooks, nice-guys, bores, his icy humour gnaws.
A friend when he sucks, a killer when he blows,
A writer loves to love, but don't eff him over,
Or you'll see yourself lampooned in print, and more
he'll have every privacy, publicly known.
And then God save your reputation of old,
For a writer never lives in a world of his own,
He seeks out the truth, then moves on alone.

(v) **EAGLES AND HAWKS**

In this country of democracy,
Who carries the branch of peace?

In the hills, in the mists,
There hides the eagle's prey
Cowering in the windswept nooks
Pretending to be free;
Is there beast strong enough
To keep a hawk at bay?

In former times dragons slept
In caves high in the mists,
But we had knights to battle on
For honour and the girl;
For there were once men enough
To combat wolves and bears.

Now the mist is ever down
And thick about the vales,
The doors are locked as nightly knocks
The eagle shaking chains;
Is there one to free us all,
To do what no one dares?

WEEK 46

(i) **LINDA**

And then there was Linda
I met at the swap shop,
Blue tank-top and bob-socks
And hair like a wild mare;
She led me to pasture
In a one night affair.

She talked of her loved ones,
Her brothers, ex-husband,
Her daughter, and mum,
All her friends in the world;
She was open, yet shy,
She was sweet, but not dry.

She was a fine English lass
Who'd tasted green grass,
Who ran on wild winds
To fly from life's grasp;
She was cheerful and free
And asked nothing of me.

(ii) **THE MARTYRS**

Robbed of good health, wrecked by sharp rods,
prodded with needles, tortured and roped,
cudgelled and clubbed, battered and doped,
naked and shamed, fingered and raped,

269

degraded and shaved, twisted and shaped,
conformed to reply, moulded to lie,
ordered to speak, slugged to be quiet,
forced to eat shit, pressed to drink piss,
coerced to suck pricks, made to ass lick,
then kneed in the gut, kicked in the teeth,
bent to say sir, beat on the feet,
gouged in the eyes, stabbed in the ears,
poked in the nostrils, choked and turn keyed,
shocked to confession, starved to comply,
denied any sleep, broken to cry,
marched to an end, hung to the sky,
put in a grave, buried with flies.

The revolution end, the rebels smashed,
the martyrs dead, the people lashed.

(iii) **THE WRITERS WORKSHOP**

Got a letter from the Workshop, them writing people
who spend all their time in talk and criticism of your work ...
The secretary wrote and said that he couldn't get the pub,
the next meeting would be held in the cinema coffee-shop.

He said "if you miss us, you'll find us down the Lane",
which of course is a bar not noted for its talk.
Then again the beer's good. It has to be
to take the sentimental love verse and the soap
and soppy pop culture of the Workshop
which drains Labour's veins -

with plays about shipyards and rusting empty docks;
poems about the miners and dustmen and bakers,
haunted ex-signalmen, seamstresses punching clocks;
teachers feeling guilty about being quite well-off,
students rambling on about some forgotten cause,
housewives driveling dry about missing out on love,
husbands droning wet about the girls they've cocked;
doleys whinging' ceaseless about not having jobs,
the bourgeois gurgling over about being in hock,
gays flowering out about being in the cold,
sexists mouthing-off about feminists and jocks,
women calling for action and their own Workshops,
men demanding order and more pints of hop,
the chairman caught unready searching for smooth words,
the secretary amused, pissing in his socks.

O what a wordy shambles during these pub Workshops,
imagine the next meeting in the cinema coffee-shop?

(iv) **STELLA'S BROTHERS PLACE**

Jerry and Carrie were happily married,
Three girls, a boy, a house on the bay -
He was a medic into obstetrics,
She was thinking about a fifth baby.

Amid the mess the kiddies had wrecked,
Stella and I drank their January wine;
We recklessly throttled six litre-bottles
And awoke hung over to the noonday sun.

(V) **IN MY BONES**

In my bones is posterity
In my blood is fame
In my flesh is glory
And the memory of a name.

In my heart is success
In my mind the same
In my soul is money
And the script writing game.

In my eyes is poetry
In my ears acclaim
In my dreams is love
And the girl I shamed.

In my hands are novels
In my fingers blame
In my arms is gone
The girl I tamed.

In my life is nothing
In my home is pain
In my brain is longing
For the girl I maimed.

In my loss is posterity
In my loss is fame
In my loss is glory
And the echo of her name.

WEEK 47

(i) **I KNOW THAT GIRL TOO WELL**

I know that girl too well ...

I'm trying to cling,
She's trying to break away,
She loves me just the same.
I talk about Rome,
She looks at me and smiles
She'd love to go I know.

I try to make her laugh,
She attempts to swerve my trap,
She's already caught in fact.

I walk her home in talk,
She's got work to do inside,
She's got me on her mind.

271

I say goodbye and kiss,
She says she'll see me soon,
She doesn't seem too sure.

I know that girl too well ...

(ii) EVERYTHING AUDIBLE

Sometimes I hear and pick-up everything:
Budgie singing at the top of his pecker;
Cars rubbering-by along our shabby street;
Neighbours swearing at each other loudly;
Postman stuffing letters through our slot;
Front doors slamming in a fit of temper;
Gas fire hissing throughout mid-winter;
Sink water draining down the plug-hole;
Electric cooker harmonising with the kettle;
Video snowing heavy on a blank channel;
Telephone off the hook and purring;
Students in the flat below playing reggae;
And all those other sounds that make renting
An upstairs flat on Tyneside far from silent.

(iii) PUNTERS PASS

I wrote a letter to Tyne Tees Television
About being just another pleb -
Queuing up outside Studio Five
To get into The Tube every Friday.

I put in some flippant poems with it,
It didn't cost a penny more to send.
I don't expect to get a Punter's Pass,
I'm grey about the temples and no Punk.

At least I don't have a beer belly
Like Jools who seems to be going bald;
I guess it must be too much coco -
It must be hard doing lock-ins every night.

The grey grimy North has its laughs,
I'm going to pray for my Punter's Pass.
Hell, come on Tyne Tees telly -
Let me have my chance just for once.

(iv) A' IS THINKIN

A' is thinkin itsa wast o tim
Neimn' a studnt writin' powtry
Fur th' sak o nuthin butt wurds
And jib's ut fulkin no-buddies.

(v) CLITSHITCUNTPISS

CLITSHITCUNTPISS was a town
I left behind years ago,

272

It was somewhere right of here
Up a clodclutclingbutt road.

I guess I won't be going back
To those asskissbrownnose folk -
Everything they steered me off
I've freakballprickdip toked.

WEEK 48

(i) **FRIDAY LECTURE**

After sitting through the Songs of Innocence,
I wit and willed an hour of Langland,
But in place of timeless lecture notes,
I felt the full impact of my hangover.

O laudee! Lectures are so boring;
Students asleep plugged into their walkmans.
O doolah! There's nothing worse than snoring
Or a fourteenth century lecturer's droning.

(ii) **SELF DESTRUCTION**

Up, over the top
He threw himself
'Till under the Sun
He baked to death.

(iii) **THE DREAMER**

The dreamer sat swimming
in an open window sea.
The wasters drifted by
on rafts of beech wood trees.

The captain waved a scarf
as he set his parrot free
which flew to the dreamer's
shutters creaking in the breeze.

He put out his hand
with a palm of budgie seed,
have you ever seen a parrot
eat that type of feed?

You can always tell a dreamer,
he's full of words not deeds,
the parrot bit his hand off
and dropped it in the sea.

The dreamer took a shotgun,
one handed drew a bead,
he closed his eyes and fired
at the parrot on the beach.

Yet when the smoke dispersed,

with sea-weed in its beak
the parrot rose and flew off
with a wild triumphant screech.

And the dreamer sat gazing
at the open window sea
for the next bunch of wasters
to come by on beech wood trees.

WEEK 49

(I) ON A TUESDAY IN DUBLIN

Wandering the streets of Dublin
On a springtime afternoon
The Book of Kells behind me.

I stepped into the National Museum.
There I found green walls
Hung with Tintoretto and Titian.

Yet half the paintings were missing,
Sent to London for an Irish exhibition;
What they'd left were twenty Magi,
Countless saints, and a dozen crucifixions.

I found nine other rooms,
One with Barrett, one with Roberts,
Hickey, Crawley, Chinnery, Barry,
Scenes of love, lust, want, desire.

A mandarin stoic and grey in age,
An Indian girl in silk unveiled.
An actor watched by two fair sisters
Caught in a comic-tragic musing.

I sat and watched their wily game
Before dwelling on Eve tempting Adam
With a rotten apple,
The poor bloke Rodan-like despairing.

Alas, we know the outcome of that tale,
I move on thinking, seeking more;
I glided on to other rooms
Mulcahy, Mulready, and Mulvany.

Then I came across the sixth apocalypse,
A Martin, Blake, Dore - all in one,
Moynan's waifs across the way
Looked well fed in view of Danby's fallen.

Then I spied Lavery's *Lady*,
Orpen's *Yeats*, O'Connor's *Nude*,
Osborne's hand at *Jugs and Dogs*,
And artist Yeats *Many Ferries* -

Its naked men and women walking

Towards a priest absolving sins,
Beehive cells behind the grief
And death before those who'd come.

And that was it, I'd seen enough,
I walked back through the many rooms;
I'd passed away two Dublin hours,
On a Tuesday afternoon.

(ii) ONLY THE POET PAYS FOR POETRY

Visiting Ireland has made me feel
I have to start a new life -
Somewhere no one knows my past
Nor kens I have the semblance of a future.

Life for me in small town England
Is a cloistered thoroughfare -
I cannot go or be alone
Nor find the time to be unknown.

In every bar, on every street,
I see to glance a face I know -
They give me nods, chance a wave,
Sometimes a frown, a look away.

Most times they ask 'How's the wife?'
And yet they know we've separated.
'Keepin' writing then' they quip,
Hoping I may have jacked it in.

'Yeah' I often make reply,
And fill them with consternation.
'Don't give up, you're nearly there!
Stick it out, you'll make it yet!'

I look at them, they look at me,
My jeans ragged, my shoes holed -
And all I think in my head
'I should have made it years ago'.

Their interest wanes like winter sun,
The conversation turns to them -
'How's your kids? How's your wife?'
And they offer then to buy a drink.

'Maybe you'll write down what I say?'
One pint's cheap payment for such hope -
No one ever pays me for such work,
A bluey for a timeless poem.

Painters get hired by the dozen,
For tons, grands, ten times over;
Poets are expected to do penance
And write their works while on the dole.

(iii) THE UNDISCOVERED POET

I must go some place no-one knows me
so I may give up being a poet,
some place where words on my tongue
are heard as me and not as work.

I long to be where things are new,
where days are bright and evenings warm.
I long to be with plain young friends
who laugh and never think of death.

I long to leave the past that binds
the present to the woes of time.
I long to turn my back and walk
from all the things that make me run.

I long to free myself from thought
to make my body feed my days.
I long to settle in a place
where all my truth is in my face.

(iv) **HEED ME, ENGLAND**

Thus I have been in Ireland but one day,
Yet strongly feel my life must change;
Time may bring me fame and recognition,
But I feel I cannot wait for fate.
I may break before my opening.
Heed me, England. Hear my warning.

(v) **DISHONEST DEMOCRACY**

Ireland has an honesty, a hope unbroken,
A spirit nor crushed by class oppression -
England is a country where freedom is dying.
Where were you when the miners were staving?

Democracy is a joke around the world,
Dictators are a product of the capitalist system;
Every movement of reform and revolution
Starts when hunger overcomes reason.

Yes, this poem is for all you capitalist pigs
Who live off the back of slave labour;
The ones who exploit youth unemployment,
The ones who do no one no favours.

(vi) **BELFAST**

The church steeples rose
against the bleak black hills
capped white and rolling
down to the stormy Loughs.

Industry's scab-coal smoke
swirled the day ... the night
cold and bitter blasted

by the wild Atlantic gales.

The black taxis snaked
Falls Road and the Shankill,
grey walled, round-shouldered,
Huddled, hidden, soldiered.

(vii) **THE BELFAST READING**

We sit in pain ... listening
Politely waiting ... our breath flaming
In the Art Centre cold.

We long for drink ... for warmth,
For happy voices singing,
For lively conversation
Dwelling not on death and violence.

Poetry readings breed discontent,
Alcohol drowns ... loud verse
Thumping politics and bible humpers,
Anarchists in ties ... Poets
singing modern dirges,
Traditional tunes sung off-key
By girls in blue jeans ...
Paddy Day short stories
Delivered by grey pensioners
Over coated, in demob suits.

Meanwhile, the cold ankle numbness
Creeping up the legs ...
Like a dog pissing on me.
Woof! Woof! The words protrude
Into the private of my life ...
See, we wait ... in abject vain,
In unprotected candlelight
We suffer on ... and on ...
Until our hell is real.

We totter in our chairs,
We pray for soft release,
We engage in harsh inertia ...
The poetry reading stretches,
Stretches far beyond the threshold
Of artistic taste.

We near the end ...
We near the end ...
We near the end ...

(viii) **ST PATRICK'S DAY DUBLIN 1985**

St Patrick's Day by the Liffey,
Green, white and gold,
The flags along the quay,
The sea-salt fresh with freedom.

The tide turned at three,
The icy winds from Iceland
Tempered by a brave March sun
Burning bright the north bank.

The parade long since past,
The girls stop to parley,
The gulls quietly circle.

There is no Sunday frenzy,
No wild mad fighting,
Only happy families,
Couples strolling, laughing.

Dublin traffic gently rumbling,
Grandmothers pushing children
Waving flags, green rosetted.

Budding elm and sycamore,
Spires, arches, domes,
The Liffey flowing out to sea
Beneath the fair bridges.

WEEK 50

(i) **TUTORIAL - WHAT HAVE YOU LEARNED**

*End of term again
And what have you learned
To make you more human,
More enlightened?*

I do not know, mentor,
I haven't read a word
To make me feel special
Or delighted.

*Never mind, my son,
What we have not touched
To get you a two-one
Is sleight.*

I do not understand, master,
I don't remember enough
To take the final step -
Examination.

*Never fret, my lad,
The world is out to lunch,
Beyond this room lies
True habitation.*

(ii) **MARCH RAINS**

The heavy March rains, washing grave stones,
Drenching mourners, weighing willows,
Pressing cypress, bending hawthorn,

Dripping on crocus.

Falling forlorn, the March rains soaking,
Spring rains pouring,
Weeping, weeping, cleansing, restoring,
Winter passing - no more snow;
No more cold - its anger going.

(iii) **PURITY**
(for Elaine)

Purity came out of the cold,
Stood on the doorstep,
Dressed in red,
Her hair in plaits.
All the way from Manchester,
She came to love,
To walk through the door
Towards the unknown.

She stayed barely a day,
A night together,
A night forever,
Sunshine at dawn.
Bus station parting,
We kissed quietly,
Turned backs sadly,
To worlds of our own.

(iv) **THIRTY ONE**

I *never thought that at thirty one*
Some people would view me as still very young.

Thirty one,
Just a young one
On the poetry scene.

I know poets sixty or more,
I think I'm just starting
In this game.

It must be tough
For those students
Who're only seventeen.

No wonder poetry's boring
And for old farts
And ugly intellectuals.

Take it from me, pal,
Thirty one is young
To be a poetry man.

(v) **THE NINE-FIFTEEN TO KINGS CROSS**

The nine-fifteen to Kings Cross!

Twelve-nineteen at Kings Cross!
The nine-fifteen to Kings Cross!
Bumpity bump bump bump!

Telegraphs and Times', Maxwell House and wines.
Clinkity clink clink. Heller to the left,
Mailer to the right. Flippity flip flip.
Durham and York. Doncaster gone.

Bumpity bump bump. Faster past houses,
Slowly on southwards. Trundily wooh wooh.
Onwards by pit-heaps, by towers of concrete.
Rumbily nock nock. Onwards to Kings Cross!

Ditches and pastures, Constable pictures,
Gulls in the trees, windmills in fields.
Humbily hum hum. Wheeliwah run run.
Swans in the furrows, horses on stubble.

Gypsies encamped by motorcross tracks.
Onwards to Kings Cross! Clickity clack clack.
Broken yard fences, dirty black bridges,
Fallen down churches, uprooted hedges.

Softly slow slip. Steadily clack click.
Grey weather breaking, tall multi's looming,
Scrap pile mountains, factory smoke streaming,
Wires criss-crossing, highways well-knotted.

People on platforms, people on buses,
People not waving, people kept waiting.
Juddery jug jug Juddery bump bump.
Onwards to Kings Cross! Midday and not far.

Onwards to Kings Cross! Tunnels and sunned skies.
Onwards to Kings Cross! Welwyn and Hatfield.
Onwards to Kings Cross! Hadley and Barnet.
Onwards more tunnels, onwards past Southgate.

Electrified cables, whizzing past Hornsey.
Onwards to Kings Cross! Four minutes late.
Onwards to Kings Cross! Kings Cross! Kings Cross!
Arrival at Kings Cross! Four minutes late.

(End of The Undergraduate – Term 5)

EASTER VACATION 1985
(Easter Monday, 7th April 1985, Newcastle)

My life is empty
Of all those things
... those hang-ups
we are pegged by
those envious and hurt
who are about us
daily and forever.

For we do not see
the harm caused,
the pain unleashed
by self admirers
and their liggers
... until too late
the cut is made
and the wound runs deep.

I am severed
to the marrow
by very little
... we are bled
by contempt and shuns
and sharp returns,
and still we heal
to carry on as ever.

THE PLAYRIGHT'S INTRODUCTION (song)
[Spring 1985, Helmsley Rd, Newcastle]

My play which is to follow
Was writ on a beach during summer
and though the plot may be hollow
I'm sure it's no bummer.

For while I lay on the sands
olive oiled and tanned and naked
I thought of grey strand England
pebble beached and oil slaked.

And with fresh winds in my hair
I gazed across the steaming playa
gulls shadowed in the glare ...
girls bronzed skins on fire ...

Unlike the peach and cream of home
a lighter shade of pale the norm -
for English skin tends to moan
in foreign sun in blister form.

JUNE
[16th April 1985, Newcastle]

June got me to smoke a cigarette
While listening to Elgar
As we kissed upon her bed.

YOUNG BILLY
[21st April 1985, Newcastle]

Young Billy and I talked into the night
Till the sun rose over Byker Hill.
We passed the jays in steady flow,
Conversed about dreams and future things,
Family ties and the passing of years,
Sleepwalking, music, and personal faults,

Rejection of love and welfare forms.
We charted the troubles of the world,
Till half asleep, we recorded the dawn –
Billy with song, I with this poem.

THE UNDERGRADUATE - TERM 6
THE STATE OF LEARNING IN ENGLAND
[22nd Apr – 30th June 1985, mainly Newcastle]

WEEK 51

As bankruptcy edges in on my friends,
I'm glad to be lost in another term.

(i) BASIL BUNTING

Where now Basil is dead,
And the crows cry alone on the Flats,
The north has lost an ageing man,
To dust now gone.

What now Basil is dead
And the wind blows seed over the reeds,
Earth to air and water fired,
Tall grass split and shorn.

What now Basil is dead
The lake heaves twigs into the weed,
The trees bend in sighing woe
Wailing 'Where did Basil go?'

(ii) WE ARE ORDERED

Too often we are ordered
To do that which we should be ordering
For ourselves, for structure comes from within
Not without. For without parameters
We allow ourselves to be shaped by others.

The commands of others represent the disunity
Within ourselves. Such disarray
Only spreads the power of others.
We are equal, but order produces
A master for each slave.

(iii) WHY IS IT SNOWING?

Why is it snowing in the last week of April?
Is this the start of the nuclear winter?

When I look out my window,
Ignoring all the red-brick houses,
I do not see a veritable garden
Of green shrubbery and protruding flowers.

It is spring, yet the verdant promise
Of a profuse summer of botanical plenty

Seems a hazy distant hope based on past
Experience of long hot summers. Sleet and

Hail three days before the advent of May
Suggests a shortish summer of heavy rain
And cool afternoons spent beneath the eaves
Of park pavilions and disused shelters.

Outdoor pursuits of tennis, bowling,
Walks along the beach in search of quiet
And isolation to go nude bathing, seems
A far mirage, a forlorn dreaming -

That paradise will come to England
While the well-to-do travel overseas
And read the British press every day just
In case they miss out on a summer heat wave.

Yes, how the tropics call to me,
To dream and idly pass my future
In a hammock on a beach upon an island
Set amidst the coral reefs of an ocean –

Coloured by the bounty of a teeming
Bathymetric sea ... But in England,
Only some folks have all the fun,
To run to the joyous ocean to escape work;

Whilst the rest grind on towards the hope
Of summer, the lucky least take off to
Asian parts in quest of drugs, of pleasure;

While a covert few depart in search of wealth
In young America, and only those discouraged,
Disillusioned, and despairing, find themselves
Dwelling on the bleakness of the weather.

WEEK 52

Everyman has deeds to do on Earth;
Ill-spent time impedes great design.

FOLLOWING MY TUTOR'S ADVICE

A poet must be brief, so my tutor tells me.
This week I bought some hash, and drove
To the Lakes on the Lit Soc outing.
Tutor's advice stops me from saying more.

WEEK 53

(i) CUMBRIA

I cannot help but dwell upon
The last few days ... and how
The Lakeland Pikes call on me
To turn t'wards their tarns,

Those strides that cradle heaven
For those earthbound creatures
Straddling dungeon gyll and airy fall
To standing stones; to mere side hosts
Round islands garlic green and yewed
That calls on me anew – till few
Remaining ripples lap me constant
In the shade of silent waters, or
In the mists upon gowned fells, or
Beneath cracked and gullied crags
Cutting cloud, piercing the sublime
To sweep along the edge of nothing
Where I long to stand and wonder
At the limit's of man's kingdom.

(ii) CAEDMON'S MIDDLE-EARTH

Now shall we hail the heavenly guard,
Metudaes might, and his mind-thought,
His world-father works, each wonder that
he our God first ordered.
He, prime poet, of men's children,
Heaven unto thatch, the holy shepherd;
In Middle-Earth, mankind's guard,
Our god, who past adorned
Life's land as lord almighty.

(iii) OFERMOD (PRIDE)

Over mind, over thought,
Over spirit, over all,
Some try to split the atom
Before the apple falls.

Pride rooted in chivalry
Killed Brythnort at Maldon,
Harold Goodwin at Hastings,
Prince Henry at Crecy,
James Stuart at Flodden.

Ofermod! Ofermod!
The kettle drum judders.
By one man's will,
Many more suffer.

Pride rooted in power
Cast Satan into Chaos,
Alexander to the Indus,
Brought Anthony to Egypt,
And Bonaparte to Russia.

Ofermod! Ofermod!
The knell bell tolls.
One man's will
Brings many more woe.

(iv) I SHAVED MY MOUSTACHE OFF

I shaved my moustache off,
Then talked to my lover on the phone,
But it didn't make a difference,
I was still the same to her.

I struggled on with *Judith*,
Hating very verb I didn't know,
My upper lip quivered violently,
Trapped in study not in love.

For my love had left me,
And fled across the vale,
Up the steps, beneath the beeches
Sloping up to Byker Hill.

There I drifted, there I lingered,
There I pined to rest,
But *Judith* drew me on to work
As darkness made descent.

No fair muse heard my call,
My spirit passing on,
Judith had me trapped fore'er
Without a thought of love.

I called upon the summer winds
To bring on cooling calm,
To wing me clear across the vale
Into my lover's arms.

WEEK 54

Ageless I find the motive of my existence
Inconsistent with the dreams I demand.

(i) **PROSE WRITER**

True to all ideals, existence bears up
To all examination, discounting art
And emotion as reasons for survival.

Prose should be the medium of poets –
Alas, would-be-bards soon turn novelist
In reaction to dictionaries and foreign languages.

How sad, we mourn ... tut, tut –
Poor England lacerating her native tongue,
And which pulp fiction hack would deny it.

Prose, my friends, is for the likes of me,
Poor man's poetry, rich man's lifestyle;
Prose is not safe for fine ideal.

Hence, an escape to freedom,
Removal from restricted reason
To digress on Kenya –

Where girls mate with strangers
And strangers have men at their feet.

In prose we swallow nectars
That middling poets have never tasted –
Poor, lone souls drifting somewhere
Between the high moors and the crashing sea.

I the prose writer, you the reader
Can twitter in a huddle to ourselves
In the recess of a fiction bower,
read words poets will never warble.

(ii) **THERE IS A WORLD OUT THERE**

There is a world out there that no wealth
Of language can express. Ablution. The life
Of an undergraduate is always taking turns
Towards the future. Likewise, his forms, his means
Of demonstrating inner motive – outer emotion
Require changing styles in keeping with the
Constant variation of his education. And so,
In streaming prose, in keeping with the wet
May weather, I the undergraduate, the drivelling
Scholar, once reviewed as a tartan Candide,
Must entertain.
        For this is too often
Is the failing of our Arts Council poets –
They rarely make us laugh, and I can only
Giggle when I see and hear such artificers at
Readings with their puffed out chests
And scraps of yellowed paper – with their
Neckerchiefs and garden-digger sweaters –
With their droll dry voices dragging out
Dreary dirges – their audience with smiles
In pain until the clapping's finished. Oh
Sad state of learning in England, must
We cry, forego the pleasures of laughter,
Exchange the literature of song for such
Versed misery?
        My tutor, a man of learning,
So Romantic, he is an expert, whispered
Quietly in my ear that poetry was dead –
'There are finer things a man may do
than waste his time upon the art of verse.'
He made me see the light – and now
Transformed, my voice speaks to you
Unmarked by rhyme, unchecked by metre,
As the novelist in me triumphs over poet
To hack me free of dogged-down verse.

WEEK 55

Text pages wet with tears, dog-end with weeping.

FANNY AND DICK

Fanny gave Dick hell for six months.
She studied art and film at the Polytechnic.
He, poor soul, struggled through Old English
And Milton, while she watched movies
In class and at home on video.

Her exams finished weeks before his;
She partied and drank, balled and smoked hash
While Dick stuck it out with *Beowulf* and *Judith*,
Hating the silence of Fanny's departure -
No one came round, called, or arranged

To meet Dick for a drink, or over for tea –
They left him to drown on *Seafarer* verse,
They left him to wallow on *Wanderer* text,
Abandoned him totally to Old English literature;
None thought to save him, least of all Fanny.

Out on the town, out in the countryside,
Off to wild picnics, off on mad trips
Down to the seaside, up in the hills,
Free as a lark, with no thought of Dick.
Fanny was happy and shot of her studies.

Dick was trapped, and fairly full sad
That Fanny forgot to ring or drop by
With a thumbnail of hash, or bottle of wine
To splash on his books – to get him wrecked
As he sat revising Old English verse.

WEEK 56

(i) **THRASHING THEMSELVES WITH NETTLES**

When the sun shines in the far north of
England, it does so usually by chance.
When the heat wave comes - the natives
Cancel their plans of two weeks in Spain
And travel instead to France by motorbike
Or thumb. The less adventurous potter
In the garden or make pots of mint tea
And enjoy the only time in England when
The climate is everybody's idea of summer.

Then the thunderstorms bring the overcast
Of cool afternoons so typically the norm –
The windows close, the doors stay shut
And everyone goes around with hard shoes
And a briskness so common of the drudgery
Of work and day to day low grey dawns
That drizzle, fizzle, pop into dull descending
Evenings leading on to another grey morning –

While the folks in Spain, turn a shade more
Olive, and the grape in France swells fuller
Bodied – the natives in north England suffer

287

the fate of Caesar's legions guarding Hadrian's
Wall – who thrashed themselves angrily with
Flowering nettles to keep themselves warm.

(ii) **RACHAEL ROCK**
for Sarah Stone

Rachael Rock – if ever there was girl
More perfectly in tune with how I felt,
Or how I wished to be, then hell, I
Don't think I'd feel this panegyric.

We met and came, and conquered all
Inhibitions at an all-night party that
Threw to dust the cobwebs from my
Boring life of going to university.

I loved her sea-green eyes and coral
Black hair, and her dark brown skin
And soft quiet voice that spoke like
No poet ever could affect.

I see her still, her talk of foreign
Places where she would like to go,
To live content teaching English
Language to the world.

Rachael Rock, a candle in a storm.
Yet Rachel is a lie, her name false –
It gives no truth to the natural spirit
Underlying her sweet exemplar.

To call her Rock is wrong ... she is an
Island verdant rich profuse with fruit
In passion ripe abundance.
Rachael Rock, sweetness profound!

The Muses sing her praise as a precious
Angel set to gift rare treasures
Of amber-gris and jet.
Rachael Rock – I cannot yet forget.

WEEK 57

(i) **PROVOKED**

Too often men find themselves provoked,
To lash out at the world and hit whatever
it is that they find most cause to hate.

Such umbrage can produce from a writer,
A satire on the fellows of his profession
Who sell themselves for everything but truth.

(ii) **THE STATE OF LEARNING IN ENGLAND**

Is it back to poetry so soon?

I thought I'd given it up for good.

But listen, which right minded writer
Would admit he's lost the knack of verse
And thrown himself to hewing hack lines
Of nonsense and tomfoolery?

Now, you may wonder at the state of learning
In England these days when its undergraduates
Are told that their verse is too long, and
That they should think about doing other
Things more in keeping with the century.
I'm sure wee Alexander Pope would turn
In this grey clay bed in the Abbey, and
Nudge the elbow of big John Dryden, and
Say 'Hey, Bayes, have you heard the latest
Gossip in the town?', and John would say –
'No, young lad, I've been dead three hundred
years and been enjoying the peace and quiet.'

But of course, his curiosity would better
His common sense, and he'd ask 'Well,
What are the hacks in town moaning on
About right now?' – And obligingly
We Alec would open his trap and blurt
That 'I've heard that goddess Dullness
Has been set above the poets that
Abound the list of Arts Council scribblers,
And that each, to get his pennies from
The State, must first of all agree not
To write the truth or say a word against
The leaders of the country, and that
All their verse must be published by the
Friends of friends of friends of government
Ministers of the Tory faction, which
Of course, so they say are the only ones
Who can afford to pay the scandalous prices
For the briefest lines of piss-pot bumf
That slides its way on to the shelves of
All the public libraries in the country where
Its ignored, as it hasn't got a thing
To do with anything that's got anything
To do with people who use the public
Libraries up and down the country!'

And Big John Dryden, listening sleepily
To the high-pitched lilt of Alec's voice
Echoing through the night of the Abbey,
Scratched his nose and offered up some
Quick advice to his young death-bed
Mate, and said 'Nothing ever changes.
Shadwells, Settles, Cibbers, and all those
Grub Street liggers, hanging on to words
Like children clinging on to sixpences as if
They were the jewels of the realm. Ne'er
Did I hear a sentence from a hack that
Did not take an hour to construct – ne'er

289

I heard a line from a scribbling poet that
Hadn't taken all of a year to compose.

They play with words and hope that the idea
Drops into place like a round peg in a square
Hole, and lo, when it does not happen
they pretend to one another that it has,
until each is slapping each in turn upon
the back at their genius – each buys each
a drink at the bar, and getting drunk
they make their lies much easier to
spin, until by closing time their words
are so inflated by bombast and farting,
they sing into the rafters of how they've
solved the mysteries of time, and can
proffer forth solutions to the ails of
common folk and half the world. And
off the go in blind drunkenness to their
shabby attics to compose their masterpieces –
where slaving half the night to find
the first word, they abandon it for
their beds like the Irish bards of old.

There they remain till afternoon and
Hunger calls them to the vertical –
Once more they totter off to the public
Houses with their pens behind their ears,
The first word of their latest masterpiece
On their lips, and safely memorised, written
Out a hundred times in case they lose it,
Or forget what it was the laboured
Half the night to compose. Aye, hear
Me, young Alec, none of this is new –
The Dunces abound and belch louder
Than those who sleep quietly at night
And rise and keep Nature's proper social
Hours. Though, I must confess, that
I have slept these three hundred years
Without seeing a single dawn, though
I doubt our enemies, the Hacks, have
Seen any more first greying than I
Since they embarked upon their fancy ships
As self-appointed captains of genius, just
because the government pays for every line.
Aye, Alec, the hacks were bad in our day –
But at least we were around.'

Woken up by Dryden, Jonny Swift, from
Over In a corner, spoke – 'You're right,
Big John, wee Alec was the scourge
To all those hacks in our time – I gave
Them hell in my *Battle of the Books*,
And you turned Shadwell's hair wig grey
With yon *MacFlecknoe*. That bit the ear
Off half the poets in the kingdom, and
Man, it was treat to see all the faces
Of the critics red and shit upon

In the very manner that they tore down
The pillars of literature we erected -
I put them all to sea with my mad cap
Tale of three rub-a-dub fools in a tub.'

The Abbey rang with their laughter, as
Now, big John, wee Alec, and lank Swifty
Garbled on about the good old days –
Till suddenly they heard a creaking, a
Groaning, then a yawning, and the voice of
Andrew Marvell – 'I remember well the hacks
Of England, and yon when I went to Rome
And bumped into MacFlecknoe; and later
When that fool Tom May died and left
Behind his sad driveling, it made me
Tirade more on him than I ever did on
Our deist Monarch! But quiet, headless
Charles lies over yonder, and Cromwell,
Thank god, is even further apart from us
Good poets crowded here in the apse.'

Then through the darkness of the Abbey
Night spoke a poet lying close to Marvell –
'Do I hear the lilt of coy Andy? I cannot
see, but I remember well every sound
I learned on my journey through Paradise
And Hell. Surely I could not have slept
So long to find my companions here
Are but mortal men?' 'You hush, John
Milton!' Marvell said loudly 'You'll bring
Damn Satan down upon our Eden!. How
Can I forget your pounding verse, in
Our time I passed as second best. Yet,
I will admit you helped me to get on,
Prosper, writing all that propaganda
For that old dog Cromwell. He paid
For every line to which I confessed –
It's just as well I hid the rest. I wonder
If they've found it yet?

Milton scratched his grave-sore bum
And said –'The Devil still not caught
Your tongue, young Marvell? You were
A cad for sure, we both well knew
How to sit on fences, ride the times
Of king's departures, lords beheadings –
I played the *Penseroso*, you the *Allegro*,
We rode our hobby-horses, not a Pegasus.
No wonder I got lost in Paradise, it
Was safer than playing politics no
Matter how much we pandered. Look
what became old Suckling, Lovelace, Carew –
feathers in their helmets, daggers at their
throats; they went public, while we held
private our own personal views. We must
have done right to be buried here. But lo,
who are those poets whispering over there?

291

Is that young Dryden I hear?'

'Hail, great Samson of English verse!
Aye, it is I, big John, you hear twittering
On to our great Augustans. We have
Been upbraiding hacks and scribblers.
Do you remember any such piss-pots
Who driveled on and made a name?'
Samson took a breath, then spoke –
'Aye, there are a hundred hacks to
every single poet of worth, so many
to recall, so few worth the bother at all.
If they are not buried here, then time
Has taken its toll. But hush! Let's speak
Softly, we don't want to awaken John Donne;
He'll sermonise us delirious, his work was
Good, but its better to let dogs snore.'

Too late! The Dean turned stone-cold over
And flew out emotion with a roar from
His mouth four centuries dry and silent.
'I heard you, young Milton – quiver
if you will, but we are in the Abbey,
and I dare not use any dirty words. These
are the stock and stave that burden hacks
and bind them loveless to the universe.'
'You old piss-prude!' another poet yelled.
'Who calls me that?? Dean John indignant.
'I know that voice. Come on, own up my
friend. I still see your Tyburn thumb
pressing up the butt of Ginger Jimmy.
You're loud-mouthed poetaster Ben Jonson!'

'You dirty old priest' sniggered Ben,
'Four hundred years and still the same –
buried in this musty mausoleum, you'd
think they'd have cleaned your grave
out once at least. I'm surprised Poetry's
pilgrims don't complain. I could do with
a wash and brush and change myself.
Our poetry is fresh, but our bodies hum.
I wonder when old Willy last turned?'

As if no one wished to disturb the
Greatest bard of them all, a chorus of
'*Ssssshhhhh*' filled the Abbey, and
everyone fell silent as they listened to
the echo carry down the aisle towards
the kings and queens, the patron of their
art, whom they had served and pandered
without being low common hacks. For
though art could be bought, genius could not
be made to order like a pudding or a pie
from a recipe concocted to guarantee a
diet of good poetry and honest verse.

So – this for all the hacks, and all

The piss-pot scribblers – let this be
A gauge of all that needs to be done
If a poet is to succeed from meager
Verse to great timeless poetry. For
In the Abbey lies our slumbering critics;
Only in the whispers of their approval
Will you hear the truth – and only when
You lie with them will the truth be known –
That you are no hack, but a poet in your own.

WEEK 58

(i) WHAT'S IN A NAME

Petra is not happy with her name.
She wishes to be someone, but cannot say
Whether Linda is better than plain Jane,
Or Debbie more common than mere Jill.

She should be called Anna or Emma,
But she has some friends with these names.
Rachael or Petra, one means the other –
I'll call her Heather, play safe.

(ii) HEATHER AND PETE

Heather and Pete came down on a cloud
And slept together in a moor land bog.
The mist provided a curtain from peepers
Wanting to know the phenomenal cause
Of the deep red glow, the blue flashing light
That covered the sky seven mornings and nights.

But Heather and Pete, unsaddled, unbridled,
Rode out their love with such blinding fire,
The peepers turned blind watching their passion.
They most they espied was one naked thigh,
Or a knee, or a toe pushed to the sky –
But never a torso, a cheek, or a face.

On the eighth day of bliss, they rose aloft,
Enveloped and wound in a celestial haze.
The mist vaporised in a steaming whirl
As the lovers sped off at a chase –
The peepers stumbled forward into the bog
Scrambled, and crawled at a loss.

They cam upon the love bed departed –
A crater shot-hot with the host;
They tumbled into the heat of the hole
To discover their vision miraculous restored;
But never again did the peepers experience
Heather and Pete making love in the bog.

WEEK 59

POETRY IS DEAD

There is little point saying something
When there is nothing to say.
Having declared that poetry is dead,
Where now can this long work lead?
If there is a resurrection, then
Who shall witness and proclaim it?
Surely not the critics, the closet hacks,
The ones who invent meaning, yet deny it!

No, if Poetry is to live in spirit, not material,
Then it is in the voice of youth we'll find it,
Not on the tongues of middle-aged capitalists,
Secure in their homes, secure in versed hypocrisy.
For were it not for reasons less important
Than a personal commitment to myself,
I would give up this diary of event –
And believe indeed POETRY IS DEAD.

For when all is said and done –
I still turn in recoil from nature
To attack all that has gone wrong
In Poetry since I began this sojourn.
Like the hour before the battle lours,
I see the hordes of hacks advancing,
Their armour dull, their plumaged jaundiced,
Smearing bile on all they trample.

Yet I should ignore all conflict,
And turn my face to gaze upon
The beauty of wild nature; seek the sublime
Hidden from the know of city dwellers.
For when man is sick of his fellow man,
He should renounce all that is material –
Travel to a landscape right for solitude,
Or seascape sedative, to reshape his hostility.

And there, on the barren hills of nowhere,
Out upon the wild waves of ocean,
Poetry may come to a listening man
And fill him with the resurrecting spirit
That eludes the urban guru – the city
Hack pounding his machine for copy.
For if Poetry is dead, there is no body,
Only a spirit waiting where few men wander.

WEEK 60

Exam results – how we tremble
To hear that we are not geniuses.

(i) **LIVING OFF THE STATE**

To hell – its summer,
Time to hit the beaches,
Forget all the book crap.

Sun, sex, and travel …
Vitamin C mornings
Chasing alcoholic dawns.

Give me stretching beaches,
Tall cocktails mixed,
Slow music yawning.

Aye, the student vacation,
No talk of work,
That's for commoners.

Greece? – no, man,
That's only a thousand off –
It's India or Oz for me.

But not this year,
Mass for this guy,
Standby to New England.

Makes you sick, eh?
Us layabouts lazing,
Living off the State.

We cares, mates –
Someone has to pay –
But not me, okay.

(ii) **NOT CLEVER**

You know, the more I study,
The more I realise I am no critic.
Someone said to me 'Anyone
Who gets more than a 2-2
Doesn't know how to think
For themselves – they're only clever.'

It makes me ponder whether
C*lever* means stupid and dumb
About the common practical aspects
Of everyday chore and habit,
Or whether *clever* means uncreative –
That is – totally critical,
Analytical, verbal and quantitative;

Or whether it means that students
Who study seven days and nights
In every week are weirdos –
Or whether people who get 2-1's
And Firsts are just into books
And not into drugs and sex.

But who cares – everyone's different –
In America *clever* means money;
There you're dumb if *clever*, but broke.

So, maybe in Britain, if you're *clever*,

Then you're into particular studies
That means more than just a 2-2.
Where as, if you are *not clever*,
You're into having a good time,
Enjoying life, and not giving a damn.

(iii) **ANOTHER YEAR ENDS**

And so another year ends.
No more exams, no more classes
Till October comes again.

The grey autumn skies
That herald another cold winter
And nights over books.

Sixty weeks gone, thirty left,
The undergraduate life withers,
Moves towards freedom.

Vacation is here, lord –
Cobwebs and bookworms
We leave undisturbed.

And what have we learned?
The echoes of masters
Go round in our heads.

We go down for the summer,
To sink in green meadows,
To forget all out trials.

We go down till autumn,
Returned with knowledge
'cept of ourselves.

(End of The Undergraduate – Term 6)

THE UMBRELLA MAN (song)
[24th July 1985, Helmsley Rd, Newcastle]

I'm living and swinging
I don't go round bragging.
I'm just one of the boys.

I'm young, I'm single,
I like to have a mingle.
I'm just one of the boys.

I don't try to hide things,
I try not to imbibe things
I'm not that sort of guy.

I'm clean, I'm smart,
I don't hang out with tarts.
I'm just one of the boys.

I'm good, not bad,
I've never had it hard.
I'm just one of the boys.

THE AMERICAN DREAM

[18^{thst} Aug 1985, Framingham, Massachusetts]

And so beginning with the trees
and all the summer foliage,
I commenced to question nature
for the answers to wild theories
formed on half-baked ideas,
never tried or put into practice
in the context of the milieu
the great American Dream.

Yet here in this vast New England
where men and women shape a land
far different from that all others know …
There is a void, a lack of life
that flows beneath the surface world
of timber houses backed by yards
that stretch in common to an acre,
deep and fenced and posted 'Private'.

For common to the rights of individuals
is belief in private ownership –
a concept in keeping with an Englishman
that his home is a lofty bastion,
from where to view the world,
to champion, to defend the Dream -
as proud hero, a stalwart of liberty
behind his mighty edifice of wood

For while Atlantis may have been a paradise
that far exceeded the beauty recalled
of lost Eden, forbidden for all time
to mortals on this earth or the next –
unlike Nirvana that lies beyond perception
to those who dwell solely on Heaven,
Utopia is a bookish premise for happiness,
offering no rules for all that's realistic.

And still, while summer grips
the conscious world of this new republic
made beautiful by a hive of industry
and the will and heart of ordinary citizens,
life slips by towards some Armageddon
taking root in the soil of America.

And while the breeze blows the tops
of old Virginia or Ponderosa pine,
and the grasses of the Plains bathe
in the sun-seas of botanic ocean –
time moves a sleeping Kali to awaken
and explode upon a guilty nation.

Yet, if truth belies stock ignorance ...
if ideal is misguided by good intention,
then we must part blame our teachers,
the enlightened leaders taking us towards
the dark empty void of chaos
filled by a blind adherence to order.

Hell has many paths to its center,
but Bardo is a place where terror reigns;
for along the road to other worlds
can be seen great citadels of pleasure
where warm blooded creatures
serve with smiles and care for nature.

Thus in this new England we discover
passion flying on the ecstasy of now,
the Dream – in that there's no tomorrow
where each yesterday is forgiven -
each sin pardoned by some saviour,
Leaves the wicked wickeder than before.

God makes his plan in each of us,
in each, in all, in everything – the Dream
lives and births anew upon America;
forever, each dawn enforces the myth,
supplants the new world doubt that
action overcomes the inner spirit.

For Paradise is a café, a diner
where good Americans feast or breakfast
before returning to the hard reality
of social failure midst material success –
where proud, fine individuals, fail to admit
the alien-ness of their fellow citizens.

Struggling to put a face on a day
that every hour is a part of the Dream,
in this new world there is hope
that someone is going to love you,
that someone is going to touch you,
And shower your life with sex.

And still ... as summer slumbers on,
the wild grass seeds blow across
a continent basking in plenty –
the sky fills with native birds
following a host of insects;
I lounge in the caverns of this England,
pine roofed, pine floored, clear pooled.

On the water, the sun reflects a vision
of perfection so much the American way.
Yet, if we cannot wish, then how
shall our dreams ever come to bear?
A penny dropped, the ripple created
is all that marks the wish never made.

Dreams are never read on people's face,
rarely found in the yellow of our hearts,
we think alone, and pass off foreign notions;
adhering to the glow of the seventh chakra,
those of the Dream are centered in the bosom
or the spine, and not on the light that matters.

Misguided in our visions, we slumber
where we should show alertness of purpose,
sleep where thought should penetrate
and manifest itself as action –
we die where concentration fosters life,
struggle where the way leads on with ease.

If the barriers to a fruitful progress
are not already mighty in themselves,
we create fresh mountains from the debris
of decaying faith and molding beliefs –
then foster a new religion, a fresh enchantment
with which to obscure the plain old Truth.

And having thus erected a mountain,
we fortify it with all our knowledge,
invest our time, our wealth of interest,
foster reverence, guard, defend, and covet
all that we jealously protect – ring it
with walls and keep out our enemies.

Loving what's within, hating all without
our code of conduct becomes enmeshed
in a struggle to subject, or conquer
all that stands against our belief -
our vision as we perceive it from
our castle on the mountain.

And thus the Dream - a sacred summit
in the mists of complex fortification -
is beyond the sight of normal man
traveling across the flat plain of Truth –
It is a mirage, a thirsty man's delusion
that life is more than what nature offers.

And here, in this new England – I see
trees swaying in a warm south wind,
smell the pine and maple in the air,
watch the wagtails flock for insects
in the long grass grazed by ponies,
shy and lazy, in the buzz of summer.

And as the light begins to fade -
the Dream is but a myth that's peddled -
each setting sun reveals its secret –
there's nothing new that is not old,
or nothing old that's not been repeated
since the first cockerel crowed.

And like old England, this new England

has men desiring to imitate the old anew -
in replica appearance, with golf and tennis,
with quaint olde world facade and fashion,
'til even those familiar with the real
may wonder if the two are so different.

In old England, the Dream is dead,
left rotten and best forgotten –
the shame of centuries chokes all swagger;
Imperialism as the perfect form of government?
With human justice so badly enforced,
who now would follow such a course?

In that old England, the Dream –
once carried around the world as a flag,
exists in this new England – in the same
clash of colour – red, white and blue.
Men marching in the name of God and nation,
overlord of all other Gods and countries.

For this is the way … the way of America,
the Dream that goes beyond imagination -
save the world, organise the universe,
shape the destiny of man by arms –
to bully on beyond the know or knowledge
of lesser mortals doomed to feed the Dream.

And I, in this new England as a guest,
what then when I return from here -
back to old England, disillusioned,
unwilling to share the daughter's Dream;
what will I say about those wooden castles -
built on moral sand and half-baked views.

EMMA
[21st Aug 1985, Framingham, Massachusetts]

As I took my morning tea,
I heard the breeze in the eaves;
Quietly, as the warm of the day
Rose on me, I lingered in the park,
Wandered there, till noon –
Listening to a bird singing 'Emma'.

As I tore myself from earnest concentration,
I caught the stream whispering softly,
Barely, as the leaves of autumn
Shed gold on me beneath an aspen
That I pondered by, at three –
I listened, and I heard 'Emma'.

As I bore myself out of meditation,
I heard the cicada call her name –
Slowly, as the cool of the night
Descended on me beneath the maple
Where I retreated after supper,
I heard it again 'Emma'.

THE BOSTON SHADE
[22nd Aug 1985, Boston, Massachusetts]

August afternoon in the Boston shade,
watching the tramps collect their booty
from the trash in Copley Square.

Lovers winning kisses with a laugh,
kids skate-boarding crowded streets
across a city doing what it does –

Despite the frenzy of nearby New York,
Boston , slow and easy every day,
Buses on as if it's on vacation.

THE MAN ON EARTH
[25th Aug 1985, Framingham, Massachusetts]

Let the peregrini travel the world,
the saddu's walk the roads;
let them find kundalini
while I stay at home.

Let the sanyasin preach the word,
the rishi guide the way;
let them have their yagas
while I dream the day.

Let the guru teach the pranas,
the saints love of god;
let them drink the ambrose
while I sip on broth.

Let pandits tap the monad,
the charkas, yantras, rays;
let them chant their mantras
while I from slumber rise.

Let the master reach nirvana,
their pupils astral highs;
let them quench their fire
while I live to die.

SIXTH CHAKRA
[late August 1985, Newcastle]

Sixth chakra – between men's brows
the fire serpent opens the third eye
which perceives cloudy visions of mountains
while watching the smallest atom dance.

SECONDARY HEART LOTUS
[late August 1985, Newcastle]

Sea of nectar around the isle of flowering trees
formed from sands of dust diamond and ruby -

in the garden beneath a kalpa tree, the deity
of personal choice sits on a platform of gems.

THE NOTES PLAY ON
[2nd Sept 1985, Newcastle]

The notes play on
down forever to the edge
and on beyond the microphone
across the room and out
towards the sky coming
in through the window
open to the night.

Chords coming on strong
and steady across the air
and straight on by and by
till they meet other chords
bouncing back off the ceiling
boards and vibrating timber
walls all through the night.

THE CULTURE SHOCK
[5th Sept 1985, Newcastle-upon-Tyne]

The culture shock of squalid England,
man pressed to man like rivals –
the open land gone centuries ago,
opportunities no longer for the labourer,
as we wait, and watch the decay
eat and fester any future we had
for ourselves or for our children.

Sent out from our homes poor and hungry
for a life this land will never let them have
the chance to search for ... as above us
rule a greedy few against all commonwealths,
the brotherhood that sets all equal.

Upon us are the laws of class
that forever cast us to the wind,
where the voices of the dead cry out,
warn us of the wrongs of servitude,
blind compliance to a dying system,
kept alive by a blind obedience
to a forceful order that breaks resistance
with the iron fist of fear.

This cruel injustice that sends policemen
To the doors of the innocent, sets soldiers
armed upon peace campaigners -
More and more the victims of repression.

These are the methods of the few,
Put in power by a people
Soft and easy in their mediocrity,
Where ideal sold for false security,

We are sick and fevered – our children
Die in this plague of self destruction.
The time for words had gone – and we
The people search for a new Messiah.
For we have no future joy – we lead
our children blindly on towards an end.
Can no man steer us from annihilation?

THE UNDERGRADUATE - TERM 7
[7th Oct 1985 - 13th Dec 1985, Newcastle]

(i) RETURN TO THE OTHERWORLD

I am undone.
Autumn steals long summer.
Take me then,
take me back in chains.
Fix the bonds of study
until I'm imprisoned.

Free my time has been.
I have lazed, procrastinated.
Racked .. my books stand dusty,
aside lies knowledge
shelved for pleasure.
Now, goes the vernal equinox.

And what has gone?
Soft long mornings,
tea and conversation,
wine upon the sands,
tomorrow hung on sunsets,
tomorrow ....

Now, expectancy is dead.
Each day takes meaning.
In a diary of engagements,
time punctuates all time.
And study draws in on
the freedom of living.

(ii) AND NOW?

Yet shall I laugh
while all others cry.
What better life can there be
than taking two thou'
to peruse and browse novels
in whimsical go-as-you-please.

You can have your two quid-
an-hour or so,
dirty snot jobs or the bru'.
The soft student life
of parties and wine
is a rich doddle and breeze.

And so when I howl,
wrinkle and scowl
at returning to varsity,
take it from me,
it's only a sneeze,
I'd rather be there than at sea.

WEEK 61

(i) **CHARLIE**

A girl from down-south
with an incredible smile
and blue eyes that dash
flash kingfisher dart
like the back of a dolphin
cutting reefed sweeps
of lapis-lazed oceans,
hung azul horizons
aglow with the blaze
of a heaven of candles
lit by the gaze,
the aquamarine glaze
of Charlie, my blue-jay
and darling.

(ii) **ALBERT**

My mate and my marra'
but no timid sparrow,
or vole off a-scurrying
through grass to burrow,
to hide in the dark
like an owl or bat;
no frightened field-mouse
turned out of house
when the harvester culls
the wheat summer ripe
for eating and storing
by hamster or mole.
He's Albert, me china,
me mate an' me marra',
me chip off-the-old-wood,
solid and rot-proof,
treated and seasoned,
sound and dry through.

(iii) **BILLY**

What's that you say?
You've got terrible drug debts!
Billy, my lad, what can I tell you
but pack it all in,
and go back to piano
or singing, or stringing
your poor gut guitar.

I heard a C minor
when you last thumbed a chord,
it's been floating around
like pollen since August,
I swear it vacationed
all of September,
I heard it come back
last week for certain.

Look ... it's under your bed,
I heard it yawning,
being on the dole
is no good for notes either,
it's starting to smell,
turn blue, and sound rotten.
So give us a song, son!
something major to rock on.

WEEK 62

(i) SOME FOLKS

Some folks are pebbles in oceans
others stones in dry streams,
some like soft limestone
wash quickly to sea,
some like black basalt
weather, fade, and erode,
others like soft clay
rain-run in storms.

but some are white marble,
pink granite, red sandstone,
others green feldspar,
blue quartz, common mica.

(ii) MICHAEL

He was a lump of schist,
hard as calcite,
and thick as pitch-blend.

Lived in grey millstone
by erections of whinsill
and outcrops of sandstone.

He was a blunt flint,
a dull scaly shale,
a soft piece of slate.

WEEK 63

(i) THE SOLDIER AND THE VIRGIN

He put his eggs between her legs
and dipped his soldier sin.

305

She was pale and yellow
as he broke the yoke within.

He beat her hard and curtly,
he whipped his weapon round.
She was warm and runny
as he gorged and finger wound.

Shelled, ash, and lint white,
he crushed her fey remains.
She chalk gone to powder,
he boiled to rape again.

(ii) **AS TALL SHIPS DEPART**

Erstwhile tall ships depart, arrive
around the world of seaboard fringe
where hearts akin to wind and wave
speed farewell and haste return
to parts dry-marshed or thistle-downed
that have not heard the call of tern
nor whale nor seal nor ocean sprites
that sail far-off beyond our ken.

And we who wait and dream of storm
and wreck upon some wrecker's rock
midst gale and tempest lashing hard
on minds beset by fear of loss,
we bar and bolt our flimsy doors
against the angry hail of night
and sleep unwary of the deep
run by ships in hunt or flight.

'Till home they come, and drop and rock
in haven, harbour, quay, or dock.

'Till tall masts sway like beeches
along the margined strand they break,
the captains on the bridge-decks sing
and tack about their sea-dog days …
and still the lubbers stand about
and gaze wide eyed-about the lee,
and shipwrecked souls roll or stroll
around the birch, and elm, and shore.

While other dry-jack-tar-chips
wistfully whistle subtle tunes,
the tall ships lean against the wind;
their flags set-out to bruise the sky
to wing like gulls afore a gale ..
to travel where no black wing dares;
till all is calm and safely back,
Charmed, and chained, and anchored there.

Where time slips by like no-one knows
and ships return like wolves to lair.

WEEK 64

(i) **WAITING IN LIMBO**

And always we must return
to the Undergraduate ... unbaptised
caught in Limbo ... his studies
like some task on the edge of Hell.

And if he breaks his chains like some Prometheus
dispossessed of Olympic fire?
Or if he overturns the columns like some Samson
dispossessed of all his strength,
will he bring down the roof of that abode
so called ... The University?

What then? Will not his Hell
become the ends of all labour?

No! Into chaos sink the misdirected
void of heart and mind to pain,
into dark and depthless chasms

fall the weary, weak, and worn
of struggle, weight, and burden laden
on them strapped great bales of straw

each sheaf a thousand lengths of timber
each fag ten chords of sawn log.

Without end, through-out time,
without time, beyond all end,
through ethered air, without grass

nor ground, nor solid living mass,
for all is dead, and black and hums
of corpses burnt, bled, or hung.

And this ... when nightmares haunt
the lax and lazy lolling student,
this is his Hell, his sinful fix
from which he wakes to find his books
closed and stacked, his notebook blank,
his thoughts unformed about his work

while stern Abe Stone his tutor broods
like Satin waiting ... set to cast
another erring student term-time down.

Yet ... in innocence of all misdemeanour
like the nightingale at dusk,
song issues from our Undergraduate.

In deference of cold hard reality,
sweet words vibrate off his pursed lips
zipped upon the latest modern air.

The refrains lilt his worries skyward
like a lark soaring free -
they lift him on the south-west breeze
rising up from out the far West Ocean
where once his childhood gamed on sands.

Now adverse to the strands of universe
that the teachings of demented bards
expound like surf upon Time's rock –
he walks ...
he mocks ...

he knocks upon the door of learning
which he finds closed and barred,
cobwebbed like some great cellar

where shrewd and greedy men hoard
the wine that unlocks the inhibitions
that block mankind from truth and wisdom.

(ii) **VINO**

If vino is the drink of Gods and poets,
there is no dispute ... men of wealth
sip the grape and swill the berry
while lesser men of fortune go thirsty
or quench their wants with hops and barley

mashed, but not strained to perfection,
not sipped and tasted unto vintage,
not aged in vaults in seasoned casks,
but served from vats like common feed
of husbandry .. with earthy modesty
and slop dispensed as honest beverage
for the breed of lower beast
cast by fate into lesser human order
maintained by those of higher birth
irrespective of genius, beauty, honour,
Pride, concern, conscience, love or learning ...

(iii) **WE ARE THE OXBRIDGE MEN**

We are the Oxbridge men.
We go up. We come down.
We end up running London Town.

Stock and state!
We take our share!
We carve it up medium rare!
We are the Oxbridge men!!

Nothing ever changes.
Beginning without end,
End without start.
Doesn't matter if you're smart,
You'll end up with nothing.
If you're nothing at birth,

You'll have nothing at death.
We are the Oxbridge men!

We have the fortunes!
We have the wealth!
Give up on money ..
Grow potatoes instead.
This is our advice -
For we are the Oxbridge men!

Bonds and chains!
We run estates!
We run the place!
So know your place,
We're not your mates!
We are the Oxbridge men!!

We are the Oxbridge men!

(iv) **OUR GODS ARE MORTALS**

Oh what dark rumblings can be heard
from behind the clouds shielding Olympus!
Today .. our Gods are all mere mortals
implementing tyranny like pseudo Titans.

Where is that fire Prometheus gifted us?
Around us dim shadows flirt in half light.
Where is the torch to guide the good man
as he emerges from the swamp of nationhood?
May such lesser beings free their will
seek their wildest dreams on equal terms?

Yet some wriggle free ...
No! The Titans interfere ... enslave!
No! The Titans doom all mortal kind to Limbo!

(v) **THE UNDERGRADUATE**

He gets his chance, his nibble
at the Stilton and the Camembert,
the reckless olives served with endive,
before his grant wanes to peas,
beans, chips, and cheap mince pies,
muesli base without nuts,
porridge oats, and lentil rice,
tahini toast, rye crisp bread,
Typhoo tea, and boiled eggs,
Pasta, paste, and boiled veg,
Lifeless, salty, starchy stew,
Madras, Bombay, Vindaloo,
he'd give a dog to chew.

While his studies ...
like some task in Hell
wait in Limbo .....

309

WEEK 65

Punctuality is the virtue of the board,
And tardiness the vice of the game.

(i) **IT MAY RAIN** ...

It may rain in Spain,
but England never changes!
It never nears the paradise we seek
when on vacation.
It never quite sustains our want
to shed our winter clothes
and bare ourselves strong and naked
on the sands of Whitley Bay,
Bournemouth, Rhyl, or Morecambe.

(ii) **WE WHALE WHITE BRITS**

We catch on time our morning trains
Yet arrive too late to catch the sun.

We wan and waste whale white Brits,
we sit before our fires and freeze,
our blotch red cheeks blue-vein cracked,
our joints arthritic, stiff, and knacked.
All wrack rheumatic, pinched, and hagged,
we huddle nursing heart attacks.

(iii) **HAPPY HUBBY HOME**

From eight to five we log and clock;
From five to eight we wait for work.

Happy hubby home to happy housey goes
to waiting wishful whole-some model wifie.
They smile sweetly with the morning separation
expecting every evening's joyful re-uniting.

What Perfect Bliss! What Bon Accord!
God made the world for such love!

Until, home hubby came one noon
and in their house found his wife
wrapped round the torso of another hubby.

Lord! What Fate! What Bad Timing!
How long has model wife been double-timing?

The other hubby Spanish brown and beetroot,
in a jiffy panted, but unbuttoned,
gathering up his tails in a panic,
said "I'm off! It's coffee at the office!"
But almost out the door he scanned
his season pass lying on the carpet.

The erring lover swift returns!

310

Folly feeds on such dumb stuff!

Angry cheated hubby cruelly quick
seized cheating hubby and did him in.
Screaming model wifie called the police
Can you imagine such a scene!

One dead! One jailed! and wife possessed!
All on account of a season-pass!

WEEK 66

THE STRAGGLER

It is so easy to fall behind
Everyone, and everything,
until there is no present
only the will to recollect
what should have been
and shall not ever be.

WEEK 67

Cold English rain upon our lips,
You chill us with your winter kiss.

KUMQUATS

Night ... it drops in half-cast grey,
the yellow street lights hazed
behind the spray of fruit trucks
bowling north to Scotland.

I watch and dream parch mouthed
and think of kumquats, guavas, avocados
rolling up to Glasgow,
to be unloaded ripe at market.

For these are things I never saw
nor tasted in my childhood dreams,
these were left 'til travelling days
took me far to luscious gardens

where resplendent fruit rained and dripped
and soaked the earth with sensual ease,
until I was taught to balance waste
as Nature's will to please itself.

For I was want to think of fruit
as Man's reward for being first
in need of Nature's sweetest food,
But soon it was explained to me -

all creatures share in Nature's gift.
And I, with Northern childhood gone,
saw kumquats as a fruit for all,
and tasted kumquat, ate my fill.

311

And as I watch the trucks haul north,
the dark November night now black;
I taste the kumquat in my mouth,
and guava, avocado, forms a part -

of all the taste my travelling taught
which ample childhood did not teach,
nor knew existed in my North
of berry, briar, and Scottish mist.

WEEK 68

THE SEVEN SISTERS

There are many things books cannot tell of.
There are many worlds poets cannot dwell in.

The Seven Sisters ... Alice, Annie,
Betty, Dot, Mary, Vicky, Violet ....
fell out from Hospital heaven
and went on a big dipper ride with me
around the snow topped Northumberland waste
in a light blue mini-bus with insignia
on the side which read 'Health Authority';
and although nobody stared in the country,
when we got to Rothbury, everybody looked
and wondered why seven old ladies
were wandering up and down the High Street
in the freezing cold of late November.

But the girls didn't notice a thing
as they sat on two park benches
and I took their photos for posterity ..
when all of a sudden, a rave-mad dog
came bulling helter-skelter across the grass
and tried to knock Dotty to the ground!
What a beast! I chased it off;
but the thing came back as Alice shouted
"Dot! Dot! Wartch out!" and I kicked it
in the teeth so hard I heard a crack,
but the thing ran on and barked,
and barked so loud, I went to the owner
standing all dumb and stupid with his chain
and said "There's a phone-box! Put the mutt
on the lead! Or I'll call the cops!",
and the bloke swore at me, and meanly
commanded his dog "Get him. Get him!",
but the smart dog, hurting in the mouth
ran circles round and round me
till the thing was spent and sore
worn out and tired and crushed
and only half the rave-mad beast
he was before he went for Dot ...
who hadn't even seen or heard him
whooshing-by just inches from her ankles.

But Alice had, and Vicky holding
Violet's arm had seen it all,
and tried now to tell her all about it.

But, well, Dot's the least with it of the Sisters.

Annie's eyes are bad, she's almost blind.
Betty's usually dreaming or half-asleep.
Mary likes to sing all the time
I could hear 'Kitty Kelly's Daughter'
as the punter's dog attacked.

But the threat was over, the punter
took his dog away on his chain.
I didn't watch him go, my eyes
were down the camera on the sisters
posing for me in the Rothbury cold.
Click! One more for old posterity,
then we joined hands, and crossed
the road to the seven-day cafe
famous in the North for being open
on Sundays all year round.

Two young boys stood at the counter
sweeties in their hands, fingers
scraping the frost off the ice-box,
"What's that say, mister?" one lad
pointed to a giant cardboard-cone.
"Cornetto" I said, and he grinned,
and I asked "No school today?"

They shook their heads and giggled
when I said "Teachers on strike, I bet".
One pointed out the window, other said
"Oh no, it snowed this morning!"
"School was called off!"
"We live up the tops. Over there!"

Both pointed out the window
beyond the Cragside trees to the bare hills,
and as the boys turned to be served
I helped the sisters slide along
the pine bench-seats of the empty cafe
while one boy asked the lady owner
for the ice-chocs on the ice-box chart
by pointing and saying "Two please".
The owner couldn't see what it was
that the young lads wanted.
She was on the other side of the ice-box.
We all laughed, and the two lads,
now red-faced, plunged their heads
into the ice-box to ease their embarrassment.

Good-natured they emerged and parted
with the change burning in their hands.
They said goodbye as I ordered
five milk coffees and three teas

313

from the lady owner eyeing the old ladies
with a look that slightly disapproved
of the Sisters sitting quietly waiting
for the drinks they'd come twenty miles
to spend their twenty pences on.

But soon she came around to view
them as the lovely Sisters that they are,
and asked me why they were so subdued,
I said "They're quiet because they're old".
This truth seemed to hit the owner
as a thought she'd never contemplated
and put her instantly at ease.

We were in the cafe quite awhile,
and as three o'clock drew closer
the cafe filled with afternoon custom
that either seemed disturbed by the Sisters
or failed to notice them at all.

Mary sang a song, I forget what.

Dot inspired by Mary's singing,
sang one of the three songs she knows.
Alice talked about her hair-do,
and Annie a little more about her eyes.
Violet, always silent, laughed,
and Betty *tete-a-tete* with Vicky
chewed on fruit pastilles she had got
me to buy with her seventeen pence
before we left the cafe and went
for a walk down Rothbury High Street
in the freezing cold of winter.

They loved it. We loved it.
We talked with three tied up dogs
and said hello to every passing child
and felt that Christmas was in the air,
and walked down to the river
where they posed by the bridge
in the biting wind for another picture
that would prove that we had been
to Rothbury one icy winter's day.

And though there were no photographs of me,
when finally we stood on the High Street
dancing to music from the cassette
recording of Glenn Miller we had along,
although we all froze and our noses dripped
as we waited for the mini-bus
that would take us back to Northgate,
I knew I would need no photographs
to remember the day I took the Seven
Sisters to the seven-day cafe in Rothbury.

And as the sun went down, and
the full moon rose out of the North Sea,

we travelled back silent, and cold,
but inside flamed a light and warmth
that matched the blazing orbs of heaven
we could almost touch as we crossed
the high moors of bleak Northumberland.

And as darkness fell, the other Seven Sisters
twinkled in the folding day, and
pointed us in the direction of home.

WEEK 69

December's here. This time of year
Undergraduates stay in bed.

(i) **BED**

Dog-down hoe raked
rough shod over ridden
black hell flat backed
cat-gut mouse tailed
cool cruel tip-toed
pit cut gob filled
dark down air caught
bed sore dead bum
numb tongue lead head
dick stiff limp legged
Bed, bed, bed!

(ii) **OTHER WORLDS**

Other notions, other times,
Sequenced, travelling on
through age predestined,
era held determined.
Movement, motion, matter
Made, destroyed, made,
Destroyed, created out
Beyond, within an end,
a destination, pre-defined,
re-embarked, disengaged
upon arrival ....

(iii) **LIFT UP YOUR EYES ....**

In the bleak December chill
the coke-smoke drifts ...

The South-West blows upon
the slate-cloud, wet and dark,
it casts a smoke-blue shadow
on the red-brick pit-rows

The miners hold their ears
to halt the singing of the wind
howling babies huddle into breasts
of mothers hauling laundry

315

Weary round-back-shouldered,
skin-sagged, puff-red tears
roll down shuttered eye-lids
and streak wind flayed cheeks.

The harsh December cat-in-lash
tan-hides their impaired hearing.

The miners dream of hearing angels
with their wan angelic singing.
Will it take a summer sun
to ease their beastly burdens?

The winter wind has no voice,
mute, it is a silent brute
bent to bend and cock-a-snoot
in mischief in the pit-row smoke.

And blow, and blow, and blow
about and on the miners going
head-on up long valley slopes
red-brick row, pit-house row.

Row, row, and row row row,
no curve, no crescent green, no park,
no tree to break the chimney line,
the grey-slate wet of time.

The miners hold their ears in pain,
who can tell what they hear?
Eyes that scrape the step of time
never climb to see the sky ...

O lift up your eyes!!

WEEK 70

(i) WHO ARE YOUR FAVOURITE POETS, LAD?

Who are your favourite poets, lad?
Whose influence sparks your verse?
Who taught you how to elegise?
Who shaped your line and length?
Who showed you how to satirise?
Who trained you in such words?

Why sir, it was God himself
Who taught me style and length!
God it was who gifted me
Gave rhythm to my words!
God it was who married me
To poetry, line and verse!

Who is my favourite poet, sir?
Why - God, the bard, who else!

(ii) GOOD MORNING ROBIN

Little robin bobbing hopping
through the white frost morning,
Charlie said your bright red breast
thawed the chilling winter.
I said I thought your chirpy song
split the morning sleep.
We slumbered on, rose, and broke
some breadcrumbs for your supper.
Oh bright red thing! How I think
we'll greet the spring together.

(End of The Undergraduate – Term 7)

NOVEMBER FOREST
[11th November 1985, Newcastle-upon-Tyne]

The lime tree lemon bitter stands
Beside the beech sandy leaved,
The chestnut reigns in the breeze,
The aspens shiver ill at ease,
The larch droops yellow in the frost,
The willows sag, and weep, and creak.

The lichen grey, and green and dark
Like carpet layers wind-chaffed bark,
And branches bare against the sky
Where spruce and pine, and fir tree rise,
Shed their needles, cones and sap,
Drift, and thud, splat and crack!

Like treasure on the forest floor,
Acorns, nuts, hard berries hide
Beneath the aural autumn glory,
Beneath the gold and amber foliage,
Scratch the mouse, rabbit, deer,
The fox and squirrel, as winter nears.

FORLORN
For Frances
[5th January 1986, Sandyford, Newcastle]

What beauty takes us from ourselves
to leave us where we've never been?
What love can make us break old vows
and make us want for purer things?
What tears may fall to make us cry
for joy at all this glorious earth?
Tell me, please, I do not know
what makes love and lovers so.

THE UNDERGRADUATE - TERM 8
COLD WINTER
[21st Jan- 27th Mar 1986]

Prologue

LAY ME THERE

There is none but what there is
before it began.

Take me down
the river of life until
time flows by like a kite
hovering over winter fields
edged by trees standing bare
in the twilight of evening.
Carry me there.

Carry me forth
upon the warm south wind
until I cross brown hills
fly over verdant pasture
enclosed by thick hedgerow
thriving with nature.
Bear me there.

Bear me along
the floor of long valleys
that stretch from a sea
gull hung to greet me from
white cliff and tide-wash
by jutting out headland.
Lay me there.

Lay me deep
where silence fells day
not far from white fall
stream banked by hawthorn
on thistle-down mountain
clover vetch crowned.
Leave me there.

WEEK 71

THE TOWER OF WORST VERSE

The worst verse
collected all together
towered to the moon
and round and back
and onwards to the sun.

Beneath that tower
eager critics hovered
dizzy at the height.
Caught short of breath,
they lit the fire.

Ablaze, the taper
crackled to the moon
and round and back.

Onwards to the sun
burnt the awful stuff.

Ten million miles
away from planet Venus,
the verse burnt out.
Earth was left
with only good verse.

The children played,
adults stood amazed
at the pile of debris.
Someone made a joke
but none were made.

They'd all gone up
in the tower of smoke,
so no-one spoke,
no-one could think
or remember any.

Worried critics frowned
nervous of their choices.
They thought of verses kept,
one's they'd burnt
or might have saved.

In panic they hurried
with pen and paper
to collect all they could
before time erased
all bad verse for good.

They talked to poets,
idiots, and old folk,
recorded every line,
noted every rhyme,
collected them together.

Until the new verse stood
towering to the moon
and round and back
and onwards to the sun
beyond, and back, forever.

WEEK 72

THE FIELD HOSPITAL

Behind each screen
lies a story,
a book of scenes
unfolded in sequence
to present the whole,
the complete picture.

With each scream

rises a confusion,
a scar of blanks
compounded out of order
to expose the numbness,
the bloody horror.

WEEK 73

FEBRUARY

The alabaster weather
drifting,
the hungry starlings descending
dropping,
on to the winter-store
dripping.

The hawthorned garden
berried,
lower branches laden,
laying,
on the white-carp-pond
frozen.

WEEK 74

LILY

A petaled flower,
who drifted at ease
upon an un-rippled surface.

Her delicate skin
when waft by the wind
was moon-white and shiny

Her cheeks fairy pink,
contrasted her eyes
the colour of envy.

WEEK 75

(i) SNOW, SNOW

Snow, snow,
fall slowly on me,
bury, bury me
deep in your quiet.

Soft, soft
lie so on me,
hide, hide me
forever in your peace.

Settle, settle,
light on me
heavy, heavy,

conceal me with your flakes.

(ii) SNOW IS COMING

If February were not so cold,
nor berries black on blackened hedgerow,
would we listen for the blackbird's
caution "Snow is Coming!".

If February were not so dark,
nor elm trees bare, oaks crack-barked,
would we laugh at our blackbirds'
calling "Snow is Forming!!".

Yet February is cold and dark,
the bare skyline is cast and stark,
we dare not miss the blackbird's
warning "Snow is Falling!!!".

WEEK 76

(i) FINALLY

As a first year undergraduate,
my obsession for poetry
was also an obsession
with study and student life.

As an aging sophomoric,
my delight was sex,
with drugs and alcohol,
and things of the flesh.

As a mature finalist,
my canon was respect,
knowledge, the freedom
to move on and forget.

(ii) WEEK SEVENTY SIX STUDIES

This week I've been pounding Arnold,
having a go at insincere elegiac,
looking at Masefield, Bridges, and J.B.,
poets of cloth, not substantially plebeian,
men of culture, not anarchy.

(iii) GYPSY DREAM

Far off, I hear gunshots ring,
and hand-held hounds barking fiercely,
I look about me, no-one's looking.

Nature wells in me like water
in a vase upon a sideboard,
but flowers drink my body
as I think upon a flood.

I am alone, an eagle on a mountain,
below me ... frozen lakes
rimmed with nature's spittle.

I groom my ruffled thoughts,
gather the flowers feasting in me
and throw them, stem rotten,
down my trash-can mountain.

They scatter on the lake,
until the thaw sets them drifting
in a toothpaste foam.

I wander the margin of shore
fern, wood-rush, garlic,
beneath the dry still oaks
I lie immortal.

(iv) **RACING ON TO MARS**

Men of war racing on to Mars.
Sickle star red banner rockets
submarines of spatial ocean
aging Argonauts birthing knowledge.

Submarines of spacial ocean.
Where the reeds? Where the coral?
Where the beasts of astral atoll?
Creatures basking in clear shallow?

Sea of stars without strand,
journey out without end,
sojourn on into dark
floating in a void of shadow.

Through the vast cosmos going
onwards daily to tomorrow
on to strange unknown border
chaos new beyond old order.

Submarines of spacial ocean,
time sits on standing shuttles,
lies in dreamy empty thoughts
fixed upon furthest harbours.

(v) **IN THIS ROOM**

In this room
I take my pleasure,
With this hand
I clasp together,
All alone
I clap forever.
Let me do or die.

In this house
I make my laughter,

With this mouth
I reap and gather,
All alone
I smile forever.
Let me do or die.

In this town
I break my anger,
With this foot
I kick and scatter,
All alone
I smash forever,
Let me do or die.

In this world
I wake my father,
With this heart
I date my mother,
All alone
I grieve forever,
Let me do or die.

In this church
I fake my worship,
With this mind
I kneel tight-lipped,
All alone
I pray forever,
Let me do or die.

WEEK 77

(i) THE FURIES

Many feasts Menara saw,
stole bread from Thesiphone,
friendship based on virtue
leads to death by vice.

The up-so-down condition
root in passionless lust,
Alecto's bow-strung arrows
pierce such hapless love.

(ii) WINTER

Winter take me from my confess
to the execution wall,
about me wail the furies
frothing on my wrongs.

Free me from my confines
at the gate of freedom's dawn,
around me woe the sirens
with hiss and spitting song.

Blow me wind in confide

to the throne beyond recall,
around me wing the cherubs
with whistle, word, and sword.

WEEK 78

(i) THE MARCH STRIKE

O Ireland! Ireland!
native Celtic blood spills
and stains humanity.

What hatred! loathing!
Love your countrymen.
No! slay them!

The shadows of the clans
haunt the 'no-goes',
death shades the sunlight.

Strike! Kill! Murder!
sick, hollow-eyed
rampage the ignorant!

O Ireland! bleeding!
heal your gaping wounds,
crush your angry fever.

(ii) DERWENTSIDE RESERVIOR

Wide, crimson-grey
breeze calm still
wild fowl cast,
larch bare margined

iced last week,
now peat-brown,

thorn-hedge wall
rain-waxed stoned
grass soft-earth
snow-hash hollow.

spring-kissed wet
bud-sprig full,
bird flight wild,
south wind flown.

WEEK 79

KIELDER

Out there ....
there is a forest
man-made, gigantic.

In here,

there is light,
artificial, comfortable.

Indoors, my heart pines.
Tired limbs, weary,
slumber on desire.

The ravens silent,
the forest creaks ...
a lapwing dips,

soars and dips,
the lichen rocks
ancient and sentinel.

Felled forest brush,
bare winter gorse
tree-line break.

WEEK 80

(i) THE EYE OF A TROUT

Time rolls on like thunder.
Imagination outstrips imitation.
Form and context
Wither in the light of summer.

Urban decay recedes
With each view of country.
War is for lesser mortals.
Peace, harmony, surrender.

Images are refracted
As pictures disjointed.
Worlds are created,
Synthesised and ordered.

Beauty and balance,
Comfort in a flower,
Love in a river
And in the eye of a trout.

(ii) WITHOUT PART

Brain without reason,
mind without body,
thought without logic,
sense without object.

Hand without digit,
arm without muscle,
foot without measure,
leg without tissue.

Middle without centre,

heart without core,
blood without colour,
flesh without whole.

(End of The Undergraduate – Term 8)

WE ARE SMALL CREATURES
[25th April 1986, Helmsley Rd, Newcastle]

We are small creatures,
The sea is our love,
The sky and the ocean,
The waves and the rocks.

We are small creatures
And we are just young.

Carry me wind, carry me sea,
tarry me not, dally me none.
Wing me away, bear me away
high over lands and far empires.

Call up cloud, call up wave,
float me aloft, soak me soft.
Blow me wild, wash me wide,
far before storm and wet cyclone.

THE UNDERGRADUATE - TERM 9
ESCAPE FROM THE TOWER
[22nd April - 27th June 1986]

WEEK 81

OLD MEN WIDOWED

Individuals, struggle on exhausted,
fatigued beyond rejuvenation.

Old men widowed, soldier on,
tend small flowering cacti,
weed beds of daffodils

with bodies stiff
and wills too weak,
they wait for late-spring
to set the geraniums,
get at the roses

while ill-mates in pain
linger in bed, dreaming
of companions waiting
in Eden or heaven.

WEEK 82

WATENDLATH ROAD
[3rd May 1986, near Ashness, Cumbria]

Rain on Ashness;
celandine, violet, and sorrel,
bullfinch call, wagtail hop,
Derwentwater in a mist,
birch trees barely leaved,
gorse-top touched yellow,
sun peeking over crag sky,
wild bee, midge, blackfly,
scent of bark, of stone,
of moss, of fern uncurling,
green in variegated brown.

WEEK 83

(i) CAESIUM ONE-THREE-SEVEN
[7th May 1986, Newcastle]

Thirty years from now,
half of what has fallen
will still be halving.

A week ago Chernobyl blew;
lovely iodine one-three-one
and caesium one-three-seven.

Today it rained thirteen times;
never saw the sun at all -
grey, grey, grey.

Couldn't drink the water;
have any milk and cereal;
rem count was hundred over normal.

Thirty years from now:
caesium one-three-seven -
half will still be there, halving.

(ii) TO WORDSWORTH
(7th May 1986, Newcastle)

Wordsworth, were you living in this hour:
England would disgust you with her marsh
Of murky waters: bomb, missile, and flash
Of fire: unwanted misdirected unheroic power
Which railroads; dictates; makes cowerers
Of her own people. We are wrecked; awash.
Corrupt men dissect our diseased nation:
Use tissue, flesh, in barter for sour
Upkeep of order; democratic freedoms.
Lake, tree, flower, creature, sky:
In your time were whole and healthy; high
Mountains once safely climbed to cloud;
Water fresh to drink; in our kingdom
Now leave us sick, unhappy, and unproud.

(iii) THE SEVENTH ART

Image on image,
language of vision,
language without words.

Montage of meaning
to guide, lead thought.

Composite pictures,
accelerated time,
parallel shadows,
attraction by like.

Each image a painting,
a thousand sounds,
aesthetic edit,
realist long-pan,
immediate copy
across imaginative span.

A hand-wave,
a fading smile.

This is the dark,
the celluloid end,
the composite picture,
the whole and the part
montage and image
of the seventh art.

WEEK 84

THE BOOK JUST CLOSED
[17th May 1986, Newcastle]

Between the book just closed
and the action of a hand
stretched to take a hold
of yet another volume,

two blue eyes stare ...

they watch me haul a thought
across my pale ploughed brow

two grey-blue eyes ...

that halts me in my labour
through the blue of summer

eyes that greyly cloud

the grafting hours I've spent
tilling miles of tract,
the long lays of text
that ruts the fields of fact.

Grey, grey, she gazes ...

Vacant, empty, back I stare,
and reach, but stop,
and rise and stretch,
and touch her hair,
her hand, her breast,
and with a kiss,
I close her eyes,
and go with her beyond my books,
and go with her to
where ..

... flowers light the earth,
and bees, and birds wing
upon the happiness of day,
and sunshine streams, beams
and plays wild upon the sound
of river, burn and stream,

and pools of weed,
reed and birch,
and ash and elm,
where turkey oak
edge a hedge
verge a road
heading for a wild coast
or some wrath ocean
of white wave toss
and salt scent breeze
on which a gull
carries free, and drops
into a boundless sea
all the books
that hang to me

The grey eyes smile,
return to blue,

Free I see
the waves of love,
books are fields
of fallow stuff.

WEEK 85

WHAT ABOUT MY BROTHER
[21st May 1986, Newcastle]

See him dying yonder in Kandahar,
and watch him starve in Eritrea.
Look at him slain in Nicaragua
while we wax fat in Surrey.

There's inequality everywhere,
everywhere I look,
I see the shame in sad men's eyes

and pity in their stare.

See him slave in Bangladesh
see him toil in barren Bolivia,
see him bend in hot Sri Lanka,
and martyred in South Africa.

There's injustice every place,
every place I've been,
anger in the eyes of men,
and hatred in their glare.

See him rich on Hampstead Heath,
and watch him stroll in Windsor's green,
see him lounge in Kentish pub,
snug and smug and warm.

Insensitive in every way,
everywhere I look,
avarice in the eyes of God,
and no God that's any good.
See men scream in every dream,
see each pass along Park Lane,
see each walk with oozing pain
the empty streets of shame.

Is this the face of brotherhood?
Is this how things must stand?
Have I rightly understood
the vision that I've had?

Is there love in Bethnal Green,
or faith in Cheney Walk,
or hope in pitch black Hackney
that men are born as one.

WEEK 86

SELECTIVE
[27th May 1986, Newcastle]

Selective,
the images emerge
within the frame
of consciousness.

Arbitrary,
without record,
visions fade
into eternity.

WEEK 87

(i) AXEMAN OR TREE?
[4th-5th June 1986, Newcastle]

Can I be the man I was

when words were blunt axes
on the trunk of other's wisdom?

Now, my blade wet keen
stands no match against
the metal walls of politics.

A life in the thickest wood
is no civil training
for survival in the clearing.

My axes stripped from me
I stand dazed
transformed into a tree.

(ii) THE SACRED MOUNTAIN
[7th June 1986, Schiehallion Rd, Perthshire.]

Burn, sun, burn,
the long summer light
drawing
behind the high Grampians.

Schiehallion, sacred mountain,
the ancient yews of Fortingall,
talk in the wind
of primeval memories.

Blazing orb, sinking,
catching the bens of Atholl,
shadowing the corries of Rannoch,
the sentinels of Erricht.

Red, silver, indigo,
sublime Swarga of the ancients,
burn, burn, and burn,
as the yew trees whisper.

White cloud lifting
from snowy ridges,
red, pink, marbled sky,
red, red, burning.

WEEK 88

COTSWOLDS - EARLY SUMMER
[14th June 1986, Stroud, Glos.]

Sun of bliss and happiness,
sunshine of my youth,
blue sky urban wilderness,
green grass, fragrant nooks,
shade of summer bower,
glades of cooling brook,
canals of duck and moor-hen,
swan, and grebe, and coot.

331

Breeze of joy and freedom,
waft of infant past,
clear-air rural tameness,
cowslip, milkwort, flag,
pools of summer eddy,
coomb's of damselfly,
vales of swift and martin,
swallow, finch, and lark.

WEEK 89

THE DEVON DAY SUBSIDED
[22nd June 1986, Bucks Mills, Devon]

Ever so meek,
the day drizzled open.
Summer rain fell.

Still, swelter noon
gave way to afternoon storm.

Sun emerged from hiding,
skies cleared, then clouded,
blackened, then poured.

Warm, chill, then cold
that's how the day subsided.

WEEK 90

THE CLASS OF '86
[27th June 1986, Newcastle]

Today I graduated.
The sun shines in all its glory,
I laze on the burn-tipped grass
while my contemporaries congregate
gowned and happy.

At last, three years strained,
I relax and feel the world before me
open like a lotus.

I gaze into the blue of heaven
so glad with joy,
I would not trade this sky
for all the world.

Let the role-call be made.
Now, no longer a class,
the class of '86,
Is part of history.

(End of The Undergraduate)

ON THE ROAD IN LAKELAND
[10.30pm, 4th May 1986, Sandyford, Newcastle]

Derwent, Grasmere, Coniston, Hawkshead,
Ambleside and Ullswater .....
roll off the tongue like a recipe for solitude ...
but 'Keep Out', 'No Parking', 'Private', 'Closed',
double yellow lines and ticket machines,
keep the cars rolling, and the hikers on the road.

I COUNT THE DAYS
[12 noon, 11th May 1986, Sandyford, Newcastle]

I count the days 'til I depart,
and who can say what's wrong with that.
My time in Newcastle's all but done,
the sands of time have had their run.

Day dream hours ill spent I sit,
but who can guess the cause of it.
Fourteen years have chained me fast,
now eddies turn, and shift, and pass.

I gaze upon the red brick rows,
and who can gauge what I know,
my footsteps vanish, the waters reach
the parts I've walked upon the beach.

THE WIDE DIVIDE
[11.30pm, 17th May 1986, Sandyford, Newcastle]

Romance is not sweet
when distance separates,
or time runs away
with intimacy.

Independent lovers
war and fight forever,
never lie embraced
in fields of clover.

Sweethearts faced with doubt
cry and tremble,
shudder, nervous
and uncommitted.

Emotion fired by anger,
rowing sleepless fight,
open-hearted whisper
across the wide divide.

LIKE A MAY MORNING IN KATHMANDU
[3pm, 24th May 1986, Ouseburn, Newcastle]

The daffodils barely gone;
thrush and blackbird song
rose higher than the sparrow hawk.
Dragonfly flirted on the hogweed.
Breeze-borne hawthorn blossom

and wind-blown nettle flower
drift-caught in the burn.

Elder swaying, bramble trembling,
dock leaf and glass-blade twitching -
bee and wasp nectar hunted
dandelion bright and blinding.
Oh what a welcome late May dawning!
Fresh air-scent, water babbling,
soil damp, sun fire-warming -
like a Kathmandu bright morning.

LOCH TAY IN JUNE
[8th June 1986, Loch Tay]

Violet and primrose,
stitchwort and bugle,
dandelion and daisy,
anemone and thistle.

FROM THE PANDON ROOM
[9th June 1986, Civic Centre, Newcastle]

From across the Great North Road,
in the Pandon Room of the Civic Centre,
I gaze sleepily on my former University,
stoic red-brick, atheistic concrete.

Old Father Tyne, green-copper rusted
Drips Kielder water from his finger,
Wind whispers through the Council dome,
The ducks' feathers ruffle in the moat.

Wearily my eyes close out the Town Moor;
The rush-hour summer traffic rumbles by
to blend the snorting of the Sea-Horse Heads
with the 'Blaydon races' of the Tower Bells.

I slumber in the D-Day heat,
The Union clock clicks past six -
The Banquet Hall echoes time
As in a dream, or sleep, I sit.

I USED TO RHYME
[9th June 1986, Newcastle]

I used to rhyme all the time
but now I try a different style,
instead of rhyme's alternate lines
I drop the metre curtly.

If this makes my verse unsound
and rough, and does the lyric in,
then the gain is in the lost and found
of accentuated meaning.

AGE DAY

[9th June 1986, Newcastle]

Sitting …
choir rising.
Waiting …
Forties songs soaring.
Dreaming …
old age on its way.

THE BOYS COMING HOME
[30th June 1986, Newcastle]

We keep the lights on,
wide-eyed we hear voices,
higher than heaven
the boys coming home.

It seems senseless at first,
men, like fine sand, run -
we move on truth,
it leaves only a few.

We hear the engines,
time slips by as light,
turn on the TV,
the nightmare is out.

They slip by beyond us,
will we blow our brains out?
Every window curtained,
may we bury our children?

We stick to our notions,
hungry men stranded,
as into our gardens
we dream of far mountains.

They won't come for us,
it is a fantasy -
our boys coming home
with their bombing done.

AN EVENING IN JULY
[11.30pm, 25th July 1986, Sandyford, Newcastle]

Where are the whispers,
the gentle sighs of children?
Is this the miss?
The thing gone adrift?
Where are the nymphs
by the pools of glass?
Hear we the pipes?
Scent we the flowers?
Where are the Muses,
the makers of music?
Where do they hide?
What do we sense in

the touch of dusk dew?
The smell of the night?
The lure of the wild?

FIVE BIRTHDAYS ON
for Laura
[29th July 1986, Sandyford, Newcastle]

Five birthdays on the summer lingers,
memories rise, but good times stay,
the Royal would-be's live and mirror
all that will be history.

While in some rotten Irish prison
lingers once what was a love,
some tangled soul caught in ideal
for a cause that's all but lost.

Every day and every rock-blow,
he sweats to serve the hated foe,
while maidenhood and pining lover
awaits for him afresh each dawn.

Where is that love that carried rivers
on towards the peace of sea?
When flowed the barge that ferried life
on the tide of kiss and freedom ?

And now, at thirty five she waits,
the river trickles, erodes soft rocks,
and still her lover, barred, imprisoned,
cannot yet break time's lock.

THE BERBERS
[23rd August 1986, Sandyford, Newcastle]

From cap-topped ridge
to valley stretch
they lead their goats to drink

with flute or sling or tribal song
upon the hills, the mountain cols
they go from stream to spring.

Their Berber blood,
their nomad lust,
their life of dust and wind.

BILLY JOE (song)
for Chris
[24th August 1986, Sandyford, Newcastle]

Billy Joe the pop idol,
tried to eat his fame,
the press shot him down
for getting on the heroin game.

Billy Joe the drug addict,
wrote all his songs in pain,
the judge sent him down
for shooting crack and H.

Billy Joe the prison convict
sang songs to the cons,
the guards beat him down
for getting it wrong.

Billy Joe the rehab hero,
shut up and played it straight,
the warden marked him up
an A1 in-mate.

Billy Joe the model prisoner,
spent a year in Durham jail,
the parole board decided
he was back on the rails.

Billy Joe the hip musician,
came out a wiser man,
and never touched the needle,
nor sniffed another gram.

WATERPITTS, SOMERSET
[4th Sept 1986, Manor Farm, Waterpitts, Quantocks]

At last, the green Quantock combes
enclose my summer days.
Chin-high nettles sway,
tap on our mobile-home.
Chickens brood or scurry,
horses snort and sneeze,
pea-fowl fuss and faddle
about us all the day.

DOWN ON THE DEVON SANDS
[9th Sept 1986, Branscombe, Devon]

And I too, lay naked there
on the beach of Branscombe,
Greece, or Spain, I'll have instead
the Devon Costa Brava!

Moaning sea and sighing gulls,
skies pure grey to yonder,
ticking breeze and breaking waves,
it was a lovely torture.

White chalk cliffs tumbled down
on chalets ruined and rotten
where pensioners transfixed by the swell
watched the bare and brawny.

Girls voices perfumed the air,
sweet laughter fed the coast,

337

cider swiggers crunched their crisps
and ice cream lovers snored.

Explorers paced the shingled shore
proud of being English,
they scowled at my naked bum
and damned the bloody British.

I lazed until the sun passed over
Branscombe's cliffs then under,
and left as clouds rose out the sea
and brought a touch of thunder.

THE BROOMFIELD BEECH
for Bridget McConville
[2nd Nov 1986, Waterpitts, Broomfield, Quantocks]

The copper beech, the Broomfield beech,
mature and tall, huge and round,
its branches latticed, locked, and stout.
Two centuries gone, aye, and more
it's whispered in the warm sunlight,
it's sighed in wind, in rain, and night,
it's creaked into the quite, cold white
of frost, of sleet, of snow, and like.
With laurel, chestnut, cypress, oak,
sprout and sprigged, specked and span,
the mighty beech, the Broomfield beech
has stood and been -strike or stroke-
a shield and screen -sheet or bolt-
by star, or moon, by twilight hour
with spread and shade, a sacred bower,
of copper leaf and silver bough.

IN HOLFORD COMBE
[4.30pm, 10th Nov 1986, Holforde Combe, Quantocks]

In Holford Combe, I climbed through oak
and made my way to Upright's hill,
and there I saw Wordsworth's Thorn,
more ancient than he saw it then.

I sat beside this tiny bush,
and gazing out, I saw the sea,
the coast of Wales beyond in haze,
the purple holms in silver mist.

And rising with the south-west wind,
I walked along the Quantock crest,
and saw to east the Parrett wynd
from Avalon to Quantoxhead.

Towards the beacon ridge I strode
Through the bracken, broom, and thorn,
beyond a cairn and Wilmot's Pool,
until the west spread out below.

And to the fore the Brendons rose
dark, more sombre than the clouds
rolling in on evening grey
from Exmoor and the Devon south.

And turning from the chill and night,
I started on the downward climb
through the oaks of Holford combe
and home towards the village lights.

THE SEVEN SISTERS OF COTHELSTONE
[3-4pm, 23rd Nov 1986, Cothelstone Beacon, Quantocks]

The sun in a beam, a flash, and a blinding,
shines upon the tumuli of Cothelstone Beacon
were like thirteen old women, the Seven Sisters
stand witnessing the acts of heathens.

The wind, in a howl, there shakes the moss
and the rain falls bitter and cutting;
the crooked sisters creak and lament their fate
crested on a hill so uninviting.

The worshippers come, but the sisters remain
through autumn, and winter, and spring,
and though summer brings hot baking days
the Sisters stand trapped in their ring.

THE FLAME IS OUT
[11.40pm, 30th Nov 1986, Waterpitts, Quantocks]

I feel like some piece of waste,
I cannot feel my inner flame;
I am extinguished, snuffed, put out,
Inside there burns no light.

I cannot yet escape my hearth -
the heat still gives a lingering warmth,
but every hour brings on chill,
I cannot yet rekindle life.

No little spark lingers on,
my fuel is black, charred, or ash,
my flame once my burning dream,
spent out, now, is gone.

THE DOLPHIN
[9.30pm,1st Dec 1986, Waterpitts, Quantocks]

The dolphin beached upon the sand,
I stood and watched and thought
I might wade into the icy waves
and set the creature on its way.

But no, I let some others come
and plunge into the winter tide,
I let them nudge the dolphin's snout

on towards the sea, and out.

When at last the creature reached
some water deep and clear of beach,
as the dolphin swam out free
an ocean welled in me.

PORTLAND BILL
[10.30pm, 1st Dec 1986, Waterpitts, Quantocks]

The spray, the spume, foamed and spat,
the black shags cracked and opened crab,
the winter wind blew and crashed
the crest and trough against the crag
and cliff of crumbling Portland.

The Channel lash, licked and smashed
the oolite lime and salt-washed linch,
the lifting gale threw and dashed
the heave and break against the link
and limb of lichened Portland.

CHRISTMAS JINGLE
[7th Dec 1986, Waterpitts, Quantocks]

Jingle, jangle, juggle, do!
Candle, bauble, trinket too!
Cards, cakes, pudding, phew!
Enough for me and you!

Got the holly? Got the tree?
Got the sherry? Got the beer?
Golly! What a lot of cheer!
Merry Xmas! Bon New Year!

THE BALLAD OF MEG GRAY
[8th Dec 1986, Waterpitts - 13th May 1988, Cothelstone]

He heard the sound of horses hooves
in the dead of night -
He tossed and turned and shouted out
'They've come for me tonight!'

His lover took him to her breast,
caressed his fevered brow -
'They'll not have you this morning light
or first they'll have my life.'

She rose and took a pistol out
and threw the shutters back -
'Who's there below in the yard?
Do you know the hour?'

The horses in the courtyard bucked,
their riders reigned them in,
but none would say who they were
or why they'd ridden in.

'Who are ye men?' she firmly called
'Who are ye black cloaked mob?
I have a pistol by my side
to use if none will talk!'

She caught the sound of whispered words,
then heard the leader say
'We look for a husband slayer!
We've heard he's come this way.'

'Who be ye men?' she asked again
'Which rich man be murdered now?
Who be this man you're looking for?
Why look you to this house?'

'We've heard' the leader of them said
'We've had it from a groom
that in your room hides John Black
who murdered your man Gray.'

'Is my husband murdered then?
I'll wear no black for him -
He was a swaying braggart man,
his love was forced and cruel.'

'Then open up this door, Gray wife!
for you have part in this!
We know you have the gigolo
behind your scarlet skirt!'

'I shall not slide a bolt for you,
be off beyond my walls!
I'll aim into the shadowed night
and one of you will fall!'

'You cannot scare us off like this,
we're here to serve the law.
Send him out before we fire
and send you to the Lord.'

'I'll gladly go' she boldly spoke
'I'll never give him up!'
She drew her pistol to the dark
but her lover cried out 'No!'

'Enough of this! I am here!
You may take me as you want,
but leave Meg Gray out of this,
she has done no wrong.'

'She is a common tavern whore!
She'll die with you tonight.
Let fire!' their leader shouted out
and pistols roared to life.

Death they brought to Meggie Gray,

341

she fell scarlet to the floor -
'O lover, do not tarry here,
they'll soon be through the door.'

'I will not leave, never, no!
No, never will I leave.
I've killed a man to have you thus
And fate has made it brief!'

'O John, O John, flee you must
or I die in vain for thee -
Leave me here upon the floor
and fly like the deer.'

'I will not leave you now' he cried
'Our fates are met in one -
Close your eyes and sweetly dream
of all our times as one.'

And as she lay there in his arms
the riders broke the door -
And as he kissed her on the lips
they took him with a roar.

'We have the adulterant murderer now!
We have him in our hands!
Take him to the oak outside,
we'll hang him good and high!

'John! John!' Meggie Gray called out
'We'll meet tomorrow morn.
We'll meet in summer sun and heat
and make love in the corn.'

'She's mad!' a rider shouted loud
'It's best we help her die.'
'Leave her be!' John screamed out
as a pistol pressed her brow.

A shot rang out through the dark
and Meggie sighed no more -
'Now take him to the hanging tree
and dispatch him to his whore.'

They took John out to the oak
and tied the noose about -
'Now we'll hear your final words
and then we'll have your life.'

He never spoke a single word,
his thoughts were all for Meg -
'We will meet in the corn
as soon as I am dead.'

They strung him up, sent him off
to spend his days in Hell -
and when cold and stiff and dead,

they threw him in a well.

Who can say what transpired
on the coming of the morn,
or whether John and Meggie Gray
made love in the corn.

But woe betide the married man
who treats his wife amiss -
for there are those who'll gladly kill
and die to have her kiss.

THE RAINBOW FARMS
[16th Feb 1987, Waterpitts, Somerset]

We are the Blue farm,
And Sapphire's our farmer,
Oh we are the Blue farm,
We're stubborn and glum.

We are the Red farm,
And Ruby's our farmer
Oh we are the Red farm,
We're silly and dumb.

We are the Yellow Farm,
And our farmer is Topaz,
Oh we are the Yellow Farm,
We're kind and love fun.

We are the Green Farm,
Emeralda's our farmer
We are the Green farm,
We're bossy old ones.

THE COTTAGER
[6th Mar 1987, Lower Terhill, Cothelstone, Somerset]

Oh Robert, need your sullen frown
Dark the days of Spring now born,
The sleet is but a passing gloom,
The wind is nothing but a storm.
Why sit you brooding by the fire?
Is it yew you burn for warmth?
Through green the evening molders on,
What is your ail? What works your thought?

For whilst you sicken by your hearth,
The laughter fills the village inn,
Though you might not liken beer,
There's comfort found in ingle nooks.
Yet sit you still, tense and bilged,
Nursing pains you self-inflict.
Tell me, Robert, I'll have the truth -
Is there sense in these dark moods?

And as your fire dims and whites,

343

The cold of night upon your back,
Do you wish that you could flee
The sleet of Spring, the gale of March,
To take upon some lengthy voyage,
A pilgrimage to some beyond?
Where gloom and wind and sullen storm
Are traded for a health of thought?

Oh Robert, will it turn you grey
To sit and pass your Springs like this?
Get you up, dowse the fire
And venture on the wind and rain.
Forget your brooding by the hearth,
Forget the yew you burn for warmth,
And though the sleet and stormy blast,
Get you down the hedge-rowed path.

See now, those hazel eyes alight,
Burn like all the northern stars,
See how a fresh kindled flame
Flares up in your knitted brow.
Here now the latch, your lively gait,
Stepping firmly off into the night;
As through the sleet and stormy blast
You set out for the village lights.

COTHELSTONE
[12th March 1987, Lower Terhill, Cothelstone, Somerset]

Cothelstone is a place for a poet -
The landscape cut with the knife of the artist,
The air has the quiet of a national park,
And the earth has the tread of the prehistoric.

I sit on the stoop of our cottage hide,
And bathe in the blaze of the first Spring heat;
The collie lies on the warm tile path
And the cat stalks a bird.

THE WILD MARCH WINDS
[27th March 1987, Cothelstone, Somerset]

On the Bagborough Road above Tilbury Farm,
One of Brown's beeches was down in the gales,
It cut off the road to Cothelstone Hill,
The old Saxon way to Seven Mile Stone.

I turned, descended by Lower Terhill,
Then on to Quelbec, past Cothelstone Arch;
A small ash lay felled by the Vicarage,
But I climbed the grade to the crest of the hill
To find a great elm blocking the road
That joined the way to Seven Mile Stone.

I turned, went down by Cushuish Cut,
Stopping to gather armfuls of kindling,
Then on to Kingston, along Lodes Lane

'Till at Broomfield Cross another impasse!
A colossal oak tree straddled the way,
Hedgerows smashed and many trees felled.

The lane, deep cut - I passed under the oak
Reached the cross at the edge of Fyne Court,
There met a lad on the Duckpool Road
Who told me - six beeches were down!
The only way out was by Broomfield Hill
By the lane that leads to the Enmore Road.

Up, then down towards Smocombe and Barford,
A huge larch lay slain on Enmore Green,
The water of Durleigh looked like a sea,
The Quantocks, now a chaos of felled trees.
Surely I'll remember March Eighty Seven
And the twenty-seventh day for the fallen.

SLEEPLESS NIGHTS
[16th April 1987, Cothelstone, Somerset]

He who takes sleep for granted
Goes through life like a dream.
He who works night and day
Suffers, pain, distress and fights
To overcome the anguish plight
Of a sleepless, torturous life.
Rest, rest from the flickering flame.
Drink, sip your phials of ethanol.

THE QUITTER
[21st April 1987, Cothelstone, Somerset]

Inside my heart, my belly, my bowels,
There is a voice that whispers 'Quitter!'
At first I could not hear the voice,
But slowly as the weeks went by
I heard the voice grow like a storm,
Until now I dread the nightly echoes,
The ringing in my ears 'Quitter! Quitter!'

Perhaps you might think I'm ill,
For I cannot say that I am well
When I have this voice inside my head
Shouting 'Quitter!' You are a Quitter!'

I cannot run away from what's inside me!
I cannot silence the voice that haunts me!
My belly cramps and knots and gags,
My mind turmoils, boils and gasps
And gives out - 'I am a quitter!'

THE QUAY
For Jane
[25th May 1987, Mumbles, Swansea]

Out on to the promenade,

We walked our love around the quay,
And there where sea and sea-wall meet,
We found a shelter from the waves.

And lip to lip we kissed the tide,
Breast to breast we lingered hours,
The breeze, the salt, the in-rush spray,
All alone the night was ours.

The city lights strung the bay
As dusk fled in from the sea,
And night fell on the quay -
We rejoined the promenade.

DINEVOR
For Jane and Dawn
[20th June 1987, Mumbles, Swansea]

By sycamore and nettle path
With wine and female friendship,
A troubled sky easing past
We climbed from Deilo's pasture,
Preceded by a wind bourn host
Bent to summer madness.

The River Towy wound below,
We skipped and crossed the motte,
Vertical to the milling sky
Ivy-walled rose the fort,
A fortress mount, a Norman keep
Enclosed by fern and oak.

In fleeting bursts summer broke
Through the violent Ambrose cloud,
Then summer plunged into dark
As showers fell on Evor Mount,
And we beneath a sycamore
Read our plays, smoked our dope.

And turning from Dinevor's walls,
The sky burst open, blue on blue
The Towy glistened in the heat'
Deilo's pasture beckoned forth;
We passed beneath the sycamores
And saw no more - Dinevor.

HOLY JUMPERS (song)
[July 1987, Mumbles, Swansea]

I used to lead a happy life
Devoid of care, devoid of strife
I thought I had a faithful wife
We qui-et were as Qua-kers!
But all my bliss has passed away
My joy has turned to blank dismay
For sad to say, she ran away
And went and joined the Sha-kers!

Oh, my cruel wife to me, she's been unkind,
Oh, my cruel wife I nev-er more shall find
Oh, my naughty wife, on my heart she's left a load
Since she joined the Shakers in the Walworth Road.

When she joined this curious sect,
I had no reason to expect
That all my hopes would soon be wrecked
Thru' their peculiar notion;
But when I tell you what I've seen,
When to the meetins I have been
You'll understand the cause I ween,
Of all my sad emotion.

Beneath the hallway arch I found
(The ladies they are kissed all round)
My wife 'all there' you may be bound
With rage I then beheld her.
For she was kissed by all the lot,
And shortly after up they got,
While I stood rooted to the spot -
She was dancing with an Elder.

The sight of this I couldn't stand
A blow on him I longed to land
So I pitched in to all the band
My wife I wished to take her.
But I was collared by the police
Who swore that I had broken the peace
But when they did poor me release
She'd bolted with a Shaker.

LOST TO THE JUMPERS
[July 1987, Mumbles, Swansea]

I lost my lad in a bad attack
of sermon and bible thumping
with shrieks and cries they carried him off
to some bethal an' brothel in London

What terrible woe, what a terrible blow
the Jumpers have stolen my boy.

I lost my lass in a moment of pride
to some wandering, preaching disciples
she deserted her home to take to the road
of religion, and prayer, and denial.

Oh what terrible days, what terrible pains
the Jumpers have cut me insides.

It's no fun that my son's on the run
with the weirdos of Walworth and Chelsea,
he hasn't a penny, to come see his mammy,
he's locked up from Monday to Sunday

Oh what terrible things, what terrible stings
the Jumpers have smitten me body.

You can see the distress, awful distress
of these parents, these mothers and fathers
it's a terrible lost, their children gone
to the Mother and God the Father

Oh what terrible tales, what terrible ails
but what can be done in these matters.

I WISH IT WAS MY LOVER HOME
[15th August 1987, Mumbles, Swansea]

Every voice I hear I think
And wish it were my lover home.
I wait, I hope, I pine
And do not know where she's gone.

I will not cry, not tonight,
I'll sit into the dawn -
How can I rest without word
Of what my lover's done.

O break, o break my broken heart,
For now I think I'll weep -
For only if my lover comes
Will I be made to sleep.

COME WIND COME STORM
[1st September 1987, Mumbles, Swansea]

I love you for what you are,
Wind, storm, and song.
How I long for your warm arms
About me 'neath the stars.

I've never had a love so pure,
Crystal, ice, and snow.
How I wish for your fresh lips
Upon my wanton own.

And though I cannot have enough
Tempest, fire, and sea,
O how I know I'll always want
The love you steal for me.

JANE AND EMMA
[13th September 1987, Mumbles, Swansea]

Jane and Emma
The loves of my life
One without the other?
Oh my, I will die!
For I cannot stand the parting
I cannot bear the grief.
Jane is my want,

Emma my need.

RUN ME OUT OF TOWN
[20th October 1987, Swansea]

I have myself a lover
But I haven't any time
For all the awkward moments
To talk about our crimes.

'Cause I'm a dodo,
No, a dirty hobo!
Run me out of town!

AT THE BOTTOM OF THE WELL
[6th November 1987, Swansea]

At the bottom of the well
If you listen quietly
You'll hear a ringing bell.

Who can really tell
Who tolls that lovely bell
At the bottom of the well.

GHOSTS IN THE LANDSCAPE
[15th November 1987, Swansea]

Wind water rush
I crave to see the blood
Some ancient Saxon shed
With his dying breath.

Howling honing rain
Sing the gasping sighs
Mail-clad Normans made
As the fatally fell.

Rage torrent flood
Flush the choking screams
Harold's soldiers poured
As they cried fleeing.

YOU'RE A WANKER
[18th November 1987, Cothelstone, Somerset]

Why don't I tell you like it is?
How I'm really pissed off.
How I don't like your ideas.
How I don't give a toss
'Cause you're a wanker.

WHEN I'M PISSED OFF
[18th November 1987, Diana's Statue, Cothelstone]

When I get really pissed off,
I climb Weary-All Hill behind my cottage,

And sit and stare out on to Exmoor.

For there's something in the nothingness
That exists when inside is full
Of hate and envy and burning anger.

I don't care about money and stuff,
All I really want is beauty,
The world and all that's natural.

I can't stand all the jealousies,
I hate people stealing ideas from others,
Doing nothing for anyone that's any good.

So I escape my hemmed-in cottage,
Flee the smallness of the human world
And sit and stare into the sun.

INSIDE BURNS A CANDLE
[18th November 1987, Cothelstone, Somerset]

Inside burns a candle
Lit for those who're lost;
Outside hangs a lantern
For those that might return.

HIGH ON MAGIC MUSHROOMS
[30th Nov 1987, Cothelstone, Somerset]

We ain't got the frickin' glib
To hustle bobs and quids
We only got the nouse for fun
We're young, and free, and fit.

We ain't got the stinking rev
To wire up our nerves
We only got our rolling wares
And nature's magic herbs.

High on magic mushrooms!
We don't friggin' care!

NORTHERN COUNTRY GIRL
[30th Nov 1987, Cotherlstone, Somerset]

All the country lads wi' their smiling faces
I'm the sort of lass to put them through their paces.
If they're after deer and birds, I'll stop them speechless
On the moors and in the woods, I protect all creatures.

I'm a' Northern lass, and that canna be bad.
A wild and carefree Northumbrian lass.
I'm just a plain Northern country girl.

PLAYMENU (North-South Divide)
[Begun 7th Dec 1987, Cothelstone, then Swansea, Monmouth,
Leeds, Newcastle, Bradford]

THE NORTH - SOUTH STORY (song)

When I begin to tell this story
about the hate,
about the system,
about the North, about the South,
about two different ways of life.

When I relate the awful truth
about the wealth,
about the poor,
about the North, about the South,
about two different ways of life.

Then you'll know, god you'll know,
you'll see it all,
you'll take it home,
you'll smack your head
and break your bones
for coming to these written poems
about the North, about the South,
about two different ways of life.

WE HAVE THE LIFE (song)

In the South we have the life,
its roses, cake, and gin ....
we haven't got no problems
'cause we've got everything.

There are a few who rock the boat ...
the South is not for them.
We like to keep them on the move
and keep them off Stonehenge.

We have our southern heritage
wot we've got's quite nice
but we wouldn't want to kid you
that nothing has a price.

Oh, it's great to be a Southerner,
rich, and smug, and loveable .....
we haven't got no problems
'cause we've got everything.

In the North they have the strife,
its thistles, spuds, and beer ...
they've got all the problems
'cause they haven't got our cheer.

Up there, they all rock the boat
and throw each other out,
and when they want to come down South
they get nowhere on their bikes.

They have their northern customs

wot they've got's for them,
we wouldn't want them living
on the Downs or by the Thames.

Oh, it's great to be a Southerner
rich, and smug, and loveable .....
In the South we have the life,
its roses, cake, and gin ....

we haven't got no problems
'cause we've got ev-ery-thing!

NORTHERN GIRL ENVY (song)

What have I got,
a couple of bob,
look at her now ....
she's all buttons and bows.
How come I'm dull
and she's all dolled up.
Is it because ...
her dad's loaded
or what?

How come I work
and I'm broke all the time.
How come a student
swoons like a queen.
Why am I tired
when she dances all night.
Is it right, is it right,
is it right?

She's taking my man!
How can I win.
What does she have
that I can't provide.
When money can buy
love has its price.
I shan't give in, can't give in
when I'm losing my man.

ON THE DURHAM STREETS (song)

Down by the bus station
you can get yourself a sniff,
you can be a vandal,
you can smash a bus-stand window
and get stoned for kicks.

I've spent my life on the streets,
sitting on benches,
hanging round cafes.
People think I smash-up gravestones
and sniff glue with kids.

I love the hills,

it's great on the hills
you can walk for miles.
you can run with the wind
take love and be kissed.

But down on the streets
you're no good to no-one,
you're in with the bums.
When you live on the streets
you run with the scum.

THE WEIRDOS OF GLASTONBURY

Iv 'ee be lookin' for that ther' place
I not be tellin ' ee where it be ...
'Cause iv 'ee be knowin how weird it be
To be zeein wizards in dar' High Street
Wu'd a man be right iv he point the way
To a town, skip, where wumen 'uv bare-feet?

No, it not be on me mind to show 'ee dar'
Where zom volks backpack evrthin' they 'av,
Rather I point ee' towards a smarter town
Arr, Taunton be alright vurst time round.
No, 'ee be staying away vrum dat weird place
Glas'an'by be lost, an' best n'eet vound.

CONSETT (song)

Last time I went to Consett
to look for a steel souvenir,
I couldn't even find a washer
from the works that once was there.

Consett's wonderful for recreation
Country walks, unspoiled views,
and dry-slope skiing ....
They shut the Steel Works down.
They shut the Steel Works down
On lovely Consett Town.

The steps led up the Derwentside
there was nothing but new laid steps
square miles of caterpillar tracks
grass seed and the wind on my neck.

Consett's wonderful for recreation ...

I turned my back on the grassy banks
and went into the town
I couldn't see an unboarded shop
the town had been nailed down.

Consett's wonderful for recreation ...

The folk of Consett aren't outdoor sports
they're a salty home-loving lot.

353

The works are now dry ski-slopes
where the doleys walk their dogs.

Consett's wonderful for recreation ...
Oh lovely Consett Town.

ENGLISH QUALITY OF LIFE

The quality of life is not in a house
is not in a job, a car, and a wife.

The quality of life is not in cash
not in possessions, trinkets and trash.

The quality of life is not pounds and pence
mortgage and rates, bills and rent.

The quality of life begins at home
not in the pub, or over the phone.

The quality of life is in the mind
in the spirit, and being kind.

TIPSY SOUTHERN SWEETHEART (song)

Would I say no,
if you let yourself go
and kissed me right on the heart.

Would I regret
such delightful caress
if you offered it so.

Would I forego
if you presented it forth
and hugged me into the night.

Would I forget
such sweet happiness
if you offered it right.

Would I say no ....
Would I say no ....
if you let yourself go ...

I LEFT THE NORTH (song)

I left the North for the South.
I heard the venom that seeped from twisted
mouths.
I'd gone over to the other side,
I'd buttered my bread on both sides.

I went South to study,
To get a degree at a pre-fab Poly.
After four years I graduated;
I got a job being somebody's Wally.

I earn good money;
I have my own warren;
I have come to think of myself
as Southern, not Northern.

I think of myself as Southern,
not Northern.

NEWSPAPERS

How can people be what they read?
Are there such newspaper breeds?
Can it be true that political creed
Is husbanded by such press-baron feed?

For what of the others; the Star? the Sun?
The Mail? the Mirror? - the regional runs
That headlines "Vicar Becomes A Nun"
Next to a picture of the Queen and her Mum.

Can we believe what the papers say?
We have to judge day by day -

IF EVERYTHING IS PAID FOR,
SELL THE COUNTRY'S SILVER

If everything is paid for
why should everyone pay again?
If everything is paid for
it should be given gratis.
For if everything is paid for
and paid for yet again,
who keeps the profit
when the second payments met?

Nothing is free in this world,
free means you've still got to pay.
Nothing is free in this world,
you've still got to pay!

If everything is paid for
who's making the dough?
If everything is paid for
who's running the show.
For if everything is paid for
and yet again,
we're purchasing free things,
we're buying up ourselves!

CHAUVO URBAN MAN (song)

He was a chauvo man ... he had no class
He thought of her as a piece of trash.
He never tried to read her mind ...
He brought to task all woman kind.

He was a pig first class ...
He was a braying ass ...
He was a brutish mass ...
He was a piece of trash.

He was a chauvo man, he had no taste
He saw every woman as a humping mate.
He tried to ignore his woman's mind
He wanted her for the bits he liked.

He was a prick first class ...
He was a dick to the last ...
He was sick and crass ...
He was a piece of trash.

He was a chauvo man ... he had no class
He was full of lust when he made a pass.
He always made her feel real bad
He always found ways to make her mad.
He was a prick first class ....

BLACKBURN BURGLAR (song)

Caught in the act
The goods are the facts
My hands are all red
I'm in a fix for sure

I'm in trouble with the law
And I'm on my way to court
O I wish hadn't thought
That I never would be caught

O isn't it a shame
That I'm taking all this blame
I really should have known
That I didn't have a chance.

And then I might have not
Had an eye on what I've got
I've been nabbed by the collar
by the long arm of the law.

I've been caught in the act
And the goods are the facts.

THE TEMPLE MEADS PORTER (song)

A porter can retain goods entrusted to him
Until carriage is paid in full,
A porter can keep a suitcase
Until carriage is paid in full.

A traveler might lend his items
And might expect to get them back
But a porter has no wages
Until a traveler pays his whack,

A porter has no wages
Until he's paid his whack.

So there we have the law, sir,
It's as plain as Jane, you see;
A porter will have his carriage
Or be first to cry 'Police!'
A porter will have his carriage
Or be first to cry 'Police!'

THE TORIES AND THE HEATHENS (song)

He had no faith in nothing
Not even the Lord above,
He didn't believe in Fairies
Or all those other things.
He only believed in nothing,
Negated all he could.

O how we felt for him!
O how we prayed for him!
O how we tried to save him
From the Devil's grip!

O Lord unleash this poor enslaved soul.
Make him see you, make him know.
Make him cower where you go bold.

HEATHEN: Tory bastards!!
Give me Marx. Give me Lenin
I want to have an earthly heaven!

THE LONDON VEGAN

I do not exist, I will nor exist
in the mist upon the hills.
I do not exist, I will not exist
with the swans on the frozen lake.
I do not exist, I will not exist
with the hiss of the rain in the trees.
I only exist, I merely exist
as a human in an urban cave.

I do not exist, I will not exist
with the stags in the autumn leaves.
I do not exist, I will not exist
with the whistle in the winter breeze.
I do not exist, I will not exist
with the trout in the river reed.
I only exist. I merely exist
amongst man and the city creed.

HEAVEN IS A SUPERMARKET (song)

We kept meeting at one of those places.
It was like Daz, and Omo, and Persil, all in one.
It was marmalade, jam, and honey.

Cornflakes, Crunch, and Wheaties.
It was baked beans, pasta,
Frozen peas, and crackers,
Rashers, buns and marg.
At every counter we encountered.
In love we touched and rubbed.

It was disgusting.
We always met there.
It was warm, it was public.
It was secret.
We could be discreet.

In Sainsburys! In Sainsburys!
The super-duper market where we meet!
Sainsburys! Sainsburys!
The only place where we can be discreet!

It is an institution,
without it we'd be losing
half the hanky panky going on.
It is an institution
where men almost equal women,
it's just the place to have a love affair.
It is an institution
with lanes of smiling women
looking at themselves in shiny cans.
It is an institution
where men thin or middling
push back hair no longer there.

In Sainsburys! In Sainsburys!
The super-duper market where we meet!
Sainsburys! Sainsburys!
The only place where we can be discreet!

ANGLE, SAXON, and DANE (song)

The Romans came and brought a name
Rule Britannia! Screw Britannia!
They buggered off to fight in Spain.
Left Britannia! Fled Britannia!
They left Britannia to the invading waves.
Poor Britannia! Sick Britannia!
Saxon, Angle, and sodden Dane.
Rue Britannia when that lot came!

ARTHUR

Arthur lies near the Holy Thorn
At rest in the earth of Avalon.
He awaits the call of the Celtic tribes
To gather his sword and ride, ride, ride!
Ride to the aid of oppressed souls,
To fight against heartbreak and woe!
To rule by right, and vanquish foes!
He'll draw his sword, unleash his bow,

And then for certain we will know
That Arthur has come to save us!

And once he has saved us,
Back he will ride swifter than wind
Rises on the Holy Thorn
Where Arthur sleeps in Avalon.

THE MASTER OF BROOMFIELD HALL (song)

Profit's the reward of those in authority
Too often it's a few impoverishing the majority.

But that's the way it is, mate
That's the way it's got to be
The pounds for me, and the pennies for thee.

It's a great old world we live in
I wouldn't trade it with Gunga Din
For all the hashish in Peshawar!
No, I'd rather be Lord of the Manor!
I'd rather be Lord of the Manor!
Toasting my bum at the fire.

THE SEX PLAGUE (song)

Then the plague came along
and struck us all down,
there were fewer of us left,
we were sad for a time,
we were sad for a time.

Then we came out of decline
everything was fine for awhile,
then, the children started coming!
O they kept coming!
O they kept coming!
'till they filled all of London
'till they filled all of England

And they never stopped coming
no, they never stopped coming
they've never stopped birthing
they'll never stop birthing
cause we cant give up fucking
they'll always keep birthing
cause we won't give up fucking
they'll be millions more birthing
so there's billions of fuckings
cause we never stop fucking
so they'll never stop birthing.

ROOTS (song)

You've got to have roots.
Unless you know where you're coming from,
how can you know where you're going to.

You don't have to go some place else
to get on in the world.
Nothing wrong with being in one place
all your life.

It breeds community ....
It makes for harmony ....
It breeds family .....

Life's all about family,
having your close ones about you,
especially in times of trouble.

I feel sorry for these poor kids who drift
about the country like gypsies.
I feel sorry for their mothers ... especially
at Christmas.

It's shameless .... who's blameless ...
Depending on neighbours ....

You don't have to go some place
to get on in the world.
Not if you've got roots.
You've got to have roots,
or you might as well look
to the ends of the earth for yourself.

You've got to have roots,
or you might as well shoot
to the moon for the source of mankind.

For if I tell you now,
while the clouds are about
that all that I know
is what I learned back home,
then you'd see why I say
you've made an awful mistake
by neglecting your roots.

You've got to have roots
and I don't give a hoot
for the fancies of wandering souls.

For I'll tell you right now
at isn't swell to find out
that there's no-one you really know

For if I show you now
while the sun's coming out
that I all that I care for
is the home that I came from,
then you'd see why I say
you've made an awful mistake
by neglecting your roots.

ROOTLESS (song)

I don't earn a thing
I don't work, so I'm thin
I live in men's homes and hostels.
I had a wife,
I had a child,
And a mother in Fife ...
But time can be hostile.

I am confined
To a bed on the ground
And roam the country in all weathers.
I get the Nashy
I need it for baccy
It keeps me happy ....
Though life could be better.
it could be better.

GOODY SNATCH (song)

If we've all to have a value,
Then it's nothing to resist,
We might as well cry 'Uncle!'
And cease to resist -

Goody Snatch, Goody Snatch,
Leaping on our backs
Goody Snatch, Goody Snatch
With her hacking sack
Sharpening up her axe
Heads instead of tax,
On our back
With one hack
Head in sack!

Goody Snatch, Goody Snatch
A price upon our heads,
Goody Snatch, Goody Snatch,
Lets have your head instead
You are such a witch
You are a fascist bitch,
You are unwell,
Time will tell.
Go to hell!

A RENTED HOUSE

A rented house is not a house
When it's someone else's home,
There's those who think rented stinks
cause it'll never be one's own.

But why do such people think
that what they've got is theirs,
I like to think that everything
Is merely out on loan.

All I know - we grow and slow
And take nothing when we go.

FOOTBALL BOYS (song)

We are the football boys
We are the champions!

We love to see our goalie dive
and save the day for us
We love to watch our centre backs
hack, and hook, and writhe.

We want to see a crunching slide
from our midfield lads,
We scream to tell our inside men
to smack and have a crack!

We cry on seeing our super star
strike it home for us
There's nothing like the after-crack
while boozing in the bar

We are the football boys
We are the champions.

THE CRICKETING VICAR

How about a game of cricket, vicar?
Nice day for the odd over or two.
Don't you think the weather's rather splendid?
There'll be no sticky wicket, for sure.
Have you ever thought of being an umpire?
My, you're wild with the odd ball or two!
You're batting is rather wicked,
You're a wretched player, vicar, aren't you??

THE THICK SCULLED RUGBY BASTARD (song)

I'm a thick sculled rugby bastard
I'm Neanderthal and slow
I like to beat upon my breast
And spit at people's toes.
I am a rugby bastard!
I am a thick sculled bastard!
I am big slow bastard
I am a sick pissed bastard!
I am a rugby lad!

(End of Play Menu)

MY MATE - THE OWL
[26th December 1987, Cothelstone, Somerset]

That owl nightly sits and who's
And woo's into the winter wind,

But as there are no summer leaves
I hear no whispers from the oaks.

That owl's my ear upon the night
Witting through the winter white,
Its who's and woo's waning slow.
'Till once again, it wits some more.

That owl and me, we're old mates,
Sometimes he keeps me wide awake.
And even when I slumber deep
That owl's in my dreams, my sleep.

BIDDY BROWN (song)
[27th December, Cothelstone, Somerset]

I used to think that Somerset girls
Were the ugliest lasses in all of England.
But then I met Biddy Brown.
Oh my! What bliss her kiss was.

Who would have thought amid the blossom
That I would meet the likes of her?
But Biddy Brown was so divine
I took her for an angel.

I think my luck was luck as such
At finding such a virtue,
That Biddy Brown knew my mind
And lay me in the hay barn.

I never knew such bliss before
At touching such a beauty,
For Biddy Brown was soft and lithe
And supple like a willow.

If you knew what sweet release
Came from our mutual longing,
Then Biddy Brown would not be mine
She'd be hunted like a fable.

For I am all of sixty nine,
Hunt master at the stables,
And Biddy Brown's just twenty one!
Sweet, and young, and able.

TO AND FRO ON THE LONG BRITISH ROADS
[30th December 1987, Severn Bridge, England]

To ... ing and fro ... ing,
Neither coming nor going,
Not in nor between
Neither excited nor bored.

What's next on the road?
What next is in store?
Hell if I know as I fro

on the long British roads.

I'VE SOWN BARLEY
[30th December 1987, Severn Bridge, England]

I've sown barley
I've sown oats
But I've never
Sown English oak.

I've sown these,
I've sown those,
But I've never
Sown English rose.

I've reaped wheat,
I've reaped kale
But I've never
Reaped in English hay.

Heed my words,
I've eaten curd,
But never ....
Fed on English whey.

THE LANDLORD'S WIFE
[8th Jan 1988, Cothelstone, Somerset]

She is sweet, she is coy,
a dream, a blushing angel,
she's the sweetest tavern lass
that man could ever fancy.

But all my hopes fade away
she is the landlord's darling;
he's a brute of plus six foot
that men are loath to battle.

I did not stay to love her, no,
because she had her hard man,
though in my mind I thought her mine
halfway through the evening.

Sometime later, feeling bolder,
I grabbed her by the shoulders,
next I knew, out I flew
chin bouncing off the gutter.

'Oh my love, where are you?
Why are you with this butcher?'
My head was broke, my back was sore,
but I loved her like no other.

When I woke, I was soaked,
and wet from too much drinking,
but I could say I'd made a play
for the darling of the tavern.

THE KNOT
[15th Jan 1988, Cothelstone]

I do not know what I have
Nor yet what it is I've bought;
The cord as yet is not taut,
It's coiled loose around me.

I will not know what I have
Nor know what I've got;
The cord binds as it knots,
It's hot-burn cruelly smarts.

I cannot know what I have
Nor yet what I've caught.
The cord continues to garrote
My knotted heart.

SHADOW OF A GIRL
[18th Jan 1988, Cothelstone]

When I look out upon the hills
And gaze into the swirling mist,
At first I see, a hand, a mouth,
Then the shadow of a girl
Who's in my head, who's in my mind
But will she end up in my bed?

A NIBBLE ON A TART
[18th Jan 1988, Cothelstone]

I cannot think what I'd like
better than a bite of you,
perhaps a nibble on a tart
or some other less exotic food.

But ban such joy, I'm on the case
for a taste of you -
you're better than a row of cakes
or a mouth of sugar cubes.

I wish to have no other muse
than have a chew at you -
so come to me, sweetest thing,
I've come to nibble you.

I'LL WAIT FOREVER
[21st Jan 1988, Cothelstone]

I'll wait forever for you, love,
till all the seas have dried,
until the heavens twinkle out
and every star has died.

I'll wait forever, and for more,
till time no longer goes,

until the exit of all space
I'll wait and love you so.

And when I've waited for all time,
I'll wait a lifetime more,
I'll wait until you're in my arms,
and your lips are on my own.

WHEN I LISTEN
[21st Jan 1988, Cothelstone]

When I listen to the beating of my heart,
I hear a little voice pleading with me -
'I must escape! Please let me out!
I'm in love, my prison's crumbling!'

Then, suddenly I find my head pounding,
my breath is short, I'm in a pant,
my cheeks flush, I'm flashed with feeling,
there's swelling where once there was slack.

And having listened to my pulsing heart,
I listen then to my throbbing mind -
'You must be nuts to feel like that!'
and once again I am torn apart.

TWO NAILS IN AN OAK TREE
[22nd Jan 1988, Cothelstone]

And though they age and rust with time,
these nails will never parted be;
likewise, though parted by wide seas,
this tree will bring you back to me.

HUA HIN
[5th Feb 1988, Hua Hin, Thailand]

The palm fronds quiver,
the sea breeze cools
the heat of the tropic noon.

Ants file across the sands,
there is an army on the march
towards the blue lagoon.

Massage girls oil men down,
peanut-boys sell their wares,
deck-chair men halt the swoon.

The sun beats evening down,
the shadows lengthen everywhere,
night comes on too soon!

KIRI KHAN
[7th Feb 1988, Prachad Kiri Khan, Thailand]

Below Mirror Mountain

and the Koes of Kiri Khan,
by the shading palms
on sands as white as pearl,
beneath the broad pandanus
and a moon of tropic night,
beside the warm green waters
on a shore as smooth as ice,
under the spell of Taurus
and the ka-ka of the black,
near an edge of ocean
where the breeze never barks.

KO PHANGAN
[28th Feb 1988, Haardin, Ko Phangan, Thailand]

The cool night breeze walked right in
with the ocean right behind.
The palms stood higher than the Cross
and drew in from all sides.

The moon two days off being full,
Scorpio flicked its tail.
Dead of night went 'ka-ka'
as deep night onwards came.

With it came the quietest calm,
a hushing of the wild,
as white sea-horses softly bucked
dawn up like a child.

CHAWENG
[6th March 1988, Chaweng, Ko Samui, Thailand]

Caught in the greyness of evening,
moon three days past full,
a stiff wind in from the east
rolled the surf over good.

In the sultry still evening,
night hung on the moon,
the palms nutted the up-draft
above the palm-thatch roofs.

In the throb of the nightfall,
the moon splintered in pools
on the hot tropical passion
in our sigh-filled lover's room.

I WILL FIND MY PARADISE
[18th March 1988, Ko Pee Pee, Thailand]

Beyond the gates of paradise
where sadness comes to bear,
I cannot face being left
in such torment there.

In search of earthly paradise

where joy and bliss are free
is a search I cannot miss
to settle down and be.

So I will find my paradise
where hope and love are one,
and I will be forever smiled
and joyed and free and young.

THE SOUTH SEA WANDERERS
[18th March 1988, Ko Pee Pee, Thailand]

On the deep-blue South Seas,
we sail beneath the Cross,
we travel on by starlight
in thought, not in talk.

We travel on in daylight
beneath the burning sun,
we rest and slumber fitful
without plan or cause.

We wander through the seasons
beneath the shifting clouds,
we pass by whole continents
without halt or pause.

PILLOCK
For Donna Catherine O'Connor
[18th Mar - 16th Apr 1988, Thailand & Indonesia]

CANTO I

Pillock sat upon a rock
the ocean washed the sand
sea-salt crystallised
on his body-tan.

O mighty ocean wash away
the meditation of the day
for who can say what will break
upon this man of clay.

And in a moment all the world
broke upon the golden shore
turquoise waters on the mind
of Pillock going round.

O mighty ocean, perfect sea
chase the shade from the breeze
for who can sneeze upon the shore
of such a pleasant bay.
....

Poor Pillock on the rock
the sun inside his head
midday heat burning

all he should have said.

O how love eats his happiness
the ocean drowns his hope
alone upon a coco beach
coping with the pain.

Should such fire eat him whole
and ash his paradise
Pillock on the rock of time
unwise he sits and pines.

Boats out on the sea crest
ships beyond the bay
across the endless oceans
gypsies run the waves.

....

Pillock sat and ate the bile
that rose into his mouth
he spat it out and cursed
and gave out a mighty shout.

Was that the cry of a gull?
Beachcombers turned and stared
all they saw was a rock
and Pillock huddled there.

Who is that wretched crying man
surrounded by the sea?
Should we proffer forth some help
or should we leave him be?

....

Pillock rose and blew his nose
then dived into the waves
walkers stopped and whispered low
Is he mad or brave?

The green sea frothed vanilla white
then settled smooth as glass
the eddy reached the pearl sands
and broke without a crash.

O mighty ocean, perfect sea
break some coral from a reef
for who can hope for the return
of Pillock from the deep!

....

Sunbathers weighed the waters
beachcombers clocked the tide
walkers stretched their metered legs
'til sunset measured night.

They searched for him 'til sunrise
not a trace was found
his love left on the shifting sands
the sea took Pillock down.

CANTO II

It had begun in the islands
on the night of a full-moon
by a gently lapping lagoon
while eating coconut-curry

Pillock met an angel!
She lifted him upwards
she carried him skyward
until they touched the stars

He'd been miserably lonely
mopping and home-sick
moaning and groaning
in off-putting tones.

She was a God-send
who came by and saved him
who took him to quiet seas
and healed him with love.

They traveled through lands
they laughed and they sang
they lay in the sands -
he adored her!
....

She was his Venus
She was his Daphne
She was his Sappho
all made as one.

How he adored her!
How he upheld her!
O how he fell!
O how he plunged!

Into her bosom
into her arms
unto her charm
he went without qualm
....

She was an angel
a beautiful angel
but I must relate
that he was unkind.

Unkind to an angel!
Such despicable nature!
I'm ashamed he behaved

like a mere mortal sole.

Failed to cherish an angel?
forget she had feelings?
thought that her smile
could never be lost?

Man can be cruel
when he lives by vain rules
and not with soft feelings
nor heart, but his head.

Man can be hard
when he orders and bullies
when he ignores all reason
in the throws of a mood.

....

And so with his angel
this beautiful angel
he clouded her smile
and damaged her wings.

The wings that had borne him
to island and mountain
that had carried him forward
from his earlier gloom.

CANTO III

What drove him East, then South
to the island where the angel
found him eating curry
beneath a full-moon?

I might suggest it was boredom
or some political objection
or that his health was bad
and he needed more sun.

But such trite reasons
for traveling from home
won't wash with Pillock
who loved to rove.

He was a wanderer
a vagabond gypsy
rootless and footless
circling the globe.

He had a restless spirit
that left him no comfort
nor property nor home life
nor such common joys.

Four-score foreign states
six continents, six seas

he'd crossed waves and highways
to fulfill his dreams.

And always one more nation
called on him. Come!
One more distant country
lured him on.

....

He loved sun and palm trees
the sands of tropic lands
and to such magic shorelines
he trekked to paradise.

He'd leave behind his stereo
his pushbike and his car
and take an endless flight
to an exotic distant isle.

He'd carry little baggage
take precious little cash
take nothing precious with him
and bring precious little back.

All he'd seek was shelter
food to keep him sleek
and sun to reach the parts
that time makes weak.

....

He certainly wasn't perfect
but sought to be himself
to find the child beneath
his adult grave reserve.

Reserve that clouds the morning
reserve that wets the day
reserve that darks the evening
and turns the spirit grey.

....

What better aim or purpose
than the betterment of self
Can all of us aspire to
on this planet Earth?

Perhaps there is a better cause
that some wiser person knows
many preach on this and that
and many follow so.

But Pillock followed his own heart
which led him all about
and this is why we first find him
in the tropic South.

CANTO IV

Pillock lingered in despair
waiting for his angel
they had parted by a lake
to rejoin on the shingle.

She had taken to the air
Pillock to the land
his journey lasted six long days
that took an hour to fly.

....

Pillock rushed to meet her
he couldn't get enough
he had never met a woman
who'd given him such love.

He crossed volcanic mountains
he trekked through matted bush
he forewent food and drink
and slept on bare wood.

He spent his last few pennies
on a boat out to the Isle
the sea kicked up a fuss
he gifted it some bile.

....

Landing on the white sands
he was broke and hunger-wracked
she wasn't there to greet him
his mood grew dark, then black.

He sold his last possessions
he prepared for her to come
somehow he'd travelled faster
than his blessed airborne one.

....

He brooded over a plain tea
and a stale banana bun
why had he let her fly off
towards the southern sun?

Why had he blindly followed
to catch with her again?
Why hadn't he turned North
to home and sleet and rain?

Why was he in torment
when he was in love?
Bewitched and so bewildered
why was love so rough?

....

The sea wiped the foreshore
coral broke the break

373

Pillock waited every boat
to bring his angel-babe.

He hoped every morning
he worried every noon
he cried every evening
and nightly swooned.

O what a sad indictment!
What a turn of fate!
Pillock and his angel
deemed never to be mates!

That is what the breeze said
into Pillock's lug ....
'You'll never see your Angel!'
'She'll not show up, you mug!'

O how cruel the breeze tormented!
how vile it played with him!
it drove him to the rock
and did him in!
....

Poor Pillock, love-sick Pillock
what a hopeless chap!
where was his fellow Man
to help hold him back?

CANTO V

While despairing on the Isle
there was one who nursed him
she was a dark native girl
who cared and tended.

She gave him shelter in her hut
fed him rice and fruit
wiped the sweat from his brow
when his fever took.

She could not speak, she was deaf
she spoke to him with touch
she tried to make him laugh
but sticking out her tongue.

She made him take swims with her
and long walks on the shore
but Pillock lost in angel love
scanned the waves for boats.

No boats came one whole month
Pillock wept at night
the dark-skinned girl put about
her arms and held him tight.

With Pillock's head upon her breast

she combed his unkempt hair
when he slept she lay by him
and watched till break of day.

She devoted all her time
to Pillock's small demands
she didn't know nor knew about
or why his fever ran.

She nursed him thru his restless
turns - his fixation for the sea
she could not guess he waited there
for Angel to appear.

....

She loved Pillock more and more
as more he grew more ill
Pillock did not realise
his cruelty to the girl.

The village talked of the cause
of Pillock's strange malaise
until at last they came to guess
sex was to blame.

The girl's father came to save
his daughter from a rogue
but when he viewed the fevered man
he quickly changed his tone.

For when he saw Pillock's face
and his daughter's hovering care
he saw that God was needed there
and off he went to pray.

But Pillock leapt from the rock
before he reached the temple
the girl put a red-tailed snake
to her lobe temporal.

Yet strange enough she did not die
but fell into a swoon
she woke to hear crashing waves
and voices in the room.

A miracle! the father cried
God had cured his girl!
which God this was who can say
but she has her hearing still.

CANTO VI

Who was this angel
this glorious creature
who mesmerised Pillock
and managed to beach him?

Was she a mortal
or some heavenly person
sent from above
to break ego-ed men?

Perhaps I should tell you
that this woman was human
she was as mortal
as woman can be.

She was all Irish
as Irish as I am
when you're raised in America
in cold Illinois.

Lets call her Chicago
sweet girl Chicago
an angelic Chicago
in her thirty eighth year.

She was no chicklet
newly out of the shell
she was a well-groomed
Mid-Western belle.

She wasn't your rough type
who tended bar
she wasn't a waitress
or farm girl dyke.

She was no nun
or schoolteacher mam
she was a lady
alright!
. . . .

Angel had beauty
she was perfect in feature
age had failed
to sag or to line.

Her voice was honey
her hair golden silk
her eyes a warm ocean
her skin like milk.

Cheerful of nature
happy of face
lively of step
she walked with grace.

A model of manners
patient to learn
careful of action
never angry nor stern.
. . . .

With no obvious flaws
nor traits to dislike
she is an angel
to all Pillock types.
....

When she met Pillock
she was lonely and tired
far from Chicago
and drained by desire

'Till under the full-moon
by a lapping lagoon
they kissed in the starlight
and a lotus bloomed.

And what was this lotus
freshly new formed?
but Pillock and Angel's
bosom love - born?

CANTO VII

Sometimes when upon the road
happy times come and go
and when things are really slow
it's sometimes best to split.

Pillock had his moody days
cold as ice, insatiable
with his own lax ways
when he couldn't get his fix.

His needs changed with his mood
and Angel couldn't understand
whether he was sad or rude
when in these mental fits.

Tired of his changing nature
she took to pen and paper
or books about romantic capers
that stole her from despair.

She loved him with increased waver
as his fitful moods enslaved her
she gave less of her favours
until they kissed no more.
....

But why discord and such rancour
when each had found safe harbour
in the breast of sighing ardour
made to foster love?

Angel never had such passion
she cherished Pillock without ration
she made with him in every fashion

377

in hammock or in sea.

They were fast at every sunset
and every morn they were wet
heavy with love's scented sweat
they rose into the day.

Each gazed into each for hours
they were bound by passion's power
Pillock brought his Angel flowers
she gave him all she had.

....

Yet time in Paradise can pass
and turn into a timeless trap
that holds mortals in the clasp
of a living Hell.

In this Hell mortals wither
idleness can turn sweet bitter
love can soon slide and dither
on the brink of loss.

Couples once so sweet united
find themselves quickly frightened
at the thought of being bonded
to one another for life.

In a way these thoughts hinder
bring on love to its winter
break pure love into splinters
before it is a whole.

Sometimes there is no prime reason
when neither wish for such lesion
when couples have great cohesion
in matters of the soul.

Circumstance can pressure all
Pillock needed time alone
Angel thought she'd get along
better on her own.

So Angel flew up and out
Pillock took the hard land route
they said they'd meet on an isle
in the tropic south.

CANTO VIII

What became of Angel?
Can I really speak
of the tragedy that befell
this perfect lady.

It breaks my heart to tell
how Angel plunged

378

was lost in the clouds
on her flight south.

Wrapped in misty garments
above the soaring birds
she was sipping coffee
when the engines cut.

What did she feel!
Will we ever know!
Her coffee spilt on her dress
as the plane plunged below.

O what distress!!
Imagine the fear!!
Imagine the panic, the screaming!
as the mountains neared.

Those mountains of death
with their volcanic smoke
craters that bubbled
and flowed!

Such serious trouble!
the entire plane shook
the passengers took
to their knees!

But Angel was calm
she took from her purse
a picture of Pillock
and laughed!

When the plane hit the ground
she was haloed in love
but her shimmering shroud
did not save her.

....

There were some who survived
but in fact they all died
those with true faith
went to Heaven.

Those who were bad
I might sadly add
had their spirits snatched
by the Devil!

Where Satan took them
is a hazardous guess
I'd rather forget
they were taken.

For to dwell on the Fate
of the unfortunate
is the vice of curates

and the righteous.
....

Angel was borne away
with the others saved
and carried beyond ...
to a garden.

And there she was cared for
and tended by fairies
and brought endless gifts
by nymphets.

There she was happy
but for moments of memory
and thoughts of poor Pillock
on the Isle in the South.

CANTO IX

What of that distant southern Isle
surrounded by a smooth jade sea
where Pillock spent eternity
waiting for his love?

It was a place of nature wild
where steep volcanoes rose above
the green expanse of coconut
that swept down to the shore.

Temples broke the undergrowth
ancient shrines fresh offerings bore
wood chimes hung on every door
and music drummed the air.

Rice fields steeped the verdant land
streams flowed ... everywhere
rivers rushed through sacred lairs
where creatures took the shade.

Brown snakes coiled harmlessly
green snakes slithered yellow scaled
(But woe! The snakes waiting there
red-tailed fork-fanged to bite!)

Sunbirds drained the pink papaya
swifts soared to sightless heights
parakeets plunged like light
into the shadowed glade.

Herons filed across the sky
white cranes waded on parade
sparrows stole down in raids
upon the seeded rush.

Lizards scurried in the ditches
insects rose in a flush

dragonflies beat the crush
with their double wings.

In the pools shamrock clustered
around pink-tipped lily rings
skeeters whizzed in reckless whim
from leaf to leaf.

Stacks of stalk lined the paths
as natives cut the ripe rice-sheaf
and winnowed chaff from the seed
sparrows swooped to steal.

Men set-to with four-pronged hoes
mud clinging to their heels
they dredged the ditches with a zeal
that drowned the heat.

....

And Pillock waiting for his love
vainly wrestling with defeat
lay prostrate completely beat
and cried all day.

'Till slowly time caught up with him
to leave him weak and crazed
the natives thought him malaised
from being bone-idle.

They laughed at him for being so
but they kept their silence
they left him on the shoreline
the ocean waxed and violent.

....

So who could blame the natives
or the girl who couldn't save
Pillock from a sea-grave
in the tropic south.

For who could muse this indolent
would plunge into the waves
when only one could save him
and she was not about.

CANTO X

Down and down Pillock went
dragged deep wards by the current
driven by the wild sea force
he went beyond all worry.

Short of breath he knew no more
sound and sight departed
some would say he left this life
but this is mortal fancy.

Two mermaids took him in their arms
ten leagues took him down
'til they broke the surface
of a cool lagoon.

Doting nymphs took him then
dressed him in shinning robes
drew him up above their heads
and in procession bore ....

Him through a singing forest
through a citrus grove
through a spice filled garden
of nutmeg, ginger, clove.

There's no beauty quite like this
no scent nor sound to match
one might say its Heaven itself
but I do not know that much.

....

They brought him to a splendid bower
they laid him in the grass
they kissed him lightly on the lips
and took their leave with that.

Pillock suddenly blinked awake
before him stood a Queen
before him in a beam of light
stood his waking dream.

It was his lovely Angel-babe!
It was his Angel-pooh!
It was his every wish in one
but how could this be true?

He rose and kissed her gently
she gently kissed him back
he took her in his wanton arms
and that was that.

At last! They were together
he ... by land and sea
she ... by air and accident
until there they are.

....

O how we try to change things
and work to shape our love
but Fate will have the last say
in spite of all our work.

And Faith will be the one hope
we have to keep our love
for without belief in someone
we haven't got a lot.

And some may say that's nonsense
we're better on our own
but perhaps they have no knowledge
of how love grows.

Yet, I have little wisdom
on matters of the heart
you should turn to authors
more expert in this art.

But now you know of Pillock
who pined for absent love
it was all a little drastic
but it worked out well enough.

....

IF LOVE WERE LIKE THE EAGLE'S FLIGHT
For Donna Catherine
[29th March 1988, Tuk Tuk, Lake Toba, Sumatra]

If love were like the eagle's flight
and hovered on a gentle breeze,
and we were fast into the night
and never thought to tease nor scold;
we would soar into the clouds
and leave the works of man below;
we would penetrate the shroud
of earth and on to heaven go.
And when we came to love's abode
where mortal coat immortal cloaks,
naked in the clouds we'd dote
and lip our days in endless bliss
until we'd filled the skies with stars
and lit the universe with kiss.

BUKITINGGI
[4th April 1988, Bukitinggi, Sumatra, Indonesia]

Crying into my tea in Bukitinggi,
an hour before my bus-trip to Jakarta,
the girl I've traveled with flies on
to cultural Java and Yogyakarta,
while I less fortunate in cash terms
must brave the broken roads of Sumatra.

Thirty eight hours away in Java,
Jakarta waits for me, and I am sad
that twelve hours on lies Yogyakarta
where the girl I've traveled with will rest
while I sleep fitful on a bus,
she will wing her way to Bali.

Eight hours on beyond Yogyakarta,
eight hours on beyond Surabaya,
I will travel on through sticky Java,
I will reach then rest in sleepy Bali,
and there I will meet my travel partner,

383

or I will cry some more into my tea.

RELEASE MY FATE
[16th April 1988, Ubud, Bali, Indonesia]

Never had I had such love
rush and gush and drain me
till I am wrecked upon a shore
where none can save me.

What can I do but take these days
as trial by Fate at work -
for if I try to fight such luck
I'll never know true love.

O heaven grant me sweet respite
from all the ails I've done -
I repent for all the times
I've made others burn.

Forgive all the sins I've cast,
the hearts I've bled with pain,
I know now that love is not
supposed to be so vain.

Age has made me realise
that love is not return,
but giving all you have to give
without a selfish thought.

I suffer now, now I know
what it is to lose
contentment with a special one
Fate was want to chose.

So break my pain, let me go
unite me with my love -
for I have learnt the hard way
that love should not be spurned.

THE UNIVERSAL BEING
[May 1988 - June 1989, Moscow, England, Scotland, Iceland]

1ST LEXICON
*I exist, therefore I am — so goes the philosophical argument.
As beings of existence, humankind is related to the whole.
This relationship is abstract — and humankind cannot make
sense of it for humanity will not embrace the Universal Being.*

EXISTENCE

1   *Ergo sum*, in being I am absolute,
     Monad in the currency of time,
     I prevail in essence and reality,
     I exist, and become to evolve.
2   I resist absence and emptiness,
     The vacuum of the nothing and the void.

Nirvana is nowhere, null and groundless,
The neverness of life unbegotten.
3   My reality is the stuff of visibility,
The matter of plenum and of things,
Substantial, concrete, and solid -
Body, flesh, pith, marrow, meat.
4   I resist vacant inane Maya,
Gauzy ghostly vague and hollow shadows,
Dreams of folly, fancy, and figures,
Figments of vain fantasy and fallacy.
5   Inherent is the inwardness of ego,
Intrinsic and generic to the self,
Essential in all aspects and features,
Implicit and autistic in the gist.
6   Outward is an accident of foreignness,
Collateral and appendaged to the id,
Incidental to the basic nub of being,
Casual to the quid per se — the ideal
7   Of State, of place, and circumstance,
The shape of things as they stand,
The way of style and high fashion,
And its relation, status, rank.
8   I am all of these ins and outs:
Of juncture, of matter, and of case,
In respect, regard, in every detail;
Chapter and verse - I am the page.

RELATIONS

9   I am kinned, and connected ....
Related, allied, and of that ilk,
To all that is pertinent, *ad rem*
And all that is relevant, *a propos*.
10 Mortals are misallied, and misrelated,
Foist in, dragged in by the shoulders,
Isolated like some outlandish alien,
Adrift from all that comes and goes.
11 Some have blood-ties, affiliations ...
With clan, tribe, nation, race:
Kith, germane, distaff, spindle,
Distant, intimate, and close.
12 Some have relationships thru' marriage
Affinity with the whole wrecking crew:
Relatives-in-law, nuncles, lawma's,
Buddies, step-kin, and kin removed.
13 Some reciprocate with interaction,
Engage and interlock and inter-tie:
With mutual or joint correlation,
Some respond, and give reply.
14 Some identify with selfsameness,
There's no difference 'tween them all:
Duplicate, twin, and homoousian,
They're six of one, and on all fours.
15 Alike or similar — analogous mortals
Match the alter ego: the mirror image;
The twin that resembles and takes after
The pea besides it in the pod.

385

16   Some are dissimilar, differ by degree
      Enough to tell the daisy from the dock;
      I'm not a bit alike, nothing of it!
      I'm as different as a prune from a plum!

17   Uniformity certainly doesn't suit me -
      Nor persistent running true to form.
      Invariably, without exception ...
      I do not tick monotonous like a clock.

18   Subtly, I am different, a far-cry,
      An apple off another type of tree:
      Like a horse of a distinct colour,
      I'm nothing of the kind, or the other.

19   Contrary or repugnant, I am not
      Counter, and opposite, and hostile.
      Such obverse, inverse antipathy
      Is vis-à-vis to all I desire.

20   Many are uneven, irregular, and each way
      Divergent, and all over the shop:
      Changeable, and varying in manner,
      Inconsistent - everwhichway erose.

21   Few are multiform and hetramorphic,
      Allotropes motley manifold:
      Of every colour and description,
      I'm diverse, and eclectic of sorts.

22   Many may mimic, imitate, and copy,
      Ape, and parrot, dupe and mock:
      Some might follow suit, and mirror
      Pattern, model, echo, all they want.

23   But I am original, and novel,
      Fresh, and unique in the whole,
      Authentic, underived, and first-hand,
      A prototype going down the road.

24   I am not a faithful photocopy,
      Pastiche, parody, or perfect dub ...
      No replica, off-print, or tracing;
      Nor cast, nor chip from the block.

25   I'm no artist model, or dummy,
      Archetypal, died, or punched
      Sample, specimen, or taster
      Made as object lessons for the world.

26   I am in accord, in perfect unison,
      In keeping with *consensus omnium*,
      I am right down everyone's alley,
      Agreeable, congenial, and in sync:

27   Not clashing, jarring, nor discordant,
      I'm no ass in a lion's skin ...
      No jackdaw in peacock's feathers,
      No sardine in a salmon tin.

QUANTITY

28   In quantity Humanity is a mass:
      Measure, strength, a force of numbers;
      Some certain sum, a magnitude,
      An amplitude, *plus ou moins*.

29   In degree Men are marked,
      Graded, notched, stepped in pitch,

Ranked and rated, status staged,
In so much, bit by bit ...
30   That some are equal, even, par,
Equiponderant, balanced, poised,
Even Stephen, nip and tuck,
Neck and neck, drawn and tied.
31   Most are at odds: imbalanced,
Ill-sorted on an inclined scale.
Thrown off, they're disquiparant
In a top-heavy lopsided way.
32   Others - mean and juste milieu,
Is in the long run middle state,
On the average, normal, standard,
Mezzo termine ... Generally.
33   Most are recompensed quid pro quo,
Peter robbed to pay off Paul -
Counter poised and bent over backwards
To indemnify and cover costs.
34   Some men are great, much, and vast,
Stupendous, lofty, large, and grand,
Colossal in their mammoth most,
Extreme and ultra beaucoup gross.
35   Most are small, slight and little,
Minute, smidge, smitch, and snitch,
Scant, and sheer, stark and scarce,
Barely not a wit, nor stitch.
36   Some are eminent, transcendent,
Superior, senior, and predominate.
Excel! Surpass! Exceed and better!
A cut, a stroke above the main.
37   Many are base, and second fiddle,
Subordinate, shabby, bottom drawer,
Tip-the-hat, understrappers
Inferior, low, and in the shade.
38   Some advance, and some expand,
Increase, gain, grow, extend,
Build up, pyramid, and parlay,
To mount and fuel the rising flames
39   Before decrease and lapse, they wane,
Downturn, fall, and fade away;
Cut down, rolled back, then shortened,
They waste away, wear and tear.

40   In addition, adjunct, append,
Attach, tag on, *cum multis allis*,
Clap on, slap on, burden, saddle
Etcetera, and so forth, affixes -
41   Mortals are addenda, and appendixes,
Supplemented to all issued things:
Codicils, postscripts, offshoots
Allonged, lapelled, suffixed.
42   Criminals are deducted, and removed:
Subtracted, tarred without rebate -
Rubbed out, ruled out and written off:
Struck off, knocked off, or erased.
43   Tramps are remains, relics, and remnants:
Odds and ends, rags and scrags,

387

Parings, raspings, filings, shavings;
Fag-ends, doubts, stumps, butts.
44 Kings smack of vestige Hybrid too!
Mixed and blended, instilled, fused,
Touch of tar, and interbred -
Hodge podge, mixty-maxty through!
45 Saints are pure: simple, plain,
Unmixed, neat, straight, and true;
Uninvolved and disentangled ...
Uncombined and absolute.
46 Demons are complex: tangled skein,
Labyrinths and Gordian knots
Snarled and fouled, confused, muddled;
Embrangled in Hyracanian woods.
47 Thus joined, hooked up in copulation,
Fastened, fixed, lashed and trussed,
Hand-in-glove, dovetailed, battened,
Firm, secure, and hung together:
48 Mankind is bound, rope and anchor,
Bowline knot and harness hitch,
Inside clinch, and hawser bend,
Couple, link, and bridge ...
49 Sectioned, parted, severed,
Ruptured, fractured, split and slit,
Non-adhesive rifted, rent and ripped,
Chipped, crazed, checked, and chapped,
50 Cohered, adhered, stuck together,
Staying close, Mankind clings -
Holding on like some old creeper:
Bramble, ivy, briar, burr.
51 So inconsistent! Non-adhesive,
Useless as a rope of sand -
Man is lax, slack and loose
Flapping, hanging, and detached.
52 Unified ... associated,
Some tie-up, fuse and blend:
In cahoots they pool their interests
'Till fortunes join in common cause.
53 Atomised ... in dissolution
Ravaged by the tear of time,
All break-up, fall to pieces ...
Crumble, wear, and waste to dust.
54 Thus, I am the whole, tout ensemble,
Each and every, be and end ....
The shooting match, the total works:
The complex jimbang, one and all.
55 Some are part, portion, fraction,
Section, segment, cantle, tithe;
Piece by piece, and in small doses,
Dribs and drabs, scraps and crumbs.
56 I am complete, all or nothing,
Heaven and earth, no stone unturned:
From Hell to breakfast, cap-a-pie,
First and last, charged and crammed.
57 Incomplete, scant, and half-weight,
Lacking, wanting, in arrears ...
Mutilated, mangled, butchered:

Most are short of what they need.
58 Embodied, constituted, made,
I am set up, formed, contained;
Factor, part and parcel, leaven,
I consist of all that's named.

ORDER

59 Before the sequel: before the trail;
Before the eddy and the wake;
Before the aftermath was tagged;
Before the after clap was tailed;
60 Before the egg; before the dawn;
Before the very starting point;
Before the onset; before the light;
Before the hour Time was born -
61 All was disarrayed, crooked,
Awry, amiss, askew ....
Huggermugger, willy-nilly,
Rant on, much-a-do.
62 Disarranged, mussed, confused,
Messed up, fouled, disturbed:
With no general order
Like tea-leaves in a mug.
63 Then, all was set to rights, regulated,
Cut and trimmed, separated,
Groomed, spruced, straightened-up,
Placed ... policed into shape,
64 Into class, rate, and grade,
Genus, genre, group ....
Subdivided - list and file,
Species, branch, and root -
65 'til Nature left us everything,
Fine fettle, jimp, and snug,
En regale, and apple-pie ...
Like flowers in a jug.

66 However - I have prime place -
I go before: I go ahead of
All afore-mentioned things
Preliminary to existence.
67 Bipeds come next, ensue, and follow
In procession behind me.
They are successful pioneers
In the order of progression.
68 They're foregoers, and voorloopers,
Frontiersmen, and voortrekkers,
Messengers and harbingers ...
The prelude to the train.
69 And that is that - subject closed.
Yet - with the last cat hung,
The proposition is not cold:
For constant flows the continuum
70 Parading, filing, marching past
Round the clock; ceaseless rows,
Caravans in cavalcade -
Columns swathing to and fro.

71 Never interrupted! stopped!
No fitful *longo intervallo* ...
The pioneers come behind me:
The ceaseless masses onward follow.
72 So - I am accompanied on my journey,
Attended by a comitatus:
A retinue, an entourage,
Fellows who blindly follow.
73 When they muster as a caucus,
When they convene as a congress,
Packed like sardines, thick as hops,
Like flies on a carcass ...
74 I demob them, I disband them ...
I dismiss them, disperse the lot -
Scatter, pepper to the winds:
And then I journey on alone.

77 Some fellows are barred ... excluded,
Precluded, purged, shut-out.
Colour, race, and segregation ...
That's what I'm on about.
78 Some revile the foreign devil
In favour of the long-nose men ...
Abroad in distant parts, or home -
I'm at one with aliens.
79 In worldliness, I am one -
Every mother's son and more:
Tout le monde, every Jack,
His brother or his far-flung wife.
80 For I am special, I'm distinct -
Your Uncle Dudley, truly yours!
The he, she, it; they, them too;
The videlicet. To wit I am -
81 The line, pursuit, pet subject,
The main interest, the leading card.
I confine my major in -
By going into minor forms ....
82 Until all men walk the chalk,
Keep in step, fall into line,
Play the game, hold the rule,
Come up to scratch when I squawk.
83 Men might dissent, get out of line,
Leave the path, go out of bounds,
Stretch a point, drive a coach
And six - but not to be undone
84 By normal, real, and naturalistic,
Usual, ordinary, commonplace,
As matter of course, expected things
Prescribed and regulated -
85 I welcome abnormal eccentricity!
Mis-creations, freaks and monsters.
Only quirks of Fate by mistake -
Create basilisks or Minataurs.

NUMBER

86 Let us figure, let us number,

digit count, cast and score.
Let us total, let us tally,
The whole including aliquot.
87   Let us reckon, let us rehearse,
Count noses, call the roll ...
Let us tell, let us tot-up,
Keep a check as we go.
88   Let us list, let us line-up,
tabulate, screen and scroll.
Let us calend, let us cadre.
Log .. roster ... poll.
89   Am I to stand alone?
Exclusive, single, removed, apart
When I am lonesome, on my tod,
A sole - per se detached ....?
90   We could be mates, coupled, matched,
Twinned, braced, yoked, teamed ...
Tete a tete, a heavenly twain,
A starry twilight pair engaged
91   Who need not duplicate, repeat,
Nor be two-sided, twice as much,
Nor double-up as much again.
If we were more like pals
92   Who need not bisect, cut in two,
Split in demi, semi-spheres ...
And half-an-half, fifty-fifty
Divide and take bipartite stance.
93   We could be tri-form, three-in-one,
Create a third from our love ...
We could triumph, deuce-ace all,
In threeness be as one in bond.
94   We have no need to triple tension,
Cube derision, and treble thought
We could terminate trilogic ...
And three times more think as one.
95   For why trisect and make three parts
Triangulate and leave three-forked,
One third this, third part that ...
Trisect one, 'til balance goes.
96   We could be four! Tetrad, quartern,
Two square one, a quartet whole ...
We could a four leafed shamrock be -
Precious, rare, and blessed with luck!
97   Not one fourth this, a quarter that,
To be nothing in this world ....
Four-fold these, by quarters those,
By quadruplication - distance grows.
98   There is no need to draw a quarter,
To make a farthing of the whole,
Create four answers to one question
When the answer isn't four.
99   We could be five! Six! Or twenty!
Sixty! Or a hundred thousand!
We could be five billion beings ...
And still be one in number -
100   Such a great number! A plurality of causes!
The majority with the excess of votes,

The lion's share, the manifold most
..... Who's who amongst that host?
101   A number .... a certain number;
Rife, abundant, copious thick .....
A million and one creeping and crawling,
Not easily stopped by shaking a stick.
102   Only a handful, scarcely a middling,
Sparsely scattered, barely a few ....
A precious little, skimp and sprinkled
Here and there push thinly through.
103   Till over and over, again and again,
Many times round ..... the echo rings
Tedious, monotone, without a ding dong:
Until it becomes a harped upon thing.
104   Into the infinite, the inclusive dark,
Knowing no bounds: bow without stern.
Thru the eternal void, they untold go:
End without end, on without term.

TIME

105   I am that bald sexton of Time,
Nurse and breeder, devourer of things.
Author of authors, spinner of all,
Summer sun and winter wind ....
106   I am timeless ... sine die;
A neverness of blue moon days.
I am the moment, the last millennium,
The era, the epoch, the aeon ....
107   I am the age that spans and stretches
The swing of season, spell and shift,
The kalpa ... yuga ... manvantara,
Day, date, duration, stint.

108   You all have your innings,
Your whack ... and your go,
Your bout ... and your stretch,
Your spell filling in for ...
109   Before the interval brings the pause,
The meantime, meanwhile, the ad interim:
The *pedente lite*, the provisional break
for the time being, for the nonce -
110   That makes you endure, last, abide,
Maintain steadfast for donkey's years
The lengthening vista of human time,
All your born days, hour after hour -
111   Till all is flit, fly, and fleet,
Two shakes of a lamb or monkey's tail;
Gone like a shadow, gone like a dream,
Burst like a bubble - short, and sweet!
112   For all's forever, constant, immortal,
Deathless, imperishable without bound
Ore a sempre - perpetually perennial
Knowing no limit, knowing no end.
113   While in the twinkling bat of an eye,
In a jiff - like a shot out of Ulster!
Afore you utter 'Goody Snatch! Witch!'

Time has been plucked by the Swooper.
114 Till what's left? Calends & records,
Annals & diaries & journals of verse,
Almanacs, chronicles, signed and dated
By Greenwich time & tolling Big Ben -
115 Both mistimed, misdated, misleading,
Prochronic or anachronously false ...
for I am true Time - I am a neverness,
I come before, and I follow all.

116 All that is new, novel, and fresh,
Newfangled modern, firsthand & vernal,
Abreast of the times, *fin de siecle*,
Up-to-the-minute latest in fashion:
117 And posterity? subsequent & later?
The *expost facto* of all presence?
I attend to that afterwhich
Sequenced to beyond past forever.
118 All that is old, cobwebbed & reliced,
Antique, traditional, primeval & worn,
Outmoded, disused, has-been & old hat,
Old as the hills; like dodos outmoded:
119 Simultaneous - in pace with the after,
As one in concert & chorus '*una voce*':
I keep in tempo with the nowness
Concurrent in the same breathe as yore.
120 All that is youth, tender, and callow,
Childlike, puerile, girlish & awkward,
Cherub, doll-like, minor and new-born
In May-morn life & salad day summer:
121 And time out of mind - *auld lang syne*
When mortals were a figment of fancy:
Days beyond recall when I was young;
When all was green and newly sprung -
122 All that is boy, laddie, and garcon,
Girlie and missy, maiden and gal,
Infant and baby, bambino and bairn,
Chunk of a kid, and unspoiled child:
123 I remember - I am sum past of all Time:
This day and hour - the here and now;
The hereunto; the as yet; the already;
The thus-far-today but not the man'ana.
124 All that is adult, woman, and man,
Darby and Joan, dame and old duffer,
Crone and hag, heffer and gammer,
Senior and dean, elder and doyen ...

125 Where flies the future on the morrow?
Which by-an-by some advent calls
life to light; which in coming,
In time is lost, by the act of going.
126 All that is years, the measure of age,
Mature and ripe, full and flowered,
Past one's prime, in the sere
With one foot in and worse for wear:
127 Until dead and off, a creature stalks
Dry or rainy, nightly comes ....

393

In solstice swing and equinox ...
Through Aries, Cancer, Capricorn ...
128   In proper time, in fullness shows.
In passing, by the by - it turns
To pinch, clutch, squeeze, and rub,
To hinge past, and push on luck.
129   Untimely, importune, half-cocked
This creature is an evil-hour
That feasts on those who miss the bus
And locks the door on those who dote.
130   It steals on those with time to spare,
It swiftly gains on those who rush,
Soon enough such said - than done!
Straight with, fore with, it overruns
131   The late, the tardy, and those behind,
Delayed, detained, those who dally,
Those who stroll, hold off, prolong,
Put on ice, postpone with red-tape:
132   'Till the morn, red-fingered dawn,
Has woke the lark at cock-light call
And noon glides on to afternoon
And moves upon the close of day
133   'Till pale pink hour of evening turns -
Grey-hooded sundown brings nightfall,
And shank of owl-light dimply draws
'Till dead and off Death it comes.

EVENTUALITY

134   Death is an accident, a fact,
An incident, a bloody do ....
Affair, matter, thing, concern,
As things turn out .... its back.
135   It is imminent ... any minute
Approaching, nearing, looming close.
An attack impending ... to be expected
Any moment ... it will attack!
136   Frequently Death prevails,
In common occurrence, oft returns:
Without cease, perpetually, constant,
Regularly I hear the fiend hunt.
137   It's rare, uncommon, unusual & seldom
I see Death doing its job.
Once in a dog's-age or blue moon,
Pro hac vice, I'll chase it off.
138   Intermittent, spasmodic, on and off,
Wavering, flicking, spastic, erratic,
By fits & jerks, snatches & catches,
Death sporadically gnashes.
139   It is a presence, an omnipresence
That permeates and overruns .....
It haunts and hangs around like mist
That always scares or chills.
140   It's always absent, non attendant,
Playing hooky without leave.
It's always nowhere to be found,
Out of sight ... but always there.

141   It lives, habituates, and dwells,
      Quarters, billets, rooms and berths.
      It camps, it bivouacs, it roughs
      Where man cannot descend.
142   Death likes to copulate,
      Couple, mate, and fornicate,
      Congress, coitus, intercourse,
      Death's beget a billion souls.
143   Mother, dam, and grand-mamma ...
      Death has had its mount and lay.
      Stock, stirps, sept and strain,
      Death has had its way.
144   Birth, blood, breed and branch,
      Death has seed in every house.
      Bastard, bantling, nobody's child,
      Death has sown a billion times.

CHANGE

145   So we need to change! alter! vary!
      we men of Earth, we savages?
      Will we deviate? revamp? veer?
      Shift and turn a leaf?
146   You status quo conservatives!
      You standpats! You unprogressive's!
      You intransigent bitter-enders!
      You brute old bulls! You farting wallowers!
147   Who are you? You fickle dackers!
      You chameleon rolling stones -
      You kaleidoscopic Cynthianan phasers
      Who blow hot and see-saw cold?
148   Who are you *a plomb* fixed Immobiles
      With your mortgaged investment-homes?
      Secure, battened, anchored, moored,
      You high, dry marooned buffoons!
149   Can we keep on, prolong the pain,
      We men of Earth, we savages?
      Drag, maintain, retain, keep going,
      Pursue the tenor of our ways ...?
150   Change, convert, transform, progress?
      Mature, mellow, melt and merge?
      Time has brought about the need,
      To renew and mend our Earth!
151   You have lapsed, regressed, reverted,
      Harked back, embraced reversionism!.
      So turnabout, escheat, recess ...
      Change your ways, you Earthling.
152   Overthrow, overturn, break down
      Without revolt, or revolution ...
      Without anarchic, *sans culottish*
      Jacobinic insurrection ......
153   Exchange, supplant, switch by proxy
      Without fall guys or whipping boys.
      Ring-in no ghosts, goats, or dummies,
      No faute de mieux in absentia.
154   Tit for tat, quid pro quod,
      This is our Earth, noble Earthlings!

Tooth for tooth, eye for eye!
As you take, you shall pay back!

CAUSATION

155   What's the cause, occasion, call,
The big idea behind the whole?
Who is the author *primum mobile*,
The mainspring, *fans et origo*?

156   What effect, result, conclusion,
Culmination, climax, end
Arises from all germination,
Stems from such development?

157   What attribution, imputation
Can be ascribed on this account,
Laid at the door of assignation,
Who's to blame, and on what ground?

158   Perhaps by chance, fortune, fate,
By fluke, by random shot, by lot,
Without design, the way things fall,
Providence provides the cause?

POWER

159   I am the power, the vigour, the force,
Omnipotent, almighty, puissant ....
Capable, competent, *vis viva et vitae*,
I am endowed, invested with life.

160   I am not impotent or weak,
Eunuched, hog-tied, done-up brown,
Out of the battle, out of the running,
Off the field and laid up bleeding!

161   I am sturdy, staunch, and stable,
Strong, sound, a stamina'd stalwart,
Sinewed, sphinctered, strapping,
Stout in stance, I stand solid.

162   I am not feeble, whimsy, or wimpish,
Frail, fragile, faint, infirm.
No delicate dainty, dodder or drooper,
Wobbly waster or weakened fool.

163   He's the kick, the zip, the zing,
The punch, the drive, the get, the go,
The pep, the vim, the verve, the snap,
The spark plug and the dynamo.

164   I am not violent, fierce, nor savage,
Fury, furore, ferment, fume.
No storm, no tempest, roaring wind.
I am no Vulcan fuelling such things.

165   I am the all of moderation,
Mildness and the golden mean;
Medan agan - the happy medium
Striking a balance, instilling peace.

166   None have influence, favour, pull,
Prestige and sway, pressure, effect,
None have the in to carry weight ...
None have a hold or gain on him.

167   You are all non influential ....
       Impotent against my immovable self,
       Unyielding, impervious to corruption,
       I am unresponsive to pleas for help.
168   I'm not inclined to lean or bend,
       Drift with trends, swing with fashion.
       Bearing, line, direction, course,
       I am in a fair way unopened.
169   I'll not go with the current,
       Fall in with fads, follow phases.
       I'll not be brought down,
       I don't believe in braving chance.
170   I'll not get involved or entangled
       Up to my neck - nor deeply ensnared
       In embarrassing tie-ups of interest
       That make for a party's own greed.
171   He'll not concur, co-act or combine,
       He alone is the Ergo Sum Id.
       He'll not go shoulder to shoulder,
       When he is the all, the whole of it.
172   He contravenes, he contradicts.
       I conflict, clash, and collide.
       I am the crosscurrent, I am the counter -
       I am creator and child.

* 173-177 removed

2ND LEXICON
The Universal Being is everything substance and non-substance. Mankind's, anthropocentric interests quickly make Man tire of revelations about time and space. Man prefers to hear of himself and the world he inhabits. Thus the Second Lexicon, is about earthlings and their place in the continuum.

SPACE AND PLACE

178   There is space and time continuum -
       From here to spheres beyond dark Pluto
       To hell and back through black holes;
       There is extent, expanse and more:
179   While Earthlings - between two Poles
       Migrate towards the torrid zones -
       In split domains of country, land,
       Of province, state, canton, shire -
180   Nations swarm, republics spawn,
       Kingdoms come, and empires go.
       Scotland, England, Ireland, Wales ...
       They are one, but they are four.
181   There is rural rustic man
       Of the clods, of the sticks;
       Provincial, pastoral, countrified,
       Hickish, boorish, and farmerish.
182   There is urban, civic man
       Of the suburbs, of the slums;
       Burgher man hived in glass ....
       Where nothing unobserved can pass.

183   Location, situation, and place,
Some strike root, plant themselves.
Some drop anchor, hang their caps,
Set up house, settle down.

184   Displaced, misplaced, dislocated,
Some are square pegs in round holes:
Some will never roost or nest,
They're out of joint with all the world.

188   It's nice to be indigenous, native,
Citizenship domesticates .....
It's harder being naturalised,
Adopted, tamed, and broken

189   By a populace, people, public,
Incumbent, *'loco tenis'* folk
With their slang ... *wog* and dago
For those newcomers making homes.

190   Homes in lodgings, digs and bed sits.
Abodes in hovels, huts and shacks.
Homes in dives, dumps and dog holes
With pig-sties out the back.

191   Nooks, corners, crannies, niches,
Cold water flats, single-ends ...
A commode as a bathroom
Beneath a folding bed ....

TOWN AND COUNTRY

192   Cities - roly-poly, plump,
Beefy, tubby, rotund, gross,
Bulky, massive, ponderous, vast,
Over sized and overlarge.

193   Hamlets - teeny-weeny, midge,
Pee-wee, itsy-bitsy, wisp,
Pint-sized, puny, tomtit petite,
Smaller than a mustard seed.

194   Towns enlarge, expand, and increase,
Spread, sprawl, span and stretch
Potbellied to the furthest shores
Bloated, forth they gassy swell.

195   Nature - in the way - contracts,
Shrinks, shrivels, withers, wastes,
Till compressed-condensed, it puckers
And gets strangled all together.

196   Wilds, distant, far, remote,
One stride from the back-beyond,
As far as east is from west
to where the parkland spreads ...

197   That's where I'd settle ...
Not near, not next to a town,
Not two whoops, not a holler,
Not a stone's throw, one spit closer!

198   Give me space! remove and break!
Let gap and gorge and gulf divide.
Keep the town and country rift!
Where's the harm in that?

199   With their rubbish - packed,
Loaded in a truck and lugged

Out to the dump, abandoned ...
Towns are ringed by muck.
200 Plastic bag, cardboard box,
Newspaper, polystyrene cup ....
Detergent bottle, soft-drink can
Mountains out of waste land!
201 Give me hills, downs, moors -
Bare steeps where desolation stalks;
Alps on Alps, sun bright summits ...
High monuments topped by hummocks.
202 Give me lowlands, the fens -
Wetlands where marsh-birds wade ...
Moss on moss, neap-levelled grasses,
Wart hung banks where water passes.
203 Give me sand flats, shoals & bars
Ripple-rung and driftwood skimmed ....
Where root & wrack get ebb-tide reefed
Where fleet shell-creatures creep.
204 Give me the deep, the ocean bottom,
The bosom of the bathyal sphere ...
Draft on draft, depths unfathomed
Below the shelf and shallows -
205 Where time shapes plains and prairies:
Flat as a board or bowling green.
Flat as a pancake or billiard table.
Flat as the belly of a skate.
206 Where weeping willows pendant droop
Cernuous as a sunflower nodding -
Pencile like a fuchsia dangling
Or gargoyle from a cornice hanging
207 Off buttress, brace and mainstay
Above rostrum, pulpit, priest ....
Great *'locus standi'* on *'terra firma'*
Beneath roofs of slate.
208 Shafts of ash, staves of maple,
Rods of birch, staffs of oak,
Stalks of rowan, sticks of hazel ...
Jamb, spar, stanchion, post
209 Which stand, run abreast ...
Correspond, match, equate ...
Co-extend in such a way
They collineate and collimate:
210 While outside at a slant, a tilt,
Slew, skew, askance, awry,
Kittycornered, catawamptious,
A churchyard guards the sky.
211 Head over heels, and bottoms up,
The soil turns and somersaults.
Who can say if fingers clutch
To keep headstones totherway up.
212 Processions reach the intersection,
The traverse of the thwartways round,
The cross point and the carrefour
Where whippletree's plough the earth
213 Around the weave of braid, and plait,
The warp, the woof, and weft of wreath ...
Intertwining, interlacing,

399

Interthreading strands of grief -
214 Sewn together, seamed together,
Funeraled by a fine drawn stitch ...
Until the cloth wears and rents
And the flowers fade unpicked.

215 This is surface, the outside world,
A facet of the great out-doors ...
The open-wide wild alfresco ...
Beyond the starry glow.

216 Not recess! Not in-ness!
The herein, therein the whole
Within the inside of the keep
Of the inner core.

217 Not the hub! Not the centre!
Not the focal point, the kernel
Midmost at the heart - the navel,
The nucleus sheaved and levelled

218 Into endless tier and stratum:
Layers, beds, belts and zones ...
Laminated, furfuraceous ....
Multiplied a zillion fold -

219 Where Nature's wrapped in a coating:
Skin, scale, shell, and tuft
Of human, snake, crab and bird
Muff, slough, scab and fluff.

220 Yet this is skin-deep information!
Desquamation might be learned:
Endermatic might be clever -
But it's dressing on the mutton.

221 Where's the grizzle or the wisdom?
The silvery livery of advanced age?
There's many wanton riddle ringlets
And cataracts of names -

222 Sure, you can tux Nature, tart it up,
Dress it in best bib and tucker ...
But strip the Sunday gad-rags off
And what have you got?

223 Nudity, nakedness, the altogether,
The state of nature in the raw.
Does nature start in Spring?
Or begin with the Fall?

224 Round and round the seasons go,
Backdrop to the hinterland.
The stage is re-set, *mis-en-scene*,
The elements hot, then cold.

225 We know no termination,
Limit to the stint of days.
Though Nature is precise, exact ....
Not partial ... nor halfway.

226 Yet there is limit to all things
Length, extent and distance,
Measure, span, reach and stretch,
The footage of two steps trodden.

227 There is a shortness, brief and curt,
Extent reduced, abridged, curtailed;
The beeline that cuts a corner
Quick and sweet and cruel.

228　Sometimes there's width, expanse,
　　　Wide and wondrous as the world,
　　　Broad arched like a church
　　　With beam that's vast inside.
229　Sometimes - narrowness, closeness
　　　Is just a hairsbreadth off -
　　　A leanness that jaws and weakens
　　　To leave a brink of brick.
230　Sometimes filament, fibre, thread -
　　　Cord and line webs the earth,
　　　To strip, spill, spin and shred
　　　A white sky for the dead.
231　There are features, outlines, contours
　　　Where sea meets sky, shore meets bay -
　　　Where brow and brim, and ledge and edge
　　　Make brink and rim the same.
232　Woods enclose, and hills shut out,
　　　And fields hem in, hedge in the towns.
　　　Cloistered, closed, confined at first,
　　　Towns have grown to fence the world.
233　But only twixt the Thames and Severn,
　　　And Hampshire east to worn out Kent -
　　　For ... only north beyond old Derby
　　　Is there some wild country left.
234　There is Scotland, some of Wales,
　　　The Pennines and the few odd Lakes,
　　　And Northern Ireland wild wind-swept
　　　Where Nature's on the gain.
235　What snoop would chose to intrude in
　　　Or trespass on these barren lands?
　　　The usual thing's to cock a snoot
　　　With less than half a heart.
236　For there are those against, opposed
　　　To weeds and Nature as it is ....
　　　Vis-a-vis they tame the wilds
　　　'Till cities grow and towns collide.
237　And there at the fore - the farmer;
　　　In the vanguard are his cows ...
　　　In the front-line are his sheep
　　　Keeping nature down.
238　At the rear gnaws the cities
　　　Coming up the trails of tar ...
　　　Through the towns and ribbon villages
　　　Growing side by side.
239　Back to back, house to house,
　　　From valley head to river mouth,
　　　Night lights lamp the wilderness
　　　Of sea-mist and hill-cloud.
240　Yet, thru' a clockwise tick of time -
　　　Through a starboard tack of tide -
　　　Through a dextrous turn and twitch -
　　　Through a right-handed twist -
241　Through a flinger out of bounds -
　　　Through a southpaw rout of bouts -
　　　Sinister things may come about:
　　　Then switch around no doubt.

242   Tiptop ... icing on the peak,
Apex, zenith, apogee -
There is crest, crown and cap
Paramount above the sea.

243   Nadir, bedrock, base and built-on
The under bellied nether side ...
The fundamental primal hardpan
That pours the magma out.

244   Erect, uprearing, to rise *a plomb*,
Palisade, cliff and crag ....
Basalt square, endways steep,
Sheer rampant to the sky.

CITIES

245   There is structure of a kind ...
Pre-fab house, skyscraper tower.
The anatomy of cities
As formed in most minds.

246   Persistent, true to form ...
Cast, mould, impression, pattern:
Leicester, Coventry or Swansea -
Are they differently fashioned?

247   Some may - say they are formless,
Featureless and amorphic -
Pity we the citizens of these cities
Living in their rough-hewn diamonds?

248   Some cities are well proportioned -
Lancaster, York and St. Andrews.
Symmetrically balanced, well-favoured,
Trim, neat, clean and comely.

249   Some cities are thrawn, distorted -
Stoke, Bradford, Leeds, and Dundee.
Defaced ... disfigured by industry,
Misbegotten by business folly.

250   Some cities are straight-lined, even
With streets unswerving for a mile -
Aberdeen, Edinburgh, Glasgow,
The Scottish straight-cut style.

251   Some cities angle off akimbo ...
Sharp cornered veer at every turn -
Newcastle, Liverpool and Bristol
Through nook and fork and quoin.

252   Some cities curve and circle ...
Durham, Bath, Exeter and Lincoln.
Cestus sashed, they loop and hoop
About their own circumference.

253   Convoluted, winding, twisting ...
Birmingham meanders crinkled.
In tortured whorl, it rolls and curls,
Corkscrews on the Midland soil.

254   Rotund and globular London splats
Itself about its hinterland -
The ice-cream cone of British towns
Drips upon the countryside.

255   These bulging, swelling cities creep
Towards mull and ness and spit.

It makes me dream of coral reefs
And lands far from this.

256   Give me a cave, a subterranean lair,
A burrow underground -
A subway tunnel to a hole
That opens on the wild ...

257   A wild of thorn, bramble, briar,
Fern, nettle, thistle barbed:
I'd run the gaff of dale and combe
To escape the city drab ......

258   The dull, blunt edged city life.
"Turn! Turn!" the grey walls cry!
"Run! Run!" they toothless mumble
At those who march on past.

259   Unbroken slip the buildings,
Walls smooth and made of glass.
Slick and sleek and most discreet
Shine the glossy polished banks.

260   Rough and shaggy, course, unkempt,
Against the grain - are you like this?
You might take the washboard road
That some already tramp.

261   That's the score, the notch and nick -
One cockscomb less won't be missed.
The city's got folks enough
To keep it on the turn.

262   In the rut, the well-worn grove;
Trench, trough, ditch and gutter.
Why carve, chisel, gash, gouge
Ourselves in much further?

263   In the fold, tuck and gathered
By a bank for a mortgage?
Wrinkled, creased, purse crumpled
To exit with what you've borrowed?

264   This is the passage to the chasm,
The break into the yawning rift:
Split, slit, crack and fissure,
Not opening to a wilderness -

265   Where banks're grass brackened slopes;
Where Nature borrows time from summer;
Where life is rock and fern and stream
And cities are a distant bother.

MOTION

266

People are motion, movement, shift,
Course, career, passage, and flow -
Travel over distant lands
For those who're on the go.

267   Stillness, quiet, peace, repose,
Resting calm on shipped oars.
Most people sleep, do not snore
Enough to rock the boat.

268   Scamper, scud, scuddle, spurt ...
The swift and swallow lightning dart.
Under press of steam and fission
Hell-bent are some folks driven.

269   Like a snail, slow as death,
        An easing off, a creep, a crawl:
        Life doesn't go fast enough
        For those in transit.

270   And so, en route, on the wing,
        On the high road, mid-progress:
        They are always on the move,
        On the run and not secure.

271   On the transfer ... car to bus,
        Train to plane, truck to van:
        They are hitching round the world
        And never looking back.

272   On the wander, roving, roaming,
        Traipsing, gadding on alone:
        Nomadic, vagrant knowledge-seekers,
        Drifting hobos ... fancy free:

273   They are bums and birds of passage,
        Knights of the road and lazzarones.
        Some are pilgrims, hadji, saddu's,
        Immigrants and refugees .....

274   They flee lands, run the wind,
        Voyage the sea, ship to ship ...
        Leg the world, port to port
        And never sleep ashore.

275   Here's to those galongee men:
        Lascars, tars, and devil dogs,
        Jacks, and pipes, and matelote's
        Steering full ahead .....

276   In their ships: spars of steel;
        In their splinters - dug from soil -
        Buoyed upon the bob of Nature
        Others sail the blue-beyond.

277   Not bound by salty favour,
        They fly, wing, and ride the skies ....
        Soar, drift, hover, and cruise
        And touchdown where they can.

278   These aeronauts, these airplanists,
        These birdmen and these aviatrix
        Jet the world - then they're back
        Well before they're missed.

279   In their jets: in their choppers
        Above the cloud to higher spheres -
        Where fighter planes loop-the-loop
        Clear of surface gazers.

280   In rockets, spaceships, shuttles:
        They are trying to get to Mars -
        We know however that these seekers
        Are - very few, of course!

281   On through space, on through systems
        Beyond the dusk of solar light:
        Cosmic rays and blackout waits.
        Who'd be a hobo now?

282   People impulsed, impelled, forced,
        Thrust, push, prod, and shove,
        Elbow, shoulder, butt, punch
        To have what others want.

283   On the rebound, on the bounce,
They flinch, whinge and cringe,
Shy and dodge, duck and kick
And bite at everything.

284   At the fore, propelled and driven,
They draw a bead on ambition:
Pepper. Pelt. Pump. Pick off.
Let fly and never slacken.

285   Some straining, dragged in tow,
Left behind, pull together ...
Take the rope, snaked and ravelled
And choke those to the fore.

286   They lever, pry for advantage,
Reel in those who take the bait,
Handspike in their flapping catches
And oarlock their brains.

287   By attraction, by allurement,
By the power of adduct awe,
Some lure the unattached
With magnetic draw

288   Then send them about their business
Repel, repulse, chase-away;
Keep at length, thus never learn
Charm or wit or grace.

289   So what direction shall we take?
Shall we drift or take a course?
Most have been north or south
But few have reached a Pole.

290   Perhaps it's easy to digress,
Lose one's way, go adrift,
Double-back get side-tracked,
Deviate - and go astray.

291   Perhaps it's hard to head the dance,
Go in the van, lead the way,
Shine the light, be the guide,
Get out and set the pace.

292   Perhaps it's fine to follow on,
Swallow dust, bring up the rear,
Tag along, be on the heels,
Join the trail of hanger-ons.

293   Perhaps it's hard to make headway,
Make up leeway, make up time,
Fight one's way, forge ahead
In strides through the crowd.

294   Perhaps it's hard to veer around,
Turn a heel and face about,
Retrace one's steps, fall behind
And turn one's back upon the world.

295   Perhaps it's all to do with chance
That some advance, get ahead ....
Draw near enough to gaining on
The get-at things they're dreaming of.

296   Perhaps it's all to do with luck
That some diminish, fade away,
Draw in their horns, then withdraw,
Retire with their dreams stillborn.

297   Perhaps it's hard to come together,
       Come to a focus, to a point
       Where folk can meet, unite together
       And fall-in with converging thought.

298   Perhaps it's easy to diverge,
       Fly off, go off at a tangent,
       Take different roads to a crossroads,
       Take separate tracks at every fork.

299   Perhaps it's hard to achieve arrival,
       Get there safe, reach one's end,
       Attain one's goal, check-in fit
       And know the journey's end is home.

300   Perhaps it's hard to take departure,
       The sending off, the last adieu ...
       The leave take and the shoving off,
       The 'Come again!' and 'Keep in Touch!'

301   Perhaps it's fine to make an entrance,
       Set foot in, come breezing in ....
       Make way into lover's beds ....
       And pierce the minds of friends.

302   Perhaps it's time to make an exit,
       Bow out, run off, and go abroad ...
       Leave a lover, weeping loudly,
       Desert a friend owed some dough.

303   Perhaps it's down to introductions,
       The squeezing in, the cramming in
       Of things inserted in our nature
       That often surface on a whim.

304   Perhaps it's all these things removed,
       Pulled up, plucked out, raked away,
       Extracted from our better being
       Rooted up and left decaying.

305   Perhaps it's how we are received,
       Taken in, absorbed, installed ...
       C'mon let's have full report
       Let's have food for thought.

306   Let's feast and wet our whistles,
       Lick and smell and do our duty,
       Eat our fill, break bread, dine
       With no wolf or whaling down.

307   Let us cheer in creature comfort
       Without resort to short commons;
       Bring on the victuals and the tucker
       So we might toast our mothers!

308   Let's sup and spoon with regime,
       Let's knife and fork with diet
       And take our nourishment complete
       To alkali our acids .....

309   For we eject, expulse, disgorge
       With a puke, or wretch, or heave
       All that is no good to us:
       Discharging - we defecate at will

310   Or once a month as nature wills
       We fly the red flag;
       Bear the trots in mid-summer;
       And flush our flux with passion.

311   For we secrete and lactate much,

Saliva with a spit or slaver....
Which might be due to hormones,
Glands or rotten guts.

312   For we are infringed,
Infested, ravaged by the plague ...
Rode roughshod over, beset, invaded,
Overrun by countless things.

313   So - in motion, people fall short,
Coming to nothing, fizzling out,
Found to be lacking, they go amiss,
Slumping, they don't make the grade.

314   People in motion - upwardly mobile,
Climbing the ladder, scaling the heights
Best be careful to watch for snakes
At the head of the slide to decline!

315   Descent is a dropping, tumble & fall,
A slumping - as the world gathers on;
A sag - when you discover the snakes
Weren't your friends at all.

316   People in motion, rampant, exulted
Like poppies paraded every November:
Fast elevators reach the top storey
Before flooring again to the ground.

317   Lower than oak hewn for timber ....
Lower than beech felled by high winds
Lower than elm pulled down, diseased -
People in motion can sink.

318   Hippity hop, skip, jump and vault,
High hurdlers can be leap-frogged on,
Pounced upon, bobbed and tripped,
Sprung upon - left standing still.

319   People in motion in the water;
People in motion brought to scuttle;
People in motion sent to the bottom;
People in motion in Davey Jones locker

320   While around & around the waters turn,
Winding & twisting as the current runs
Put a girdle around the world?
Would those in motion falter at all?

321   For things whirl, and reel, and spin!
Rotate, revolve, gyrate, wheel!
Like a horse in a field .....
Tethered up and left to feed.

322   If this is evolutionary growth ...
Progress through advancing time,
Are we blossom still unfolding?
Opening up to flower?

323   To and fro - people go -
With a flourish, flaunt or wave.
People in motion, back and forth
Move through every day.

324   Are you petrified, disturbed?
Should you quiver like an aspen leaf?
No. Look you quietly to yourself
For the things you seek.

3RD LEXICON

Man has not created the universe. Mankind is part of creation and is bound by it. Man's attempt to explain creation to himself has developed a science lexicon which reveals his ignorance.

325   There is belief in natural theory,
Atom chain, ring and cycle ....
Neutrons, protons, fusion, fission
Governed by law and reason.

326   There is belief that creation
Flash-burned, waved & mushroomed out -
Charge-exchanged ... cascaded forward
As a speeding blur of cloud.

327   Alpha, beta, showers of gamma ...
Ray to particle, X to Vee ....
Irradiate - charge invested
The cosmos came to be.

328   Yet, whence stemmed the firstborn light?
Prime creation, blaze and glow ....
Radiating ... stream and glimmer
Across the veld of all that's known.

329   Whence stemmed the flame that lamps
Moon, sun and flambeau stars?
Whence came the force, the power
And the corpse of atoms - matter?

330   Or darkness - the palpable obscure,
Creation in a pitch-black shade ...?
What has fuelled the heavenly luminance
To light and fire day?

331   What screens and shields and filters?
Veils the day with blackout curtains?
What awnings drawn cover, shade
'Till all is overshadowed?

       *

332   Objects, lucent, lucid, clear -
Chiffon, silk, and cellophane;
Onion skin and tissue paper;
Panes to liquid windows ...

333   Do these frost light - milky opal?
Put mother pearl on all creation?
Beryl, diamond, moonstone, quartz?
What forces - glaze such crystals?

334   Creation is ... opaque and cloudy,
Misty, fogged, smoked and murked.
Dirty, turbid, obfuscated .....
Like a wolf's dark mouth.

335   There is hue - colour tint,
Bright, gaudy, rich and gay ....
Exotic, intense, florid, vivid
Chromatic coating, pigment grain.

336   Pale, dim, faint and sallow ....
Pallor ghastly ... haggardness.
Livid, sickly, pastel, blanched ...

Pasty, wan, white as a witch.
337 Silver, frost, chalk and pearl,
Alabaster, eggshell, hoar.
Kelt and buckra, lily, snowdrop,
Fair jasmine and albino rose.
338 Jet black sable, ebony, ink;
Pitch, tar, coal and soot.
Raven, rook, and night dark crow ...
Noir, schwarz, dhu, negro.
339 Gray, taupe, slatey ash ....
Dove, mole, mouse and squirrel.
Dappled, spotted, salt and pepper ...
Steel, lead, zinc and iron.
340 Cocoa ... coffee ... coconut,
Chocolate, chestnut, cinnamon.
Bay, dun, fawn and tawny ...
Hazel, olive, autumn corn.
341 Rose, rouge, scarlet, crimson ...
Blushing bloom, flush of flesh.
Damask, puce, stammel, murrey,
Cherry, carmine, ruby red.
342 Orange, ochre, peach and carrot,
Morning sun and marigold ....
Marmalade and tangerine ...
Mandarin and apricot ...
343 Lemon, daffodil and primrose,
Saffron, amber, citron gold.
Dandelion and sulphur yellow,
Beige, buff, sand and yolk.
344 Emerald, jade and olivine ....
Fir, grass, leaf, and sea;
Yew, apple, leek, and pea -
Shamrock, moss, myrtle green.
345 Azure, turquoise, sky and sapphire,
Electric, steel and cobalt blue.
French, Dresden. Prussian, Persian ...
Hyacinth .... forget-me-not,
346 Pansy, violet, lilac, thistle;
Plumb, raisin, damson, grape;
Orchid, lavender and mallow,
Mulberry, mauve and bilberry.
347 Multi-coloured - variegated.
Poly chromed - kaleidoscopic;
Creation is a striate prism,
Rainbow plaid mosaic daedal.

348 Day on Earth - heat and hotness,
Fervour, ardour, steaming warmth.
Atacama .... Kalahari .....
Sheets of fire, seas of flame
349 Like - the fierce Sirocco flare
Birch-brand burning - auto da fe;
Or the blow-torch blast and blister
Of the Baha scorch and sear -
350 With its basting and its broiling,
Roasting, grill and barbeque;
The Gobi fry and frazzle ...

Bake, cook and sand caboose.
351   All that heat: fuel and feed,
Torch, taper, faggot, fuse,
Thunder caps and detonators ...
Tinder, touch-wood, amadou -
352   Against the night, against the chill,
Against the glaze of jokull cold.
Against the raw-frost feathered snow,
Depth of winter, berg and floe -
353   Of Alaska - of Siberia -
And the kvef Icelandic white.
Creation sleeps in wolf's attire,
Glacier capped or crowned -
354   Sugared by layers of cloud,
Light, weightless, buoyant, airy,
Feather, thistle-down and fluff:
A bare touch, a cobweb's worth
355   Of dense, solid, thick, compact;
Body, block, cake and mass.
Clotted, lappered, bonny clabbered,
Serried, heavy, firm, intact.
356   Oh so rare - attenuated ...
Refined, purified and cleansed.
Defecated, filtered, winnowed,
Subtle, tenuous - sublimated.
357   Cloud catching on callous mountains,
Rigid, firm, stiff and tense.
Inelastic, quite unbending ...
To torrent gullies, o'er becks
358   As soft, gentle, pliant water:
Tender, mellow, tactile, lax:
Lithe, fictile, supple, limber -
Over rock and shingle ....
359   Across the Earth's surface grain ...
Jurassic wale, Cambrian weft,
Course or rough or linsey-woolsey,
Dainty, thin spun, fine and filmy.
360   With weight, gravity, tonnage, heft,
Sinker, lead, plumb and bob.
Avoirdupois, troy or metric ....
Running on and on.

361   Yet, there is a stream, a current
Through a field where no men go.
A circuit, path, loop and break,
Cable, cord and coil.
362   No machines can take Man there ...
Image matched, output retarded.
Should we drone on about it ....?
When it's so dull and boring.
363   Folk would rather don headphones
And tune-in on their radios ...
Play a tape, or flip a disc
Upon their personal stereos.
364   Or watch T.V. - their V.D.U's,
Relay link and simulcast ...
Than wrestle with the facts beyond

```
      Reflectors, discs, and telescopes.
365   Electric boffs try their luck:
      Radar pulse, and microwave ...
      Huff-duff, sniffer, cat and mouse ...
      Jam and spoof, sweep and scan -
366   With mechanics, statics, kinematics:
      Hydrodynamic engineering ...?
      Man exits by tools and instruments,
      Power machines and locomotion.
367   Knife, fork, spoon and chopstick ...
      Movement, action, motion, work.
      Machines are geared, wheeled & driven:
      Combustion, cam and piston rod -
368   Automated, self-pro pulsed ....
      Self-controlled and regulated,
      Robomatic, cybernetic ...
      Self-winding: moving freely -
369   Rubbing, scraping - scratching,
      Abrasive, grinding, rasping sounds.
      Machines with gnashing of cogged teeth
      Wear creation down .....
370   With elastic, flex, and rubber!;
      Whalebone, baleen, spring and gum.
      Vulcanised, strain and tension ...
      Give, yield and snap return.
371   Things - tough, resistant, stiff;
      Tenacious, viscid, fibrous enough,
      Even leathery, stringy, ropey ....
      For when the goings rough.
372   Things - fragile, brittle, frail,
      Easy crushed, easy cracked ....
      Shattered, shivered, splintered quick
      As light - through a pinprick hole.
373   Until to chalk, reduced to powder,
      Pulverised, churned to meal ......
      Beaten, pounded, thrashed and mashed,
      Creation's querned to dust.
```

4TH LEXICON

Bound by matter, Mankind has no knowledge of matter beyond his own solar system. This is reflected in the crude and small vocabulary that tries to equate that all known life is embodied in matter.

MATTER

```
374   Rotating constellations, times & tides
      Inverted dish we call the sky,
      Surrounded by such golden fire
      Revolves a globe where we dwell.
375   Material, matter, substance, stuff,
      Ball-bearing in the cosmic hub,
      There exists ... length and breadth,
      Our flesh and blood ...
376   Bound by corporal mundane fact,
      We mortals live to disembody.
      We dabble in the unsubstantial,
```

411

The psychic and the supernatural.
377 We are crazy! We are mad!
We are brick, plaster, lath.
We are lumber, timber, wood.
We are textile, plastic goods!
378 We are oxygen at base ....
Organic elements in trace.
Atomic mass, molecular weight ...
We are chemical in every way.
379 We are fat, grease and oil.
Lubricated, waxed and soaped,
We are lard, blubber, ghee,
Tallow coated, bees-wax daubed.
380 We are resin, rosin, gum,
Shellac joined and mastic tarred.
Lacquered, varnished, and veneered
We are hand-glued souvenirs.

LIFELESS MATTER

381 What of all lifeless matter?
Azoic, brute - the mineral kingdom
Of regimes contained inert in
Atom chains and rock crystals?
382 Is there life? We do not know!
A mortal's interest is in gold,
Silver, platinum, uranium ore.
Men melt worlds to cast their own.
383 Rock, stone, gravel, shingle,
The cosmos in a grain of grit ...
What more to scoria, breccia, schist
Than tombstones, shrines, & pyramids?
384 In *Terra firma*, we are rooted,
Sod, clod, dirt and clay ...
On this Earth, we are bound ...
Shore, coast, strand and bay.
385 By ocean ... we are margined,
Sea girt in an insular way;
Island, key, reef and atoll,
Isolated ... salt and wave.
386 By continent ... we are divided,
Bordered and barb-wire walled;
Behind strings of pointing missiles
In defence, we fence off.

387 Man is O ... or A ... or B,
Ab ... Rh ... plus or minus.
Blood, gore, claret, ichor ...
Such liquid is our water.
388 Creamy, milky, semi fluid ...
Curd, clabber, goo and gunk.
When male and female get together,
Sperm, semen, gamete run.
389 O liquids racing, mixing, fluxing!
Through the eons in suspension
Evolution turns ... resolves
In solution ... *Luxivium*.

390   Wet and moist dew-beads drop
Seed of earth and sky begotten,
Showers soak and impregnate
Mortals tearful for the sun.

392   Arid, baked, parched and scorched,
Too much sun or not enough.
Burnt, shrivelled, seared to dust,
Never drought. Always flood -

393   Rain, drizzle, scud and mist,
Cloudburst, downpour, deluge, storm,
Dogs, polecats, tadpoles, frogs,
Dagger drencher, pitchfork drowner.

394   Rindle, beck, gill and burn ...
Headwaters run, race and rill,
Jets spout, whirlpools gush,
Cascade, force, linn and rush.

395   Aqueduct, canal, and ditch ...
Channel, trough, drain, sluice.
Eddy, gurge, surge and swirl ...
Clear of weir, the waters billow

396   To the sea ... the bounding main,
Neptune's realm, soaked with salt,
The wavy waste where men thirst
Upon wild waters wound with wind -

397   Where millpond days, few and far
Allow sick-travellers lakish hours
To dream of lax lacustrine life
By loch, lagoon , mere, or tarn;

398   By inlet, estuary, gulf, cove;
By bay, bight, firth or fjord ...
Where homesteads by the harbour stand
Where men are want to be land-bound

399   By the salt marsh, quicksand mud,
Bogged down in conventional mode,
Where humans tearful for the sun,
Sink, and slough in their abodes.

400   We humans are prone to vapour; gas;
Fetid air; and choked damp smudge;
The reeking fumes and plumes of smoke
We breathe in leisure and at work

401   Should we not enjoy our air,
Alfresco go and fresh breeze take;
Weather-beat our bloodless faces,
And think about the ozone layer.

402   Should we not inhale the wind,
Boreas, Notus, Zephyr, Eurus ...
Eager stand their howling rage,
And welcome gale and hurricane.

403   Should we not, shroud in cloud
Enjoy the nebulous, sleepless sky,
The wool pack banks, the cirro-tails,
The pillows, curls, stripes and snails

404   That froth, foam, and bubble up,
Spume, surf, and spindrift boil,
Seethe, simmer, cap-cloud cream

'Till culled of smog - the air clears.

MATTER ORGANIC

405 We are ... protoplasmic,
Organic, bion, morphon, zoon,
And like all flora-fauna
We die too soon ....

406 A bridge across a burning stream,
We are chased by fateful forces.
A ladder infinite climbed to safety
Is fiction made from fact imagined.

407 Death follows life without arrest,
There is no tribute cancels sentence.
Across the bridge, the burning Styx,
There's only sleep not more adventure.

408 There the Beast dwells eating mutton,
Drinking wine knee-deep in water.
No abattoir ... no aceldama ...
All is quiet, there is silence.

409 There are no graves, no catacombs -
The earth's grassed & sweetly flowered
The Beast is all that's left of us,
'*Hic jacet*' on it's tattooed arm.

410 There is flora, plant and herb,
Seedling, evergreen, perennial.
Legume, cereal, fern and shrub,
Tree, woodland, grove and scrub.

411 Botanised, it is vegetable,
Thallus algae, fungi, moulds;
Lichens, worts, rusts, mosses,
Smuts, fuci, wracks and more ....

412 It is husband 'd .... cultivated,
Gardened, lumbered, tilled and farmed,
Nursed, hot housed, cold frame forced,
Grown, cropped, cleaned and stored.

413 There is fauna ... creature, critter,
Creeping thing, brute and beast.
Lion last, and foul mart first,
A cuddy Jack ... a neddy ass.

414 There is insect ... vermin, louse,
Bed-bug, tick, chigger, midge,
Cootie, skeeter, gadfly, nit,
Leech and worm ... such lovely things!

415 What's wrong with worms after all?
Platyhelminths ... anneloids ...
Nemathelminths ... what a mouthful!
Don't let the name put you off.

416 Let's love worms! Let's love worms!
What pleasure's found in such words.
You cannot herd, drive, or goad
Five billion worms to rule this world.

417 Mankind, mortal, human Man,
Biped .... homo sapiens.
A false God made us as we are -

A breath, a shadow, nothing more.
418   Our peoples, cultures, ethnic groups
Are skin-deep to the cosmic whole,
Like ants we swarm, our greed succeeds
In keeping each racing each.
419   And were it not for *OOMPH* and IT,
The facts of life, the birds and bees-
The phallic male and vulva woman,
The heat, the burning, and the itch:
420   Blokes and guys, bucks and chaps ...
Penis, gonads, testes, sperm;
What point would there be to men
And all their lust, desire for flesh
421   Without *femme*, and *frau*, and dame,
Rag and bone and hank of hair ...
What appeal would IT have ...?
If the OOMPH became unknown.

5TH LEXICON

Through the senses - Man feels the Universe. Such sensations effect Man's mind and body - and often when Man speaks of it, he uses a lexicon of love.

SENSATION

422   We all have feeling, conscious or not,
Sense of awareness, perception, response
For all experience sensuous or nerval,
Keenly exquisite, poignant, or raw ...
423   'Till we faint, swoon, succumb .....
Numb and dull ... fall out of love;
Dazed, stunned in *dammerschlaf*,
We return dead to the world -
424   Where suffering hurt, distress, pain,
We pang, ache, fret, shrink ...
Inflamed, festered, sore tormented -
'Till time salves the sting.

TOUCH

425   We contact, touch and feel
With a whisper, breathe, or kiss;
With a brush, graze, or stroke
We run our fingers over ....
426   With a tickle, tingle, thrill,
We titill, goose, and vellicate
With tactile paw, wield and ply
We palm, massage, manipulate.

TASTE

427   With taste, relish, smacking tongues,
Wooers sip, sup, lick and lap
The savour flavours love supplies;
Sample, specimen, and bite.
428   Goodness, zest, gusto, *gout*,
Sapid season, sauce and spice,

Provocative, piquant, larrup,
Luscious, gratifying love!

429   Not nasty, foul, vile nor acrid;
Not pungent, sour, bitter, gall;
Not icky, rank nor nauseating ...
Love sucks deep and savours on

430   Manna, nectar, *eau sucre*;
Syrup cloying honey dew ....
Mellifluous fancy, sweetened fervour,
Rich sugar-candy bill and coo!

431   It does not feast on sour grapes,
Tart crab-fruit, acid diet ...
Astringent vitriolic fare,
Fermented citric pickled food.

432   Love does not nip the hungry tongue,
Pepper hot and ginger kick ....
Lively, tangy, racy, brisk,
It pierces - but does not prick.

433   So, pull, puff, draw, drag,
Chew, chow, dip, inhale ...
Take the pill, spit and run,
Through the smoke feed on love.

SMELL

434   There is an odour, ... a scent,
A whiff of fragrant perfume.
Strong, heady, and suffocating
That stops all lovers dead.

435   For is there aromatic equal ..?
Attar, essence, balm or oil
Of jasmine, musk, frangipani,
Sandalwood or bergamot?

436   Malodor, fetar, stench, stink
Of skunk, stink-horn, rotten corpse,
Offensive, reeking, fetidness,
Stops all bipeds short.

437   So lovers fumigate and lime
With sachet, spray and pot-pourri;
Deodorize and ventilate ...
Rose water, cologne, bay *pastille*.

SIGHT

438   With bedroom eyes we lovers stare,
Gaze, gape, gawk and glower,
First blush, wink, *coup d'oeil*,
We steal and spy and look.

439   Through a glass darkly mote,
Mope-eyed dim, we boss-eye view
Men as trees walking past
And forty ways Sunday note.

440   Blind we ken not hair, nor hide.
O bats! Amid the blaze of noon!
Eclipsed without a hope of day.
Dark, dark, we play at peek-a-boo!

441   Bystanders watch, behold as seers,

Observe and witness our blind love,
Spectate and see us lions slum
And rubberneck like cooing-birds!

442 Bifocals, pince-nez, goggles, specs,
Blinkers, lorgnette, contact lens,
Horn-rims, monocles, glims and shades,
Love is clean-cut, sticks out plain.

443 Perceptible, prominent, pronounced,
We lovers live in homes of glass ....
En evidence, exposed, outcropped,
Crystal clear, love's not blurred.

444 Invisible, faint, *'a perte de vue'*
Hazy, misty, foggy, fuzzed .....
Escape the notice, lie hid, dim?
Blush unseen? .... don't kid us!

445 Love's own air, mien, demeanour
Betrays itself, comes to light ...
Bearing, garb, complexion, colour
Flushes forth, flares into passion

446 'Till time dissolves, leaves no trace,
We lovers cease to be, fade out,
Melt away, depart or flee .....
Leave no shape or form behind.

SOUND

447 Listen drumheads, conches, luggies!
Hark, you cock-eared, long-eared house!
Hear, you acute lappet audience ....
Eavesdrop on these lips of mine!

448 For you are deaf or hard of hearing,
Dull-eared to the sound of song.
Attend! Oyez! you adder stoppers!
Heed you now the voice of love.

449 Love is sonant, stressed, accented,
Poly phoned, vowelled and thonged ...
Timbre, tone, key and note,
Lovers voice then voiceless turn

450 Silent, still, quiet, and mum.
Mute, muffled, deadened, lulled,
We save our breath. Cheese it. Choke,
So hushed you'd hear a feather drop.

451 Faint and soft, dimly veiled,
Voce velata, we lovers sob ....
Mummer, whisper, sough and moan,
Waft a sigh ... *sordo* ... low.

452 Love resounds, echoes, rings,
Peals and tolls - in hollowness
Vibrates, rebounds in repercussion
On all send backs, all returns.

453 So thump! Beat the lovers' drum!
Rat-tat-tat! Tom-tom-tom!
Tattoo a ruffle, rub-a-dub!
Kettle, snare, and tympanum!

454 Thunder clap, crash and crack!
We lovers take our knocks and taps;
Burst, blast, bang and boom!

417

Rumble, roar, roll and *rale* ...
455   Love hisses, fizzles, whistles out
To snooze, snore and saw on logs,
We lovers sniffle, splutter, lisp,
Wheeze, sneeze, don't kiss but spit.

456   For love can be a shrill, course rasp,
A croak, a caw, a growl, a snarl,
A screech, a shriek, a scream, a whine
A high-pitched, jarring, grating life.

457   A cry, a call, a shout, a hoot,
A bawl, a yelp, a yap, a howl ....
Love can be a *view halloo* ...
A cruel sport - hunting you!

458   So you may gaggle, crow, or squawk,
Cluck, clack, gobble, coo ......
Love is not just ... chirp and cheep!
It's not a tweet or twee cuckoo!

469   Love can be discordant, flat
Sweet bells jangled out of tune.
Above the pitch, sharp and sour,
Chiming harsh and toneless hours.

460   Love is a melody, a Lydian measure,
A mosaic of music, a canto of verse;
A lay, a ballad, a carol, an anthem,
A rondo, an aria, a lyric motet.

461   Arranged, adapted, harmonically tuned,
We lovers vibrate, tremble and trill.
Metrically cadenced - rhythm & pulse
We scale and run. Minim and rest

462   We make music ... nightly perform
In tin-pan alleys, where neckers know
That no-one need play second fiddle
To catgut scrapping troubadours.

463   So harp and lute, viol and flute,
Zither, banjo, cello, horn,
Guitar, bassoon and tambourine ...
Love is string, and wind and drum.

6TH LEXICON

Of all the things in the Universe - it is supposed that Man knows the workings of his own mind best. He has intellect - which he believes to be unique and singular in the Universe. To demonstrate that intellect - he has compiled a modest lexicon. The modesty of the lexicon reveals the modesty of his intellect.

CONCEPTION OF MIND

464   There is intellect, sense and psyche,
Sconce, reason, *vernunft* and wits.
Faculty of mind, gifts, talents ...
Pate, noddle, noggin, nouse.

465   There is intelligence and savvy,
Verstand, comprehension, reach ...
Astuteness, acumen and foresight,
Canny cunning, *geist*, esprit.

466 Thus are sages ... Plato, Nestor,
    Soloman, Manu, Buddha, Christ!
    Sensible, prudent, knowing, wise,
    Oraclers, luminaries, shafts of light.
467 They are sober, sound and sane,
    Right in mind, *compos mentis*.
    They get things in proportion,
    Bring to reason all that's bonkers.
468 They know - with ken and savvy,
    Acquaint, grasp, master, grip,
    Have it pat, dead to rights ....
    Have it at their finger tips.
469 Brainwork, head-work, mental labour,
    Workings of the mind ... ideas.
    They weigh, muse and ponder all,
    Profoundly think ... deliberate.
470 Rational, logic, dialectics ....
    Deduction, debate, deliberation,
    Argument, premise, postulation ...
    They don't break the bounds of reason.
471 Thus they're wise not ignorant, blind,
    Stupid, doltish, dense and thick -
    Chowder-blocked and turnip-headed,
    Foggy in their numbskull brains.
472 Thus, they're not inanely silly -
    Witless, crazy, goofy, daft;
    Wacky, batty, mute and dumb,
    Loopy, screwy, inept and mad.
473 Tom-fools, nincompoops, noddies,
    Zany, gaby, sops and sots ....
    Dolts, dunces, dopes and dullards,
    Drivellers, doters, dunders, dummies.
474 Some conjure up their own psychosis,
    Schizophrenia prepossessed ....
    Maniacs well demented - with
    Rats and spiders in the head -
475 For some have bats in the belfry ...
    Others have a button missing ...
    Some have water topside (ugh!)
    And demons in their upper stories.
476 They are strange! odd and freakish,
    Eccentric, queer, crank and kinked,
    Non-conformist, nuts - screw balled,
    Quirked, twisted, beed and quipped.
477 Eggheads, highbrows, savants, pundits,
    Gents and scholars, men of letters ...
    Pedants, blue socks, dilettantes ...
    Triflers - who know no better!
478 Blind and naked, empty-headed,
    Vague of notion, ignorant, green ...
    They are cooks of half-baked ideas,
    They are wise in their conceit
479 Of notion, fancy, concept, image,
    Impression, statement and opinion:
    Recept ... abstract or principled
    By slant or twist of inspiration -
480 They are fallow, vacant, empty,

Vacuous. blank, with no idea.
Pushed from their hollow thoughts -
Riding in on hobby-horses,
481   These vague ghostly dreamlike shadows,
Don't perceive the things unseen,
They do not see themselves around us -
These 'little birds' live by hunches,
482   Claptrap, moonshine, pussyfooting.
Such camel gulpers, hedging dodgers
Beat themselves around the bush
And beg no questions later.
483   All their talk is caption headings,
Topic leaders, banner-lines ...
It's the pabulum of the day!
It is what the papers say!
484   Inquiry, search, quest and hunt,
Rummage, ransack out the muck ...
Question, quiz, grill and pump,
Poke, probe, pry and plumb -
485   Press men don't allow reply,
Riposte, retort, repartee ...
They receipt response rebukely
With quotes of butchered précis.
486   Not allowed answer, reason,
Explanation, real denouncement ...
Issues addressed to the public
Remain unravelled, unresolved.
487   Thus HEADLINES - Caught in the Act!
Caught Flat-Footed, Caught Off-Guard!
Caught Out Napping, Pants Down - Off!
'GAY VICAR HANGS SATANIC BOY!'
488   So - flying in the face of facts,
Misjudgement warps, miscalculates,
Misconstrues with mis-conjectures;
Over-reckoning leads to censure
489   Till mountains out of molehills rise
Because the most is made of least.
Some overrate the worth of dung
And under prize the worth of meat.
490   Some undervalue and underrate ...
Minimise, make little of .....
Think nothing of, set no store,
Make light of all they do not know;
491   While others experiment and test ...
Try it on the dog for size,
Fly a kite ... just to see
How the wind blows, how land lies.
492   Others measure, gauge and estimate ...
Load luck to the plimsoll-line.
Apply the yardstick to chance ...
Square off - and with wide eyes -
493   Compare, contrast, and check,
Match dope, stack up, note
That candles melt in the sun
And shipped water can sink boats.
494   Others - discriminate with tact,
Know a poop from a prow ....

Pick and choose, be diplomatic -
Know the walrus from sea-cow.
495   For indistinct is half of twelve,
And one half dozen of indiscreet -
For those promiscuous, muddled up ...
See their ships sink on reefs.

496   But let us not judge, presume,
Surmise, imagine, fancy .....
All things considered - on the whole
Taking one thing with another ....
497   That preconceiving, presupposing,
Going off half-cocked in pre-decision
Is prejudice on the trigger
By leaping to conclusions.
498   For suppose, I had a theory, guess ...
An inkling, a hint, a notion, an idea,
A shot, a stab into the dark
And took a fancy into my head
499   That philosophy, that love of wisdom
Was the summation of all folly in man.
Would my supposition be preposterous?
And deemed untrue - rather than a lie?
500   For some have belief, faith, a tenet
They swear by, take an oath upon ...
You can bet your bottom dollar,
Bank on them, give them credit,
501   Trust that they will not swallow,
Take the fly, hook, line and sinker,
Or think the moon made of cheese,
Believe in cats or broken mirrors.
502   While those from Grantham disbelieve,
Doubt, mistrust, don't buy a word -
With a "Now, now ... I know better!"
Take them with a grain of salt!!
503   They're the ones to turn an ear,
Disposed to be no-one's fool ....
Sceptical - and hard to swallow
They kid themselves they're ungullible.
504   Such folks need proof of all belief
To bring it home to prove some point -
To make a vessel hold great volume
They make a hole in it first.
505   What confute have we for blind faith
That takes the ground from under us?
Lets knock wind against the sails
Of those who won't shut up!
506   Some would say we should exempt,
Make proviso for their sconce ...?
Mitigate, concede and temper ....
Make concessions sine que non.
507   But with no ifs and ands or buts
To certain express clear beliefs,
With no strings attached outright
There can be no fixed proviso.

508   Yet - as luck may have it -

By off-chance, all things considered,
It's conceivable - on the cards
Imaginable and remotely possible -
509   For some to weave a rope from sand;
To catch the wind in a net;
Go fetch water in a sieve;
Gather thistles, think them figs.
510   It is plausible to believe-in
Probability and '*ben trovato*'.
I dare say one can assume ...
Ten to one that everything's equal -
511   Some can in two places be;
And make cheese out of chalk;
Catch a weasel fast asleep;
And gather grapes from thorns.
512   Certainly, sure thing, it's a cinch,
Rain or shine, sink or swim .....
No buts about it, without doubt,
Sure as fate, some are liars.
513   So - in a maze all turned around,
Who shall decide when all disagree?
Who will leap into the dark ...
When up a tree or out at sea?
514   When the certain seems improbable,
Some go blind, take pot-luck;
Some buy a pig in a poke -
Nil lay down, nought take up.

515   Some hit the nail on the head,
Some hit it on the nose ....
Right as rain tell the facts,
The truth, the real McCoy.
516   Phrases coined, said before -
Dictum, adage, proverb, gnome ...
Slogan, motto, moral, maxim ...
Hummed tunes and quoted songs.
517   Errors, faults, untruths, wrongs.
Boners, blunders, slips, *faux pas's*'.
Lapses gauged without one's host ...
Aimed at a pigeon - wound a crow.
518   It's all a trick, a gross deception,
A wrong impression, a warped illusion,
A will-o-the-wisp conception ....
Imagination and hallucination.
519   O rude awakening! Disenchantment!
The bubble burst, the truth exposed.
With one's eyes open, un-blindfolded
With it comes the dawn for some.
520   So, let us assent - some are smart,
Give the nod, our validation ....
Put our Hancock to the thing
And carry it by acclamation.
521   Let's not dissent, protest, object,
Put up a squawk or a howl ....
Raise our voice against the charge
That some are sometimes clowns.
522   Let some avow swear and pledge

To tell the world what they know,
Maintain with their final breath,
That they have taken an oath.
523   Let's not deny, disclaim, dispute,
Not for love or money sell ....
The issue some are joined on
If we cannot help.

STATES OF MIND

523   Outlook, attitude, point of view.
From where I sit, my bent, my bias
I'm warped by the way I feel
In the climate of opinion.
525   I am broad minded, open, free ...
I swear no oath to any master.
I forbear to hand out judgment.
I live, and let others breathe.
526   If I am narrow-minded, blind,
And do not protest to aid a cause ...
It's not because I shut my eyes
But because I'm ill-informed.
527   I'm as curious as a snooping cat,
Quidnunc & questioning as Lot's wife,
I would brave the Gorgon's eyes
To get inside her mind.
528   Elizabethan born, and heedful ...
I look right or left with interest.
I don't want to be indifferent
Pursuing an easy life.
529   With attention, thought and ear;
With observation, note and care;
With concern, regard, respect;
I'll smile while bored to tears.
530   Without disregard, distraction;
Without unwatchful inadvertence;
Without unwary, dismissive yawns;
I'll bear the dullest simpleton.
531   And when my mind's made to swim -
And when my head reels and whirls -
And when I'm really made quite ill -
I'll bear the jokes of bimbos.
532   I'll take care to groom my image -
I'll take time to be most vigilant -
I'll keep alert, take an interest -
It pays to know others' business.
533   I'll not neglect to heed my needs -
Nor disregard my own hushed voice.
Muddled, fuddled, hazy, fogged ...
I'll not let others knock me back.

534   Flames of figment, fumes of fiction,
All the dreams romance is made of -
High flown turrets, flights of fancy,
The rainbow's end, cloud-nine fantasy.
535   Some are staid, stuffy, dull ...
They keep both feet on the ground;

They burst balloons and say that stars
Do not shoot the moon at all.

536   Blind with hearing, deaf with sight,
        We forget things, and erect monuments.
        We collect trinkets, cherish treasures
        Like diaries to review in retrospect.
537   Blind with movies, deaf with music ...
        There's lots missing and loads burdened.
        Bygone's - trickle through a sieve
        Like water - consigned to oblivion.
538   So wait! And watch! Bide your time!
        Or we will say 'What did we tell you!'
        That's how things are, the way it goes
        When something turns out as expected.
539   With a start, a shock, surprise ...
        We do not expect some things to be
        Unforeseen - dropped from the clouds
        Like cats and dogs on Christmas day.
540   It blights our hopes, leaves us blue,
        Frustrated, foiled and all forlorn.
        Let-down, it makes us sad and glum,
        We zip our mouths and bite our gums.

541   Sometimes we feel it in our bones
        To see our way into the future ...
        There were no spacemen when I was born
        I was seven when Yuri flew.
542   I never thought I'd foretell
        Of men on Mars before my death.
        But who needs crystal balls
        When the Big One's overhead.
543   Warnings, portents and omens imminent,
        There are foreboding presage signs ...
        But I harbinger in the Space Age
        And proclaim auspicious times!

COMMUNICATION

544   Word for word to the letter,
        We learn to grasp sense and meaning.
        Purport, import and implication -
        Not everything need be verbatim.
545   More than meets the eye sometimes
        That makes no sign, escapes notice.
        Unexpressed, unsaid, unmentioned ....
        Latent things can be suggested.
546   Sounding brass but tinkling crystal,
        A bunkum tale told by an idiot ...
        A load of bosh blabbed by a bumpkin ...
        Is something almost inexpressible.
547   For to get the idea, get the picture,
        To get it into our thick heads ...
        Some speak volumes of high English
        When single syllable words are best.
548   There's much Greek and Double Dutch,
        Way over my head and beyond me -

549 Enough to puzzle a Law Lord judge
With the word LOVE in the language.
Unintelligible too much of the world,
Ambiguous and inequitably duplex ...
Love's meaning is a four-letter word
Or a five lettered one if you're French.

550 As a rule, in a manner of speaking ...
Figures of speech make it difficult
To partition parable from paraphrase,
And to separate fable from rendition.

551 In other words, strictly speaking ...
Explanations can be all wrong.
To read between the lines is fine
But not when sense is lost.

552 Abuse of terms, misuse of words
Puts a false construction on
All that strains or stretches sense
Or perverts, distorts the meaning of.

553 I took a walk into winter ...
Then came back, began to write
A letter to the girl I love.
We keep in touch across the miles.

554 We've learned to talk 'tween the lines
She lives in the English south ....
Open, out-spoken, we tell each other
Of the traffic we've encountered.

555 We wear our hearts upon our sleeves,
We face the day, bare and naked -
Plain as the path to the parish church
We lay our cards upon the table.

556 We confess, concede, own-up ...
Cough-up our soft impeachments.
I get it off my chest, she her breast:
Without disguise - we plead guilty.

557 Kept informed, kept up to date,
Made aware of all small changes -
We give notice of impending strain
Progressive love acquaints us with.

558 And here's a piece of news for you -
We've no time for small town talk:
The gossip sailing in blabbers' mouths
Is filth to the normal child.

559 And I pronounce - We are young!
Write in the sky - We are in love!
Let it be seen the length of Britain
And publicised by sandwich boys.

560 For when we're on the telephone,
I can hear the call-girl's sigh.
A long distance toll call signal
Is all that keeps us silent ....

561 And in the chill of a winter day,
I dispatch ... this newest letter.
By van, by bus, by rail, by plane -
We'll keep in touch forever!

562 Teach a cock to crow, a dog to bark.

Teach a hen to cluck, a fish to bite.
Sometimes the blind lead the dumb
When the dumb are born with sight.
563   From time to time, we're all misled
And fall foul to the propagandists.
Laputa leads the pack of wolves -
Goody Snatch follows close on after.
564   These quack philosophers - so absorbed
In extracting sunbeams from cucumbers;
They turn students from high ideals
And make them dwell on vulgar matters.
565   'Till education is a live and learn -
Lessons in the school of hard knocks.
To burn the candle at both ends ....
Means a Goody Snatch help yourself.
566   For we're in the hands of Coryphaei:
We're witness to the New - Old Order.
Our tongues are tied, we cannot chorus
This schoolmam'ish kind of drama.
567   It's fee-boy stand and free-boy fall.
It's fee-girl laugh and free-girl cry.
One is privileged - Ten are not -
Why teach worms to walk or talk?
568   Public, private, boarding, free.
Fees! Fees! Fees! Fees! ......
See those mud holes by the road ...?
Where state schools used to be!

569   With a gesture, with a nod,
Di gave Charlie the hots ....
Maybe they haven't such a lot -
What have we got ...?
570   We've got regalia, emblems, badges,
Lions, eagles, crosses, sickles ...
Flags starred, barred, tri-coloured,
And Liz and Philip.
571   We've got records, rolls and annals,
Memo's, memoirs, notes and minutes,
Catalogues, lists and registers ...
But give me hugs and kisses.
572   We've got clerks, scribes and writers,
Ledgers, books, journals, logs.
You can have my private diaries ...
All I want is love.

573   We're all dolls, puppets, dummies,
Manikins and men of straw,
Models, marionettes and statues
In a spitting image show.
574   We're all mis-drawn, falsely coloured,
Disguised, distorted by all art.
Actors give the wrong idea -
And painters camouflage.
575   Yet art is commonplace perfection,
Time captured in a gasp of air.
Meaning caught between two rhymes,
Sense tossed between two lines.

576   Science is a still-life flower ...
Man made man a crafted chore ...
Sculptors tooling at their marble
Till gargantuans roar.

577   Potters work the fine fire-clay,
Shape and throw, turn and bake.
Glaze the world in a kiln -
Day after day.

578   Snap-shooters shoot mugs and places,
Blow up the world in their own way.
Stop in the bath as a solution ...
Before the picture fades.

579   Engravers needle, point and etch,
Scratch, hatch, stipple, burr ...
But like all high and noble artists
They infer what they concur.

580   For artists conjure up illusions,
Consent to dream the actual world.
They cannot note how things are -
But how things might become.

581   My language is the speech of Time,
My father's talk, my mother's tongue.
I speak with a Northern *Rrrrr* ....
And patter is my idiom.

582   My alphabet is Roman through -
My script is cursive, sometimes print.
My spelling isn't very good -
My signature's a squint

583   My stock of words is very small,
I use catch phrases when I can.
I use slang and pick up fads.
I swear and curse when mad.

584   My Christian tag is very formal,
People call me mate or pal -
And 'cause I like my granddad's name
I use that as my handle.

585   What's in a name anyway ....?
Is it wrong - being unknown?
What's with being you-know-who?
Such-and-such? Or so-and-so?

586   I'll never learn how to express
In good set terms the way I feel.
But I wouldn't trade all my *Rrrr's*
For a world of *Quuu's* and *Peee's*.

587   Grammar rules parts of speech -
Subject, object, case and tense.
Some can parse and conjugate
And that is very nice.

588   Some misuse, murder English -
Caco on, lax and loose ...
They misconstrue and malapropos
But that is not abuse.

589   For diction creates wide divide -
It is the garment dressing thought.
The wealthy - clothed with fashion:

427

The educated - hung with language.
590 But O what elegance! Grace and taste
In those who master language ....!
The right word in the right place
Upstages the snob or bastard.
591 Barbarous, uncouth - plain vulgarity
Is most offensive to the ears!
Well, is it not? Crude and rude
And in bad taste, or what ...?
592 Far better we hear plain speech,
Household words, dull and dry -
Than bear a string of in-decorums:
Low stuff shrilly laughed-off.
593 Far better to be brief and curt,
Crisp and terse, compact, succinct.
Within a nutshell, all compressed
The soul of wit's - a wink.
594 Far worse it is to gush out words -
To circumlocute with longiloquence;
Expatiate ..... speak at length
With circuitous protractedness.

595 With wag of chin, yap of jaw,
With a prattle, gaff or gab -
Man may conceal the dawn of day,
While breaking light upon the dark.
596 With bat at breeze, bump of gums ...
With raise of voice, get in a word -
Man may buttonhole a friend .....
Or take the floor in self-defence.
597 Others - less articulate -
Broken voiced, speech impeded ...
Might stumble, hum, hem and haw,
Stammer, stutter, falter, halt.
598 Others - loose tongued, idly glib,
With a twaddle, tittle-taddle ....
Might varnish twattle with a rattle,
A jabber-gabble-gabber-blabber.
599 Others converse, have intercourse;
They sweeten the banquet with chat;
Feasting on emotion, each conversation
Feeds on the fruit of the heart.
600 Others stand aside addressing walls,
Hamlets .... apostrophise loud
Soliloquise on - alone in the world.
As life's monologue clowns.
601 Others - orators mounted on soapboxes,
Lecturing, haranguing, tirade on apathy
on sin, spending, and world concerns -
Apartheid and the killing of whales.
602 Others - ride the tide of eloquence
With ideas that breed, words that burn.
They have tongues in their heads ....
Going double-four at eight-to-one.
603 Such prose run mad - the gift of gab
Turned *sesquipedalian* highfalutin -
Is pompous bombast, rant and bunkum

That's balder dashingly platitudinous.

604　There are hacks and penny-liners,
　　　There are many mad *scribendi* ...
　　　Writers drafting *'coup de plume'*
　　　Black and white calligraphy.
605　Much is written - little's published,
　　　Proofed, set, plated, pressed,
　　　Left to run, pulled, reissued
　　　Or printed time and time again.
606　Few are fussed to write a letter,
　　　To communicate with those they love.
　　　The most they'll do is send a postcard
　　　When they go abroad.
607　Yet nearly all ... peruse books,
　　　Flick through art and fashion mags -
　　　Read the comic strips and stories
　　　And headlines in the daily rags.
608　But few review, write-up, report,
　　　Run a commentary on the world.
　　　There seems to be a billion views
　　　But few of any worth.
609　Perhaps we cannot compend life,
　　　Survey it in a few short lines,
　　　Abridge mankind in a draft
　　　Of words, condensed and rhymed.

610　Many fictions, sets of lies,
　　　The memory of man is gossip form.
　　　Legend, myth, and fairy tale
　　　And scrolls of wild romance.
611　There is poetry, verse and song -
　　　Emotion recollecting beauty;
　　　Painting with the gift of gods;
　　　Expression of exquisite feeling.
612　But poetry - that knot in the gut -
　　　The unison of man with nature:
　　　Is for all who love and feel great truth
　　　While cheering their own sweet solitude.
613　And prose - words in the finest order,
　　　Grand - can be plain and common place,
　　　Matter of fact and unromantic
　　　When written in a truthful way.
614　Then there's drama - prose at play,
　　　Poetry masked to stalk a stage ....
　　　Tragedy the art of masters:
　　　Comedy the fun of knaves -
615　Actors puffed and self important,
　　　Prima donnas primped with paint.
　　　Extras always out of work ....
　　　Like Pimpernels when paid.

616　Other times, there is a mute silence,
　　　A reticence, a Laconic calm .....
　　　A tight-lipped, remote detachment
　　　I cannot understand.
617　There is a veil, a dark concealment,

A screen of fog before my eyes.
So I play dumb, put the lid on
The coffins of my past.

618　I hide *perdu*, lie in wait,
In the shade eclipse myself.
From sight retire, and undercover
Watch for tell-tale signs.

619　Signs of falseness, tarradiddle,
Fib and flam prevarication;
Cock and bull exaggeration;
Bosh and bunk and drivel.

620　With much cry and little wool,
The tempest in a tea-pot poured -
I come it strong and stir
The truth with a silver spoon.

621　But I don't deceive, delude or dupe,
Trick, jape, kid or spoof .....
Play a bunko game of bilk
Nor sell gold bricks to boobs.

622　I am no double-dealing Janus,
A Judas or a Machiavelli .....
An Artful Dodger or a Diddler,
A cockatrice or Indian giver.

623　For I'm no gull, duck, or pigeon,
Goat, cat's paw, mooch or chump,
Fool, monkey, jay or coot ....
Do you hear me? …. Good!

7TH LEXICON

Humanity is gregarious, but each individual has a will that distinguishes him or her from the rest of humankind. This is commendable - but it also produces folly and madness which is counter-universal. Recognising this folly, and learning from it, requires Man to be familiar with the seventh lexicon.

WILL

624　With a will, a wish, a fancy,
With a mind to have one's way,
Some take the law into their hands
To have their own sweet way.

625　Some ... far less grudging
With willing heart and happy cheer
Takes it ... on their own freewill
To gladly volunteer.

626　Others ... more demurely scrupled,
Balk, beg off, shrink and shy.
With recoil, and an ill-grace
They protest ... then fly!

627　Fly, flee, cut and run,
Abscond, elope, welsh and truck ...
Take it on the lam, scram!
Lead the world a pretty dance.

628　Slip the collar, shake the yoke,
Smartly leap into the lifeboat.
Get off cheap, go Scot-free ...

By the skin of their teeth.
629 Abandon, forsake, leave, desert,
Throw in the sponge, wash their hands,
Azzle out of all commitment,
Bid a long goodbye.

630 Some do not know their own minds.
They flounder between will & will not;
They wait to see how the cat'll jump -
Call the shot once the coin's dropped.
631 With a coolness - neutral air,
Without a care, a hoot, a scat;
Nonchalant, spineless, cold ....
Desire can turn all black.

632 Some have cause to incite, goad,
Blow the coals, apply the torch,
Wake the rabble from their sleep,
Nettle, irritate and prick.
633 Others throw dust in the eyes -
On some pretext or lame excuse
Find a peg to hang their cloak ...
Or pretend they're drunk.
634 Some allure with sex and glamour,
Angle with a silver hook -
Gild the pill, give the come-on,
Vamp you with a wicked look.
635 Others bribe, corrupt and purchase,
Soap their palms with all they grease,
Oil the pan with all the graft
They've sugared-off from thieves.
636 Others dissuade, dampen, deter,
Play it cold, chill the air -
Whoever they are, or their ends,
They're a bunch of pains!

637 Intent, purpose, design, aim ....
The be-all end-all *raison d'être*.
Some take it in their dizzy heads
To take no heed of progress.
638 Scheme, device, plot and plan,
Many sketch out their whole life
But few make arrangements for coping
With the problems they'll encounter.
639 On the track, on the scent ...
Some bend each step to shape a course;
Others chase the hounds in full cry -
In hot pursuit of what?
640 Business, occupation, work ....?
Task or stint, chore or job?
There are careerists in the world
But most are just employed.
641 Yet, there's a choice, a selection -
You have a vote, a voice to barrack ...
You have a yeah, a nay .... two hands
To nominate your ballot winners.

431

642   You can reject, disown, rebuff,
        Do away with all those appointed.
        You have the right to brush aside
        Those who serve you badly.

643   And if you are compelled, obliged
        To make a virtue of necessity ...
        Then, the die's cast, it's in the cards,
        And you must act with urgency.

644   For all is preordained, foregone.
        Who can swear it is not so?
        Rough-hewn Time shapes your end,
        While some say that God is dead.

645   How would I know if it were true?
        A case is still being made for Him.
        Some say it is a put-up job ...
        Please put me up there too!

646   Some make the most, turn to account,
        Apply themselves beyond all price.
        They'll not impose, presume themselves
        More profitable than their worth.

647   For others consume, expend, waste,
        Finish, eat up all the cake ...
        Light their candles all at once,
        Burn incense in a gale.

648   Some misuse, abuse, pervert,
        Persecute, do their worse ....
        Misapply their witch-like talents
        To profane and desecrate.

649   Others cast off, throw away,
        Adopt the order of the day,
        Rid themselves of all the trash
        Consigned to file thirteen.

650   Others labour on in vain,
        Take part in the great goose-chase,
        Whistle waltzes to the walls
        Shine their torches at the sun.

651   Such custom comes as second nature,
        Habit, practice, *dastur*, rule -
        There is a pattern that is fashion,
        There is the well worn groove.

652   Some break the mould, cure themselves,
        Buy a frock to dress old lines ...
        Do old things in a new way,
        Rid themselves of inured self.

653   Some glossed up in spiffy ideas,
        Adorn themselves in the latest thing.
        Stranger still - they keep in step
        With Jones - who's up-to-Dick.

654   Rather odd, but quite conventional,
        Good form, really proper, right ...
        They shop for things on Main Street,
        As that's the approved style.

655   Some stand on ceremony, outward form,
        Prim and rigid, civil be .....
        Place social grace on par with riches.
        Well, on the surface, dear!

656   Deep down most cherish - *sans facon* -
        A free non-tight be yourself ....
        So let your hair down - *en famille* -
        Do things as you might.

657   There is a path, a track, a trail,
        A road that leads to a door.
        To what extent the journey's light
        Depends upon the load.
658   You have resources, means and ways,
        Devices, measures, methods, steps,
        The wherewithal to get therewith
        If you are equipped.
659   Room and board, and the keep
        You eke each week to get by on ...
        Clothed, fitted, rigged and heeled,
        You're ready then for fun.
660   But what if you have no reserves?
        No stocks or shares to trade for cash?
        No nest-egg for a rainy day?
        No savings in the bank?
661   It is very nice to be sufficient
        And satisfied with what one's got.
        A wallet oozing milk and honey,
        The cupboards choked with grub.
662   But when you're woefully insufficient
        With none to spare ... short of change
        Poor and hungry, lean and starving ...
        Shit! That's just tough luck!
663   It must be nice to have plenty,
        To have a cup running over ....
        To have the gold to gild the lily
        And the scent to dowse the rose:
664   To have all one can have ....
        And not have piss-all any more -
        To have one's fill, be satisfied
        Without being overdosed.

CONDITIONS

665   Sometimes it's expedient, *pis áller*
        To make shift, manage, get along,
        Eat one's cake and have it too
        As a stop-gap, last resort.
666   Sometimes there's drawbacks, damage,
        Discommode to overcome .....
        Out of place, unfit things
        Not worth the hurt.
667   Sometimes mugwumps make ado,
        Ascribe importance to sine qua non,
        Parade their greatness, make a fuss,
        Play fiddle with the biggest frogs.
668   Sometimes trifles light as air -
        A paltry feather on the scales;
        A hundred years hence or back -
        Is counting hairs, splitting straws.
669   Sometimes the good (as good can be),

433

The cream of the crop, the pick,
The flower of the flock, the bunch,
Are conditions well received.

670   Sometimes some endure all ails:
The slug in an English rose ...
The wasp on a Scottish thistle ...
The flea up Ulster's nose.

671   Sometimes plague, blight and canker,
Locus, fungus, moth and rust ...
Toxins dumped into the ocean
Are worse than any worm.

672   Sometimes perfection beyond praise,
Sans peur et sans reproche ....
Is quintessence - *ne plus ultra* -
Polished, pure and highly-wrought.

673   Sometimes, defect, flaw and blemish,
A hole in a brand new coat ...
A crack in a piece of china ...
Devalues the whole.

674   Sometimes scars, pocks and birthmarks,
A freckle on a cheek of cream ...
A mole on a snowy breast ...
Add interest to the common.

675   Sometimes low grade, second best,
Namby-pamby, milk and water ...
Neither tripe ... neither offal,
Doesn't mean it's awful.

676   Sometimes - there's improvement,
Things turn out for the better,
Some seem on the lift, the mend
And making up for lost time.

677   Then all of a sudden, things worsen,
There's a slump, some hit the skids,
Things get out of joint, go wrong,
A plane-load hits the drink.

678   Why this destruction? Ravage, ruin ...
How can some strike at the root?
When the axe is aimed at the trunk
After the branches are removed.

679   But, snatched from the jaws of death,
Some live to live again ......
Having weathered the storm
They pull through - to err again.

680   Refreshed, pure and sweet,
Their strength returned for a new life:
Perked and chipped, cheered & bucked,
They join a reconditioned world.

681   And then ... relapse! They revert,
They regress, backslide, sink,
Eat their deeds, apostate crow,
Turn about, and fall from grace.

682   So seizures follow - fevers, throes,
Cancers, tumours, Cupid's itch ...
Heart disease, Aids and MS,

Infirm - and on the danger list.
683 Remedy, relief, narcotics, balms,
Cure-alls, heal-alls, *elixir vitae's*.
Knock-out drops or Mickey Finns,
Expectorants or stimulants.

683 Some wouldn't mind a Turkish bath
To purify their washed-up skin.
How they'd love a pretty boy
To scrub and rub them fit.
685 If you think that's impure,
And their bodies are a dump ...
That's why they need that pretty boy
To scrape them clean of muck.
686 No doubt, it would be good for them.
Can you deny this truth?
Most think it's fine for one's health
To care about one's looks.
687 And with full pep, a burst of health
(Helped by the pretty boy)
They'd eat their oats, and of course
Enjoy the country air.

688 The healing arts are nine-tenths sense
And ten percent of medicine ....
A bunion on some's big toe joint
Is a fashion victim's paradigm.
689 So treat yourself, diagnose yourself
Or end up like them- beneath the knife!
It's not so nice to have a slice
Cut away because of pride.
690 Perhaps we all have mental blocks,
Obsessions sent to try our health.
So wear broad shoes or be psychotic!
You smoke and drink corned-neurotics!
691 For there is danger, peril and hazard
When one sleeps on a volcano ....
If one sails too near the wind,
Or skates on ice that's thin.
692 For when one's name's on the list;
When one totters near the brink;
When one dangles over a viper pit -
It's too late to run for it!

693 There are those picked to guard us.
There are those who watch and ward.
And there are beasts sent to cordon,
Sent to beat us up.
694 In retreat some need a rock -
An ivory tower aloof from life;
A refuge in a time of trouble;
A door that they can lock.
695 For there is need for preservation,
Conservation and all that stuff.
There must be more reservations
And sanctuaries for you lot.
696 Sanctuary - in a place of salvage

435

Where you may be *tirer d'affaire* -
Where you may be unobligated ...
Free - and well at ease.

697   Do not wait for the red flag.
Wait not for the yellow jack.
Attacks advance the raised alarm.
Read the signs ... or be undone!

698   With dismay, disquiet, distress,
The cry of the wolf is clearly heard.
But few believe that wolves exist
Until the chicken's dead.

VOLUNTARY ACTION

699   What's doing? What's up?
What's cooking? What gives?
What's happening? What's with it?
What's buzzin', cousin?

700   Not a hoot! Not a stir!
Not a sausage! Not a thing!
Just some twiddling thumbs
Leaving things as they stand.

701   Well! Where's the enterprise in that?
Where's the itch to get ahead?
Don't some have fish to fry?
Other irons on the fire?

702   No - they bum and loaf about,
Eat the bread of idleness ....
Swing the bat, whip the cat,
Waste what waking hours they have.

703   They see no need to hurry, rush,
To scammer, scud, scuddle, spurt;
To bundle on and make short work
In hot haste against the clock.

704   They have spare hours, time to burn
With a creep and a crawl.
Every tick they take their leisure
Every tock they live for pleasure.

705   For them - it's all sweet repose,
A take-it-ease sprawl and loll -
Every day's a - *dies non*;
Every week's one long hol'!

706   They sleep - make darkness brief;
Knit-up the ravelled sleeve of bliss;
Gently don the hood of grief -
That cloak their idleness.

707   They have no wakeful nights,
Restless, sleepless moonlit hours.
They don't toss and turn 'til dawn
To rise ulcered, tired and worn -

708   Like they who strive, struggle, strain
'Till they are black in the face ...
Breaking arms, breaking legs ...
Breaking necks, to do their best.

709   Why undertake a task, a venture?
Put your hand to the plough ..?

Take the bull by the horns?
Do all that's in your power?
710   With great effort, pain, and labour,
Free the dog - the donkey Briton!
Free a slave, navvy, kefir!.
You workers try to pull together!
711   Fighting fatigue, wear and languor,
Without being tuckered, beat or pooped.
Battling tiredness like a lion ...
Without collapse, or dog-tired look.

712   Hail you workers, makers, doers!
Perform your tasks, do them well!
If an actor, author, artist -
Be a master, do things - else
713   Find your workplace, house or parlour;
Install your skills and be yourselves!
Hive away and work your engines,
Be geared for life! Try now!
714   So why do men make no provision
For tomorrow, live hand to mouth?
Go unprepared in this world
They haven't a clue about?
715   If they had skills and knew their stuff
If they could tell the hawks from doves.
Would they be stinking rich like some
Who cut a coat to suit their cloth?
716   They're unskilled, without the knack
To start a business. Yet they're not daft,
They have brains, but what good's that?
They haven't got a credit card.
717   They're not cunning, crafty, sly.
They can't outwit the blue-suit men.
They'll pay their poll tax and their rent
And watch all wealth elude them.
718   Though they are artless, simple, frank,
They can look men in the eye ....
They can trust their honest selves
But not a blue-tied world -
719   Where all that might have - is undone,
Not carried through, left half-hogged,
Not implemented, nor finished off -
Not even worth a shout or bawl.

720   All that fails, flops, collapses,
That starts off like a rocket,
Takes it on the chin, and sinks
Falls to earth like a stick.
721   All that's ruin, rout, defeat,
Overturned, crushed, reduced ...
Drubbed, licked, whipped, thrashed,
A cooked goose served as hash.
722   All that's adverse, hapless, hard,
A shock fall from one's high estate,
To come down heavy in an ill-wind
And left to bear the elements.
723   What a hindrance! What a shock!

To have one's beak put out of joint.
To have one's wings clipped so short
That flying is a skip and hop.
724 All that's difficult, arduous, tough:
To walk on eggshells, tread hot coals,
To dance on crocodiles - what suicide!
The end of the rope!

725 Give some a world where that dispatched,
Is not by halves brought to pass ....
Realised, accomplished, done,
Wound up, closed, capped and crowned.
726 Where all that comes good - succeeds,
Makes headway on a raging sea ...
So that which goes beyond all dream,
Cuts a swathe through a world
727 Where all's comfort, well and fat -
A cuckoo's life in a sunny hedge.
Born beneath a lucky star ....
Living high in a feathered nest.
728 Where all that's effortless and smooth -
Catching tadpoles in a goldfish bowl;
Stealing candy from a baby's mouth
To live the life of Reilly's folk.

729 To be good, be nice, behave, act well,
Deport oneself with perfect manners.
Easy said - hard to do.
Perfection is the mien of few.
730 Mischief makers, rogues and devils,
Pixies, pucks, minxes, rascals.
Most people are a little elfish
About their voluntary actions.

AUTHORITY

731 The government, authorities, them above,
Old John Bull and Uncle Sam ....
The past brought us Goody Snatch
And her *argumentum baculinium*.
732 On the throne - on her broomstick,
Potent, lordly, influential ...
At the helm, puissant, powerful,
Ex cathedra - magisterial.
733 Lawless, nihilistic, rule by lynching,
Doing as disorder pleases ....
Mice will play when Puss's away
And eat the moldy cheeses.

734 You had no Lords, no Lower House
You had a parliament of mice ....
With one big rat on the floor
Logrolling laws with Christian no-no's!
735 You had the UN, the IC laws,
The EEC .... the IMB.
God saved you not from crushing rule
That changed to suit just one.

736   You were the pawns of dismay science,
The guinea pigs of party line ...
Nineteen-Eighty-Four come true
By Nineteen-Ninety-Nine.

737   You were the biggest chumps to date,
The greatest number ever sold ...
And what you bought in exchange
Won't help you when you're old.

738   And who's to blame for your greed?
Who led you to get round God?
Whose assets were such liabilities?
Whose strengths were your own faults?

739   If you were properly guided, steered,
Directed where you'd like to go.
You would not let dictatorship
Drive you to war.

740   If you were managed, stewarded, chaired
Governed as you'd like to be ....
You would not have been over-seered
By an Iron Moll.

741   If you were mistressed by a good wife,
Matroned by a gracious dame ...
You would not need governessed
By a Madam T.

742   If you were served, chambermaided,
Cinderella'd or Abigail'd ...
You would not need Wizard Man
In to take her place.

743   We sometimes fear terrorists,
But only when we cannot hear
Words of reason from their mouths
On our own TV.

744   Why is there so much censorship?
Phone taps and ID checks?
We do not know from day to day
The real from rumoured in the press.

745   Are we traitors to question these
Precepts, maxims, canons, codes
That hide the true facts of life?
We have a right to know!

746   And if it's said we have no rights,
Then now's the time to fight for them.
Some want a Bill of Rights, and then
A constitution to go with it!

747   Some want a free elected Lords,
Ten year seats for all the shires.
Some wish to phase out birthright peers
And join the modern world!

748   Some want a senate, free, impartial,
Instead we have a bunch of cronies
All roped together by the Whip
Of Goody Snatch the Witch -

749   Now conjured by the magic wand
of Wizard Man the Rich -
It is a sort of horror story,
Putting claims upon our rights.

750   Sixt'n Scots peers, twelve from Ulster,
The rest from England, dukes & earls.
What right have they to govern Britain
Or we to think them wise?

751   Send them back to their estates,
And call elections for the Lords.
And if a duke desires to stand,
Well, let him if he wants.

752   But let folk have their parliament ...
Not some junta bashing god.
No committee in a huddle
Deciding for them all.

753   By force of arms, coercion, violence,
At point of gun, hijacked, dragooned,
Put under screws, duress and pressure,
The fist, the big stick and the boot.

754   With rod of iron, stern austerity ...
With heavy hand, grimly harsh ...
With Spartan shrift, hard and rigid,
Roughshod rode, no holds barred.

755   With rope enough on a free reign,
Lax and slack, loose, relaxed ...
With remiss and pliant head
With plenty yield and give ...

756   With lenient favour, mild forbearance,
Easy going, decent, kind .....
Pampered, spoiled and mollycoddled.
Some would think that nice!

757   Fettered, hampered, trammeled, shackled,
Constrained, controlled, curbed, checked;
Hog-tied to the ways of men .....
Some have had enough!

758   Captured, charged, confined to care,
Consigned to a custodial cage ...
Cordoned off, cooped up, committed.
Some wish they were a birds!

759   Free to be at liberty!
The right to live and live well right.
Go unrestrained, run the wind
Be free in will ... and wild!

760   Set loose, free to go ...
The wish to want to and want to wish ...
To whisper sweetness to the world;
To whistle down the wind!

761   Serf, vassal, thrall, slave,
Bondsman, odalisk, villain, churl -
Dare not call their souls their own
And who can really blame the sods.

762   Offer, proffer, presentation ...
Submit, propose, bring up broach,
Make a move towards advancement,
But ... you, don't volunteer!

763   Appeal, cry, call, plea,
Entreat, implore, beg, beseech ...

If you please, for goodness sake,
Don't cap in hand proceed.

764 For if you acceded - acquiesced,
Surrendered to the rule of men,
Bent a knee, bowed your head;
You might as well be dead.

765 If you submitted - suit and service,
Pleasure, nod, beck and call ....
Had to lie down, roll right over;
You would kill yourself.

766 To disobey, revolt, rebel,
It is your right to counter cruelty,
To fly in the face of tyranny ...
Instead of dying cowardly.

767 To observe, respect, comply with
All that's wrong in humankind .....
With faith in justice, law and order,
You'd have to be a hypocrite.

768 To disregard, infringe, transgress,
Take the law into your own hands ...
You would, because the law's a bitch!
Life has taught you this!

769 Promise, pledge, word of honour.
Oath, vows, marriage contract ...
There was two ... some time ago
They slipped the ring ... oh bother!

770 Signed, sealed, arranged, settled,
They broke it off, went their ways ...
They had a bargain, an agreement.
Instinct engaged their reason.

771 Deposit, stake, monkey money ...
They had none - with none to sell.
No insurance, bonds or stocks;
They only had themselves.

772 Consent, assent, deign, comply,
Turn a willing ear, approve ....
Some voters have no objections, none.
They nod their heads without a hoot.

773 Refuse, decline, reject, turn down,
Repulse, rebuff, deny disclaim ...
Some landlords up their tenants' rents
And go off winter skiing.

774 Permission, leave, *imprimatur* ...
Permit, license, warrant, pass;
On sufferance archbishops vouchsafe,
Things they cannot authorise.

775 Ban, embargo, veto, bar,
Forbid, prohibit, enjoin, preclude;
Some governments license misery
By making happiness taboo.

776 Repeal, revoke, recall, rescind,
Retract, renege, reverse, abolish;
Nobles null and void agreements
That peasants have to swallow.

777 Select, they choose their nominees,

The Party Man, committee backed ...
Oh how many wish they could have
A candidate with heart.

778 Each Party Man's a go-between,
An advocate of Party line ....
A mouth piece for the Party boss
And the Party mind.

779 Can folk respect a Party Man?
Promoted for the Party cause?
Christ! Some do not have a vote
They can't pay their pole tax.

780 How can folk remove the Party
When they've removed folk's voting power.
Deprived of rights, the poor can't oust
An incumbent oligarchy.

SUPPORT and OPPOSITION

781 How can a boy aid, help, support
A girl four hundred miles from him?
Foster, sponsor, back, abet?
Give manna in the wilderness?

782 How can they ally, join hands,
Cooperate, club together
To get her through her college course
Without a grant to keep her.

783 Must he consort, confer, collude
To find a patron, friend at court?
Is this how time has worked on him -
On all who need support?

784 Must he join cliques, clubs & circles,
Belong to clannish social groups?
Must he enrol or be invited
Without a pedigree ....?

785 How can he without connections
Ignore the set, avoid the lodge?
What hope has he in aiding well
A girl who needs his love?

786 There are those in his way
With bayonets crossed, daggers drawn.
Yet, the boy make his stand against
The fiercest queen or pawn.

787 Opponent, adversary, antagonist,
Assailant ... rival on the field;
Up in arms he'll do his worst
And advance like a fiend.

788 He'll kick against all the pricks,
Put up a fight to frighten God!
He'll resist, repulse, rebuff,
And stand on his tod!

789 He'll toss his glove into the ring,
Pluck a beard, slap a face ...
Raise his fist, bar his teeth,
But take it at his pace.

790 Such *guerre a mort*, *a outance*
Are struggles of the last ditch kind;

442

791
Hand to hand, contention, strife,
A free-for-all, knock-down, drag-out!
Violence is an insane epidemic;
A brain-bash wind-pipe slitting art;
A feast of vultures; a waste of life;
A by-product of the arts of peace.

792
Violence is the art of bullies;
The trade of traders in ideas ...
It does not determine who is right:
Victory goes to those who survive.

793
Attack is for - the dogs let loose!
Bloodhounds seeking out their game;
The hunter stalking on his prey -
Brought to bay, slain and eaten.

794
Defence is for the ready primed,
Those who beat the yelping curs -
The hunted, shielded, armed and waiting
For the attack to begin.

795
Combatants, soldiers, warriors, veterans,
Rookies, draftees, and plain regulars,
Mounted troops, reserves on foot,
Fleets of forces, flying or floating -

796
Big guns; small shot; cannons; pistols;
Munitions - ammo, missiles, bullets;
Polaris; Trident; fission-fusion
Nuked-up megatonned plutonium.

797
The world's a stage, a coliseum
For slingshot, shrapnel, high explosive;
A hippodrome of TNT,
A theatre steeped in tragic hope.

798
Instead - let the boy seek fellow feeling,
Affinity, sympathy, harmony, union.
He needs rapport to cement community
With people of the same mind.

799
He does not need a house divided,
A rift within the lute, discord.
If there's a crow needing plucked
Leave him out the quarrel.

800
For peace of heart; peace of mind;
Follow that which makes for peace.
Be at peace, boy, with yourself;
Vade in pace! *Pax vobiscum*!

801
Wave the white flag: play the pipes;
Shake hands on the truce agreed;
Raise the siege; play in tune;
Pour waters on the waters smoothed.

802
Settle troubles, boy, come between;
Intercede and referee -
Negotiate, and arbitrate;
Bring to terms a lasting peace.

803
Impartial be to point of means:
On the fence; half way trim;
Be neutral, boy, strike a balance;
Not hot, nor cold, just in between.

804
Be compromising - fifty-fifty,

Adjust to steering a middle course;
Make some virtue of necessity;
Make it your measured most.

POSSESSION

805   Nine points of the law - possession.
        Tenure; holding; ownership ...
        Mine; yours; ours; theirs ...
        Puts one's name to it.
806   Finder-keeper, those who have:
        Master, mistress, holder, host -
        From year to year the lessee pays
        The bank the leaser owns.
807   For property is one's real estate,
        The visual proof of all endeavours,
        It does not show the inner wealth,
        Nor account for mental assets.

808   Acquisition through take and profit:
        Make a penny turn a pound;
        Rake off gains, net the gleanings,
        Have money on the brain.
809   Retention through: holding on;
        Gripping firm to what one has;
        Clinging on as if for dear life:
        By always sitting tight.
810   Loss through waste, expense, depletion:
        By the board; into the red ....
        Out of pocket; cut off; bust;
        Without a single cent.
811   Relinquishment through: giving up;
        Letting go without a fight ...
        Disposing of, kissing goodbye to
        All chances to be rich.

812   Commerce, trade, traffic, truck,
        Bull and bear and all that stuff ...
        Buy and sell, outbid, haggle.
        Mercury keeps his shop in London.
813   Share the snack, take your whack,
        Have your finger in the pie ...
        Divvy up, halve your part
        And have a jolly laugh.
814   Parcel out the cake, allot,
        Cut the melon, portion, piece ...
        Save a pittance, stave some crumbs
        For those who're having none.
815   Buy up, buy in, buy off, buy back -
        Bee Tee was a yuppie granny ...
        But Sid Gas was a come-on con
        Who got the suckers bidding.

816   Transfer, convey, hand over, sign
        Seven years on before demise ...
        Why should Charlie pay death tax
        When Mam's estate's so fat?

444

817 Donation, present, gift, grant,
   Largess, gratuity, bounty, favour!
   Hand outs are the fad of gentry.
   Begging is the poor man's legacy.

818 Who shall now inherit the earth?
   Receive? Accept as beneficiary
   The birthright passed by primogenicy
   That has displaced the many.

819 Beneath the sign of three gold balls,
   A line of desperate *wallahs* queue ...
   The needy in the loan shark's jaws:
   The way it was between the wars.

820 Pawn; hock; - debtor's borrow,
   Raise the cash on credit, trust.
   They never pay the interest off;
   They soar like birds before they drop.

821 Sell up, sell out, sell the lot!
   That's fine if you've got some spare,
   But not when hunger knocks it
   Under the hammer of despair.

822 Sharks catch, grab, snatch, hold,
   Hook, snag, snare, spear,
   Strip, fleece, shear, skin
   You out of house and home.

823 Do they restore, return, give back?
   Make restitution and amends?
   Remand the wrong? Reclaim right?
   Atone for all their wolfishness?

824 They pilfer, filch, purloin, swipe,
   Plunder, pillage, loot and sack ...
   They disregard the 'me' and 'you'
   And lift what they like.

825 Crook, gun, chor and prigger,
   Sneak thief - poacher, prowler,
   The biggest bandits of them all
   Are the stock market dealers.

826 Illicit business, racketeering ...
   Fair trade? What a piece of crack!
   These swag-looting marketeers
   Moonlight on your backs!

827 Perhaps some need business kings,
   The egg and butter job tycoons -
   Merchants, salesmen, brokers, traders
   And the hordes of lesser mongers.

828 Perhaps folk need their merchandise,
   Their goods for sale, products, ware;
   But need they take the dividend
   They hand out as pay?

829 Perhaps - if there were ten-pence stores,
   Pound-post houses with all needs ...
   The open-market would be fair,
   Not fouled-up by greed.

830 Most are not - me first - speculators,
   No wheeling-dealing operators ....
   They mount no raids, rig no killings,
   Nor wash cash like dirty linen.

831 Most have no stocks or shares,
No big Nats, Gas or Oil .....
They could have bought their piece of State.
Instead, it was sold for them.

832 Many had a share in this country ...
A dividend from National wealth,
But Goody Snatch has stolen that
And sold it to her friends.

833 Money, cash, all legal tender
Is at the root of most things wrong:
The eagle on the dollar bill;
The monarch on the one pound coin.

834 Financing backing, sound, substantial;
You'd all like that, it's only natural,
But there are greedy Midas types
Not sharing El Dorado.

835 Made of money, bloated, pursed,
There are those flush with wealth:
Stinking, filthy, lousy rich;
Who are also wadding sick.

836 There are those on narrow means
Pissed off at not possessing much:
Not worth a rap ... the going hard;
They're walking in the crap.

837 Of course there's credit, trust and tick,
But nothing's free, that's for sure.
The interest compounds every month
And doubles every year.

838 It's no surprise that there is debt
Up to here - and in arrears!
Repossession .... what a price.
Death is not as dear.

839 Who will pay a living wage
To clear and settle up accounts?
Stand the shot? Recompense
For Goody Snatch's work?

840 Who'll wipe off the Welsher's slate?
Cancel out the bankrupt's bills?
Who'll pick up the debtor's tab
Before the system fails?

841 Spend, expend, disburse, outlay ...
The cost of living rising daily.
The boom is over so they say -
Who now can spare the price of day?

842 Profits, earnings, gains, receipts,
It's not enough to make ends meet.
The yield brings in scant return;
Expenses out-gross net-income.

843 Accounts outstanding, statements, debits
Banks gnaw life like diseased rodents.
Accountants gobble at the cheese
And leave the mousetrap open.

844 The damage done, the quotes accepted,
Tax and duty, vat and pole ....
Direct tax, progressive levies,
And tax to fill a hole.

845   No discounts, cuts, deductions,
        No rebates, reductions, none ...
        Perhaps the odd set-off concession
        And allowance for a child.

846   Precious, dear, and far too much,
        Overcharged, inflated, steep ....
        Through the nose; you onward go
        Without a wink of sleep.

847   Cheap, low priced, marked down, slashed;
        The cost of life's a piggy bank ...
        A bargain-basement crock of chalk
        Cracked from being robbed.

848   Where are the Annie Oakley shows?
        The on-the-house Scot-free gifts?
        The free-as-air get for nothings
        Life presents you with?

849   Now-a-days it's economics ....
        Frugal prudence, nothing free.
        Skimping witch-face Goody Snatch
        And her gobbling few.

850   Clean and smiling Wizard Man
        Is no miser, is no match
        For Goody skinflint-pinch fist Snatch
        And her venal pack.

851   She spared no expense,
        She lavished wealth with her wand
        On the backs of those who kissed
        Her butt and felt her hand.

852   There is waste, a down-the-drain
        End to all that you have known.
        Close your eyes, make a wish ...
        And dream the nightmare gone!

8TH LEXICON

Mankind is affected by a weakness - emotion. In sympathy, humans support one another. Yet, there are those who employ the lexicon of morality and religion to hide their weakness in order to foster their own superiority. In truth, there are no superior beings - there is only one Universal Being.

PERSONAL FEELINGS

853   I have talked in brief of love:
        Of beings ruled by taste and touch;
        Of feelings roused by sight and sound;
        But not about what passion does.

854   Now I'll speak of lesser love:
        Emotion locked within the heart;
        I'll try to strike an inner chord
        Without pealing raw.

855   For there are those numb to feeling,
        Poor creatures lost: hard and cold
        With hearts of stone; callous; brazen;
        We must keep them warm.

856   We must not let them shirk excitement.
        We must help them get some thrills:
        Make them tingle, tremor, quiver;

Let them thaw their icy selves.

857   And if we can't? Then we'll become
Just like them ... sober, staid,
Calm, composed, stiff and starched.
We'll become straight-lace faced.

858   For what's the peeing point
Of living life with a Rodin look
With dark Da Vinci staring eyes
And mouths forever crooked?

859   That is a pose meant for art:
Not for people who have nerves;
Not for those highly strung
And living on the edge.

860   No! I shall forbear, brook, abide,
Take it like a man, resist!
I'll lay in the lap of good
And make the best of it!

861   What's the point of being impatient,
Fretful, restless, in a sweat,
All hopped up and in a lather,
Too breathless to submit?

862   For life is balmy, sunny, bright,
Delightful, pleasant, sweet and nice,
Divine, sublime, fetching, fine
..... Most of the time.

863   Sometimes life's unpleasant: sour
Enough to make a preacher swear;
So bad, that it becomes more
Than flesh and blood can bear.

864   But let's be happy, just like larks
Soaring high in joyful bliss.
With -*joie de vivre*- pleased as Punch!
Let's be four times blessed!

865   There's natural shocks enough to wound
And ghost our lives in misery,
Without arrows barbed with trouble
Aimed at our closet histories.

866   I have no belly for such tosh!
It shouldn't happen to a dog.
Of all the ills, the sickest pill
Is a dose of vile gossip.

867   For ease of mind, I'll not flirt
The shadows of my own dull past.
Instead, I'll now be reconciled
To be well satisfied.

868   I'm not a grouch, a crank, a crab,
A grumbling, griping malcontent.
Why be displeased, vexed of spirit
In a world that isn't bad?

869   It's not hard to raise a smile,
By being chipper, crouse and canty.
As merry as the day is long,
The blithe will chase off melancholy.

870   Let the demure, grave and grim,
Not be you, or who we know ....

For who enjoys a staid long face:
Morning solemn, evening sober.
871 There are those with heavy hearts:
Penseroso; soul-sick; blue ...
In the doleful doldrums; dumped,
Sad-eyed, and forever glum.
872 Sometimes a sadder man is wiser,
Wild with regret - the better -
But what a pity when remorse
Turns into a penance.
873 Worse still are those unrepentant,
Unsorry folks - hard of heart -
Who untouched by their own impenitence
Are without any qualms.
874 And there are those wailers: weepers
Who beat their breasts, and fall about;
The ones who cry their eyes out; bawl -
The world will end tomorrow!

875 Until at last there is a laugh!
A rah! rah! ray! A hip hur-rah!
A haw-haw! hee-hee! tee-hee guffaw!
A whoopee! hoopee! yippie! Wow!
876 Such celebration deserves: a fanfare;
A *feu de joie*; a gun salute -
But wait a mo! I'm blowing the trumpet
For no reason worth a hoot.
877 This verse is but a small amusement,
A diversion from the waiting world.
It is a game, a sport of words
To drive the hours on.
878 It is a dance: a Terpsichore;
A hoof around the lexicon;
A reel around the dictionary
In lines of four.
879 Perhaps it's all a bit absurd
That I should make fun of words,
But after all - we're all fools.
It's ludicrous to think we're gods.

880 I'll admit, there are wits
So quick their lips merely twitch:
They tongue tunes like violinists
Fiddling on a Stradivarius.
881 Such banter as a joke is fine -
Kidding; ribbing; ragging; razing.
Such jesting as a give and take
Might lead to fists in faces.
882 But is there worse than those who are
Weary, stale, flat and dull:
Who pass through life switched off
As dreary lumps of lard?
883 What's more tedious than a bore?
Ho hum! Heigh ho! What a life!
Humdrum dead and near extinct?
How do they survive?
884 And what of those who sow the wind?

449

From bad to worse see things increase?
Those who might round Cape Wrath
To come to Pentland grief.

885   What would they give to have relief:
To smooth their ruffled brow with rest
Like lion fleeced to tempered lamb
Meek with sighed short breath.

886   We all seek comfort from distress;
So let's rejoice with them that do.
Let's weep with them that weep!
And laugh with them too!

887   There are those when things are bad
Who declare that all is well;
Those who will come what may
Say:- The blackest hour's heaven!

888   These optimists make the best
Of all the worst thrown their way:
They knock on wood, trust in God,
Make promises from air -

889   Which is no worse than those of gloom
Who fancy clouds - where no clouds are:
Who dash the cup from the lips
Of all *enfants perdus*.

890   For I have thoughts, troubled, chafe,
That vex, beset and plague me:-
Worried sick, disturbed, distressed,
In dead of night; I leave my bed.

891   Sometimes it's fear, a cowardness,
A qualmishness of cold misgiving ...
An afraidness brought on by years,
A diffidence of shivers.

892   Scared to death, I stand in terror,
Cowering in the black of time:
Paralysed, pale as ash -
I bear the pass of panic.

893   Dare I admit such dire fears!
And still proclaim myself an adult?
Be strong: quit yourself a man.
Be bold! Beard the lion!

894   How can I, paper back-boned,
March up to the cannon's mouth?
When my courage's made of glass
And broken in a moment.

895   Yet advance I must, timid go
Safely forward, right foot cautious:
Tip-toe slow, across the floor
Back into bed before the dawn.

896   Often I'm overcome by life,
The pernicketiness of urban folk,
The nothing of their finickiness,
The up-turn of a nose.

897   Dainty judgment - discerning airs,
Good sense pertly put in force:
Such culture of the conscienced soul

Leaves the spirit low.
898 So base in fact, an angel dies!
Such folk can be vulgar Goths:-
To err is human, sin divine,
And they submit to both.
899 What ugliness in refined taste;
To see a clock stop a face
Wry and baboon-made by art
Like something a cat has pawed.
900 True beauty is without a name:
A something caught with half an ear;
Something glimpsed with a flick
Or felt without a hand.

901 Ornate array is *foofarow*:
Make-up on a small girl's cheeks;
Tinsel round the head of Christ,
Or rings on every toe.
902 Unadorned natural beauty
Illuminates the common world.
Fair is the lily gilt ...
Fair sweet the wild rose.
903 Such air! There is no pretence:
No posy in a piano vase;
No bouquet breakfast jug arranged
That we might love if wild.
904 For vain our species seems to be
With all its trump and solemn pride.
We may act the grand seigneur -
The rose grows beyond all time.
905 Yet, what is pride? Self-esteem?
Napoleon on a beggar's horse?
Mussolini flying high?
Or Hitler cross-armed posed?
906 Too few like Garibaldi, Gandhi,
Descend to sing the small man's song;
Too few with humbled hang-dog looks
Stoop to conquer all.
907 Nay! Who would be in servile chains!
Who would drain their every vein!
Who would kiss the hem of Cain!
Unless they were a saint.

908 The modest violet outshines the rose:-
With bashful blush it finds its fame
In the shade beneath an elm
Where timorous lovers play.
909 But oh beware! Also there
The pansy in self-love - in bloom!
Conceit and swollen cockiness
With which to please a fool.

910 Braggarts on their trumpets blow
Louder than the big-talk daffs
Along the shore - where Wordsworth
Strode - head into the windy blasts.
911 Chatter, chatter, June to May,

They rave and rage, fuss and fury.
They are bound, yet sway free:
Bluster, bluff and swagger.

912

Let he - whose arrogance values pride
And all false traits so admired -
Let him ride his high horse home
Eight hands above the mire.

913

And those - whose insolent reply
Gives the world a curled lip -
Let them be the rose, the bud -
And not the prick of it.

914

Perhaps some forfeit our good opinion,
Disgraced they fall from high estate.
Exposed to infamy's black respect,
They bid farewell to glory.

915

Honours lauded, credit given:-
How the cited can be sullied!
By disgrace, stripped of ribbon,
Branded bad, and shamed.

916

Distinction made with a title:
Your Grace, My Lord, or just plain Sir.
That conferred - can be annulled
When favour shrinks.

917

And what of those born to rank?
Those sceptred, orbed and crowned:
Those exalted in an age
When republics blossom.

918

The common man, the third estate
Cannot fall - can only rise
From out the waving multitude
Where future kings are spawned.

919

Such wonder! Will such things be?
Marvel! Miracle! and prodigy!
Blow me down when such things occur.
God bless me!

920

Unastonished - not a blink!
History will accept new things.
Of course! No wonder! but why the stink
When queens spawn queens, not kings!

SYMPATHY

921

What sympathy have we for friends,
Our comrades in the common cause
For fellowship and family joy
Hand in hand familiar joined -

922

When snakes coil snug in the shade
And spiders watch and web aloof,
And scorpions wait self-contained
To join the masquerade?

923

What know we of those forsaking
A world forgot by those forgetting
The kith less few fair forlorn
Far upon a foreign shore?

924

How may we keep a light
Or catch the latch in these times,

925
Or greet our friends with a kiss
When we're not home ourselves.
Our door is barred, we are out:
Displaced, we derelict move about;
Proscribed, we pass the black ball
Round - and sign the robin blind.

926
Friendship stems from fellow feeling,
The love of fault in spite of virtue.
A friend in need is a friend indeed
And who'd dispute such wisdom!

927
Thank God, said Kipling, for a chum!
Someone with whom you are yourself.
A pal with whom you are sincere,
A mate not scared to give you hell.

928
For who needs folk to bear a grudge!
Who needs fools with bones to gnaw!
Who needs guys who throw a punch
When you come to odds!

929
Who needs hate, dislike and odium!
Who needs detest, wrath and loathing!
Who needs abhor, adverse ill
Eating at them like a poison!

930
Love is the potion of my passion!
Love is the fervour of my fancy!
Love is the ardour of my enamour:
Sweet, appealing, charming!

931
But O! La! La! *Faire yeux doux*!
Coquettes flirt and dig for gold.
Philanders wolf and whisper sex:
Osculate - do not propose

932
To make themselves like man and wife.
Would you have that if you were wise?
Well - many tie the knot - unite!
And take for worse a better life.

933
And some - the lone wolf on the prowl:
The bachelor girl blissfully wild;
The monks, the maidens on their own;
The misogynous world - all alone

934
The widow wearing dowager weeds;
The widower grassed and weak;
The lost divided by divorce;
They're in need of love and warmth.

935
A nice and very perfect gentleman
The mirror and pink of courtesy:
Regards one well, gives his love
And always keeps a civil tongue.

936
A nasty vile and utter scoundrel
Rude and scant of courtesy:
Cuts one short, tries his luck,
Cheats and never counts the cost.

937
There is luxury in doing good:
To friend the friendless, vice a foe;
To help give the sick man health;

453

To do as would be done to you.
938 There is no good in ill-will
In man's inhumanity to man.
No delight in sharp-toothed cruelty
Nor kindness found in spite.
939 All misanthropes are anti-social,
They're misfits ill disposed to man.
Befriend the unkind? Hard of heart?
Is like asking for a cold.
940 But I will don my public spirit
For love of man, extend my hand,
Embrace all hard malicious persons
Until they stab me back.
941 I will - be their benefactor;
Be their present help in trouble;
Be their patron - help, assist
Until they're saved from this.
942 How brave I am! Befriending ruffians,
Hoodlums, thugs, monsters, demons.
It's just as well, I'm a saint
And not a friend of evil.

943 'Tis a pity she's a whore!
'Tis a pity he's a bore!
Have mercy on all erring souls,
You never know who's next to go.
944 There are some who give no quarter,
Those who claim their pound of flesh:
The heartless folk who turn an eye
And cruelly call in debts.
945 Yet, why side with them that weep?
Why weep with those who grieve?
Why grieve with those condoled?
Why console the weak?
946 Forgive and let all things pass?
Rub out marks? Clear the screen?
Exonerate all affronts ....
And wipe the slate off clean?
947 Congratulate the desperado?
Compliment the woman bruiser?
I've pity for the bore or whore,
But no sympathy for losers.

948 So get down on your marrowbones,
Thank your Gods, you are alive.
There's many friends in the grave
And many soon to die.
949 Bless the stars that we are here.
Je vous remercie tres beaucoup!
Do not forget the gift of life
And the life that's gifted you.

950 For the monster begot, born itself
The green-eyed worm within us all.
Suspicious, we distrust the world,
And more so - those our lover knows.
951 Such pain of mind our neighbours cause,

Our envy like a sickness gnaws -
It eats the fibre of our souls
And leaves us hungry all the more.

952
So ghosts of the great! Immortal fame!
The most recorded of all recorders!
The name on everyone's tongue & lips!
The pride of all posterity!

953
Let not ill-humour be your game.
Bad nature is the trade of sulks.
Hot tempers are the quick of shrews
When a quarrel brews.

954
Resentment is a sport of teeth.
Offence is a spray of words.
Umbrage is the clash of fists
When the humour hurts.

955
Until we take an eye for eye;
Give in kind for that sustained;
Pay off old scores *en revanche*
And take reprisal for each wrong.

956
And brooding on our open wound
We plan revenge before it scabs.
We breathe vengeance, take an oath,
And think not how vendettas start.

MORALITY

957
People and the ten commandments.
People and a code of ethics.
People and their inner conscience
Twinged by right and wrong.

958
What is right or proper, mate?
The seemly thing's not always decent.
Some will steer clear of scandal,
And some will have no shame.

959
The right of suffrage: that's justice.
The defence of sex: that's indulgence.
Some men knock their girlfriends up,
Then sure enough, they do a bunk!

960
One must reap where one has sown!
Do you believe this? Not me, nope.
All that comes our way is Fate,
And Newton's third is Karma, mate.

961
Give an inch and take a mile.
Do you think I'd stand for that?
All the gear we have for free,
Cost our friends very dear.

962
We have a duty! But to whom?
Friends pass the buck themselves.
We have to lump it when we're conned
And hoof it when we're wrong.

963
To hell with those who lay on hands?
Impose themselves, palm off, fob?
What respect have I for mates
Who take advantage of a pal.

964
I respect - the setting sun;
The wind and the tide that turns;

The lightning in the April sky
And all the creatures in this world.

965
Young Adam's sensual way with Eve
As voluptuous carnal-minded girl -
Was hedonism at its height
Before the fall from Eden.

966
Then sometime after Plato thought
That love should be virgin pure -
Diana, chaste as un-sunned snow
Chased the morning dew.

967
Then Jezebel, that queenly hussy,
Her free-love an easy virtue -
Strump't her way through Ahab's court
In the service of Israel.

968
Yet men, in their obscene state -
Lewd, bawdy, ribald, impure.
Bring temples down upon themselves
For loving living idols.

969
Perhaps it's well that some abstain:-
The yogi in his mountain cave;
The fakir in the cazzba shade;
The monk in the vaulted nave.

970
They let passions dry to reason;
Look not at wine when it's red;
They mortify all fleshly lusts,
And say no to excessivism!

971
Too many indulge, debauch and orgy,
Dine not wisely - but too well;
Carouse; run-riot; squander health
And wealth without intemperance.

972
And worst of all - the greedy eater,
The swinish glutton wolfing down
Every morsel in the house
And remaining hungry-minded.

973
Thank god for those who care to fast,
Who dine with Humprey, Duke of Lent -
Who share a crumb with Tantalus
And make a feast of bread.

974
You'll not find them intoxicated,
Soused and crocked on whoopee water.
Not a dram you'll find them lip
From the still burns of Scotland.

975
Sober as a judge they'll march,
Beneath the Hope and Glory banner.
As tipsy as the day they're born
They'll teeter to the *terra firma*.

976
Except for man, I have no scorn,
No disrespect for all that's known
Or all that which I cannot fathom
In the universe beyond our own.

977
I look cool upon mankind
Which cannot curb its arrogance.
It is young and cares not for
All the fruits in paradise.

978
Bah! Pah! Phoo! and all that boo!

Some don't give a toss, a wink:
With scoff, mock and caustic taunt,
They laugh and jape at all as twits.

979　Not so I - I'm more concerned
To praise, applaud, endorse, accept.
But who's to say I'll not regress
To smirks and jibes and jests?

980　For who's not prone to be a critic,
A give-what-for Jesse or John?
I'd be hanged if some could stop
Their gobs from finding fault.

981　Is there worse than blarney-mouthed
Sycophantic taffy-talk?
Or the patter of the urban snob
Troweling on the butter?

982　Tell the truth and shame the devil?
Be honest as the day is long?
Be noble, upright, sterling, worthy?
I try to all-the-while.

983　But, in each man, betrayal lurks:
He parts on some a Judas kiss;
He breaches trust with the thrust
Of steel between the ribs.

984　So be fair - do the handsome thing,
See justice done, and all that's due
With regard, respect or fear
For persons near and dear.

985　For iniquity is a way of life.
Injustice can be worse than death.
As long as nepotism's rife,
The wrong will judge the right.

986　Dogs in mangers! Mean self-pleasers!
Fortune hunters, hogs and toads!
How I dislike such self-considerate
Self-absorbing bores!

987　Give me large-heart princely virtue:
Do as you would be done by too.
Put yourself in place of others;
Make a sacrifice.

988　Do unwitnessed what you should
Like to do before the world.
Resist desires that have no virtue
Of health - good or moral.

989　For vicious vice is not so nice:
Bad habit is a devilish fault
That leads to weak and wicked sin
And shameless loss of pride.

990　Such malfeasance, such scarlet foible,
These deeds without an act I name -
Transgress the laws of decency
With a crime clenched fist -

991　They wash their blood-stained hands
With looks like cats who've ate a bird
Shame-faced they guilty-conscience
Smile in a show of innocence.

992　It is said that there are those

457

Pure of fault and not yet stained:
I would like to think that - Yes!
That some were clean of blame.

993 No end of fellows, likely lads
And perfect lasses nobly planned,
Salt the earth and pearl the world
As jewels of paragon.

994 For who has time for ne'er-do-wells,
Wastrel, worthless, human wrecks -
Radically foul-mouthed whore-son knaves
Who'd see us all in hell.

995 Such lampooners knock and slander,
Rake the muck and sling the slur.
They give a bad name to a dog
And tongue the blackest words.

996 They swear until the air is blue:
They curse with candle, bell and book;
They blaspheme! Blast! Effin! Dang!
Their way to Billingsgate, goldarn!

997 Why disrespect canon, law,
Regulation, dictate, bill;
It's *Lex non scripta*, *jus civile*
And *jus commune* for all.

998 I'll not say that laws are right
Or those who make the laws are wrong:
Many set the law to nought
And take it in their hands.

999 Perhaps there's need for bureaucrats,
For ministers and secretaries,
For magistrates and mayorships
And all the sheriffwicks.

1000 Perhaps we need courts of law,
Circuit, County, High and Lords;
The mercy seat, the woolsack bench
Where privilege confounds tort.

1001 Perhaps we must respect our 'Honours'
As Musselmen respect their Mullahs -
And like a Solomon or a Pilate
Accept their weighty judgement.

1002 But what of lesser legal men?
The green-bag mouthy friends at court;
The slick-silk QC's, stiff-gowned men:
The sentence never falls on them.

1003 In their suits of deposition!
In their suits of litigation!
In their suits against the world,
At the bar they please each other.

1004 Should they make their impeachments?
Accuse and charge and lay the blame?
Should they cry out? Should they cast
The stone that starts the fray?

1005 Many have learned to shut their mouths
To let attorneys rest for them;
To allow advocates to speak for those
Who tend to pay them best.

1006 No legal man is above acquittal

The law is not the right of lawyers.
The law's no ass though attorneys ride
It with a stick and carrot.

1007   Come, you lawyers, if you will,
Denounce, condemn and sentence me.
Let the punishment fit the crime.
Convict - be rid of me.

1008   Come, you stiff-necked legal priests,
Vacate your temples, view the light,
Do not handicap yourselves
By giving justice price.

1009   If you must play right from wrong,
Do it with an unmarked pack.
A stacked deck against the poor
Is a game non-rightly bought.

1010   Take me to the scaffold now
If I must live in a corrupt state.
Better dead and half-way pure
Than alive in a rotten system.

1011   Let me atone for all Man's faults
At the gates to the world beyond?
Let me beg pardon from those -
Fit to judge me wrong.

1012   Such louring does not menace me.
I thumb my nose at clenched fists.
I turn and watch the setting sun
As in warmth - life moves on.

RELIGION

1013   Upon the Almighty the world seeks
Allah, Khuda, Kami, Dieu!
The universal life force - Lord!
The supreme soul - God!

1014   Whichever gods that there may be,
They are one, and one with us.
Too many names flood the mind
In the universal see.

1015   If there are Angels, then I believe
That good will come of such belief.
If there are heavenly beings -
Then let them come to me.

1016   If there are Devils, then I believe
That bad will come of such belief.
If there are demons leashed in Hell -
Then set the creatures free.

1017   If there are ghosts - and there may be
Such spirits trapped 'tween two worlds
Then help such spectres right the ties
Of wrong that chain them there.

1018   But take Man to the happy land,
The place of mansions in the sky
Where mortgages are all arranged
And on the never-never.

1019   Do not leave Man in the pit,
The nether-abyss far below

Where rents are always overdue
From years and years ago.

1020   Religion, cult, sect and faith,
        Every one is stamped 'Man-Made'.
        There'll never be one reply
        To all that Man has questioned.
1021   Oh, there are scriptures, vedas, writs
        From Moses down to Joseph Smith.
        Words of prophets heat our thoughts
        The way the sun warms the world.
1022   Amos, Daniel, Joel, Isaiah,
        Confucius, Laotzue, Zarathustra.
        Many tongues, and many founders,
        Vates sacer, saints, disciples.
1023   There are creeds to shift mountains.
        There are beliefs to move large hills.
        There are doctrines to mount hummocks,
        And dogmas to level dunes.
1024   All, of course, are orthodox,
        The faith as given from above.
        Religion thrives on being right
        When the competition's wrong.
1025   And oh what names! Infidels!
        Pagans! Goys! Zendiks! Papes!
        How can truly holy men
        Belong to any faith?

1026   What is this holy business then
        That's so ineffably inexpressible?
        What makes redemption and salvation
        So unutterably venerable?
1027   Why the bad press for things unholy,
        Unhallowed and temporally mundane?
        Why the bad crack about things secular
        Non-sacred and plain?
1028   For many fight the good fight:
        Stand up for Jesus - Hip hip hoorah!
        I don't mind being saved by a saint -
        I'm heavenly-minded and sane.
1029   But I don't like sanctimonious zeal:
        The saint abroad who's a devil at home.
        Look at Tartuffe - need you more proof
        Of cant made sniveled and snuffled.
1030   But hush my mouth blaspheming out loud
        About irreligion sacrilegiously sworn:
        Piousness ill-suits irreverent ranters
        And is wasted on those who have faith.
1032   Atheist sin and wicked agnosticism,
        Clover & dock in the field of mankind:
        Undevoutness and skeptical scoffing -
        Are as common as weeds in the wild.

1033   So with a latria, dulia, hyperdulia!
        Praise the Lord and his hosts.
        My God? I think I must be nuts
        Kneeling on the floor.

1034
    But my, my, my, she ain't half nice
    That goddess statue over there.
    If stone could speak, I'd find strength
    To strip the idol bare.

1035
    She does not touch the inner man,
    The vital spark that fires life.
    She is no psyche divinely breathed
    With telepathic mind.

1036
    Yet, this idol is no voodoo doer,
    No juju jigging vampire doll,
    No hex or hag or witchcraft moll
    Charming me - into a warlock!

1037
    This idol casts no evil eye,
    No mumbo-jumbo leaks from her,
    No hocus-pocus makes her dance
    To place me in a trance.

1038
    She is all stone, quiet and still,
    I see her, but she not me.
    I may touch her when I wish
    And leave her when I please.

1039
    And to the end I come at last
    To take my vows, renounce the world,
    To take the church, cloth & robes
    Of an ecclesiastic father.

1040
    I take the ministry as a priest,
    A black coat Holy Joe styled life;
    For I have come into the light,
    No more will I go hungry.

1041
    You, laymen, do not write me off,
    I will still be in your parish;
    For I am in every being
    And in every part.

1042
    And should your rituals leave me sad;
    And should your service make me laugh;
    And should an unction be your last -
    I'll be with you - always.

1043
    So let me don my robe and cloak;
    Let me take my staff and orb;
    Let me raise my cowl and smile
    And bless you - and mankind.

1044
    And when you meet in your kirks
    Or meeting houses, mosques and kiacks:
    Remember who you are with –
    The Universal Being.

(END OF THE UNIVERSAL BEING)

NUDE TO LOVE
[17th September 1988, Flateyri, Iceland]

Tomorrow strives to be tonight,
Love is on the lips of dawn -
Between the greying and the day
We are fast, entwined, ensnared -
Our lips bare touching, naked rest
We are one in shy caress.

461

Daylight stays to end the night;
Our mouths match the parting clouds -
Between the haze and hue of sky
We have heaven here on earth -
Our sighs heave fresh, pared to touch
We are open, nude to love.

MOSQUITO
[12th – 16th October 1988, Coventry Cathedral & Glasgow]

In the east, and in the west,
In the south, and all points north …
There is a buzz, there is a hum,
There is an airborne host of birds –

Bees and flies and crowds of gnats,
Swarms of midges, swirling black.
In the spring, and in the summer,
In the autumn, before the winter,

All the world is thick with life,
There is a creeping insect sea –
Cockroach, beetle, ant and worm,
Earwig, spider, tick and flea.

There was a worm called George Facker
Who stuck to his woman Heather;
He was a wimp until his friend Pete
Turned George into a sucker.

George was in love … it wasn't enough
For Heather ran off with new lover Pete –
And George midst the tears, swore he'd get even
On all the women who'd treated him rotten.

Alone in his bed, the full moon rose
And strange happenings took place in the light –
He turned and tossed and dreamt he'd lost
The use of his limbs overnight.

When he awoke, it wasn't a joke,
He nearly choked at the sight of himself –
On his back he had sprung two lengthy wings
And his nose was the length of his arm.

He couldn't believe the state he was in,
Or the thirst that strangled his throat –
Before he knew what, he'd straddled his cat
And drank all of its blood with his nose.

George passed out with the cat's last meows
And awoke to discover it gone –
He looked in the mirror and sort of remembered
The pair that had done him the wrong.

He vowed there and then to do what he could

To take his revenge as the cuckold –
George then knew what Jekyll went through
Now that he was a bloodsucker.

Some mate he was, George cursed Pete,
'I'll get the bugger back somehow!'
And as his anger grew, his wings grew
And his nose sniffed for blood.

George headed for town to get himself drunk,
His head was rushing with thought –
'I'll get my own back on them both!'
He had no time for sociable talk.

He frazzled his brains on McEwans ale,
Until the landlord had him thrown out –
He straggled and swayed along the high street
Shouting 'I'll murder them both with me hands!'

At last he calmed down, smoked his last fag
And fell over in a heap on a bollard –
Someone helped him up, gave him a shove
And he stumbled on towards the disco.

There he met Stella, a bit of a piss-head,
Together they boogied, rocked and rolled;
She booked the taxi, he paid the fare,
And together they went to her hole.

Stella would not let sleeping dogs lie,
So George did not transform but performed –
Morning came, she drew him up,
Then threw him on to the floor.

'Sorry, darling, I've got to rush,
I've an essay to write for my course –
My tutor's talking me out tonight,
I'm tied up all the time. *Adios*!'

George went home to his flat ...
The cat was still not back –
'Where the hell have I gone wrong?
Christ! The cat's crapped on the mat!'

He ate dry bran and drank black tea,
And smoked a pack of fags –
The nearest George got to work
Was looking at the ads.

The cat came back just after noon
As George was having a nap –
The cat went up and scratched him hard,
Then shot into his lap.

George stroked the cat and mumbled things
As he watched the kiddy shows –
Both were glad to have respite

From being on their own.

Evening came, the cat went out,
George hummed quietly over tea –
And then as he did the dishes …
He said ' What's come over me?'

'Oh my God!' He said aloud –
and then he buzzed, and buzzed about,
then folded back his wings in pain
as he pushed his nose back in again.

He took control, blurted out
'I've got to have a woman!
I've got to have some female blood!'
And off he went to hunt.

Drunk once again, back at the disco,
There he met Linda, a tart with heart –
He sweet talked his way into her clothing
And spent the night at her flat.

Linda awoke with George at her breast
Sucking her blood up his long nose –
She started to struggle, but all that was audible
Was suck and a slurp and a croak.

George was flapping about trying to draw out
As she swatted him one with her fist –
He staggered away in a lip-smacking daze
Shouting 'What's got into you, bitch!'

'Get out of here! You bloodsucking male!'
Cried Linda in a fury and rage.
'There's enough of your type wandering the night
You pervert! You keep away!'

'You're far too rough for my kind of love'
Linda continued to fly at dazed George –
'I'll need a transfusion after this evening,
 I'm weak, and feeble and faint!'

Linda passed out and George sneaked off,
Back to his flat on the far side of town –
The cat heard him coming and started to run,
It was learning to say out the way.

George threw himself down on his bed
And sobbed himself into a bad sleep –
He had a dream about Heather and Pete,
A dream that made him quite sad.

The sun came up, George didn't get up,
He somehow passed and wasted his time –
Cleaned his toenails, scratched his bollocks,
The cat watched, keeping it's distance.

Thus he spent the whole day in bed,
For the night before he's been amply fed –
He groomed his wings, blew his nose
And slept until the half-moon rose.

He slumbered on and dreamed some more,
The cat came and went, meowed for food –
George flapped his wings, spat out blood
And the cat hid under the cushions.

Time went by, and George remained
Lodged in bed in hibernation –
His cat pined and moaned and gurgled,
hung around in hope of a meal.

George awoke – he was hungry,
He hadn't had a suck for weeks –
His cat was ill and anorexic …
George got up prepared to hunt.

He prepared himself to find a girl,
He no longer cared about freewill –
He was now a dirty Devil!
A dirty laughing fiendish insect.

The cat lit out broken hearted.
Escaping through a broken window,
George tried to grab it by its tail,
The cat screeched, took a leap of faith.

It leapt down into a pile of snow –
disappeared into the whiteness
George thought him lost forever,
And broke down in abject remorse.

George grew worried, put on his coat,
donned his wellies, braved a blizzard -
Searched for tracks, called for the cat,
In the street, the park, and the lanes.

In despair, George threw himself down,
Lay in the waste, would surely have died,
If a girl called Lily coming out of the Chinese
Had not seen him lying covered in snow.

She dropped her trash, stooped to discover
That George was a man she had admired from afar –
A regular customer in his days of sobriety
She had liked his looks and his charm.

She helped him home, put him to bed,
Started to clean his mess of a flat -
She nursed him daily with chicken soup
Until the pain he had - left his heart.

George had no desire to attack his saviour,
He had fallen in love with this Lily –

465

For in her arms she had his lost cat
Wrapped up in a bundle of woollies.

She struck George dumb with her beauty
As he lay in his bed like a wally –
She took his hand as he started to cry
And tell her about Heather and Pete.

George agreed to go for treatment,
Discovered his wings and nose were figments –
His emotional distress of being deserted
Had made him imagine himself an insect.

Such low esteem is common enough
For those who sustain emotion rebuff;
His need for revenge - manifest thus
As a weird desire to suck human blood.

His counselor said the cure for his pain
Was to find a good girl and love again –
And sure enough George quite agreed,
He rushed home - gave Lily a squeeze.

A squeeze? George was a changed man;
No more sucking ladies breasts -
Well, not in revenge. We'll say no more.
They got married. Isn't that nice.

BRIDGE OF FEUGH
[4th November 1988, Banchory, Aberdeenshire]

In the weak November sun
On the Bridge of Feugh,
An icy autumn downward wind
Whites the raging burn.

Stumps of brackened birch,
Fir and copper beech,
Twisted mountain ash,
Banks of lichened schist.

Depths of black slow river,
Cascades of swift foam white,
Parts where violent rocks
Push up where ripples fight.

Leaves down on the water,
Needles on the stone,
Debris smashed and carried
Along and seen no more.

CASTLERIGG
[12th January 1989, Keswick, Derwentside]

The black clouds swirled about the stones,
Across the fields a rainbow rolled,
Sepulchered the grey day moaned

Hail, and sleet, and snow.

Greenhouse winter blossoms withered,
Silver birch and thorn bush quivered -
Ravens rode the dry-dyke currents
As sheep lay cold together.

THE BLACK DINNER (song)
[1989, Glasgow]

Twenty-fourth November, fourteen forty O,
The Black Dinner night, fourteen forty O!
Black Douglas brought the boys at night to the Castle Rock,
He left behind the Douglas might and their many loyal lords.

Twenty-fourth November, fourteen forty O,
The Black Dinner night, fourteen forty O!

As they ate an autumn fayre set out on the boards,
Crichton ordered in - the black head of a boar.
The Douglas boys saw the head and looked to their host.
The king of Scotland - Fiery Face, was barely ten years old.
Black Douglas raised not a hand, nor Hamilton a nod,
Livingstone denounced the boys, then cut their Douglas
throats.

Twenty-fourth November, fourteen forty O,
The Black Dinner night, fourteen forty O!

JAMES II

The age of the king had come, once more a Stewart ruled,
he was young, and fired guns on the grass of Holyrood.
Douglas - back from France found his power curbed,
in a huff the Earl took James's action as a snub.

In contempt he made a league with Crawford and with Ross,
these three earls swore to join with each in every quarrel.
James - mad about this league, which threatened open war,
sacked Crichton for bad advice and asked Douglas to his court.

Douglas, seeing Crichton sacked felt safe from any plot -
he did not know that James had a Black Dinner heart.

THE STEWART CHILDREN (song)

Papa's gone away to fight,
He's taken the whole army south.
He's left us all here behind
To play and muck about.

Some think Papa's pretty tough,
He's taken all the bombards out,
Enough balls and powder stuff
To blow ten castles down.

Will he do it? Surely not?

467

You're too wee to understand.
Will Papa bring back lots of dolls?
Yes, he will, lots of toys.

We're all soldiers! Where's my sword?,
Where's my armour? Where's my horse?
Who'll be king, and who will not?,
A sister and four royal boys.

We're all children, Papa James,
We'll want our Mama in the morn!
James, Alex, David, John,
And little Mary - sleep til dawn.

NEVER THESE DAYS AGAIN
[6th May 1989, Glasgow]

Enclose me in your eyes
Or just forget about me -
Never will these days return.

Love, love secret, no one knows -
Think, think blush, I have found
A sweet dream - the touch of love.

Within my heart I'll hide you,
Truth, let no omen be on you -
Slave I am to your eye.

These cool breezes, join our sighs,
These clear springs shower our joy,
Sing a song to flower the world.

Without you here I cannot smile,
My eyes are never tired of you -
I never can forget, you my muse!

TAM TAR TIN (a fragment)
[19th May 1989, Glasgow]

Tan Tar Tin, the Mac of Man,
Made in Scotland, so its thought
Without the consent of the clan
Without the tying of the knot:
This boy, on Lady's Day late March
Was born, weighed, wrapped and brought
By a stork starched and large
And put into a foster's arms.

No clocks rang out, 't was that time
Between five and six past twelve
When all the clocks are spend with chime
And once again renew themselves
Except one clock - St. Thomas's Church
Behind the hour began to bell
With thirteen doleful blows struck true
And never struck again till two.

SAUCHIEHALL STREET BAR
[May? 1989, Glasgow]

Here in the bar on Sauchie' Street,
Tapping our fingers, stomping our feet,
Pretty girls frumping under the lights -
I think it's going to be a good night.

Hot is the air on this August eve,
Hot is the passion pumping the heart,
Hot is the body next to mine -
Looking divine and ready.

Don't know what to think of this,
Who can say what it is -
Who can argue with the truth
Or the passing of youth.

On and on into the dark,
Hard is the way coming back,
Round the world ever which way
Standing still in the day.

Sun coming up on the trees,
Blossom falling on my hair,
Breeze in the branches of thorn,
Around me friends travelling on.

Over we go into the morn,
Over we go into the future,
Beyond the horizon eternity stretches -
Dancing to mark time's passing.

MIDSUMMER SPEEDS
[18th June 1989, Glasgow]

Midsummer speeds to aural height
And we are caught in the heat
Of days that bring more than rain
And wind that is the norm.

WE MUST THINK AGAIN
For Dawn
[18th June 1989, Glasgow]

Two years ago on Dinafawr
We wined and toked and read our plays
And all the world lay before
Beyond the green Welsh valleys.

Now we've come two summers on
And know not what waits ahead
Beyond the Scottish urban life
We must think again.

LITTLE INDIA

469

[27th June 1989, Halt Bar, Glasgow]

Can I watch the world go by
When I am part of it?
The man who sits and views the world
is of no use to it.

URBAN LANDSCAPE
[27th June 1989, Halt Bar, Glasgow]

In the urban landscape north -
North in the haze of summer,
Jazz steals through the rainy nights
And music thieves all culture.

Here - the north west light of Europe,
A throbbing bursts the strictured brain:
Love is on the lips of strangers;
Art's in the mind of dreamers.

Here - no structure, only chaos,
Anarchic freedom to be oneself.
Here - no pressing common order
Forcing denial on its people.

Why? Should pressure come to bear
And force us all to be prostrate?
Here - the weak sleep through the night
And the strong embrace the day.

WOKE UP THIS MORNING FOR REHEARSALS
[28th June 1989, Glasgow]

Woke up this morning - window open wide.
Summer's here for sure - June-time.
No festivals this year, just performances
Taking place all over town.

Rehearsals drag out in the east -
The dandies dress up in the west -
The hours turn slowly on
To the performance in the south.

MAISIE MADRAS
For Isadora Mann
[28th June 1989, Glasgow]

Darker than a gypsy girl,
Nimbler than a ballerina,
A quick-tongued shrewish lass
With a hot curry temper.

Who would cross Maisie's path?
Who would chance to kiss her?
Who would lay a hand on her
And not regret it?

In all the wide theatre world,
No leg or eye's like Maisie's.
Take heed, boys, she's too hot
A dish to have for starters.

THE GREENHOUSE SUMMER
[26th July 1989, Glasgow]

If this is how the future is,
Then lets be thankful of our past;
Summer once was rain and cloud,
Now its drought and fire.

THE FIRST JOURNEY OF THE WANDERER
[Composed Aug 1989 - Nov 1990]

At seventeen, the Wanderer leaves Scotland to discover the world. He passes through seven European states, sleeping where he can, learning what he will, before returning home. Seventeen more years of travelling, he moves back to his native city for good. Re-establishing contact with a childhood friend (The Narrator), he arranges to meet him in a bistro in a bohemian part of the city to tell him about his first journey.

SCOTLAND

NARR: It was summer and the sun was going down:
Northward, the multi-storey windows glared
Above the chimneys; but to the west
Beyond the Clyde at ebb, the evening sky
Reflected by the waters round Strathclyde's isles,
Glowed red and created shadows eastwards
To shade Glasgow from the august day.

I met the Wanderer by the riverside
Beneath the Kelvin Bridge, close by the subway
Where friends and folks from different walks
Of life relax by the breaking Kelvin waters
And talk their troubles out over drinks
In a bistro-cafe well-known to beggars
Who block the pathway to the cafe entrance
And ply their trade, take their chances
With the intellectuals and the artists
Who patronise the bistro out of habit.

I was late and the Wanderer had gone:
Then I saw him standing on the bridge
Staring into the Kelvin water, which barely
Trickled as it had been a scorching summer,
So hot in fact, it had been the hottest
Summer of the century; but there he was
My childhood friend, just now returned
From seventeen years of wandering perpetually.

At first I thought it was not him -
I looked away but soon turned about to see
That he had noticed me standing there

471

Thin and greying from a life half-lived;
And he - elbows perched upon the parapet,
Hands cupped beneath his chin, his eyes
A piercing mystery of a thousand tales
That I would never get to hear -
He stepped forward and took my hand
And pulled me to his bosom in a movement
That made me put my arms around him.

He made me feel that we had never parted
All those years ago when we were seventeen
And fresh from school.

We were friends again: in a Glasgow vale,
At a table, we relived our schoolboy days
Of how we two had faced the world
Of childhood and never lost a fight,
Nor failed a test; how we had spent
Our time together playing games, chasing girls
the names of which we could still recall,
One of whom, I had engaged, and who
As my lover had given me one child.

The Wanderer smiled, and said he envied
Me my happy home and family bliss,
And when I protested that it was not so,
He cut me short and began a tale
Meant to make me cherish all I had.
But I would not let him start his cant
Until I had laid my troubles out before him -
How city living was a mental drain,
How family life was dull and boring,
How children ate into a father's soul,
How a job for life made life a job -
But my friend laughed and called me
A happy man searching for unhappy joy,
And as I disagreed, he began his tale
But I stopped him short with my all.
"While you were traipsing the world,
I was bettering myself the best I could."

WAND: "Do not feel threatened,
travelling is not a life to envy.
If I were to live my youth again
I would not take the road to freedom -
For freedom is an ideal manufactured
By individuals shackled by their upbringing."

NARR: These words passed on top of mine,
and I recalled the faces of his parents -
His patient, warm and endearing mother
And the father who adopted him as son.
For it was common knowledge as boys
That he did not know who his father was,
And thus half of him was a mystery -
Half of him was secret and unknown.
And now my interruption had silenced him,

472

He rose and said that he must go -
I pressed him for his address,
But he stated that he had no home.
I gave him my card and made him promise
That he would come and visit me soon.

The hottest summer of the century passed,
Autumn came as autumn always does -
The leaves lingered high until December
When the grey of winter finally closes in.
Cheered by the lights of Christmas,
New Year came, and a new decade too,
And with it floods and gales so severe
That thousands were cut-off, marooned;
Vast tracts of land joined the ocean.

It was on the eve of Saint Valentine's
With a howling storm ripping at the eaves
That there was a soft knock at my door.
It was the Wanderer!
Without hesitation he entered my home
But did not speak until tea was served.

WAND: "People blame others for the depletion
Of the Amazon and the ozone layer. Why?
And why do people pay this evil Tax?"
He banged his fist on my coffee table.
"Like rats cowering in holes!
Like rabbits in fear of a fox!
Educated to live like cowards
frightened to face the hunter's dogs!
Fear makes people cunning and devious,
They cannot face losing what they have,
Nothing makes them relinquish possessions
Though they arrive with nothing in the world
They shackle themselves to wealth."

NARR: The wanderer looked me in the eye
Then cast his eyes about my house
I thought I lived a modest life.

WAND:"You have enormous wealth -
Wealth of education and a solid house,
In my travels I have been in palaces,
But most of the world lives in huts
And shacks or homes less grand than this -
In wealth you are a fortunate man.

Once I saw a holy man in India
Beneath a date palm in the shade,
Cross-leg seated in the dust, bowl in front,
Eyes fixed on the great above -
A crust of bread, dal or rice,
Some fruit or nuts - a little cake,
Students flocked to him with food
But none could make him part his lips.
Every dawn - the crowds collected

473

And swarmed about until night fell,
They slept by him or talked til dawn,
They would not leave him on his own,
They asked him questions, begged replies
To things that any man could answer,
They pleaded, but were met by silence
Or cruelly jeered by the attendant throng.

Too often violence riddles heaven
And breaks the brittle bones of children;
Too often pleasure eats the perfect
And pain feasts on the discarded;
Too often destitution steals
And richness robs all happiness.

I too wished to ask that holy man
Many things - find great truths,
But I could not ask those things aloud:
I was filled with my own lies -
Lies that shut me out from beauty,
Beauty flawed by my existence;
My craving for each moment different,
My need for every second quickened.

We all have wealth shut within us,
Locked within us, trapped within us.
I have tried six years by six
To steer a painless course through life,
But I have suffered more for this
Than those who tightly close their eyes
To all out there - the pitch-black void
Where lurks the total of our past."

NARR: I could not comprehend his drift,
He seemed to contradict himself -
But something in his traveller's words
Made me see all there was -
Killer whales snatching seals
Off the sands of Patagonia;
Squibs bashed on the rocks
Of Mykanos and Kos;
Turtles netted and de-shelled
On the Pondicherry coast;
These were the kind of scenes
I thought I'd hear unfold
As I listened to the tale
Of his first sojourn abroad.

WAND: I first left these British Isles,
when I was seventeen, naive and innocent
our shores were all I knew;
our mountains were all that I had climbed;
Our people white-skinned and Lalloned
was the world of a boy taught to know
that out there lay an empire once so vast
that one third the globe was British.
Those days were gone, and none knew

where Britain stood in the minds
of Sikhs or Kenyans or any nation freed
at last from colonial rule.
The memory of the Third Reich years
was still imprinted on a new built Europe
twenty six years after Berlin fell
and the Allies split - East and West.

ENGLAND

I began to journey south -
Through England I travelled by thumb
to leave Dover on the midnight tide
like Harry Four on his way to Agincourt.

BELGIUM

I first set foot on foreign soil
four o'clock one morning late July.
I slept with young folk like myself
beneath an up-turned boat on the shingle.
Daylight came too soon from behind the town
beyond which lay continental Europe
stretching eastwards to the Orient.

In that Belgian channel port, I knew
nothing of the world beyond.
I left my pack in a luggage kiosk
and went walkabout in Ostend.
With my friends we hired bikes,
but a puncture cut short our time
on the cobbled alleys of the town.

We spent our afternoon on the promenade
drinking coke, baring chests
to the scorching sun of summer.
I tried chatting up a local girl -
she was tall and dark and pretty,
she spoke in stilted French to me
until her boyfriend appeared on the sand
and broke our friendship in its infancy.

Such is the life of travelers:
We ate our bread and cheese for tea
then shuffled into a crowded bar
where drinks were too costly to get drunk.
In sober hunger we returned to the station
and in possession of our belongings,
we cooked sausages on a beach fire
and spent the night on the Channel sand.

Passing through this Belgian world,
I knew nothing of Flemish customs
beyond that which I had read in books -
books weighed with facts and dates about
the creation of Belgium as a buffer state
to protect the French against bully Germany.

History repeats itself despite the will
of men bent to make sure it does not.
Life turns full circle within a lifetime
though men believe they travel a straight line.
Now the Berlin Wall is down - new fears
spread in France that Germany will rise.
Europe, close to being one, shrinks from unity -
the ideal of a community with no frontiers dies.

When I was seventeen, no date seemed
fixed for the end of European fellowship.
Ours was a continent of young ambassadors,
a post-war generation free of death and hatred.
I vowed I would join no army,
nor take a rifle in my hands -
I was a new breed of man.
I was not alone - all across western Europe
the youth were on the road,
hitch-hiking to discover our new world!

A shower woke us from our slumbers.
Full of hope and belief in human nature
we tried to hitch lifts from cars
driving off the channel ferry in from Dover.
Two ferries - no success,
we took a train to Brussels,
on arrival at the Gare D'Nord,
we found a nearby hostel.

We went in search of the Pissing Boy;
we made our jokes well heard to others
then took ourselves to a cafe for drinks.
We ran out of time -
the hostel barred the door at eleven,
we forsook the demon alcohol for bed.

Next day I passed on through to Flanders,
and I should remember more than I do ...
At Bastia - I rested by a rusting relic,
a Sherman tank cemented by the roadside
left by Patton of the Bulge.
How could I forget the movies,
the comics that depicted war,
the tragedy of dying in a foreign land,
sermons preached to the young.
Show me the man who has no enemies,
I'll show you that man has no friends.

I was educated - had no enemies -
except for the Russians and the Pact;
I was warned about the yellow peril.
But Marxist life remained intact,
Clydeside lived on strikes and sit-ins.
Overthrow of empire was everywhere,
there was no-where left to plunder,
no-one to exploit except ourselves.

The hills of Scotland came under the plough,
swathes of moorland given to the tree,
I endorsed the arrival of forestation,
regretted the loss of scenery -
barren waste and bog, aesthetic beauty.

There are those who might have left
our country naked for deer and grouse,
blood splattered gumshoes -
wiped upon our Scottish soil.
We Europeans - a sky covers us,
the same sun lights us in turn.
The same rains make our blood.
What is race? We are one.

LUXEMBOURG

I hitchhiked on to Luxembourg,
through battlefields of past misery,
through landscape once battered by artillery.
Quiet now, the summer fields lay
stretching peacefully on to Alsace.

Past a grove of trees, the Duchy's frontier:
A pleasant country caught like a pea
in a mattress shared by Germany and France;

Enchanted by fairy castles and bridges
I spent two days wandering the City,
I shared a dormitory with two Quebecois,
spoke with some citizens of the world.
Kenya? India? Brazil? or Alaska?
What dreams had I - a boy from Glasgow?

In Luxembourg I drew breath -
I sat out in the hot August night
listening to the homesick talk of strangers.
Captured by the white tales of trekkers,
journeyers fresh from Greece and Italy,
drifters up from Spain and Portugal.

New codes of conduct for the young -
part imported from the new world:
anti-violence, anti-foreign wars,
abhorrence for hunger in Bengal.
There had to be more to life,
there had to be more than death,
there had to be something to it all?

Such questions never leave the lips
of those born to see the world -
youth rushes at us all ablaze
before old age snuffs the flame.
The answer is plain,
the answer is always the same,
the answer comes with the pain

by asking the question again.

A travel-weary Californian,
too old to make the draft for Nam,
had lived the beatnik life in San Francisco
on the Golden Park side of town.
Haight had flowered into hippy love
when a singer gifted weeds into a crowd.
Drugs became an aspirin to violence,
love became the solution to war.
A composer became more popular than Christ,
and a President more hated than the Devil
who had butchered a Hollywood star.

Outcast - but reborn,
the circle of life going on and on.

Californian Bob was the first of many
I met from the new Atlantis -
a state where dreams come true
like some Disney tale of fancy -
living legends and self-made fortunes.
And I lily-white from my parents care,
fresh from a council house in Pollokshaws,
I swore I would reach the furthest shores
or die within along the way.

Time grants the wish of those determined,
fate takes those whose time is wasted.

My future was already charted -
I was to be - a civil engineer.
I had the choice of two universities.
Which one? I was still undecided.
I had no idea of the great cosmic whole,
I was traipsing where will had no authority,
I was journeying where I was welcome
and arriving where I had - no home.

At seventeen I had no awareness,
I had no notion of my own self,
I had no concept of inner forces,
my mind was set on the here and now.

GERMANY

When I crossed into Germany,
I cannot tell you what I felt,
a cloudburst sent me scurrying
beneath a railway bridge for shelter.
I hitch-hiked eight kilometres,
walked seven to the outskirts of Trier,
nightfall dropped like a curtain,
I kipped down on a railway embankment.

In the morning I awoke blackened,
I had bedded down on burnt grass.

I looked into my pocket mirror -
I was black. A child pointed.
I was too filthy to hitch-hike,
I entered Trier looking like a tramp.

I was young!
A night on the road beneath the stars,
a night in a bag on burnt grass,
a night outdoors like a bum.

Eight to one, I exchanged marks for pounds,
booked into a hostel for a scrub -
wanderers must take refuge where they can
or sink to being hobos short of luck.
For the now - I was in ancient Trier,
a Roman town with splendid baths and fountains.
All gone to ruin, modern Germany
stood brash and imposing on the past.

I looked for signs of history -
no spirits spoke, no voices whispered
as the Moselle rushed to join the Rhine.

BAVARIA

Next day I set off for Munich,
three hundred miles at the whim of drivers,
left me stranded in the heart of Nuremberg.

I dined out that night with a Dane
who spoke of home life in Copenhagen.
He was going on to visit Prague,
just a thousand days since Dubceck
had been toppled by the tanks.
Revolution fights regression,
independence fights oppression.

In Nuremberg's rebuilt square
destroyed in nineteen forty-five,
we watched the figured clock strike twelve,
then slept within the castle walls
and rose with the dawn.
I headed south and outside town
I met a blonde-haired Berlin girl,
We hitched together, got a lift -
then another - we spent the journey
eyeing up each other.

An English lecturer from Reading Uni'
took us to the fringe of Munchen.
He was on his long summer break
making the best of his substandard pay.
He was on his way to Salzburg and Vienna.

We hitched into the city centre,
we parted with a kiss,
since then I've met Berlin girls

around the world canning fish,
playing chess, or being chaste
while chased by unchaste pricks.
Kim in the Alaskan wild,
Ula on a Carib isle,
Bettina in sweet paradise -
What I've come to miss!

Faded images of imperial Munich,
cobbled streets, parks and tramcars,
a touch of coldness in the air
brought on by Scottish gibbering's.
I found the hostel fully booked.
With Dublin bhoys, Pat and Ger
and Joel, a Californian guy -
I went to eat, then returned
to sleep in the public park.

At midnight the cops came by
said - we may sleep upright
but lying down broke the law.

We climbed a metal fence
into a small sports ground,
and dozed beneath some limes.

In the morning we awoke
a herr with a shepherd dog
silhouetted over us.
We explained our restless night,
the janny let us use the showers
in the school sports house.

With my friends I spent the day
in and out the Munich stores,
we made a meal of rolls and cheese,
then ran to the hostel grounds
to escape a heavy downpour.
Later, hot dogs and bier,
we squeezed into a photo-booth:
I have a photo of us four -
all hairy heads and beards.

That night it was too wet to kip
out on the sports ground grass.
We slept beneath a building arch
on a slab of marble.
Stiff - we awoke, played in the park,
shared our yogurt and our choc-o-milk.
I spent all my marks on ice-cream.
Another night on marble followed.

In the morning, I regretted
spending all my change on ice-cream.
Breakfast-less, I hitch-hiked to Austria.
I saw no point changing sterling
into Deutsch marks just for breakfast.

I swapped addresses with my pals,
and set-out for the Salzburg road.

An hour's walk took me to the autobahn;
I joined the hitchers on the ramp.
The traffic was ferocious, in no time
I was halfway to the Austrian border.
Then it started - three hours passed,
a short lift of a few kilometres -
three hours more, and another ride
dropped me on a deserted slip-road.

Darkness descended, hunger gnawed,
Salzburg was a distant dream.
I took my stove from my pack
to heat some soup in a pan;
I stuck a match -
A car pulled up, a door opened,
a long-haired youth got out
to take me to his house.

Eric was the local doctor's son.
Life in a tiny village in Bavaria,
not a stone's throw from Berchtesgaden,
was dull and boring much of the time.
He was soon to do his army service,
he did not relish the cropping of his hair,
he saw no need for a German army,
he was against all things military.

The house stood back from the road,
there Eric had watched me wait
an hour in which three cars had passed.
I had eaten nowt all day,
I was weaker than a mouse,
I would've ate horse that night
if he had set it out.

Out came the rye breads and bratwurst,
the salami's and an assortment of cheeses -
I eat a donkey-full and brayed contently.
"My father is still marked by the war,
scarred by Stalingrad and Warsaw,
he feels the hands of six million Jews,
resting on the shoulders of his generation.
Now, there is an ashamed silence
there is a numbness - a self-humiliation
that makes me believe we should forget
and forgive the crimes of the past.
Germany went to war - and lost;
East and West and Berlin walled.
Never again will the Reichstag rule
the West and East as one."

I spent the night on the surgery couch
Dachau and Auschwitz on my mind -
I was clear about right and wrong,

bible class lessons and the Boys Brigade
had made me a righteous snob -
I was as Presbyterian as they come;
I would borrow ten pee and pay it back,
I was an irritating sod.

In the morning Eric gave me breakfast,
drove me back to the Autobahn.
He gave me some Austrian schillings,
to buy a coffee on the other side.
How many people have helped me since?
Stuck in the Saharan waste and dying,
tired and lonely on the Baha coast,
broke and hungry in the Transvaal,
miserable with love in the Bali hills,
ill and trapped in a Lucknow hotel,
swept out to sea in a Brazilian ketch,
under arrest in Panama city,
alone and afraid in a Kurdish village.

What use has such travel been to me?
Where is my wealth? Show me my riches.
Memories do not make a man secure.
Stories do not shut out the cold.
Twenty years on - I am a loner
living in the damp of a Glasgow basement.
I am here, but my mind is on -
the waters of the Victoria Falls.
My eyes are on the Taj Mahal,
My heart is in a dozen countries,
I am spread across the globe.

This is the price I have paid:
experience feeds on variation,
variation has ruined contentment,
ambition steals every second -
There is always one country more;
one more sight left unvisited,
one more temple to explore,
one more beach to stroll.
My eyes are bigger than my mind -
the cupola on a minaret;
the turret on some ancient fort,
the arch into a black bazaar,
the inscription on a soldier's grave
"Here fell a man no-one knows,
May God safeguard his faithless soul."

In a dark Glasgow bedsit,
February's light, short and fading,
the blue skies of mountain Spain,
the green canopy of Siam's bays,
the red hue of Sudan's plains -
I am home to stay.
The season's pull my heart apart,
I want to up, leave, depart -
throw off the chains of urban life,

trade in my all for cash - and run
to haunts where happiness exists,
return - to life in paradise.

Who does not crave for perfect days?
Who does not dream of sand and waves?
Who does not wish their life away?

Here now - I stay to quietly rot
in my Glasgow hobbit hole,
I struggle on to find my place
in the cosmic whole -
Despair creeps-up on me at times
and lingers as a festering sore.

Now Spring rushes, summer fades
til autumn golds wash the earth,
there they melt into the soil
or cover the grey clay walkways
between the rows of graves.
Not so when I was seventeen!
The snow capped Alpine peaks
traversed the length of my horizons.
Over those mountains lay fresh prizes.
I had the faith to chance my luck
in search of love and fortune.

I knew nothing of transience,
I believed - youth and exuberance
would carry me to greatness!

AUSTRIA

That night I slept in Zell-am-See
beneath the span of a roadway arch:
it was cold - the mountain air;
the ground was dirty, damp, and hard
as I lay my head on Alpine stone.

I rose at six hunger-pinched,
I marched into the sleeping town
twee with schloss and austro-kitsch,
I waited for the banks to open.
I changed ten pounds into schillings,
I bought some yogurt, bread and cheese
and hitchhiked on up the Pass -
Gross Glockner at eight thousand feet,
mist about it's sheeted peaks
five thousand feet over me.

I felt small 'neath nature's wild
rugged edge revealed that day -
my mind expanded with each view,
my heart pounded on each curve
that left me gaping at abyss.
There was no earth as we turned
and wound our way down the pass,

483

a mile beneath us - pasture land,
while in the distance, mountains rose
not as high as those we'd crossed
but breathless still - to one so young!

A family bought me lunch at Dollach,
and let me out at quaint Lienz.
I found shelter for the night
in Gastof Neuwirt - with outside loo
and wash-room in the yard.
I settled in, washed off the grime
of traveling three days with a pack,
I toured the town as tourists do
and listened to the town's brass band.

It had been a pleasant day -
I slept between linen sheets
beneath an eiderdown.
I awoke to a deluge of mountain rain.
I made a cup of tea on my stove,
and I thought of the road before me.

The downpour stopped, I set off south
I opted for Venice as my goal -
I had counted my cash and concluded
that Venice, that ancient merchant city
was to be the turn-round of my sojourn.
Who can say if I chose wisely,
tradition has the grand tour end in Rome,
but I was not versed in culture then
or the ways of Oxbridge men -
I am still not acquainted with the latter,
they're not acquainted with me either.

A German family - their son hitch-hiking
in Denmark - took me short of Sillian.
I walked three miles, reached the village
where an old man took me to the hostel.

We waited patiently until it opened,
myself, an Italian cyclist, an Irish couple
with another - an Austrian from Vienna.
The cyclist's shorts were brown
but such details do not matter now;

ITALY

Friday morning - thirteenth of August -
I walked two miles to the Italian border,
and two rides later I was in - Cortina.

Perched high in the Dolomite mountains;
ringed by rugged arete-edged peaks;
summer's snows melting in the heat -
alpine blossom blooming on scree.
I waited by the roadside
longing to be by the Adriatic sea.

484

Two hours of Italy passed me by,
I had no shade from the mid-day sun,
the mountain air was thin, but warm.
My dark Celtic skin, once pale - now burnt,
my hazel eyes more green than brown,
my auburn hair part streaked blonde,
my body changing each hour abroad,
my mind absorbing all it saw.

On that hot Ampezzo road!
What cared I for future life?
I had the there and now
high upon the Dolomites!
I pushed my thumb out at cars,
none would slow, none would stop;
an hour more passed me by,
then - to my shock - a biker!
a Dutchman on a Bayern bike -
"Where you go?" "Venice" I said.
I clambered on the back -
and we set off south!

A hundred miles downhill we raced,
cliffs and curves and devil bends,
a hot-rod ride towards the sea,
six hundred cc's taking us
through village towns like Langarone
and Ponte Nolle Alpi, Vittorio;
on highway fifty-one we sped
to join route thirteen near its end.

I was dropped eight miles from Venice,
seat-sore, stiff and weather beaten.
I hitched a lift into the city
along the Ponte del Liberta.

Venice

A vaporino from Piazza Roma,
took me down the Grand Canal -
some say - the world's finest street.
We passed beneath Sealzi bridge
by the ancient church of St .Jerome
wherein the relics of St .Lucia lay.
Then a palace gazed my thoughts,
my eyes fixed on its balconies -
the port where Richard Wagner died.
Beyond the fifteenth century Ca d'oro,
the smell of fish caught my breath.
It was the Pescheria!

I disembarked at the Rialto Bridge,
found a hostel, booked in for two nights.
Some potash des legumes did for supper,
banana ice-cream as a sweet -
I was tucked away in bed by ten,
no lover in a gondola as in dreams.

485

Is there something wrong with me
that I experienced so little at that time?
Is there something missing in the man
not living life while he can?
What was I searching for in Venice,
naive and young and seventeen?
I did not find it, or for sure
I would recall what it was.
Perhaps you do not see importance
in noting that I ate ice-cream.

Next day I marched to St.Mark's Square,
cheese and bread by the Procuratie,
I was impressed by the Basilica,
it was an architectural jewel.
I still see the paneled doors,
the hush of the baroque interior,
a rival to the grandeur of St .Sophia
I was to visit one year later
barefoot and broke in Istanbul.

Let not the mutterings of a wanderer
reduce Venice to a nothingness,
I saw too many things to tell
as the midday heat did me in.
Ninety three degrees, give or take,
I retired to the hostel shade
to watch young Venetian boys
retrieve coke bottles from the canal.
Five liras for every bottle cashed,
the water was polluted with oil;
foul smelling and algae green,
they dived head-first into the deep.
Cheerful loud-mouthed dark-skinned youths
performing for the likes of me.
I saw these young Venetian boys
without the eyes of Thomas Mann.

Lost in my self-made world
I planned my route for the morrow -
Up the Po valley to Milan,
then back into the high Italian Alps.

Short of company, and tired,
I took another early night,
my mind upon the day just gone
and not upon the years ahead.
For had I fixed upon a big house,
a house so grand I filled twelve rooms -
I would not now have wandered, no,
not spent my youth in exile.

I know better now - a wiser man,
maturer in my thoughts, my looks,
these give hint of all I've done.
Now I've come to some dead end

where my spirit climbs a wall
in order to be free of what?
Caged I cannot live out life,
behave as though I'm civilised,
I cannot smile nor greet my friends
nor live with purpose or with point -

Four billion years of history -
I am just thirty six.
I've not seen nor felt a thing
worth passing on to anyone.
All you'll hear from me
will find its place in the wind
and pass round and round no end
with no start to it.

My time in Venice is small worth,
my journey fruitless to the hungry,
I cannot say I enjoyed burnt hours
hitching west on the Pisto Quatro -

Como

Happily I said goodbye to Padova,
the slip roads of Vicenza and Verona.
Night descended as I flew past
Brescia, Bergamo and then Milano.
About two a.m., I found lodgings
on a park bench in Como.

This is the life of the traveler,
this is the way of the wanderer,
weary miles across vast lands
to sleep wherever time allows.

I awoke to the still blue waters
of a resort the rich possess -
the beauty of the lake - spectacular
after the hot dusty plain.

The mountain air revived me greatly,
I felt at home in the mountains -
Dear is the Highland blood in me
passed down the generations,
I hear the skirling of the pipes
when danger presses in on me.

I heard no pipes on Como's side,
I left my bench, went into town
and booked into the hostel there.
Drowsy from lack of sleep, and heat
I found a spot beneath a tree
and slept a couple of hours.

I tried to rise, but with no strength
I lay until late afternoon
wrestling with some sort of pain.

487

In my gut was diarrhea,
I stole some public-loo sheet paper,
in case an accident ensued.

By nightfall, I was normal,
I shared a pizza with Johnny,
a youth from outer London.
Next day I washed all my clothes,
my jeans, my four tee-shirts.
and dried them in the sun.

I had my lunch in a park,
sunbathed, then ambled back
to talk with Pete from Coventy.
Jean, Jenny and Israeli Ehud,
more like names than faces now,
they became new friends.

This is how time's a swine,
it leaves you nothing worth a dime.

SWITZERLAND

Next morning Ehud hitched with me,
we planned to travel to Luzern,
but who can plan anything
when you're at some driver's whim.
We found ourselves on foot for hours
dwarfed beneath towering mountains,
at last a ride took us on,
but left us short of Lugano.

Late afternoon, hot and tired,
Ehud took a train to Luzern,
I could not afford the fare,
so I hitch-hiked on alone again -
Six hours I waited, walked, and passed
trying to circumvent Lugano,
til at last I reached the town
and met Graham 'Hockey' Henderson,
the ex- vice captain of the Academy
that I had left that summer.

Accompanied by his girlfriend,
a girl who'd been forms above me!
we chatted for half an hour or so,
then they went south towards Milan,
heading for the artifacts of Florence
and the great monuments of Rome.
I was mere pleb to such a hero -
Hockey Henderson four years my senior,
he had seen half of Europe's treasures,
all I'd seen - two thousand miles of road!
If there was be some justice
then "God" I prayed "Let me see more."

That night I slept on a wooden bench

in the waiting room of Lugano station.
I was comfortable, considering -
An early start saw me outside Bellinzona,
but four hours followed in blazing sun.
It all seems so innocent now
when we are faced with war -
a half million Christian men
against a million Musselmen.

Stupid pride will bring about
needless deaths to aliquot.
In time - shrines will rise
to glorify those who died.
I will not justify aggression,
I will not back imperialism,
I will not put my voice to war
or call for retribution.

It is no joy to fry in the sun,
he who waits blisters and burns.

A ride at last! south of Lichtenstein;
three lifts more left me near Zurich.
I spent the night in Rapperswil,
between bug-free hostel sheets.

Bern

I was in Zurich for breakfast,
then in Bern, just in time for lunch.
I studied zoology at the Bear Pit,
studied history in the national museum -
I re-met Robert, an Australian
who'd been in Rapperswil the night before.
I befriended Christian and Liz,
and Jimmy, a boy from Bishopbriggs,
I visited an exhibition on pollution
'*Uberleben*': I left somewhat touched.
Survival, I was into that - depicted
as the dove of peace Picasso drew.

That night I felt alive, aware;
I walked the streets of Bern glad
some folks were trying to 'Save the World',
I knew not how they would succeed
but I endorsed the whole ideal.
And now? I am a trash of past,
I consume and waste and junk,
I contribute to the filth
that floats or sinks to slime existence.
Who is God? Where is he now?

Lausanne

I left Bern for Neuchatel,
quaint and old and not so new.
On I went - to Lausanne

489

where Eliot wrote his Wasteland -
where Spender penned his first lines
on the shore of Lac Leman -
Placid in the summer haze;
south, rose Mount Blanc.

I pre-ambled in the hostel garden,
and spoke to a pretty girl,
at first I thought she was Swiss,
but she was from San Diego.
Yet, we were young and knew not
how to bridge the wide divide -
I, from my land of rain;
she from a sunshine State.
Our bodies were athletic, yes.
She was twenty one -
I kept quiet about my age.

In the fall of evening cool,
we shared our yogurt, cheese and rolls,
we gazed into the lake land depths
and coyly flirted - innocence!
Youth flushed our faces, in a blaze
we rushed into a quick embrace
of minds; our bodies never touched,
my finger tips never brushed
nor touched a hair of hers
though we were made for love.
Respect and fear, hand in hand
kept the two of us apart,
yet we both knew, felt desire
tug at us, but we were strong.

We walked to the railway station;
enraptured by her sunshine voice
I gazed into her deep blue eyes
concealed behind her straw blonde hair
flowing down her woman's back
where it was tied by a clasp
used to the La Jolla sands
and the courts of Kellogg Park.

She was not from Chula Vista,
La Mesa, or El Cajon -

I knew not then what I know now
of girls from such foreign lands.
Abe Lincoln! You may rest -
your girls are among the best!

Late, we wandered slowly back
to the hostel by the lake -
all the while we talked and talked
and still we did not touch.
We said goodnight, and as we went
we shook each other's hand.

Romance? I hardly think so now,
who knows, it might have worked
if I had been some Don Juan
or some modern William Tell.
I was just a Glasgow boy -
that doesn't ring so well.

Wrapped in folds of eiderdown
I woke to heavy Sunday rain;
mingled thoughts of getting drenched,
thoughts of San Diego Teri.
I lay in bed made my plan
to stay another day.

We walked to a boulangerie,
rolls, tomatoes, broke our fast,
bananas as an after course,
we squatted on the harbour wall;

Out of wind, out of rain.
We played I-Spy, observed the lake.
We put English names to things.
Far away - snow covered peaks -
Mount Blanc hidden in a mist;
I know we should have kissed.

Side by side we espied all
except the souls within ourselves;
Greek and Latin poets speak
of the myths we make from dreams;
Delusion feeds alternate worlds
that no-one knows for long.

So too - as I re-live
and tell you of my young life,
the truth will out despite desire
to make it more than it was.

On the shore of Lac Leman
I had no interest for the Swiss,
all my thoughts were centred on
the girl I was with -
All the wishing in the world
cannot change this little truth.

So let me take you back again
to the wind and rain that day -
I was glad that I had found
a girl to share the break;
Far too much sun without some love
cannot make the difference up.

Cold and damp we returned
to the hostel hand in hand -
No! we kept ourselves apart,
desire gnawed at our hearts.
By then in fact, we had no hope

491

of being more than friends.

Two hours sitting by the lake,
our dreams had not matched,
Teri was a language student
with plans to teach high-school kids;
I hoped to be an engineer
to live and work in foreign lands.

Our worlds were - poles apart -
I cooked some soup, gave her some,
then spent the afternoon in bed;
alone, and tired, and worn
from traveling Europe like a bum,
my home upon my back -

Years of wandering were to come
though I was not aware of that,
when I awoke, I was fed
by a little bloke from Brum.
Macaroni cheese for tea!
I'd never had such food before;

I was a simple Scottish boy
brought up on beans an' toast;
lunches of soup and pudding,
evening meals of pies and spuds.

I was born in fifty-four,
reared three miles from the Clyde
in a Southside council house.
At seven - too big for the sink,
I went every Friday with my dad
to the public baths.

At eleven, we were re-housed
when they pulled down old Pollokshaws;
we got a toilet and a bath.
I was angry - my childhood
was erased by bulldozing men
who then put up high-rise flats.

They filled them with families
decanted from poor Govanhill,
the Gorbals and Kinning Park.
I was a native of the Shaws -
and baited by new inner-city indians,
wars erupted, battles were fought.

It brought me many victories
before I sustained defeat
at the hands of Glass-Eye Gillespie!
What a name! Even now I shake
when I recall his steel toe-caps,
his shoddy tweeds and freckled face.

Ginger hair - like Irn Bru,

his one good eye fixed on me
as he aimed his hob-nailed boot
towards my sweet angelic face.
Innocence itself - a Shaws boy
standing up to all he could
in the name of good!

Where were my pals on that day
outside wee Pollok Annexe school;
Hamilton, Houston, Mackay and Kennedy,
cowering like wee timid beasties!
Not a word to spur me on
Glass-Eye grabbed me by the throat,
I fought to catch my breath,
my face turned beetroot red.

Like a ton of church roof lead,
Gillespie pinned me to the earth.
Twelve years old and I had lost
my first fight since I'd punched
Gibson's nose and made it bleed
when I was seven years old.

I had never lost before,
ten years of scraps, kicks and bites
since my first success at two
when cousin Hughie caught my blow
and cried because I got to ride
on his sister's three-wheeled bike.

Cousin Marjorie says I was an awful child,
until my battle with G-Eye Gillespie;
there I was - bruised and hurt
and in a heap against a wall,
jibed and jeered to go on home
to let my mammy hear my cries.

Such things flood back on their own,
and in Lausanne as I drank tea,
the pain of defeat shadowed me,
for I had had a violent youth;
now I wished to turn my back
on acts that made men beasts.
There was more to life I sensed
than the confrontations found
daily in the Glasgow that I knew.

I walked to a patisserie -
and bought a bag of broken sweets,
nabisco biscuits, dry and crumbly -
how I craved for real shortcake.
Then thoughts of Teri came to me,
I returned to search for her,
to kiss her while the night was young,
but it was not to be -

The warden sent us all to bed,

I fumed and cursed at hostel life,
it was only ten o'clock,
who could call that fun.
So love was ruined - next day we parted,
Teri Sher of San Diego - (sob!)
She is just a memory now,
a name on a diary page

There is a note - Fell in love!
Left unkissed! End of tale.

Geneva

Through Narges, Rolle, Nyon,
I thought of love - it of me;
I hitch-hiked past Fournex, Versoix,
by midday I reached Geneve;
the city where John Knox heard
the truth and gained the light
with Calvin and the Lutherites.

I found the hostel closed,
but a helpful passer-by
informed me of a place near there
where drop-outs had encamped
in a hospital no longer staffed.

Off I tramped to dump my pack
in this novel makeshift place,
and there I made my peace
with some cool cosmic freaks –
and secured a space on the floor.
I went outside to lie about
and sleep upon the garden wall
in sight of the Jet d'Eau -

That night I ate a heavy meal
promenaded by the lake,
I ambled on the cobbled streets.
The old town spoke to me -
history mingled with the now,
this part of Switzerland I liked!

I forgot all the miles,
the nights sleeping in the wild,
the days burning on the road;
I enjoyed some pleasant hours,
not a traveler any more
but a tourist on his rounds
strolling as a happy person might.

Even then the past was catching up;
I ran into Shaun I'd met in Bern,
he was looking to kip for the night.
I lead him to the hippy place
now candle-lit and Indian incense.
Half the road seemed bedded down;

We found ourselves bagging by
three blokes from Glasgow -
knocking back the vino tinto.
Oh well, such is the wandering life
to sip wine with one's compatriots
while dossing in a foreign country.

FRANCE

I rose with the dawn - in blazing sun
I hitched to the French frontier;
on to Gex, and then - mistake!
I crossed the high Faucille Pass
in a fast car with a rally driver.

He put his foot to the floor,
and deafened by the whining engine
we crossed the Jura Mountains -
even now I still shudder and think
of how we might have come a cropper.

Alive and shaken at La Cure,
I thumbed a sedate ride to St.Laurent,
on to Champagnole, then ill-luck,
a woman took me to Arbois
and left me stuck outside a farm.

Between Mouchard and Besancon
This was France - cow dung and straw,
rural life - pigs and chickens.
I loved the sense of openness,
despite being stranded by a dung heap -

Three hours later a farmer stopped
and took me into Besancon,
and there I spent another night
underneath the summer stars,
off the road, in a field –
I slept beneath the sky.

During the night a heavy dew
settled on yon poor hobo,
he awoke wet and hungry
as factory workers filled passed
along a lane some yards away.

Faces peered over the hedge.
Red-faced I gathered up my things
and scrambled back on to the road;
I hitched through Marnay to Gray,
took buttered bread for nourishment,
then thumbed on north to Champlitte.

My luck broke - mid-afternoon -
a ride with a girl from Geneva;
she left me off in Verdun -

Who has not been to that town and not
had white crosses etched in their mind.
Criss-crossed with neat white crosses,
everywhere one looks - white crosses,
white crosses to the ends of the earth.

No trees grow on the hills of Verdun,
white crosses grow with each new sun.
Lest we forget those white crosses,
buy poppies to paint the white crosses
that criss-cross the hills of Verdun.

Sombre, I walked far beyond the town
shadowed by the Great War dead;
A lorry stopped, and in six hours
we chugged into the outskirts of Paris.
A few hours rest, the driver in his cab,
I kipped in the back with the cargo.

We drove on to Rouen - where dropped
I slept under the porch of a restaurant
avoiding the fierceness of the rain;
fueled by a storm in from the Atlantic.

Daylight came and on to Abbeville.
My luck held out as I took a ride
with a lecturer from Croyden Tech
who took me to Bologne and Dover.

ENGLAND

Up to London, and deposited at Brixton
I caught the tube across town to Hendon
where the M1 once began, and where I
could hitch-hike back to Scotland.
I'd visited seven states in Europe.
It was only the start of my traveling,
I'd had a taste of the life
that was to make me a wanderer."

SCOTLAND

NARR: The Wanderer stared into his empty glass.
I looked to the clock - it had unwound,
We knew not the time, nor what day
Or if it were night -
Or if time had halted or sped on -
We had traveled through the seasons
And it was now Guy Fawkes.
I could hear fireworks outside,
Yet he had begun on St .Valentine's night.

And while I pondered how and why,
He rose and said he must go.
Go where? He would not say,
I must assume to his hobbit home

496

Or to his parents house,
Three miles south of the Clyde.

He said goodbye, and off he went
Into the crisp November night,
I wondered if I would see him soon,
I was not convinced he was home for good.
I regretted that I had not been
To the furthest corners of the globe;

There was wisdom in my friend's rebellion.
I had to seek him out, make him stay
So I might use his knowledge to advantage.
For if Scotland was to be a nation again
And independence taken in the lion's jaw -
The wanderer was needed for the cause.

(End of The Wanderer Part 1)

MORNING ROWS A BOAT
[11.39pm, 9th October 1989, Ashley St, Glasgow]

At ease my mind floats beyond
To dream of things to come -
There is no past to recall
Or years of troubled words.

Time soothes the turmoil's of youth,
Emotion falls with the leaves -
Rain dowses any thoughts
Of wishful drifting, free.

Clouds carry off balloons of dreams,
Sleep sends off bottled hope -
Darkness brings the rainbow out
And morning rows a boat.

ART IN PLACE OF REVOLUTION
[7pm, 11th November 1989, Glasgow]

Art drives the world crazy!
As world walls crumble -
People throng through streets!
Elsewhere freedom marches.
Democracy bungles, tumbles
As taxes fuel the grumbling.

TOWARDS THE END OF DINOSAURS
[11th November 1989, Glasgow]

I wonder where time has gone -
How much time was spent
When reckless mankind marches on
Towards the end of dinosaurs.

Active minds still the feet
Of those bound to rule us all,

A finger pointed like a wand -
Presto - and the world jumps!

I'm not one to wave a stick
Proclaiming peace in our times -
Never were the times so rife
To split us with black magic.

Fragile is our grasp on life -
A movement here - then a flash!
Gone like sulphur in a fire
Shot from volcanic vaults.

Still, our idle rulers sit
And watch the worlds collide.
No man can shape his own end
Nor God forgive his crimes.

SWIFT AND SHORT
[10th December 1989, Glasgow]

At the centre of the universe
We find ourselves conditioned,
Ruled by inner forces
And all that yet may be.
We are pressured by great powers
Weighing down on us -
Yet still we will ourselves
To be above - and free.

At the end of our being here
In our reconditioned slums,
There will be no reckoning
Of all that has passed.
No time will be spared
(To list the rights and wrongs),
Our departure will be swift
And the journey short.

SO THAT WAS CHRISTMAS DAY
[25th December 1989, Glasgow]

So that was Christmas Day Eighty-Nine.
Twelve hours in bed.
Twelve out and about.

No Christmas comes easy -
Each is crammed with prior obligations,
Arrangements with family.

Escape from conviction is painful
When mothers weep for sons
Not yet home.

I cannot be more hopeful than I am
That Christmas staves off isolation
Bourn all year.

Now almost over - the goodwill shared
Will not last the week ahead.
Bring on the New Year.

POETRY COMES EASY
[Midnight, 13th January 1990, Glasgow]

When poetry comes easy to the lips,
Words slip out that should not be heard;
Meaning takes a back-seat to melody
And sense rides uneasy on the metre.

THE SECRET CUPBOARDS
[13th January 1990, Glasgow]

I try to unlock the secrets kept
concealed behind large bolted doors.
I have a set of keys weighing me down
and a thousand locks waiting to be opened

There are no markings on the key chain
there are no numbers on the locks -
I have only luck and desperation
before time rusts the unopened doors.

I AM NUMBERED AMONG THE DEAD
[14th January 1990, Glasgow]

I am numbered among the dead.
I exist but I do not exist.
I am at one with the dead
But I am also part of the living.

Everything I do is already old,
Though everything to me is fresh;
I measure the past with the now
But the present has no length.

GETTING ON FOR THIRTY SIX
[14th January 1990, Glasgow]

I am numbered with the dead.
I exist, but I do not live.
I am at one with the dead -
But I am also partly flesh.

Everything I do is already old
Though everything is fresh.
I measure the past with the present,
the now I measure by the then.

This is why I am with the dead,
Here I am, but I am gone.
I am awake to nothing living.
In sleep I cannot raise the dawn.

THE MIDNIGHT STORM
[12.35am, 18th January 1990, Glasgow]

It rained until the cows came home
and then it rained some more -
The grey city met the sky ...
so grey they merged as one.

The lightning grazed the black rooftops -
peels shook the walls ...
the January gales howled wild
on the midnight storm.

A STUDENT OF LAMBRUSCO
[27th January 1990, Glasgow]

It all began as little sips
to get his mind off exams,
and would you know it, soon enough
the exams passed he never sat.

And why? you ask. What transpired?
A student once so ardent minded?
What made the laddie leave his books
in search of El Dorado?

Was it chance? No, not at all,
it wasn't fate that brought him down.
It was - it is fair to say -
his love of vino blanco.

No woman could have brought him lower.
No drug could have doped him more.
He bade farewell to book utopia
once he was on the blanco.

So heed! You wayward scholar types,
stick to books - and don't imbibe!
The student of Lambrusco drowned
in a vat of vino blanco.

AN UNOPENED BOOK OF MASTERS
[27th January 1990, Glasgow]

It fell open at Milton on about Shakespeare,
a few pages on, Keats, Byron and Shelley
weren't far away from Blake and Wordsworth
and Robbie Burns chasing Highland Mary.

Not all these names are names to a pleb,
Perhaps they're like a stick to a donkey -
Beaten too often, open wounds fester,
until a past master becomes a dead ass.

THE HOWLING NINETIES
[12pm, 5th February 1990, Glasgow]

February - and the gales blow
ships on to the shores of disaster.
Storms rage on the warm winds
howling up from Africa.

Floods and melting Arctic waters,
greenhouse effect and ozone destruction -
who can say if God exists
or if this is man-made weather.

Tying down the attic windows,
roofs rip off Barratt houses -
sixty-degrees to the blasts
wild nights bring disaster.

Welcome to the howling Nineties.

RACISM IN GLASGOW
[13th February 1990, Glasgow]

Militants and Nationists clash at St.George's Cross,
They rip the faces off the foe;
They smash the limbs and crush the skulls
Of those opposed.

THE ST. VALENTINE'S TRAMP
[1.23am, 14th February 1990, Ashley St, Glasgow]

Another day for lovers comes,
I find myself alone ...
Not on some craggy mountain peak
but alone in my home -
a rented room, an attic box
containing all I own.

Dawn filters through the yellow blind,
I curse and turn to sleep ...
not slumbering on a tropic beach
I sleep on dirty sheets -
a bed in a Glasgow slum
the wine inside of me.

THE CIRCUS
[2am, 25th February 1990, Glasgow]

Laugh comic, laugh, laugh, laugh.
Circus makes the world burlesque,
Parody pokes the Satire's ribs,
Pantomime tickles laughter's lips.

THE FLOW OF THE FLAME
[12.36am, 28th February 1990, Glasgow]

I can't decide too much about life,
where it will take me, when it will stop.
I go along with the flow of the tide -
to see the eddy out when its time.

I can't believe all that is happening,
I have the luck, the chance to be free -
free like the fleeting moorland deer
to run in the wild breeze.

Perhaps I can see the light in the tunnel,
the candle that burns in the howling gale.
I nurse the spark that ignites the fire
that fuels some inner flame.

AYE AGAINST THE POLL TAX
[1.28am, 1st March 1990, Glasgow]

It comes to me in these days of business
That we ride the road to revolution.
Pressure bears down on us!
Who will snap first? Regret later?

Tighter the screw is turned and turned
Until there is blood.
I can't back off ... this is destiny.
I must stand as counted.

With the sheep march the cattle,
I must face my own conscience.
My back is now against the wall
With the Bruce and Wallace.

TODAY I FACED A SHERIFF'S OFFICER
[11.48pm, 1st March 1990, Glasgow]

Today I faced a sheriff's officer
eviction writ in his hand,
repossession order number blah blah
seven days since notice served.

I'm not a man of broken finances,
how could I be stern with him?
the roof above my head remains
even if ownership changes.

Not any more - no more rights,
eviction - no appeal, no protection.
Property is number one today,
a sheriff doesn't argue.

He came alone and left quietly
warning me to make provision -
who can live through these times
without a revolution.

WHO IS GEORGE
[3.39am, 4th March 1990, Glasgow]

Pushed into a corner full of drunkards,
backed against a wall by a mob -

Speak up now - or be dead tomorrow!
Don't mess with me - George's a murderer.

Who is George? Who is George?
The cavern echoes 'Who is George?'

George will kill you in an instant,
inside him sleeps a tired warrior -
inside George Prometheus rages,
his fire stolen by ignorant forces.

But who is George? Who is George?
Mock the ignorant so-and-so's.

George has witnessed Armageddon!
He has killed - escaped oblivion!
George has faced a thousand horrors.
Let him be - condemn him not.

Who is this George? Who is he?
He must be guilty. What's he done?

George has harmed none but himself,
his nature is to give not take;
alcohol blunts his wits -
who is not a slave to something?

But murder is not mere mistake!
It is crime - it is horror!

George is flawed - unto death
guilt's a noose around his neck -
George has been the pawn of innocence,
the weapon of the righteous living.

Who says George should be forgiven?
Who can wash the sin of criminals?

George has paid for us all,
he has lost so you might gain.
The soldier home from the wars -
Feel his pain and not his shame.

LOST SINCE CHILDHOOD
[1.48am, 13th March 1990, Glasgow]

Such fantasies come my way.
I cannot turn or turn again.
Home is found in every street
And gone just as quick.
Lost since childhood days
I cannot halt to think.

LIGHT WILL SHINE AGAIN
[1.01am, 15th March 1990, Glasgow]

Sometimes life runs away

with all the things dear to us,
in it's place it leaves a hole
that none but past can fill.

Most lament the race of time
that leaves them staring at themselves,
but nothing quite gives a shove
like the hand of death.

Sunshine always follows rain,
life is ordered night and day,
the downpour might be falling now,
but light will shine again.

ELIZABETH
[1.29am, 16th March 1990, Glasgow]

Today I met Elizabeth -
Young and free and seeking help,
I could not shut my eyes to her -
And now we're friends.

GLASGOW GIRLS (song)
[March?1990, Glasgow]

East Coast girls are good with talk
And Northern girls are slim and tall
And Southern girls have got the lot
But Glasgow girls are warm.

Highland girls can do the fling
And Geordie girls can dance and sing
And London girls - they know it all
But Glasgow girls are hot.

ABLAZE THIS SPRING
[12.41am, 30th March 1990, Glasgow]

The streets are ablaze this spring:
Burnt out vans in alleys;
Mosques set on fire;
Fascist arson and beatings.

Here in Nineties Britain
Things are going wrong.
The wrong corner turned -
I welcome police protection.

There are no innocents:
Children doping up on stairways;
Alkies passed out on the pavement;
Dossers begging spare change.

No-one here pays the pole tax:
Barricades in tenements;
Demonstrations every day;
Fascists on the black-hunt.

Blue is a dirty ideal:
Masons with funny handshakes;
Try finding honesty in men
When poverty's on the gain.

I predict no happy end,
I foresee no coming utopia.
I take no interest in the future
When hell gapes before us.

APRIL FOOL'S HAS COME
[1.45am, 1st April 1990, Glasgow]

Narcissus in the window
Peeking through the curtain
Resting in a water jug.
April Fool's has come!
Spring has sprung!
Winter now is done!

BALMAHA (LOCH LOMOND)
[1.43am, 2nd April 1990, Glasgow]

Wagtail at the water's edge,
Driftwood dry upon the bank,
Tree-roots bare to the shore,
Garnets in the pebbled stone,
Narcissus edging on the bay,
Wood-smoke in the gladed shade,
Ancient rocks perched to drop,
Footpaths washed away in part.

Ash, elder, bramble, gorse,
Holly on the highest hilltop,
Hawks hazed against the cloud,
Gullies gashing through divides,
Crags and cliffs every place,
Spring in a skylark's craze,
Fossils in the softest shale,
Crystals in exposed quartz,
Contentment in the still collect,
Peace down by the loch.

THE OLD RUSTS ALL THE MORE
[1.18am, 8th April 1990, Glasgow]

Time marches on like some Goliath
Trampling on the smallest things.
I am an ant in creation,
I huddle in a hole.
Blow breeze, blow fresh air
Before suffocation wins.

Down wind success gathers,
Fame clears away barriers.
No girl comes to me from America,

505

Nor any place I know.
Rain washes nothing new -
The old rusts all the more.

NO MORE WORDS
[12.11am, 9th April 1990, Glasgow]

No more verses for posterity
No more verses for prosperity
No more lines for infidelities
No more words from me.

ITS NOT WITHIN MY POWER (song)
[Glasgow Girls, 2.40am 18th April 1990, Glasgow]

If you think I can
Then think again, my friend
You must think I'm a fool, alright.
Can't you forget all
The talk that you've heard
And see me as more than just a man.
Its not within my power
To make you mine.

BARBERS SONG
[Glasgow Girls, 3.07am, 18th April 1990, Glasgow]

I shoo the sun
I shoo the stars and moon
I yeah I do - O yes, I surely do …
My heart smiles
When I'm sure of her
Sure that she's fine, oh yeah
For sure, fine
For I'm sure of that girl of mine.

THE PUPPET MASTER
[from Glasgow Girls, April 1990, Glasgow]

In the morning I've a booking
Then two more in the afternoon.
I can see the children's faces
Lighting up the gloom of adults
Briskly going to and fro
Trying to make a living -

Up and down the Merchant City
People rush as if on wheels,
While I - in my tethered booth
Move both hands and squeek,
And cry, and laugh, and croak
To make ends meet.

I move the world with my hands;
From every continent they come
To stand and watch in awe;
My puppets bow - they applaud.

They throw their coins into my hat,
I wave goodbye, and they are gone.

THE ARTIST'S AGENT
[from Glasgow Girls, ? April 1990, Glasgow]

To see him take his high percentage
Makes me boil - I want to - Phah!
Would I drink the wine of leeches?
Suppose I would - when it suits me.

When you're alive no-one knows
How many paintings you've done,
How many copies you've made,
How many you've stored away.

Life treats me like I'm dirt,
I don't care - that to them!
The world can be a pile of dung
With flies as thick as .....

Have you seen the starlings swarming
above Jamaica Bridge in autumn?
The pigeons flocking in George Square
like agents at an opening?

THE ARTIST
[Glasgow Girls, ? April 1990, Glasgow]

Is this the price of one week's work,
gone for less than half its cost?
There are those who rule the arts
who think artists have no worth.

I'm not one to paint a cause,
I see the universe as dots:
Within each dot - a million more
Specks of life elude my vision
Til I'm blind - beyond myself
I cannot view a new horizon.

It's then I turn to booze and fags
And drown and burn my talent -
For when the musics plays –
I'm free of all that's bad and nasty.

THE BOBBY AND THE BUSKER
[Glasgow Girls, ? April 1990, Glasgow]

I know it's not a crime to play a tune,
And it's certainly no offence to sing to the moon -
And it's hardly illegal to stand in the street,
But to ask for donations is not the law for sure.
Know what I mean.

I'm a Glesca polis, I take pride in my job,
There's hooligans and ruffins around every block.

There's drunks and drug abusers and those that give the eye,
I just nab them by arm - just like that!
Get my drift.

I'm waiting for this lefty to stick out her cap,
I've heard she did it up the street right behind my back.
I'll catch her at it one day, sure enough,
Then we'll inform the Tax man, the Brew, and she'll be done.
Know what I mean.

YOUR PICTURE DONE
[Glasgow Girls, ? April 1990, Glasgow]

People going up and down
Round and round the town,
And all those faces going past.
'Heh, mister! Your picture done?'

Everyday I come down here
And sketch this and that, you know.
Sometimes a tourist comes along
'Heh, darling - I do portraits!'
Faces pass by .. zip .. and zap,
Then someone stops, I look the part,
And just as they're about to ask,
They run. 'Come on, come back!'

For sure I'll never make it pay -
For sure most days it always rains.
This is all part of fame ...
And being a struggling artist.
'Be done by a struggling artist',
Why do I cheapen myself like this?
Well, it's better than office work.
'Oi, special offer! Three pound only!'

Silly way to make a living.
I must be mad to consider it.

TAKE WHAT YOU CAN (song)
[Glasgow Girls, ? April 1990, Glasgow]

If you're ever going to make it,
Take what you can when it comes.
No-one's going to give you favours
If you can't give any in return.

You've got to be nice in a hard sort of way;
You've got to be firm, but polite.
Even if its' Come back another day'
Take what you can when it's right,

For you'll never get to make it that way,
So take what you can and run.
No-one's going to give you favours
If you can't give any in return.

Any chance you get - take the whole thing,
Snap it up, squeeze out the life.
Don't throw it away when it comes your way -
Take what you can when it's right.

LET THEM BREAK IT DOWN
[1.18am, 8th May 1990, Glasgow]

Once more the bailiffs at the door
like the curs of robbers.
Is this life in the hands
of tomorrow's doyens?

No sense comes of homelessness -
people die in the streets.
Around the world resistance leads
to a loss of freedom.

What place is left - what peace?
Hounded out of home by crooks,
men without moral thought
in the name of duty.

Tired of talk, tired of niceness,
against the wall prepared to fight.
Bailiffs at the door - pounding.
Let them break it down!

LEFT TO ROT
[19th June 1990, Glasgow]

The world is going at a crazy pace,
No place to hide, no escape from thought.
Where will tomorrow go and what found
When all is left to rot.

SANDRA
[3.24am, 19th June 1990, Glasgow]

One cannot pursue the sun, the stars;
One cannot pursue the wind, the sea;
One cannot pursue the fleeting day
Or a Wexford lass running away.

BODIES AND MINDS
[1.17am, 25th June 1990, Glasgow]

What are bodies to those of minds?
The flesh comes apart in the hands.
The eye grows weak with time.
Beauty of form turns to memory.

Scars across faces and broken backs.
Scars with no traces containing no past.
Scars where smiles hide bad luck.
Scars where love has had no return.

What are minds to those with bodies?
Those with muscles? Those with health?
Those who ridicule life's pale bookworms
Those who cannot flaunt themselves?

MY LOVE IS LIKE A COFFEE (song)
[1.25 -1.41am 26th June 1990, Glasgow]

My love is like a coffee
sitting on its own -
My love is like a rainbow
just beyond the road -
My love is like an angel
hovering above -
My love is like a mountain
never big enough.

But when I see my lover
I am not alone -
And when I see my darling
I have my pot of gold -
For when I kiss my angel
just lay me down -
For my love is like a fountain
and I shall not drown.

My love is like a bottle
tossed upon the sea -
My love is like an apple
fallen from a tree -
My love is in the heavens
too far to see -
My love is spring blossom
raining down on me.

IN BED WITH YOU
[1.52am, 26th June 1990, Glasgow]

And when in bed I am yours,
And in the dawn's glitter'd dew,
Curlew's cries say it all,
To close our eyes to love.

THE BELL TOLLED
[2.13am, 26th June 1990, Glasgow]

The bell tolled loud beyond the wood,
A taxi ticked into the gloom,
A drip of wax trickled through
To mark the dark hours passing.

TOMORROW'S A DAY
[2.54am, 26th June 1990, Glasgow]

Tomorrow's a day and a half behind!
Question each hour to find lost time!
Forward the workings with all haste!

Wind up the past to now.

A SOBER MAN TALKS TO THE LIVING
[June 1990, Glasgow]

McDiarmid, Burns, Morgan, Muir,
I cannae talk with youse nae mair,
I'm up tae here wi' pritty wurds,
Youse auld boys must move owr,
Gie the living life again,
Let Scotland's gobs wance mair roar.

THE NEW GLASGOW FAIR
[15th July 1990, Glasgow Green]

O Yea, you old fashioned fair,
back now to haunt the new,
try as we might to dance,
we sing the same old tune -
puppets beat the children,
clowns play the fool.

THE FOSSIL GARDEN
For Germana
[11.50pm, 2nd August 1990, Glasgow]

In the fossil garden, I thought of you -
You whose perfume fills my heart,
You whose fragrance lingers fast,
You who has me in your grasp,
Till I am crushed and spent aside.

IF EVER LIFE
[12am, 3rd August 1990, Glasgow]

If ever life were less confusing -
If ever love were less a losing -
If ever fame were less elusive -
I would be less choosy.

If I had all I'd be contented -
If I had nought I'd be without -
If I had something in between -
I'd only be part right.

OUT OF THE FUTURE
[10.39pm, 15th August 1990, Glasgow]

Out of the future-winter came
Rain on the roof of human decay,
Love running down the gaping drain
On a night mid-August in Scotland.

Where in eternity will faith enter,
Hope in form of happiness arrive?
Out of the wet when will need falter
And not be turned down again.

511

NANCY NOBODY (song)
[10th September 1990, Glasgow]

Nancy Nobody was going somewhere,
Everywhere she went - people stared.
She was held back by Tom's and Dick's;
She was held back by all sorts of pricks;
She was hassled by the weird and the sick;
Nancy was a nice girl at heart.

Nancy Nobody went cheerfully to church,
There she was safe from all the nurds;
There she could hide behind holy words;
There she could feel she belonged to God
Until she discovered God was a man!
Nancy gave religion the shove.

Nancy Nobody cared for her country,
She was patriotic to her undies and bra;
She was true blue and honoured the Queen;
She respected the police, justice and all;
Until the appearance of the horrible witch!
Nancy couldn't stomach the bitch.

Nancy Nobody was trying her best
To buy a flat in the trendy West-end -
Rents were too high - she wasn't dejected;
Her earnings were half of what was expected;
She wasn't a liar - she was just selective
And coy when asked awkward questions.

Now Nancy Nobody's living somewhere,
Everyone wonders how she got there -
She has everything a nice girl needs;
She has it all without the greed -
Nancy Nobody will not go to seed!
Nancy's a girl born to succeed.

DREAMS
[3rd November 1990, Glasgow]

What man does not dream
himself a Caesar or an emperor.
And what of those foolish men
who believed such dreams possible.

DOWN IN THE BASEMENT
[2.43am, 9th November 1990, Athole Grdns, Glasgow]

Down in the basement
The window facing south
Trees as a morning view
Voices of children going to school,
Leaves on the pavement,
The traveler home from abroad.

Across in the gardens
Behind the old pailings,
Cascading seclusion -
Voices coax a kite into flight.
Air stiff with a frost,
Not a leaf on the tops
I'm lost in the wild.

IN THE CHILL OF NOVEMBER (song)
[12.14am, 11th November 1990, Glasgow]

We sat alone in the chill of November
We talked of things that we could remember,
And when we forgot why we had argued
We couldn't recall why we had parted.

We kissed in the dark - it was romantic,
We looked to the future across the Atlantic,
And when we returned both broken hearted,
We couldn't resolve why we were angry.

Entwined we stretched out across the mattress,
We touched the edge of our own circumference;
And when we dressed, we were strangers -
We grew cold, then you departed.

AS THE END IS BEGUN
[1am, St. Andrews's Day, 30th Nov 1990, Banchory]

In bed in a daze brought out by pleasure,
Lost in the waves of evening and winter;
Embracing the play of time in the hours;
Who would trade life for another's?
Who would fade and not be a stranger?
Who would crave that which is possible?

Into the depths of night we journey -
On through a tunnel to emerge for eternity,
Sleep for posterity, and dream for tomorrow;
Scream for the past, and laugh at the horror.
Who would go forward knowing the outcome?
Who would begin as the end is begun?

KNAPPACH (BANCHORY)
[1.04am, 5th December 1990, Glasgow]

Four on the floor before the fire,
Exploding coal atop Scots pine.
Where went the hours of the full-moon night,
An hour's walk from a Deeside town.

Whistle down the wind without return,
Fleeting flames - December turns
Rooks on currents that seabirds sail
On the tail of an Indian autumn.

MARCH IN THE NIGHT

513

3.14am, 6th December 1990, Glasgow]

March in the night, my best friends -
File through everything old age brings.
Look back in anger at bad luck,
Curse the fleeing of youth and love;
Find no beginning in goings-wrong,
Search for the key to unlock it all.

March in the night, thunder, rail!
Unraveled questions unanswered remain;
Lost is a scene never explained;
Perdu is all gossip lacking detail;
Request an audience with my past,
Travel the distance, march, march, march!

LONELY PEOPLE
[12.32am, 23rd December 1990, Glasgow]

Hey! All you lonely people,
I've been there too -
Nights in the rain alone,
Dinner on the stove for one,
All in bed on my own
Before twelve o'clock.

I've been there more than once,
Its not fun, not at all -
Coming home, empty flat,
Feeding coins into slots,
Watching tv close to dawn.
Still breathing, and carrying on.

THE WAY WILL OUT
[2.14am, Christmas Eve 1990, Glasgow]

The way will out when there's a will
To succeed beyond the dreams of others;
Fantasy exists in the slumbering of hopers;
Reality comes to those who are workers;
Gambling is for those used to losing,
Sure-bets come to those used to choosing;
Don't say that wealth is not for you -
Happiness is now, not in heaven!

THEY'VE HAD THEIR LOT
[1.54am, 27th December 1990, Glasgow]

Beyond, between, there is a view
I cannot see, cannot hear,
Something which you sense or feel,
Not something they can use.

I wish I could work it out,
I dream that we share - that thing;
I hope you get my gist,
And don't ignore my drift.

For I cannot say more than this,
We must not think less of it,
You will not carry on unheard,
Or they will think it strange.

Still - within a drumbeat pounds,
Outside we think that all is sound,
Beyond you bobs to the swell
All they make from the tide.

I pray you understand my thought,
Bent, we make time of nought;
You wait - all will be revealed.
They have had their lot.

NEW YEAR, NINETEEN NINETY ONE
[6.30am, 1st January 1991, Glasgow]

Six a.m. on New Year's Day,
Full moon one hour from the west,
Six full swings from Uni-tower
This side of the Kelvindale.

THE SECOND JOURNEY OF THE WANDERER
[Composed 1st Feb 1991 - 13th Jan 1992]

It is 1991, the night the Allies invade Iraq. The Wanderer
sequestered in his bohemian hovel in Glasgow is visited by the
Narrator. Against the backdrop of world news, he hears the
story of the Wanderer's second journey to Europe, aged
eighteen.

THE GULF

NARR: It was the night the Allies bombed,
massacred a ten-mile column -
January was all but gone
and February all but come;
ground frost made the evening cold
for war! war! war!

There is no escaping blame -
wells pouring flames and smog;
treatment plants clogged with oil;
all in the name of God!

Will we forget those bloody hours!
those bloody weeks, those bloody months!
those bloody deaths without count!
those bloody wasted lives!

Is it dharma brings about
slaughter to cleanse our guilt?
Is it greed that leaves us nowt
but blood on the butcher's knife?

515

Each answer given prompts a question:
each question asked meets with silence.

Career the wild on to war!
Push the weak to stop them short!

I, meanwhile, in Scotland,
relaxed by the fire reading Crawford,
kept warm by North Sea gas
I thought of my oil-rig days -
the wild howling winter gales,
the ninety foot wrecking waves.

Snow fell that evening. Perplexed,
I set-out for the Wanderer's.
I had been to see his mother,
a woman of retirement age,
she had told me of his place
on the slopes of Dowan Hill -
basement bed-sit, dark and damp,
the type of room students take
in over-crowded terraced streets
let to Scots by prosperous Greeks.

I found myself at Atholl Gardens,
wet and dreary from the trudge;
I climbed the icy-sandstone steps
and pulled on a big brass bell -
behind me on Gilmorehill
the college clock chimed half-ten.

A student came to the door,
I enquired about my friend -
invited in, she led the way
through the house, down stone-stairs,
to the right, along a hall,
the smell of dampness pungent, strong
until we came to a door
the scent of incense masking mold;
the student smiled, wished me well
and left me there all alone.

I put my knuckle to the wood,
tapped as lightly as I could;
I chapped again, silence reigned,
then came a muffled cough,
but no-one came to the door -
I waited some minutes more,
turned the knob, entered slowly,
and there! sitting on the floor
limbs crossed, in a trance,
mind non-conscious to the now,
his back to an old gas-fire
the tell-tale signs of simple life
effused in the subdued light

The Wanderer!

I could hear a sitar dancing
with a tavla in a rag.
Oh church of Scotland kirk men cry!
Krishna lives! Christ has died!

What place had my faith there
in that dim-lit heathen room?
I had intruded on his prayers,
I tried to turn and get away
but I stood there just the same
to spy and gape and stare.

I had not seen such a place,
not since my student days,
that which comes out the past
some call fashion, some call art,
candle in a Buckfast bottle,
incense ash on the rug.

I was older than I thought,
I tip-toed to the wee recess,
I put the kettle on to boil,
a ritual no-one minds at all.

The Wanderer came out of his trance,
saw me, smiled, rose and coughed,
pulled the curtains in one draw
"Earl Grey, Robert. One's enough."

He was older than he thought,
we talked about by-gone times,
we had no common present,
we made a present from the past.

"And Chrissie Campbell?" he asked me,
"Where is she - about or not?"
I replied "We're divorced -
I love her though we've lost touch."

"And Jilly Hickman?" he inquired
"Lorrie Irvine? And Jean Love?
"Ruth Young? And Lyndsay Rourke?
"And Dorothy from the Tennis Club?"

We drank our tea, and chatted on
about the girls at school we'd known,
about our wait to be eighteen
and what we did to look much older.

WAND: It was the wait that done me in,
made me idle, made me a dosser.
After Venice, you might remember,
I worked with you at the Bank of Scotland,
six months of short-hair, tie and suit,
saved nine pounds, spent three a week.

I'd got my place at university,
An English one, I felt good,
I couldn't wait until September,
the bank-job was such a boob,
I wish I'd done something else,
I was such a stupid fool."

NARR: And so began a lengthy tale,
which in part I will retell -
about the Wanderer's second trip
which in all took sixteen weeks,
which led barefoot to Istanbul
and changed his life for good.

ENGLAND

WAND:"The Ides of May, my eighteenth year,
with ninety pounds, I set off
down the A1 in a pick-up
in the back with two Yanks.

Eight that night dropped in Brixton,
I walked south to Blackheath,
I got a ride with Mister Quine
who thought I was his long lost son.

He let me stay the night in Bekesbourne
in his Jacobean home,
I had never seen such wealth,
oak beams and Persian carpets,
leather uppers, crystal cabs,
paintings older than the house.

Mister and Missus Q were very nice,
they were lately from Mauritius -
diplomatic service - ambassador she said,
home at last from foreign climes.

Oh what I'd give now to live
in quiet Kentish countryside!
Orange juice, toast and eggs,
Mister Q wrote his address,
I pledged to drop him a line
from some place that he'd like.

That afternoon, down in Dover
I found my passport stolen!,
Or lost! I did not know -
Left in Bekesbourne? Dropped in Brixton?
I spoke with Q on the phone.

I waited til nigh on six,
the police had nothing to report,
and with a new passport form,
and snaps from a photo booth
I hitched north back to Bekesbourne.

That night I watched T.V. with Dave,
the son who looked a lot like me,
long-haired, tall and thin -
Mister Q slept in a chair.

Mister Q drove up to London,
with Missus Q, me in the back,
parking close to Petty France,
we went straight to Clive House,
and with his diplomatic manner,
I got a passport - twenty minutes!
Oh Mister Q, my hero forever!
swore he'd known me all my life.

How different then, eighteen and free,
from thirty six and going grey -
Vietnam was raging on -
I cared, but it was far away.
It seemed a crazy senseless war,
unlike the liberation of Kuwait.
No sense is made of human strife
without some loss of life.

Back to Blackheath - by bus,
on to Canterbury, beyond and south
to Dover spilling over cliffs
forever England to the last.
Who has not crossed by boat
the silver streak that makes G.B. different.
Who has not had a glimpse
of France in the distance.

FRANCE - Calais

Eight that night the rain poured down
as we docked in old Calais;
two Bangor girls said goodbye,
a Scottish pusher pushed on by,
skipping bail for Amsterdam,
his goods inside his bag.

Stamped and checked beneath the lights
I asked a couple "Que route Paris?"
"A Paris?" .... "Oui, soi Ecosses."
They took me in for the night.
They were Chris et Marie,
they made an omelet thick with cheese,
oozing with fresh young brie,
something odd and new to me.

On the stroke of half-past-nine,
tucked in bed, hot-bottle too,
I awoke eight next morn
to Calais shaking off the world
invading it from dawn to dawn.

NARR: Carried by the Wanderer's words,

I saw myself rising out of bed
I gazed out that French window,
the May rain came on again,
cherry blossom fluttered down,
narcissus drooped beneath broad elm,
magnolia buds opened up
to bleed their sweet scented musk;
a thrush emerged from a hedge
that edged a walled-in back.

I love beauty, art and good,
distaste all that's evil, bad,
all that which corrupts a child
or turns the tender hard -

I am a man reading books
who's turned his back on the world.
How can I assess the words
of my friend - so vastly miled?
How can I doubt his encounters
when my own are so short?

Taking refuge in my garden,
weekends and evenings in the soil,
I bury my hands in memories
and let time pass, as uninvolved
with all but my own thoughts,
I dream of being by the Taj Mahal,
or on the steps of Macchu Picchu
above the lost Inca world.

Such romantic thoughts are the norm
of those, like I, meant to die
where they are born, like a flower
root-bound in a pot.

These days, I am in bloom,
open to the night stars,
open to the morning dew,
wind and water, sun and earth.
I am one with nature and myself:
until I am taken from my world
by the words of a friend;
a friend not tied to homely things,
a friend long lost to wandering.

WAND: What did I find, or indeed
did I seek from the nomad's life?
End to end the countries stretch,
end to end, until back they come
til memories are all but hazed
by the doubts others have -

For who can say yeah or no
unless with their own eyes
they've seen a leper with no nose
or a dog roasted whole.

I am a man of peace, not war.
I have gone where tourists go.
I have been where life is sweet
and stayed where pleasure grows.

Paris

In France, then, to be undone
I left Calais for the world;
three lifts saw me reach Paree,
I came upon the Arc D' Triumph.

Down into the bowels of Paris,
confused by my own bad French,
I made friends with Steve and Pete
with whom I shared a dorm.

Thirsty that warm May night,
we bought three two-litre beers,
gutter-sat, as wide-boys do,
we drank and watched Paris move.

We drank Stevie's lager too,
he was too engaged in talk
with a tall Finnish blonde
with whom he hadn't a hope at all.

He said he'd like to give her one,
we just laughed him off,
we went to our hostel beds,
I dreamt of girls all night long.

Up at seven, showered and dressed,
I was off to sunny Spain,
our football team, the Glasgow Gers
had made the final of Cup Winners Cup.
The game was in Barcelona.
Up the Gers! Here I come!
Or so I thought at the time,
odd how life takes strange turns.

Breakfast in the Kellerman Park,
Steve told me all about Mannheim,
three days of rock extravagance
at a village called Germansch.

I may have been a Rangers fan.
I may have been football daft.
I even had my Rangers scarf!
But it was not to be.
Fate steered me then to Rock-an-Roll,
I was ready for the road,
no more going to Barcelona,
but the road to rack and ruin.

I took the Metro to the suburbs,

and hitched with ease on to Meaux,
half-an-hour - on to La Ferte,
then minutes late on to Metz.

Metz

Nine o'clock and in Lorraine
by the Moselle yet again,
now one year older, wiser too
I wandered Metz's platzs and rues,
twice German, French for now,
I spent two hours touring round.

In the station, washed and clean,
my long hair normal for that year,
a traveler bought me two cold beers,
then left to catch a train. To where?
I could not say - I left the gare
to find a park-bed for the night.

A cool May breeze with a bite,
I perched on a wooden bench
in my feathered sleeping-bag
with newsprint round me tight
to stop me getting sodden wet
and drenched by morning dew.

I woke at five cold and damp
and hitched a ride into Deuschland.
Two French freaks picked me up
they were driving to the festival.

GERMANY - Germansch

In Mannheim by nine o'clock,
we got directions for Germansch.
Three days of bands had been arranged
by some G.I's. fresh from Nam -
The Second British Rock Show - man!
that's what a road-side banner read,
we waited two hours in a jam
paid twenty marks at the gate.

Through a wood to the field -
I lost the Frenchies in the squash.
I pitched my tent within sight of
the biggest stage I'd ever seen.

Remember I was young, naïve,
a Glasgow boy from the Shaws,
I wasn't used to seeing culture
or being close to hippy stuff.

A German boy from somewhere north
asked if he could crash with me -
sure thing, love, peace and dope,
Franz spent three nights at my abode.

Oh life was so simple then,
an easy life - quick made friends,
no need to find next month's rent
or pay off a decade's debts.

I found a place stage-front left
to listen to the rock-an-roll -
Max Merritt, Linda Lewis, Quiver,
Beggar's Opera - and Pink Floyd -
flashing lights and zooming rockets
to the dark side of the moon -
I dozed off - hitchers sickness
and dragged myself off to sleep.

I rose at ten, took a wash,
then wandered round the site;
a seething mass of hair and sweat,
naked bums in the sun.

The music went on all day long -
Chicken Shack and Lindisfarne,
Osibisa, Mungo Jerry,
Uriah Heep, Rory Gallagher –
The String Band folk, Tom Paxton too,
Spencer Davis, and many others,
names past, names forgotten.
All music is a passing fashion.

In the evening, shy and tired,
I lay in my tent in thought
listening to the sound of drums,
guitars with their Clapton runs,
the smell of hot dogs in the air
being cooked by Frankfurt freaks
who gave me some hund to chew
before I fell asleep.

Next day I rose at ten again,
washed as the day before
at a small slow flowing stream
in a clearing in the woods -
me and a hundred other dudes.
And there - while half-dressed,
besides me, almost in the nude
was Pinky, a peach from New York,
long dark hair and slightly plump,
but formed in such female ways
she made my boy's heart thump.

She was all of twenty-two,
and as the stream ran-off her skin,
I saw how dark she was, and firm -
She eyed me with her charming looks,
and soon she had me in her arms.

That quick? No, I lie ....

it took all day to get that far:

We spent the afternoon with Sandy,
Pinky's boring Queens companion;
we smoked the hash the G.I's passed us,
and sat and ate their army rations.

A sergeant with a headband on
with his platoon, all ex-Nam pals,
had a hash connection chain
that went Kabul-Saigon-Weisbaden.

Stoned, we missed Humble Pie,
the Riders of the Purple Sage,
Wishbone Ash, The Kinks .... The Doors
who didn't show with Country Joe.

But as the night finally fell,
Pinky came back with me,
we got to touch and kiss and play
before the drugs did us in.

Pinky helped me pack next day,
no fond farewells, no sweet adieus.
I said I'd meet her in Karlsruhe,
and sure enough, we rendezvoused –

She was distant, cold, withdrawn;
she said we were two different folk
with very different needs and wants.
But what use now are memories –
now in business I find myself at war
with my office landlord - Harry Singh,
small time garage owner, who thinks -
a cow shed's prime space in the West-End!

What a joke! Four months I went
without a door to my cubby hole,
no window to the outside world,
an asbestos roof hiding me from God.
Every nail, every screw - my own hand -
not a bit of help from miser Singh.
There every week for his sixty pounds,
six weeks now I have not paid the rent.

In response, the electricity is cut;
what use is an office without power?
I must now call it quits.

NARR: The Wanderer left me in a rush,
that was the last I saw of him
for some weeks, when by chance
I saw him one mid-May Sunday
in Kelvinpark lying in the sun
between bush myrtle and gorse.
And almost as if no time had passed
he began where he had left off -

Southern Germany

WAND: Pinky shunned me in Karlsruhe,
there and then I quickly learnt
how hard it was to make firm friends
with those you meet on the road.
You may be bosom pals one day
then not recall their names at all.

Still friends, we all went for biers;
two Yankee boys, the girls and I -
and after tea we smoked an orange,
a hashish pipe of hollowed fruit –
before the rain coerced us in
from the jugen-herberge lawn -
alas, in German youth hostel fashion
we were all in bed by ten.

As I was on my way to Greece
I changed my plan to go through Munich,
Olympic year and full of tourists
it was no place for me; I missed breakfast -
hitched to Stuttgart, then travelled on
to Ulm in a Coca-Cola truck.
I struck Kempten, stayed at the hostel
where I met Mike and sister Doris –

The warden, mistaking her for a boy
had put her in our small dorm,
and there, with her clothes shed off,
blonde, fair skinned and seventeen,
the prettiest German thing I'd seen,
more lovely than the upper Rhine,
more divine than Reisling wine,
I discovered she liked me -

But I was shy, reserved and quiet,
a Shaw's boy to my very quick
that night at least I was warm
in that dorm with angel Doris.

In the morn we took *frustucke*,
said goodbye, and travelling on
two lifts later I came to Fussen,
crossed the frontier post by foot.

AUSTRIA

Two German girls - Heidi and Rene
swept me up in their beetle,
carried me forth to Heiterwang,
Lermoos and over high Fern Pass;
down through Telfs, Zirl and Innsbruck
to climb again the Brenner Pass,
through the checkpoint into Italy
on the south side of the Rhuetian Alps.

The beetle coasted down to Brixen
and beyond the turning east ...

NARR: The Wanderer went on and on,
but by this time I was thinking
'Where was I when he was there?'
and then it all came back to me –

I'd been on the Campsie Fells
with my girl whose mother had died
the day before aged forty five.

It had been a warm Spring evening
the waters in the burn were clear,
we saw the sky in the pools
and talked of swimming there some day,

but not that night late in May,
there to take the clean fresh air,
we walked a mile up Campsie Glen,
a dead sheep lying by the stream.

Death! My girl, Cindy, quivered
as up ahead a black crow hovered,
picked a morsel 'neath it's claw,
saw us, flew up, circled round,

then settled on a grassy mound
and gazed at us, sideward glanced,
then foraged in the wild morass
as we approached it from below

it swooped up, circled round us slow
and watched us as we turned to go
down across the Campsie knolls,
the dark eyed creature hovering low,

we, three souls, all alone.
Re-incarnation touched our every thought,
Cindy talked of spirits freed,
of cremation, and a need for God.

As the Wanderer in Yugoslavia
passed through Lubliana and Zagreb,
we lamented the loss of her mother.

We walked through the blue bells
near the Forth and Clyde canal -
off its tow-paths of matted reed,
we cried in an aspen wood -

We were eighteen in lowland Scotland
while my friend was on his way to Greece.

Serbia

And as he recalled his won past,
I ignored his trivial passings by train
through Beograd, and south to Skopje
where he had become shadowed –
by Findlay - a boy from Kilmarnock!

Was it fact that we had once been
the closest of childhood friends -
biking through the Pollok woods
or hanging over Cartcraigs bridge
that spanned the Glasgow-London line
spotting trains and looking up
our Allen books to underline
Robin Hood or Princess Caroline.

The days of steam! We were happy then,
racing up the Greenknowe road
to the cow fields that overlooked
sleepy Pollokshaws and the Kirky Hill
with its wild plum trees, now concrete
little boxes served by orange buses.
Childhood days on Shuggies milk-float
along the Auldhouse road to the dairy
where Davie MacMillan's dad's garage
was a place that smelt of grease,
where tyres could be rolled down the road
and lobbed into the Auldhouse burn.

We had no cares, but if I had known
my friend would spend his adult years
traveling to discover what? Himself?
and leave me behind to struggle
and to carry on day to day with existence
among those also, likewise bound,
who do not know what it's like to leave
home behind - then, be damned!

Suddenly I was aware of silence -
The Wanderer stared at me intently;
I felt that my mind was being read.

WAND: "Don't despair. No place
is more sacred to me than home.
This you will discover if you listen
to the tales I have to tell of towns –
where no man would wish to live
unless it was the place of his birth.

For now, I will not name such places,
for when I was eighteen, optimistic,
I did not wish to spoil too soon
my belief that I was pure and uncorrupted.

But traveling changes a boy -
the world must make him a man
or he has no purpose for the world.
How I resisted! I was a Spartan!

Strong willed, I slept where I could,
Hardy made, I ate what there was.
I had no thoughts for home -
I was looking forward all the time.

I lived for tomorrow! Not the present.
Ahead! That is where I lay in wait
for my own arrival. My dreams
were of distant lands, their treasures –
the secret monuments of men,
the mysterious mountains of nature.

I was glad to leave behind
the repetition of life in Glasgow -
There on that second journey,
I encountered something I had not;
evidence of a world that was hostile -
Serb, Croat and Montenegrin,
Macedonian and Bosnian
Slavs living Tito-ised as one.

I was in Belgrade barely an hour,
at midnight aboard the Orient Express,
at the rear in a second class carriage
with Findlay I'd met at Zagreb station.
Along with two Kiwi's - Gale and Carol -
we'd been with Croat musicians
eager to learn John Lennon's songs
to busk on the streets of the world.

They put us up in their rented home,
we smoked from a bong, as hippies did,
until the church bells of a Zagreb morn
brought up the Sunday dawn.

Four in the morning we halted in Nis,
the Orient Express sped on to Bulgaria,
we recoupled, chugged out of Serbia
and into the wine lands of old Macedonia.

Macedonia

There was no time for breakfast in Skopje,
Findlay went hitching with two guys from Brum,
I hiked for two hours, left them behind,
trekked six more miles onwards to Greece –

Three Ozzies stopped, took me to Thessy,
I booked a bed in a room with a balcony,
re-met Findlay boring an Albertan,
who skinned up and gave us a puff.

NARR:The Wanderer rambled on about hashish,
I yawned, and thought about sex -
I gazed over at his bedside clock
which stood on his Mockintosh desk.

Heavens! if only it was original Tosh,
a work by Glasgow's Jesus of Art -
He, who had a penniless end,
is priceless now he's dead.

GREECE

WAND: I sold blood in Thesalonika.
Do you think I'm not aware,
that you are bored by my talk?
Perhaps you don't want to hear
that I was too young to sell blood,
or that night, on a bar veranda
I watched Ajax beat Inter Milan.

Football, you ask - the European Cup,
who has interest in such things?
Not those who's life is art -
not those who's hands are soft –

But let me tell you what I know,
football is the common man's art,
not the Parthenon on Acropolis Hill,
nor bronze Poseidon on display!

Art is posters of guys like Gazza,
magazines with strikers on their covers.
Art is not the national costume,
the tourist gifts and homemade trinkets –
I saw when I arrived in Athens
down on the stalls of the Plaka.

Eighteen then, thirty seven now,
I had only thoughts for the Aegean islands.
Findlay was whinging in my ear,
chasing me round Omonia like a flea,
I liked him well, he was a Scot,
but he was from Kilmarnock after all,
and there we were - in sunny Greece -
the time had come to go our ways.

I took the subway for Piraeus,
and met a Tahoe boy onboard,
his name was Henry French the Third,
a Nevada lake boy going on twenty one.

Mykonos

We took a ship for Mykonos,
seven pleasant hours passed on deck,
we palled up with a Gail and Sue
though I was pure and virtuous still
despite attempts with Dot, a Hutchie girl
who I had met by the cricket ground.

Dressed in whites, she should have been
on the courts of Poloc Tennis Club –

instead, her racquet behind a bush,
we rolled in the grass by Pollok House.

She was such a proper spoken girl
castled in a mansion in High Shawlands,
we met several times without friends,
and hand in hand, we styled the fence,
to be among the Hielan' cattle herd.
Wary, their piles of dung, we climbed
the old stone dyke beyond, and made
our way through private grounds
to where the ancient beech tree stands
on a massive mound of earth -
made by the tree itself it's said
eight hundred years of leaves being shed.

We carved our names into the bark
and through the bluebell copse of birch
we came unto the garden path
that led us past the honeysuckle
and on beneath the rhododendron,
so thick - the petals fell on us
like winter snow on Cairngorm.
And on we went beneath the willow,
copper beech, scarlet maple -
hedgerow bound on either side
at last we came upon our spot
sheltered by a garden wall
beyond which fell sandstone steps
topped by nymphish statuettes.
There, secluded, not a sound
would penetrate our secret lair -
perhaps a blackbird would pip,
a robin would lightly ribble,
but Dot and I, just sweet fifteen
had no time for the birds.

One hand upon her tennis blouse,
one against her pearl skin,
her fingers on my blue jeans,
five others lost in my hair,
we touched, kissed, lingered there
her eyes closed while I stared,
her eyes open, mine now closed
I trekked my hand beneath her blouse
soon to climb her little mounds
while she descended mine.
Then our youth would spoil things,
embarrassed by our own desires,
panic forced us oft apart
to talk about our adult acts
'til soon the guilt of being alone
in the woods of Pollok Park
would make us both insecure,
unsure if we should pursue
our trysts beyond that hour -

our youth in its finest flower.

O Dot Fleming! tall and blonde!
we showed each other what we had,
but we knew from the very start
that love was never in our charts,
and thus annoyed, we disagreed
and argued as we left the trees
fell silent through the field of dung
'til parted at the Tennis Club.

And after that we met but once
at Shawlands Church on Christmas Eve,
you coyly smiled, looked away
as your friends nudged and winked,
our friendship well at its end,
our reputations made by then,
we were older than the rest,
but hungrier in our youthfulness.

Three summers later, there, aboard
a ship out on the blue Aegean,
I conversed with Gail and Sue
with the hope of union.

The barren Cyclades to the south,
the cliffs of Paros within sight,
we rounded Thermia, slid past Seriphos,
and rugged Naxos by her brother's side –

We came upon the Golden Isle.
Delos! isle where Apollo dwelt
to be adorned by Mykonos men.
Where men are boys, boys are toys.

There - on that isle of Delos,
long robed Ionians once gathered
to dance and praise Apollo
on the soil of his godbirth -
tyrant Pisistratus, chronicler of Homer
had purified the sacred earth
removing the lesser mortals buried
to the island's sandy edges.

Such a place is a robin's cry
removed from the weeping daisies
and the sighing of beech and sycamore
by Crookston Castle's remains
where Mary Stuart fled Langside
through the Shaws and Pollok trees,
through the dark of Crookston Wood,
to harbour in the Maxwell keep.

NARR: There now, the Wanderer told me
that he had moved to the suburbs,
left his seedy West-End room
to live life as others do - in Crookston

with a girl, all but half his age,
in a three room re-con'd flat,
hot water, carpets, car bay, grass
out front, grass out back.

How time takes care of things.
It makes the poor think their rich.

WAND: Ten nights I spent in Mykonos.
At first we slept on Bruce's beach,
the west-bay sands outside town -
with Tahoe Henry as my pal –

we watched U.S. Navy ships
anchor half-a-mile off shore.

In droves came these navy boys
from their nuclear warhead hulks
with grilled steak and burger pats
they barbecued on the sand.

They partied all afternoon
and left us with so much food
we took twenty hippy folk
to eat with us at Spiro's –

a taverna on the rocky shore
below the west bay windmill.
Who knows or cares to visit places
to see them as I saw them so;

few would recognise my world
and fewer still would go
to many of the towns I've found
off the track tourists trek.

Not Mykonos! The Windmill Isle
where pelicans are sacred birds,
where life is made from the sea,
fish, and squid, and lobster claw,

where Apollo's sons gaily dressed
hand in hand walk bare-chested,
where old men sit playing cards
sipping ouzo by the glass,

while the women make baclava
and children ride donkey-back
along the dusty vineyard tracks.

Idyllic Greece in fascist times!
The Junta ruled with heavy hand,
no-one spoke with foreign folk
unless a stranger spoke out first -
plain clothed police checked passports
and spies hung on every word.

Too young to fully understand,
I was a happy tourist lad –

Eighteen and free of all commitment,
I shared my tent with Tahoe Henry,
and Gail and Sue from Houston, Texas.

Gail's eyes were iridescent blue,
sparkly like a Transvaal diamond,
yet something was amiss with her,
as if there was no mind attached .

I have seen that look in others,
that glazed-eye stare they have
in common with a salmon.

Beware, you boys, of such women!
You may pour out all your love
to find a sieve-like bottom -
You may empty out your soul
and never fill the chasm –

that void between Timbuktu
and the shores of the Sahara

The girls went B and B,
two wild boys, they'd had enough,
we brushed our teeth in the waves,
wished them bon voyage!

I lay on the beach and talked
to B.C. Glenn, Ash and Steve -
while Henry slept, Sue arrived
to see how we'd survived -

That evening we met the girls
they took us back to their room -
we downed four pints of white rum,
Gail, of course, threw up, then swooned.

We left her in, hit the bars,
slammed the ouzo with a vengeance -
Henry propositioned Sue,
she clung to me and shouted 'Rescue!'

Next day, hung over, Henry slept
'til the girls came on the beach,
sunned their bones until time
to meet the tourist policeman.

Policeman? Gail was seeking work!
Henry and I went slinking off
for toast, fried eggs, Turkish,
but soon the girls caught us up,
made us eat with them - spaghetti!

Gail had got herself a job

in a bar, she 'trusted Greeks' -
That night we ate stuffed egg-plant
and drank another bottle of rum -
Sue once more led Henry on,
Gail spoke of the guy she loved.

On the beach next day they came
to be with us - they always did.
We were pissed off, told them so,
gave them what for, made them go.

That evening we dined alone,
we climbed the hill to Billy's club
stayed 'til we were well past bored
then built a fire on the sands,
and lo, our lives changed after that.

While wandering through the narrow streets
I met Lynn, a Glasgow girl,
we talked a while, met again,
then made our way to the beach,
kept a fire until there was no wood.

That night Lynn moved in with me,
while Henry was out chasing Sue,
but he came back just as we
were on the point of being one.

And thus we two, three became,
three young adults making plans,
Lets all hike our way to Morocco!
We bought our tickets for the mainland.

We relished our youth and nerve
at crossing the length of the Med!

What did I know at eighteen?
Full of my own esteem -
God might as well have been in space,
as within every being that tenth of June –

for soon the Bader Meinhof would kill
the spirit of the Olympic dream.

NARR: The Wanderer's eyes glazed like Gail's,
he drifted off on some low cloud,
he was stuck between hell and paradise
between this and that and Grecian life.

I meanwhile had been working nine to five
in the Bank of Scotland Ibrox branch
stamping cheques and licking stamps,
and inking figures in ledger files,

taking home twelve pound a week
when a pint of beer was all of ten pee;
I hated my short hair, shirt and tie,

534

and my suit that made me look a pratt.

I worked to live my weekends for Cindy,
we'd walk on the hills, in the glens,
Lomond, Glencoe or Aviemore
or the sandy duned Ayrshire coast,

to the fells of Tay or Killin,
the Forest of Jed, or Rannoch Moor -
there we took our wandering souls
with our pals, or sometimes alone.

But, my friend, that far-flung sage
counted time by clocking miles -
a postcard from a Grecian isle
mentioned distance, food and girls.

There were no insights, inner thoughts
we average folk daily truck - no
Who are we? What's life about?
that whose we're close to often sigh.

How life turns full circle like a wheel,
we find ourselves upon a hill
viewing change that time has brought
but which, despite all that's past,
has left us nought, changed us not.
We are no different from our youth.

Upon our hill, our native land,
layers of dwellings upon the old,
that is all that time has built.
Let them dig and find a church,
a primary school beneath it all.

All that marks my churchyard now
is an elm tree - gone the holly,
or poplar that lined the dyke
which faced upon the old school yard

sunken from a century of children
playing above the old mine works
that fueled the print field looms
that bleached the old Shaw's fields.

By church and school ran Maida Street,
bare twelve feet wide wall to wall,
across the road, Station West, where
we would wait for trains to come –

trains that went on south to England
through the station with a roar,
or if they stopped, we would peer
into ill-lit coaches at weary travelers

from other countries, and wave,
not out of recognition of their foreignness,

535

but to let them know we existed,
that we were boys from the Shaws.

On they would go hauled by Excalibur,
or Lord Clyde, or the Queens Own Borderers.
It is from those trains we learned of Fiji,
Sierra Leone and Mauritania - lands we
later looked up on the map together,
the Wanderer and I, thirty years ago.

Scoff not at those who tick off names.
A name is knowledge, the first seed
out of which experience grows,
for without a name, nothing's known.

The railway linked us to the world.
Trinidad, Aden or Singapore -
Through Pollokshaws the world roared!

On Maida Street, between church and school,
we crowded up this narrow vestibule,
squeezed through railings beneath crab apple
to see tiny snowdrops droop their heads –

we marveled at such wilderness.

Almost seven, I remember still
the beauty of that first wild sighting,
in mid February's luke sunlight
such welcome prelude to the Spring.

And then! tragedy on our young lives,
a smoggy lunchtime February day,
Neil Dickson ran across the road.

We never saw our pal again -
run down by the bus to Ayr.

In the smog his soul remains
For we were three at that age,
The Wanderer, myself and Neil;
In the class we were tops –

except for swotty Leonard G
who couldn't run or kick a ball.

Neil was the fastest one,
I was the smartest one,
the Wanderer the tallest
and the leader of us all.

After the death of Neil we were lost,
we hung out with older boys
like Specky Smith - train spotter
who was all of ten and a bit!

What a drip! - he tried to bully us,

but we ganged up, kicked this shins,
pulled his ears, renamed him "Specky Git!"

Then we joined the One Seven O,
the Life Boy group in our church,
there we found new things to do.

Most boys were at our school –
the Hammy Twins, the Hutchie Boys,
Houston, and a few Home Boys
in the days before Gillespie arrived.

And those above us - Primary Five -
Gordie, Fishy, Nivie, Bean,
and those in lofty Primary Six
who taught us knots and discipline.

They made us march two abreast,
the Wanderer learned to march the best -
A left-handed, left-footed boy,
they never broke his natural stride,

so he would lead us round the hall;
and for eight years he led us on
through into the Boys Brigade
and out into our Higher Grades.

And yet despite his leadership,
his natural flair to lead us all,
at school I was the teachers' choice
for prefect and the honour roll.

They knew not of our boy's world,
or saw the Wanderer as we boys did;
I got the prizes for my brains,
but the Wanderer was our champion.

And now years on - at thirty seven
he sat there greying, thin on top,
the boy who'd been around the world
and knew not when to stop.

He spoke with a distant voice
of leaving Greece and Mykonos.

Adriatic Sea

WAND: The night boat from Mykonos
docked six o'clock in Pireaus;
we took the subway to Omonia,
wasted time having breakfast –

missed the first train for Patras.

Five hours on the Ionian Express,
four hours on the Patras docks,

we set sail on the 'Appia'
across the dark blue Adriatic –

that I had glimpsed the year before
from the steps of St. Mark's, Venice.

I washed two weeks from my hair,
remembered how soft a mattress felt,
meanwhile my pal Henry, my girl Lynn,
were getting on far too well.

Morning brought Corfu into view,
we anchored half a mile outside
the hidden reefs a million sails
had lightly skipped in over.

H and L were tete a tete,
there and then I read the signs,
I knew not then what I know now
about how fleeting love can be.

Sometimes love fades away
'til nothing's left but the grave
filled with partners long time dead
who haunt the romance newly laid.

Time and time again they rise,
lover's cherished, partners dumped
'til every kiss becomes a cross
to hang all past lovers on.

Criss-cross they ever onwards come
every face of every love -
until the last becomes the first
and romance and death are one.

ITALY - The South

We steamed towards the Bari coast,
starboard Brindisi, we veered to port
and docked and cleared all controls
to pass into a shiftless town,
grey, asleep, and like a fool
I let myself be split from Lynn,
she hitched on south with Tahoe Henry
so much for pals upon the road -

I was left to hitch alone.

In Taranto I checked the station
to see if they were waiting there;
they had said they'd meet me there
and I believed their every word.

On the road south-west to Reggio,
two baccalaureates transported me
to a beach house in Lido di Cass.

There we picked up some vino,
went next door to a villa -
where three pretty Roman girls
attended by a hag of a matron
swooned us with their flirtation
and graces until the hag grew wary,
and waved us out into the midnight air.

It was a dream I barely recall.
Awake at nine, they dropped me off
on the road that went from Heel to Toe.
All day I travelled the Sole of Italy,
five hours to travel thirty kay,
lunch a half-baked calzone -
three hours by a Fina station
before a tanker ride to Crotoné.

That night, assaulted by mosquitoes,
I slept in a ditch by the road.
Half-five I rose into the fog,
packed my stuff, hitched anew
a trucker slid to a halt,
took me somewhere near Reggio.
I hitched on to Giovanni,
crossed the Straits of Messina.

Sicily

Sicily looming ever nearer,
I felt the hairs on my back prickle,
I fingered the hilt of my hip blade
and mentally prepared for a fight –

but it was all just silly self-delusion,
I was frowning, but I began to smile
as I passed through Sicilian farmland
on the last Palermo train of the night.

In Palermo I dined on the waterfront,
bread and tomatoes, nothing else,
I sat legs dangling over the water-break,
industrial, smoggy, and polluted,

I fought to cope with the Etna heat,
for it was the Ides of June,
the hottest night I'd ever known,
the ship for Tunis delayed for a day,

it shimmered in the dockland haze
though it was dark, the moon was up
as I stretched out on stony ground
behind the bright lights of a fair,

but I turned and tossed all night,
slept and dreamt in fitful fear,
I clutched my knife in case
some Sicilian ventured near.

That night was all thick sea air,
mosquitoes darted everywhere,
night gave to damp cold day
in old Palermo.

No music in my head -
no poetry to make it memorable,
my only thoughts were of moving on,
across the wide blue Med.

What did I know then! Senseless
way back - so many years ago,
eighteen and floating aimless,
like seaweed wrenched from rock.

How was I to know someday
that youth was the treasure,
not the search for some hidden truth
that only time could unravel.

You out there - listen well!
I have seen the four corners of the world
but I have never found the edge
to all that has no whole.

Look! but you will never find
an answer to it all.

Yet I arose that Palermo day
hopeful that life would bring
some joy and laughs as I
progressed on my way.

My way! How now I laugh
that I saw my journey then
as a route from town to town
in one straight line.

At eighteen - I saw clear,
my young man's logic made me believe
that I was right, I was educated
too much, too quick, too Calvinistic.

I knew nothing of Italians,
my Latin was no use at all,
I had to learn to wave my hands,
move my tongue around new vowels –

I was less learned than a child.
I wandered down to the quay,
lodged my rucksack at a kiosk,
slept awhile by a road,

ate some breakfast - bread and milk,
returned mid-morn to the quay
to find pal Henry cuddling Lynn.

Oh what tales they told me –

about their night in a barn,
in a haystack with each other
fending off the farmers brothers
who wished give Lynn their love.

A likely tale - it made me jealous,
it made me doubt them as friends;

Lynn with her brown eyes smiling,
I smiled back, but she knew
I could see right through their sham -
She couldn't fool a Glasgow man!

Lynn was from Newton Mearns,
three miles south of Pollokshaws;
six months later she would come
to my parents council home

to tell them she was back for good,
she had joined the Renfrew Police.
So much for the hippy life -
she grew up far too soon.

But there on that Sicilian quay,
Lynn and I, and Tahoe Henry,
were still resolved to reach Morocco,
and we were joined by Brighton Pete
who'd traveled in from distant Crete.

Now a band, we grew worried,
we'd be turned away at Tunis.
Why I said? We're not Hippies,
we're all under twenty-one.

The ship cast off at six o'clock.
Concerned that I looked so rough,
I shaved off my fuzzy beard,
tied my hair up with a clasp.

I looked tidier in the face,
despite the jeans and tie-died shirt
and their four weeks of dirt.
Oh Southern Mediterranean -

the fresh open sea -
what now is sea to me!
Chained to these Northern days
of mist and sleet and rain.

Where are the years fanned by breeze?
the scent of brine, the feel of spray,
an untamed sea in my sight,
the taste of waves and free?

There are moments in our lives

when we are free of all mankind,
when we are on our own and glad
no-one's there to rein us back.

How many times have I felt so?
regretted not a single note,
called the tune and listened not
to any but my own.

TUNISIA

Most mornings dreams dissolve,
and so it was when we arrived
in Tunis harbour where dolphins swim,
to discover we were Freaks!

I, and Lynn, and Hen, and Pete,
and a guy called Jurgen from Koln -
they would not let us go ashore,
aboard they kept us under guard.

We were they said 'Filthy Hippies!'
The captain had to take us back.
Back to where? No-one cared,
the ship set course for Sardinia.

I watched astern, Africa fade,
I vowed one day I would return.
I have since fulfilled that vow,
I shall not talk about that now.

Sardinia

Thus we arrived in Cagliari,
against design, without plan,
we disembarked and in disgust
drowned on red Sardinian wine.

Sardinia! Drunk we all agreed
it was no place for the young.
I was angry, needed peace,
I opted for return to Greece.

Lynn and Hen and Brighton Pete,
older, richer, than poor old me
had set their hearts on Marrakech,
via Marseilles and coastal Spain.

And thus we finally parted ways.
I hitched with Jurgen, good enough,
seven rides took us north,
we reached Sassari close to dusk.

We kipped out beneath the stars
in a haystack - it was warm.
I felt all my worries go,
I listened to the evening song.

I felt the on-shore breeze come up
and fan the hay we slumbered on;
the sea now dark - the sky aglow,
above - Orion's Belt and Bow;

I slept the best I had in months,
what I dreamt I can't recall.

Perhaps dreams come, another kind
that later years bring to light -
How I had turned my back upon
the culture that was my life –

Scotland - how proud I was,
yet restless to see the world
to find my fortune there - abroad!
to turn my back upon my home.

And now? matured by that search,
I discover not by chance
that which I have so long denied -
that I am home at last!

Reconciled to live and die
where I entered from the past,
I have traveled earthly lands,
I have come to know of man.

I am ready now to pass,
let atoms split, let stars be born,
let new things take shapes unknown,
let unknown things known become.'

NARR: My friend began to glow with light,
his Eastern ways had spaced him out,
candles, incense, music, fire,
had made his brain run wild.

We were back in his basement,
Ravi Shankar blasting loud.
I heard no more about the trip
that left him on Sardinia's shores.

WAND: You think I'm mad, a little crazed
living life as I do -
what chance have I without profession,
poverty is an endemic problem!

Do you think it is my choice
to live life at the bottom?'

NARR: I offered help, but he was proud,
he said he'd fund his own salvation,
he'd survived past misfortune,
his present life was a dawdle.

On this he took out a pipe
and put some hashish in the bowl;
he lit the stuff, took a puff,
then spoke with softer tone.

WAND: Judge not a man by his surroundings,
what you see is not his -
time destroys all he has,
all he's gathered soon decays.

All he has acquired or stolen
when he goes shall have no use,
but is baggage on his back
as he tramps the heavenly road -

guided by a clever sod
whose wealth is in his soul.

At eighteen, thinking wealth would come
I fought off creature comforts,
for how could I be a man
if I was over-weak from over-eating

or lazed in baths, avoided exercise?
Thus, not ready to surrender
I had to go - see the world!
I had to go in search of fortune

before I could take a wife,
have myself a child,
a boy, a girl, one on the side
in case of war or accident.

So much of myself unknown,
I began now on the real sojourn -
the exploration of my being.
Who was I? Boy from the Shaws?

The answer was no clearer then -
we slept late; a cock crowed,
we left Sassari, hitched to Osila
ate salami, fruit and dry bread.

Jurgen, in his stilled German manner,
restless to be on his own
shrugged his ringleted shoulders
and lit-out on up the road.

I waited by the kerbside pensive,
counted out my dwindling cash.
In Tempio Pusania, we met again,
Jurgen in the back of a Fiat –

I joined him, backpacks on our laps,
onwards went to Santa Teresa Gallura
where beyond the Bocche di Bonifacio
crumbled the white cliffs of Corsica.

We spent the night on the rocks,
hungry for hot Italian food -
we met Lynn and Henry in the village,
where having bought some pizzas -
we made our way to the beach
and ran into Brighton Pete.

So once again we were five
about to depart another island;
we had a swim in the Bocche;
I visited the castle ruins –

briefly won by Totila the Goth,
re-won by Justinian's Belisairus -
lost five centuries later to Saracens,
lost again to Pisa, then Genoa.

Who can say how many Princes
occupied Sardinia before Spain
gave the isle to Austrian Savoy
in exchange for the riches of Sicily.

Napoleon freed the isle from Savoy,
Garibaldi claimed Sardinia for Italy!
Restored it to Savoy's Victor Emanuel
by making him first King of Italy.

I felt something of that history
as I sat by castle Santa Teresa;
I still see this image now,
the sun setting on the western Med

and ancient ships slipping by unseen;
but what did I ken of ghosts then
as I slept on Sardinian bedrock,
I was a Jacobin, not a Jacob.

Corsica

Sixty pence to cross to Bonifacio,
fifty minutes, cold, but pleasant.
Jurgen didn't like the town much,
he hiked out shortly after –

Pete and I, bread and cheese for lunch
spent the afternoon on the beach,
a rock quarry doubling as a dump.
What about Lynn and Henry?

They caught a bus to Ajjacio
to catch a ship for Valencia;
Pete - on a tighter budget
Took the ferry from Bastia.

And I, poorest of them all,
had to wait for five days

to take a cheap ship to Livorno.
Jurgen hung-out with me.

That night, kipping in a field,
we passed out on the vino.

Midsummer's Day in 'Seventy-Two,
or Christmas Day in 'Ninety-One -
I am as I always was -
journeying on, not yet home.

It is rest I seek from debt,
favours spent I cannot pay;
if there is profit from my life,
I've made no savings from the labour!

In me, there is an echo ringing -
'Fifty years left to get ahead!'
A plaque in a crematorium,
is this to be my only mark?

Then, all is well, I am free
to live without fame or fortune;
I will love my fellow man,
I will not rise above my birth –

I'll be third part commonwealth,
part God, and part of Earth.

Alas, hitching through Sardinia
I had no philosophy as such,
a driver gave me his in French
as I sat nibbling some bread.

A lorry took us to Bastia,
we had sausage, beans for lunch,
we met Jurgen in the street,
we all camped out on the beach.

So mundane, but oh so free!
God watching over me.

NARR: Did you not miss family ties?
You were gone for seventeen years,
no Christmas union with your kin,
none you knew when you were wee?

WAND: I had to break the family bond,
so I took on foreign ways -

Yet I was always looking in
like some keeker at a window;
I was there, but not in spirit,
dining with a world of strangers;

it was never to my ken;
Christmas lacked the love of childhood,

surrounded by those who're dear.
Not so this year, home for good,

my Auntie Mary licked her lips
and Cousin George in paper hat
read aloud the cracker jokes
while Cousin Nan sucked a bone.
Yet all the while the world whirled,
we ate and wined to the news
of Gorbachev's last Kremlin hour
as Soviet Russia finally died –

the red flag lowered into hell
and Yeltzin's dream just begun.

Who could have foretold such a thing,
when I was sleeping on a beach
waking to the sound of waves,
bananas as the fasting break,
our bags at a beach cafe
as Pete left for Marseilles?

Hands in pockets - promenading,
we watched striped men beneath the palms
throw their boules, inhale gauloise,
laugh and joke and swig cognac.

We took some citrons from a park,
bitter fruit, but we were glad
of something free in that land;
we returned to the sands,
read books 'til it was dark,
then lay and watched shooting stars.

At dawn I found Jurgen gone,
to re-appear with two French loafs,
a bag of fruit - we ate the lot,
then I washed beneath a tap.
It was early, it was quiet,
I brushed my hair free of knots;
I was young, I was free,
I didn't care who saw me.

That morning on the beach, bored
we tried to hitch to Sant Florent.
It wasn't very far at all - no-one stopped
so we returned, ate two loafs.

We walked along the harbour wall,
looked back upon the town and saw
bonfires on the highest slopes.
What the hell was going on?

A celebration? I asked a man –
The Feast of Jean Jacques! Who was that?
And to this day I do not know
though I believe he is well known.

Ah well, another day, nothing done,
more dirty, one more day less young.
Next morning I woke to find
my rucksack missing from my side.

We searched about, found my clothes
scattered all about the beach,
my passport, travelers cheques and maps
lying with them in the sand!

As for my rucksack, tent and stove,
my camera, torch, cape and shades,
my spitfire knife, toothbrush bag?
Gone the lot! I nearly cried -

The police wrote down the particulars,
gave me a typed claim certificate -
and that *c'est ca*, we returned,
searched some more for my things,

found nothing else that was mine.
I went to cash a travelers cheque
and woe! The pound was going down!
I cashed a fiver just in time.

I bought an ex-French legion pack
that set me back thirty francs.
I sat awhile in the square,
then I returned to the beach.

I was running out of funds,
enough to get to Greece - not back.
I brooded, watched the grey Med lap,
then Jurgen came, in his hands

a bag of goodies for our lunch -
bananas, bread, tomatoes, yeah!
My spirits soared, but later fell;
I walked the water's edge a while.

We wandered through the town again
eating bread as we went -
Another night on the beach,
this time our packs beneath our heads.

Half-six I rose, washed my jeans,
my t-shirts too, in the sea
and waiting for these things to dry
I washed my hair beneath a tap.

It was Sunday, the shops were closed,
we made do - one loaf each.

The ferry for Livorno came,
among the disembarking folk
a German hitcher spoke with us,

then off he went without a wave.

Half nine that night, we gave in,
the smell of grease luring us;
we each bought a bag of chips
and a sandwich with meat in it!

What a splash out! Five francs each!
All day we'd spent ninety centimes.

ITALY - The North

At ten next morn we set sail,
left Corsica and France behind -
soon Capraga Island rose
white and cliff-sheer out the blue.

Then, we saw a light aircraft
circling off the ship's port-side,
and soon we came upon a boat
drifting in the Genoa tides.

The crew and boat winched aboard,
the spotter-plane veered to land,
we docked Livorno high-tea time,
lost an hour to Italian time.

Because the pound was going under,
the banks would not cash my cheques.
I changed six quid with a lender
who made quite sure I lost out –

I paid off Jurgen what I owed,
and I was left with just six bob.
Money! How it comes between good friends.
How money makes life a hell!

Jurgen bought my evening meal -
two pizzas, pan-e-torte, cider;
I bought a loaf and a banana.
I was preparing for the morrow

and the road that left Livorno.
We walked five kay, parted ways,
tired of each other's company -
I made it to the autostrada;

a sea-breeze brought some dampness,
darkness came, and feeling tired
I kipped down by the highway.
Oh God - when I woke up –
my face was one mass of lumps -
the mossies had done their stuff,
my lips were swollen, my eyelids shut;
no frog would have kissed such bumps.

No better than a dirty tramp,

a priest took pity on my plight.
He stopped and took me in his car
via Pisa's leaning tower –

He left me outside Lucca town,
and on I went to outskirt Florence;
four hours by a service station
with twenty hitchers - Italians, Germans;

I prayed for clouds to screen my bites
as I blistered in the midday sun.

Yankee doddle-dandy day!
Two G.I's rescued me -
dropped me off at Padova
and on I went to Monfalcone.

I walked a bit; bought salami, bread;
took a ride for ten kilometres,
then found a lonely spot to sleep
just off the Trieste road.

That night I slept really good
but paid for it - mosquito food!

YUGOSLAVIA - Croatia

I rose, waited for a while,
a lift took me to the border.
My last lira spent on bread.
I crossed into Yugoslavia –

that part now known as Croatia.

The sterling crisis still full blown
no bank would change my travelers cheques,
so I hitched on without dinar
towards the resort of Rijeka.

I trekked uphill out of town,
the Adriatic on my right -
towards Karlovac I journeyed.
It took till night to reach Zagreb.

I plodded mile after mile
to escape Zagreb's lights,
but tiredness came upon me quick,
I stopped to sleep in a ditch.

Serbia

Next day, hunger gnawing at me,
a driver bought me some lunch -
another bought me a coke,
before a Lebon man picked me up,
bought me a coffee every stop.

The windscreen of his car had gone,
we got smeared with flies and gnats,
and when we got to Belgrade -
oh my god! he tried it on!

I told him there and then 'Piss Off',
I only kissed pretty girls,
I kept away from guys like him
with his strange foreign ways.

What'd he take me for I asked?
My hair was long, I was lithe
but I was not a nancy man.
I was an A1 Scottish lad!

Still no money, I couldn't eat,
no-one wanted Scottish cheques.
I trudged south towards Nis
and slept in an urban park.

Woe the tramp who dares to stop;
dark is no protection from the law.

Half-past four a policeman nudged me,
told me to be on my way -
He trailed me through the morning streets
tailed me down along the side-walks.

Eventually, tired, I had to stop,
but with his stick he coaxed me on
out his patch and well beyond
and on towards the edge of town.

Tired from too many nights outdoors,
weak from far too little food,
I slept on the table of a closed cafe
until the cleaner shoo'd me on.

I had no rest that morn as the birds
sang up dawn on the Balkan world.
Was it fun to be alive?
I felt fit for nothing but to die.

Seven o'clock work began,
the shutters of a bank went up.
I went in, tried my luck
and sure enough, crisis over –

I changed two pounds into dinars,
bought a loaf, two tubs of paste,
a pint of milk for twenty pee
and praised the Lord for manna.

How life can turn on three dimes,
life once more became a triumph,
a Dutch pair took me on to Nis,
I crossed the road, bought a loaf –

and heh, another couple stopped;
I had re-found hippy luck.

Jurgi and his love Marina,
he - German, she - Italian,
were into Pink Floyd and the Dead.
We spent the night at a campsite.

I remember now, how bright the stars
shone that night south of Nis,
how content I was with life.
I had found two fellow souls

who were pleased to share with me
the simple comforts of the road -
bread, coffee and free chat
that views the world for all its worth.

I loved all my time with them,
I helped them pack away their tent;
we ate well, hit the road,
and past Kumanova, we turned off,

went down a dusty road -
found the church of Saint George.
What piety it evoked this church,
the relics enshrined in its walls.

Of all the churches, I believe
this is the holiest of the lot.
Don't ask me why. I was touched.
Religion is about belief after all.

GREECE

We drove to Skopje, ate mousakka,
crossed into Greece, passed Katerina,
put up the tent at the coast -
I slept out beneath the stars!

No dream is sweeter than the one
forgotten with the rising sun.

Fifty miles short of Athens,
we parted ways, said goodbye.
On to Eribus they went,
I picked up by other friends –
a pleasant Greek and teenage son
who bought me a mousakka lunch.

Athens

An hour's walk I reached Omonia,
I carried on towards the Plaka -
and first, resting at the bottom,
I climbed up to the Acropolis.

A young boy spoke with me,
bought me a pineapple crush;
all we could speak about was football,
the universal sport of the world.

I continued up the winding road
to the stairs of the Pantheon -
I clambered over the ruined shrine
and let its history become mine.

At eight they threw me out;
on the Agora, looking down
I smoked the hash Jurgi gave me
and sat content for two hours,

the lights of Athens far below,
the journey of three weeks over.

Out there in the dark Aegean,
lay the Mykanos I'd left.
Since then, I had changed,
I could survive anywhere now;

I was back in sunny Greece.
I slept on the Acropolis without a care.

Mykonos

I stayed six weeks on Mykanos,
on the beach east of town -
fifty pence a day, I ate eggs,
soup, spaghetti, and green beans,

drank ouzo, chatted up the girls,
behaved as any youngster might.

The days passed, the nights went,
friends were made - Glenn, Klaus,
friends lost to time - Dave and Jan,
who cannot be had back- Carl, Darryl,

they were a beginning and an end.

For struggles may rack Tblisi,
fighting may divide Osijek,
faith may split Beirut
and people see no end –

end is beginning it is said.

The end came on the glorious twelfth,
I had all of two pounds left.
Glenn, Carl, Darryl and I
said goodbye to Dave and Jan,

and on a stormy Sunday night
leaving from Saint Stephen's beach -

a small boat thrashed through the waves,
wet we stepped aboard the Patras,

and below the stars Homer charted,
I found a place to sleep on deck.

Though thousands go every month,
all these years - I've not returned.
Mykanos remains unspoiled,
and as it was when I was young.

I have no wish to undo life
by seeing again that lovely isle.

The Road to Istanbul

Athens; I gave blood, got three quid;
saw Glenn and Darryl off to Crete.
Carl fronted me five pounds
as I was going to Istanbul –

he wanted one gold, one silver ring,
the puzzle types that interlock;
he was flying out for home,
a house he rented Bromley Road;

he was just an Aussie bloke
who had a job by Earls Court.

I walked miles out of Athens,
my sandal broke just at dusk;
I had lost my walking boots
while sleeping on Bastia beach;

now I found my sandal bust
I was barefoot hitching north.
I met two French girls and a guy
and kipped beside them in the dark.

Morning - dirty, hot and hungry,
I tried hitching with my pals;
no good came of that -
three hours on, a Greek took pity

and then a London couple stopped,
looked at me, my dirty clothes,
my matted beard, my bare feet,
and muttered 'Jesus Christ British?'

'What size sneakers do you wear?'
Threw me out a size ten pair.

Newly shod, one size too big,
I reached Larisa, got a lift -
a French couple with two young kids,
a caravan attached behind,

they left me out near Thessalonika.
The rest of the way by scooter
behind a Greek who tooted everyone;
a hearty meal of rice, green beans,
then a trek through the centre -

to the road for Istanbul
where I slept on stony ground.

Next day, five hours in the sun,
I waited for a ride to come,
the ride that would take me on
to where Constantine had sat,

where Justinian's Byzantium
gave way to Sultan Ahmet's rule,
then Suliman, then Ottoman,
had given sway to modern Istanbul.

An English couple, twenty-odd,
with their trendy hippy look
took me in their 2CV -
through what was left of Greece;

we suppered on bread, soup and tea,
and camped off the road in peace.

An early start across the bridge,
one side blue, the other red,
the days of fighting not long done,
the tension of the past alive;

we crossed the frontier pretty quick
and drove pell-mell on to where
the roads to Istanbul-Izmir split.
They went south, I went east;

I have their London address still.

On I went with some Swiss,
we arrived at six at the city;
they mucked about, darkness fell,
they let me out at a hotel –

the Gungar, near the Pudding Shop
between the city's two great mosques.

TURKEY - Istanbul

I had a wash, combed my hair,
descended to the Pudding Shop -
a place where travellers going east
talked with those new returned.

With their many tales of woe
and stories that had all enthralled,
these travelers bent my young ear

with scores of Asian city names –

Tehran, Herat, Kabul, Lahore,
a Canadian with talk of Delhi -
his friends about Kashmir and Bombay;
I listened till they grew weary,

the shop lights dimmed, the shutters closed;
I shook their hands - they were heroes!
They were the knights of the road.

I slept in room one-o-seven,
in a bed - the first for months,
but in the morning, hot and bitten,
I changed my room to the roof –

to have the most splendid view;
Saint Sophia left, Blue Mosque right,
and in between the Golden Horn.

I meandered through the Grand Bazaar,
searching for the gold ring shop;
dazed for hours in it's maze -
copper urns on human heads,

donkeys whipped, flies on fruit;
it all seems so normal now,
but then - at eighteen, young and green
I was a naive European -

Time teaches what tales cannot,
and tales are nowt but idle talk
until you've seen the lot yourself.

At last I found the factory shop,
a first floor room up wooden stairs,
and there in three metres square,
hunched fifteen boys on three leg stools.

Candles lit the tiny room,
charcoal smoke filled the lungs,
the smell of sulphur, silver, gold,
the tap of hammers, snip of shears,

the grate of files on the ears;
the look of boys, tired, scared,
and I amidst the rag-clothed throng,
a tramp amongst my own kind,

bought from them thirty rings
for little less than seven pounds,
one year's wages for a boy -

I returned to the Gungar,
washed my long flowing hair,
brushed it dry on the roof
listening to the muezzin's call -

carried over from the Blue Mosque,
one of Islam's most treasured shrines.

Barefoot I crossed to the mosque
that Sultan Ahmet built so well;
I washed my feet at the fountain,
covered my flesh the Muslim way.

At the door, armed guards stood;
they turned me back, my feet were dirty;
I went to the fountain, washed,
but by the time I'd reached the door
my feet were dirty yet once more -

the guards shook their sticks at me
and chased me from the sacred grounds.

That night - a meal of rice and beans,
simple fare for most Turks,
I was at the edge of all I knew;
I'd been wayfaring a hundred days,

there was more to life than being alone;
in the morning I would turn for home.

Thus began my homeward journey,
fourteen days of trampish existence;
south-east edge to north-west fringe,
four thousand kay across Europa.

It all began six next dawn,
I bused it to the city walls
where I hitched for three hours,
picked up by the Swiss again!

TURKEY/GREECE - Macedonia

At Terkidag, I hitched anew,
a lorry stopped to load some straw,
the driver pointed to the back,
he drove me six kay short of Greece.

A taxi-man took me free of charge
to the frontier's painted bridge,
I walked ten kay in the heat,
and just before onset of dusk

met a Frenchman Athens bound;
we shared some bread, a little water,
slept the night in an orchard.

We woke at four to pouring rain;
the sky had opened, torrents fell;
I scrambled out my sleeping bag
and as I did, the downpour stopped!

557

We slept an hour, then got up,
dried our bags, picked some plums,
said goodbye, then split up.
This is the way it is with bums.

I hitched on to Alexandropolous;
nine hours passed 'neath blazing sun,
then a scooter, next a three-wheeler
took me to Makri five kay further –

where sunset came, and I found sleep
in a Macedonian field.

Next day turned out a little better,
some Germans dropped me off in Zanthi;
three Italians - to Salonika
and on beyond some twenty kilometres

where I waited till it drew dark.
I pulled out my sleeping sack
just as a Swiss-reg beetle stopped
a Bavarian with the name of Axel –

took me towards the Yugo border,
but he ran out of petrol.

He waved down a passing car,
bought some gas to reach the frontier,
filled her up, and on we pushed
to a bar near Tito Veles.

We ate meat-bean soup with salad,
drank black coffee and biscuits,
put down some shots of slivovich,
and slept in Axel's car.

YUGOSLAVIA - Macedonia

It pains me now to think back on
the next few days we were together;
Axel - wearing contact lenses,
woke to find his eyes infected;

he could not drive on that day,
we spent the day in Tito Veles;
Axel slept, while I more restless
wandered that Balkan hillside town

that overlooked the Vardar river;
the hills were dry, the soil poor,
it's people rustic, dull-clothed, sincere.

Kosovo

Next day, Axel's eyes improved,
on we drove Skopje, Prizren,
on through Dakovic to Pec

and up the Cakar Pass we went.

Forty miles of dirt track road
though the forests to Murino;
this region known as Kosovo,
they have their problems with the Serbs;

Albania's mountains to the west,
past a frontier post we flashed,
border guard and wilderness,
on to Andrijevica we sped –

dust and trees and broken road,
a part of Europe so remote -
though I have made it not sound so.

Montenegro

At Kolasin we turned south
on Highway Two for Titograd;
Tito was alive those days,
he was the father of the nation –

The Yugoslavic federal state
which in the year ninety-one
became a war-torn ruined place.

We made Petrovac by dusk,
we stopped for coffee and some booze;
drunk, we slept in the car
above the Adriatic cliffs.

Dalmatia

On we went to Dubrovnik,
ate salami, bread and honey,
toured the ancient city walls
and marvelled at it all –

Here was a city time had loved
and left intact despite the wars.
Up the Dalmatian coast we drove;
Split, Rijeka, Trieste - the West!
We left the East in the wet.
Stopping once for some tea –

Vicenza's roughly where we slept.

SWITZERLAND - Zurich

Dawn we traveled on - Milano,
and sometime in the afternoon
we reached Axel's cosy flat
in the heart of modern Zurich.

Oh rejoice! what a trip!
Four nights, five days on the road.

Washed and shaved, in clean clothes,
Axel took me on the town.

I met his friends, told my tales,
they wondered at my nerve -
to sleep in fields, live carefree
when life cost so much these days.

Axel laughed, told them off,
they were just a bunch of snobs,
he said they should chuck their jobs
to be like me - they all agreed!

Three days I spent in Zurich,
Axel and his friends were warm;
they treated me as their own;
they gave me money for my trip –

northwards home to Scotland;
I was sad to go.

GERMANY / BELGUIM / ENGLAND

Another night outdoors, near Koln,
next the boat Ostend to Dover;
I got to London around mid-day,
found my way to Bromley Road;

there I gave Carl his rings
and spent two nights on his floor.

SCOTLAND

September First, I hitched home,
back to grey stone stoic Glasgow;
my parents were relieved to see me,
I was a shade near black -
which came off with a bath;
and thus I was back.'

NARR: Here, the Wanderer stopped
the story of his second trip;
to a point I knew the rest,
three weeks later he had gone off
to university in England.

The candles had gone out,
it was late, he showed me out.
The snow had gone, I was amazed,
he looked at me with his gaze,
there was something strange in his face.

I felt as though I'd been bewitched,
and sure enough, when I got home
I found a year had passed
since I had gone to see him.

How this was, I do not know,
the year was nineteen ninety-two.

Yet, life is too short to dwell
on things that take place in the past.
I knew intrigue would have
me speak with him again.

When that was to be
I could not say or guess.

[End of the Wanderer Part 2]

THE BONNY FALLS
[2.23am, 18th March 1991, Glasgow]

Up the Bonny Falls we climbed
Beyond the slums and the power,
And on we climbed beyond the linn,
And on a crag overhead,
We climbed up through ash and heather,
Beneath a pine we lay together,
Rush of fall and words together,
Sundown raining on forever.

In the bracken, sky and river,
In the wild, tree and lichen,
We let the world go down river,
We let the future fly to heaven,
Forgiven not, forbidden never,
In the new moon's silver glimmer
We worded wishes to the stars,
And listened to the roaring river.

IN YOUR ARMS
[1.45am, 21st March 1991, Glasgow]

In your arms I will not cry,
a seagull on a wild March wind,
a curlew on a bleak moor hill,
I'll lie there 'til all the world
and all the stars no longer are,
'til all there is – is all there was,
and all I know is all I have.

DEAD POETS FORM NO SOCIETIES
[March 1991, Glasgow]

Eliot lies in ashes in Coker yard -
Betjeman rots not far from Harrow Hill;
Thomas haunts nightly the shore of Swansea Bay;
McDiarmaid pushes daisies where thistles used to be.

ESCAPE INTO THE MOUNTAINS
[Journey 7th - 11th September 1991, West Highland Way]

(I)

Leave the grey city streets,
leave the office work behind;
leave the sleepless nights - go!
Escape into the mountains.

On by bus to the foothills;
on by foot into the woodlands;
mile for mile along the footpaths -
deep into the Highlands.
On through Mugdock, to Carbeth,
to the standing stones of Goyach;
beneath the shadow of Dungoyne -
hay rounds and dry stone dykes.
Smell of whiskey, pine and moss,
through Gartness, near Killearn -
the Endrich burn bubbling on:
north - Loch Lomond shimmering.
Into the trees Drymen fades,
the forest gobbles all it sees;
silent, still, the Scots pine squeeze
the oaks out of existence.
In Woman's copse - Garadhban,
storm dead the past is strewn;
In the hot September sun,
the hottest Scotland's ever known -
Dusty leads the Western Way
dreams and debris blown.
No fire has pyred the romance yet,
perhaps one day before too long.

In such heat Strathclyde scorches,
ground dry like the Gobi waste;
woodland plants limp and brittle,
dwarfed blackberries hanging shrivelled.
Out on the open moorland,
across the ebbed Kilandan burn,
on past hikers puffed and blistered,
on and up steep Conic Hill.
Aye! the view across such country!
Ben Lomond snowless to the north,
Balmaha beneath in oakwood,
Loch Lomond sail-lite hued.

Across the water - Alps of Arrochar,
the Argyll peaks beyond Loch Fyne,
to the south the knolls of Bute
just beyond the Renfrew Heights.
There! - the Clyde, distant, white,
where Arran's sleeping giant aye rests -
where Celtic legend outlives life
in names, beliefs, and rights.
But there, below on Lomond loch,
man-made islands, three thousand years;
the Isle of Old Queens - built upon
cranogs we'd like to know about.

Our history! know we ourselves?

Us Celts, our trust is in the past -
See that rock by the road?
It's a cyst for the dead.
Yet, bathers swim in Craigie's waters,
speedboats brave Inchcailloch channel,
windsurfers skeet by Arrochymore,
and flaunt their city manners.
Have they been to Mallorca?
Have they done Waikiki?
Have they sunned in Cancun,
and lain on Bondai beach?.

Such is the drudge of urban life -
while sap seeps from a weeping pine,
silence heals the shed of tears
in the hollow of Amair ...
Glimpse of pasture, grazing land
along Sallochy's oakwood path,
tumbling over sheer-drop crags,
stumbling over fern-crowned rocks.
Ross Wood, Black Tarn, Rowardenan,
beyond - respite, human comforts -
black beer in a hostelry;
a broad-bed of white linen.

(II)
Red Robin sitting on a fence,
Rowardenan left behind -
through the trees to Ptamigan Lodge
then steep down to the lochside.

Hereabouts Rob Roy roamed,
his prisoners kept on a crag;
he was more a nationalist
than any Campbell swine.
Thus his fame outlives his deeds
despite being a cattle thief;
in the Rostan trees he hid
and lived his secret life.
He knew Rochoish and Cailness burn,
the gnarled root way to Inversnaid
where the Campbells did their worst
to put the chiel in chains.

And still - something in these woods
makes the past come alive -
Loch Lomond lapping on block-rock
that some ice-age dislodged.
Until at last - at the Snaid,
a bridge high above the falls -
this darksome burn, horseback brown,
this rollrock high-road roaring down;
This coop and comb fleeced in foam
to the loch falling home -
takes the traveller to the Lodge
for tea and morning scones.

Tired, yet the legend lures
the trekker on to Rob Roy's cave,
a crevice in the fallen rocks
above the Lomond waves.
What waves? such calm days
man-made from speed-ski tows;
a blonde-haired lassie scooting on
I Vow Isle's shores.
And there, watching from the beach
beneath the Fritihich crags,
a lone hiker bathes himself -
his lunch a slab of cheese.

While through the trees the way leads on
through a cull of fern,
burns dry to their boulder beds;
ten days since the heavens bled.
The reckless carry on regardless
along the River Falloch track,
and on they go for their reward
to drink from Falloch falls.
Such are the waters from Ben More,
three thousand feet above - a source
first a trickle, then a gush,
then a roar towards Loch Lomond.

Further north - across the river,
the way meets the Military Road,
the road that General Wade constructed
to bring the Southern hordes.

I will take the Highland cause,
though I am but a Lowland man,
to hell with better British life
the breaking of the clans was wrong.
Wrong? One wrong made another wrong;
cruelty in the name of progress.
Exiled by English law,
the Highland man exiled the Redskin.
And on this old military road,
trekkers now traverse the West,
on they trudge to rest the night
in Crainlarich beds.

(III)
Through Herive wood from Crainlarich,
the morning dew still on the ling;
munros peaking through the mist:
skylarks, swifts and swallows.
Sun breaking out on Fillan glen
up the strath to Tyndrum's gold -
If there are other lands like this
they must be up in heaven.
Down the braes to Fillan's side,
shallow, clear and flowing south,
banked by the old lead mines:
there's gold in Fillan's waters.

564

Celtic history is all mounds,
more ancient ruins oak-tree bound,
where Saint Fillan, Ferdach's son,
built his chapel by the burn.
Five relics of that holy prince,
five durach held his holy parts;
Bruce sent for Fillan's arm
on the eve of Bannockburn.
Thirteen-fourteen hundred years,
Fill's parts have healed the sick,
now glass-cased in Edinburgh;
all that's left of him - his limbs.

The fate of all famous men
is to have their parts preserved -
Westminster kirk or some museum
how saintly can such action be.
So onwards - past Fillan's well
where once the insane were made well,
until the magic was destroyed
by throwing a black-bull in.
Such Scots there shall always be -
Scots who'd have us all believe
that doing good is a disease -
Thank god for old Saint Fill.

Past Auchtertyre, across White Bridge,
Cononish stream tricking on -
through the fields of Dalrich
where McDougall beat the Bruce.
In the woods of hewn timber,
along the banks of Crom Allt,
past the bridge of croft Glengarry
by lower Tyndrum's walks
where Wordsworth walked in a storm,
crouched on naked rocks rain-swollen,
saw the cloud sequestered heights
and marvelled at mountain life.

Still not a town, a village yet,
big business now is moving in,
tourism fostered on the back
of the nation's gold-mine boom.
If this is Scotland here and now,
a Scottish accent hard to find,
then Scots must ask themselves -
Can we call Scotland ours?
What have we lost? Our history?
Our lochs now lakes? Our bens now peaks?
We are a nation of three kinds -
Celt, Pict and Anglophile.

Too few can claim Pictish blood;
Too few wholly Celtic thrive;
Too many now of Angle tongue
buying-up and selling.

565

Yet, still the munroes tower above,
impulsing those far below
to climb into their shrouding clouds,
wild about them churning.
Til pangs of nationalism ease,
the world beneath beyond control -
the rain lashes down the glen -
God has no existence then.

And on the trekker treads his way
along the route by Ben Odhar;
along a way time has passed
and left it's scarring mark.
Dorian shades the whole terrain,
the larch of Auch to the west,
Horseshoe Bend across Auch glen
and the Allt Chonoghlais.
Dorian's crags roll with scree,
to crash into the Coire Chailein,
and climbers with their mutton feet
descend the leacann side.

And on towards Bridge of Orchy,
The Clach-a-Ben on its own -
a rock the size of a house
in a moor of bleached sheep bone.
And on, in cold to the clachan,
Twilight on the western sky,
no stars out above the bunkhouse;
rain to come before the dawn.

(IV)

Mist hanging on the Tulla hills
of white-beak sedge and clubmoss -
the smell of myrtle in the air
by asphodel and sphagnum bog.
Between Mam Carraigh and Doire Darach,
the rock-cliff pap and wood of oak,
down the hill to Inveroran
to a mound goes the road.
A shot rings out from the woods,
a gunman stalking his wild prey;
past the Forest Lodge and up
towards Black Mount and Little Beag.

Towards An Torr, then Ben Toiag,
Wade's old road twists and turns
until it crests the watershed
to cross the Rannoch waste.
Few men have ever made a home
Though out the world on land like this,
where in an instant mist is down
and summer turns to howling gale.
Deergrass, sundew and tormentil,
bog pondweed and cladonia spore;
this is the world of Rannoch Moor
ringed by rugged bleak munroes.

To the east - Schiehallion,
sacred peak of the Pict,
towers over a small yew wood
containing Europe's oldest tree.
No trees stand on Rannoch Moor,
bog, bog, peat, peat, peat;
water flows in off the hills
to saturate brooding fen.
Hence, The Moss and the Ba,
where Wade bridged its raging burn,
a few rowan in the lee
or on the rocky brink.

And there upon a sheep-gnawed knoll,
trekkers rest, make their tea
until the midges drive them on
towards windswept Chaorach.
Past Raven Crag and Wailing Knob
where deer rut in the booru winds,
where cairns stand for the dead
that death stalked on the moor.
And on towards White Corries tow,
into the valley of Glen Coe,
into the shadow of Shepherd Mount -
the black rock face of Etive Mor.

And those weary of the wild -
shelter in the Kingshouse Inn
until they gather up their strength
and march towards Ben Beg.
Up the slope of Rocky Hill
to reach the Cliff of Extent
down which seeps the Boggy Loch
from off the Little Ben.
And once again on Wade's road
across the West Highland hills,
snaking up the steep cliff side
of the Devil's Staircase.

The way climbs MacMartin's Stob,
descends towards the Sallow stream,
rounds the nose of Odhair Beg
and on towards Loch Leven -
Down to where the myrtle's tall,
where rowan's fruit, heather crawls
down to where the waterfall
washes Kinlochleven.

(V)
Is there land like this on Earth -
Loch Leven in the morning sun,
birchwood giving out to ash
beyond old Mamore Lodge.
The wheatears chatter up the glen
where Lairig men had their crofts.
Ruins now - a silent place

567

where Lairig stream trickles on.
What clan of men homed the mor?
Stob Ben as their high munro -
where have all the children gone?
Mamore ridge no longer crossed.

The house of the mountaineer -
Ben na Caillach - Old Woman's Hill;
the Great Pass between the Ranges
is quiet and deathly still.
Time moves against those who try
to tame the land for their needs;
the ruins of Lairigmor are stones -
stones once more the glen's.
And over these stones, trekkers go
in the burning Highland sun -
they have never known such heat
in this end summer month.

Until the Moor of Rowantree Hill
meets the Loch of Wooden Quern,
the way in line for Callous Cleft
beyond the round of Hollow Ridge.
Down this road fringed by ling,
down the banks cross-leaf heathed,
down the way bell-heather lined
to where the cinquefoil gives.
And there, above, the highest crest
Ben Nevis broods with cloudy eye
as trekkers drop through pine and spruce
below Tuft Pin' and Eagle Peak.

And there by the banks of Nevis burn,
the journey ends for the few -
An Garrisan looms tourist bright
and the seals of Linnie sing -
'You who've trekked the Himalayas!
You who've climbed the High Alps!
You who've hiked the Central Andes
Welcome to Lochaberside!'
 And there a hundred miles on -
and a hundred more after that,
lies Knoydart, Assynt, the Gaelic Isles
where few are want to wander far,
escape their inns for the wild -
the wide beyond the city grey
far beyond the Highland Way.

THE WORLD FREES BUT WE ARE CAUGHT
[14.37pm, 18th Sept 1991, Banchory]

There is no quiet, only storm
And gale where peace was found;
A place where tranquil calm hung out
Is but a sphere of violence now.
For shifting sands and changing tides
And dunes all drift with time -

Waters frozen on winter's lakes
Thaw to turn winter out -
And where silence held supreme
Chatter echoes through the trees;
Stillness in the undergrowth
Stirs awake and loudly breathes.
Oh where can rest now be sought?
The world frees - but we are caught.

LYNDA
[11.26pm, 23rd October 1991, Glasgow]

Oh sweet gentle sniffling faun,
Winter comes as Autumn falls
Into the future no one knows
Or where or when a cold goes.

We are left with tissued days
That leave us duvet-sofa bound -
Ah for perfect summer walks
And sweat upon our brows.

For now we itch, scratch and flake,
Our noses stuffed - we are weak,
We cannot work, we cannot sleep
And soup is all we eat.

Oh is there answer to it all?
Why those we love bug us most.
A kiss upon a cheek - then woe!
Their germs strike us low.

Yet we bravely smile and sneeze
And break a laugh before a wheeze.
We will not give into the foe!
We fight on until it goes.

And so sweet dear Lyndy love,
Kiss goodbye your sniffs and bugs.
Greet the world with all your must
And get you now back to work!

NEW YEAR'S EVE
For the Lyons of Hull
[11.30pm, 29th December 1991, Glasgow]

I am old beyond my years,
I've seen time pass me by,
I've seen many left behind.
I've seen the road many trek
Without a look or backward glance –
Yet here you see, I stand!

Older still I am by years,
I have lived through war and peace,
I've gone through famine, feast;
I have thirsted, I have supped,

I have praised and I have cursed;
I am as you see me, thus!

Middle in all things I am,
Neither one nor other thing –
I have steered a centre course,
I'm neither young, nor old,
Neither small, neither tall,
I am between and halfway so!

I have all things recent done,
I live for now, for the present –
I have no use for the past,
The future is beyond my grasp;
I take all things as they come,
Take me now, as I am!

I am young, bright eyed, fresh,
I am full of life's full breath –
Give me sun and wind and rain,
Give me hills and lashing waves;
I've no time to waste or lose,
I am free to pick and choose.

Younger still, I am growing,
I am sapling, supple, lithe –
I will bend, I will flex,
I will make many friends;
Tomorrow will be better still.
Better that, if you will!

Soon the old will be the new,
Soon the recent be the past,
Soon the present will be recent
Soon the now will be the bye;
Soon the future will be here –
And the new year come!

MY NAME IS MARY
[11.59pm, 10th Jan 1992, Santa Ponsa, Mallorca]

I went stand-by to Palma, to buy me a beer bar,
I wanted some sun, sand and air -
Instead I got lonely, went on the bottle
And reflected on all my lost years.

Then one night, on a bar stool in Paguera,
Alone I sat counting my change -
A voice at my shoulder asked for a vodka
And I turned to look at her face.

There what I saw I'll always remember
Was a lady with a suitcase and coat,
She sat down beside me, lit up a menthol,
And these were the words that she spoke.

"My name is Mary, I'm alone and I'm lonely,

Do you think I could buy you a drink?
I've left my husband and kids back in England,
I don't know if I'll see out the dawn."

We went down to the beach, sat on the cold sand
And spoke of the partners we'd loved.
After awhile, we went to a hotel
And took a room for the night.

We lay together sharing a bottle
Until the coming of dawn and the first light -
Then up she got without saying goodbye
Picked up her case and lit out.

I watched her get into a cab for Palma,
She looked up, and then she was gone -
An hour later, I saw a plane pass over
And recalled the first words she had said.

"My name is Mary, I'm alone and I'm lonely,
Do you think I could buy you a drink?
I've left my husband and kids back in England,
I don't know if I'll see out the dawn."

VALDEMOSSA
[8pm, 14th Jan 1992, Santa Ponsa, Mallorca]

Bitter is the olive flesh,
Tart the orange and sour
In the terraced fields and groves
Of Mallorca winter time.

Rotten is the almond nut,
Dry the black fig fruit,
Shrivelled the Valdemossa vine
And pomegranate seed.

Yet never have I seen such
Sweet melancholic beauty -
I close my heart and die
When I think of Glasgow's grey -

Walnut, date, palm, lemon,
Apricot, rose and elder flower
Where green oak, carob, pine,
Poplar, cypress, all entwine.

Varied hues in leafy tangle,
Perched above the deepest chasm -
I will chew the olive flesh
And smell the almond blossom.

SON MORAGUES
[8.50pm, 14th January 1992, Santa Ponsa, Mallorca]

Ancient walls, ancient trees,
Lined ancient roads to ancient ways;

Almonds in the valley bottom,
Olives terraced to the sky;
Mountains rearing into void,
Tumbling into wild ravines;
Secret paths, secluded parts,
Shaded regions beneath ramparts;
Cellars, tunnels underground,
Earthy soil, ancient footprints
Of soldiers long departed.

SANTA PONSA
[15th? January 1992, Santa Ponsa, Mallorca]

Who would not winter wisely
Where wind and wet are winkled,
Where weather will not wicked be
Or women need wear wrinkles.

Santa Ponsa - you have rescued me,
I see the way life should be -
Not a head of greying hair
But a life of sand and sea.

Grey city life wears man down,
Makes him chase the buck -
Leaves him sleepless every night
And further into debt.

Money! Root of death, decay,
Wasted lives led astray -
He who has - has all the say
With those who want the same.

In this place, ice-plants droop,
Date palms hang the squares,
Eucalyptus line the roads
And pine trees hem the bay.

THE LADY IN THE FUR WRAP
[16.24pm, 4th Apr 1992, Pollok House Library, Glasgow]

In a fur wrap by the fire,
April rains on the green chestnuts,
Wooden beams masked by casts,
Bare floorboards worn by hordes.

They tiptoe through the *par terre*,
Through the window bays they pry,
To see the lady in the wrap,
The coy Goya of Pollok Park.

She listens to their shaking steps,
Their creaking flirting with the past,
Their whispers knowing not what is,
Claims for this, or that, all false.

Four hundred years of vigil thought

Of viewing backs from other lands,
They gather 'neath her sneering gaze,
They know not who she is or was.

Silence never comes 'till five,
After which the park owl howls,
She looks at me, and I at her -
She'll outlive me she smiles.

THE THIRD JOURNEY OF THE WANDERER

[Composed 6th April 1992 - 20th March 1994]

The Narrator, walking in a park in which he spent much of his childhood is surprised when The Wanderer emerges from the bushes and greets him. His appearance is changed and there is something in his tone that suggests that all is not well.

SCOTLAND

NARR: Two nights before Election Day,
I took a walk through Pollok Park,
saw narcissus 'neath a beech,
my name carved in it's bark.

Red rhodos edged the path
that led down to the River Cart
where crouched beneath cherry blossom
I watched young anglers cast.

My eye carried to the west
where grey cloud merged with red;
I wandered through the *par terre*;
paused by the beggar's tree,

then broke upon the Highland cows
head to head in youthful play;
heavy drops of April thumped
upon the fresh hoofed clay.

Images from movies, destruction, war,
Eastern Europe still in turmoil,
I'd crossed that dung-filled field before,
the year Armstrong took his leap.

Now, I lent upon the fence,
a fresh-leaved chestnut overhead,
one with all, and all forever,
no winter chill, no winter shiver.

Spring had come, banished winter,
hither came the songbird quiver,
I heard the murmurs of the river,
saw the last hint of a glimmer –

before the evening star's faint glitter.

Then I heard a crack! a break!

the rustle of a laurel bough;
in a spin I turned and saw
a hand, an arm, then a brow;

and with a shock that took my breath,
the twilight catching his wild eye
that gave no flicker of surprise -
there before me stood my friend.

The Wanderer!

His handshake firm, his greeting short,
we quickly fell into talk;
he brought me up to date with life -
he had moved to the Southside.

WAND: I'm living with ageing parents,
sleeping in their small front room;
I cannot say that I am rich,
nor say that I am poor –

my mother cooks every meal,
my father slips me cash.

Times are hard - not just for me,
it makes me sick to see the gap
between the have's and those who don't
bridge the shark-filled gulf.

So I have been to George Square
with my saltire and my voice
to fly a flag for our Scotland,
for common cause and freedom!

I have been to Calton Hill,
to meet the six who came from Syke;
I have clench fisted raised my arm
and held aloft a burning brand.

NARR: For what? For who? I asked;
after all this time a Brit,
had he awoken from a sleep
to find himself a nationalist?

He would not look me in the eye,
and hung his head as if the world
had passed from others' troubled backs
to rest on his.

WAND: At last I am for the cause!

NARR: What cause is that? I replied,
I could not quite grasp his drift –

A cause that frees us from oppression?
One that redistributes wealth?
One that makes our children strong?

One that makes us one with God?

We walked the drive from Pollok House,
up the slope to Bluebell Wood,
o'er the brow into the field
where now the Burrell broods.

WAND: Man preserves the things he makes,
yet cannot store the cherry blossom,
nor the harebells, nor himself;
in my own way, like the rest,
I keep mementos of the past
I hope that will survive -
for memory is a flickering film
with a live sound track.

NARR: My friend, obscure as ever,
took me down through Nether Pollok
and out upon the south by-pass,
into the Old Swan for a jar.

I bought the drinks, for he was skint
though he was doing puppet shows
for kiddies groups - for forty quid
schools and parties where he could.

ENGLAND

WAND: I wish I'd stuck with Civil Eng
and got my degree at the uni -
but when I quit, I'd had enough;
seventeen years of education,
nineteen years, four months old,
I couldn't wait to see the world.

My tutor said I'd have to change,
switch to Mining Engineering -
I said 'No way', I wasn't daft,
'Two years down the copper mines!
Get someone else out to Lusaka.
I'm a Scots boy, not a mug!'

Looking back, I blew big bucks,
I'd be living high by now -
but money's not the only thing,
I made sure I lived while young;
for all the money in the world
cannot make youth return.

A drop-out, unemployed. I signed on,
shared a flat with Barnsley Steve,
Barnsley Tony, Barnsley Nora,
ended up with Barnsley Mo.
I fell in love, I met her parents,
but she ran off with a sailor.

Renamed Maurice, she had his baby,

it broke my heart. I needed saving.

Oh transcendental meditation!
it raised me to another station;
self awareness, one with one;
two was a crowd, three a mob;
O*m* became a sacred word
that promised me eternal love.

Soon my troubles blew away
like balloons in a gale.

It came to me as a vision -
India - the land of wisdom;
I would seek my fortune there;
to hell with the English way,
for I was not an Oxbridge boy,
I was a Scot fae the Shaws.

I'd reached lesson thirty three;
I was earmarked for their ranks,
they'd booked me for their Zurich class,
summer season in the Alps -
a disciple of Lord Krishna.

I quit the Transcendental school,
forewent the rules of Natural Law;
they were sorry when I went,
yet what knew I of yoga life,
how could I take the path
leading eastwards to the Alps?

I'd been there! Twice and back!
on my tod without mishap.

No, I had to find my own way,
head out East all alone,
turn cant dreams into knowledge,
go in search of myself,
not in search of a guru;
for many lead, few guide,
and fewer still get on with life.

Oh Maharishi Mahesh Yoga
are you to blame for my roving?
Not at all! I am Scottish!
I was meant to see the world.

So, eleventh August, seventy-four,
six months conducting on the buses,
off I went with Maggie Slack,
a clippy from the Fenham run,
hitch-hiking south from Low Fell,
standing there with all our gear.

We waited on the old A1,
ten hours later arrived in London.

Tubular Bells in Petty France,
Maggie clipped her long toe-nails;
We stayed in an M.P's flat -
James Whyte, the Pollok Labour man;

I read the Anti-Room that night,
chewed my toothbrush thoughtfully.

FRANCE

Next day on the Dover Quay,
with some francs from a bank,
we put ashore in Calais, France;
we hiked out, and near Arras
I took my stinking gutties off
cast them in a field of corn.

I ripped my shirt off my back,
I was white, but France was hot.
Maggie bitched. We walked a lot.

Two days later, Marvejois,
stuck out on the Massif Central -
the air was clear, the water fresh,
but hitching was a nightmare.

Next day, Pezanas, Cote d'Sud,
Maggie felt like getting drunk.
What an alky, what a pig,
she sipped, then took to swigs,
the vino ran down her lips.
We spent the night in a ditch.

SPAIN

Vive Catalonia! Barcelona -
in those days under Franco's power;
the city was an army town
and not a tourist haven.

On towards Madrid we hitched;
a truckie stopped, took us west,
tried to get in Maggie's vest,
her pants and all the rest,
but I declined his money.

We had ourselves a room that night,
Hotel Espana, in old Lerida;
floors tiled, walls white,
beds mattressed, sheets pinstriped;
Maggie smiled, joked and laughed,
she was happy, so she said;
we slept sound till midday.

Madrid

We reached Madrid, went to stay

with some Divine Light Mission folks;
we weren't allowed to drink or smoke,
eat meat, fish or dairy produce,
or wash our clothes with washing powder,
or have sex within their walls.

Sex? As if we would -
with Ma-Jee watching us?
He was the Lord omnipotent;
we were guests at his lodge.
Oh praise the Maharaji!

I'd heard it said on T.V.,
he was a dwarf who'd kidnapped God,
but there was good in Ma-Jee,
that's why he had such devotees
who were too good for me.

I little knew ten years later
his wayward clan would woo my wife,
whisk her from the family home
and make her see the Light -

This is another tale itself,
for in Madrid I was free,
I could stand back, pick and choose
what I thought was good for me -

Now much older, Maastrict rules
my head and chokes my national voice;
while across the blue divide
Clinton takes the purple robe.

Time moves on and freedom stales;
things of conscience get in the way;
clashes against our rulers rise
and wither, then remain as pain.

The seasons change, bring forth rain;
life falls brown on potholed roads;
those who're rich splash the poor
and the downtrodden sleep all alone.

There are no answers in revolutions,
no happy smiles on history's lips;
caught in the maelstrom of hurricane time
we perish to rebirth again.

Traveling in circles, passing through hoops,
You have no answers, nor do I;
you follow my journey, I shadow yours;
someday we'll meet down the road -

You will be me, and I, you of old,
and between us we'll make the same mistakes.

Soup kitchens open in our towns

as more and more die of cold -
is it fair to feel self pity
when Major's world makes us old?

The youth within me, shrivelled, wan,
the sun has left this gloomy land;
I find that only in the past
did dreams come true (though did not last).

NARR: The Wanderer was on a tangent,
we stood beneath the Shawlands bridge
on 'Shaws Road, and cleared his chest.

Winter, yet again, had come
and bonfires lit up the sky.
A firework knocked out a star,
it fell at our feet and glowed.
We stamped our boots, rubbed our hands;
Guy Fawkes night, I was sad.

That afternoon I'd been to see
a girl in Greenhills, East Kilbride;
her house was filled with warm sunlight,
healthy plants on every sill;
we talked intense one whole hour,
I could have talked into the night.

But with her husband due home soon
she was anxious she'd be found
and took a harshness to her voice
that made me ask her the time;
we both agreed I should go
before her husband found us so.

What now I asked as I left,
not of her, but of myself;
had I invaded her fine world
to covet someone else's wife?
Had I transgressed the tenth law?
Would I try to break their bond?

Knowing what I did was wrong,
Oh god of Gods! I needed help.
Did I turn my back on love?
Was there better judgement found
in making friends, and not divide?
For he whose anger unjoins vows
can find no peace in return.

WAND: Love and bible clash like steel;
like red and green do not mix,
like oil and water ever split,
like two poles that never meet;
the heart warm, full of fire;
the head cold like icy water;
and in between, accused of sin;
first you'll burn, and then you'll sink.

579

NARR: The Wanderer in his own void,
making light of my turmoil,
driveled on about the rain
that fell when he was in Spain.

WAND: Britain seemed a long way north,
Scotland, Glasgow, Shawlands Cross,
the rain brought back many thoughts
of youthful times I'd forgotten;
the days when summer came and went
and winter passed on to Lent.

I had no cares, gave not a toss
if it rained or if it poured.
The rain always cleansed the streets;
I'd tramp about them with wet feet,
Mum tried to keep me indoors
saying I'd catch my death of cold;

I'd disagree and off I'd bolt,
a thing I'd later much regret
when Dad cuffed me on the head.
Kept in, I'd have to pass time
by the Burgh Hall quarter chimes;
I'd watch the rain-drops steady fall.

Ripple puddles, pools and holes;
the steamed window my artist's pad
where I drew pictures of our dog;
sketching the world of an infant
which I believed unimportant,
but prepared me for the world.

The rain stopped, childhood faded,
I found myself back in Madrid;
the sun eased through heavy cloud
and splattered rays upon the sands.
Once more free to move outside,
I chose instead to stay inside.

I read about Gerald Ford -
Nixon barely gone, resigned.
Now nearly two decades on,
Bill Clinton in the Oval Office,
no doubt there sits in wet Madrid,
a Scottish guy mulling over –

all that has and been before
and all that will become in time.

Ibiza

When we set eyes on the Med
which we saw from Valencia's shore -
where young Don Juan's ship was wrecked;
where Twelve Night left Shakespeare's head;

- we met Flock and Hanni,
two Fräuleins from the High Tyrol;

They had come from Algeciras,
escaping from Moroccan thieves.
Their tales of woe were so exciting,
sex, and drugs, and near death misses -
Maggie sat with open mouth;
I let the sand slip through my fingers.

In Spain I was eager for the morrow,
I knew nothing much of sorrow;
big the world, big it's fortune,
small the problems there before me.
Simple needs, simple life,
and Maggie with her simple smile.

We shipped out for Ibiza,
out to the Balearic Isles -
for we had enough of guards,
of Franco's strong-arm bully boys,
for we had tried to share a room,
we were shunned at every turn.

Perhaps if we had not slept rough,
love with Maggie might have blossomed;
yet we sensed we were friends
who felt our friendship near it's end.
She was such a pretty girl,
full of life, a lovely smile.

Her hair was black just like night,
her eyes a rich chestnut brown;
her nose petite, her skin milk-white,
her mouth sensuous, straight-toothed, wide;
her chest broad, her breasts round,
her waist slim, her belly tight;
her buttocks curved, her hips broad,
her legs and ankles like a horse.

A horse! I can hear her voice now,
the high-pitched lilt of Eyemouth town.
And when I think, just twenty then,
she must be all of forty now.

We landed on quaint Ibiza,
crashed out drunk on the beach.
In short - Ibiza was a dump,
a place where all the hippies went
out to swampland Formenterra.
We hung out on Sabana beach.

I wouldn't give a fig for it!
It rained, it shone, it rained, it shone,
it rained, it rained, it rained, it rained;
we spent the night cold and damp
and in the morning - the cops arrived

and told us all where to go –

a hundred poor bedraggled souls,
they shipped us out on a boat
back to Barcelona.

NARR: The Wanderer droned on and on,
my mind was many miles away;
for suddenly, I had recalled
an evening in the Fintry Hills -
fireworks, bonfire, drugs and booze
on a farm near Carronbridge.

There I met a gymnast girl
with whom I strolled beneath the moon,
we kissed, embraced so tight
her body stretched to equal mine
before her toes left the ground
and we went spinning round and round –

until the cold conquered us
and we once more went inside.

WAND: What is there to life but giving love?
What is worse than none at all?
All the traveling in the world
cannot make life love more.

NARR: And with that quip he passed on
to talk about his wandering world.

Perpignan

WAND: At Perpignan we said goodbye
I put Mag's on a train for Lyon
accompanied by two German boys -
Andy Steiber and his friend.
I waved her off with no regrets
Though Maggie didn't want to go.

But I had plans of my own -
She was already short of cash,
and unless I set out alone
I wouldn't get to Istanbul,
to start on the Hippy Road.,
and the long miles to India.

Focused and selfish, both are true,
my dreams were made by lonely choice,
I started north upon the road
but found myself going west -
a couple in a Citroen bedstead
took me to their Toulouse home.

A tenement flat, sun-washed, old,
they gave me cheese, bread and meat.
Bad luck! I broke a china cup

but spent the night in a bed,
safe in France as August went;
I never had such sound sleep.

How months pass with no recall.
How seasons fly, do not return.
How lives exist, then cease to live.
How all that's known, repeats itself -
for few can understand, or see
What is now is all there'll be.

Which rivers did I cross next day?
Garonne? Lot? Dordogne or more?
Towards Limousin I hurtled,
twisting through cobbled villages
to wait in Brive, to wait in Tulle,
for a ride - that ended in a ditch.

I should have left him to his dent,
I helped him change a tyre instead.
He bought me a meal in Ussel sur Diege,
I spent the night in the Auvergne -
beneath the shadow of Mount Dore,
I slept on stone in a tenement close.

Next morning I met Phil from New York,
we jumped a train to Clermont Ferrand -
hotfooted it out at the terminal station,
showered and washed at a hostel.

NARR: The Wanderer gave me mundane facts,
I tried to keep my thoughts on him,
But I could not concentrate that well,
I dwelt upon my gymnasts woes.
The night before, at her small house
two bricks came through her front window.

Passion driven, chard glass flew,
showered us both on the sofa.
The police came and took away
the two bricks marked exhibit A.

How did such a thing come to pass
in sleepy little High Blantyre –

where fog hangs on the lights
and people huddled move about.
Was it something in the sky?
Was it Venus sectoring Mars?
Was it the Moon on the wane?
Or the cause a quart of Ballantines?

No excuse is good enough
that scares a woman to the quick,
the hidden hand of a beast
quick to chide and slow to cease
the torment of the poisoned tongue

twisting every decent thing -

no good comes from such words,
evil eats all honest love.

And when insults no longer whip,
the hand becomes the spoken word,
it wraps around a fragile neck,
chokes resistance, gurgles up
two dead eyes, a lifeless stare
giving into all but faith –

a faith that keeps the mind intact
after each cruel attack.

Hate, the product of blind faith,
how are such things resolved?

In dead of night, evil lurks -
for when the police were finally gone,
And all the glass was hovered up,
with the windows boarded over,
the door locked, a silence reigned -
every sound become a nightmare.

Every creak a shot of fear,
every trick of ear a terror -
Until the grey of dawn appeared.
I bared my worries to my friend
but the Wanderer, he was ranting on,
without a clue about my world.

WAND: On by Lyon, north to Thiers,
up the Rhone alone to Geneva -
to sit upon the hostel steps
with two young Welsh Medeas.
Chit as chat, and chat as chit,
they talked about planting mint –

about the garden they would grow,
about work permits, things like that,
and books in vogue - Catch 22 -
I promised them I'd write a book
And put them in it!

They laughed and kissed me on the cheeks,
I blushed and read aloud to them
From a book I carried with me -
Jonathan Livingston Seagull.

NARR: There I had to interrupt,
he was out of touch with people:
Europe was much different then?
Now revolt is everywhere,
we have the wall at our backs.
The Maastricht Bill stumbles on.

They listen not to countless calls
to dump the old dead ideal
of Europe one, and one for all,
new times have come these thousand days
since they took down the Wall.

East looks West, and West looks on
as Europe prepares itself for war.

WAND: Not then.

NARR: He smiled smugly, made me angry,
I had to give him my own view.

Time becomes Time that halts,
for still the politicians stumble on -
their power crazy fool ideals
leading us into Europe,
when we an island people, different,
have no borders to contest.

The cliffs of Dover are our frontier,
the Cape of Wrath our last domain,
the white sea waves bounding us,
we know the lands of our birth.

WAND: When I left Geneva for Germany-
Crossed the frontier near Lorrach,
did I think that I was European?
Not I, a young Scottish guy
in a town where people frowned,
the old looked rather trodden on.

A Germany not yet awakened,
non-one idle, the young polite.
I could not see a driving spirit,
work was the only guiding light.

Munich

Once more I came to Munich,
twenty seven years after the War,
took the S-Bahn to Ammersee.
Andy Steiber - at the station
drove me to his Hersching home -
his parents were such perfect hosts.

I stayed three days in Schillerstrasse,
with Bach playing softly in my ears,
Her Steiber set out his onyx chess
and badgered me to play my best.
Somehow I tried too hard,
I beat him with such success –

he took huff and puff with me,
demanded a rematch immediately,
but I feigned tiredness, fatigue,

in truth I lied, was selfish, yes -
and he with Bavarian pique
took himself off to bed.

Frau Steiber took one look at me,
eye brow arched as if to say -
'You young folks must always win,
have your way and pay no dues'.

And with a wink of an eye,
She led me to the grand bathroom,
handed me a spotless towel,
ran the bath - I got the message,
while I soaked in the suds
she threw my clothes in the twin tub.
Oh such was life in those days -
who would wish them fade away.

In reflection my weekend stay
at the Steibers of Ammersee,
merited my best behaviour,
brought out in me my finest nature.

We went to Munich in the rain,
sat in a nice clean restaurant,
drank coffee, ate choc-cake,
listened to a jazz quartet
playing fine Dave Brubeck,
made pleasant conversation.

We went to Andechs Monastery,
where the monks brew black beer -
and there we saw a nun,
ambling on the verdant grass,
a monk on her arm -
and smoking a long-tipped fag.

Geoffrey Chaucer would have smiled
At the halo round her head -
not from doing pious work,
but from the tiny little puffs
emitted from her pink pursed lips;
flirting with her courting monk -
fingering her necklaced cross,
her rosary dangling from her belt.

This is the way of the world!
Let no-one think it is a lie.
Andechs beer-brewing monastery -
I could not quite believe my eyes.

I bade farewell to the Steibers,
left Herrsching, thumbed for Saltzburg,
hitched a lift that went onwards
deep into the Austrian night.

AUSTRIA (again)

The driver offered me a bed,
I said yes, then found out
he wanted ten marks for that right,
I said no way, got out the car,
and found a haystack, crawled inside.

At dawn I woke to driving rain,
poked my head through the hay -
I was in Bad Mittendorf,
a scant populated rural place.
I slept a few hours more
then rose to get out on the road.

The rain drove down, the cars were few,
I took shelter from the storm
close against a cabin wall,
I huddled, watched the mist roll down
the steep hillsides to flood the vale.
Not unlike a Scottish morning
I lived in hope for a lull,
three hours passed, I huddled on.

YUGOSLAVIA

Evening saw me in a hostel
close to the Yugoslav border.
Next day a lift from Graz to Zagreb
left me where two years before
I waited more than one whole day,
burnt and eaten by mosquitoes,
ignored by the Croat people.

I dreaded now an awful wait,
contemplated going by train,
then to my joy, a Jordanian stopped,
offered me a driving job -
he had eight cars for Amman,
a driver short at Istanbul -
I could drive to Ankara,
no more sun, no more rain!

He waved a car down, it stopped,
I drove with a Turk called Yas,
he'd been picked up in Bavaria,
he said the Chef was a big-shot
who bought cars at German auctions
and ran them to Amman for resale.

Was he a crook I asked the Turk,
he smiled and shrugged his shoulders;
we drove Belgrade, on through Nis,
all night we rode the Eastern road -
crossed the frontier into Bulgaria,
drove until the red sun rose,
we hit the cobbled streets of Sofia,
all but dead to the world.

Across the main square we clattered,
Soviet flags on every pole,
thirty years of Soviet friendship
since September nineteen forty-four
when the pro-German regime fell
and the communists staged a *coup*.

TURKEY

Two hundred kay from Istanbul,
The Chef finally caught us up,
eight vehicles once more grouped,
we set off for the Turkish border;
and there somehow I found myself
with the car stamped in my passport -
I wondered why this was so?
The Chef told me not to worry,
I could drive on to Syria,
he'd pay me once we got to Jordan.

Jordan? That was not in my plans,
we reached Stanbul two hours past noon,
and there Yas left me with the car
wishing me the best of luck.

I nearly died of sheer shock
right there at the Golden Horn.
I crunched the car off the ferry
with alarming jerkedness -

I had no time to meditate,
I was now in Asia Minor,
the Chef's face was thunder-clapped,
I waved, almost ran the battery flat.

We convoyed slowly out the docks,
the noise and smog left behind,
we reached the open Ankara road,
I hit fourth gear, cruised 'til dark -
then WHAM! I ploughed into a truck.
SMASH! The windscreen blew out -
I woke to find two train rails
either side of my head! Six inches
this way, or six inches that,
I would have been decapitated.

I sat there stunned. Miming prayers,
God had watched over me -
Then in a FLASH, I felt my breathe
leave me with a gasp of air!
And there, leaning through the screen,
his hands about my constricted neck,
the Chef with his popping eyes,
trying to choke me to death,
while all the time, foul breathed
cursing me in Arabic.

Well, what a to-do, I must admit,
I sat and let him squeeze me blue,
I could not believe I was alive,
I'd been to Hell and back again.
I had cheated certain death,
and seconds later, death again!

A crowd pulled the Chef off me,
and checked to see if I was injured,
they carried me from the car,
and marveled I had not a scratch.

I was till in deep shock -
I couldn't hear a word they uttered,
they put me in the Chef's own car,
he drove me to a close-by motel,
a seedy joint by the highway -
he checked us into a room
and had a man bring us food.

I lay on my bed, shocked, exhausted.
Until a hand reached up my leg,
the Chef was having his revenge
by taking it out on my flesh!
I fought him off with all my strength,
the greasy toad ran out of breath,
rolled over on to his own bed,
and lay there panting in the dark.

Surely I was brought up right
to put up such a manly fight!

I feared the Chef would slit my throat,
I gripped my knife between the sheets,
stayed awake 'til first light broke,
prepared to tiptoe out the door,
but Chef awoke, coughed and spat,
and said t'was time to hit the road.

My battered car brought up the rear,
we stopped five kays short of Ankara,
the other drivers and the Chef
ate lunch and pointed directly at me.
They spoke with vile contorted mouths,
spat their words with crooked smiles,
then finally huddled heads together,
plotted murder, planned my end.

I left the keys in the ignition,
took my pack, and started walking,
the Chef shouted, I ignored him
from the Turkish tavern garden,
a public place with many watching,
I kept on walking up the highway
towards the blazing midday sun.

Five kays I walked to forget death,
all the while expecting Chef
to chase me, to have his way,
but instead I found I was free
I'd left the West, embraced the East
on a Friday, thirteenth day,
month nine in a year with a seven,
hardly an auspicious time,
yet I lived to tell the tale.

NARR: The Wanderer broke from telling me
about his Turkish misadventures,
by now we'd sheltered in a pub
to escape the rage of a blizzard.
Gale force twelve battered hard
every window, every nook
where friends together mulled events,
shook their heads about the Braer
breaking up on Shetland rocks,
spewing oil upon the shores
of Sumburgh Head to Ninian's Isle,
shag and salmon, other, seal,
poisoned by the killer slime.

The Wanderer was in his own world,
the blizzard but a small diversion,
he could feel the Turkish sun,
the Turkish dust in his throat.

Ankara

WAND: I was going up Cankaya Hill,
a stranger stopped me, with concern
asked me if I needed help,
he sensed my distressed condition,
took me in a shared *domush*
to his parents plush mansion house.

Haldun Ozen, an Ankara boy,
went to school in Washington D.C,
he was studying world economics,
planned to be a big-shot on day,
his dad connected with the government,
his mom stayed home the Muslim way.

He smuggled me into his basement,
I could stay the whole week-end,
his dad had gone to Istanbul,
left him as the head of house.
His playroom, out of bounds to parents,
with Jimi Hendrix on his stereo
blasting out *Star Spangled Banner*,
he spoke about D.C life
in stilted Maryland hippy jive-talk.

I met his sister, she was nice,
he showed me how to play *tabla*

590

'til it went well past midnight,
he set out a canvas bed,
said goodnight, went upstairs,
and in the dark, tired, worn,
I could hear the scratch of rats,
but it was Asia after all,
where man was closer to the world.

Half-nine a servant brought me breakfast,
then I set out for our embassy,
a journey full of winding turns,
a long trek of sun and dust.

Yes, no visa needed for Iran,
but one needed for Afghanistan
and Nepal, but not Pakistan,
not India, where if I wished
I could stay ten years or more!

Those were the days,
not so now, and rightly so,
three month's your whack
then out you go!

I *domushed* to the railway station
to buy a ticket for Tehran.
The train ran once a week,
four days and two thousand miles.
A ticket four pounds, second class.
Bana bar! Tesekkur Allah!
That was what I called value.

Walking back, I was euphoric,
the trees swayed in the wind,
too few birds to make for song,
the children's cries echoed loud,
I fixed on the distant clouds.
I watched a man hose his lawn,
the sun still warm, going down,
people going past, heads lowered,
caught up in their daily chores.

Haldo made me take some pills,
and off we went, out on the town -
he took me to the local whore-house,
but she was on her business rounds.
I felt sleepy, awkward, shy,
I didn't want to wait around,
I was desperate to read a book
to feed my empty Scottish mind.

Too late the lady returned home,
a bulky, well-worn, pot of flesh,
her hair was matted, her breasts huge,
she advanced, and Haldo fled,
escaped the thrust of her embrace,
and we returned to the house,

smoked some hash, played chess.

Next day, for my Afghan visa,
I tried to pay in Scottish pounds,
the Consul's staff shook their heads,
Bank of England, marks or dollars.

A Danish guy helped me out,
bought two from me as souvenirs,
he was one of forty kids, paying
to travel east in six old buses
some Afghans bought in Munich
to start a service Herat – Kabul.

They'd got aboard at Istanbul,
some had paid less than others,
ten pounds to get to Kabul -
they were on the Magic Bus,
they were from around the world,
Stockholm, Dublin, Rio, Texas,
drop-outs, students and Nam dodgers
like James Ballou, Keene, New Hampshire,
or Retta Ratts of Weatherford,
like me, they were on the road,
heading east, full of hope,
the world seemed a better place,
by going east than staying at home.

It was the start of Ramadan,
the month of fasting, dawn to dusk,
seven morning 'til seven at night,
few would pass food or drink,
but being a silly Christian boy,
and not prone to Muslim ways,
I ate bread, drank black tea,
for I was young, knew not how
to respect the fine Islam faith,
that wiser now, I accept.

Carsamba went, Persembe came,
I said goodbye to Haldo Ozen,
he was off back to school.
Is Haldo Ozen a big-shot now?
Who can say if he survived
or got himself a Yankee wife.

I got aboard the Tehran train,
found a carriage full of freaks …

NARR: The Wanderer rattled on and on,
while I had drifted off myself -
I heard a voice on television
talk as if the world were fine,
that ll the evils of our day
were not the fault of politicians.
He said the poor hold us back,
the unemployed must do something,

no longer can the state provide
for those who live on state hand outs.

Of such is the woe in our time,
this land one hand above the mire,
we've sold out future out to fools.
Citizen John! We cannot laugh,
out train-set's run right off the track.

I'm too disgusted to expressed
the way I feel about our times,
we live in a free-for-all
where the weak get trodden on.
If this means that to survive,
we have to draw in our horns,
then Scotland rise! People power
speaks where silence haunts.

At Bannockburn Bruce's statue
against the skyline, facing south,
modern Scotland plays football,
girls in jeans, four-a-side,
snow upon the western Bens,
coal smoke ringing Stirling town,
the castle there in our times,
our nation lives – the winter sun
warmer now that springtime comes
upon the echo of the birds,
punctured by a Piper Cub.

In the past, repeats our future,
on which side the Langs and Stewarts?
for whose rights Forsyths and Frasers?
Is all mankind doomed to failure?

In the land is oput deliverance,
take it back from individuals?
Divide it out to politicians?
For their friends, to their minions?

On Bannochfield, alone in February,
back against the Bruce's statue,
the white granite feels not cold,
no wind blows, the sky is gold
in parts where silver cloud
catches the last rays of day.

A mackerel sky to the west,
the north one large school of whales,
the east herring-boned and blue,
the south a clear ocean view.

For what ails our sick land
when we have skies as rich as these?
Our bare hills weep their snows,
pine-sap zaps the peaty floor.

Children – not yet in servitude,
ride their bikes on Bannockfield,
they may smoke a fag or two,
they have hopes, all children do.

Yet, can I, an ageing man,
tell them that all life is fair,
that they will stand equal chance
of being equal in this land?

Forgive me – the wall grows cold,
the sky grows dim. It is an omen,
the future for our raped land
is in the sword, not the tongue.

No talking now will change minds,
the gun, the bomb, and the knife,
they too can have no effect
for we are infected from inside,

Diseased, infiltrated by 'good souls'
who fool us long enough to finish
our resistance, eat our thoughts,
undermine us with their talk.

The enemy remains the same,
we have one border with the world,
across that frontier comes disease
unless we close it, we will die.

Mister Bruce, you did your bit,
where shall we find the likes of you?
Across the seas in Ontario,
or in a village in Lochaber?

Where is the new Scots Messiah?
Is he a soldier or a minister?
Or must we find a foreign general
like Bolivar or Che Guevara?

And while I thought on this matter,
my friend made a pot of tea,
we were in his mother's house,
it was the tenth of February -
time had slipped yet again,
Spring was but a month away.

Kurdistan

WAND: When I reached the Iran border,
I was taken off the train,
my passport was not in order.
Where was the car? Sold for profit?

The guards marched me up a hill,
I turned to see the train departing,
my heart sank as it went,

594

bare hills and open wilds,
there I was in Kurdistan
facing years in Turkish jail.

They took me to the Kommandant,
a captain – he spoke good English,
his lieutenant, fluent too,
listened to my woeful tale
about the Chef and his car,
how I wrecked it, nearly died,
and how Chef in his anger
put his hands around my throat,
then took me to a seedy room
and tried to get in my pants,
how I'd escaped the evil man
and spent six days with Haldo.

They asked if I could find the car,
I said it'd now be in Amman -
They called a guard to take me out
while they discussed the situation.

It was midday and baking hot,
it was the summer equinox,
I kicked up dust on the drill yard,
baked hard earth – top layer cracked.

It was a well-manned army post,
in all, perhaps, forty regulars,
out on patrol most of them,
keeping watch on the Shah's men -
who could have guessed five years on,
the Shah the richest man on earth,
would flee Khomeni's black-clad clerics,
and abandon Iran to Shi'ite rule.

They didn't keep me waiting long,
politely offered tea and cake,
the captain stoked his chin, smiled,
the lieutenant winked, stood relaxed.

The captain said "Here in Kurdistan,
last night a Kurd set off on horse
over the mountains into Iran -
but we are honest Turkish men,
we both agree you cannot leave
unless you find the car you lost …
But if you lost your passport too
who would know the car is yours?"

I could not believe my ears,
"My passport lost? It is done!
If I go back by bus to Ankara,
I could get a passport in a day" -
as I had done two years before
when Mr. Quine had saved me.

They clapped their hands in delight,
broke out a bottle of araki -
I had a shot, it burnt like hell,
Kurd whisky from the nearby hills.

As dusk was falling on the camp,
the village elder led me out,
a few dust covered steps north-east
to a house owned by a Turk,

A crooked looking shady fellow,
wrapped from head to foot in towelling,
his lazy eyes slyly rolling
across his broken crook-hooked nose.

I was well-advised to leave behind
my back-pack, money and my boots,
locked safely in the captain's office,
the only safe place in those wilds.

And so it was, I spent the night
on some ancient Kurdish rugs
between four walls of Kurdish daub,
beneath a roof of thatch and clay.

Cold the night, though hot the day,
the lamp tuned out, there I lay
with half a dozen Kurdish folk,
exhausted by the day's events.

I slept as sound as any might
below a sky aglow with stars
fringed by a ring of mountains,
few boys like me had traversed.

Too many stars in my life,
not enough bright moonlight,
dark is the universe to its end,
a bit like life in old age.

Next day the captain bade farewell,
warned me not to return by rail,
an army jeep took me west
to a village where I caught
a min-bus on to Van,
where by the shore of the lake,
I caught the ferry at a run.

Ten hours across the placid lake,
night fell as we reached Tatvan,
a muessin called the end to fast
as all broke from their Orug,
ate like no tomorrow mattered.

The coach horn signaled all aboard,
the bus for Ankara filled with folk,
filled with smoke, farewells made,

loved ones embraced, parted sad
as luggage sagged in the racks,
and still we waited as mothers cried,
and sons declared they'd be back,
until at last we departed,
and Tatvan's lights gave to black.

Eighteen hours through half of Turkey,
we reached Ankara next afternoon.
I hurried to the British embassy,
a consul clerk took my details,
and in a polite official tone
said return the following morning.

Next day I had my new passport,
outside I chuckled at my fortune,
planned to ditch my old papers.
Should I throw them, burn them, what?

I scratched my head, then remembered
a week had passed since I had washed,
that's when I met Quebecois Jacques
who took me back to his hotel
where we talked dope and girls
and about the days we had to come.

New passport in my neck-tied holder,
old passport kept close to my chest,
I went by coach to Erzerum,
on the way saw from the window
a flag draped coffin pass by
sticking from an old car's boot,
the way a bodger carries wood -
no ceremony is less becoming
than going luggage class to heaven.

Dogobayazit, beneath Aratat, where
Noah docked his home-made Ark,
cows idled on the road,
ducks waddled where they pleased,
goats gnawed at all things green,
and trucks ran horse-carts off the road.

Day and night merged as one
as East I traveled to Iran;
Eastern Turkey, dust and chaos,
barren land and stony fields,
so poor a man may sell his soul
and receive a bill for his chores.

IRAN

Oh what a difference in Iran,
fertile, green, with long straight roads,
the land of Shah Palava's oil
on which the Persian lion roared
while all around her, Afghan, Iraqi,

597

ran before it mighty claws.

Proud Iran, how it has fallen
from mighty power to friendless nation;
if there is hope for its future
it's in the history of its people.
Allah has found his disciples ready
to spread his teachings and the life,
yet failed to quell their warlike minds
on Aryan people like myself.

Let not the British judge them bad,
The British are by far much worse.

NARR: Here I stopped him in his rant,
his reasoning and his kind of kant,
I'd thought hard about the ails
our country suffered under Major -
the selling of our forest lands,
the privateers and speculators.
I was angry at it all -
I felt powerless and small.

The summer was almost gone,
the worse for almost fifteen years,
the sun had barely shone at all,
it had rained May and June,
July cloudy, cold and grey,
most of August much the same.

All the kids were back at school,
it grew dark by nine o'clock,
every day seemed the same,
I was bored and boring back.

My friend had moved to Garnethill,
two-up left, in a slum,
the windows rattled, floorboards creaked,
but what a view from the lounge -
the Campsies and spired West-End,
the sun going down every night
the way it had four years before
when I'd re-met my friend in Kelvinside
staring darkly into the Kelvin water.

Now was not the century's hottest summer,
I shivered, sitting by his window -
below the motorway traffic stuttered,
nose-to-tail through the rush-hour.
I had come to tell him of Sarah,
how we had parted, gone our ways,
how she as one of many
was no just mere history,
but he wasn't really listening,
he was busy pouring vodka.

I talked to him about the house

I was trying to buy in Dunoon,
it was all of half a villa, nigh
on Cowal shore at Sandy Beach.
It looked to the north Ayrshire coast,
the Bute and Arran ferries plying past,
and in the sea-walled garden,
stood a giant Californian sequoia,
largest living thing I'd ever seen.

At the mention of California,
he took an interest in my words,
he had spent a year in San Francisco,
seen the Sierra Nevada peaks,
he had walked around great sequoias,
and drunk their sweet sap neat.

"A redwood in your garden" he howled,
"Buy it, man, I'll move in!
I hate this grey shit-hole city
where everyone is so insincere.
It's the worst town in the whole world,
all you meet are waster dead-beats!"

I dismissed his simple observations
as that of a man without a wife,
or perhaps a traveler without a reason
for getting off his idle backside,
or was it, that now close to forty,
he was at a crisis in his life -
though once I'd had a vodka or two,
I began to believe that he was right.

Maku

WAND: I mean, take Iran for example ….
no sooner over the border and hiking,
some kids started hurling rocks at me.
It was something straight out the bible,
a stoning – and I was the victim
because I was long-haired hippy.

It was just another happening,
four thousand kay in a week,
army camp, Ankara and back -
I survived, went on my way.

Traveling on by bus to Tabriz,
dear, pal, what a thrill -
I saw a herd of camels!
Me, a young man from Pollokshaws
finally in the Middle East.

I took the train for Tehran,
eight of us in a carriage,
trundling across Qezel Owzan,
through Zanjan and Takestan,
shadowed by the Rashtek Mountains,

bloating out the Caspian Sea.

At Qazvin as the train pulled out,
an train inspector came onboard,
a young man in my carriage
hid beneath the seat duckboards -
we shuffled up, all sat straight,
draped tribal shawls across our knees.

The inspector, with an armed guard,
peered into our smoke-hung void,
drew back the door, stepped inside,
one by one checked, and scored
our third class ticket stubs -
but woe, he dropped one on the floor,
stooped – but just in time,
an old man stamped his foot on it,
the inspector snapped bolt upright,
the old man held the ticket up,
the inspector looked, with a huff
backed out, pulled the glass door shut
just before the fare-dodger coughed.

We helped him come up for air,
dust in his throat, we banged his back,
offered water, but he would not drink
a single drop, he'd rather die
than offend God during Ramadan
which was now but half way gone.

Argyll

WAND: My friend went off at a tangent
about religion, and all that stuff,
Time passed, now mid-September
he traveled with me in my van,
up the old Loch Lomond road
as we drove towards wild Argyll
on a dark overcast night,
we parked the van in a lay-by,
had some hash, then we crashed.

It'd been months since I'd slept well,
we didn't rise 'til ten o'clock -
we set off down the Loch Fyne road
to fed ourselves in Inverary.
I made a call in Lochgilped
to the lender for my house,
and all the way to Tarbert
I talked about my move to Cowal -
the Wanderer listened, staring out
across the choppy tops of Fyne.

After coffee and a snack -
(it was too wild to make a fire),
we trundled down to West Loch pier,
their catch loaded on a Spanish truck,

we watched the fishers stow their nets
aboard their battered west-coast ketch,
no name upon her rusty bow,
white letter-number on her side,
T T Two Sevens, her harbour mark,
her three man watch hauling chain,
pulling on their drift net weights.

We met friend Kenny in Ardpatrick
who toured us round the laird's estate,
the house walls cracked, sashes wormed,
the garden overgrown, forlorn
we walked upon a broken road
by broken walls and broken posts,
to come to the fishing shore
of broken sheds, huts and boats,
doors flapping in the north-east wind,
decay, neglect, and nature winning
over all that man had built.

Ardpatrick – once a thriving village,
now a wilderness of privilege,
all the land under patronage
and not a penny spent on maintenance.
And there upon the swelling loch,
a yacht moored to a buoy,
the third son's toy anchored there
awaiting some mighty gale
to wreck it upon a shore
people-less beyond his know.

That night we stayed with our friend,
loyal to the cause of freedom,
we talked into the early hours
about the fight for independence
while on the elderberry wine,
our passions ran and never dried.

And in the morning before we left.
we were no closer to our dreams,
the sky was clear – an azul blue
except for one cloud above.
A white cross "Jings oh, Lord!"

Of us three – who was the prophet?
Our friend, the Wanderer, or me?
An Argyll man, two Shaws boys,
I looked for another sign
but there were none I could see.

We journeyed on to Dunadd,
climbed up its mossy ramparts,
I put my shoe in the footprint,
declared myself King of Scots -
the Wanderer killed me with a look,
declared himself my overlord.

Onwards north to Kilmartin,
sacred place of ancient times,
standing stones and bronze age cysts,
cairns quartz white in the sun,
stones on which no moss grows
unlike the crosses in the churchyard,
broken, mismatched, spiked together
to record the Protestants displeasure
and angst about the Celtic church.

We made a fire by dark Loch Awe,
cooked fish, made some tea -
the Wanderer took a pipe of hash
and floated off to other lands -
left behind, Loch Awe and me
while he was back in Tehran.

We came back down to Carradale,
took some tea at Izzy's van,
listened to her old wife's tales
of fishing in Kilbrandan Sound
as her tears rolled down her cheeks,
reliving the Antares drowned,
a nephew lost, son's friends gone,
pulled down by a nuclear sub.
Oh such waste of life for nowt.
In Carradale the wound was raw.

The shellfish gatherers, waders on
by Davaar, loch of Campbeltown,
accompanied by their joyous dogs,
dug into the sea-pool sands,
a harvest in their honest hands,
as cockle-catchers stretched their backs,
shivered in the autumn blast,
turned towards the town at dark.

Next day Land's End, Columba's caves,
his footprint carved on a rock,
seals basking in the sun while
beyond the break – Mallin Head,
Rathlin and the Giant's Causeway,
Ireland but a stone's throw off,
we upon the Kintyre sands
cooking simple Scottish fayre.

What of Kintyre's well known Mull,
known through song to all the world,
a lighthouse midst a barren waste,
the ruins of Balvicar shore, now
but lines of rough hewn stone
where wind was once a source of power,
fish and wool a crofters life,
and for a view the Emerald Isle.

Further up the coast we lingered
to stretch our legs, view the seals,

parked upon a private road,
towards us with a dog, approached
a man who shouted at us thus -
"This road is private, don't you know!"

He was a Dalmarnock man, and
really couldn't give a toss -
"This land is owned by a Brummy,
I can' stand his English ways,
destroy the signs if you want,
it would make me more than pleased."

Eddie X – ex M.O.D,
told us all about his world,
he took us to his house for tea,
told us of the owner's plan
to build more houses by the sea,
and turn this idyll spot on earth
into a rented-village dream.

Oh wild west sea, waves of seals,
how many dreams have you wrecked
on your barren rocky fringe?
How many come to rue their ways
in the grave left behind,
their dreams of Ozimandi's kind -
desert sands but for a sign -
Private. Keep Out and Beware.

Back upon the Lock Fyne side,
we waded through a Clachen stream,
made a fire on the drift,
watched the oyster-catchers home,
viewed the twilight coming down
on Drisaig's dark Ben Buide shore.

"I am home" the Wanderer said,
"I've refound the place I love.
These past few days I am whole,
once more Scottish in my heart.
How could I have been so lost,
to lose sight of this wondrous land.
This is the home I left behind,
I can now forget the past."

The Wanderer let some tears escape,
went down on his knees and cried.
"What can I say of foreign lands,
I've been a fool to go away.
What use has all my roaming been
when here before me in these hills
is all there ever was for man."

I could not see what he could see,
I did not have his worldly vision,
he rose and put the fire out.
"I'm ready to depart to heaven."

We went past Luss, where at eighteen
we got smashed as wild boys do -
beer, and girls, and naked joy
swimming in the ice-cold loch.
And when we hit Glasgow's lights
I found out what I had lost -
Paradise in Argyll's beauty.
Hello crime, deceit and bedlam!

Welcome Hell! I'd crossed the Styx.
I said goodbye to my good intentions.
The Wanderer's mood went to black,
he was back in the past,
on a bus to old Mashad,
and onwards more to Herat.

AFGHANISTAN

WAND: At the Afghan border post
the customs guy handed over
a lump of hash to a guy called Bob
who'd been along that way before.
Welcome to the land of hash!
Party time! Goodbye Iran!

Travelling on to old Herat
where Alexander built a fort,
the walls still standing, mud and clay,
a score and three centuries gone -

For three days I got smashed
with Bob and Minnesota Doug,
a frontiers boy from St.Paul,
check-shirt, jeans, hiking boots,
a backpack bigger than a moose,
his mind fixed on the Himalayas,
the Everest trek from Katmandu,
his blue eyes dull, his speech slow,
the nicest guy you'd ever know.

But sometimes niceness belies plainness,
produces awful boring folk
who make you want to grab them,
shake some sense into their brains.
For what is worse than Mr. Nice Guy,
whose niceness makes you fall asleep?
What is worse than lovely fellows,
who cannot swear, nor scream?

Oh yes, we all seek a nice life,
but Jesus, take some names in vain,
curse the world, act insane,
for every hour is not the same.
We take our knocks, soak our pain,
what goes in comes out again.
I'd rather hear a lover rave

than have her stare into space.

I'd rather have my friends go nuts
than have my friends say they love
everything and everyone!
For he who loves all the world
sees none of the world's flaws.

Doug McCoy was so perfect,
he was fruit for every conman,
yes – he could climb snowy mountains,
he could kayak down white rapids,
he could hunt and trap wild animals,
he could light fires though matchless,
he could lumber with an axe-blade,
he could do everything single-handed,
he was Minnesota Man -

Big and strong, tough and spartan,
and there he was – Afghanistan?
Desert waste, and rocky nothing,
not a tree, stream nor cabin,
he was Minnesota Man -
defenceless without his gleaming axe,
his kayak and the moose-outback.

We talked on the bus going south,
to the north the Hindu Kush,
Doug slept, dreamed about Nepal,
the temple city of Katmandu.
Afghanistan – dry and barren,
for him was not the real McCoy.

Kandahar

Into the sands of Pashtun tribe,
we arrived Kandahar – the Peace Hotel,
those heading west, laden with beads,
gods in their wisdom and daily deeds,
no longer travelers on the road -
but the children of Shiva and Krisna's love,
in their cotton pants and lungi shirts,
modern day Christs in latter day robes,
rings on fingers, bells on their toes.

Hearing music in the singing of birds,
the rustle of leaves, the bark of dogs,
flying higher than the circling hawks,
dowsed in phials of jasmine and musk,
they placed every movement, picked every word,
passed chillums round "Dum Dehra Dum!",
muttering "Shanka" for the world they'd lost,
India behind them, the West to come.

Kabul

We entered Kabul on October the fifth,

605

aggressive dogs in baking bouts,
woodmen chopping, their echoes bouncing
back and forth across the mountains.

I re-met Jacques, Bob and James,
and many others on the trail -
the way that stretched from Istanbul,
onwards forever around the world -
there seemed no end to the road,
into the sun every morning we strode,
for well we knew where it set
but not where it rose.

Green grass and calling birds,
acacias swaying in the wind,
I mounted a camel in the bazaar,
an Afghan slapped its behind,
it bolted in a fit of spitting,
I fell like a kite in a spin.

When I rose covered in dust,
they laughed, offered me tea,
a smoke on a pipe, and the camel
for the price of two ugly wives.

I was just a boy from the Shaws,
they were men of the Hindu Kush,
tall, good looking, erect and proud,
holding their heads higher than generals.
Bowing to those who were their elders,
not one beggar among their number,
no man so poor he had no rifle,
no boy so poor he had no sandals.

They were men from Bamian and Kyber,
men from Pamirs, Hunza and Wakhan,
men from the hills and valleys of Helmand,
men from the towns of Sharif and Baghlan.

I, a boy from the Central Lowlands,
drew breath at their colourful vestments,
their flowing beards and Afghan caps,
they were heroes from my boyhood past,
they were the sons of Kubla Khan,
in them flowed Iskanda's blood.

Kyber Pass

Four whole days in Kabul passed,
Down we went into the Kyber Pass,
we headed on to Pakistan -
down past lairs perched on high,
slits for windows, fortress built,
the Kyber Gorge a fortress still -
every home an eyrie post,
every bend a bottleneck,
every twist a dice with death

as down into the plain we went -

There beyond the sheer cliff-edge,
the desert fringe of the Indus Valley,
a great black smog in the distance,
Peshawar! Den of vice and virtue,
the mecca of the hashish business.

PAKISTAN

In Peshawar I awaited the 'Pindi bus,
I watched the locals thronging by,
now and then one would stare,
but most would politely glance away.

Doug drank tea, hubbled on a pipe,
the air was heavy with petrol-cide,
the fumes from kerosene open-air cooking,
three wheeled taxis puttering for custom -
this was Pakistan on an October evening.

They say that first sight forms opinion,
but what I know of that great nation
I learned on return eight months later,
for I was in a hurry to be in India,
a bus, a train, and into the Punjab,
ancient Lahore in all its squalor,
the last of Pakistan before the border.

NARR: The Wanderer stopped, as if reflecting
upon his experience of that far place,
I meanwhile looked towards my future
having bought that house near Dunoon,
where now we sat by the window
looking out towards Wemyss Bay.

The January winds blowing wildly,
I nursed a coffee 'neath my chin,
listening to the Wanderer's wisdom,
thinking of my lover in Kilbirnie.

I was to be married in the Spring-
upon the morning of my fortieth birthday.
We were to be married by Reverend Conkie
and have the reception in the house.

It was to be a modest do,
fifty folk with a sprig of heather,
kilts, some whiskey and a blether,
escape to Rothesay by ferry
for our honeymoon in Bute.

And there I sat with the Wanderer
droning on about Amritsar -
he was twenty in India
and searching for a personal guru.

INDIA

WAND: Of all the places in the world,
there is none to match Bharat -
I have been to the furthest parts,
I have seen many mighty lands,
but deep within my heart, the jewel,
my treasured India!

All I've told you to this pointing
is but a preamble to the months
I spent in my endless quest
to find myself in India.

Is there a need to tell tales
about the daily toil and trouble
surrounding me every hour
in painful heat-ache India?

Or the bliss, days of joy,
high or in the deep abyss
of meditative happy thought
in carefree sunny India.

There I undid twenty years,
rewound to my infant days,
recalled the moment of my birth
while in ancient holy India.

Amritsar

Yes, there I was in Amritsar,
down three days with the trots,
holed up in the Golden Temple
deserted by that weasel Doug -
he was a Minnesota boy,
he wasn't going to be a nurse!

Illness shows us all the truth,
I lay fevered in the heat -
but I was young, strong within,
I fought the fever for three nights
on the pilgrim's-refuge floor.

And on the third day I rose,
went with the many pilgrimed horde
sat cross legged upon the marble,
banana leaf laid before me,
I received alms from the Sikhs,
a little rice and chutney.

I let my heart fill with joy
by the shrine of Guru Nanak;
I'd been deserted by my own kind,
six thousand miles away from home,
but I had found a better friend
in faith and hope and in mankind -

in all the world, ne're again
would I believe I was alone.

My illness gone, my hunger stayed,
I traveled on to the north,
went by bus to Chandighar
by fields of wheat and rice
until the bus – with a BANG,
shuddered, veered off the road
came to on a grassy slope.

We disembarked as the crew
threw a tyre from the roof.
I sat upon a little knoll,
watched them labour in the heat,
punctured wheel thumped and knocked
sticking fast despite the kicks.

I saw an old man pick some leaves
from some plants by the roadside,
he had found a ganja patch
and I likewise helped myself,
picked my fill of sticky leaves,
filled up my woolly hat.

Woolly hat? In such heat?
I was just a young Shaws boy
who knew not what to wear
or where to buy the right gear
without at first feeling silly,
or learning to discard discretely.

The tyre changed, and on our way,
near Chandighar we stopped again,
street protesters chanted loudly
"Power Workers! Stand United!"
A doctors strike! A student strike!
Half of Chandighar was out,
the other half without lights.

Indira Gandhi versus worker rights,
it was the same back in Britain -
it was the Heath years afterall!

Himalayas

On into the Himalayas -
the night sky hemmed by shadows,
white chevrons marked the edge
of plunges to the deepest chasms.

Until at last the Tata stopped
upon the crest of Simla town
where once the bastards of the Raj
had escaped the summer drought,
built a hill-town for themselves
and lived upon their Indian wealth.

609

Colonial patronage, racial power,
they gifted snooker to the world,
the white ball striking all the colours,
a metaphor for all that's wrong
with empires throughout the world -
Thank god ours is dead, and gone!

I passed the night at Lords Grey Lodge,
woke, went off into the world,
I had not then such fixed views,
for what I saw was not a system
but mountains beyond all description.
The Himalayas! Oh such beauty,
beyond, above the cloud
wrapped in glittering, brilliant snow,
twenty peaks that dwarfed the Alps,
made Nevis but a lump of rock.

Monkeys in the hillside trees,
Tibetans, sacks upon their backs
from truck to shop, shop and back
up and down steep sloped streets
filled with chanting army squads,
merchants crowding Grindlay's Bank,
sunshine filtering sublimely through
clouds six thousand feet above
roads that hair-pinned on a dime.

Beneath great chasms of space
I traveled on in Himarchal Pradesh.
Came to the market town Mandi,
perched upon a hilly exposed outcrop.

Under the shadow of the Sivalik chain,
it rained there nearly every day,
torrents from Swarga filling Bhakra
mixing with the rainfall from Kailas.

Drenched by the vapours, I sheltered,
then ran for the oasis of a nearby hotel;
six rupees for puke-pink walls,
bile window shutters, sea-puke door,
scraps of food on a dust layered floor,
a room alive with kitchen sounds,
clattering dishes, kitchen staff,
the waft of culinary concoctions
that turned my stomach to its core.

But I was well, fit and whole,
and despite a damp sleepless night,
From that hell, next day I entered
paradise upon this earth -
The Kulu Valley! Apple heaven,
green and filled with ripening fruit,
the scent of blossom in the nostrils,
the clear sweet air in my hair

as the bus climbed towards Manali.

NARR: Thus so my friend prattled on
as we cleared away rotten wood -
the ides of February gone a day
we were still at Hazelbank -

Burning stumps and severed limbs,
stacks of sycamore just felled,
briar and holly on the fire,
it sparked and flew into the sky,
hazed and humid from the snows
which lay upon the seaward grass
driven in the day before
blizzard fashion on the shore.

We had stood on the Point,
counting seals in the blast,
sipping coffee from a flask,
the Rothesay ferry ghosting past,
stormy days at their last,
Spring a month away at most.

The Wanderer spoke more of India
while I gazed out on Inverkip,
scanned the long Ayrshire coast,
Cumbrae and Goat Fell's white slopes.

Manali

WAND: In Manali, high on hash,
I met my Minnesota buddy.
He had rented out a shack
in the pines high up the valley,
shared the space with two guys,
New York Jack and Bernese Karl,
I joined them in their rustic home
where we all slept on the floor.

The nights were growing bitter cold,
we made fires with windfall wood,
we rubbed and took the ganja weed,
comatosed – we fell asleep
to awake upon the golden sun
breaking through the shutter slats.

We'd boil tea, have a toke,
wander on the valley slopes,
through the terraced paddy fields,
along the narrow hamlet ways,
where children barefoot played with us
and adults shouted "Namaste!"

We roamed, wandered where we could,
took our baths in a stream -
on days when overcast or grey,
we'd trek and bathe in a hot spring,

inhale the hot sulphuric vapours,
emerge pure and chaste again,
the weariness of life washed off,
the mosquito and bed-bug mites
gone but for a few red marks
soon lost in the bright sunlight
as we wound down the mountainside
to eat fruit or go inside
a little hut full of smoke,
be served a bowl of *tupa* soup,
prepared by an old Tibetan man
exiled from the Forbidden Land.

Back at our own humble shack,
an old haggered crow sold us milk,
she was the owner of the shack,
we bought her *dood* every morn,
every night took the can back.

In exchange we gave her cash,
listened to her biting bark -
Was it Punjabi? Hindi? What?

But we understood what she meant,
we were four backward boys
who made a mess wherever we went -
at the stream, out the back
when nature called, which once we'd gone
would n'er be left the same again.

We cleaned our act up very quickly,
we learned the local social order,
as guests when on the terraced slops,
we used no soap at the stream
from which they also drew their water.

We used no tissue for our toilet
but cleansed ourselves with water,
brought no tins and left them lying
where animals might ensnare themselves;
and cut no wood from the trees,
but used twigs to make out tea.

Such simple things thus observed
made life simple there for us -
our old hag began to smile,
left the milk can overnight;
we smoked our dope, twigged our fire
and lived as rustic ancients might
if they were living now.

One whole month in that nirvana,
passed like one long sunny day.

NARR: The Wanderer lost in time's mist,
brought me back from despair,
for my marriage, now, was off,

the girl of my dreams unsure,
had packed her clothes in poly bags,
left for her small Ayrshire town,
moved back to the council house
her mama kept in old Kilbirnie.

Listening on to the Wanderer,
sitting now in her best chair,
I thought of all the things I said,
the many things I'd forced along,
the silly things I had done
knowing not where I'd gone wrong.

Gone, two weeks before the nuptials,
and I two weeks just off forty -
I could not sit there any longer,
listening to my friend the Wanderer.
I had to act, go in searched
of my frightened, scared, lost fiance.

But the Wanderer carried on,
describing his journey to Delhi,
how he fell in with some crooks
in thronged, squalid Pahajang;
dodgy deals and crooked barter,
three weeks later Katmandu -
he was ringed by snow-capped mountains
in a valley close to Swayanbu.

I could not comprehend the beauty
of such a foreign far-famed place,
my thoughts were all for my Jean
on the Heights, Glengarnock way.

I had to rise, leave the Wanderer,
go and see her right away,
the Wanderer said I was foolish
to chase someone, let love escape,
but on the phone my brother said -

"If you love her – seize the day,
do not give up just because
she'd lost her will to say 'I do'.
Go after her! Take some flowers!
Tell her you need her, just the same".

So I rose, the Wanderer with me,
caught between Nepal and Bengal;
we took MacBrayne across the Clyde,
drove through rain, sheets of sleet,
and crashing waves Skelmorely way,
until we reached the lights of Largs.

The way bent above the bay
as I raced on beyond Kelburn,
snow-hemmed in by roadside banks
towards the mists of Muirhead dam,

613

then down into Kilbirnie town,
screeching through the cobbled streets
I turned into Bankfaulds estate,
halted outside Jean's mama's gate.

All this while the Wanderer rambled,
the journey making his tongue wag,
he spoke of reaching cold Darjeeling,
eating Christmas dinner there,
tucking into turkey roast,
brussels sprouts and all that stuff,
fruit pudding and a whiskey toast,
which made him ill, made him boke.

I knocked on Jeanie's Ma's back door,
and fell into Jeanie's arms -
we hugged and cried, and cried some more,
declared the fighting now was over.
I took the ring, clasped her hand,
put it on her curled third finger -
I put my hand upon her breast,
we kissed with such tenderness,
no words would give full express
of what it meant to be with her
instead of with my wandering friend.

I left Kilbirnie all alone -
for now I'll finally tell you that
the Wanderer is not a friend,
he is but part of myself -
I am the Wanderer! He is there
inside me, he shadows all I do;

And on the way back to Dunoon,
he talked to me about Calcutta,
the squalled filth of Sutter Street
where he had stayed for a week,
smoking hash, eating opium
before going on to holy Puri
to battle with the Indian surf,
to lie about getting burnt,
eating peanuts, sucking melon.

Outside the gates of the Temple
where Jaganath, Lord of Heaven
hauled juggernauts in procession
in honour of the three great gods -
Brahma, Shiva and his favourite
Vishnu, lord of all creation -
the Wanderer leaned that
God may never enter man,
for man is godless, sinned from birth,
he cannot be a god within,
but must instead let God in.

And as he traveled south in India,
and I along the Clyde coast road,

however much we are told
about the void beyond the whole,
about the quasi mass of holes
like caves in the cosmic glow -
we know nothing of this life,
we are ants marching on,
going nowhere in our march.

Oh yes, I may talk of India,
dwell upon my learnings there,
a boy, all of twenty years,
rolled up mat as a bed,
canvas bag beneath my head
containing all I possessed
except for the money round my neck
resting against my bare chest
in a purse beneath my vest.

And now, heading back to Dunoon,
almost forty, greying, balding,
home, car and own employment,
time to spare for enjoyment -
I felt empty, lost and scared
of life without someone there
to share my days, and my nights,
the lover I had left behind -
Jeanie Boyd of old Kilbirnie,
who had awoke, run away
across the bonnie banks o' Clyde.

To say her love for me had gone,
that I was now to carry on
without her smile, without her eyes,
without her in my daily life,
while all the time she wouldn't say,
she loved me dearly, for she was proud,
so proud she'd rather go to hell
than say she needed any help
with all the things troubling her.

Dear God, how love hurts,
how love is blind at times -
how clear it all becomes,
how murky it can turn
'til all one's hopes are burnt.

Not so in India, in Madras,
in Pondicherry, then Madurai,
where on the twenty fifth of March,
my twenty first year arrived -
I celebrated with a flight
from Truchi to north Sri Lanka,
landed on the Jaffna airstrip
happy to be alive.

For I was full of joie d'vive,
enjoying all things Ceylonese,

the world was an uncut jewel,
as I went about that garden isle.

From coral costed Hikkadua,
to the misty heights of Adam's peak,
here was a land seeped in culture,
painted caves and sculpture rock,
and Buddha's boa, planted there
by his wandering holy men,
declaring he was mere mortal -
that God was in everything,
and everything was part of God.

As I crossed the brooding Clyde,
looking over the ferry's side,
I saw what Siddhartha saw
in everything, and chided myself
for having been where I have been
and having not put aside
the torments of the inner self.

I'd lost myself in perfect love -
lost myself in Jeanie Boyd.

I knew then the time had come
to bury all my pasts for good.
I said goodbye to the Wanderer,
then cast him into the Clyde,
watched as he bobbed, then drowned
as the ferry docked at Kirn.

As I drove towards Innellan,
I knew he was gone from me -
at last I was once more free,
the weight of all my past now gone,
I looked towards a new dawn.
I'd fight to win back Jeanie Boyd.

I was finally home to settle,
to take my place, pay my taxes,
spend weekends in the garden,
have my Jeanie make me bairns,
have our home full of friends,
take long strolls on the sand,
climb the hill behind the house,
look out upon my native land,
bless my luck at being Scots;

home now the wanderer, once a boy,
home to settle as a man.

[End of the Wanderer Part Three]

FRANKIE BLACK (kids song)
[15th June 1992, Glasgow]

Frankie Black went for a walk,

He could barely even talk -
He saw the gate wasn't shut!
Now he's in big trouble.

Frankie Black the tiny tot
Escaped while his sisters fought,
Sitting on a tip, he coughed!
Now he's in big trouble.

Frankie Black the bully boy
Liked to make the girls cry.
He didn't have pals at all.
Now he's in big trouble.

Frankie Black was rather wild,
He liked to swing through the sky.
He couldn't sing but he could fly!
Now he's in big trouble.

Frankie Black was really tough,
He liked to jump, kick and run.
He didn't listen very much.
Now he's in big trouble!

VIEW FROM THE BRIDGE
[8.45-9.00pm, 10th Dec 1992, Pollok House Bridge, Glasgow]

Gone are the fishers, gone are the visitors,
Gone are the lovers, blossom and west wind -
Instead runs the river, northwards in winter,
Wearing the weir-stone and walls of the mill.

PRIDE
[3rd February 1993, Glasgow. ?]

Fair is the lily gilt …
Fair sweet the wild rose.
Napoleon on a beggar's horse?
Hitler cross-armed posed?
Too few like Garabaldi, Gandhi,
Descend to sing the small man's song;
Too few with humbled hang-dog looks
Stoop to conquer all.

Nay! Who would be in servile chains!
Who would drain their every vein!
Who would kiss the hem of Cain
Unless they were a saint.

The modest violet shadows the rose:-
With bashful blush it finds its fame
In the shade beneath an elm
Where timorous lovers play.
But oh beware! Also there
The pansy in self-love - in bloom!
Conceit and swollen cockiness
With the itch to please a fool.

Braggarts their trumpets blow
Louder than the big-talk daffs
Along the shore Wordsworth strode -
Butting the windy blasts.
Chatter, chatter, June to May,
They rave and rage, fuss and swagger;
They are bound, yet sway free;
Bluster, bluff and fury.

Let he - whose arrogance values pride
And all false traits so admired -
Let him ride his high horse home
Eight hands above the mire.
And he - whose insolent reply
Gives the world a curled lip -
Let him be the rose, the bud
And not the prick of it.

RIGHT, MATE
[3rd February 1993, Glasgow?]

What is right or proper, mate?
The seemly thing's not always decent.
Some will steer clear of scandal,
And some will have no shame.

The right of suffrage - that's justice.
The defence of sex - that's indulgence.
Some men knock their girlfriends up,
Then sure enough, they do a bunk!

One must reap where one has sown!
Do you believe this? Not me, nope.
All that comes our way is Fate,
And Newton's third is Karma, mate!

TRALEE
[1.30am, 10th Nov 1993, Tralee, Ireland]

The streets were empty
on a chilly Tralee night -
talk was of the fair Rose
etched on the Green Stone.

In search of a Kerry wife,
an old boy thick with the brogue
laid his wealth on his tongue
for a lass from Barrow.

Beneath James Street, the river flowed
whispering tales of ancient Ireland,
running west to the Atlantic,
'cross which half of Kerry departed.

Two girls born to every boy,
neckers in the burger bar,

618

petters up against a wall,
snoggers in a glass call-box.

Goodbye to the western world
on an iced November night,
sleeping in the county hotel
with a lassie by my side.

GEORGIE
[7.42pm, 5th June 1994, Hazelbank]

She came to me in her red clogs,
took me by the hand and led
me off into her velvet bedroom,
laid me down without a word,
stripped me of my raiments,
took me on a lover's voyage
across the wildest seas of anger,
through gale and fervent storm,
out into the brilliant moonlight
where all about was utter calm.

THE OLD PUPPETEER (fragment)
[1.45am, 1st February 1994, Hazelbank, Innellan]

Once upon a time in our land,
When times, like now, were very hard
And life most times was very sad,
A kind old fellow with a good spouse
Who'd lived all his life in the same house,
In the same bed with the same wife .....

WHERE HAVE YOU BEEN?
[midnight, 17th May 1994, Hazelbank]

She said she went for a walk on the beach,
she said she lost her way, went to a cafe,
she said she met a guy, went to his place
she said she got drunk, spent the night there.

CLAUDIE AND ME
[6[th]July 1994, Hazelbank, Innellan]

In Oban and in Inverness,
me and her were best of friends.
On the gold Lochinver sands
we bathed together, stood upon
Clochtoll broch, walked the strand,
hand in hand through the land
we travelled where no other had
thought the thoughts we two shared
in Smoo Cave's chasmic depth
or on Edinburgh's Castle steps
we meant all that we said
in Lochalsh or in Durness
or by Europe's oldest tree.

We were not Swiss, were not Scots,
we were lovers first and last
at Inverewe or Fort Augustus
we entwined, exposed our hearts
to the Scottish summer sun
thanked God for being young
and whole enough to take our fun
through the glens, up the duns,
to laugh louder than the rain
to take joy from the grey -
the grey wet of Inveraray,
where we first fell in love.

More quickly than a hungry gull
can swoop upon Kylestrome's waves
more swiftly than fleeing deer
can cross the East Ross moors
we came to test ourselves
as we passed Dalmally by,
renewed ourselves in Dunoon
and in Glencoe's Clachaig Inn
went onwards out into the wild,
sharing all we had to spend,
meaning every word we said,
knowing that the past was dead.

For we had just begun to sing
the song of the Toward seals,
the tunes of the doodlesack
we heard in every street -
This was mine and Claudie's Scotland,
a time so lovely we did not cry,
we did not pass one bad word
or do a single thing of harm,
we embraced the whole wide world
and it became part of us,
I became some part Swiss,
and she became part Scots.
This was our love.

IN THE RAIN
[8th Sept 1994, Sissach, Switzland]

In the rain the world stops,
it doesn't pour out it's heart,
it dries up like a desert,
sand blows across the land,
all that's living hides,
all that's open cries.

In the rain the mind closes,
it doesn't hear the singing,
it cannot smell the roses,
petals drop upon the floorboards,
all that's pretty's covered,
all that's beauty quivers.

THE SECOND KILLING OF THE WANDERER
[11th Sept 1994, Jungfrau (2,350m), Switzerland]

It was the time the Cubans came
in boats and rafts to Key West,
it was the time Rwandans died
in thousands in make-shift camps.

It was the time I made time
beneath the Eiger and Jungfrau,
high upon the warm Swiss Alps
mid-September on my own.

It was night, the rain came down
while upon the Wengen heights,
above Grenwald's fairy lights
far beyond the world I knew.

I drew upon a cigarette,
listened to the wind that blew,
for I had nothing else to do,
in Switzerland time passed slow.

Then the ghost that haunted me,
returned to me on the wind,
howling into my hollow brain,
once more ate into my soul.

That shadow ever at my back
who will not let the past depart,
who will not let me grow old,
or let me be a common man.

For that is what I wish to be,
no-one special, no-one important,
to let life run its course,
let it end without note.

I am torn, made unhappy
by this friend I once had,
he made my young years fun,
now he makes my mid-years hell.

For just when I think he's gone,
out of me for all time,
back he comes with his torment
to laugh and mock and scorn -

'til I am once more a wreck
who cannot settle for the norm.

It is of course, the Wanderer,
the devil part of my own self,
who I believe I had drowned
when pushed into the River Clyde.

But no! I was deluded,

by my own better self,
that I was ready to have kids
with Ayrshire Jeanie – my bride.

But she jilted, cut me off
from seeing her for all time,
and I was left bereft and ill
until well into summertime.

Then lo, I was saved by Claudie,
a village girl from Rheinfelden,
hitch-hiking on the Oban road,
I picked her up, we made friends.

We kissed, we touched, we made love
on an Oban hostel bed -
then spent ten days touring north,
the highlands and the island glens.

Making fires, bathing naked,
sleeping where nature bade us sleep,
until she flew back to Basle -
need I say she was Swiss.

Two months later there I was,
but now she had another boy,
and I was a forgotten joy
left to take my luck elsewhere.

So up the Jungfrau I went,
to go and start life afresh,
and there again, I don't regret
I killed the Wanderer.

THE WOODEN BRUCKEN
[12th Sept 1994, Luzern, Switzerland]

Bats on the black night waters
beneath Luzern's wooden brucken;
a bum drinks his budget beer
waiting for the swans to come
with their white angel-wings,
to carry him carefully up
from the cold concrete quay
to a bed made in heaven.

What hope has he in hell on earth
as the rain runs down his face;
his bottle empty, made from sand,
he throws it willfully at a swan -
but with a splash the waters part,
all is lost, his hope departs,
he flees his wet worthless life
across the ancient brucken spars.

DOWN A DUSTY ROAD
[11.45pm, 16th Sept 1994, Grez-sur-Loing, France]

Down a dusty road the way all travellers go,
That's how I saw life in Grez-sur-Loing -
Off the beaten track, no back-pack on my back,
I was on the slippery slope and didn't care.

I had beer to my lips, I was tobacco finger-tipped,
I had the stars above as my light -
It was Friday night. Should I dress for town?
No, be damned! To hell with Fountainbleau!

The moon peered thru trees like a big French cheese,
I ate it up as if I were Ben Gunn -
I was happy having fun, singing out my lungs
Down that dusty road all on my own.

THE LAND THAT WE LIVE IN
[4th- 8th Oct 1994, Hazelbank, Innellan]

What do we know
of the land that we live in
of the soil that we turn
the earth of our ancestors?
as we dig with our shovels
as we scrape with our fingers
as the leaves of the trees
drop on our dreamings? -

I see a ship sailing this way
sail of the Dugall
shield of the Fingall
an island offshore no longer there
washed by the tides
swept off by gales
the beach is all empty
where once there was fighting.

Beneath the clods of drowning clay
bones still fresh from yesterday
the sky moves like shifting sea
but the earth spews it's history.

What do we know
of the land that we walk on
the burnt open heath
the wilds of upland?
where forests took fire
where oceans ran dry
where seed on the wind
fell on our future? -

I hear a voice growing much louder
tongue of the Gael
song of warm welcome
pipes and drums gone to the grave
drone of the pibroch
rap of the snare

623

the hills are all forests
where once they were bare.

The worms traverse the embalming caves
rabbits warren where badgers lay
the rain descends upon the raised
walking and sharing the invisible.

What do we know
of the land that unites us
of the boundaries we guard
the mainland and islands
where sentries long dead
still patrol the eternal.

TA, DA, TA.
For My Father's 60th Birthday, 18th Oct 1994
[11.08am, 16th Oct 1994, Hazelbank, Innellan]

I have a dad, a great dad,
This poem is for his sixtieth birthday -
For when I think back all the years,
The things he's done to make me - me,
I cannot help but smile and say
'Ta, Da. Cheers!'

He taught me how to kick a ball,
How to fight, how to swim,
He even showed me how to row,
To use a hammer and a drill,
How to mend a leaking tap -
'Ta, Da. Cheers!'

So many things come to pass
Between a son and his dad -
Too often son with outstretched hand
Has his dad rescue him
From hunger, debt and foreign places -
'Ta, Da. Cheers.'

So here's to you, Da, thanks again,
Without you here I'd be lost ...
Oh by the way, my cistern's leaking
And the bank are on my back -
You couldn't just help me out ...
'Ta, Da. Cheers!'

THE CROWN COURT KARAOKE
[Friday, 21st Oct 1994, Crown Bar, Dunoon]

This is the place for karaoke –
Try and tell a simple joke
An' people break into song.
How can a man compete
With women singing 'Baby, baby'
Or guys like Perry crooning 'Rock-an-roll'?
Oh God, put me out on the road

Where I can find stars above me
Before I reach another pub.

THE KARAOKE SINGER
[12.47am, 24th Nov 1994, Hazelbank, Innellan]

Sing into the rafters, mate,
No-one knows, no-one cares,
No-one guesses you are sad,
No-one sees that you are down,
All about them's in a dance,
You are but the moment's voice
Belting out cheap romance -
A tune that makes someone cry,
A song that makes someone laugh -
While in the back-room of your mind
You are taken through a door
Leading out into the past,
Where you once stood in light,
Where someone once held you tight,
Where you were once left behind,
Left to get on with your life -

The crowd may not know it so,
Your song is not a string of lines,
Your voice is from another time,
Your thoughts are sunk in your sublime,
That place where all your memories go,
The sad, the bad, the untoward,
That guilt has hidden far within,
Where pride has covered up the sins
Which each of us will not admit
Except through songs others wrote -

So sing, mate, without reserve,
Sing your tears without reproach
While the world about applauds
Your song - dredged up to mask your voice,
Your misplaced thoughts in a song
Upon your lips in the pub!

You are alone before the world,
No-one knows, no-one cares -
All about you's in a dance
Listening to your cheap romance,
Inside you are a mixed-up mess -
What'd you mean it's my turn next?

OUT OF LOVE
[3.58am, 26th Nov 1994, Hazelbank, Innellan]

Out of love, no special one,
no girl to keep the winter warm,
no tressed-head upon my chest
no sweet lips pressed on mine
no whispered words willing me
to do what I have not done -

625

I sleep alone, content and sound,
I rise and naked go about
all the things I might hide
if I were in love again -
I may miss the warm caress,
I do not miss the arguments.

MRS HAUSER
[1.03am, 1ˢᵗ December 1994, Hazelbank, Innellan]

If I were to say to you
All the things I felt inside,
All the beauty that I see
In your eyes and in your smile –
Then I would talk about the stars,
The bees about the honey flowers,
I would wax about the moon
And wane upon the changing tides;

I would chase the free-born deer
And run upon the linged brae-sides,
I would catch the breeze-borne seed
And dwell beneath the towering pines;
I would swim below the linns
And come to shore on lochan isles,
I would touch the spreading fern,
Inhale the breezes from the south.

For if I were to kiss your cheek
And tingle as I surely would –
All the troubles of the world
Would melt and never freeze again,
For I would feel your soft skin
Against my face, upon my lips,
And I forever smote by you
Would never kiss another then.

I would for all time be charmed,
Bewitched beyond a heavenly earth,
I would softly kiss your brow,
Your eyes, your cheeks, and your nose,
I'd gently kiss you to your toes,
And whisper through your scented hair,
Then listen for your whispers back
Like drifting smoke upon a gale.

SHE WAS THE AGE OF BYRON
[10.12am, 27ᵗʰ Dec 1994, Dunoon]

She was the age Byron died,
Burns too when he went
to that happy land of bards
where poetry's never dead.

I must admit she wrote no verse
that we might view now she's gone,

she left no marks upon a page
we might judge her for.

Her poetry was in her touch,
the way she reached out and loved;
a single word whispered low,
barely more than a moan.

Yes, now she's gone – up to
get the kids dressed for school;
she'll be back at five to nine
with poetry on her lips.

FRAGMENTS OF TIME
[11.57pm 15th Jan 1995 Dunoon – 10.36pm 29th Apr 1995
Hazelbank, Innellan]

Let no man say he's found
God in the eyes of his wife –
nor any wife declare aloud
that her spouse despises love –
too few are here a hundred years,
too few are wise enough for us.

Ten years ago Roderick announced
that he was free from his bonds;
he was done with family cares,
free of all the twosome ties.
The time had come to finally live
to do and try the yet undone,
yet none of those he'd befriended
liked or shared his new lifestyle –
they abhorred his evening jaunts,
they discussed his fickle wants,
they whispered in the lowest tones
behind his naked back.

The bells still ring every Sunday,
and every Monday sure as rain,
the children pull on their black tights,
tuck their blouses into waistbands.
All those sleepy puffed eyed faces
splashed and made bright and shiny –
there goes the future up the hill,
lunch-boxes swinging in the wind.
Ba ba blacksheep, Jack and Jill …
no man can sing such honest tunes;
time passes like a speeding train
across us lying on the track –
we lose a limb, perhaps a hand
until we are beyond repair.

Lord! If you are out there somewhere,
Don't hide away like some recluse;
There's folks down here need some help,
who haven't had a chance in hell,
snatched from the void of birth,

627

thrust into the dark of life –
who knows where to find light
when all about is deathly pale.
Mystics, yes, but missing too;
gurus, yes, through and through,
knowledge enters, knowledge leaves –
the wisest men are also fools.

Susan laid her tarot cards upon
the carpet when the light went out –
and by the candlelight she read
the future through the night.
The wild wind blew gale force twelve,
the river broke the sea-wall front,
cars washed over the watery edge,
their headlamps, to the turmoiled depths
sunk into the briny waste
while Susan dealt out Death.

Know we nothing, nothingness –
Empty is the human head.
Stand upon the highest hill –
See you the distant universe?

Maxwell smoked a cigarette,
tossed it half-done in a bin,
gulped his coffee, rushed his lunch,
burped and paid the hotel clerk.
His brief case sagged in tiredness,
his suit hung like Frederic West;
he crashed through the one-way door
out into the wilderness.

Tuesday always brings the same –
children staying home from school;
mothers take their headache pills,
go screaming through another day;
while on the phone officials moan
that they're hated by their peers,
that they are grey, as others spend
the tax they should declare –
such envy in their petty words,
malice in their righteous airs.

Who is honest now, dear John,
point him out, or her, and croon
that out there - who's never tried
to cheat, nor steal, not told a lie
in this land of broken numpties,
where broken things are never fixed.

On the ghats of old Benares,
bodies for the pyre await –
the flies are warded off by incense,
harm is bayed by mantric chant,
pensive mourners cleanse their ills
as holy helpers beat on drums.

Mr.Watson packed his bin-liner,
left behind his pile of bills,
he ran off to a Russian mistress,
promised her he'd go straight –
but time repeats itself like Accurist;
he ripped her off, fled to Spain.

Such episodes are all too common,
we shall not speak of him again;
life is shorter than a toothbrush,
a little longer than a pen –
toothpaste tube squeezed, discarded,
ink running dry before the end.

Lovers know what others don't,
that time is short, running out –
they cling despairingly in tears,
count the hours they are apart,
send intruding friends away,
walk in wind and rain, and go
where few seldom make a path
upon the edge of a cliff –
a ledge above a violent gorge
beneath a pine by raging falls.

Lovers know the fruitless aims of man,
they give themselves no false hopes,
they breathe, the wind, the rain and laugh,
catch time in their clasping hands,
pass their eyes across the sky,
across the wide world expanse,
they return to walk and move
from wooded wild to windy moor.

Time makes all drift apart,
this is the way of all things –
the Sun deserts the day at dusk,
the Moon denies night at dawn;
for when the morning rays come over
the hills beyond the ebbing tide,
the evening sinks into the waves
beyond the other side of life.

Meanwhile on this side of time,
Bobby rubbed his pot-marked nose,
Daphne laid him on her bed,
wrapped a towel about his face,
made him lie still and quiet,
squeezed his blackheads one by one.
He cried in pain, thrashed his legs
as she cleansed his filthy snout,
wiped it raw with a cloth,
then daubed his agony with ice,
eased the hurt with natural oils,
kissed him softly on the mouth –
made love to him for an hour,

then made lunch while he dressed
and went to look at himself –
skin gleaming, face now cleansed,
except his beak was totally red.

Beauty in the seeker's eye,
mirrors rarely every lie –
what you view is what you know
about yourself however dark.

Children never know themselves,
they change, grow, daily learn
that what they were yesterday
can be altered on a whim –
a few tears shed undoes wrong,
a sideways look defeats authority,
a simple 'sorry' earns more love
than any adult lover claws
by care or service to a mate.
For children are raw creation,
animals born to be instructed
with all our foolish human traits -
we take their wildness, break their will
and substitute their good with guilt.

We were once children too –
we know what was done to us;
we need not dwell on such things
for it makes us mostly sad.
For sad are many folks always,
never shown or offered joy,
lost in some murky past,
they through life stagger on –
some waiting for a Prince to show,
or fearing a knock at their door.

There are those in fitful sleep
receiving visits from the dead –
a grandma's scowling angry face
scolding them for guilty deeds;
its little wonder they are ill
and fear the coming of the night
when every sound is a ghost
come to haunt, rob their rest,
leave them useless in the day,
racked with pain, terror ridden
they cannot function, smile or laugh,
they are tortured every thought,
brought so low they crave love
to save them from pointless death.

Not so James with his hammer,
making shelves with his toys,
tools that boys dream of owning,
electric drills, saws and sanders,
cleaned with care, love and thought,
used to hone and dress hewn timber,

endless hours in his shed
shaving down boughs of lumber.
Each piece is James's Mona Lisa,
or products of his misty faith,
such as a Christ on a cross;
for James is sick of facing life,
so he hides in his shed –
enjoying the rest, his quiet pursuit
shaping bits of forest wood
that harms none, so no one cares
he puts his shelves up, places there
all the artifacts he's made –
while all the time his house is bare,
lacking carpet, curtains, chairs –
a simple life is all he craves,
and so he lives day to day.

Meanwhile in far Macedonia,
Trevor teaches what he can;
eager eyes and cocked head kids
listen to his English words -
for he could not speak to them
in Greek or Serb or Albanian.
He is there 'cause no one else
wished to work in distant Skopje,
and now in all his thirty years
he's never been quite so happy –
he is free of all his past,
he's got himself a Veles lass,
he has plans to let time pass
in love in Macedonia.

Walking to the beauty parlour,
swept before a north-east wind,
Madge has made another boob –
she's dyed her hair shocking blue.
Quick rinse set from a tin,
she pulls down her floppy hat,
and 'cause she is a size eighteen
her mink coat bulges at the hips.
She really must get rid of it,
place an ad in the Gazette,
exchange the beast for a car -
she's had enough of taking cabs,
she'd rather risk a heart attack
than have a cabbie make a quip.

Then in a gust, her hat blows off,
tumbles down the crowded street;
all the world turns to stare …
poor Madge in complete despair
runs into a baker's shop
throws some flour in her hair.

Now she looks more her age,
white from years of toil and wear,
a pensioner lifts his hat to her

631

as she wobbles on her way
a block or two to the parlour
to have her hair re-dyed grey.

Time shows on our faces
Time leaves all its traces
Time cannot be evaded
Our time is now.

DEAR LOVED ONE
[Spring ?1995, Hazelbank, Innellan]

A thousand kisses on your lips,
A thousand hands upon your hips,
A thousand thoughts when you're missed -
I am yours, oh loved one!

THE ALBANIAN TRADER
[10.36pm, 22nd March 1995, Piraeus, Greece]

Cold blew the wind across Attica
North-east down from frozen Russia
The coastline grey and uninviting
The sea cruel, the tide-line garbaged
As evening darkened the horizon
The ill drove to buy their medicines
Taverna owners washed their salads
Widows mopped their floors of marble
The lonely clenched their packs of Marlbros
Curators locked away their statues
As I flew into dismal Athens
On my way to far Tirana.

I missed the kids and their mother
I remembered all past horrors;
Life upon the road is empty
When love is traded for a hotel
And the whine of cars and buses
The pain and shudder of the city
I could not hear the lapping waves
Nor the gulls I'd left behind
At my home, by the sea
In tranquil, quiet, sweet Argyll -
Where horses pound along the sands
Where seals bask upon the rocks
Where redwoods tower to the sky
And garlic grows upon the cliff.

Instead, I had picked Piraeus
To spend a lonely night in Greece
In a spartan Attic room
Waiting for the time to go
Recalling slowly all I've done
To bring about all that's passed
To make me leave the perfect dream
Of life in an idyllic land.

Hazelbank! My cottage house
Where every day is happiness
Gazing out upon the sea
Out across the Firth of Clyde
With the kids and their mum
Who I loved more than Greece.

I always knew I'd come to lose
That which I knew I had
When at home in the garden
With the children in the mud
Trying to tame the mountain burn
That gushes from the rocky cliff
That we hoped to bring to flower
To plant and make work for us
Which in our hearts we did not want
We were doing it for the fun
For in Argyll, nature wins.

And now, discontent with happiness,
I had come to the Balkans
On some wild business scheme
Some mad idea to make a fortune.
And if this meant a night in Greece
In some wayward room in Piraeus,
It was not for myself, but for the future
So we might someday tame the burn
Girth with rocks, guide it seaward
Make it gurgle, sing and sparkle
Make it babble over stone
Let it travel fully noticed
Let it not seep and leach
Into the earth of Argyll.

Too many men seep into the unknown
Lives lived that never sparkle
Existence sinking without trace
Seeping in and never running.
Therefore, a night - a Greek hotel
Was a journey to the beach
To gather up, carry stones
Over which I might run.

If not, it was with the knowledge
That I did not desire change
But had to prove to myself
That what I had was beautiful
By the shore of the Clyde
Far away in far Argyll.

TIRANA URCHIN
[Midnight, 24th March 1995, Tirana, Albania]

In the folds of the mountains
Neath the peaks of Dahti high,
An urchin slept in a doorway
Nowhere home, nowhere to go;

Left behind his childhood dreams
Beyond a distant mountain pass.

LOST
[10.22pm, 25th March 1995, Tirana, Albania]

I am a child in search of a mother,
I am a boy in search of the child,
I am a man being a father,
I am a father being a boy.

HOXHA'S BUNKERS
[2.27pm, 25th March 1995, 7km from Tirana, Albania]

Sitting on a Hoxha bunker
On my birthday in Albania,
Tirana spread out below
Like Kathmandu or Managua,
Nothing big on the horizon
Ringed by mountains, grazed by goats,
Third world housing in construction
In a nation long cut off.
Europe where is your compassion
For a people few of us know?

Here a people poor and hardy,
Here a nation hungry cold,
Here a people warm and friendly
Like the Afghans and the Poles.
Here a nation with no tourists,
Here a people badly clothed,
Here a nation full of smiles
Despite the Hoxha years of old.

In Albania on my birthday,
Far from my own wealthy land -
I have money in my pocket,
One year's wages here at least.
Is it right that I am rich
In a land, dusty, poor?
Europe, where is your guilt?
Albanians are one with us.

All through time, Greek and Roman,
Turk, Italian, German too
Have trudged across Albania's soil
Taken what they wanted, gone.
Communism gave them nothing
But a system doomed to fail;
Where now Albania? What future
With your new dawn?

Here in Albania on my birthday
I have no answers to the past,
I have some questions for the future,
Man is never equal born.
There is no succour in religion,

There is no faith in politics,
Yet I can hope for better times
Though many doubt an optimist.

Oh Albania, free of Europe,
Perhaps its better to be lost
In your mountains, on your beaches
Which still yours, are not yet sold;
For once the sharks, the piranha
Arrive from Europe with their bucks,
A few of you will surely profit
But most of you will suffer loss.

Loss of what? The open question,
Time has shown you are naïve,
A nation open to suggestion,
You've fallen foul of foreign greed.
So beware the Anglo Saxons,
The Italians, French and the Greeks,
Remember Hoxha's concrete bunkers
And why there was once a need.

STOLEN LOVE
[12.41am, Easter Monday, 17th Apr 1995, Hazelbank, Innellan]

Too soon in love, yet not quick enough
I fell in love with a lady –
On the arm of a man abusing her charm
Without any qualms, without a delay
I said to myself 'She is for me!
I'll set her free!' and hatched a plan
That only a man in love understands.

For there before me across the floor
At a table she sat, unable to laugh
With the man with his hand on her wrist.
With a twist, he took the blood from her face,
Blackened her eyes with a snide aside,
Made her lips colour like an icy river
Forever shivering over a frozen weir.

I was right in deciding to fight –
A beautiful woman being slowly destroyed,
A toy in the hands of a childish man.

NAPPING
[10.52pm, 29th Aug 1995, Hazelbank, Innellan]

Let no man know a single sound
That he has not some knowledge of,
For if he comes upon a crash,
A bang, or some unprepared smash,
His heart will jump and fain attack
At having thus been caught out.

LOOKING FOR A DIRTY WORLD
[11pm, 29th Aug 1995, Hazelbank, Innellan]

There is more than I can say herewith
About the months I've let pass –
I have left the ink pen down …
Instead let my fingers type
A novel spanning twelve decades
In which I barely reach the truth
Of all the things I want to clean
From my cluttered inner cave.

I have not missed my verse,
Thought or pined for its loss.
No! I am free to fictionalise,
Break from true poetic mood;
For who has want of trite confession
When there is sex within a book,
Who would not read of murder,
Deceit and fortunes made from war.

Poetry's for corrupted spirits,
Cleanser of the wild debaucher;
Prose is for the clear of conscience
Looking for a dirty world.

THE SECRET WATERFALL
[1.56pm, 12th Sept 1995, Hazelbank, Innellan]

There is beyond my house a hidden glen
Down which a tumbling stream cascades,
With sides so steep it takes a man
From brink to brink of gaping death.

No fool would lightly scale down there
With outstretched arms descend by choice,
Except in search of what he'd heard,
But what as yet he had not found.

There is – so village folk recount,
A secret pool below that fall –
An enchanted lair of ages past
Where lovers hid and murderers drank.

I descended, found that pool -
Stood mute beneath the thunderous spray,
Half blinded, saw the cascade foam
And curdle all my senses.

NEIDER SACHEN
For Nadine and Vanessa
[15th September 1995?, Hazelbank, Innellan]

When the days were not right,
We crossed the sea, we three
Drove into the night, six days
We slept out upon the moors,
Turf stacks, across the fields
Deer hid in the aspen.

NO ONE TRAVELS ALONE
[1.07pm, 14th Sept 1996, Route 90(84) circa Sturbridge, Mass]

No one who travels alone, travels alone,
There's always someone to meet on the road.
Speaking in Spanish to grey-haired Italians,
Or listening to Yale grads talking in Gaelic;
Busing from Mass, thru Rhode to Conn.
If you travel alone – you're not on the bus.

RUNNING FROM THE HURRICANE
[1.36pm, 14th Sept 1996, Mile 77 (84) southbound, USA]

Boston to New York, the green slips by,
The scoured bedrock blasted by time,
The pre-autumn trees touching the hem
Of the hurricane clouds marching by.

What is beyond the grassy soft shoulder
Edging existence mile after mile?
Signposts hint of satellite cities
Beyond the aspen, cedar and pine.

Rolling black tarmac bridging brown springs
Flowing from sources still not found;
Out of the green New York rises
Into the grey of the hurricane night.

WASHINGTON CATHEDRAL
(for Maisie Gordon Whitman)
[17th September 1996, Washington DC]

There on a hill in the white water rain
flooded in light, the evening song -
the swish of a tyre, the pull on a brake,
a cut of an engine, and a headlamp fade.

High heel upon limestone steps
beneath vaulted arch and buttressed nave -
beyond the trees on Capitol Hill,
Congress wrestles with the devils's ways.

Conscience weary and heavy souled,
shoulders wet and hurricane blown -
as the choir recants a godly tune,
a lost soul prays by Wilson's tomb.

Embalmed in a mantle of cathedral stone,
shed of sins and skinned with hope -
presidents seek and senators uncover
a higher law than the laws they order.

There on a hill in the spiraling rain,
tail-end to another hurricane,
above the flood and Washington's ways
a whiter house prevails.

SILENCE
[1.03am, 4th April 1997, Priesthill, Glasgow]

Never is the quiet moment so silent,
So still that life is stagnant;
For always there is a stirring,
Somewhere there is a movement,
Somehow there is always something
Not quite settled, nor married
Enough to tarry, or stay.

POPPING OFF AND LOST
[10.54pm, 16th June 1997, Priesthill, Glasgow]

Waiting for tomorrow in the twilight hour,
Summer on us now as in younger days.
What becomes of time in the silent fall;
Heavy dyed clouds heading this way.

No one can remember the minute just gone,
Who will have recorded it all anyway?
Life's a button hanging by a thread,
Popping off, and lost on a rainy day.

SHOPPING TROLLEYS
[Near midnight, 23rd July 1997, Hazelbank, Innellan]

From the Auldhouse Burn near Newlands
To Levern Water, just past Crookston,
A dozen little streams feed and nourish
The River Cart edging on to Renfrew.

Somewhere between Pollokshaws and Paisley,
Out of Barrhead, drops Brock Burn,
Draining Barrhead, Nitshill and Darnley,
Its shopping trolleys rusting in its mud.

TOWARD POINT
[12.49am, 24th July 1997, Hazelbank, Innellan]

Sand through the hands on a rocky shore,
Altars for prayers near standing stones,
Crystals of coal washed by the sea,
Sharded clay icons on black feathered scree.

Breaking of boulders lodged by white ice,
Mountains of pink cliffs atop of debris,
Walkways of paving, child like created,
Below strong lights shadowed by techno.

War in the distance on a ferned slope,
Cone gatherer silhouetted under Welsh slate cope,
Hatless cyclist and coat-less barefooted wife
Search the seal-less water for signs.

DOON VALLEY - DUNASKIN

[3.29pm, 14th September 1997, Dunaskin, Aryshire]

The legacy left by spirits now gone,
Pit-rows demolished traced by moss,
Wind mixed music scraping the rust
Of machines and structures abandoned.

Deep in the dark of watery faces,
Deep within the empty brick kilns,
On the slag slopes overlooking vast acres,
The waste of man's labours remains.

Hot are the hills steaming in winter,
Owls nest snoring in craters of flux,
Green is Doon Valley hedgelessly gardened
Out of the ashes of work.

NIPPED AT
[11.12pm, 1st October 1997, Priesthill, Glasgow]

Lost in the anger of unfinished business,
Left to the torment of bitter exchanges,
Red-faced and tempered, over-extended,
Reaching for objects to signal distress -
Such is the outrage of patience that's ended,
Such is the outcome of lovers at odds.

EL NINO'S YEAR
[15th January 1998?, Hazelank, Innellan]

Marked by memories, turns another year
obscured by cluttered recall, void of resolutions.

Gales lash south of wild isolation,
sandbags discarded, lie in doorways;
the Little Bay calm, swans in ceilidh;
second-hand shops empty of all rain-wear;
mist halfway down the snow-topped ridges
ice-aged and scarred by all that's passed.

Lerag Cross shattered in three pieces
stands iron girded guarding Kilbride glen;
moody vapours swirl the crippled chapel;
the roofless tumble stoned MacDougal graves
stacked so high the churchyard gapes upwards
to engulf the overtired blue Argyll sky.

Near to distant whispers reach the ocean
traveled by those dispatched by angry hands.

Time offers no escape nor solace in this landscape
from city life's grubby deals and money grabbers;
seas and lochs and tumbling mountain chasms
do not erase an old year, and bring another -
time is mindful, minds are full of time,
times of failure, times of doubt and sorrow.

A fish box grinding on the loch-side gravel
by shore paths tread for centuries, now uncharted;
mated herons skimming outbound, homeward going,
carrying the crofting ghosts of Ardentallon.

Sleep contains no cave to hide from history;
closed eyes hold visions worse than living;
faces rising out the night marsh, gatecrash oblivion.

Grey rising dawn, grey falling evening;
wet scud morning, wet dreary gloaming;
the driving drench of Western kenning.

Bridges built to belittle mighty oceans
cannot save the damned from Christian forces;
rock wracked slatey Easdale is St.Helena.

No escape from destiny by moral action;
doomed to failure by a labyrinth of choice;
New Year brings no new beginning.

Kilmelford churchyard shuttered, fenced, locked;
salvation in the rain there shall not be.

If there is hope in the wail of winter
within the shadow of black mountained Mull;
if there is faith in the fists of Morven
or the fissures of Ossian's fabled world -
ruin stands between ambition and fortune
in the shelter of Kerrera's horse-shoe coves.

If darkness ends in the caves of Olaf,
respite must ripple back from Lismore;
Dunollie bleak, broken, haunts the treeline;
Dunstaffnage black and barren haunts the shore -
it's bleach barked beeches limed on buried bone.
Sunlight breaks through on Ben Cruachan;
Ardchattan repels the wrack and fuming loch;
in a near-by glen, a white spate falls.

Out beyond the mainland, island driven
the future runs between Aros and Tobermory;
cliffs of road, and crags of single highway,
plunge and rise double-crossed by tomorrow -
Christ-crushed by Columba of Iona.

Rock-wrecked smack at Creuig Point,
broken pier and derelict houses rubble ruined,
minor shadows flirting in the lichened oaks,
sirens screaming in the wind by Dutchman's Cap,
deadly pools and eddy's round Staffa's stacks,
deserted Ulva haunted by Kilninian's ghosts -
wailing for the return of the young.

Sleep is no escape from weary winter,
upright standing sentinel guarding Lonan,
ancient birch and alder ripe with catkin,

oak and larch, and one lone red Scots pine -
all that's left from Bonawe's charcoal smelting,
pig iron for the ploughs, post Culloden.

January blows and spring has passed -
Sirocco breezes buffet as El Nino comes.

Falls of Lorn, silent running, black and brooding;
Linn of Avich, cascading, raging lochwards;
crannogs and causeways long since out of usage;
drover roads traversing Loch Awe clachan strewn;
Carncassie Castle tower, a virtual ruin;
Kilmartin's cysts and cairns stripped of treasure;
ring and cup marks, on the march to Dunadd.

In the landscape, only ghosts can hunt -
in our time, the dead are large in number.

There in the fields with their tumbling dykes;
there in the streams, in the forests, on the lochs;
there in every boulder, stone or rock -
there in the past where our ancestors dwelt;
the living and the dead jointly walk.

LEAVING HAZELBANK
[1.22pm, 18th March 1998, Dunoon-Gourock Ferry]

A house where laugher rung,
Empty now with death is hung,
A garden filled with children's singing,
Now's overhung with brooding laurel -
Sands where lovers took long strolls,
Now are strewn with wrack and litter.

Time puts its hand upon my shoulder,
I dare not turn and look behind
At all that's withered during life;
For still ahead lies the hope
That what I want is still to come,
And that which comes will bring me joy.

FAR AWAY FROM THE FUTURE
[8.20pm, 16th July 1998, Cayton Bay, Yorkshire]

Why fret away the future before today is gone?
All about is finer than it was …
My house of ill-repair is rightly sold,
I stand upon the threshold of a new abode.

Welcome friends come bearing lucky charms,
The composer, countess and banker laugh -
My duchess lover climbs the stair to bed;
I linger on as master of all past debts.

Fortune winks at me in the evening sun,
Warm winds flow through favoured haunts;
Children's laughter covers all my cowering doubts;

Today is with me now, and tomorrow walks.

AELLE'S POEM
[9.50pm, 30th November 2001, Tyndrum, Argyll]

Wounded by warring, worn with walking
High in the hills, hankering for home
Wrestled from women, wrenched from wenching
The weary warrior stands alone.

Blooded by battle, axe blade broken
Spear shaft smashed, helmet hewed
Chanting war cries, stirring the sleeping
The warrior waits, bereft of brew.

Thirsty for fighting, hungry for hunting
Slinging of shields, singing of swords
Proud in his posture, brave in his bearing
The warrior wishes to fight his foes!

AERIC'S POEM
[9.03am, 3rd May 2006, Camden Market, London]

Sailed from shore, shipped from storms.
I sought and slayed my kin's killer
Avenged in anger, Aeric's axe
Fell foully on Aeric's foes,
Cruelly cleft Fingal's naked neck
Claimed his land with Woden's sword.

NOT TO BE SEEN
[12.13am, 1st October 2008, Crick Bung, Denham, Bucks]

Not to be seen, not to be heard,
The voice of the naked, the face of the child,
Wandering the alleys and lanes of the West,
Straggling the roads stretching no end.

LEAP NOWHERE
[12.17am, 1st October 2008, Crick Bung, Denham]

Leap nowhere without faith
And never look back
On the deeds of the doer
Or the sins of the pack.

THE ROAD OF NECESSITY
[10.01am, 4th April 2009, Crick Bung, Denham]

The road of necessity is the way of despair,
The need of the poor is the want of the rich:
From heaven to earth, mountain to sea
The traffic is heavy on the path to the cliff.

SHE LIKES TO RUN
For Suzie
[11.19am, 4th April 2009, Crick Bung, Denham]

She likes to run in beautiful places
Far from the cry and hue of the city,
Where she can be ordered and perfect,
Her breath the wind wed to the wild.

QAWRA
[1pm, 12th April 2009, Qawra, Malta]

Free in the sun to swim and run,
To pound the sand, brave the surf,
Take the shade in the terrace trees,
Stare at the stars in the midnight breeze:
Find the dawn in the rising east,
Kiss your lover and feast till lunch.

SEVENTH DECADE
[10.15am, 3rd Jan 2010, Crick Bung, Denham]

Each decade turns the pages of time
Between the sheets the sun revolves:
The heat of the day, the ice of the night
I wake to eat, I wait in line,
I walk the moors, I wade my brooks,
I whittle every passing hour -
Watch the waves turn the sand,
Wish and want my fading child
To turn, retrace the wandering road
I first trod so well alone.

SUZIE
[7.54am, 7th July 2011, Estonia]

I am an island in a sea of dreams
Caught in a storm - harbour with me.
I am fresh water, shelter and calm -
A rock in an ocean of wild drowning fear.

I'M STILL BREATHING
[10.24am, 20th January 2014, Denham]

Today I woke up and thought –
I owe forty thousand,
I can't pay the rent this month,
In two months time I'm sixty.
You know what – who cares!
I'm still breathing.

[END OF MIDDLE WORKS]

SIXTY
[1.40am, 26th March 2014, Denham]

Today I return to poetry
Like I said I would twenty years ago –
I am ready to fill in the gaps,
Re-find my purpose in life,
Throw off the trappings of comfort,
Strip the veneer of convention from myself,
Re-discover my reason for breathing.
I am sixty – I have made it this far –
How much further is there still to go?

ALEX THE COUNTESS
[2.13am, 26th March 2014, Denham]

A talent with a voice and a smile –
A woman on a mission, but no nun.
The world owes her nothing, so she fights
Her corner – every round brings some hurt.

Her courage takes her the distance –
On the ropes or punching above her weight,
She covers the ring like a dancer
And is on her feet at the ringing of the bell.

AT LAST THE SUN IS HERE
[12.20pm, 29th March 2014, Denham]

At last the sun is here –
The wind has dropped, and Spring
Like the heads of drooping daffodils
Floods our garden with colour.

Once more I can sit in the yard,
Catch the early ultra-violet light
As our planet whizzes round the sun,
And our days lengthen.

Wet the winter may have been –
Yet I did not miss the snow,
Nor the cold and icy Northern blast
Endured last year.

Joy! It comes on us thus –
The birth of new and better days,
The hope of better times before me,
And an end to all decay.

EASTER MONDAY
[10.15am, 21st April 2014, Denham]

The resurrection and the life,
Blue skies clear to heaven,
Schoolboy days of boiled eggs
Rolled down parkland knolls.

I laze in slumber mode –
Through the haze of condensation,
The ticking clock counts down
The hour to morning mass.

I will not attend or pray –
Age has not destroyed my will.
If God exists, then I know
I will keep him to myself.

A BETTER MAN
[10.32 am, 21st April 2014, Denham]

If I were a better man,
And not some flimsy artist,
I would have made my mark,
Done something to be proud of –

Instead I've spent forty years
Engaging in self-absorption,
Soaking up my own persona
In a series of dramatic acts.

A better man would have done
A single feat of outstanding merit,
Instead I've been hacking on,
Making little headway through the jungle.

A better man is plain to all,
Stands above, leads the crowd,
Moves us on to better things,
Asks for nothing in return.

Instead, I think on myself -
Preservation of my own lifestyle,
Protection of my worldly goods
The hoarding of my next twenty years.

WOMEN
[10.38am, 21st April 2014, Denham]

Women are creatures of fickle nature,
Prone to blowing with the wind –
Reason does not wrestle with them,
It bullies them into submission –
Cursed with worry, they give up,
Throw themselves into the nearest arms.

OVER THE HORIZON
[11.27pm, 29th April 2014, Denham]

When you get older you start looking back
At where you have been, not where you're going.
It's easier to turn and look over your shoulder
Than to face the future shortening in length –

Whilst the past is longer and getting longer still,
What waits ahead is nearing each day –
It takes some courage to greet it warmly
For it does not offer comfort or certainty.

Whilst the past contains days of hope,
Times of joy, lost summers of plenty –
The path before us goes over the horizon
Where those we knew, never turn back.

LOOKING BACK ON LETTERS
[11.10pm, 30th July 2014, Denham]

Looking back on letters written forty years ago,
I didn't like myself as I was –
But after two days of depressed reflection
I re-read them all in posted order –
Realised that – out of context
The actions of my past were ordered.

The fear brought on by the rediscovery
That I was a wild thoughtless youth,
Had been groundless. I was nineteen,
Full of life, and energy, and lust –
A boy who couldn't get enough excitement,
Nor restrained by the obligations of love.

MADE HOMELESS BY COMMITTEE
[11.22pm, 30th July 2014, Denham]

I'm being made to vacate my bungalow
By a heartless bunch of capitalist democrats –
By committee my life has been decided;
By cold letter the order passed down.

At first, I thought to fall on reason,
Request an answer as to why?
Deaf ears and cruel cynical rebuff
Followed on my cries for redress.

Now I fight to some soon-end
That must come somewhere down the line;
In the sand is drawn my destiny,
And in my heart the battle lost.

Yet still a small flame burns –
Perhaps justice will be done?
I'll be rescued from my homeless future
by a new enlightenment.

It is small beer for seven years –
A home's a home, home is here;
Uprooted at the age of sixty
Is not a tragedy I predicted?

I will adapt, depart my idyll,
Like I did from far Argyll –

646

For life's a wheel ever turning,
Rolling on to other lands.

FUCHSIA SAGS IN DISARRAY
[11.17am, 7th September 2014, Denham]

Autumn draws us to our windows
To dwell on the summer now lost,
The hope for sunshine breaking through
And warming us with some love.

The cricket field empty now
Reminds us of lost hot-days –
Apples droop from bending boughs,
Fuchsia sags in disarray.

THE 45
[1.31am, 21st September 2014, Denham]

They made their mark in ordered fashion
Without allegiances to a single party –
They registered their voice for freedom,
Showed the world how it was done.

The Brits threw in the kitchen sink
And half the contents of the living room,
Yet still they could not shake belief
Their lies, their peddled ware.

The vote to separate is over –
An aftermath of unchanged ways,
An emptiness that leaves Scots nothing,
Turns now to renewed effort.

Scotland our land, beloved by all,
We fight to free it from its past,
Not what we were, but what we'll do
Dangles before us within our grasp.

16th NOVEMBER
[11.21am, 16th November 2014, Denham]

The bastards still don't have me out,
And Christmas is on its way –
A court date will not be set
'til well after Hogmanay.

So for the now, I live rent free,
Get to think about my future –
Get the time to enjoy small things
And triumph over small adversities.

IT IS TOO PEACEFUL
[11.33am, 16th November 2014, Denham]

The leaves hang on the trees like no tomorrow,
The birds sing as if it is Spring –

What's happened to our usual weather?
Or are we lulled into complacency?

It may be damp and muddy underfoot,
But flowers blooming as if it is summer?
Squirrels scurrying here and there
As if it is the month to find a mate.

It is too mild, far too peaceful,
Something's up? What's about to happen?
Whatever comes, the now is restful,
The calm before the storm arrives.

AS BEAUTY PASSES
[9.49pm, Wed 19th November 2014, Denham]

Do I still have the will to say
The lovely words that she wants to hear?
Or am I void of all endearments,
To talk only of my own sad decay?
For if I dwell upon her beauty,
Not the wrinkles that I perceive,
Her façade would surely be
The Taj Mahal of all my days.
For if by some brief encounter,
I chanced upon her some thirty years ago –
I would have taken her beauty,
Trapped it in a world of my own –
For such is life as beauty passes,
I need to praise her beauty more.

DRUNKS
[1.05pm, Sun 23rd November 2014, Denham]

Watching drink ruin the lives of others
Is like watching water going down a drain.
It's a waste of time cleaning the water,
Preparing it for everyone to use.

Likewise drink ruins the drinker,
Wastes their bodies better than worms,
Half-way to the grave they continue
To kill themselves with their habit.

I am no saint, and I like a drop,
But knowing no limit is the want of some.
Children cry, and spouses quiver
Before the terror of the drunk.

Diseased, these bums lumber on,
Leave their wake of self-destruction,
No words can halt or make them change
The course of their own oblivion.

TASKS UNDONE
[9.05pm, Wed 3rd December 2014, Denham]

The hurly burly of the day is over,
Evening eats on what is left,
Scraps of moments litter my leisure,
Make me doze in recollection –
But only in the tasks undone,
Those remaining for tomorrow.

YOU ARE THE ONLY READER
[9.24pm, Wed 3rd December 2014, Denham]

The alternative to reading is to write,
Create your own book to read,
Discover the truth of who you are,
Uncover the lies you tell yourself.

Why falsify your own inner-story,
The one place others cannot view?
Yes, show that you may be clever,
But deception is mere conceit.

Honesty of thought is hard to sum up,
It is easier to spin a web of tales,
Conform to an awful notion,
Write what people want to hear.

The point of writing for yourself -
You don't have to entertain others,
There is no audience to please –
You are the only reader.

WE TOO ARE WATCHED
[9.55pm, Sat 21st December 2014, Denham]

The outdoor man, once so wildly active,
Lies on his bed sipping beer:
The movies play in one long continuum,
Flashing through images of his times.

Where was he when Vietnam ended?
Where was he during the Miners' Strike?
Where was he on Nine Eleven?
For now he's idle every night.

Life is not about great moments,
Time is not about being there:
Reflections in our history's mirror
Should not be our measured worth.

Individuals, linger, always wear out:
We can't recall what we have done:
Our skins are scarred from adventures –
That's all we notice as we wither.

We are watchers as we age,
Wrinkled with each setting sun,
We view each dawn in wishful thinking
Knowing our time has overrun.

The outdoor man drains his beer,
Flicks his wrist in search of worlds,
New connections with his past,
He did not know walked his path.

SLEEP LIKE YOU HAVE NEVER DONE BEFORE
[11.40pm, 13th January 2015, Denham]

Between the winter and the shadows
I will look for sunshine –
Brightness in the wasteland of rocks
Under which hides the unknown,
That part we hide from –
That fear we shrink and cower before.

There is no shaft of light round corners
That leads towards the sun –
Waves roll like earthquakes,
Sands shift like a black volcano,
Ash obscures our vision of Elysium -
The land beyond our woes.

Great parks outlive the largest monuments,
Skeletons tell of lives –
Evidence is the body of our truths,
The dark secrets buried deep,
We slumber like granite monoliths
Perched on the edge of a cliff.

Light. The craving of the damned
Chained in dungeons –
Shut the door and enter freedom.
Discover the path across the mountain,
Find the circle of enlightenment –
Sleep like you have never done before.

TOW PATH
[5.17pm, 24th May 2015, Hillview, Denham]

Canals and life in flight –
Why talk now of wildlife?
Curiosity in the mayflies,
Wonder in moor-hen wakes –
What now fills the void?

Apathy is the world of old age
And days lived to the max –
Where now are the new kicks?
Walking blindly into each day
Without a lover at my side.

IVER GROVE
[12.50pm, 15th August 2015, Iver Grove, Bucks]

The clock counts the cunning pass of time
Stolen from us like candy from a child –

We're left in tears for what might have been
And angry that we wasted what we had.

ALIENS ARE STALKING OUR STREETS
[6.32pm, 18th August 2015, Iver Grove, Bucks]

The darkness that descends upon the world
Is not my world, it is alien –
It is the nightmare of others,
It is the dream of the rich and empty,
The purgatory of the slaves to religion,
Those who … those who you know.

Everywhere there are traitors, puke-balls,
Snakes rustling through the average day,
The snails leaving trails of slime.
You see them in their black cars;
You see them hiding behind menus;
You see them looking in estate shop windows,
Envy burning up their eyeballs.

Heaven knows nothing as it does not exist,
Just as haven from harm is an illusion –
For those aliens feed on every fear,
These aliens feed on other's illness,
Supply them with their cartels of drugs,
Fill their cabinets of despair.

For out of the darkness comes the evil
Seeping into every fissure,
Filling every sinew of weakness,
Taking over, sinking all resistance,
Draining blood out of everything –
These aliens are stalking our streets.

POSSIL GIRL
[12.18am, 7th September 2015, Earls Court, London]

Knock down the walls, throw out the piano,
Break up the sofa, and bin the kitchen sink -
There's a Possil girl at my front door,
and I'm going to let her in.

Lunch is her dinner, and dinner is her tea,
Give her a jeely-piece, cocoa for her supper -
There's a Possil girl in my bedroom
And she's kissing me.

Let the thunder roll, the rain piss down,
The rough tempest roar, the seas run wild -
There's a Possil girl making out
And we're on the floor.

The drums are beating, the pipes skirling,
The churches are empty, the chapel bells silent -
There's a Possil girl dancing naked
And its still not dawn.

651

INTO THE DARK
[11.30pm, 19th Sept 2015, High Wycombe]

Vikings raiding through the night,
Cycles wheeling on to nowhere,
Children lost and always crying,
Reckless trains speeding westwards,
On and on into the dark.

No-one knows what is right,
Planes crashing into Babel's towers –
Mothers weeping, never smiling,
Thunderballs rolling onwards
Out and out into the night.

Hordes migrate, slip the barbed wire,
Zombies wield empty power –
Chaos reigns and anger triumphs,
Danger dances with the lonely,
Spins them off into the dark.

HIGH WYCOMBE
[5.43pm, 20th Sept 2015, High Wycombe]

I live in a town where the rivers are brooks,
The woods as tame as a parrot –
The trees are filled with the voices of children,
The breeze as fresh as a daisy.

It is a town of back to back houses,
Pristine and smart like show homes –
Kerbs for skateboards, ponds for minnows,
Cars straight out of a sales room.

Kites crest the crowns of misted heights
Rising up, hiding golf courses –
Trains depart every quarter of an hour
To carry the folk to the Big Smoke.

On the edge of town hypermarkets sprawl
By the ramps of the superfast highway –
Escape is easy, arrival a slow crawl,
But time goes by very easy.

It is a town of alms houses and learning,
Proud of its past and the new –
A town where Sundays are always Sundays
As quiet as a cat in a dream.

It's the town my childhood once was,
Family life and everyday happenings –
A town that knows its place in the world,
As suburban, proper and clean.

BACKWARDS IN TIME
[5.57pm, 20th Sept 2015, High Wycombe]

I live in these times, backwards in time,
Traveling by foot on pathways …
That lead somewhere ahead of me
On the wind along with the kites.

I know where all these byways lead;
I worry that I've come to an end –
The storm has ended in a dead calm,
But I will fight on, my friends.

Renewal comes from getting good rest,
A door to lock, a bed to lie in –
The suitcase put away in the cupboard,
A sofa to put your head down.

Open the curtains, watch the sunset,
Open the windows, feel the air –
The way to the west waits, of course,
But I'm in no hurry to tramp there.

WAITING FOR NEWS
[7.19pm, 28th Sept 2015, High Wycombe]

Waiting for news for our ship to come in,
Loaded with cash and goodies and good times.
Who would take poverty and ill-health
As legacy for living out their last years.

SOMEWHERE SOMEONE IS WRITING GREAT POETRY
[8.52pm, 20th Sept 2015, High Wycombe]

In Stornaway, someone is writing poetry
About the stones of Callenish, the clouds,
The rocks beneath his feet, the red moon,
Eclipsed by the earth on a clear night.

I am too weary to rise at three a.m.,
In the dark to look for rivers on Mars –
Whatever the tick that tocks in my heart
Is the beat of a drum that is silent.

Try as I may, I am worn by events,
By comets, and stars I can never reach.
The excitement of youth, the sparkle of space
Is a glass of wine, and a broken sleep.

Somewhere someone is writing great poetry,
Words to inspire, to change who we are;
Once he was me, youthful and angry,
Not an old man searching for peace.

How we all turn into our fathers,
Into the men we once railed against –
The pigeons will fly to the crow's nest,
The eagles will plunge to the sea.

Change turns full circle as scriptures foretell,
The meek indeed inherit the earth –
The angry die or run out of anger
'till all that is left is the shell of oneself.

Cry as we may in our sad lonely flats,
Our empty houses harbouring time's shadows –
We older ones are the survivors of anger,
We've come to know passion as ignorance.

Had youth shown me much better purpose,
Guided me better to use my time well,
My pages of poetry would be as void …
As the blank eyes of an owl.

ALL OUR LIVES WE WAIT
[11.54am, 1st Oct 2015, High Wycombe]

All our lives we wait, we try to do,
But thwarted by the procrastination of others,
We wait, and wait.

Life is far too short, too short to wait
For others to get their lives together,
So we wait.

Try as we might as we try to do,
We are blocked by the inertia of others,
So we wait, and wait.

NEVER TODAY
[1am, 9th Oct 2015, High Wycombe]

Never today, never tomorrow,
Dwell on sorrow, never be sorry,
Always reflect, never fret.
Always be sure, and don't regret.

THE FLAKE
[11.59pm, 16th Oct 2015, High Wycombe]

Three times I waited like a young man
For an older woman who was a flake –
Eager in her desire to date me,
Three times I waited to be snubbed.

Tis easy to make excuses in hindsight,
To brush aside the actions of the flake –
So earnest was her pressing desire,
Three times I lingered to be ignored.

Three times is enough for any man,
No matter how humble his expectation;
No words can ease the wounding –
Three times stood-up by a flake.

THE MISSING COAT

[11.07am, 20th Oct 2015, High Wycombe]

Where's my coat? Where's my coat?
Its raining, its cold out there –
Find my freakin' coat, sonny,
now get out of my face.

Listen, sonny, you little tosser,
I'm going to slap ya! There I've done it!
Where's my coat, you tiny prick …
Find my coat, you wanker.

Don't touch me, mate, I'm warning you,
Get your face out of mine –
What? Get my coat, you dickhead.
You want me to punch you out?

Okay, biff! There you go –
Don't ever asked to be punched.
Now find my coat, you little cunt,
Its raining, and its cold out there.

MARY OF THE STAG
[10.31pm, 27th Oct 2015, High Wycombe]

In the quietness of The Stag,
Two days before the workers get paid –
There is a moment with the barmaid,
Old as the pub, and Scottish,
A stoic lady from Dundee -
Called Mary.

Many's the time in that pub,
A walk away from Pinewood Studios,
Mary has poured me a welcoming pint,
With her lovely Dundee smile,
Her soft Albion nature,
Her convivial warmth.

Whatever the hustle in progress,
The night's raising to the rafters,
Mary's had time to say hello,
To engage and exchange,
Smiled and made welcome,
One of her own.

THE DOOR TO THE GARDEN
[11.09pm, 27th Oct 2015, High Wycombe]

Try as I might to do things right,
Getting things wrong is being mortal –
Life ebbs away towards decay
Of everything once that was fine.

Try as I might to make things stay,
Things change, are never the same –
Wrong things bloom, right stuff fades,

All that is black is now grey.

Now as I hope to somehow cope,
To turn the dark into light –
Somehow I hear the creak of time
Closing the door on life.

LONDON
[15.44pm, 1st Nov 2015, High Wycombe]

From the smallest to the grandest,
They are all greedy for gain …
People and politicians alike,
They all act falsely ...
Declaring all is well,
When nothing is well at all.

RETRIBUTION
[3.53pm, 1st Nov 2015, High Wycombe]

Every nation oppressed when freed
Cannot resist becoming the oppressor –
It is the nature of us all,
To seek retribution formerly denied
By slavery.

Apartheid breeds long term hatred
That is never vent 'till the oppressed
Triumphs over the oppressor –
Then the barbarity of the barbarians
Is outdone by the savagery of the victor.

This latent inhumanity is everywhere,
Dormant in the consciousness of us all –
Directed at our bitterest enemies,
It extends beyond our borders
To all our foes.

I AM SILENT
[12th Nov 2015, High Wycombe]

I will remain silent.
Many questions have been asked,
answers given on my behalf
while I have remained silent.

What news from me – nothing
about the hollow promises of peace,
the shattered lives and the untold dead
whose voices echo across the Aegean;
baby corpses float like flotsam;
shell-shocked misery, lines of fences
erected by their saviours.

What peace is this? Detention camps,
tramping innocents of the destitute -
forced marches of the hungry,
angry anguish midst callous apathy.

Others have spoken for me,
self-interest has overtaken charity -
I remain silent.

Who then speaks in my name?
Which hero can I trust?
Which heroine has made me believe
that we are governed fairly?

Our times are dominated by weakness -
moral force has no moral basis,
perverse greed and avarice ...
glass edifices, and sharded structures,
the epiphany of all that's wrong,
all that's built, the epitome of our times.

Corrupt ... or not at all, but amoral,
the surface seepage of the Arab sands
finds its way into private pockets -
through the holes, deep caverns of influence
drip down the leg of capitalism,
soak the thirst of bankers,
loosen the tongues of judges,
water the gardens of politicians
who speak for me, my conscience,
while I remain silent.

And I will remain silent ...
I will go with the flow of time,
I will bite my tongue ... choke
on the meat on my plate,
drown on the wine in my glass,
but I will not worry ...
for others will speak in my name.

Yet I will not sleep soundly,
nor dream of some reached utopia,
for there is no comfort in silence,
in my blindness to the hurricane.

I will rise, shower in hot water,
eat my warm cooked breakfast,
go to my heated, tidy office,
do my work, make my living,
and remain silent.

For I will owe nothing to the world,
or be owed by the world -
I live as I please, how I want,
say what I like, go where I choose,
have no corporal restrictions placed on me ...
for I answer to no-one ... others
answer for me, and I am silent.

Can this be the way life is?
Missile firing drones, online videos,
entertainment, modern war games?
Silent war games, never a sound,
always done in our name, for us.

For us? If we are not for ourselves
then who is for us? If not for us
then they must be against us?
Just one more enemy, just one more,
and always in my name -
for I am silent.

I need not fear my future ...
it is being secured for me -
by stealth and prudent use of weapons,
I am protected from all invasion;
safe from all loss of freedom,
I am free to sleep soundly,
free to dream of utopia.

For I am silent.

IT WAS NOT A GOOD DAY
[12.44am, 14th Nov 2015, High Wycombe]

It was not a good day for the world.
Paris blown up – the coffee massacres;
Jihadi John eviscerated by a drone,
Russian athletes banned from all competition;
A murderer convicted for dismembering his sister.

The world in a violent turmoil –
The devil turns the soil as we watch.
A dark night precedes a dim dawn ...
The candles burn for all our wrongs.

THE SMOKE FROM THE FIRE
[4.34pm, 15th Nov 2015, High Wycombe]

The smoke from the fire engulfs Paris.
Who started the fire? Who will put it out?
The arsonist cannot turn up in disguise,
Be allowed to throw oil on the flames.

Madness takes the form of sainthood,
Self-interest comes in the cloak of charity,
Debt is hidden in the supply of weapons.
And fear makes the unwilling collude.

Yet the fire still burns brighter,
The smoke goes half-way around the world,
No-one tackles the blazing inferno –
As we choke on the acrid smell.

PRAYER FOR SYRIA
[12.51pm, 28th Nov 2015, High Wycombe]

Shoot down the plane, behead the pilot,
Throw grenades at the wall –
War zips over broken glass.
The jagged edge of our horizon
Filled with smoke and screaming,
Our eyes burn – in the name of what?

Cut down the meek, slaughter the lambs,
The wolves are baying at our door,
Cast the babes to the lions,
Feed the vultures their rumps of meat,
Make no mention of God.
In our name – revenge or what?

Scatter illusion, shatter the mirage,
Place laurels on the victors' heads.
Shoot the vanquished, bomb the cowering,
Tear down the mosques and minarets.
Destroy all light, return to dark
In our name, or that of God's?

DREAMS ARE BEING MADE
[1.23am, 29th Nov 2015, High Wycombe]

Gone are the nights of the broken man,
The destitute lost in the defeat of his past –
Death is not the career of his future,
Failure is not the sum of his all.

Long were his days, beaten and down,
Until there was no further to go –
The lonely times with not much help
Except a friend offering shelter.

A little voice whispering 'quitter',
A nagging pain laying him low,
A languor making him hide away,
And a despair eating his hope.

Gone are those times, he never surrendered,
Never gave into the terrible doubts,
He never gave up on his own self-belief,
Never gave up on his life.

Out of misery, through his hard work,
Given the chance and a barrel of luck,
Success once more within his grasp,
His sadness changed to a life of laughs.

There is no number to life's chances,
No matter how many times they fade,
The sun comes up every morning,
And dreams are being made.

MY WONDERFUL LOVE (song)
[12.32pm, 13th Dec 2015, High Wycombe]

When the sky is grey,
And the rain comes down,
Despite the wind,
Despite the storm,
I think of you ....
My wonderful love.

When the sun comes out,
And the rays are warm,
I'm full of hope,
I'm full of joy,
As I think of you ...
My wonderful love.

When night-time comes,
And you are here,
In my arms,
Close to me,
I think only of you ...
My wonderful love.

YOU ARE MY PEARL
[10.08am, 14th Dec 2015, High Wycombe]

You are the pearl in my oyster,
The bit of grit I can't get rid of ...
I secrete my love in you ...
As you become more valuable.

The risk I run is incalculable,
How precious you could be to others ...
I fear you will be discovered ...
And I discarded.

So I hide you, my darling,
Shed no light on your beauty ...
Have you trapped, covered, smothered ...
I keep you guarded.

A FISTFUL OF BEER
[21.48, 15th Dec 2015, Uxbridge]

I used to believe - sitting in a pub
with a girl when I was twenty two -
that I was wasting my life.

How stupid I seem in my lonely years
watching nervous lovers -

envious of their youth.

Passion is an evil worm that wriggles,
makes the young man believe
that out there is a better world.

Over my pint, and my solitude,
I tell that young man -
seize what you can with both hands.

A fist full of beer and liver spots,
watching the lovers laugh -
youth is so wasted on the young.

GOZO SPARROWS
[15.56pm, 22nd Dec 2015, St.Lawrenz, Gozo, Malta]

Sparrows stalk the evening light,
Chase the dying of the day –
Their chatter fills the fading heat,
Then fades with dusk to silence.

GOZO
[22nd-30th Dec 2015, Gozo, Malta]

Down beneath the clean cut stone,
Under layers of ancient living,
Deep within the cysts of ages
Dug away, exposed to daylight –
There lies the truth, the past,
The sum of all endeavours,
The anchors and the vases,
The jewelry and the day tools,
The clay, the flint, the bronzes,
The fragments of Gozo's tomorrow.

Citadels rise on every escarpment,
Churches stand on every hillock,
Terraces run along every slope,
Houses perched on every road.

The sun goes down into the sea,
Red into the dark blue Med,
Black isles of cloud, wisps of mist,
Silver glints of distant stars –
Cool night settles on the pines,
The palms quiver in the winter solstice.

The sandy soil turns on the plough's blade,
Eases over like good earth should –
Into the ground goes the seed,
The future of all that is to come.

Twisting ancient roads descend,
Yellow-walled, cut-stone hemmed,
Pathways lead over cliffs,
And step-ways end at hanging rocks.

Into deep chasms gullies race,
Into fissures, rain filled pools,
Age washed limestone, fossil pock-marked,
Pitted and ragged, serrated and jagged,
Caverns cut into sandstone walls,
Grottos wind-gouged with every squall.

Hidden bays and sea-cut harbours,
Shelters from all wicked storms –
Caves etched into the landscape,
Dwellings abandoned by Egyptian times,
Phoenician traders of oil and wine,
Passing galleys and marauding tyrants,
Running after dark, - the curfew
In the cellars of the church,
Refuge found on the hardened floors.

What life was this? Slavers chains,
Pirates raiding at a whim –
The knights of St. John as saviours,
Their fleets fighting off the Moors.

From east to west ten miles long,
North to south five miles wide,
Africa a day's sail away …
Sicily a half day the other way …
Mighty empires have come and gone,
Left their ruins on Gozo's soil –
Punic, Carthaginian and Roman,
Aragon, Sardinian and Sicilian,
Turkish, French and British –
gone, all gone to history,
Lost in the yellow stone, sandy fields,
The memories dripping with the rain,
Into hidden caverns, caves of wonder.
The sub terrain beneath the normal.

Giant monoliths, and stone circles,
Grand edifices, smashed and crumbled –
Osimandi's world found, and buried,
Not more knowledge, just more questions.

Christmas Eve's bells ring loud,
Deafening the café drinkers in the square –
The children's choir before the altar,
The priest placing baubles on the pulpit,
Holy water pressed against a forehead
Under the tenth station of the cross.

And outside everywhere – ruins,
Land lent to rubble.
Hillsides strewn with history's dereliction,
As the ringing of the church bells
Summon Gozo's children from their dwellings
Into the sanctuary of the Lord.

2015 - THE YEAR OF THE DAMNED
[11.40am, 30th Dec 2015, Golden Sands, Malta]

Another year comes to its conclusion,
A footnote to the calends of history;
Many think it a year of misery,
Wars, displacement and ugly death.

Yet, are we not cruel to ourselves?
Injustice breeds insurrection and chaos;
So we reap the wind of time,
And cry for the wrongs committed.

But we cry for ourselves, not for others,
For the shame of being the culprit,
For being the perpetrator of hatred,
For being superior to the unfortunate.

We are not absolved by our aloofness,
While distant from the woes of anger,
We were the root of the problem -
We paid for the year to be damned.

AS STORIES GO
[12.50am, 24th Jan 2016, High Wycombe]

So as stories go, this is another one.
It begins with a fur coat on a chair,
Ends with a dryer tumbling damp clothes,
Wet streets and memories of football matches,
A girl with a dog, and face cream –

There is no order to this never-ending tale.
The middle is a jumble of mathematics,
A car journey down a long straight road,
A music box meant for outdoor playing,
A guru in training on my mobile phone.

So I will start again, finish off –
The sound of laughter in the night,
A letter waiting to be posted last week,
A lost hat never to be found,
A yarn mined from this mind of mine.

WORDS HAVE LOST THEIR DOMINANCE
[11.15pm, 28th Jan 2016]

While the world goes round ...
Somewhere in India a theatre troupe performs
Romeo and Juliet to a student crowd
Who squeeze backstage to praise -
The foreign actress who has been in films.

If Shakespeare were alive, or Tagore ...
The candle in the wind would flicker -
When the lights went off, no power plant
Could provide the playwrights needs –

663

Darkness put an end to his imaginations.

Is sound a greater frightener than light?
Listen to the words, the tales they show,
The wonders of the past, the fancy concepts,
The cache of ages caught in syllables,
Not with moving images, nor snapshots.

The language of telling has morphed –
Now made for the eyes, not the ears,
Blindness renders the story intelligible,
We listen but we cannot see –
Words have lost their dominance.

IF I'M IN LOVE
[12.21am, 4th Feb 2016, High Wycombe]

Is love a state of being, or a state to be in?
As big as a county and as wide as our memories,
Emotion plays with the spinning of the world,
Endless 'takes' on the bundle of our wealth –
What is really going on with my brain?
Am I wired to self-destruct?

Want is coupled with a desire for need,
Help is something that we all can give,
Acceptance is a novelty constantly cherished,
Apology the foil to deflect the strong –
Give me half an hour with honesty,
I'll give you ten hours in return.

When minds meet in an equal understanding,
No earthquake can shake the firm belief
That down the line, created by encounter,
Only good can come from such commitment –
Worry then as if there is no tomorrow,
And comprehend there is none to heed.

Selfless we may think we are progressing,
Yet endless we recede into ourselves,
Passion flares and lights the room for seconds,
Smoke lingers longer, but will disperse –
If I'm in love then love has no answer,
For the question will give answer to itself.

MY COAT ON HIS KNEES
[11.41pm, 4th Feb 2016, High Wycombe]

It's never too late to dream before dawn,
To stumble beyond your allotted departure,
The time set by the sum of your past,
Or by the will of your thought.

I'm not professing that I am immortal,
Or I will outlive all of mankind –
But perhaps by holding on to my dreams,
I can put off the inevitable knock.

Life is full of unfinished business,
And I'm not ready to get up and go
Out of that door and into the darkness
Without completing the last of my goals.

And every day I dream up new ones,
Schemes of thoughts, and plans of ideas,
Things that keep the devil waiting,
With my coat on his knees.

THE ITALIAN GIRL
[10.02pm, 28th Feb 2016, High Wycombe]

She said she really liked me,
Her eyes were dark and deep,
She looked into my shallow heart
And touched my crippled soul.

She slid her hand into mine,
Pushed her head on to my breast,
She spoke with Italian words,
Then took me to her bed.

Her hair curled about her head,
Her almond skin lit the night,
On never-ending sheets of silk
I traveled on her lips.

AS WINTER DEPARTS
[1.10am, 2nd Mar 2016, High Wycombe]

As the winter passes warmly,
As the future fills the mornings,
As my hopes open doorways,
I am on my journey.

Others wait on the morrow,
Friends believe in only sorrow,
Workers search for their saviour,
As I take their burden.

Life is but a bag of dreams,
Breathing's such a simple scheme
For getting through a troubled day
Is but a common theme.

Let the clouds grey the sky,
Half the world is in the black,
I am feasting in the sun,
But hungry in the dark.

Spins the world to its end,
Life is but a nest of eggs,
Dare we break with our past
To progress to our end.

Canter on the muddy track,
Do not take a backward glance,
Ahead is all we need to know
As winter now departs.

OUR DREAMS
[12.57am, 4th Mar 2016, High Wycombe]

Our dreams are but fairy dust,
Willows in the wind –
Headlong we rush on our whims
With hope and love –
Our faith like bubbles blow
Us out to sea –
We bob upon the deepest depths
Looking at the sky –
Waiting for the night to fall
To catch a star.

AROUND THE CORNER
[2.14pm, 3rd April 2016, High Wycombe]

Never is life so fraught as
When success is just around the corner
That you cannot see beyond.

Look all we want but still
The unknown better life is a step
Too far to reach just yet.

Try as we may to quicken
All ourselves towards that place
We cannot yet achieve it.

Left to ponder our own folly,
We take each painful hour
As our dose of poison.

FRUITLESS JOYS
[10.05am, 10th April 2016, High Wycombe]

How we waste our lives
In pursuit of fruitless joys.
How we wander off
The path of barren hope.
How we wish and wait
In our fields of idle time –
To reap no laughter,
Nor joy of any kind.

MAIDA VALE
[3pm, 16th Apr 2016, Maida Vale, London]

In the depths of Maida Vale,
Drinking wine with gusto –
Gone the day into night,
We look towards the morning light,

To have our moment in the sun.

A BELL TOLLS IN THE FOG
[10.36am, 19th April 2016, High Wycombe]

I try to look forward,
But I want to look back,
For the future is shrouded in mist,
While the past bathes in sunshine,
And rings out in laughter –
Ahead a bell tolls in the fog.

I want to see into the future,
Beyond the trees in the way,
But as I put my foot forward,
There is no light falling ahead,
The path is dark and dead –
I hear only a barking dog.

LITTLE ENGLANDER (JOHN BULL)
[12.35am, Tues 26th April 2016, High Wycombe]

Run, John Bull ….
Run and hide your face in shame,
The world watches your brexit posturing
As refugees remain … rotting in vile camps
While you don your whites,
Play your games.

Curse all those with foreign names
Marching on your cherished lawns –
You vote to keep England English,
You huff and puff your racist cant
For all to hear loud and clear ….
You selfish twat.

THE LONG NIGHT INTO DAY
[12.51am, Thurs 5th May 2016, High Wycombe]

The long night into day comes slow
Through a dark narrow endless tunnel,
At its end a meagre breakfast,
A cup of tea to wash the sorrow.

Daylight breaks upon my labour,
Sleep deprived I stand and shiver –
I shift the burden from my knees
To feel the weight of my existence.

Chained to notions above my station,
I seek escape and exultation –
There is no haven for the troubles,
Nor peace of thought for the restless.

The darkness brings on many doubts,
Sleep is but a fitful lull –
The narrow tunnel binds me in,

Leaves me hostage to the dawn.

GOING DOWN TO GLOUCESTER
[12.32am, Tues 10th May 2016, High Wycombe]

Broods the Brecon bluebell vales,
Castle straddled, dark and ruined –
Deep rut scarred to Offa's Dyke,
Tintern Abbey barren stands ….
Broken fords, lost Roman roads,
Every step steeped in time.

Black coal glaciers bleakly spread
Along the vale from Ebba's hell –
There is no music in the hills,
A stalking kite sails the blue …
Battered cliffs hedge the valley,
Thin haze hangs above the highway.

Brazenly the land upturns its dead,
In blazing shafts, joy returns …
The Severn slithers like a snake,
Smooth and brown to Gloucester –
As dragons race to beating drums,
The choir soars in sunset song.

VANISHED KINGDOMS
[3.55pm, Sat 28th May 2016, High Wycombe]

Broken skin split in broken dreams
Pounding on the sands of silent screams –
Blackbirds parade the promenade,
Kiss and tell their tarty tales …
Slip between the sodden sheets,
Sing their songs of freedom –

While tired, the old soldiers march
To the trumpet tunes of old,
Tell their tales of tawdry tarts,
Their priggish lusts and honky pasts,
Beat their breasts like wild apes,
Wail for their vanished kingdoms.

MORE TEASE THAN CAKE
(for Angela)
[11.02am, Sunday 29th May 2016, High Wycombe]

She flashed her eyes and showed her breasts,
Warm, inviting, but hardly chaste,
She teased me with her puckered lips
But did not give me cake.

I smiled and focused on her eyes,
I did not look below her chin …
No matter what she offered there,
I was not going in …..

She downed her whiskey with a gulp,
She pranced and danced into the dawn,
She led me to her plush abode,
But I could not bridge the gulf.

Life offers many tempting treats,
The best sometimes over tea ...
But in the night with drunken belles,
The cake can be a tease.

THE COLD LIGHT OF DAWN
[10.33am, Sat 11th June 2016, High Wycombe]

What is this life we live?
A dance around the maypole ...
Making love in the long grass,
Wrapping scarves around our necks
And hiding from the cold in bed.

What is this merry dance?
A long walk in the woods ...
Holding hands in the afternoon,
Kissing under a full moon,
But empty by the cold light of dawn.

GREAT NATIONS
[12.29am, Sat 1th June 2016, High Wycombe]

The greatest nation in the world,
Is the nation that does not know its great –
The people who do, not only talk,
Who give, and think giving is normal ...

No bombast, trumpeting, or grandiose fanfare,
No beating of drums, no parade of arms –
Immense with humility, small with pride,
Greatness is by acclamation, not by shouting –

Thus the great nations of the world proceed,
Ahead of all those nations bent to conquer.

THE ARTIST
(for Agata)
[11.23am, Monday 13th June 2016, High Wycombe]

The artist danced her hands into the paint,
The music played a Maltese rag –
The colours poured like summer rain
Down her fingers to the floor –
Drenched her canvas with her art,
Showed the door into her heart.

BREXIT
[13.35pm, Sat 25th June 2016, circa Preston]

What tears and lamentation ....
Dragged into the abyss by demons,

Beasts and ugly monsters screaming,
Grins that show their yellow fangs.

Innocent of their vile world,
We become the new inhabitants,
Immigrants to their foreign ways,
Hostages to their ravenous destruction.

ANIMAL FARM
[14.01pm, 25th June 2016, near Carlisle]

Our new days start with introspection,
Anger, pain and disbelief –
Snatched from our land of Eden,
Deposited on a huge dung heap –
I do not like the smell of it,
Nor standing in it ten-fold deep.

Packed-in with the dispossessed,
Twenty-seven different tongues,
We look towards a distant shore,
Beyond the fence, beyond all harm …
Instead we stand in the rain,
Trapped inside this animal farm.

A NEED FOR GOD
[17.01pm, Tues 28th June 2016, near Locherbie]

The rancour and enmity,
The anger and the ache,
Nothing heals a broken heart,
No beer can make the mind forget –
Folk who embrace the devil,
Make God more needed every day.

BREXIT 2
[17.07, Tues 28th June 2016, train – Carlisle]

This is no Dunkirk,
It's the end of Empire,
The death throes of a nation
Totally obsessed with itself.
Fly the flag – empty gesture –
Mob rule at its worst.

OUT OUT DAMN SOUND
[13.00, Sun 24th July 2016, High Wycombe]

Distant times chime in my mind,
crash in on my present state,
discord with my inner self
and my majesty of grace.

Out out damn sound!
The pounding of the waves -
leave me with the butterflies,
my birdsong summer days.

THE GREAT WHEEL TURNS
[12.21, Mon 1st Aug 2016, High Wycombe]

The great wheel turns …
burns the evening sky -
how my eyes carry into the sunset,
my back to the eastern blackness
as each night eats my days,
shortens my mortal coil,
fades me out, blocks my light
from this wonderful life -
propels me over the horizon
to bring on the inevitable dark.

THE SAND IN MY HAND
[01.07, Fri 19th Aug 2016, High Wycombe]

The sand in my hand -
I strain to understand …
why God made my brain
so small that I struggle
with faith and beliefs.
Where is he?

Each day starts well -
the sun brings us light …
and light is good,
without it I am cold,
left in the dark
would I meet the Devil?

One speck of crystal
turning in my palm …
holds my ignorance of life,
contains my fears,
why am I here,
how did I get here?

Facts are not enough -
sand is just silicon …
glass-like it sparkles,
where did it come from,
how did it end up
mixing with my sweat?

I cannot fathom it,
get to the bottom of it …
as hard as I stare
up at the Milky Way,
plot the arc of the stars,
the sand remains.

Smash it with a hammer,
it will multiple in number -
if I heat it up,
it will turn to glass.

I can't make it disappear,
how did it get here?

God is the only answer,
God is everything -
yet still I ask myself ...
Is God a grain of sand,
the sun, the universe
beyond the void out there?

What is in between?
I have no answers -
no quantum mechanics,
no wishful formula,
no simple logic can explain
the sand in my hand.

I CAN SMELL THE PACIFIC
[17.05, Sun 21st Aug 2016, High Wycombe]

In the breeze today is the Pacific -
Alaska fireweed, forget-me-not,
tall pine trees touching clouds,
wild rivers of thrashing salmon.

The scent of moose in the wind,
hot springs and sulphur bubbles,
lone bears crossing glaciers,
rotting kelp on the tidal fringes.

Brown fern, blackened bracken,
blueberries ripe on the slopes,
bark-sap carried on an updraught,
carried to the furthest shores.

The day turns cold in the shade,
four quarter chimes, four full bells,
as I stroll an English park
of rose, yew, fresh cut grass.

Old age does play tricks with me,
makes me switch between the decades,
yet I swear I can detect ...
the perfumed wild Pacific.

AUTUMN EQUINOX
[23.52, Thurs 22nd Sept 2016, High Wycombe]

Day and night in equal measure share
in equal balance hold the turning tide -
summer lingers in the humid haze,
autumn tints the cool bright stars;
on the edge of change we hang ...
to wish for time to be suspended.

RAGS TO RICHES
[22.07, Wed 28th Sept 2016, High Wycombe]

I am obsessed with my days left,
not the days gone, or my glory years -
I look ahead with the same dreams,
the same hope I've always had.

I know others – with their lottery bets,
artists with visions of discovery;
none give up their inner faith
that life will be fair before they go.

With optimistic hope of success,
mankind is naive like an animal
seeking to find a winter store of food
to stay life's eternal struggle.

Some pray to their chosen God,
others to messianic over-lords,
many simply bank on stars and luck -
yet believe they will have their day.

Likewise I keep my dreams alive,
won't give in to what's gone before -
the present is where I make my plans
to win my riches, shed my rags.

LIBERAL ELITE
[22.41, Tues 4th Oct 2016, High Wycombe]

Those who do not wish to change their way of life,
hope that things will last their time -
after that let happen the tragedy that will come,
for they are blind to the chaos drawing near.

LOVE OF POWER
[22.04, Thurs 6th Oct 2016, High Wycombe]

Love of power does not go with goodness,
in all its aspects, it is pride, cunning and cruelty;
but to rage against a regime that is violent
is to replace one set of tyrants with another.

IF WE LET DAYS PASS
[00.48, Sat 22nd Oct 2016, High Wycombe]

If we let days pass without recording them,
then – we have never been here, not existed
for ourselves, nor for our memories of ourselves,
- we are only the persons we are now.

Who can see themselves in the mirror
without the shadow of time behind themselves
contrasting the false image we project
that obscures who we are are, and who we were.

I AM WORDLESS AGAIN
[01.04, Sat 22nd Oct 2016, High Wycombe]

My own silence baffles me -
empty of anger or burning passion
to rage against the world's woes -
I sip my coffee, eat my cake,
sit warmly in my neat abode
numb to all the distant killing,
detached from all the fleeing migrants.
The world is awash with chaos
and I am wordless in response.

WHEN THE POET DIES
[10.50, Sun 23rd Oct 2016, High Wycombe]

When aged forty the Poet dies,
the passion spent, the cynic born,
his anger changed to selfish rant,
all writing but a heap of kant,
rubbish piled upon himself,
his inner-soul lost to verse -

now lost in self-importance,
pinned by such to his past,
tied down by dogmatic lines,
chained to his clichéd lines,
the echo of his former truths,
on every page the dullest thud -

liberty once the gleaming goal,
truth the target of his barb,
when no coin could buy him,
when no romance could tie him;
free in thought, deeds and wants
living life with a God -

causes filled his wakeful hours,
his rage waged against the times,
his work flowed like the tide,
swept the beach of his mind,
drifting words made him distinct,
timeless in a wasteful world -

now – all washed up,
soiled by his own survival,
the cynic as the status-quo,
seeks approval from his foes,
goes to bed every night,
basking in his own betrayal -

so the burnt out Poet dies,
drops his pen to join society,
accepts corrupt immoral ways,
condones untruths for personal gain,
backs wars as doing good,
behaves blind to all injustice -

better then that he dies,

lets the mantle fall on others,
that we forgive his latter failings,
remember his poetic railings,
his anger, angst and accusations,
the truth of his youthful pennings.

I HAVE LOST NOTHING
[00.33, Sun 3rd Oct 2016, High Wycombe]

When I reflect on what I have lost,
I have lost nothing -
I may swat a bug with my finger
but there is no memory of cruelty.

Many have not found what they are seeking -
I cannot say that I am wanting -
along the path I have taken,
I have collected my dreams.

I have never exiled myself,
turned my back on the things I love -
I have never abandoned my vocation,
though many friends have been lost.

I don't pretend to be short-sighted
in order to cut out painful reunion -
I just quicken my pace to distance
myself from untimely encumbrances.

Regrets only come with reflection,
yet changes nothing, cannot undo -
loss is not a thing to dwell on,
there is more to find than to lose.

ELEPHANTS
[00.14, Thurs 3rd Nov 2016, High Wycombe]

What cruelty there is in man -
greed, avarice and self-survival;
civilisation is just a game,
the cunning ringing our territory
with brick walls and wire fences.

Not so our big-eared beasts,
roaming their ancestral plains,
making their elephant walks,
towards their elephant graveyards
to be visited by us.

SIRENS ALL DAY LONG
[14.53, Mon 7th Nov 2016, High Wycombe]

What is wrong with the world?
Accidents and incidents,
heart attacks and crashes,
lights flashing on and off!
It makes my pulse race,

my blood pressure soar.

TEN MINUTES
[14.55, Mon 7th Nov 2016, High Wycombe]

I have ten minutes ....
should I write a poem
or should I exercise?

I'll do both ...
have a cup of tea
and find ten minutes more.

NO TWO DAYS
[23.47, Thurs 10th Nov 2016, High Wycombe]

No two days are the same-
its river deep, river high ...
storms rage every hour,
news pours on us like a deluge;
who is Noah in these times
with the foresight of the flood?

WE WILL DEPART BY DESIGN
[00.56, Mon 14th Nov 2016, High Wycombe]

Life has no answer to anything.
It comes as a gift ....
Ahead of it is the taking away,
but who can grudge the departure;
we have arrived by accident -
we will depart by design.

TO LOVE TOO MUCH
[00.02, Thurs 17th Nov 2016, High Wycombe]

To love too much, but not too well
is like gambling everything on one horse -
odds to win, but no sure bet
that its going to be first past the post.

CRISIS YEAR
[00.50, Sun 18th Dec 2016, High Wycombe]

No snow falls on this crisis year,
no cosy fires or jugs of warm wine -
little cheer to bring in joy,
looking back – an anguished task.

Yet forward pushed we will proceed
at our rate, not that of others -
we will falter all along the way,
marching to the tune of robbers.

What becomes us will be sorrow,
every day, and every morrow
until we house, feed our brothers,

sisters, children and our mothers.

These careless times will excel
a cruelty beyond our reckoning,
we now must bear the screaming
of our own distressed reasoning.

HAPPINESS IS NOT GUNS
[00.34, Wed 28th Dec 2016, High Wycombe]

Happiness is not guns -
firing them ... watching them fired,
people being killed,
animals, birds ... killed.

How can death be fun?
Or violence joyful?
Or mass murder give pleasure
in real life?

Spear, bows and arrows, swords,
bombs, weapons of mass destruction?
I cannot see the good times,
nor the benefit.

THE WINDOW IS OPEN
[00.58, 28th Dec 2016, High Wycombe]

The window is wide open -
every possibility exists.
Will the sparrow be lured
or a robin tempted?

Roll up the blind,
pull back the curtains -
anything can happen,
the day may rain.

Nothing foretold, nothing expected,
anything imagined may occur.
December may melt,
replaced by May blossom.

RAGE AGAINST THE LIGHT
[2nd Jan - 23rd Mar 2017, Bucks]

It began with a big bang,
an almighty roar, not a whimper,
no stifled sobbing in the night.
The sound was clear, distinct
like the roar that thunders,
like the beat of the Parana
falling on the mission rocks below.

How then did it start ...?
This epoch of uncertainty and violence,
this age of deafening chaos,

this time in which we live
with its wailing and shouting,
the endless cacophony of noise
disturbing our restless sleep?

The answers rest in the future,
that place ahead, that quiet zone
given to the babbling of brooks,
the listening to bird song bursting
on the gaggling of beasts,
the snorting of surface creatures
cruising off the coast.

There ... in that heaven ahead,
the solitude of certainty awaits -
all transgressors who trespass
shall find a rock to rest,
shall take the sun ...
shall shed their naked guilt,
re-find their days of innocence.

The present presses on the chores
that wastes the waking hours of thought,
garbage fills the streets of reason,
sewage seeps disguised as wisdom,
rubbish leaves a littered conscience,
fills it with a heap of nonsense,
exhausts the mind beyond all logic.

The epoch marches to a tune,
in step strides, does its duty,
no tearful sorrow for its actions,
unlike Arjuna in his chariot -
his bow slung, his arrows quivered,
questioning the choices given
and his own existence.

Reflection in a placid pool,
the snapping of a selfie image,
Narcissus lurks in the background,
few can see beyond the mirror -
Aristotle perceived the worth of idols,
little more than human folly
dressed up as art and drama.

The door of perception opens
out into a plain of grass -
this idle life of grazing,
foraging with the huddled herd,
Elysium shimmers in the distance,
crickets mix with the wind chimes,
chirp into the dawn.

Forests cover up our history,
plough-shares slice up our past -
once there was a city here,
over there stood a temple ...

Avebury now a line of rocks,
a wisp of what it once was
to a God.

Pagans plod through every age,
star-ward gaze with their dreams,
their feet planted in the soil
preventing them from flying off.
Beam me up! their eyes implore,
seeking more from life than this ...
earthbound erstwhile, just the same.

On the plains of poor Albania,
Ilyria lies beneath the dust.
Lost in ancient Latin texts,
locals know where it exists ...
point to where the ruins lie;
yet who has time for the past
when time is in short supply.

And fly it will, all too quick
until we find our sand has run,
our moon is full of shifting cloud
blotting out the evening star -
the steps worn, the way steep,
we'll slip and slide very stride,
stumble, just to stave the journey.

Thus each day becomes more precious
as we horde the hours we have -
yet we waste the one resource
that will depart, escape our grasp,
leave us silent in the dark,
without a hint of what to think
or what comes next.

Through each day we will slog,
tied to our pagan rituals -
routine as a vital virtue,
companionship as a constant vigil,
loyalty an essential ethic,
truth a fundamental element
of who we are today.

The fog comes down ...
the ice crackles underfoot,
dim lamps yellow in the mist,
pines stand on the ridge
drenched by the swirling dew
an owl wits its evening tune
above the traffic.

In the Okovango swamp,
rhinos wallow in the mud -
a river flows very slowly,
snakes its length to Mozambique.
Who can stem the predetermined?

Who can pause all momentum
or halt the inevitable?

Marked by time, scarred by fate,
tempests hurricanes and gales -
forced by forces beyond our know,
no man of science can explain,
no priest of thought can declare,
no argument, no simple faith
can unmask the mystery.

The polar ice breaks away,
drifts, melts, fades to nothing -
rain drops, seeps, then dries,
till it seems it never came -
sun heats, warms, cools,
dissipates to leave us cold,
to wait in the dark alone.

Solitary in our skins we sleep,
lonely in our minds we breathe,
snow drives on the mountains,
ice coats the city side-walks -
and somewhere a president is sworn-in
against the will of the people
he will divide.

This is the time we endure,
rock-an-roll a sideshow drug,
movies in staggering violence
splattered in expansive scope -
refuge behind new Chinese walls,
lessons never learned, bottles thrown,
smashed against urban sprawl.

Where is the eternal hope ...
the child with the open arms,
the parent with the loving smile
masking out the looming world.
Can innocence be preserved,
can goodness be untouched
by the doubts of age?

Life takes its turns ....
anger comes and goes -
the tide of passion wanes
then returns again to haunt
each waking second, and in sleep
the worry builds its walls
against its troubles.

Such seas swell each storm
bearing on the coast of angst,
no rest from the howling wind,
no shelter from the constant blast -
the light burns to the wick,
the heat turns to freezing cold,

sweat wets the pillow.

Terribly we live like this
in constant torment, fevered fear
of all there is to lose -
Has progress come to nought
but ticky-tacky little boxes
stacked in terraced rows
like lines of Lego?

Once three score and ten
is now four score and five -
the lengthening span of sorrow
increased by five thousand tomorrows.
Has this brought more joy?
Should we sing ecstatically
at our fortune?

Time will tell with each tick,
the liver spots marking age,
aches in the tender parts,
creases on the weathered skin -
yet inside the child hides
blowing bubbles at the world
with a wicked smile.

Slumbering lies the secret eye
beyond the sight of natural vision -
wisdom flirts from soul to soul,
knows no limit to its visit.
Somewhere in the Himalayas,
somewhere in the human jungle,
there is an answer.

For most, the days stretch on
without a clue about existence -
give us each our daily bread,
we shall breathe, give our thanks,
trespass not upon our brothers,
our sisters, or on any others
if we are righteous.

Yet, we fail, flawed we fall,
don't reveal our foulest sins -
in the dark we flail and flounder,
shut away our filthy deeds -
as fickle to our foulest thoughts
we deceive our better selves
and die alone.

Who is that inner struggling self
so tiny in this universe?
Frustration vent as modern art,
reveals little of this vital spark
of life, of being, this individual
trapped within the cosmic whole
without a reason.

To bear the pointlessness of existence,
too many end their engagement early,
burn up in one great rush
to get to their own Nirvana -
youth becomes a blaze of light,
ends as a martyr's life
or as an icon.

Victor or victim, it is the same,
they are gone from our presence,
perhaps to a better sphere -
we are left in our rotation
around the sun uninterrupted;
we wake, we sleep, wake to weep
at our existence.

Then the light through the window
whitens the black dog night -
I am alive, I am breathing,
I am joyous in my fortune
as I travel into the dawn,
the curtain drawn morning
of glorious day.

Down to the sea I go,
down to where the travelers sail,
to exit off to sweltering lands,
to lie beneath languid palms -
lost to cocktails on the beach,
lost in many lapping waves
washing me.

Simple sultry senses simmer,
contentment gives to deep desire;
lust fills the flickering mind,
each and every waking hour -
longing enters every bone,
want weighs every thought,
erodes all moral.

There my imagination stays,
lingers on a fresh corruption,
enters into darkened hollows,
descends into deeper chasms,
chases shadows into caverns,
catches air in clutching spasms
all for nothing.

The hunter soon hunted is
pursued until he finds the light -
the dark dog howls his fright,
the child knows no delight,
the adult in us seeks perversion,
the sinner in us tries coercion
on the weak.

No escape from inner dreams
tearing at our selfish selves -
we sip our tea, gulp our gins,
take a spin in our cars -
beat to some secluded place,
bask at some beauty spot
and seek redemption.

And still we try to laugh
at the absurdities, the banal,
the pointless and the pitiful,
at those who pontificate, seek
certificates for some knowledge,
or affirmations for some talent
or insecurity.

The wrongs of this world
cannot be healed by sociopaths -
politicians are merely policemen
maintaining social order -
they can't fix our illnesses,
mend our broken hearts,
or heartless minds.

Televisions cannot feed us,
nor books dress us warmly;
art is a drab distraction
meant to dull our dissent -
music is the people's opium,
movies a corporate commercial
selling pizza.

Then life brings love so pure
it need not speak its name;
love that is silent in its stealth,
so overwhelming in its honesty;
beauty in the dark lit eyes,
lips lightly pursed in laughter -
there is no crying.

Souls meet in distant circles,
entwine in unknowing worlds;
there is no reason to such connections,
it happens without plan or purpose -
eyes meet across a crowded room,
attraction draws each together
without restraint.

We wait for something to go wrong,
the bubble always bursts somehow,
yet love transcends corporal things,
survives somewhere beyond ourselves,
takes root in our deeper being,
saves us from our own deception
and inner evils.

Then death strikes like lightning,

no warning, a flash, a nephew gone;
the noise that follows is anguish,
anger that he was in his prime.
There is no time to lose -
each day must be taken now,
not wasted.

And though the times are hard,
the chores are dull and tedious,
there is hope in the smiles of strangers,
laughter in the face of bad news,
endless joy in the eyes of children,
calmness in the walk of widows
and their carers.

There may be cloudy times ahead,
but through the damp swirling mist
there is the longed-for open land,
where opportunity has no fences
nor barriers to advancement -
where dancing is the stimulus
to burst into song.

Destiny drives its own car into town
and parks on double yellow lines -
there are no rules or stipulations,
no limitations to its boundaries;
the predetermined waits to happen,
will come about come what may
for certain.

The tired wait with the condemned,
have nothing else to do but linger
between this world and the other;
between sleep and the suffering,
they flit between the light and dark
uncertain of the way ahead -
the lonely journey.

The sunny upland hills are waiting
to ring with the call of youth -
long strides atop the ridges,
bounding steps in gladed woods;
clear streams to quench a thirst,
long grass to rest and dream
of things to come.

As time presses on each day,
gnaws away at our conscience,
chokes and stifles all contentment,
strips the essence of existence -
duty bound to serve survival,
commitment eats our *raison d'etre*,
our *joie d'vivre*.

We march to different kinds of tunes,
the piper plays for all of us -

the soldier home, the traveler safe,
the flowers fresh on their graves;
we mourn the valiant and brave,
as we reflect and stare upon
our own mortality.

The sun sets on the cold horizon,
the crisp air turns to chill,
a calm descends on the churchyard,
the village clock strikes six times -
time is marked with precision,
marked by means so familiar
we lose count.

But count by count time runs out,
pours away, drains to empty -
we are done, spent of force,
we cannot change or fix our course;
no magic word can will our wish,
our want to somehow carry on
beyond our hour.

We face the truth in our mirrors,
in our friends lost to us -
yet we want to fool ourselves
that we are somehow made immortal;
we put off all our dreams,
put off all our best endeavours
until tomorrow.

We hear that ticking ebbing sound,
ignore it as an irritation -
paralysed by our own deception,
we blindly drain our inner doubts;
today will never come again,
tomorrow will never come at all,
the past is dead.

Truth is for the brutally honest -
when mothers die there are no lies,
all the wounds once so hidden,
now become bare and healing;
scars buried in the psyche,
secrets locked in the memory
told to all.

What of that mother gone to heaven,
her shame also gone with her?
Why she felt she had to hide,
hold her tongue all her life -
love can be a cruel deceiver,
love can be a vain protector
of our dignity.

Still the rivers flow on freely,
each new rain washes wisdom,
knowledge lost with the aged

finds new lodging with the young -
a child soon a mother is ...
a mother shields her precious child
from pain.

How big the cosmos wheels about
above our heads beyond our reach;
what joy there is in the stars,
where man for sure will never go -
God is safe from our greed,
God is safe from our desire
to conquer space.

Happy then, content to prosper,
I conclude that I exist;
I march through my final days
with a limp, not a whimper -
I will not go with a bang,
I will not go with a song
but with laughter.

A PICTURE OF ISABELLE
[14.14, Fri 20th Jan 2017, High Wycombe]

She had my mother's name -
Hair golden in the winter sun,
Her eyes sparkling in the frosty hoar -
Her voice free in the forest light.

The artist in her shone brightly,
Radiated from her excited thoughts,
Glowed against the darkened wood
Set against a clear blue heaven.

She sometimes trembled with emotion,
A glimpse into another time .....
But most, she jokes, simply spoke
About her love of life.

She painted her own picture ...
A snapshot, a blink of an eye;
In profile she was Hellenic,
Full faced – curious as a child.

In a click she was gone,
Back to her other world .....
Where beauty tries to blossom
And escape becomes a joy.

ANOTHER DONKEY ON THE ROAD
[14.30, Tues 2nd May 2017, Kalahari, Botswana]

Another donkey on the road.
Another elephant waiting to cross
to a distant waterhole.

The Kalahari stretches forever,

flatter that the Indian Plains -
the bush is lush with rain,
the season near its end.

TODAY WILL NOT BE RECALLED
[19.50, Sun 14th May 2017, High Wycombe]

Wet the British Spring dowses hope -
loud voices drown out the birds,
an argument over nothing but pride,
a chorus of unrepented shouting.
The quite of Africa so far away,
the heat of the setting sun -
tomorrow will be but a memory,
today will not be recalled at all.

THE BALLERINA
for Henrietta
[noon, Mon 29th May 2017, High Wycombe]

She appeared from nowhere ….
I looked up and she was there
sitting in the soft light,
her warm eyes fixed on me.

She offered out her hand -
and as I accepted her approach,
something inside opened,
a lotus blossomed.

How these things are mysterious -
We are not prepared for surprise,
moments counted in one hand
that last forever.

IT WOULD BE HER
[00.54, Tues 30th May 2017, High Wycombe]

If heaven sent down an angel
to remind us of all our wrongs,
to let us gaze on perfection
to gauge our own ugly forms -
it would be her.

If art drew on all beauty
to sculpt the perfect form,
to paint the perfect picture,
to express art's high ideals -
it would be her.

If the eye saw no blemish,
the ear heard no flaw,
our fingers touched the skin
of the smoothest of them all -
it would be her.

For when love is blithely blind

and hears no evil from itself,
that love is perfect love
a love that has no end -
that is her.

AND STILL SHE IS SILENT
For Teresa May
[10.55, Sun 4th June 2017, High Wycombe]

And still she is silent ...
We will turn the other cheek
and reiterate our superiority
over the tenets of another faith.

But we will still sell arms
and bomb the shit out of others,
though not in our name,
for she is silent.

Life will go on, the election -
she will defeat the enemy,
she will lock up the innocent
in case they are guilty.

Oh Sunday Sunday, pray for us,
that she is silent on the threat
we are to others far away -
blown up every day by our bombs.

Weak and wobbly we continue
into the abyss in silence -
a silence that does not work,
a silence that does not become us.

Silent we stand waiting for leadership,
but silent she remains,
as silently she turns her back
and dwells on her own silence.

A TOWER OF TRAGEDY
[1.07, Fri 16th Jun 2017, High Wycombe]

A tower of tragedy burns
into the souls of everyone.
A single spark ignites anger
and dismay at its enormity.
No words can describe pictures
that will haunt until eternity.
We weep for those now missing,
and cry for those in agony.

THE SUMMER OF OUR CONTENT
[17.07, Tues 17th July 2017, High Wycombe]

This is the summer of our contentment
caressed by our days of sunshine,
long afternoons of perfect bliss,

short shrift given to our cares -
short shadows cast on our past,
our talk is of the future.

PASSCHENDAELE 2017
[09.28, Wed 2nd Aug 2017, High Wycombe]

A hundred years on and Hell on Earth,
the dead still lie where they fell.
Ypres haunted by Australian spectres,
shadows on the old town walls.

Miles of rows, and rows for miles,
the white gravestones scar the ground
where half a million men lay down
and never rose to stand again.

Sombre, silent, poignant, sober,
a city lies beneath the soil -
there are no streets, only trenches
that house soldiers far from home.

Lest we forget, lest we forget
the names etched on all the walls,
the gate to Hell is open still
for whose who march to war.

23,163 DAYS
[08.33, Thurs 24th Aug 2017, High Wycombe]

Born on a Thursday, today is a Thursday,
three thousand, three hundred and nine weeks old;
I stumble on towards my glorious future
knowing the number of days since I was born.

Seven hundred and sixty months or so,
sixty three years with sixteen leap years,
one hundred and fifty two days added on
to get to today – a fine summer morn.

How many weeks, how many months,
how many leap years remain to be counted?
My days are numbered in various ways -
I live each one as another day saved.

YOU JUST HAVE TO SAY GOODBYE (Song)
[01.44, Thurs 16th Nov 2017, High Wycombe]

He said I was an angel,
but I have a brittle halo,
and everything he gave me
turned to bad -

sometimes when you're in love
its just not enough
you just have to say – goodbye.

Now he's gone I'm empty,
no-one else can tempt me
to cross myself, and
pretend I'm good -

for when you lose your lover
and sadness overcomes ya',
inside you die, you cry.

No angel, I've not fallen,
I have my inner calling
and everything I've got
will come good -

for though I'm on my own
once my tears have gone
I'll get over all my woes.

CHORUS

Oh lord, how I miss him,
his sweet talking whispers
and his kind of loving
every night -

sometimes its not enough
when the sun comes up
you just have to say goodbye

ANOTHER BOOK OF NOTES
[17.06, 19th Nov 2017, High Wycombe]

And so to another book of notes,
of poems penned between the light
that exists squeezed from the dark
of sleep and dreaming.

DITA AT KEW
[17.29, 19th Nov 2017, High Wycombe]

We walked round Kew in the sun,
the golden brown of all the world
at our feet, crisp and dry,
the canopy of autumn's cull.

We took our tea and almond bun,
we talked about our recent past,
she produced a tin of sweets,
I a birthday card.

The hothouse left far behind,
we wandered in the Himalayas,
squeezed down a Chinese path
no monkey ever favoured.

Until at last, three hours gone,
we left by the turnstile gate,

she went to buy some fish,
I, to drive away.

WHERE ARE MY FRIENDS NOW
[27th Nov-26th Dec 2017, H Wyc-Marbesa,Spain]

The hour is late, I am alone,
given time to quietly think,
to dwell upon my nine lives,
my passing through many towns,
places where I made friends
in countries where few travel,
but also here at home.

Where then to start, to tell,
when memory plays all its tricks,
makes us want to fondly think
that every friend we have found
was someone lost along the line -
but is this so, maybe not,
I'd like to know.

My early friends were my cousins,
Hughie, and his brother John;
I lived my youngest years with them
in a small council flat -
as children do, children play,
get to know each other well,
too well some would say.

At nursery in Pollokshaws,
Muriel MacDonald was my friend,
in later years her brother John
became my early teenage mentor;
Muriel, shy, coy and sensible,
I, wild, bold, unreasonable,
we parted at the nursery gates.

Then with John, aged thirteen,
a summer spent playing cards,
I teased Muriel about her breasts,
growing out, firm, erect -
tried to kiss her, did just once,
but she was younger by four months
and not as grown up.

In nursery there was also Linda
who next I saw aged sixteen,
she sided up to me at school,
stated boldly, I was the kid
who'd been to nursery with her
and changed his name.
I denied it.

Why, oh why, did I lie?
What arrogance ruled my heart!
For she was such a lovely lass

in a lower class than me -
I was such an awful fool,
we had grown up together
in the same slums.

Years later, when I went home
to live and marry yet again,
Linda lived along the street
though I did not get to see her
my daughter knew her youngest one,
through her passed the message on
to say hello.

How could I not have visited,
made the effort to make amends,
taken the chance to reminisce
about our times at nursery -
Too late now, the years gone
to renew the friendship bond
made in infancy.

How we waste our worthless lives,
blind to our own shortcomings.
What have I squandered thus
by being so un-empathetic?
I cannot turn back time,
I cannot reclaim the friends
I've thrown away.

Let this not be a reminiscence,
not a tract to make amends -
I have no reason to regret,
no grounds to frown upon events
that shaped my life, that of others,
whose I've met along the road
of my existence.

The pages turn on all us mortals,
on those we knew now passed on -
we each retain a part of them
in our own conscious self;
a special part we might recall
or feel it is a point of truth
we touched upon.

But to the present – my current
friends who populate my being,
my being here, present in my mind,
in my daily actions, there,
here and now, not back then
when such friends are mere stories
not now so real.

Is it polite to name these souls,
those dearest ones close to me,
when they are still around, about
me in my daily deeds and chores?

Should not I be respectful, churlish
in revealing such faithful friends
to my foes?

There rests my deepest reservation,
to let loose on my many secrets,
the things once told, never mentioned,
the whispered words, the tiny actions
that make for lasting friendship -
the greatest stories ever told
lost to history.

So safer then to recount the past,
to dwell on those lost acquaintances,
for this is what they become,
shadows on life's long wall,
flickering lights dancing in the mind,
leaves rustling in the breeze
that time blows on.

Neil Dickson, what a boy -
lost in my childhood smog,
aged seven, taken, just like that,
his desk empty, my tears dry,
to have your best friend killed
without a single goodbye
is a travesty.

How I have dwelt on this loss,
fifty odd years of bereavement
for my closest, dearest friend,
still not replaced, or dislodged
from the core of who I am,
of who we were together
at school, invincible.

His friendship taught me that
together two can conquer the world,
whilst alone we can only wish
for better days ahead, better times
than we currently get by on -
that man is an island of misery
without companionship.

And so, my friendships thereafter
became a competition, a rivalry,
a need to be better than my peers,
not their friends, but their leader,
not their equal, but their master,
with no need for love, just respect
through dominance.

Such admission, such woeful sin
to have led a life of pride,
to have lauded my being thus,
over those on whom I triumphed,
not out of love or friendship,

693

but out of loss.

This may seem a retold fabrication,
but no, the loss of master Dickson
so affected me – no-one knew,
no-one understood the deep bond
young lads place in one another
as they build their house of adulthood,
stone by stone.

At seven the man is made -
the child has begun to depart,
leave behind the crying for good,
to get on with being a boy
who cannot wait to grow up,
find adventure, seek his dreams,
and leave home.

With Neil's death, friendship became
transient in every friendship made -
Was I to lose again a friend somehow?
Would he be taken, gone too soon?
I learned to break friendships off
before the pain of separation
left me bereft.
[Unfinished]

SCOTTISH SUMMER
[15.52, 24th Dec 2017, Marbesa, Marbella]

It is a Scottish summer sun
though it is Christmas Eve -
in six months the Earth will spin,
turn some forty six degrees,
and bring back again the warmth
I know as Scottish summer.

Meanwhile here in Andulucia,
Scottish sun rages with its breeze,
its crashing waves on the shore,
the cool character of the shade,
the evenings of overcoats, some hats,
but dark, not light like Scotland.

There lies the Spanish difference -
the night time sky is black,
the moon is not behind a cloud,
there is no rain coming down,
there is no eternal twilight
to run free with friends on open hillside.

CHRISTMAS LUNCH
[13.34, 25th Dec 2017, Marbesa, Marbella]

What a feast! What joy!
Lunch – avocado, salami, cheese
on wholemeal bread, a glass

of Temperanillo as my champagne.
Palm trees drooping with rain,
the clouds shifting like pirates
in the wave-laden sky -
How dear is life so cheaply
paid for on Christmas Day.

HOW FAR MOROCCO LIES
[13.44, 26th Dec 2017, Marbesa, Spain]

How far Morocco lies is not far,
a mere gulls fly, a dolphin's swim,
yet for us it is an ocean's width,
a stretch too far for weary legs.

The day turns on its usual axis,
the idle sit and drink their coffee,
labour labours on it's chores
on numbers few, serving many.

The clouds drift like desert sands,
shade the sea, shift its hues,
the sun hides in the southern sky
beyond where far Morocco lies.

REFINDING WHAT IS LOST
[17.03, 27th Dec 2017, Marbesa, Spain]

What new is there to learn when
most knowledge has been forgotten.
It seems that nothing will be discovered
unless we re-find what is lost.

WITHOUT THE SUN
[17.24, 27th Dec 2017, Marbesa, Spain]

Without the hot Sahara sun,
I am in Nicaragua or Dunoon;
the winter shore shed of light,
a wild stretch of breaking white,
at my feet the thrown shells,
the pebbles wrenched from the depths,
my footprints in the dampened sands
unbroken for a thousand steps,
the wind in my weathered cheeks,
my lips closed devoid of speech -
how, now so like other times
I find myself retracing life.

MARBESA IN WINTER
[18.14, 28th Dec 2017, Marbesa, Spain]

How slow it all seems to be -
nothing but the sound of the waves,
the rustle of the wind in the palms.
It is cold now – no hot tiles
radiating their evening warmth,

no crack of the settling timbers,
no wet mist on the night lawn,
just a biting southern draught
swirling about deserted balconies,
empty wrinkled pools of blue,
colourless in the twilight hue.

MAIJA
[18.25, 28th Dec 2017, Marbesa, Spain]

It started with a zing, then a pop,
a simple tick, then a quick hello,
now its blossomed into a long exchange,
pics, and talk of art and children.

How easy it is to be open to strangers,
those we have never met, may still not -
we have no fear, for they do not exist
as real, but fantasies of our making.

Distant voices that we never hear,
we will never really know for sure
until we have proof they are flesh
and blood, and there before us stand

real after all, and full of frailty,
with flaws and everything we imagined
and hoped they would not be
mere mortals just like ourselves.

THE BULL IN THE FIELD
[12.36, 29th Dec 2017, Marbesa, Spain]

The bull in the field chased the chicken,
the goat and the sheep watched on,
the chicken clucked, jumped a fence,
the bull stopped short with a snort.

The goat turned, made eyes at the sheep,
the sheep looked back vacant eyed,
then started to twitch as the bull turned,
the chicken crowed at the fun.

The goat took flight, climbed a tree,
the sheep found a hole in the fence,
the bull fumed, circled the field,
the chicken stuck out its neck.

The goat bleated from a high branch,
the sheep ba'd stuck in a hedge,
the bull wallowed in a pool of mud,
the chicken made off for its shed.

The farmer came, just shook his head,
rescued the goat, untangled the sheep,
gave his prize bull one of his frowns
and collected from the shed his eggs.

THE IDLE LIFE
[14.58, 29th Dec 2017, Marbesa, Spain]

Why do some do all the work,
while others shirk, lay about?
Is there something wrong with this
or can the worker learn to live?

Live to work and die too soon,
work to live, enjoy life's fruits?
Busy hands make busy lives,
empty hands enjoy life's spice.

So what are you, my dear friend,
a worker or an idle wretch?
Wait you until the day is done,
or sit you all day in the sun?

MANDY
[00.23, 12th Jan 2018, High Wycombe]

Mandy had four fingers on her right hand,
four toes on her right foot,
but her smile was six fingers to the world,
and her eyes six feet deep with warmth.

She was small but boiled with life,
childless, but full of joy and spirit,
normal in a pub of freaks and clones,
more unique than all of them combined.

COME BACK INTO MY LIFE
[23.18, 12th Jan 2018, High Wycombe]

I want someone to come back
into my life to complete the circle.
The girl in the polka-dot dress,
the son of the mysterious secret agent,
the nurse who I could not fulfil,
the bigamist I loved despite his flaws.

Where are they? How I wonder,
how I search when memory returns -
a name is not enough to reunite,
friends must want to be found
or all the searching of the world
will uncover nothing of what remains.

It is the saddest of ironies that
we sing of - don't know where,
don't know when, but someday
we will meet again somewhere,
knowing not *ca sera sera*,
or the words of *auld lang syne*.

I am of an age of wanting closure,

a tying up the ends of friendship,
the need to know how life works
on those who once were close -
so close I cared, care still
for them to come back into my life.

WHAT HAPPENED TO ME (Song)
[00.39, 5th Feb 2018, High Wycombe]

My lips need time to recover,
my legs are like rubber,
what happened to me?

I was pulled out of my bubble,
and now I'm in trouble,
'cause that girl got to me.

My head's in a tail spin,
my heart's been done in,
what happened to me?

I'm free falling with no chute,
its not looking too good,
she was too cute for me.

I'm a dodger and weaver,
I'm an artful deceiver,
what happened to me?

I was just that one look,
I was totally hooked,
how did she do it to me.

My lips need time to recover,
my legs are like rubber,
what happened to me?

EXCHANGING TIREDNESS
[00.07, 13th Feb 2018, High Wycombe]

That moment the eyes close ....
I am tired, worn out by repetition,
witness to mundane happenings,
I just want to shut life out,
fall asleep, float off in dream,
flee every day routine -
exchange it for jumbled fantasy,
make-believe nonsense -
in exchange for the desire
to wake rested and renewed.

BACK FROM AFRICA
[22.30, 18th April 2018, High Wycombe]

I am back, but knowing not
what I am back to.
A month in Africa has passed,

and so too has my past.

I am not longer that young man
so eager for adventure and risk;
the old man has arrived
and the rocking chair beckons.

THE HOLE IN THE HEDGE
[08.01, 25th April 2018, High Wycombe]

I am told 'just knock it out',
but its been knocked out of me,
the stuffing, the omph, the substance
that makes me, me.

Through the hedge backwards,
I feel I've been thrown, landed
not on my feet but my neck
in a head-banging heap.

'Pick yourself up' I'm told;
I need a wheelchair today,
and someone to shove me back
through the hedge hole.

MY RUSSIAN SPY
for Lana
[23.02, 25th April 2018, High Wycombe]

I spoke with my Russian spy,
it was a distant voice,
but she spoke sweetly -
I forgave her all her flaws.

I urged her to get a suntan,
buy dresses for the summer,
told her to rest her mind
and ignore the FSB.

She was on the Riviera,
being chatty and carefree -
I loved her for her boldness
and her time for me.

APPLE
[21.55, 29th April 2018, High Wycombe]

The little Chinese dancer moves
as a flicker in my eyes.
Such beauty in a perfect form
of movement that is joy -
emotion and understanding
that straddles all divides
and cultural differences.

TAO GIRL
[23.30, 20th May 2018, High Wycombe]

ROBBIE MOFFAT

She speaks with symbols,
she sings her song,
moves without a shadow.

No plum petals fall,
no weeping stains the earth
through the bewilderment of life.

No left-over consequences,
every step is traceless,
a bird darting in the night.

CHINESE IMAGES
[23.50, 29th May 2018, High Wycombe]

I'm all words, not pictures,
the sounds I make, not images,
the crude sentences of ink,
do not paint, do not colour.

All I write is black and white,
characters with little character,
a repetition of plain information,
transcriptions to be interpreted.

If only I could draw Chinese,
use a sweeping brush, not a pen,
real images, not mere letters.

TWO SIDES OF LOVE
[00.02, 30th May 2018, High Wycombe]

What can another person offer,
give of themselves you cannot take?
In reverse what can you give
that you do not need returned?

Love is two sided like a coin,
it has an edge that can be rolled
until it falls flat to reveal
which lover has the upper hand.

A RIVER NEVER FALTERS
[23.50, 8th June 2018, High Wycombe]

My life runs its course -
like a river that knows its way,
edging past fields containing shadows
that I wave to as I pass.

It is not too late to extend
a hand towards the bank,
to take hold of a lover
and float onwards together.

We will part on the journey,

I will surely float on alone;
my river is running swiftly
and I detect the nearing shore.

It is as it should be,
I am at peace with myself -
a river never falters
on its journey to its end.

A KISS ON THE LIPS
[23.56, 8th June 2018, High Wycombe]

Can love exist as words
without touch or scent or sight?
Can the object of desire be real
without a kiss on the lips?

MY LITTLE APPLE
[00.08, 9th June 2018, High Wycombe]

She is beautiful, just perfect,
there is no need to look for flaws,
she is human, has her moments,
don't we all doubt our actions?
My task is to love her, need her,
make space, let her into me,
make changes to my being, soul,
throw off my ways, my reservations,
say things I've never said before,
pack my bags and be prepared
for the journey along love's road.
For ahead lies joy and laughter,
a life better than the old.

JANET PRICE
[00.37, 11th June 2018, High Wycombe]

And so our good friend Janet Price
passed away today, aged ninety five,
a child hood friend of Richard Burton,
a poor boy who came to her house
to receive soup and bread from her mother,
the doctor's wife.

We will clearly miss Janet Price
who only put champagne to her lips,
who lived on the sunny Riviera,
who knew everyone who knew her,
a favourite of the mayor of Cannes,
her confident.

The Valley's will remember Janet Price,
the Welsh girl with her Chanel style,
who took in artists and poets,
who befriended stars and princes,
in Monaco and Nice, on radio
with that Valley voice.

I will remember dear Janet Price,
a true friend in hard times,
a true friend in every sense,
a wizened soul wisely wise,
a saint to all film-makers,
a blazing star.

MY BODY HAS CLIMBED MOUNTAINS
[13.58, 18th June 2018, High Wycombe]

My body has climbed mountains,
crossed deserts, sailed oceans,
trekked jungles, faced elephants.

It is still my temple,
the house of my Gods,
the home where I reside,
the library of my thoughts,
the dwelling place of my being,
where my soul is imprisoned,
unable to escape yet.

TEXT MESSAGE
[01.27, 15th July 2018, High Wycombe]

Its the little things, the little thoughts,
however short, however brief,
that brings joy, brings happiness.

I want for nothing more, nothing,
for the little thoughts are enough,
they fill my weary days with light.

Bless the sender, bless her again,
bless every little thought expressed,
I am blessed.

LAKE VICTORIA
[16.24, 6th Aug 2018, Entebbe, Uganda]

The waters once more lap on my memories
of distant shores traversed barefoot -
between my toes, experience lies
filtered by the waters of the lake.

The echo of those years still ring,
refracted in waves of constant noise,
I travel with the circling seabirds,
sail on into the far flung wild.

DUBAI
[00.45, 8th Aug 2018, Dubai Airport]

Thirty five degrees and McDonalds,
Dubai is one big shopping mall,
the palm trees are made of brick,

the carpets all untrodden by camels -
carrots don't grow in the dunes
walked by donkeys in a daze.

A HUG, A KISS
[23.38, 28th Sept 2018, High Wycombe]

The days go by with friends I love,
lovers past and ones who love
the things I do to ease their lives,
to bring joy where sadness lurks.
I cannot give them everything,
just a spark to light the way.

Age teaches us to be more kind,
to couch all differences with a smile,
a hug crosses all divides,
a kiss plants the seed of trust,
a whisper in an ear brings warmth,
releases secrets never heard.

The inner soul pines for embrace,
the longing mind seeks full union -
no being truly desires seclusion
or abandonment within themselves -
we are made to share our lives
with those that chance provides.

There is no great master plan,
there is no fantastic after-life,
there is no hidden super-being,
guiding us across the stars -
we live our days, sleep our nights,
wake thankful for what we have.

If I am not a normal being
who loves his friends who love him,
then what am I but a fool
who thinks only of himself -
I am blessed to be surrounded
by those who take me as I am.

JULITA
[23.55, 28th Sept 2018, High Wycombe]

As yet I have not spoken of her,
her quiet, steady way,
her secret life of emotion,
that smile of hers, that look
that stares into the abyss;
her tender nature, caring eyes
for the little things missed -
her loyalty, her companionship,
her beauty that she thinks is flawed,
that reveals her worries,
her fear of the unknown -
that makes me take her youth,

take her in my ageing arms
to tell her all is well.

GISELLE
[23.35, 3rd Oct 2018, High Wycombe]

A rediscovery of someone thought lost,
a realisation that I knew her not,
an awakening that she is a dark horse,
a slender expression of someone with heart,
a woman of spirit, fun and warmth -
someone to love without any remorse.

LIGHT AND DARK HOLES
[23.24, 10th Oct 2018, High Wycombe]

As light travels at constant speed,
or is created by artificial means,
the electricity wired through our brains,
moves along at the same rate.

What theory binds this all together,
ruled by gravity – time displacement?
One hundred billion little galaxies
connected by a web of pulses.

Wave or a beam of particles?
Our minds a single universe?
Bent by magnetic forces
and filled with dark holes.

CROCODILES, HYENAS and VULTURES
[23.00, 20th Oct 2018, Phalborwa, S.Africa]

When all the elephants are gone,
the predators and scavengers left,
crocodiles, hyenas and vultures,
how ugly will the wild be then?

Evil will circle the veld,
chaos will ensnare the savannah,
fear will fester the waterholes
until the world ends.

I GO TO BED FULL OF FAITH
[22.43, 21st Oct 2018, Punta Maria, Limpopo, S.Africa]

I go to bed full of faith
with all my hopes tightly tucked
wishing for the dawn to come
so I can rush into the day
to set about all my tasks
to make my dreams come true.

WINTER IN BEIJING
[20.20, 11th Nov 2018, Beijing, China]

The house was large, cold within,
the evening dark in old Beijing,
each sound amplified like ice
cracking in the winter night.

May Long made the cabbage soup,
chop sticks and a long-sup spoon,
the dumplings steamed on a plate
as we delved into our bowls.

The kitchen gave the one respite
from the freezing clinging chill,
we sat huddled with our broth,
coping with our silent thoughts.

FILTHY WORKS and BARBAROUS ACTS
[22.33, 16th Nov 2018, Xicheng, Beijing]

We struggle with our modern days
uncertain of where our futures lie,
no leadership from our elected,
only woes and unprotected
we sway in the wind like wheat,
bend like stalks of barley.

Time sings its own refrain,
the chorus every time the same,
we reap what is badly sown,
go against all that's known,
go not well into the dawn
and pass beyond all parley.

We stick our heads in the sand
while all the while we understand
our selfish aims bind our hands,
blind us to our dire demands,
leading us towards foul deeds,
filthy works and barbarous acts.

WHEN I LEFT
[08.55, 19th Nov 2018, High Wycombe]

There were leaves on the trees -
now there is bareness,
a sense of Christmas coming,
the air filled with frostiness,
crisp chilly-morning, grey afternoon,
scarf-clinging evening,
and dark icy night.

INACTIVITY CREATES NO TOIL
[09.31, 20th Nov 2018, High Wycombe]

I do not wish to get out of bed,
there is pleasure in being idle,
of dreaming away all reality,
being warm, content with thinking.

Unwilling to rush headlong abroad,
without profit or purpose at all,
what point is there to such action
when inactivity creates no toil.

A ROTTEN LOT
[01.24, 14th Dec 2018, High Wycombe]

The folly, the farce, the pantomime,
what are we all to think,
a parcel of rogues in parliament
and us outside looking in.

Is there any sanity in politics,
is it still a game of dismay -
whatever we think is irrelevant,
but we will have our day.

The clock ticks on in Westminster,
the leavers will do their worst,
the remainers will just prevaricate
and we won't be better off.

No answers every news at ten,
number ten answers nothing at all,
the clowns are running the country
and we are the prats of the fall.

Its disgraceful to watch such antics,
to be part of things going wrong -
such fools governing the country
with all of us going along.

Rogues and idiots and madmen,
what folly they have wrought -
two fingers to the lot of them,
the fig-leaf rotten lot.

BACK IN ANDALUSIA
[15.30, 20th Dec 2018, Calahonda, Spain]

Back in the Andalusia sun,
the peace of Spain in winter -
some carp at such convention,
yet know not why its thus.

No grey here, just white, blue,
the hue is one of yellow -
scent hung with pine, sea
breeze ever in the air.

Sleep comes as a no tomorrow,
no worry for the thing to come -
life to live, enjoy, unwind
to rest while the world runs.

TIRED
[19.36, 20th Dec 2018, Calahonda]

Tired, very tired, yet only
now I find this as I stop,
stop to think, just reflect,
relax without the need to
go somewhere, do something,
or be on the move because
I am relied on, needed
somewhere by someone else -
less self reliant than myself.

THE SUN
[10.58, 21st Dec 2018, Calahonda]

Sun is the order of the day,
sun, my son, heals all decay,
with no delay go into the sun,
feel the healing power it gives,
stretch naked in its rays,
let its energy enter your core,
take its light into your being,
store its power in your loins,
go into today charged once more.

THE FRUITS OF IDLENESS
[11.08, 22nd Dec 2018, Calahonda]

The fruits of idleness are many,
some too ripe to take much of,
others too rich to palate -
there is an abundance of choice,
the wrong choice, a hazard,
the simplest the most rewarding.

Yet which is which in Eden,
that forbidden or that on offer?
The idle man is indecisive
in his own indulgence.

BETTER NOT TO WONDER
[10.32, 24th Dec 2018, Calahonda]

Every day I wake up, wonder
what has changed. The sun is still
shining and the sea still laps
on the shore of my existence.

Perhaps it is I who has changed
into someone different from the night-time,
for the moon has come up
just the same as Armstrong found it.

Better then not to ponder
what has changed. The wind blows
on the tall ageless palm trees

reaching for the sky like yesterday.

FAR DISTANT PASTURES
[10.55, 25th Dec 2018, Calahonda]

Morning rows a boat once more
down the quiet back canal,
the sleepers neither wake nor stir
as I rest upon my oars.

All around me all is still,
the shadow shafts all are long,
the bridge ahead now is gone
as I pass beneath its arches.

Where I go I do not know
drifting on without a sound
to some place not yet found
in far distant pastures.

MY ONLY CHANCE TO BE HERE
[00.24, 28th Dec 2018, Cabopino, Andulusia]

What worth, what value
does any artist possess
that is not thought frivolous
or unnecessary as others struggle
with poverty, with death.

It is not comfortable nor pleasant
to be valued as a liability,
an addendum to real life,
to things that matter,
that are deemed important.

How did we come to this?
Slavery, the drudgery of thoughtlessness
permeating from the downtrodden,
those put upon the most,
the victims of circumstance.

Thus I am, circumspect,
understanding, but also dismissive,
for I too am a human being,
given only one chance
to be here too.

AT PEACE ONCE MORE
[00.44, 28th Dec 2018, Cabopino]

Meadows of flowers, fields of colour,
a child again in a familiar world,
when eyes saw every buzzing insect,
every petal plainly etched in focus,
the wonder of each new experience -
what joy, what curious interest aroused,
nothing could arrest me from when

I became an adult, set my eyes
on more wondrous things.

Now I realise the field of flowers,
the meadows of colour is my life,
my interest, my deepest love -
those childhood smells, observations,
who I am, the child, the adult,
the man I know myself to be,
a creature of the wild, the outdoors,
the wanderer to be, now home,
at peace once more with himself.

WHEN THE STAR IS BORN
[12.45, 28th Dec 2018, Cabopino]

When a star is born, another dies,
is this the order of all things ...
heavenly bodies or movie icons
with each birth space is made
by snuffing out another light.

The cycle of external lifestyle
is not something just for India,
our connectivity concerns all
things joined by unseen forces
so fast we dare not blink.

If I am deluded in my thoughts
then explain to me how it works -
is energy not a fixed amount
held together as one fixed mass
we are just a small part of.

I tell you now, no-one knows,
will never know, will never fathom
how it came to be like this,
the world as we know it now
when a star is born.

NEW YEAR BALLS
[15.20, 1st Jan 2019, Mijas-Costa, Spain]

The music mixes with the fireworks,
the dancing goes on all night;
my right ball is inflamed
as I jiggle to familiar tunes.

What agony to have such swelling,
a melon resting in my pants -
my left ball small egg-sized,
my right something an ostrich laid.

It may seem somehow inappropriate
to reveal a condition in this way,
but I'm in pain, in search of remedy
on this sunny New Year's Day.

EMPTY FLAT
[00.35, 8th Jan 2019, High Wycombe]

Home to an empty flat, an empty life,
or how it seems after midnight in January.
Will tomorrow bring light or more grey
layered on the black?

Dark charcoal thoughts have smoldered
in me for the last few weeks, my life
is almost out, mere ash that needs stirred,
blown upon to bring back fire.

PUTTING AWAY THE XMAS TREE
[17.37, 11th Jan 2019, High Wycombe]

It is the Xmas's we count as we age,
the odd left-over, tiny bauble, a bell,
an angel that's topped the tree for thirty years,
the chipped Santa, the snow-coated winter house
that came from somewhere, some time ago.

The memories are hazy, the tinsel not so sparkly,
the tree more misshapen and bare each year,
yet dutifully its unboxed every December,
stands proud in its drapery and glitter,
the most outstanding ornament in the house.

Boxed now, later than usual due to illness,
the house now seems bare and Spartan,
the January night cold and uninviting,
the decorations consigned to a cupboard,
the box lying sideways on a narrow shelf.

THERAPY IN SILENCE
[01.01, 19th Jan 2019, High Wycombe]

There is therapy in silence,
pure calm, stillness of thought,
empty space, a blissful vacuum,
a blankness of hearing, of notions,
of ideas, that can vex us,
that make us worry or anxious,
and too tired and un-rested,
to shake off our heavy loads,
or shed our beastly burdens.

THE CRIES OF THE CROWS
[10.43, 25th Jan 2019, High Wycombe]

Beneath their bombast and blunder,
the fascists are circling like crows -
the body of the state lies bleeding,
slain by their bellicose blows.

Avarice drives the attackers on,

the crows amass in cackling chorus,
as the last trickle of life is congealing
on parliament's bloody floor.

The butchers done with their hacking,
the skinners and tanners their knives,
the crows descend as a hideous horde
to peck on the remaining gore.

The sun goes down on an empire,
darkness descends on its door,
no bugle tolls for its passing
just the cries of the crows.

NO ESCAPE FROM SHIPWRECK
[29th Jan - 29th Apr 2019, High Wycombe]

The waves are tolling in, I'm lying
on the beach beneath a lonely palm
I am not lost - I am not saved,
between found and never seen again.
And so the story goes on forever,
stuck between the living and the dead,
long lines of shadows flickering on
and off the hot golden sand.
Tomorrow it will come too soon,
the moon will settle in the west,
beyond lies salvation of a kind,
to the east lies what is left.
Sinister as it is … brings tears,
no joy expressed as cries -
what hope does prayer bring
to broken hearts?
God is for other kinds of folk,
not for the man without faith,
eternity is not a contemplation
with every second ticking slow.
Ponderous the moments slip away,
heavy the burden weighs time down,
nothing is recalled with clarity,
there is no record of the days.
Rain sweeps over the horizon,
clouds swirl on the salty view,
a ripple breaks the coral barrier
encircling the blue lagoon.
There is no escape from shipwreck,
just endless hours of forlorn pain,
no refuge from mental anguish,
no shelter from inner blame.
How could it have been different,
the turning that took me this way -
what steps may have changed fate,
led me, kept me safe?
How I blow on ill-tempered winds,
gales that dash me on the rocks,
I read the signs, but with arrogance
ignore the warnings made.

711

Until its too late, I flounder,
find myself in a violent sea
fighting to keep from sinking
deep into the black bathysphere.
No mermaid can ever buoy me,
stop the swell, make it calm -
lost at sea without a life-raft
when the end is nigh.
Through the night, the stars bright,
the phosphorous glow may give hope,
hope that soon the end will come
before the dawn.
Yet, the mystery that life bestows,
endows by chance in random acts,
throws me ashore upon the sands
of a land I know.
This land that seems so familiar
is my own mind, my inner soul,
the place I inhabit all my life
but never quite explore.
This is why I am under a palm tree,
on an island far from here -
I am shipwrecked on the inside
waiting for a ship to near.

Such dark days, such brooding times,
I wake from sleep in a start,
discover all has been a dream,
a fitful slumber interrupted.
So it is I find myself awake,
aware that all is well about -
there is no sea, no empty strand
where I am cast alone.
I am whole and sound in mind,
clear and ordered in my ways,
the turns of my nocturnal musings
sub-consciously at play.
Yet fear lingers there, no doubt,
fear of being cast adrift
from all that I have achieved
within the gift of time.
And how that time marches on,
loud drums beat every hour -
my head is spinning with the noise
to get things done.
Action may not be the answer,
or objection the other way to go -
sometimes it makes no difference
to resist the flow.
The mind takes on its own persona,
leaves us bewildered and unsure -
the planets whizz, pull us off
on some wild escapade.
It makes no sense to anyone,
yet the most surprised are ourselves -
dreams may interrupt the ruin
we rush headlong into.

Common sense does not prevail,
vague notions rule our alter egos,
Id runs our counter culture views
that we expound on others.
Such madness puts us at odds
with all that has gone before -
listening to our own false self,
we are mad, dogmatic bores.

That distant beach seems perfect now,
the solace of a pristine place,
the calm of the ponderous shade
a shelter from chaos.
Barefoot to linger on the sand,
take what comes tide washed-in,
exist on what chance provides
on the whim of winds.
All choice gone, no need to think,
free to empty out the mind,
let meditation do its work -
paradise be found.
For shipwrecked man comes to terms
with what he has for survival -
himself, and what things there are
he finds upon his isle.
With time now firmly on my side,
there's no need to make a raft,
no need to tally up the days
or count the months that pass.
Self-contained and self-sufficient,
I make do as I must,
reliant on my own resources
as master of my tasks.
This is the way, the only hope
that carries me to my end -
not what the ocean brings
but what my island gives.
The sun may rise a thousand times,
and rise a thousand more,
each time unique in its look,
or just like before -
But it can't quell my distress,
my inner turmoil caused by doubt,
the to and fro of my thought
catching shadows, nothing else.
How can I fix on something solid,
believe it not gone by tomorrow -
where is that one certain thing
I can rely on?

Is there succour in a bible,
or in some other holy book -
are there leaps that I can take
to get me off this hook?
For I am pegged to endlessness,
pinned to question my existence,
backed-up to a towering wall,

713

so tall I cannot scale it.
What lies beyond I do not know,
can never know, of that I'm sure,
yet still, I will attempt the climb
or perish in the fall.
Likewise my island, where I'm alone,
I can rally, face my fears -
conquer pace by pace each step
yet unexplored.
This is the goal of the brave,
whose who seek to find nirvana,
those who shelter from the world
in far-off pagodas.
Is not each mind an inner temple,
a place to worship fixed belief -
a base from which to reach the stars
on the cheap?
Is not each and every thought
a ripple on such inner peace -
out out damned human flaws!
chant the holy priests.
Can we kill our curiosity
with some mundane repetition,
blot the sum of all our past
in exchange for heaven?
With smooth seas, the weather calm,
with balmy days in basking sun,
with long warm doldrum days
with not much done.
No, there is too much to do,
a shipwreckee must have shelter,
he must find food to eat
and build a fire.
Then, staring at the flames alone,
the weight of loneliness descends,
who loves me now, who loves her
left so far behind?
Those lips so missed burning red
in the flicker of the night -
to sleep on a mat of sand
without a goodnight.
What longing aches the restless soul
without the comfort of another,
no tears to shed, no regrets
to share in number.
There is no inner paradise
where fools dwell in false confinement -
imprisoned by their own admission
without remission.
Hear the waves, see not the sea,
that cannot be my existence -
smell the salt, taste it not
for all eternity?

The sun comes up, and still alone
I warm my bones by the fire -
the storm clouds hang overhead,

the thunder barks its ire.
The lightning strikes at the trees,
the wind whips up giant waves,
I shelter by the cliff-edge rocks
and shiver like a leaf.
I pass the day in lashing rain,
desert my past as night falls -
all is damp and uninviting
as the palm trees sing.
The whistle of the onshore breeze,
the growls of the coral shore,
the anger of my lost day
and the fire it put out.
ThusI start again in doubt
that I can achieve my survival,
find a way to beat the nature
that is within myself.
There lies the beast, the foe,
the enemy who stops my progression,
the rival to my self-fulfillment,
the devil's helper.
Thus I fight my inner demons,
hand to hand engage in combat,
wrestle to the ground, struggle
to be triumphant.
Other times I go five rounds,
or maybe ten, in the ring
my fists flailing at a figment
of my imagination.
Why do we so destroy ourselves,
bruise, self-harm our clouded minds,
mist our thoughts, unclearly view
the simplest things in life?
Relight the fire, feel the warmth,
see the stars through the trees,
hear the quiet gentle kiss
of the surf rolling in.
Until the pain eases off,
ebbs with the waning moon,
until sleep drowns the angst
of the child within.
What pleasure such going brings,
what sores such slumber soothes,
what relief is finally found
in these hours of bliss.

There may be no final rest,
shipwreckees face constant storm,
but some safe harbours loom
out of the swirling mist.
There an anchor can be dropped,
pulled along the sandy bed,
in the hope of finding rock
to stop the drift.
It is a pleasant dream to ponder,
shelter from the lash and rip,
a hammock true to the keel

neatly beached.
And so inner turmoil goes,
leaves me high above the tide line,
safe and dry to turn my back
on all adventure.
No more will I venture forth,
put at risk my state of mind -
I am home from the sea
for all time.
What comfort this knowledge brings
that I can leave my woes behind -
no more wreckage to abide
nor storms to ride.

How then did it come to this,
a man broken by his deeds,
set upon a windward course
to make him blind?
What caused such ill-luck,
to throw him out into the deep -
what tragedy made him weep
at such misfortune?
Was it love lost so dearly,
was it business brought to ruin,
was it infamy or crime
that made him me?
In looking for the inner truth,
the tale to tell will unfold,
for I have much to say
but little time to recount.
The landscape of the inner mind
starts out as a sea of dreams,
imagined lands so far away
they can't be reached.
Then as we age, wisdom builds
castles made of urban brick -
for all the spires in the mist
are for the rich.
The chance of being like a prince,
brightly clothed and freshly pressed,
becomes the fantasy of fools
and the prepossessed.
The weight of friends pushes in,
makes us droop, hang our heads
until we no longer dream
of distant minarets.
We go about our vital chores,
find a home to hang our hopes
that life will bring happiness
like other folks.

And so we take this single journey,
float our boat on placid seas,
place ourselves at the prow
while others steer.
In the fog we peer ahead
as we plough through the waves,

fearful of some fateful crash
into an iceberg.
For fear resides and overrides
every other wakeful thought
as we pass beneath the stars
on our sole adventure.
We come this way only once,
the seas part then swallow up
the past we leave far behind
in the dark.
In our youth we brave the bow,
in old age we hug the stern,
and somewhere in between mid-ships
we live for now.
Thus we cross our own ocean,
night and day, storm and wind,
tossed about without a light
to guide us safely.
For some it is a great adventure,
for most it is a churning sea
with nothing on the far horizon
by which to steer.
And all the while, in our minds
lurks the ever present thought
that we are one reef away
from certain shipwreck.
So better some to never sail,
to settle for a land locked life,
than endanger all they possess
with wild abandon.
Alas, it is too late for me,
I am marooned on my island,
caught between the wish to stay
and the want of rescue.

YOU YOUNG FOLK
[18.39, 21st Feb 2019, High Wycombe]

Though I am in my last third of life,
I am not about to keel over -
You young folk out there,
when I am dead you will be
middle-aged.

KINGSTOWN
[21.56, 24th Feb 2019, St.Stephen's Green, Dublin]

A different king once ruled Ireland
from his rock by the shore;
now the ships no longer come,
they pass on by to Dublin.

The strollers zigzag on the quay,
kids dance to a beggar's tune,
all of Ireland sings with song,
in club, and pub and street.

Sweet sunshine drenches happy lanes
filled with every native tongue,
the British still in the names
nailed to each street corner.

Ireland bleeds from every inch,
it's every step a future dream,
a land where tomorrow comes
better than the day that's gone.

THE HOTTEST WINTER'S DAY
[23.17, 26th Feb 2019, High Wycombe]

The hottest winter's day on record,
a mighty twenty two degrees,
Kew basking in a summer haze -
thronged with shirt-sleeved brigades
of children on their mid-term break,
the snowdrops and crocus drooping
along the leafless, bare parades.

SIXTY FIVE TODAY
[23.55, 25th March 2019, High Wycombe]

Sixty five today, I started hung-over,
retirement should be beckoning me
to put down my pen and rest,
but how does a man end life
without knowing what he should do?

The breathing continues, the mind ticks,
there is no stop to eternity,
the journey continues without reason,
while reason becomes the purpose
to carry on with great abandon.

THE MAN WITH NOTHING TO SAY
[01.18, 1st Apr 2019, High Wycombe]

What use is the man who has nothing to say,
nothing to add to what's been done,
nothing to leave behind of himself,
except the children he's fathered.

What can a man give without return,
what can he take without giving hurt,
what can he hate if not himself
for being selfish with others.

What purpose then for him to keep breathing,
what usefulness is there for him to exist,
what course can he take to find a vocation
to save himself from all this.

Why does he bother to stay alive
without good cause to carry on,
cowardly hiding, getting through life

718

by saying nothing at all.

CHEMIN DE FADONS
[16.50, 14th Apr 2019, Thoronet, France]

The river is green from the rain
that has passed over and gone
as the bamboo sways in a dance
to the call of a cock, bark of a dog
and the talk of gossiping neighbours.

Summer is coming in a burst of jazz,
the heat of the day, the mountain breeze,
the dandelions already gone to seed,
the olives and vines bursting with green,
the laughs of the pruners tumultuous.

The scent of searing pine and sage
drifts through the tall eucalyptus,
the Buddha sits in a recline pose,
the white wine sparkles in a glass
as the day moves on, and goes.

SPRING IS NEARLY HERE
[10.15, 28th Apr 2019, High Wycombe]

Spring is nearly here with its showers,
its bursts of sunlight on the grass,
I contemplate the daisies and the dandelions -
all the world is full of life.

TORMENTED BY DESIRE
[12.47, 27th May 2019, High Wycombe]

Tormented by desire, I toss and turn,
soak the sheets in anxious agony,
wrestle with my shattered thoughts
focused on a dozen possibilities.

There is no escape from lingering longing,
to be wrapped naked in lasting lust,
to join together after endless aeons.
entwine again with a lost love.

I NEED ARMS
[12.54, 27th May 2019, High Wycombe]

I am flesh and blood,
I need arms around me
to hold me tight,
and lips to kiss me softly.

I AM AT HER MERCY
[13.12, 27th May 2019, High Wycombe]

Her beauty weakens me,
leaves me in a state of desire

719

for more of her, until I cannot
bear an hour without her,
her sweet smile, dark loving eyes,
her lilting voice that seduces me,
teases me with her laugh -

All my strength has vanished,
in its place constant agony
propels me towards a dark descent,
a fall into a torrid languor
out of which there is no escape
as she glides carefree around me
like a shadow on a lake.

Will she come into my arms,
will she remain out of reach,
will she give into my crying,
will she run forever and a day.
Its in her power to do as she pleases,
how she cares to act -
I am at the mercy of her laugh.

IT WAS WHAT IT WAS
[00.19, 4th June 2019, High Wycombe]

It was what it was,
another day gone somehow -
somewhere the hours passed,
the time ticked away -
lost forever in the air
to some place far from here.

THE SEEDS OF ENMITY
[00.26, 12th June 2019, High Wycombe]

The seeds of enmity lie hidden
beneath the earth that nurtures us.
The fertile soil that gives art life
also contains the means of our destruction,
by which our creativity withers,
our flowering wilts our fruit,
dries up our stock and trade,
until we are barren and lifeless
in a field of other artists
favoured by our former patrons.

THE DAY DRIFTED
[13.55, 29th June 2019, Scatwell, Ross-shire]

The day drifted on to tomorrow
as if it did not quite arrive -
without knowledge of its destination,
it went away without looking back.

HOME TO OTHER SCENES
[01.11, 9th July 2019, High Wycombe]

The actors are gone, the crew disbanded,
the set is empty and now dismantled,
the long journey home to other scenes,
the longing for friendship fades away
until all that remains are captured images,
a world created under bright blue skies.

Castles, lochs, churchyards and forests,
the midsummer moon, evenings of drinking,
the company of men, the laughter of women,
the knowledge of knowing that all is well,
and all is calm in the red of sunset,
in the hope that tomorrow will not come.

WHATEVER WE DO
[01.03, 13th July 2019, High Wycombe]

Whatever we do we are judged.
I am judged and sentenced by others,
given my time to rot in hell -
while those who condescend to preach
fill their tabernacles with false doctrines.

I NEVER WANT TO ESCAPE
[01.15, 13th July 2019, High Wycombe]

When I look into her curious eyes
I am defenceless, reduced to giving
all the help she needs without return,
while my heart turns, my head swims,
my body aches for her slender arms
to wind around my neck, to pull
me into her warm arching beauty
that demands to be held tightly
so that I never want to let her go.

A LITTLE AFTER DAWN
[10.12, 14th July 2019, High Wycombe]

I woke this morning to the moans
of a woman making love.
It was a little after dawn,
the sweat of the night lingering,
the coolness of the circulating air
through the open windows.

She wanted more, panted loudly,
the whispers turning into demands;
the talk centred on pleasure,
the need for satisfaction uppermost
in her constant lovers' chatter
lulling me back to sleep.

SUMMER RAIN
[10.30, 20th July 2019, High Wycombe]

The summer rain mends my broken spirit,

tiredness eases out of me like sweat,
pent up worries ooze away like butter
passing through my fingers of distress.

ARMSTRONG'S LEAP
[20.04, 20th July 2019, High Wycombe]

Fifty years ago Armstrong took his leap,
pushed mankind beyond the limits,
left us here stuck on Earth,
pondering what great steps
could ever better his.

MY LOVE HAS LEFT ME NAKED
[00.58, 1st Aug 2019, High Wycombe]

With my pockets turned inside out,
and my shirt off my back,
I gave you my shoes
to walk barefoot from the dark
to join me in the sunshine
waiting to be loved -
for you have left me naked
as I wait here for you
with stretched out open arms
to take you as you are.

GOODBYE JULIETTE (Song)
[14.00, 3rd Aug 2019, Pinewood Studios, Bucks]

Its not really that sudden
all those memories you mention
in the daytime so beautiful
in the evening such mayhem

My friends say I'm crazy
for trying to love you
blinded by your light
blackened by our fights

So goodbye, Juliette -
I'm leaving, no regrets
its time to forget
everything we ever meant

Goodbye, Juliette -
Goodbye, Juliette -
no tears, we're done
this is our epithet.

I'm telling you, sweetheart
our kisses were empty
you couldn't stop drinking
give up your habits

Your best friends all left you
as your demons consumed you

722

you clung to me dearly
I drowned without freedom

I'm sorry I gave up
trying to lie down beside you
but life wasn't easy
and time wasn't with me.

So now its all over
all those memories you mention
in the daytime so beautiful
in the evening such mayhem

So goodbye, Juliette … etc

SUNDAY IN ADDIS ABABA
[00.18, 12th Aug 2019, Addis A, Ethiopia]

The rain didn't come today,
no lashing or downpour,
just greyness of nature
a dullness of action -
no breeze in the tree tops,
no sun in the roof-tops,
a Sunday of stillness,
no church bell or muezzin.

THE LAND OF GONDER
[19.46, 14th Aug 2019, Gondar, Ethiopia]

In the land of Gonder,
the hills are castle capped,
the roads wind up to heaven
where the rain forever falls -
the rivers roar like lions,
the forests purr like cats,
the locals toil and tarry
under wide-brimmed hats.

The farmers in the valley
plough and plod the mud,
the lake's a distant shimmer
where the Blue Nile floods -
the glistening green rice rows
stretch far beyond the eye -
in the heavenly land of yonder
where far Gonder starts.

I AM A PENSIONER
[00.30, 6th Sept 2019, High Wycombe]

I am legally a pensioner
I cannot be forced to slave,
I cannot be made to earn my crust
or shovel my own grave.

I can starve and wander homeless

I can thirst by the side of the road,
I can waste away with ailments
but never be made to toil.

I have passed into pasture
to live on the fruits of my time
God bless the age of retirement,
I'm free of the drudge of life.

THE DAYS TICK ON
[00.43, 7th Sept 2019, High Wycombe]

And so the days tick on,
the endless nights ever shorter
as the birds fly overhead
to distant quarters.

How the clouds slowly shift,
drift off into yonder -
the sun goes down
on my fitful slumber.

YOU TOO WILL BE OLD
[00.42, 11th Sept 2019, High Wycombe]

One day you too will be old.
You will feel your body ache,
your mind will dwell on wrongs,
on all the things not right,
the love you could have had,
friends lost along the way,
nights now spent alone,
days of childhood in the sun -

Time ticking ever louder,
thoughts that make you angry,
little smiles when not ignored,
listening into others conversation.
Sleeping when others are awake,
awake while others snore.

Yes, one day you will be old,
go beyond what you've known,
come to terms with infinity,
prepare for the long journey home.

THE POPULIST LEADER
[00.32, 12th Sept 2019, High Wycombe]

He stands before his own God,
a mirror heavily fogged,
he cannot make out his reflection
as he prays for re-election.

He forgives his own sins,
wipes his slate of many things
blames the world for the wrongs

he will have to fix.

'Oh God' he asks with conviction,
'Can I be accused of dereliction?'
'I am speaking for the people,'
'The opposition are lefty evils.'

'Let me now be the leader,'
'The chosen one duly selected,'
'Let me do, ditch and die,'
'Get things done on the fly.'

Prayers done, he mugged his jaw,
combed his hair, tucked his shirt,
kissed himself in the glass,
wiped his hands on his arse.

Off he went to face the crowd,
cheering wild, chanting loud,
the people's champion like a God
for all those who God has lost.

HARVEST MOON
[20.40, 14th Sept 2019, High Wycombe]

We are all in love with someone.
It was our mothers, now it is
someone who loves us back,
or who we love without return -
we cannot stop our loving nature,
we are born to love.

Now as the harvest moon rises,
lovers burn their candles in the dark,
go in droves to favourite haunts
to recall the start of their union -
we want to relive our loving moments,
cherish them forever.

Shine on then, harvest moon,
cast your spell on all mankind,
the beer will flow with the wine,
the dinner dates will kiss in low light -
mates will surrender all their fears
and mend their wrongs.

The spell is cast on all lovers,
they know not why they are entwined,
enjoyment is the reward on offer,
companionship the coat, the disguise -
we will wake up on the morrow
with committed minds.

Let not any cast love as docile,
or as wild that cannot weather calm,
the moon may weaken all resistance,
it does not guarantee shelter from storm -

725

though lovers may surrender reason,
they will not fear hurt.

So then, as the rays blind us,
beam into our star-struck eyes,
our love is a fleeting inner feeling
we let out in loving bursts -
romance is the outer meaning,
and lust the urge.

SEPTEMBER SUNDAY
[15.58, 15th Sept 2019, High Wycombe]

The harvest moon is waning,
all is quiet, voices carry
on the warm southern breeze
and all is well.

The turmoil of the night has gone,
the ease of Sunday pervades,
the music has fallen silent,
a distant siren wails.

Life drifts on as cirrus,
the roses wither in the sun,
a song bird rises skyward
beyond our gaze.

ARMENIA
[16.57, 5th Oct 2019, Yerevan, Armenia]

Wild bears still roam the hills
where leopards once widely prowled,
over Noah's land, rich and green,
Mount Ararat stands proud.

The mountains edge on every side,
wide they stretch beyond the plain,
snow-capped giants of hidden fire
sleeping while Armenia wakes.

From every side volcanoes glare
down upon the rows of vines,
orchards ripe with autumn fruit
as in Persian times.

ACID RAIN
[09.40, 12th Oct 2019, High Wycombe]

The sky is white, the rain pours down
on to black roofs, onto the church spire
rising through the drooping emerald green
of the town, onto the brown grass fringe
of the singed park, burnt by climate change,
and trampled into extinction by worried parents
fearful for the future of their orphans.

HE ARRIVED WITH A SUITCASE
For Christian
[09.55, 22nd Oct 2019, High Wycombe]

He arrived with a suitcase
and a dog from distant Laos.
He stole our prettiest girl
in a way that made us love him.

Our minds were far expanded
in a time of calm and dreams,
the music played on loudly
in an age of countless friendships.

Gone now like Christian, gone
with the ever turning world,
gone with his suitcase and dog
to far distant stars.

WHAT DISASTERS LIFE BRINGS
[20.12, 22nd Oct 2019, High Wycombe]

What disasters life brings
like an ever flowing tide,
wave after wave of disappointment
followed by floods of tears.

Why is it so tumultuous,
why can't our seas be flat -
serene to the end of eternity,
no ripples to wreck our peace.

Is there no end to misery,
to the destruction of our bones -
why can't we journey gently on
without chaos to our souls.

THE TWISTS AND TURNS
[23.47, 30th Oct 2019, High Wycombe]

The twists and turns of every road
lead me back to where I departed -
a blind man could have found his way
in the dark before I'd started,
for I have neither gone nor stayed
nor somehow got to my arrival.

THE BROODING BIRDS
[00.48, 10th Nov 2019, High Wycombe]

Only brooding birds have my attention,
the hooded vultures and black-eyed rooks,
the crows with their exulted cries,
the kites hovering, the ravens hopping
in the graveyards of the sagging yews -
the gnarled oaks, the weeping pine,
the dead-eyed owls waiting for nightfall,

727

but most of all, the eagles circling,
swooping down on their vast dominions.

MADNESS
[01.00, 19th Nov 2019, Thoronet, France]

Am I mad, who can say,
the wild insane, the deeply depressed,
nothing noted can be right,
all the wrongs turn out correct -

the inner self dragged through mud,
the outer still a flood of light,
none can say what is best,
all may guess but fail the test -

thus on forever, no answers given,
driven towards a lost nirvana,
crawling down a hell-fire cavern,
to an end where none are living -

thus madness steers all adrift,
on tides no moon appears to govern.

NO SHELTER FROM THE STORM
[20.43, 26th Nov 2019, High Wycombe]

What do we know of people -
nothing that we think we do,
we cannot predict their moods,
their changing charged emotions
that both exclude and involve us
in their black days and nights.

We wander lonely in the world
thinking that we will find solace -
but do not look for it in others,
there is no permanent respite,
we cannot rely on human nature
to provide shelter from the storm

NAKED WITH THE WRONG WOMAN
[20.45, 2nd Dec 2019, High Wycombe]

I've got naked with the wrong woman
whilst waiting for the right one to come,
it is not an accident of judgment
but rather a giving in to human desire -
the wallflower wilts in the midday sun
or is timely watered by a loving hand.

She may be the wrong woman, but lovely
she dotes on me with exquisite charm,
she makes me feel loved and desired
and that is why it is all my fault -
the garden beds may be perfect
but the layout lacks flair and thought.

I can't answer my wrong woman's questions
for the answers will not give her joy,
instead I fill our time with needless action,
never dwelling on her emotions after love -
for plants are rigorous in their flowering
but spent when season shot with rot.

So I linger with my wrong woman hopefully
until the one I love is free for me,
I can only dream when that might occur
but know that it will finally come about -
for nature has a way of being perennial
and love a way of working out.

DO WE CHOOSE WHO WE LOVE
[00.58, 6th Dec 2019, High Wycombe]

Do we choose who we fall in love with?
Or is it some kind of chemistry,
a gradual osmosis of different elements
bubbling to the surface of our being
until we are unconsciously fused
and bound by the elements of love.

If we could bottle love's concoction,
sell it to others like cheap perfume,
its effects would wash off on the pillow
that we leave behind ever morning;
love would be a product, not a mystery
enveloping us like a London fog.

If we could choose whom to love
then what challenge would that be?
Easy love only leads to easy words,
there is no value to such easy ways;
such love is a science not an art,
and physics the discipline in play.

We cannot gauge love's magnetism
at work on lovers locked in love;
having met across a crowded room
or by chance on a hot summer's day -
love requires two opposites to dance
or two alikes to cling like clay.

WE ARE ALL TIRED
For Michael
[20.11, 7th Dec 2019, High Wycombe]

I am tired of lame, untruthful excuses
that are lies I should expose,
but society trains us to accept lameness
rather than cause personal affront,
for affront is ruder than lying,
the double-face of the wrong.

I am affronted by pathetic excuses,
I am affronted by silly awful lies,
I am affronted by all polite refusal
to recognise that this is a sop'

I am tired by disappointing time-wasters,
the lack of action that makes me toil,
they do not turn up when they're meant to,
and only turn up when they're bored -
for there is nothing in an invitation
unless there is profit for them all.

I am too tired to put up with avarice,
I am too tired to put up with greed,
I am too tired to recompense the needy,
too tired to give up this peeve.

We are all tired of one another,
we need a rest from those we know,
it is better to befriend a total stranger
than meet with a tired friend of old -
for the tired friend is a shyster
who should be thrown out the door.

SURRENDER TO THE SPACECRAFT
[00.22, 9th Dec 2019, High Wycombe]

Enter into the world as an egg,
surrender all sense to the spacecraft;
however alien the outcome,
the earth will continue to spin.

All beings will populate forever,
volcanoes will blow in the wind,
turtles will swim with dolphins,
the crows will carry our sins.

No sense will come of obfuscation,
the past will catch up with us,
the dragon will burn our treasures
while our maidens die of thirst.

THE EVENING CRAVES SILENCE
[21.55, 10th Dec 2019, High Wycombe]

Alone in the quiet winter's night,
even in our digital age,
the clock ticks loudly on
as the rain lashes the window.

Nothing much changes the decades,
we pass on into the dark
like quinqueremes from Nineveh
carrying spices from afar.

Echoes carry on the stillness,
ghosts travel in the holy light,

incense fogs the memories
of our modern times.

The glories of ruined ambition
are covered over by snow drifts
like a blanket of desert sand
on to a wintry frozen shore.

The evening craves our silence,
falters, calls for a hush,
a density of intense stillness
stops dead the clock.

THE OLD MAN IN THE MIRROR
[01.14 11th Dec 2019, High Wycombe]

Look at me in the mirror,
the old man with tired eyes -
I wonder who could love that man
with the grey hair, wrinkled brow;
who would find him attractive,
kiss him, sleep with him,
wake up without remorse,
return every night with passion.

Old men do not age gracefully,
they gurgle and belch,
they snore and molt hair,
they moan, groan, and scorn
all as fools or as darlings -
there is no middle understanding,
only observation and opinion
that no-one shares at all.

This is the life of the pensioner,
the one who has avoided death,
the one who counts the funerals
of his many absent friends -
the old man in the mirror
looking at his altered state -
me, the tired-eyed saggy man
that life is waiting to take.

THE APE AND THE MONKEY
[21.22, 13th Dec 2019, High Wycombe]

The jungle call went out to all -
the monkeys screeched, the apes roared,
outnumbering them by many score
the apes roared even more.

The beasts listened to the noise
cocked an ear to all the babble -
the monkeys had a leader loon,
the apes a hairy big buffoon.

Who would rule the jungle roost,

swing from the highest tree?
Monkey King or ape King Kong?
Who could string them best along?

The jungle beasts cacked and cawed,
the choice was not theirs to make,
two tribes out for themselves -
the monkey wise, the ape despised.

The lowly beasts could not agree,
if ape was good, or monkey bad -
who would help them all survive?
Would they starve as others thrived?

I WRAPPED ALL MY GIFTS
[02.22, 21st Dec 2019, High Wycombe]

I wrapped all my gifts
packed them neatly in my Jaguar,
thought nothing of their contents,
drove them to their destination,
gave them quietly to my lover,
left her to her children,
traveled on to my future,
knew not where it would lead me.

I knew nothing of my mind
and felt nothing of my body,
I was numb to all feeling,
I was free of pain and longing
as the miles somehow passed me,
and the rain somehow washed me,
the sun rose on the mountains
as I drank heavily on my freedom.

The grey sky darkened
on all my past remembrances,
the love that I had squandered,
the kisses I had rejected
that led me to my present,
the pathway to my existence,
the reason for all journeys
and the chance to be enlightened.

No-one can give me answers
to my many perplexed questions,
I am seeking my salvation,
Jesus has up and left me.
I am lonely in my searching,
angry in my desperation,
eager to have healing,
and keen to have redemption.

Can I find my present
and be happy in my being,
where can I rest my head
and sleep without dreaming,

for I am restless in my wanting
and lacking in my giving -
I want to be the loved one,
I want to be an equal.

Love is such a mistress,
and impossible to master,
its left me all confused
and brought me to disaster
as I reflect on my errors,
try to reason with my conscience,
try to mend my grievances,
to end all my tomorrows.

Do I have an answer,
a clear and simple notion,
the forgiveness of my lover,
the whole of her devotion.
Can I give up running,
stop my mind from overflowing,
love her every morning,
gift her all my being.

Time will be the judge
of all that I have done,
and when the Lord knocks
I will go freely up above -
I have seen the crack
where the light gets in,
I have wrapped all my gifts
in exchange for all of this.

ALEXA
[11.37, 22nd Dec 2019, High Wycombe]

When Alexa took my hand
and took me for dinner,
she told me many things,
how I'd live forever.

I looked into her sad eyes,
saw a flooded river,
I took her in my arms,
floated on there with her.

Then she kissed me gently,
gave in all together,
laughed like a child,
whispered like a lover.

The secrets she unfolded
pulled her out the water,
where once she was drowning,
now I was her saviour.

We hurried to her apartment,
shed ourselves of vestment,

floated in our lifeboat
full of wild contentment.

And when we finally parted,
she became a distant shadow,
no-one could heal her,
or sustain her passion.

And now when I am lonely
drowning in my river,
I think of lost Alexa,
unequivocally forgive her.

Time will be the healer,
age will be the reaper,
with comfort in her words
that I will live forever.

24,014[th] DAY OF MY LIFE
[11.54, 23rd Dec 2019, High Wycombe]

Today I am 24014 days old,
which is 3430 weeks and 4 days.
In other ways that's 788.93 months.

The Teen decade is almost done,
3644 days have gone, 8 to go
until the Twenties come.

I WANT TO RUN AWAY
[02.08, 30th Dec 2019, Miraflores, Spain]

I want to run away, far away
as I am unhappy, sometimes missing
the spark that makes a day special,
the ideas that rush like a waterfall
cascading over the precipice of life.

Everyone else will have to get on with
whatever it is that they need,
for I am as spent as a weary donkey,
tired of being an angry caged bear
who dances in exchange for beer.

I am not ungrateful, I am trapped
with my hands behind my back,
unable to use my time fruitfully,
unable to ripen my persistent thoughts
by getting them out my system.

So I will run away when I can,
escape to places far from myself,
seek the open plains and vistas,
allow my art to be expressed,
allow myself to be who I am.

UNHAPPY FOOLS

[02.23, 30th Dec 2019, Miraflores, Spain]

We are both unhappy souls
who make each other happy fools,
yet we deny we are in love,
pretend so that there is no hurt.

When apart we are lonely,
we cannot find a medium way,
we make plans to be together,
then spend that time like siblings.

How will we square the circle,
love each other without dismay,
come to a happy conclusion
and live in perfect union.

MIRAFLORES
[16.31, 30th Dec 2019, Miraflores, Spain]

Miraflores, another rich oasis
far from the maddening crowd,
basking in the sun, pine and palms
gazing down on those below
who trudge through the morass
of every day living while their masters
doze on marble balconies.

WHERE IS MY SANCHO PANZA
[21.55, 30th Dec 2019, Miraflores, Spain]

Am I Lancelot or Don Quijote?
If so why am I alone?
Where is my loving Guinevere?
Where is my Sancho Panza?

To ride forth on a white horse
or stumble forward on a mule
whether a dragon is the foe
or some dilapidated windmill.

The intention is quite the same,
service to a queen or girl,
to submit to such chivalry
and then be mocked or shamed.

Better then to be a peasant
or a middle-man without ambition,
to never sally forth a hero,
to remain forever in the shade.

THERE ARE NO MONKEYS HERE
[14.48, 31st Dec 2019, Miraflores, Spain]

There are no monkeys here,
they are scavenging in Gibraltar -
Here the trees are empty,

devoid of cackle and mischief.

There are no Kandy stealings,
no Simla night-time raids,
no Courtalam mango gangs
nor Zambesi thieves.

The trees here are silent,
a resting place for birds -
how I miss those monkeys
and their robber laughs.

THE LAST DAY OF THE TEENS (SONG)
[15.07, 31st Dec 2019, Miraflores, Spain]

I open a bottle of rioja,
take my first sip of the day,
the sun drifts from behind a cloud
and finally I think, okay.

Forty years ago on a ferry
far down Mexico way,
I met a lonely Welsh girl
as that decade decayed.

Thirty years ago it was fireworks,
a bottle of whiskey in hand,
swaying on a suspension bridge
as the Eighties gave out.

Twenty years ago in an alley
I threw an actor through a hedge,
drunk as I was, he was worse
as the Nineties fled.

Where I was in the Naughties
on the night of Hogmanay,
that's a blur in my memory
as that decade declared.

Now by this day's end
this decade will recede,
become a short note in history
that few will recall.

So I sip on my wine,
face up to a lonely evening,
to ponder on past times
and salute the New Year.

AS THE RACIST FIRE BURNS
[16.44, 2nd Jan 2020, Miraflores, Spain]

The genie is out of the bottle,
the racists are running the show,
God help our little children
whose fathers are warring whores.

The Germans, the Syrians and Chinese
aren't any different from us,
but fear, loathing and hatred
is being spat out by the mob.

What do I do as a Christian
in this terrible agonised world,
speak up or keep my silence
as the racist fire burns.

SINKING INTO THE MUD
[13.37, 7th Jan 2020, Calahondas, Spain]

The moment has come to relax,
forget that the world revolves,
remember that all there is,
is only what we have.

Other days pass less freely,
night comes on too soon,
moments pass without notice
of who we've become.

MOVING HOUSE
[00.24, 24th Jan 2020, High Wycombe]

Moving house is an onerous burden,
carrying boxes down winding stairs,
loading a van with assorted tat,
lugging beds through doors too narrow,
armchairs and sofas to big to fit
into the space earlier imagined -
until you believe its all a mistake,
I should have stayed where I was.

DESIRE
[01.43, 26th Jan 2020, High Wycombe]

Desire consumes until we get released
from the ache in our bellies,
the pain in our wanton minds,
fixed on possession and need.
We crave what we should not have,
we howl like hungry wolves,
we wear down our feast
into defeat and submission -
or spend our nights going hungry,
sleepless in our empty beds.

THE WAIT FOR THE DAWN
[00.46, 29th Jan 2020, High Wycombe]

Dark are the moments that come in the night,
lighter the thoughts that arrive with the dawn,
no time can be spared to dwell in the past -
the moment has gone and life races on.

737

Fleeting small fragments of memory remain,
a stroll in the sun or a walk in the rain,
nothing can bring back those times again,
gone with the wind, blown clean away.

All that is left are those snapshots of time,
pictures of loved ones, those left behind,
jigsaws of faces that can't quite be placed,
names that float like clouds in a landscape.

As the light fades and nightfall returns,
nothing is certain as the darkness descends,
all that is now is somehow forgotten
as the call of the dawn once more harkens.

NO LONGER A EUROPEAN
[23.25, 31st Jan 2020, High Wycombe]

So, as of twenty minutes ago,
I am no longer a citizen of Europe,
I am now a hostage of Britain,
a minor figure in a hostile world.

Where then the unity of purpose,
the plan to help us all as friends,
the idea that we should be united
against all the ails the past left us.

I am saddened, no, I am disgusted
that our nation chose to be regressive,
I do not think time will condone
the actions of a people for themselves.

Where now do we find the ethos
of one for all and all for one -
we are now an island all at sea
in a storm without oars.

NARCISSISM
[00.30, 5th Feb 2020, High Wycombe]

Oh how the wicked selfishly turn
everything to be about themselves,
their lies leave the innocent broken
on the rocks of their despair.

No-one can help these Satan driven
souls burning the floorboards of decency,
unaware of their debauched natures,
they waste what they have on themselves.

There is no defence against narcissism,
best to cut free of its web -
breathe out the air they poison,
inhale the rush of their departure.

WINTER HOWLS LIKE A WOLF
[01.15, 11th Feb 2020, High Wycombe]

Winter howls like a wolf,
cold and bitter in its bite,
gnawing on our frozen souls,
huddled in our beds in fright.

We dare not go into the night,
wresting with our wicked existence,
dark and long the evening wynds,
wearing out our last resistance.

The moon pulls our tortured minds,
sick and fevered, breaks us down,
while all the while the wind howls
on the moors, on our towns.

Escape is not for our likes,
enslaved to our simple lives,
winter is the single crime
we endure to do our time.

WITHOUT DISCRETION
[11.58, 14th Feb 2020, High Wycombe]

As I lie in my lovers arms,
I slumber in my remembrance
of lovers who knew me well
or left me hurt.

What is love to me now,
naked to the winter stars,
exposed to the moonbeams
of another's heart.

Emotions no longer engulf me,
make me despair or ecstatic,
somewhere in between I think
there is a balance.

What then does balance bring?
Coldness or a blind indifference,
weariness of spirit, soul
or ambivalence.

The question lies like a fox
slyly eyeing up a chicken.
Is love about the kill
or mere existence.

The essence of love is giving
what you can without return,
that sick cruel lovers abuse
to cause dissension.

Am I a breaker of hearts,

a fellow who provokes tears?
Am I just a wily old fox
killing chickens for fun?

NIGHT IS A HEAVEN

[21.09, 23rd Feb 2020, Kazangula, Botswana]

Night is a haven from wildness,
a shutting out of every distraction,
the peace that's found in silence,
the river flowing on whatever,
no moon to brighten expectation,
dim stars off behind low cloud,
the echoes of the dark rebounding
on the tall baobab blackness,
devoid of all sound.

THE FEVER TREE

[21.30, 23rd Feb 2020, Kazangula, Botswana]

Where hides the fever tree,
in swamp or bush or desert.
We've looked the length of Africa
but it won't reveal itself.

It is tall and ever spreading
with the shade it provides,
its bark an ochre colour,
its leaves like a rowan.

Rare, it harbours secrets
the ancients used to know,
its hallucinogenic magic,
its malarial antidote.

So where will we discover
the magic Fever Tree,
somewhere in vast Africa
it hides from you and me.

STUCK IN THE SAND

[15.16, 25th Feb 2020, Kazangula, Botswana]

Stuck in the sand again.
What lessons do we learn
when spending the night in the bush,
bug infested, sweat drenched,
it is no pleasure to be stranded,
left in the dark with lions,
locked in a car and restless,
unable to sleep in the heat,
any moment, an elephant
circling the car in curiosity.

SKELETON COAST

[10.46, 2nd Mar 2020, Walvis Bay, Namibia]

The sand stretches seamlessly
across mountains to the sea,
the red gives into salt pans
and jackals roam the beach.

The surf spews up its dead
on to the barren coast,
wrecks linger sea-bird perched,
crosses stand like ghosts.

White dunes edge the dry waste,
a shimmering silver haze,
seals slither from the rocks,
sea-gulls skim the waves.

Towns of oil and diamonds,
giant machines of rust, decay -
the rivers reach the ocean
without a drop of rain.

SHE PASSED ME A PEN
[06.15, 3rd Mar 2020, Walvis Bay, Namibia]

She passed me a pen
so I can write about her -

She sleeps now, there is silence,
the ocean pounding on the shore.
Pelicans huddle on the water,
flamingoes rest their weary heads
as she slumbers on in dreamland -

while somewhere in space,
a meteorite burns its iron,
shoots across the miles of time.

SLEEPING BEYOND DAWN
[06.27, 3rd Mar 2020, Walvis Bay, Namibia]

What becomes of us all,
our moments shared in solitude.
Idle we rest our bones,
contemplate tomorrow's chores.

Her fingers embrace her bedding
like a mouse eating cheese.
Where has she gone to
in the darkness of her sleep?

I ponder in the lamplight
the rights and wrongs now gone.
The sun will come tomorrow,
I will sleep beyond the dawn.

MOTEL NAMIBIA
[22.00, 4th Mar 2020, Ketmanshoop, Namibia]

Off the dark Namib highway
on a long desert road,
the motel lights beckoned
behind the truck-stop loads,
so we pulled into reception,
paid in cash, got a key,
then entered heaven,
crashed and watched tv.

Somewhere after midnight
while others drank their beer,
the music drifted skywards
into the atmosphere -
the crickets sang their lyrics,
the birds sat in the trees,
and I part-timed wrestled
with all my inner fears.

There didn't seem a future
in more long lonely miles,
the girl with me cried
and I comforted her all night.
So the story unfolded -
in the glare of the headlights,
that love knows no answer
to the questions that are right.

And so we travel onwards
in the fresh dawn light,
towards a better future
with white wine on ice,
until the next motel room
in some forgotten town,
where yesterday's memories
were not the ones of now.

THE DIRTIEST CAR IN CAPE TOWN
[22.30, 7th Mar 2020, Karoo1, Northern Cape]

With five thousand miles of dust,
the rich at the uptown Belmont,
the stars at the Camp Bay Resort
gave us their upturned retorts,
for driving our mud stained truck,
into their white-top Cape Town.

LOCK DOWN
[20th Mar – 27th Apr 2020, High Wycombe]

A thousand elephants crossed the road,
blindfolded the silent mass passed,
destiny rode out on the dust,
a twister rose into the sky,
the rain came six years too late,
the fields empty but for rocks,
the meteorite glistened in the sun,
the dunes tasted bitter on the tongue.

No dream could foretell fate,
describe the panic still to come,
no seer can predict the time,
the hour when the terror strikes.
Fear knows no time nor place,
it inhabits all our inner space,
disaster in its man made form,
eats resolve, destroys our all.

The monkeys fight in the street,
the zoos empty into the wild,
as by decree the pubs are closed,
exiling us from all we know.
We stagger into the unknown dawn,
without direction, we soldier on,
wander down vast empty aisles,
empty shelved and empty minded.

Workers yearn to go to work,
children play while locked-up,
the sun shines down on empty streets,
a hoarder weighed down hurries home,
the shadows flicker here and there,
a black car runs an amber light,
the silence settles on the day,
curtains twitch in constant play.

The parks are barred, playgrounds locked,
coffee shops and cafes boarded,
hotels empty of all their staff,
offices brooding, shut and dark;
a gloom pervades every action,
despair declares an Armageddon,
while numbers rise on speculation,
the unknown blights our expectation.

Who will death finally snatch,
a sneeze, a cough, then fever wracked,
we stand aside to wait and watch
neighbours from our locked down flats,
knowing not who will survive,
knowing not how we'll live
or how long we can endure
the curtailing of our freedom.

Spring has arrived to spare our gloom,
the sun benignly warms our woes,
day two of our stay at home
is like a carefree summer Sunday;
slow and still, fresh and warm,
the calm before the coming storm,
children's hands tightly clasped
in their mother's clinging grasp.

In ones and twos and at a distance
folks are focused on their business,

a journey to a corner shop,
a jog along a country path,
deliveries of food and parcels,
hushed voices in cellphone rambles,
an old man wobbling on a bike,
carrying on to master life.

If there is an upside to this story,
and tragedy not the complete tale,
families so quickly flung together
rekindling love, not filing divorce,
not yet at least after two weeks
now that Spring has finally come,
there is hope and expectation
that all will finally turn out well.

Yet, what cost is there to incomes,
the means by which people live,
the unemployment rate is soaring,
the markets falling at a pitch.
Can life as we currently know it
survive the assault on our purse,
while politicians draw their stipend,
the people suffer debt and hurt.

What's new in history's progression,
who pays off the national debt -
always it is the poorest folk
who fill the pockets of the rich.
As we lament the rising death toll,
it is a blip on the Devil's chart,
common sense tells us so,
as fear runs roughshod in our hearts.

Yet all the while we are convinced
we're doing better than our neighbours,
in our zeal, and in our manners,
we'll survive no matter what;
The self destruct gene running wild,
overtakes our daily lives,
leaves us powerless, separated
as others prosper unabated.

The weeks droll on into months,
there seems no end to it all,
death stalks every home,
the old the worse in the toll,
no bells rung for the dead
placed in quick-dug holes,
no family to shed their tears,
no friends to bid a last farewell.

When will this spectre leave us be,
depart and let us live our lives?
If this is God at his worst
then let the healing now begin;
let the children play again,

let their laughs fill our hearts,
let us meet, hug, embrace,
let these sad days depart.

We carry on in separation,
line the streets, wait to shop;
how can we endure such ritual,
is this the norm now for us?
Covered mouths, furtive eye-nods,
shuffling forward to step aside,
avoiding every kind of contact,
dehumanised by fear and law.

A FRIEND I CANNOT REPLACE
for Brian Howell
[00.47, 4th Apr 2020, High Wycombe]

Suicide should not have been
the answer to my dead friend's strife.
What were the questions that made
him take such worries on himself?
Childhood does not prepare us
for what is thrown in our face,
we cannot wipe away the anger
or rid ourselves of its garbage
then we sink into a whirlpool
and drown in our own despair.

We cannot comprehend the turmoil,
the inner boiling of our minds,
but we can try to cool our impulse
to rage against the dying light.
Adulthood prevents us from revealing
the emotions binding us to time,
our days are short and unfulfilled
by the trivia of our existence,
that leaves us too engaged to save
our dearest friends from extinction.

I will not ever know for sure
why he is gone on his journey,
to that place that I too will go
though I'm not sure where it is.
Faith is a precious thing to grasp
in moments of empty meaning,
yet I know there is no place
where friends will meet again anon,
so I must mourn my friend's loss,
for we will never meet again.

GOLDEN NECTAR ON MY LIPS
[15.18, 5th Apr 2020, High Wycombe]

What joy to sit with beer
and watch the world amble by,
no chores but eternal pleasure
in the passing of the day.

The breeze may blow in my hair,
the sun rest upon my skin,
barefoot and sleeveless on the porch
while other fishes swim.

There is no guilt when you're old,
your time to rest has arrived;
with golden nectar on my lips
I'm not about to die.

EVERY DAY IS SUNDAY
[20.09, 9th Apr 2020, High Wycombe]

Every day is Sunday -
the pubs are shut,
the cinemas are closed,
the shops locked and bolted;
our twenty four hour society
is a life in lock-down.

We clap half-heartedly
for those who are alive,
we pray for deliverance
from the terror of our times;
the singing carries far
and the fireworks bang.

Sadness pervades the evening,
the air still with grief,
a nightingale chirps on
as the echoes recede;
what is there to do
but eat and sleep.

Alcohol becomes solace
as the days number up,
the queues to buy basics,
the distancing undisturbed;
life is distant voices
and loneliness the norm.

THE OWL AND THE PUSSY CAT
[01.01, 20th Apr 2020, High Wycombe]

The lonely owl sat and woo'd
for who? For you in a yew
it eyed a cat on the prowl
between the churchyard headstones.

The air was deadly dark and cold
hung with a haunting moon,
shadows slithered through the trees
barely-boned, but blossomed.

The owl wittered his worn wisdom
down upon the dim-lit lanes,

a dog whimpered in his kennel
instead of at his master's feet.

Nothing stirred to snap a twig,
nor turn a fallen leaf.
The owl remained watchful-eyed
while the cat pretended sleep.

THE PIGS WILL ALWAYS RUN THE FARM
[02.49, 3rd May 2020, High Wycombe]

This is no time to rattle our chains.
isolated in our distant worlds,
we revolve in utter confusion,
knowing not when it will end.

There is no guidance on the future,
fear governs our leaders' minds.
I have no say on these matters,
I am a sheep in the crowd.

The pigs will always run the farm,
they make the rules to suit themselves,
we lesser beasts may bay and grumble,
but power is beyond our grip.

Thus we suffer their imposed misery
as if it benefits us all -
deep down we know it is their folly
we will pay for down the line.

For the present, we endure uncertainty,
hope for better times ahead,
the pigs will always run the farm
but their time will end.

IS THERE A MOMENT
[19.46, 23rd May 2020, Vila Bled, Slovenia]

Is there a moment when we are free
to roam the world without restriction;
locked in our rooms in every land,
caught in the panic of mass extinction,
the sensible always keep their distance,
the reckless bent on self-destruction,
we somehow manage to co-exist
without the joy of former freedom;
we now somehow live in limbo,
knowing not what is the future
or when to celebrate our survival.

THE FIGHT IS NEVER OVER
[20.35, 26th May 2020, Porto Roz, Slovenia]

It was over. Eight thirty-five
and the sun passed into the sea.
She bent her legs, her hands locked

747

between her floral covering.

The twilight crept into the villa
as she lay on the chaise-long,
her eyes were droopy, drowsy
for a day without photography.

She was cold before being old,
restless in the failing light,
the years sitting on her hips
as she rose to stretch again.

There is no stopping time,
we age as the sun goes down,
we wake with hope eternal
and sleep knowing no tomorrow.

But the fight is never done,
the halting of advancing age,
she stood in the gloaming,
a silhouette on the scarlet sky.

LIPICA
[22.40, 2nd June 2020, Lipica, Slovenia]

The horses stand unimpressed,
they fill the fields unperturbed,
nurse their foals as mothers do
without the worry we humans have.

The swifts nest in the yard,
dart to feed their crying broods,
the stable doors wide ajar
in the oppressive summer heat.

The thunder rolls across the Karst,
the limestone caverns echo loud,
ancient tracks wound round walls
that stone age men erected.

Black pines tumble to an abyss
topped by a lofty spire,
the meadows stretch speckle-flowered
as the rain squall passes.

THE SECRETS OF MONTENEGRO
[01.06, 7th June 2020, Bar, Montenegro]

Th rain lashed the windscreen
of their sleek black car
winding on the coastal road
of the sun baked Adriatic -
the apartment towers were shuttered
the beaches forlornly lonely,
the mountains grey and brooding
above the snaking road below.

They exchanged their anxious hours
for a sushi shaded terrace,
followed a power boat to Kotar
with their focused camera lenses
as it went between two islands,
a church and mosque opposed,
not knowing which side won
or when they'd been divided.

The black clouds descended
as the many towns receded,
the flood lights of the stadium,
the walls of lost imperialism,
the mysteries of history's making,
the masks of present living,
the road wound on southwards
to dispel their misgivings.

They held hands just briefly,
they hugged above the calm sea,
they exercised their surly manners
and forgave their moody reasons,
they were equal partnered vagrants
on a wild far-flung coast
that revealed its many secrets
while they concealed their own.

THE GIRL IN PINK
23.29, 9th June 2020, Igomentista, Greece]

The woman in black in Montenegro
is now the girl in pink in Greece,
she carries her phone like a javelin
to pierce the hearts of her lovers.

She presses the buttons of her menfolk,
creates pure joy out of the pain,
she never dances to any tune
nor kisses the lips of pure strangers.

Caught in the trap of independence,
she does what indy women do,
she creates chaos in a timely manner
and makes sense of the confusion.

Her politeness is a desire to please,
her smile the foil to all arrows,
while her javelin rests on the table,
her shield is the barb of her eyebrows.

There is no defence against such arts,
the flick of an eye, crease of a smile,
the girl in pink cannot conceal
that she is the woman in black.

CORINTH SEA
[10.33, 11th June 2020, Selianiki, Greece]

The breeze blew through the olive trees,
vines hung with a coat of salt,
a young girl carried her schoolbooks
towards the beach and sun.

The laughter of children echoed,
the waves lapped on the shore,
geraniums sat in their clay pots
as the sunflowers gave a nod.

Clouds thinly veiled the blue,
cafes closed, their shutters shut,
the smell of coffee faintly lingering
since the plague has struck.

DAYBREAK IN SANTORINI
[09.30, 14th June 2020, Fira, Santorini]

The dogs barked into the night,
blanked out the constant chatter
rising from the hotel below
before day broke on the cliffs.

Greeks flags merged with the sky
as the breeze turned onshore,
the church bell struck once
then broke into a roar.

The sun dried out the bikinis
g-strung on a pegged out line
as their weary wearers rose
from their dreams in paradise.

HYDRA
[00.24, 20th June 2020, Hydra, Greece]

I don't know if today should end
or that tomorrow should come,
whatever gap remains behind
will soon be only me.

The birds fly high in the wind,
the boats sail across the sea,
the harbour fills with travelers
but none are here for me.

The stars hang on the clouds,
the windows open for the breeze,
who knows if God will come
and let me flee.

The traps we make for ourselves,
the choices that divide our lives,
the sheets on our double beds
that shield us from our love.

No man can seek his truer self
than to find it in his lover's arms,
how fleeting all those moments are
as time turns on the tide.

No memory can ever savour
the seconds lost, the minutes found
when night is about to go
and dawn brings tomorrow now.

SILENCED
[22.45, 22nd June 2020, Belgrade, Serbia]

Silenced, the voice in my head
deserted me, left behind rubbish,
images that were never mine
floating on top of my memory
like plastic in the ocean.

Caught in the seaweed anchored
to the floor of my soul,
like a net of knotted debris,
I am trapped by the waste
that has ensnared my happiness.

To cut free I need help
to clear my endangered deep -
with a desire to cleanse,
to rid my once clear blue
of all the filth I've collected.

MY TORMENTED HOUR IN VIENNA
[22.50, 24th June 2020, Sussen, Germany]

In St.Stephen's church I wrestled
with the demons chasing me.
I prayed they would leave
and my answers would come clear,
but God somehow left me sitting
on a pew looking up,
the stain-glass windows shone
as the heavens drifted on.

I spent an hour in torment
as my girl sat in the shade,
she watched a child fall over
and get up, to fall again -
God still refused to reply
on my anguish and my lows
as I struggled with my conscience
in a crippled bent repose.

I sought my own redemption
as a churchman swept the floor,
the lofty fresco restorers
brushed on their leaves of gold,
while I in tearless abjection

751

wrung my hands in woe,
asking God for his guidance
as God only knows.

HALFWAY THROUGH THIS VIRUSED YEAR
[23.24, 1st July 2020, High Wycombe]

Halfway through this virused year
and all my dreams are shattered,
not broken and ready to be fixed
but fragmented and unrepairable.

Such years come rarely in life,
most years drift by as time does -
but this year is one of misery,
woeful goings-on everywhere I look.

With heads down and no good news,
despair pervades into our souls,
the expectation of more bad tidings
steals the laughter from our lives.

The hidden war that is ourselves
as we are the carriers of death -
a bomb dropped from high-above
is something we could comprehend.

For the now we bear the silence,
the stealth that takes folks away -
the corridors of life are empty
and we are the shadows lingering there.

LOUISE
[00.45, 18th July 2020, High Wycombe]

Many people interested, none of them interesting
as we strolled the alleys of fame -
She told me of times madness struck
at her dreams of living a life -
free of the demons pulling her down,
shot of the whispers filling her mind,
rid of the lies rotting her brain
making her think she was insane.

Fear is a weapon used upon her -
the threats of a mother bent on death,
the whims of a father never at fault
using her guilt to get what he wants.
Tiptoeing between suicide and violence,
a ping-pong ball batted back and forth
in a backhanded spin or forehand smash,
the child is broken or learns to resist.

JULES (song)
[23.40, 30th July 2020, High Wycombe]

I love her like no other,

I cannot give her up,
I must have her forever,
or I will forever weep.

I love her like the mountains,
I love her like the sea,
I love her every movement
and I love her close to me.

I cannot bear our partings,
I cannot be alone,
I need to have her love
and kiss her all the more.

She is my only lover,
she is my sole respite,
she saves me from myself
and wrongs all my rights.

I cannot live without her,
I perish at such thought,
She is my only solace,
and she is hot!

FILM STARS
[01.52, 9th Aug 2020, High Wycombe]

In their heyday they are great,
young, athletic, in their prime,
glowing like a burning star
with no end to their brilliance.

Then life takes its payment,
tarnishes what it once promoted,
dulls the shine once so bright
to leave an empty black hole.

All fires must burn then die,
have their flames finally spent,
the warmth and comfort they provide
will as ash scatter wide.

Yet we still love these stars,
immortal in our own dull times,
blazing through our short lives
like Gods in ancient paradise.

THE FAITHFUL TEMPTRESS
[00.25, 12th Aug 2020, High Wycombe]

How secret are the secrets kept,
the dual world of the faithful temptress,
the flash of her flirtatious eyes,
a smile to quell pent up ire,
a way with words but not enough
to let the mask fall away.

How can a man deal with this dilemma
but to run away to Samarkand,
ride a camel into the storm,
hide in some far-flung hovel,
for nothing else will save him from
the temptress he cannot have.

I JUST GOT LUCKY
[00.42, 18th Aug 2020, High Wycombe]

Not a genius, just lucky,
the millionaire told me on the phone.
I was in the right place, right time
and the money flooded in the door.

There was no design to my actions,
no plan to get rich quick,
I just happened to be lucky
and now I am extremely rich.

HABITUAL SPEECH
[00.15, 21st Aug 2020, High Wycombe]

Over the top a century ago
was equated with death at the front,
now it is an online platform
delivering war films at a price.

As our language changes every day,
we are the victims of old age -
lines that were funny just yesterday,
now are the phrases of bigots.

Who can be certain of their vocabulary
that it will not fall into disrepair.
Ever watchful our tongues wag,
whisper the things we want to say.

Who can keep up with each new mote,
abbreviations or slick catchphrase -
all of us succumb to habitual speech
until we are part of a bygone age.

I WILL SLEEP WITHOUT HAVING DOUBTS
[00.06, 24th Aug 2020, High Wycombe]

At the centre of the universe is a black hole,
a darkness that no-one can describe -
a shooting mass of gas and heat
that has birthed the whole of the cosmos.

But who really knows if God,
that eternal being we'd like to meet,
exists in some parallel dimension
that will always be beyond our reach.

Always these same damned questions,

754

that the scientist nor preacher answers,
they give us their qualified viewpoints
but always fail to satisfy somehow.

So for the time being I will gaze up
and read my bible in the failing light,
thus armed with the tools of understanding,
I will sleep without having doubts.

A FUTURE TO POLICE
[01.59, 30th Aug 2020, High Wycombe]

Yesterday Julie went back to Poland
and when I arrived back from Heathrow,
my bus pass was lying on the mat.

How time has flown like pollen,
scattered are my years now spread
to leave my seed floating in the wind.

There is still a future to police,
a chance to order what is right,
to plant new ideas in nice neat rows.

NORMAL DAYS, AVERAGE HOURS
[23.19, 30th Aug 2020, High Wycombe]

Some days are just meant to pass
without any thought of remembrance;
these normal days, these average hours
of nothing special, or worthy of note.

BACK TO THE TREADMILL
[23.34, 30th Aug 2020, High Wycombe]

It is the end of summer -
the rain has stopped for now,
darkness has fallen on the town,
the streets are empty and silent.

Next week the schools reopen,
overcoats shaken and brushed,
the adults forced back to work,
lamenting the summertime lost.

Trying hard not to feel hard done to,
the treadmill mounted once more,
Christmas becomes the focus
before thoughts of some rest return.

NOTHING OF VENICE
[21.52,,1st Sept 2020, Palanca, Venice]

Whatever is said about Venice
has been said before in prose,
in poetry and in visual art.
I cannot add one iota

755

to works that fill libraries
and museums around the world.
Such is the knowledge on Venice
only a fool would add more.

Yet I will, as I am foolish
and cannot still my pen;
I must make mention of beauty,
of decay and views to die for.
But perhaps this short poem
is not the place to say a thing.
I will leave off here now
and not begin again.

MEMORY
[01.19, 10th Sept 2020, High Wycombe]

And so time goes like a freight train at night
to wake in the morning further down the line,
a bird on the wire chirping its song,
heard long after the rain has gone.

The eyes of a lover the following dawn,
the cries of a child moments ago born,
the feel of the wind on a bare back
bent in toil over newly dug soil.

The clouds wizz by like a galloping horse,
free like a tramp with no fixed abode,
the days gliding by like a boat on a lake
lost to our gaze in a fine summer haze.

THE WORLD STOPS TO SAY HELLO
[00.33, 30th Sept 2020, High Wycombe]

The world stops to say hello,
then it moves on, leaves behind
those who cannot step with time
to the march of history.

Thus standing still without a plan
gives no place to shelter from
events that make them unprepared
for the dance of destiny.

And so they wait ill at ease
in the hope of a chance
to carry on beyond their fate
to escape their dull reality.

TO FEND, MAKE DO, SURVIVE
[01.03, 8th Oct 2020, High Wycombe]

The warmest September on record,
the world burning up with fires,
the virus raging on unstoppable,
no-one knows when it will end.

Here the rain still comes down,
a week of storm, violent flood;
if Noah were alive just now,
he'd be sailing down the Thames.

Life seems to be so chaotic
without a steady guiding hand,
we are adrift, on our own,
to fend, make do, survive.

THE MANY HOURS TO HARBOUR
[18.35, 15th Oct 2020, Brindisi-Igumentista]

The dark falls on the windy sea
as through the swell the ferry rides
the waves towards the Grecian shore
still distant in the gloom ahead.

Onboard we sit in empty hope,
a ship devoid of any souls,
behind us now Italy's shore -
a hazy fuzz of night lights.

And so we pitch into the void,
the Adriatic chop and roll,
sip our coffees, chat or doze
the many hours to harbour.

OUR BAGS ARE PACKED
[20.52, 7th Nov 2020, Hydra, Greece]

Our bags are packed, our ship has sailed,
yet we are trapped in a raging storm,
the island soaked in winter sun
while we're marooned to walk the shore.

The world closes down around us,
the cafe chairs stacked, the tables bare;
the wind howls on the awnings,
whipped, lashed, and cracking loud.

Abandoned to a double fate of helplessness,
the curfew curtailing all our escaping hopes,
companionship's fraught hours of boredom
makes me hopeful, my companion full of fear.

Elsewhere a new president is elected,
the rancour of living a distant worry,
the solitude of our island existence
a contrast to the world's bitter woes.

Make-believe should be for film-makers,
not real life in this present unreal world,
the actors here made their timely exit
but we remain here to pick up the tab.

How difficult it is to end enjoyment,
to return to a norm that is not normal;
this paradise in Greece called Hydra
is rightly only half of what's required.

There is no place to find true salvation,
no place where the head and heart can rest,
for one pulls this way, the other t'other,
until discontent builds into strife.

And still the wind howls quite foully,
as if the roofs are going to fly;
the sea a black swell of darkness
and the sky a black void of hell.

The hours tick away as they dwindle
into the late hours of the wild night,
an orange light offering some warmness
as the humid cold numbs our sleep.

Ancient houses creek with every new blast,
floorboards crack and shutters bang,
the lanes ghostly empty of locals
except for the cats patrolling the town.

The donkey men have gone to their lairs,
the carpenter lathes are eerily silent,
the shops boarded up, restaurants closed,
the times we have are not the best.

This is life in these unfortunate days,
the plague compounded by a winter storm;
trapped we find ourselves for many hours
but always is the hope of dawn.

I LEAVE BEHIND
[23.59,19th Nov 2020, High Wycombe]

Every place I go, I leave behind
a thought, a deed, a footprint in the soil.
I leave something of myself each time,
on every pillow, on every sandy shore.
What I leave is in the air -
unexplained to others and myself,
there is no need to quantify or tally,
things that no words can describe.

Yet, something, is there left unseen,
something you could not put your finger on,
something your hand cannot touch,
yet your mind knows, senses the ghost
that has passed by, lingered there,
taken action, somehow changed the place,
just by having once been present -
a living being you have never met.

How many living souls, most now dead,

758

have walked the streets I trudge,
here trod the grass, the meadow-lands,
the mountain pathways of many foreign parts,
sat on chairs, in cafes and in bars,
drank and eaten, laughed like children,
left their palm-print on a door-knob
while walking through doors into oblivion.

Will I be discovered when I am gone,
my presence felt, my shadow detected;
will my thoughts be relived, experienced
by those who will be many after me.
Will they see what I have seen,
will they touch where I have been,
will they think like I oft do,
about those who walked in other times.

I have no fears, I've had my fun,
far-flung has my shadow fallen
into the shade of other's presence,
I'll let my being fade away.
For this is life, we are mortal,
passing though beyond such shadows
into the light, the warm calm place
where I can rest, and worry none.

POSITIVE
[23.42, 21st Nov 2020, High Wycombe]

My test came back positive
just as I am back on my feet;
eight days of fever gone,
the anguished dreams banished,
my stiffness of limb lingers,
fatigue grinds me to a halt.

Otherwise I am on the mend,
gone is my stifling cough,
I have survived the pandemic;
I pray for those who've not.

VACCINE
[00.19, 24th Nov 2020, High Wycombe]

I'm out the other side of Covid,
but now I'm itchy, covered in spots,
my right leg is stiff and limp -
how much more can go wrong?

The spots – its like having measles,
a rash across my back and midriff,
and that cough, still underlying
every time I think it's gone.

No chance of seeing a doctor,
they're still locked down and scared,
I'm waiting on the national vaccine

to get me back to any kind of norm.

THE DEVIL WAITS TO SEE HIM BURN
[00.27 6th Dec 2020, High Wycombe]

What now as the Trump years end -
that horrible excuse of a human being.
Has there been his like since Adolph Hitler,
he's not far off, he's full of hatred -
for all the sins of his father,
for all the pride of his mother,
he is a failure as a person,
despite his rise to being President.

Bringing his country to such division
by his inaction, his texting quips,
the damage goes around the world,
returns to wreck all moral code.
His lies, his barefaced bragging bouts,
his tongue tied tales he fabricates,
can such a man be made for heaven -
the devil waits to see him burn.

IMAGES
[01.11 9th Dec 2020, High Wycombe]

Sometimes when I think.
When nothing seems to fit -
a rain dogs, cycle sort of thing;
I love the one I'm with,
the villain and the kid,
the falcon and the dove all mixed.

I think I know myself,
but the heckles always hurt -
the dark side of heaven remains.
Finding fortune in my friends,
seven crosses as their end,
islands in a crab filled sea.

Inside I've got to run
from the number runner's sums -
so long to all that puppet stuff.
The rose has lost its bloom,
as the warrior takes the nude,
the hunter lays down to sleep.

The axe raider sails away,
the beast departs his lair -
fingers part the water for good.
The stone is going green,
the right bus leaves unseen,
as the sisters wave a sweet adieu.

HUMAN FRAILTY
For Neil
00.46 12th Dec 2020, High Wycombe]

Friends will always disappoint
as they are flawed and human
to the point that their existence
is more important than my own.

Naturally I must sometime be
a disappointment to my friends -
I do not see it, only feel it
when love goes out the door.

Too often it is our values,
our upbringing forming our view -
the disappointment our expectation
of how others should be.

However hard the hurt hits -
causes pain to hearts and minds,
acceptance of all human frailty,
a lesson Christ taught well.

GOD HELP US
[23.29 12th Dec 2020, High Wycombe]

When will the light shine bright again
so we can go about our business
with smiles, and joy, and happiness.

The politicians are playing silly games,
gambling our future for their ideals
while being paid from our taxes.

Is there a glimmer of future cheer,
a time for celebration and laughter
that for now evades us all.

I will not pray for our deliverance,
I will bring no superstition into play -
but please God, give us hope.

WHO KILLED THE ALBATROSS
[15.59 19th Dec 2020, Marbesa, Spain]

Who killed the albatross,
brought this time of bad luck -
someone shot it down,
watched it cruelly drown.

All our hopes disappeared,
sank with the albatross -
one moment freely roaming,
the next a frightful omen.

Fate is as pre-determined
as the planets round the sun -
the albatross our conscience
of all we do wrong.

We all shot the albatross,
took part in its demise,
until left with a horizon
and a bare empty sky.

POTENTIAL
[23.18 19th Dec 2020, Marbesa, Spain]

Some say I have not reached my potential.
What would my parents say?
I believe I exceeded their expectations
and those I set for myself.

Yet others always want to push,
get me to go beyond my limits,
the limits I think exist within myself
that seem impossible to breach.

To excel without being dishonest,
lies, or the deception of others -
How do we reach our potential
if we don't know what it is?

TO HAVE SUCH PEACE
[22.15 20th Dec 2020, Marbesa, Spain]

The child skated in the moonlight,
drifted into the dark sultry night,
the streets deserted by the seaside,
the vacant villas all without light.

There was peace to be found there,
the waves lapping without fear,
the stars twinkling in the blackness,
the way the sky ought to be.

No human speech, just the shore fall,
the lapping waves on the beach,
the bliss of having reached there
to have such peace.

DRINKING CHAMPAGNE IN THE AFTERNOON
[15.14 23rd Dec 2020, Marbesa, Spain]

Drinking champagne in the afternoon
is not the socialist norm -
but at sixty-six such concerns
are merely for the birds.

Our politicians are morally bankrupt,
corrupt and mentally holed -
sheep are far better fellows
to follow than government blokes.

Reading Jean Brodie in sunshine
as the stock market goes up -

old age offers some hindsight
on how society works.

Now I've tumbled the methods
that always made me poor -
'Its up your bum, you wankers,
and fuck your Brexit too!'

The sun will go down as always,
come up again for sure -
lets hope for a better future
and a proper covid cure.

So I'll continue my drinking,
champagne in the Spanish sun -
don't judge me for my values,
I've done my socialist work.

THE ZOOM MEETING
[15.31 23rd Dec 2020, Marbesa, Spain]

Middle class and middle aged,
they cackle on in babble,
relieved that Xmas had arrived
and work was off the table.

Its no bad thing to take rest,
get all worries off their breasts,
sipping on their tipples,
gaggling on quite tipsy.

Talk of husbands, turkey roasts,
charades played with little cries,
shared confessions, little cries,
laughter breaking through the sighs.

Questions asked, answers given,
bonding in their tearful havens,
lonely, but somehow driven
to bridge the rules of lockdown.

As Christmas comes at a distance,
the ladies have their little party -
sweet and kind and understanding,
the hours pass in part oblivion.

EVE OF CHRISTMAS
[12.32 24th Dec 2020, Marbesa, Spain]

The pancake sea, donut sun,
the hot bun sand, ice-glazed pool -
all is ready to consume
as party-time is with us.

But this Xmas is not cake,
not chocolate, not party hat,
no cracker jack, paper jokes,

763

no friends around us.

The pancake sea remains unswum,
the ice-glazed pool ripple-less,
the hot bun sand sandle-less
this year's eve of Christmas.

PROBLEMS
[01.21, 26th Dec 2020, Las Chapas, Marbesa]

Whatever problems people have
I have my own. Loneliness
is a disease that eats life,
makes ending life a good way out.

When you get to the end of the road
and find that it ends at a cliff,
you look in the mirror and decide
that you won't go back the way
you came.

The pain's too much,
its too full of pot-holes and traffic,
so you turn the engine off,
get out the car, walk to the edge,
stare into the abyss,
and jump.

LAS CHAPAS
[23.39, 28th Dec 2020, Marbesa]

Here the leaves do not fall,
scatter nor drift into a pile.
The day ends, the night descends,
with no sound other than the pines
catching the breeze inward bound
from the silent sea.

WHAT IS THERE TO SHOW
[00.29, 29th Dec 2020, Marbesa]

What is there to show for another day,
showering, shaving, the breakfast consumed,
the photos taken of my closest friends,
the beer drunk, the wine devoured,
the book bought, the forest walk,
the groceries bought home for tea?

THE DRUNKEN JOURNEY HOME
[29th Dec - 2nd Jan 2021, Marbesa-Malaga]
[5th Feb 2021, 25th July 2021, Iver Grove]

The moon was full of chaos,
on this cold Spanish night,
we drank to all the werewolves
and howled in wild delight.
We laughed into the marshes

with swaggering bottled hands,
we straddled countless ditches
and frog-jumped boggy land.

We took relief in a churchyard,
between the silver-frosted graves
we rested on a headstone,
and cursed the Devil's mates!
We did not believe in witches,
in goblins, warlocks, nor more,
we were high on vino tinto,
and free of nonsense lore.

We were men of the morrow,
not the type to cower in fear.
Our motto was 'Up them!'
to all who'd venture near -
until a chill came upon us,
stilled our bombast shouts
the moon obscured by a mist
descended like a shroud.

It covered the entire graveyard,
hid my friends from me,
and when the vapour lifted
I was alone in that lee
where not a soul was human,
alive, or able to say -
"Hello, my sweet drunken fellow.
How was your full moon day?"

For it was night and eerie,
as I sat with the dead,
I began to doubt and wonder
if I'd be home by first crow.
Can you imagine my bravery,
alone with the spirits of old,
some of them my ancestors,
but many my enemies' folk.

I swigged on my empty bottle,
threw it against a stone,
it smashed with a violence -
I wished I'd not done so
as a moan, and then a murmur
shook the frozen ground,
and a ghost appeared before me
and I was mortified!

My heart gave out – stopped –
as I died a hundred times,
the spirit eyed me sideways
then sank into the ground.
I gasped and gurgled loudly
as my life somehow returned,
I careered to my feet
despite my limbs being numb.

An owl wittered loudly,
a bat went past my ear,
a spider crawled up my leg,
I stood frozen full of fear.
I recalled the beers I'd drunk,
the wine I had consumed,
the spirits liberally poured for me
by my friends who'd disappeared.

What now could I imagine,
was it the drink doing me in?
Or was I in this graveyard
for all my dreadful sins.
I crossed myself threefold,
then again, three more times,
for when you call on God,
no-one is keeping count.

A wind got up, blew off my hat,
left me staring at the moon,
I was betwixt blue heaven
and the Devil's motley crew.
Was I now part sober
or caught now in a trance?
I knew not June from January,
nor October now from March.

Where was I now I wondered,
so close to home but far,
how many miles still to go
until I reached my hearth?
For now I had a vision
of my wife before the fire,
my dinner cooked and ready
and her welcoming loving arms.

Suddenly, a cold blast shook
this idyll from my thoughts,
as I knew my wife was angry
and nursing her vilest wrath.
That is the lot of the drinkers
who reject their wives for booze,
when they come home merry,
her tongue's their only muse.

How had I let it become so,
in love so long ago -
I'd traded in companionship
for the demon alcohol.
How now then to get home -
to plead my deep remorse,
my legs were like jelly
and my head a sea of words.

I would beg my wife's forgiveness,
pledge to give up drink,

help her with our home-life,
and pay my debts on time!
I'd seen the road I'd traveled
as a wicked wild highway,
led up the garden path by many
and down many broken lanes.

Done now! I was a changed man,
standing straight and clear in mind,
I looked at the glaring full moon,
and saluted the grinning swine.
I was not going to be seduced
by any celestial rays,
I was a man by my own rights
whatever my wife may say.

I staggered out of the graveyard,
left that ghost of mine behind,
carried on to my nearby village
where I came to the stile -
that long since had been broken
and required a difficult climb
over a fence, trailing a ditch
where a dead witch was found.

That was all just hearsay,
and well before my time,
but still when we were children
we never crossed that stile.
And as I stumbled, clambered
o'er that crooked fence,
my foot caught on a post
and I fell into the mire!

The stench was all country,
thick and caked on me,
I swore at all creation
and damned that wife of mine,
for had she not been home,
I'd have slept in the mire -
Now I was a scarecrow
covered in rural slime.

The rooks all laughed loudly
as I passed beneath the boughs,
onwards then I staggered
without a thought of time.
For I knew when I arrived
I'd be tried for my crimes,
jury, judge and hangman
all in her combined.

So I tarried under an old oak
where we had first entwined,
and I recalled a little vaguely
where it had all gone wrong.
I welled with such emotion,

the tears poured down my cheeks,
great fountains of self-pity,
burst the dam on my deceit.

Perhaps I was not perfect,
the sort of man who's loved,
more the kind of fellow
well met but somehow shunned.
I'd had my share of hard knocks,
and times when things were rough,
but my wife had stuck by me
though I was often drunk.

I resolved to end my bad ways,
and somehow sobered up,
I bade the rooks a farewell
and set off for better luck.
The night light in the window
cheered my withered soul,
as I peered through the glass
at my wife on her own.

My love for her swelled greatly
as I strode through the door,
I bent down to kiss her
and she stuck me on the nose!
I went reeling off the cottage wall,
and landed in a heap -
and there I slept the whole night
until she broke my sleep.

She handed me a porridge bowl
and a mug of stewing tea,
she said it was time for me to go
to work in the fields.
I kissed her on her reddened cheek
she blushed and wiped her nose,
a little tear drowned her eye,
then she cried out loads.

And as I set off out to work,
I vowed to swear off drink,
I loved her more than all the world,
she believed me so I think.
With happy plod I ploughed a field
knowing all was well with me,
one drunken night behind me now,
it was the moon, not me.

MALAGA
[13.57, 4ᵗʰ Jan 2021, Malaga]

The beer glistened in the sunlight,
the soup warm against the cold.
Picasso left here for Paris's lights,
left behind this ancient town
the Phoneticians built so long ago.

The fountains babble in the squares,
the orange groves are everywhere -
the narrow streets marble worn,
the churches reaching for the sky,
bluer than the bluest eye.

HAPPY DAYS
[20.19, 14th Jan 2021, Iver Grove]

Happy days have returned.
Without happy days we are dead,
useless to the world,
useless to our friends
and everyone we love.

Thank God for happy days,
for when all is done,
happiness is the best -
it lets the heart soar,
the sad mind unwind,
makes friendship a bliss,
and each day a joy.

THE KISS OF A LOVER
[23.56, 15th Jan 2021, Iver Grove]

With a kiss on the lips,
we parted for the first time
in a way that was different
from all the years before.

The feel of her softness,
the sensation of her touch
that lingered long on me
as she smiled and left.

What had we just done,
we had not done before,
something different had occurred
beyond that we had known.

It was the kiss of a lover,
not that of old friends -
why is love so guarded
and a mystery without end.

THE ALLUSION OF LOVE
[00.35, 16th Jan 2021, Iver Grove]

I admit – I am in love,
but at my age I am guarded.
There have been many old fools
made to be mistaken by looks,
enamored wholly by youth,
taken in by guile and flattery.

I prefer then – to say nothing,
keep my feelings to myself,
show my love in small gestures,
collect gestures in return,
balance my hopes with caution,
keep my feet on the ground.

How age warps the emotions,
somehow, not worth the exposure,
playing safe to avoid commotion,
keeping the peace at all costs,
stability the guiding purpose,
and love a lost cause.

FORGIVE ME, FRIENDS
[16.20, 16th Jan 2021, Iver Grove]

For all those I've misplaced,
forgotten, or haven't had space -
forgive me for my disloyalty.

Better now to understand friends,
hard to find, harder to replace,
forget me not in your prayers.

Time throws egg in our face,
our actions can be a disgrace,
please forgo my many mistakes.

Dear friends, let us retrace,
find new ways to embrace,
I apologise for my past ways.

Signing off on gone days,
I ask you to retrace,
retake the path of our friendship.

So thank you for listening,
yours sincerely, R M,
this end is just the beginning.

OUR FUTURE IN THE BRIGHT BLUE SKY
[14.13, 25th Jan 2021, Iver Grove]

The snow was down around us,
Simon sang his song for America,
the sun flooded the stable eaves,
the music faded into memory.

All our troubles were beyond us,
gone without the smallest care,
hope was in the crisp air,
our future in the bright blue sky.

MY LIES CONCEALED
[00.11, 12th Feb 2021, Iver Grove]

Is truth the words I set out
here upon this cream page,
or is truth the lies I tell
somewhere further here below.
I cannot tell if I am deluded
or blinded by my own deceit.
Are my views somehow tainted,
somehow tarnished by my lying?

How can I remain truthful
on matters that are personal -
my ego will not permit my faults
to be revealed in their entirety.
Part of me remains unexposed,
covered by a blanket of words -
my truths are lies in disguise,
my lies concealed in verbose.

SPRING ARRIVED
[23.36, 20th Feb 2021, Iver Grove]

Spring arrived today with warmth,
the first glimpse of yellow spotted
in a shallow trough of earth
up against the old garden wall.

WE DANCE TO NEW COMPOSITIONS
[23.59, 20th Feb 2021, Iver Grove]

Dutifully we dance to new compositions
tailored and cut to suit our gait -
so we as cripples can take part
in the waltzes we try to imitate.

Into the dark, out into the light
we cruise across the uneven dance floor,
spinning our partners, whispering our worries,
listening for secrets, and so much more.

The music plays on, night follows day,
we find new partners to wildly spin,
until we are giddy, tired, exhausted,
we end our hoof with a parting kiss.

But the music plays on, an endless record
as the wallflowers wilt, and others get up,
the tunes fade from our pounding heads
and our dancing kicks are yesterday's licks.

CONSPIRACY OF SILENCE
[00.44, 22nd Feb 2020, Iver Grove]

When great men are greatly wronged,
condemned by a conspiracy of silence,
they carry the falsehood to their graves
with no reply to all who've shamed them.

771

Only when such men are buried,
and only once their accusers die -
does the truth emerge from the silence,
and others speak to clear their names.

Thus great men are often set up
by greater men seeking revenge,
and being greater, and in power,
false witness is at their command.

Perhaps the folly of all great men
is to put pride before common sense,
to have their honour on their sleeves,
so that their wounds don't heal.

For those who go along with wrongs,
knowing that a wrong's been done -
these are the lesser kind of men
whose silence tarnishes everyone.

ART HAS SHUT DOWN
[00.39, 23rd Feb 2021, Iver Grove]

Art has shut down like in Shakespeare's times,
the plague closing theatres, artists hungry
to feed themselves, not just their art,
taking labouring jobs to make ends meet.

When times are hard, food, clothes and shelter
are the means of survival, not plays,
not comedians letting off steam in hot rooms,
nor musicians blasting out their rock and roll.

Disease and death is about health and welfare
of the human body, but not the mind -
all effort goes into preserving tissue
with nothing spent on dreams of any kind.

This is art, the wasting of endless hours
by artists trying to make us all understand
that our bodies will succumb to disease
and our minds are indeed who we are.

When the plague leaves us, gets controlled,
audiences will flock to their favourite shows,
for they will want to lightly recap, recall
what they have suffered, to laugh at it all.

SHE CAME BACK TO ME
[00.39, 26th Feb 2021, Iver Grove]

My sweet friend, came back to me,
with a text, a warm loving note
that sparked, rekindled the fire,
relit the room, cleared the gloom
that had descended on our friendship.

772

THE HOBO'S PRAYER
[00.25, 28th Feb 2021, Iver Grove]

I've tried to forgive them,
her brother, her sister,
but I can't quite give in at all.
Though I pray to my saviour,
and do good without favour,
its just not coming along.

I somehow still hate them,
cannot quite face them,
they are the low, of the low.
But I do it for her sake,
try not to look fake,
yet she know's it's all a show.

And when we get gone,
and we are alone,
I wipe the tears from her eyes.
For her brother is cruel,
her sister's a fool, both
easy to loathe and despise.

We've said our goodbyes,
packed up our bin bags,
gone back out on the road.
Her family's a lost case,
there's no hope of some grace,
taking on some of our load.

I hold her hand tightly,
walk with her nightly,
looking for some place not cold.
Its not coming easy,
its not light and breezy,
the worry is making us old.

Its tough on our bodies
as we search for somebody
to rent us a cheap room.
When you're down on your luck,
and don't have that much,
you inhabit a world of gloom.

All the folks up against us,
I try to forgive them,
but its hard not having hope.
Lord, please answer my prayers,
save us from this despair,
for she's at the end of her rope.

But before I leave off,
though I want nothing as such,
don't leave us on the streets all alone.
For I've had enough
for a man sleeping rough,

without a home of his own.

BIG THINGS IN LITTLE PACKAGES
[22.44, 10th Mar 2021, Iver Grove]

Big things arrive in small packages
carefully wrapped, beautifully bowed;
expectation is in the content potential
as the outer coating is peeled away.

Now as I open what is concealed,
I understand what I have been gifted;
a priceless object I cannot describe
for I am dazzled by its richness.

And so it is with my little treasure,
my big gift in a small package;
lost for a time in misunderstanding,
feeling somehow she'd been wronged.

Not so, my love, not so at all,
time has a way of being cruel,
sowing discord instead of unity,
dividing souls, and causing wars.

Not us, never, friends for life,
we will love and never fight;
there will be no divide,
just kisses where hurt is found.

THE SULTANS SING IN THEIR PALACES
[23.40, 17th Mar 2021, Iver Grove]

The sultans sing in their palaces,
the dog-leap stairs lie bare,
money is free on the tv
as others nurse despair.

Days like these are not rare,
they are common average times,
local heroes so hard to find,
sip on gin, suck on limes.

The roses bloom in early Spring,
news of cancer makes us shrink,
fear is hidden in our dreams
while others turn to drink.

Bed is for the early starter,
while dark is the killer's heart,
some progress with their art
despite all that binds us.

The cars race into the night,
round the corner lovers fight,
comets whirl beyond our sight
as time goes on without us.

TILL DAWN BRINGS UP THE STORM
[00.25, 23rd Mar 2021, Iver Grove]

All is quiet in my western world,
the guns are silent in my house,
the clock is ticking like a bomb
but inside there is no dynamite.

The day departed with a whimper,
a barking dog at a window,
a whiff of curry in the air
and angry voices simmering.

All is now peacefully calm,
there is no sense of due alarm,
there is no fear of coming harm
till dawn brings up the storm.

AS OTHERS LEAPED
[11.15, 27th Mar 2021, Iver Grove]

I had many lovers,
very few chose to stay.
While the kites flew high
and the moles dug deep,
I carried on dreaming
as my lovers leaped -
fell to their fate
while I remained asleep.

THIS WASTELAND, MY HOME
[30th Mar - 9th Apr 2021, Iver Grove]

This wasteland, my home,
this place destroyed by many hands,
my village, ravished by greed,
demolished stone by stone,
made derelict by demolition.

There is no beauty in decay,
no stop for the eye to rest,
all is gone, removed
or left to fall down -
day on month on year.

Snow, rain and wild wind
do their worst on my memories,
replaced once, replaced again,
bulldozed into non existence -
my village I call home.

The river no longer stops,
rushes on without a flood,
the weir broken, long unused,
the mill now just a hut
for storing rust and debris.

Hope of lost things returned,
faith in finding new beginnings,
a roof put on the church,
the school children all returned
to their abandoned classrooms.

No such charity exists -
the fountain lies in pieces,
the headstones in the graveyard
lie sideways in a ditch
where derelicts piss.

That place that made me!
Is there no shame?
Are there no tongues wagging,
no wise heads shaking,
fingers pointing at the rot?

Is the decay like empire?
Tennis courts green-slimed,
bowling greens just puddles,
my memories of greater times
before the nation regressed?

The park swings gone,
the public baths demolished,
the chip shop boarded up,
the Italian cafe shuttered -
no ice cream for the young.

The pavements uneven, broken,
the cobbles coated in tar,
the poplars lining the road
cut down before the lime trees
gave up the ghost.

What shadows lurk there
in the lanes of the past,
the voices of congregations,
the chatter of infants
coming out of Sunday school.

All the laughter long blown
away on the south-west wind,
carried on to barren mountains,
scattered on the sodden moors,
drained and left to wither.

How can life return anew
when all is almost dead,
the village barely breathing,
its last cough a gasp
of trembling and shaking.

There is no place to rest,
nowhere to sit, to reflect,

no tree to put a back to,
no wall to wind protect
the weary and the old.

My home is a wasteland
made so by many hands,
the village that I loved
has left me homeless
in a bitter world.

CRITICS THERE ARE MANY
[13.35, 10th Apr 2021, Iver Grove]

Critics, there are many,
doers, there are few -
the critics in their armchairs
sipping on their wine -
while the doers climb their mountains
and chant their songs.

WE ARE WILD ONCE MORE
[23.00, 19th Apr 2021, Iver Grove]

The cage is open, we are free
to leave our narrow perches
and fly into the trees.

What joy to have our freedom
to drink the perfumed air,
chase the cherry blossom.

We can sit and warble,
make our nest the best,
hatch our little eggs.

No more bars, kept indoors,
left to trill and tweet -
we are wild once more.

WHY DON'T I HAVE A LOVER (song)
[from The Beehive, 24th Apr 2021, Iver Grove]

Why don't I have a lover
who has a great hunger
why don't I have a hundred
or thousand or so.

Why cant I have a lover
who has seven brothers
why do I have to suffer
til I'm wrinkled and old.

Why have I no lover
who's handsome and clever
why must I serve beer
to dirty old bores.

O give me a lover
who brings me flowers
O give me a true love
before I grow cold.

YOUR HUSBAND HAS GONE
[23.3, 10th May 2021, Iver Grove]

Your husband has gone, you are alone,
you are free to share your love at last
with me, for I have loved you always,
adored you in a hundred different ways
that you have pretended not to notice,
though I know you have suspected
that I have waited for this moment
to arrive, and now its come.

I MEASURE OUT THE ROPE
[23.59, 18th May 2021, Iver Grove]

Some people just take the piss,
try to get what they can while they can
without any thought for your feelings -
well, they're wrong and stupid!

They think they are God's gift to you,
stupid to believe that they are entitled
to tramp on your respect and morals,
and then get a way with it!

If you are meek you might whimper,
cower before such selfish tyrants -
but I quietly measure out the rope
I'm going to hang them with!

I CRAVE SILENCE
[00.22, 19th May 2021, Iver Grove]

I crave silence from the noise
that people make with their mouths
the roar of their wheeled-machines,
the rattle of their humdrum lives.

I want to hear the birds,
shut out the fume-filled skies,
close my tired sagging eyes
and listen to the rising lark.

What luck to have such sound,
the ecstasy of the moving air,
the pleasure of it on my face
with not a whisker out of place.

To lie still undisturbed,
to slumber with no ticking clock,
to dream like no dream before,
deaf to all the world's woes.

SUNSHINE
[23.32, 30th May 2021, Iver Grove]

Sunshine heals all our woes,
gives us life we had forgotten,
restores the lost and terminated,
revives the tired and irritated,
makes us forget our miscalculations,
renews us with determination,
provides us with exhilaration
to conquer all our trepidations.

NATIONAL BANK HOLIDAY
[23.42, 31st May 2021, Iver Grove]

Has summer come, I hope so,
the icy Arctic wind eats us up,
freezes all our good intentions,
makes us huddle in our misery.

Not so now, this day,
this national holiday enjoyed,
made use-of as it should,
meeting with friends from afar.

Taking walks by old canals,
breathing the freedom of rest,
lounging without counting hours,
making plans beyond tomorrow.

This is a good time -
the reason to be breathing,
the essence of existence,
the purpose of our lives.

BANNED FROM FOREIGN TRAVEL
[23.32, 3rd June 2021, Iver Grove]

The misery of lock-up continues
to restrict our personal freedoms.
We are banned from foreign travel
out of fear of mutant variants.
God forbid that aliens will arrive
and zap us with their ray guns.

The Martians are here already,
the white men forbidding our futures,
the children of Empire immigrants
interning refugees and asylum seekers;
concentration camps in rural Kent,
and God knows how many other places.

Crypto currencies continue to tumble
as house prices rocket through the roof,
wages are stagnant and inadequate,
workers are too few to staff the schools;

the rich are running off to Cornwall
to live off their home-rental loot.

The Prosecco perches on the verandah,
the sun sets into the pristine sea,
the well-off stroll the shimmering strands,
eat prawns for lunch, sea bass for tea;
they have sworn off foreign travel -
they should be happy to let us leave.

A DAY GONE WRONG
[00.05, 8th June 2021, Iver Grove]

Not every day runs smoothly,
the bus is often not on time,
it rains while the sun shines,
with none to catch our falls.

Failure may be the only option,
the table may be bare at lunch,
but somehow, no matter the solution,
there is no answer at all.

GOING TO BED
[23.30, 22nd June 2021. Coalpits Heath, Glouc]

Eleven o'clock is heaven,
midnight is just right.
By one o'clock we are done,
two o'clock should be one!

COTSWOLDS COTTAGE
[23.47, 22nd June 2021, Coalpits Heath, Glouc]

The ash falls upon the table
as the laughter shakes the rafters
of the medieval Cotswold cottage
nestled on the chalky uplands
in a village near to Bristol
but closer to old Bath -
where the vicar is a nuisance
and her churches always barred.

The garden falls into the combe
like blossom on a summer breeze,
the pear and the cherry tree
offer shade from the Wiltshire sun.
A wooden chair, a rusty axe,
the bunting o'er the bower path,
the crunch of gravel underfoot,
exotic flowers and verdant grass.

IVER GROVE
[23.27, 5th July 2021, Iver Grove]

Back to the sound of rainfall
on the stable yard cobbles,

the running of the flood
down the internal wall drains.

Old buildings echo older sounds
once common, now long gone
with the clatter of the hooves
across the stony courtyard.

The rose petals wash away
down the cast iron stank,
as the rattle of thunder
shakes more rain from above.

ANNA
[14.01, 11th July 2021, Cannes]

We drank into the early hours,
danced to wild Irish songs,
planted kisses on our lips,
caressed with our finger tips.

As dawn came up we lay down,
slept beyond a decent time,
rose to find our two clocks
ticking to a different chime.

THE ACTRESS
[13.00, 13th July 2021, Cannes]

She came in her red robes
and filled me with long tales,
she lay on the white sheets
naked and longing.

She performed all her horse skills
and submitted to my will,
she moaned my name softly
into the pillow.

She passed into the evening
white robed and red scarfed,
held on to my arm firmly
then went up the red steps.

SILENT IN THE CORNER
[20.00, 18th July 2021, Le Thornet, Var]

He is invisible, silent in the corner,
sipping his red wine and watching
the night pass well into the dawn,
the revellers oblivious to his presence.

So time passes, silent in the corner,
the old man wrestling with his thoughts
with each sip of wine an old memory
returns to shadow his present existence.

SHE IS BACK
[23.44, 27th July 2021, Iver Grove]

She is back to haunt all my thoughts,
beguile me with all her charms,
engaging me with all her tales
of home life and adventure.

Like a fool I'm taken in -
entranced, bewitched by her smile,
tricked by all her little looks
that rip my heart asunder.

What hope have I against such arts -
the darting of her flashing eyes,
the pursing of her sensual lips
on words that hold my wonder.

Can I escape her web-like spell
that binds me like a coiling snake,
or are am I doomed to my fate
of unrequited blunder.

Time will tell if she succeeds
in keeping me so betwixt,
for such strokes can turn the tide
and sweep the swimmer under.

THE LIVING ROOM LODGER
[23.25, 2nd August 2021, Iver Grove]

She wears her red shorts to bed,
her black hair cascading on her skin,
her long brown legs stretched on the sheets,
her dimpled chin resting on her hand,
the bareness of her shoulders inviting kisses,
the arch of her back prepared for giving,
her smile full of warmth and longing,
her eyes full of life and living.

LIFE TAKES ITS TURNS
[23.10, 9th Aug 2021, Iver Grove]

Life takes its turns on the merrygoround,
the horses bobbing up and down,
the lights flashing at blinding speed,
the chatter of the croud incredible loud,
the senses all dazed and in a whirl,
all feelings numb, all emotions swirled,
by the wurlitzer music drowning out
notions of guilt and lingering doubt.

TIN SOLDIERS ON PARADE
[23.44, 9th Aug 2021, Iver Grove]

The same circle drawn every day,
the routine that comes without thought,

the endless hours spent in ritual,
nothing changing but the clouds
passing overhead without influence.

This is the daily bread of God,
the repetition of all daily chores,
the never-ending tale to tell,
the ever-binding chain we wynd
link by link around our frames.

This same circle our fathers made,
the routine that our mothers taught,
the endless rules to be obeyed -
the everlasting commands we salute
like tin soldiers on parade.

There is no escape from such order,
tablets fetched, scrolls unrolled,
laws to make the circle whole -
no gap to somehow wriggle through,
no escape from growing old.

DAYS GO BY
[00.23, 21st Aug 2021, Iver Grove]

Days go by like pennies through my fingers,
spent on nothing much to remember -
then along comes a day of pound notes
and I find myself creating requerdos.

By surprise comes a fifty pound note,
a day that refuses to be cashed -
a day when everything is free and easy
and makes me happy to be alive.

TUMOUR ON MY BRAIN
[00.17, 28th Aug 2021, Iver Grove]

Today I was told
I had a tumour on my brain.
It was all rather surreal
and impossible to equate.

It was twenty months ago
I had my MRI scan,
Covid in between
and doctors on the run.

What will be the outcome
of this turn of events -
life will be the question
and my life the test.

DESPAIR AS MY ONLY THOUGHT
[21.59, 28th Aug 2021, Iver Grove]

I've had a lucky carefree life,

yet I've learned nothing of this life
except cruelty and a little generosity
to light up the world's wicked ways.

As life ends, surely as it will,
I take stock and chastise myself
for my ignorance of others' suffering,
my lack of compassion and my pride.

Even now as millions in Yemen starve
and thousands face Afghani persecution,
I feel sorry only for myself,
for my own self-inflicted misery.

How the weight of time depresses,
makes the world dark and forboding,
casts the lonely down into hell,
leaves despair as my only thought.

SUMMER ENDS TOMORROW
[23.19, 30th Aug 2021, Iver Grove]

Summer ends tomorrow, will be gone
leaving us with autumn at our heels,
the return to thoughts of winter
that will in time approach.

It was not a great summer.
It contained too many unknowns,
the continuation of the plague
the orders to stay at home.

What kind of summer was it,
other than one we will forget,
short, and wet, and passing
and gone with no regrets.

EMPTY LONGING
[23.30, 4th Sept 2021, Iver Grove]

When the women you love like no other
leaves loving you more than ever -
the feeling inside is one of empty longing
that lingers endlessly until she returns.

ALL THINGS ARRANGED IN A ROW
[0.10, 6th Sept 2021, Iver Grove]

All things arranged in a row -
the car parked up in the bay,
the shelves stacked with the essentials,
the laundry washed and dried,
the plants watered, carpet swept,
the flowers arranged, dusting done,
dinner cooked, the bedding fluffed
and the day all run.

ANOTHER'S DIRT
[20.00, 22nd Sept 2021, Iver Grove]

I left school fifty years ago
to grovel, bow and scrape,
to make a living in a world
not made for me.

I've sweated, toiled and laboured
with nowt a thing to show
except my blistered knuckles
and my broken toes.

Had I been a smarter man,
what tales I may have tell't,
adventures on the high seas,
the wealth I'd spent.

But none of that transpired
in the life that I have led,
despite my dreams of respite,
God has held his breath.

This is not how I foresaw
all those years since I left school,
rising early in the darkness
and trudging home at dusk.

Now Im old and luckless,
I have grovelled quite enough,
the dirt I've dug to live
is now another's work.

WHEN YOU ARE DRUNK
[00.17, 2nd Oct 2021, Iver Grove]

When you are drunk,
drunk as a skunk,
you don't see anything
except the spinning lights,
the stupid conversation
making your head light.

You make jokes and stuff,
try to pretend you're sober,
but the harder you try
the more you keel over -
even at my age
I can't escape closure.

THE DRUNKEN PHILOSOPHER
[00.31, 2nd Oct 2021, Iver Grove]

Another month tells me nothing new,
though it tries to say – listen,
there is still much to learn
on this road with a view.

I'm not interested in looking
at what's up ahead,
it may be pretty pictures
but I'm already dead.

Yet my voice is still whispering
'You cannot give up yet,
all that you have experienced
is the sum of all regrets'.

I may fight those opinions
as I want to come to rest,
but the doubts of existence
make me question what is next.

So if I want to tally
all that I've come to test,
then I reckon it is likely
being pissed is not the best.

DAYS LIKE THIS
[20.25, 4th Oct 2021, Iver Grove]

There are days like this -
when I want to get on my donkey
and ride off into the sunset.
To hell with responsibility,
to hell with the people in my life
fading into the night!

THE WHEEL I CAN'T GET ON
22.32, 9th Oct 2021, Iver Grove]

We play our songs, carry along
as if nothing is going wrong,
but underneath the cloak, the hope
has long gone, gone up in smoke.

It's all maybe a joke for some folks
with their life in order, free of bother
and all the little piddly things
that make life hard, disordered.

The grass appears greener, bellies leaner
on that side of the street, a cheat
of a place to be, to be seen
getting on in life, with no strife.

I try to be, but its not me,
its how it is arranged, displayed
before my face, the rat race,
the broken wheel I can't get on.

LOOKING FOR THE LIFE-RAFTS
[22.35, 17th Oct 2021, Iver Grove]

The winds of change are sweeping
through the corridors of our institutions,
our banks and our computing systems.

Nothing is the same as it was,
its all topsy turvy and awash -
afloat on a sea of chaos.

Politicians look for the life-rafts
they have thrown into the sea -
they are going down with the ship.

Holed with their reckless-ness,
they will drown in their own folly
and we will be left adrift.

FORGOTTEN ART
[23.37, 20th Oct 2021, Iver Grove]

Forgotten art, forgotten artists
who made a living from their craft;
their work moulds in damp attics,
turns yellow in the summer sun,
either hidden from the world
or ignored in frames on faded walls.

Brilliant colours once so dazzling,
bodies etched and superbly shaped,
gone now to hidden vaults
beyond the gaze of the public -
what tragedy awaits us all
when we view what's gone before.

Dwell then not on the future -
those artists lived for their time,
worked to please their paying clients,
somehow kept their souls intact;
for they have left a little something
many dreamt of having done.

ALL SAINTS DAY
[00.22, 1st Nov 2021, Iver Grove]

Halloween ends with an icy blast,
the arrival of November at its heels,
the turn of the clock back an hour
brings on night by late afternoon -
the memories of summer in the chill
of winter, laid bare before us.

I AM A STRATHCLYDER
[00.22, 2nd Nov 2021, Iver Grove]

It is said that I am a Celt,
but this may not be so.
I am from the Damnonian lands,
the Alba people of Strathclyde

where the Rock Kings ruled,
where the people dug the earth,
for coal - and smelted iron
to shape their swords.

There is nothing Celtic in this.
Daanan and their tales,
their four sacred treasures
they carried in their ships
through the Pillars of Hercules
and unloaded in fair Ierne;
which they easily conquered,
but not so in green Strathclyde.

Perhaps I have some Celtic blood,
but what part, what share
of me is that post-Milesian race?
For I cannot see it -
I cannot see it in my eyes,
in my statue or in my gait,
I don't fit the mould …
I do not look Celtic.

Perhaps some Roman intermingled
with my people two thousand years ago.
Some Norman perhaps, some Norse,
some Gael from the Highlands.
But I do not feel it …
I do not believe it …
for I am from Strathclyde,
it is in my bones.

Perhaps memory tricks our thoughts,
makes stories from our desires
to be that which we are not.
But not so with me -
I am a Strathclyder …
I have my sense of belonging,
of knowing that my people
were the first settlers.

It is a fixed, inherent feeling
in a world of flux and chaos -
to know where I am rooted,
where my seed was spawned,
where my ancestors had laboured,
where my own kind has toiled,
where life has been continuous,
and that I belong.

IT TRICKLES AWAY
[23.32, 15th Nov 2021, Iver Grove]

It trickles away, no matter what,
it trickles every second, every day,
every moment of our existence,
it runs through our lives,

it passes through our hands,
it disappears followed by itself,
in a never ending trickle,
never stopping, just trickling on.

MOTHER
for Valerie
[23.41, 15th Nov 2021, Iver Grove]

She died of cancer -
quickly she passed away
as if life had gone,
the reason to live, departed,
the desire to see the dawn
not in her gift to have,
so she faded quietly,
went without a fuss,
so no-one would notice.

THIS LONDON LIFE
[18th Nov 2021, Iver Grove]
[19th Nov 2021 Train to Penzance]

This London life, what life is there
for those living on the streets,
for those who live to pay the rent,
for those who struggle with their health.

Where are the mountains & the seas,
the fresh green uplands, golden beaches,
the places where normal humans heal,
where eyes lift up beyond the concrete.

This London life of toil and greed,
this town of anguish and broken dreams,
this place that offers no relief,
that shakes the core of self-belief.

Lost, not found, in every borough,
the city oozes wealth and power,
eats the soul each languorous hour
of all who live and work there.

Lured by riches beyond the grasp,
seduced by fame that never lasts,
sucked in by flashing clubland lights,
the doormen bow, the waiters laugh.

And laugh they do with tired eyes,
thinking of their late night bus,
the life they thought of passing by,
today dismissed with a sigh.

This London life, its double lines,
the rules that keep all in check,
the rules that often seem to warp
for the few that bend them best.

789

This life, this town of workers,
these hordes of slaves and toilers
from distant lands and furthest corners,
having left behind their fathers, mothers.

This town, this place of sorrow,
this city of Sodom without Gomorrah,
its church spires and museum domes,
its stone palaces, and forbidden walls.

Each passer-by with glazed eyes,
each step a step just too far,
each look a furtive glance,
each bump or touch just pure chance.

Every moment the Bow Bells ring,
"Where is God? Who is he?"
Is God some conjured myth,
set to keep us turning cheeks.

What thoughts churn on every face
passing by at such a pace.
Where are these folks going now,
have they arrived, or hurry still?

Who can judge, make prediction
of others' aims, their life's religion.
What goals are such actions for,
what door will open, to what land?

This London life, grinding on,
day to night, dusk to dawn,
while others sleep, others yawn
and pass into another dawn.

WINTER STORM (ARWEN)
for Stuart
[19.55, 27th Nov 2021, Iver Grove]

The winter storm has reached shore,
pounding on our battered doors,
howling at our shuttered glass,
creaking at our timbered floors,
seeping through every crack,
bringing cold and driving snow.

YOUTH & KNOWLEDGE
[23.01, 28th Nov 2021, Iver Grove]

Memories brought on by cold
can drown us in their depth,
leave us floundering and gasping
at why we were so inept
with our youth and knowledge
that now seems so wasted
on the young we watch paddling

in waters infested with sharks.

THE FIRST SNOW
[10.05, 2nd Dec 2021, Iver Grove]

The first snow arrived,
lay on the rooftops
like confetti at the church.

It blew in the wind,
the yellow sun blazing
on the frozen fields.

THE 2AM TICKING
[01.50, 5th Dec 2021, Iver Grove]

The two a.m ticking of the clock,
all is quiet, there is no talk,
only breeze racing through the trees,
rushing on to somewhere next.

What know we of this world,
never silent, earnestly at work,
spinning on through time and space,
while we hang on to what we've got.

The void of night, long and dark,
the clock ticks on, the wind howls,
cowers the meek to turn to sleep,
to hide away until the dawn.

PRAYING FOR PROSPERITY
[01.10, 10th Dec 2021, Iver Grove]

Prosperity eludes the wanting,
happiness is lost on the wild,
envy is the disease of the wealthy,
greed is the worst kind of crime.

Hope fails to rekindle kindness,
pride loses the man in himself,
love is the refuge from despair
when anger is abroad everywhere.

Lessons never learnt are forgotten,
minds that are broken are hurt,
healing is time's only blessing,
wealth a gift beyond words.

MAY THEY ROT IN HELL
[00.35, 30th Dec 2021 Marbesa, Spain]

Wealth, power and money is nothing -
without morals the individual is bankrupt,
nothing more than a pimp of depravity,
an exponent of corruption and abuse,
a defiler of dignity and integrity -

a pariah on society and individuals
destroyed by association and connection;
all they touch is tainted and despoiled
by the involvement and influence
they waste to make our lives hell.

LITTLE SECRETS
[00.31, 31st Dec 2021, Marbesa, Spain]

Time will come again to save
the moments I thought lost for good,
found again to be renewed,
reunited by somehow freshly viewed,
each moment really something new
that comes into existence.

With each loss space is made
to occupy the vacant slot,
empty plots of unmarked time,
endless in the emptied mind
seeking moments to be refined
and kept as little secrets.

THE MARBESA BIRDS
[14.00, 2nd Jan 2022, Marbesa, Spain]

The Marbesa birds are full of chat,
back and forth from branch to branch,
they hop with all the joy of Spring
though we are in the winter months.

What joy to hear their endless chirps,
to watch their everlasting play,
devoid of all our human traits,
we are slaves whilst they are free.

THE WOLF MOON
[22.01, 17th Jan 2022, Iver Grove]

It hung overhead in the freezing cold,
cobalt shadows in the winter gloom,
the dogs were silent in their makeshift beds,
nothing stirred, not a leaf fell -
the hoar glazed the sheets of slate,
covering the night in a misty haze.

BENEATH THE MILKY WAY
[20th Jan - 9th Feb 2022, Iver Grove]

What is important in life -
bananas, sunshine and sleep,
simple joys, essential oils,
a lover on your knee.
No endless journeys going nowhere,
no dark nights all alone,
no egos getting in the way
of truth and love.

Why then is it not so,
not plain sailing on a breeze?
Why is there always strife
and companions full of fear?
Is there something in the air,
the planets playing with our heads,
pulling on our darkest thoughts,
revealing all our faults?

Why can't we just be happy,
grateful for the life we have,
accept that this is what it is,
and this is our given lot.
Is that too easy to accept,
to have a humble life of joy,
to ease through days with a smile
and never be at odds?

No, something in our stubborn nature
makes us rail against the norm,
forces us to wail and cry
that the world is unfair.
Unfair of what, or with whom,
the Earth rotates around the sun,
the sun drifts where it might
through the cosmic storms.

Do we know what that means,
what it does to our thoughts?
Can we control the sky above,
or beneath the earth we trod?
Can we grasp the air we breathe,
or touch the sky up above?
Do our dreams exist at all,
are we real or not?

What forces then guide us on
to do the things we always do,
the things we repeat each day,
the blood coursing through our veins,
our ever beating fragile hearts,
our breathing done without thought,
all that's taught, or learned along
the ever winding way.

Day in day out we carry on
as if we have a special plan,
as if we are in control
of all we think we can -
Our schemes, so ably laid,
too often are of a mould,
a dozen times done before,
a hundred times or more.

Our genes dictate who we are,
what we will in time become,

our fate is what our fathers were
or what our mothers bore -
a timeless pattern to observe
the warp and weft of humankind,
we are the fabric of the past,
the cloth of time.

You may say it is not so,
each and all are unique,
I protest we are clones
with mutation sequence flaws.
The flaws that give us our quirks,
give us all our different looks,
leave us with the oddest views
that destiny ignores.

And so with our hidden secrets,
strewed across our wrinkled brows,
there are no tales to unfold,
they have all gone before.
We present nothing new,
our actions are just as tame
as those folks now long gone
who thought the same.

The danger lurks in belief
that this time round we are special,
somehow different from the past,
a breed somehow set apart.
But what folly in such talk,
blind we walk towards the cliff,
without a glance up ahead
we come to grief!

The sun will spin around the skies,
we will spin around the sun,
the Milky Way will always be
the place where we come from.
Two hundred million years or more,
our planet whizzes off and back,
our lives are but a single blink
of the cosmic eye.

What wisdom can we add to that,
to know we know not a thing,
our mindsets fixed upon ourselves,
not what has made all of us.
It is not some woolly thought up God,
conceived and watching us with love,
it is not some unseen hand
turning us back to dust.

If we know what life's about,
we would loudly shout it out,
but timid as we are at heart,
there are some convinced they know
that life is one endless wheel

where conscious thought is not real,
it is some long waking dream
we must escape from.

If so, then why all our fuss
to etch and scratch, make our mark,
record our time with our pens,
erect tall buildings with our names?
Why put our dates on our tombs?
Why etch in marble *lest we forget*?
Have all our rituals set in stone
while our planet spins?

Can we not see beyond the stars,
blinded by all that glimmer,
the black we think is a void,
that void containing what we are?
And what we are is not clear,
its something strange to ourselves,
that all the knowledge in the world
cannot explain.

And so we spin none the wiser,
hung in space going nowhere,
well, not in any cosmic terms
rooted here on planet Earth,
with our lovers on our knees,
our endless journeys somehow stayed,
no dark nights on our own
beneath the Milky Way.

ALL THE TRAINS ARE BOOKED
[23.52, 9th Feb 2022, Iver Grove]

All the trains are booked,
all the flights are full,
I'm going nowhere fast,
I'm stuck here for the now.
The country's on the move,
and I'm not in the loop -
folk are acting busy
and I'm a Betty Boop.

Winter is hard upon us,
I'm pressed to understand
why folk are whizzing off
with all their travel plans.
Its not our British nature
to go to and fro
when there is cold weather
and the threat of snow.

Perhaps I'm missing something
broadcast on the news,
perhaps I am muddled,
somehow most confused?
For all the trains are booked,

all the flights are full,
and I'm stuck here sitting
on my suitcase like a fool.

Oh well, I better unpack,
take off my winter coat,
hang my woolly hat
and scarf behind the door.
I won't be off to somewhere,
countryside or coast -
for all the trains are full,
and all the flights are booked.

HOMEWARD BOUND
[00.25, 22nd Feb 2022, Iver Grove]

The stag stood on the crest of the hill,
the loch below flat and still,
the afternoon sun on the mountain tops,
snow on the peaks, sleet on the slopes,
the air cleared by yesterday's storm,
the winter halted just for the morn.

Homeward I traveled on snaking roads,
southwards as rivers flooded and rushed,
broken mud banks, green meadows engulfed,
washed away fences, floated off trees,
felled by the fury of the gale force winds,
from far far out on the wild west seas.

TWENTY TWO, TWO, TWENTY TWO
[22.22, 2.2.22, Iver Grove]

Twenty two, two, twenty two,
the hour clicked on to twenty two,
the minute hand ticked to twenty two,
and all the twos aligned as they do,
but never again will the twos read,
forwards, backwards and upways too!

WAR
[01.10, 26th Feb 2022, Iver Grove]

What does war do for every man
but steal his freedom, rob his plans.
What does war do for women
but kill their children, make them cry.

War offers nothing but wild despair,
anguish, grief and endless mourning,
loss of faith that God exists,
debates on whether life' worth living.

War smashes all that's in its way,
does not distinguish right from wrong,
orders passed down are obeyed,
chaos defeats, leaves us decayed.

War destroys all our highest hopes,
makes us flee from all destruction,
makes us turn our back on those
who are not us, who now are foes.

This is war, that thing we dread,
that thing we cannot stop once started,
for we are led by idealists
whose pride prevents a fresh departure.

Thus war rages on with no end,
with no solution but tanks and guns,
this is the way men proceed,
while children pray for lasting peace.

INSTAGRAM
[00.00, 8th Mar 2022, Iver Grove]

I picked up my phone,
I felt incredible calm
as I looked at my babe
I knew she would come,
to pull me in closer,
hug me, and hold me,
and love me forever
if I could forgive her.

ZELENSKI
[20.18, 10th Mar 2022, Iver Grove]

I am not responsible for your problems,
all I want is guns and planes.
I don't care if you somehow starve,
go cold and cry into your borshe.
I believe I'm in the right
and you are all just talk.

I am not the one killing children,
bombing schools and our care homes.
I am not firing missiles,
shelling whole apartment blocks.
I am standing up for freedom
while you won't let me in your club.

Yes, I will take all your warheads,
line them up and face them north.
Yes, I will take all your aircraft
and load them up with nuclear bombs.
I am not the biggest problem,
I am the righteous of us all.

THE ORPHANED CHILDREN CRY
[22.20, 3rd Apr 2022, Iver Grove]

I will keep my counsel,
withhold my thoughts in public,

for I fear I am out of kilter
with a Western world bent
on destroying all our futures,
believing it is right,
and I am wrong.

The lambs will always baa,
for that is all they know,
they will follow the flock,
fall in line as they always do,
the dogs nipping at their heels,
the shepherd with his crook
hooking out the lame.

We are all lambs to slaughter,
knowing not our futures,
led off to war's abattoir
without the slightest whimper.
We are lost and helpless,
hostage to our leaders
and their talk of freedom.

If we were somehow free,
there would be no conflict,
surrender would be victory,
avoidance of all misery
would be the end of war;
the intelligentsia would cry,
the workers thrive.

The root of freedom is love,
love for one's native land.
Bound to a piece of Earth
by some magnetic force,
we give up our lives
for each blade of grass,
each gram of soil.

This is the folly of war,
the means by which we destroy,
obliterate all our progress,
return to the self same soil
as corpses turned to dust;
in the name of freedom,
we destroy.

Call an end to this cause,
lay down your arms,
pack away your bombs and missiles,
disband your soldiers, go home.
The weeping mothers wail,
the orphaned children cry
for those who're missing.

OUR DREAMS
[22.20, 3rd Apr 2022, Iver Grove]

Our dreams are as fragile as ice,
they melt on our aspirations
when we discover we are not in control
of anything at all.

THE ANATOMY OF MY WORLD
[9th Apr - 16th May 2022, Iver Grove]

When I go out into the world,
I fear not what I will meet,
nor who I will greet freely.
I think not of what is out there,
nor of what I will encounter
in the street of pub.
For as a man of our times,
I enjoy the comfort of companionship,
the beauty of the human form -
for what better is there to look on
but the fair complexion of youth
or the twinkle in an eye.
Thus is conveyed the secret of life -
draws in our attention as such,
as we look to find the uncommon,
the rareness of human nature,
the unique individual of thought
who does not hide their knowledge.
Who does not enjoy the human
who reveals their inner nature,
who happily shares their companionship.
What more can a stranger want
than to receive a nod to their existence,
that we are alive, living now -
not in some ideal world imagined,
nor some dream like member's club
where I am not welcome, for I
seek the company of open friends,
individuals with no inhibitions,
with talk that transcends conditioning.
How else do we know one another
if we live with a false perception
of who we should be, or act like,
for acting is the human condition,
the means by which we lie -
tell our untruths to protect our egos.
Not so when we are well met
to confide with a total stranger;
we discover that we are not alone,
that we are only lost, looking to be found
for who we are as beings -
children wandering, looking for a home.
This home that we have lost,
that we left without knowing where
we were going, or when we would
return to where we started -
that child without preconceptions
of who we are, or will become.

So goes life, and how we revel,
discover the joys and pleasures;
how we love to indulge,
take hold of what is delivered,
served to us without payments
or expectation of some return.
Thus the greatest gifts are free
of consequence and commitment,
given to us without cost,
enhanced and loved with loss,
or pain, or remorse for enjoyment
of being alive and happy.
Oh how these times sustain us,
prevent the Devil from succeeding
in warping our hold on existence.
We discover what we do, not know -
we unravel the complexities of nature,
behold the wonders of the Earth.
Seeing these wonders for the first time,
we comprehend their meaning,
the hidden essence of their structure.
Such joy is always short lived
as we crave some new experience
to lift us from our worries.
For do we not crave distraction
to free us from our concerns?
Our concerns of war, of poverty,
of suffering when it is needless,
the cruelty of men on children,
the neglect of mothers for their sons.
There is no escaping the human condition,
that throwback trait we all harbour,
the cave-man, the tribal traditional
that makes as resentful of strangers,
that makes us suspicious of outsiders,
those who are no different from ourselves.
We make outsiders with our words,
with our imagination and indignation,
our indifference and our behaviour.
So we crave laughter, hide such thoughts,
embrace those we know with warmth,
trust those who are just like us.
We can fall into a sense of well-being,
put up with bad behaviour from some,
the enemy within, those who subvert us,
those who are envious of our ways,
want something from us, some gain
they can take away to profit on.
Who needs rancorous friends,
such shallowness will always out,
will always reveal itself to others,
be made plain and in full sight,
for us to condemn, or forgive,
depending on the severity of the slight.

Is this not the Christian way?
Our capacity to be hard done by

that somehow we willingly overlook
to make allowance, to offer pity
when it is not deserved, even then
we still find some saving grace.
This is the trap of the meek,
the flaw that permits exploitation,
the state of mind that repeats mistakes,
until all self esteem is eroded,
whittled down to loss of status,
diminished joy, and unhappy stasis.
All around us are the broken,
the lost, the seekers of redemption
who stretch for a reaching hand
that we will not refuse to take -
for today we can offer help,
tomorrow we may need the same.
How life turns back on itself;
we climb our hills, take our views,
then homeward, we reach the woods
and lose the path in the dark,
until at last we find we're lost
without a light to guide us home.
Many times and many places
I have found myself thus lost,
yet always there comes a time
when the darkness falls away -
shows the path out the woods
towards an open sunny place.
There the breeze freely blows,
there the sun warms our face
there we find some respite
from all our personal strife,
far from all the inner fights,
the anger and the doubts.
For homo sapiens that we are,
with our warlike take on life,
why do we create our saints?
Why do we present our art
as cultivated, thoughtful, loved
while we destroy all other life?
How can we lie, be so false,
promise those requesting help,
offer up our arms and bombs
to any nation fresh invaded,
when we know that such supplies
will lead us to our own destruction?
We are led by vane idealists
caught up in their need for fame,
drenched in their sense of history,
we somehow will get the blame,
for such leaders lead us down
a path that's in our name.

Is this how we treat our foes,
how we evolved so long ago -
wiping out our Erectus fathers,
erasing evidence of their triumphs,

by discarding their advancements,
leveling all their grand achievements?
I do not know, my life is short,
so short that there is little time
to find out why life is cruel,
so that all I achieve is to survive
until I'm robbed of that spark,
my brief flame before its snuffed.
How nature saves us from ourselves,
glares back at us on darkened pools,
knocks our senses with perfume,
roars at us with spray and fume,
until we know we are small,
and we as humans are such fools.
If I knew how to right all wrongs,
to lead us to the promised land,
then delusion would be my fate,
I'd lead you up the garden path,
line my pockets with endless gold,
write my memoirs before I'm old.
I'm not fit for public office,
who then is qualified to lead us?
I scan the horizon, do not see
a leader standing tall, erect
who I would follow with my heart
and want to vote for with my head.
Am I alone in my disenchantment,
this notion that I'm badly served,
that all we get is fibs and lies,
rogues who justify their acts
with half-spun truths, weak alibi's
they somehow think we will buy.
How delusion blinds the blind
to all but their own self interest,
life repeats itself in endless fashion
like nature reborn in the Spring -
with all its glory budding forth,
envy poised to stunt and choke.
If we cannot weed good from bad,
then one bad apple taints us all,
such rotten fruit at the top
should be discarded before the rot
permeates to those below -
me and you and countless more.
Our only friend is the sun -
our saviour with each coming morn,
dark forces cannot hide from it,
it reveals all mankind's wrongs,
though we are trying to blot it out
with carbon fuels, atomic bombs.
We are the losers in this fight
to save the planet as it is,
while far off in the distant dark,
a billion light years from now,
destruction lurks beyond our know.
So worry not, ignore such woe.
I say, cherish this life we have,

make it sweet, not a sweat,
not a toil to make ends meet -
live not for your children born,
live not for your selfish wants,
live to laugh, cry, enjoy.
For there are those wrinkled brows
warning us of all life's ills,
their whispers echo in the streets,
rebound along the prison walls
that they try to bind us with -
do I give into their talk?
And health? This will fade from us,
drain away with the years,
pain our gut, bow our legs,
bend our backs until we stoop -
with wretched aches and countless ails,
life will be a long travail.
Will we give up? We have our minds,
to guide us through our later life,
our strength will be in our talk,
our gestures and our kindly acts,
these will soothe our body pain,
help to numb our nightly turns.
While in some far distant land,
an actor squares up to a bear,
a boxer paces round the ring,
the circus crowd blankly stare -
the thud of shells loudly blares
from the backs of elephants.
War is never too far away,
though we may never see the carnage;
death is never in our face,
yet death is going all around us -
the Irish know how to atone,
to wake the living gone.

Someday this will be our end,
yet still we carry on mundanely
to scrimp and save in penny jars,
squirrel pounds, save in tens
saving for some rainy day
that will not someday come to pass.
For pass we will, there is no doubt,
to burn or rot in the soil,
to leave behind our piggy banks,
our treasures, and perhaps a house
bequeathed to our kith and lot,
deserving, or deserving not.
Thus we'll speak beyond the grave,
to sow resentment, strife and anger;
for what is our life's labour worth
but labour unspent in our life -
and with our wills we divide,
calculate our total profit.
How so then, born naked, poor,
do we not depart just as clean?
How have we acquired wealth,

objects hoarded, retained in bulk
just because we've grown attached,
because we've spent a lot of cash?
Wealth is an abstract notion,
totted up on our balance sheets,
how it reads defines statistics,
does not reflect our true worth -
for each life has equal value
in the eyes of us all.
Who does not think this is so,
for if they do, strike them down,
there is no place in our world
for life to have no worth at all -
yet we see at every turn
that this indeed is what unfolds.
Can there be justice in refugees
being carted to some foreign land,
corralled into fenced off camps,
saying it is for their good.
Are we blind to human misery
and to the love of brotherhood?
I wrestle with such noble notions,
how to be the perfect man,
and time and time again I fail
to be the kind of man I can,
or perhaps become, now too late
to help all those in my past.

I struggle with my Christian faith,
not the God bit, heaven forbid,
I tussle with my moral code,
which laws to breach without cause -
the ten commandments are my guide,
that I have broken many times.
Not all, not many, not that often,
I am loathe to state my flaws;
yet I admit I have fallen,
made selfish choices, indulged in sin,
made profit from my neighbour's weakness,
my neighbour's wife, and forgone Sundays.
Yet, I keep only one God,
do not take his name in vane,
I have honoured both my parents,
and never never have I killed -
I have refrained from common stealing,
I do not lie, nor falsely name.
Perhaps then, I am bound for heaven,
or some variation on that theme,
who knows what's beyond that point
if there is such a place at all -
I do not seek to have such comfort,
I'm strong enough for when I'm called.
But och, my head is full of things,
nonsense I need not share aloud,
the sort of stuff that dulls all sense,
the stuff that makes the world turn -
the spin of such minor things

that topples a much bigger world.
What know I of others' thoughts,
of how they think day to day?
How do they cope with God?
What things are in their prayers?
I look about and only see
people working, not their thinking.
Is this the world we inhabit,
a veneer of human concentration,
hands moving in rhythmic action,
completing tasks in automation,
robots in a mindless system
existing in a mindless vacuum?
Perhaps not, not all the time,
the deeper self gets revealed,
spills out in gushed emotion,
opinions shared midst high elation -
then too soon external pressure
returns the robot to safety mode.
Heartless, you may dismiss me cruel,
senseless in a fragile universe,
that I am somehow out of whack
with mankind and mankind's acts
of goodness, kindness and remorse
that I somehow cannot grasp?
Alas, I have no swift defence,
I am bare of all my armour,
I have revealed without pretence
all the thoughts I can present
within the time I've been given
before my time is spent.
For what is a man without a beer,
his loins bared to his lover's quim,
his passions built on his ideas
as he accepts his lover's kiss,
as she offers all that's bliss
to take him off to Timbuktu!
Returning from such fetching journeys,
I realise that life is such -
that moment when in a gush
life is summed up in a rush,
all that's wanted, all there is,
that nothing else matters much.
Enlightenment, how gurus search
for that same thing with their OM's,
and yet its clear to every man,
the reason that we're meant to be -
to carry on, make life continuous,
the purpose of our entirety.
When I forget, my *reason d'etre*,
my mind gets foggy with silly things;
before I can help myself, I have
convinced myself of higher purpose -
I am here to combat wrongs.
I am above all human flaws.
How we delude ourselves,
time and time, and time again,

forget the lessons of our loins,
the clarity of such special joy -
until we once more search for love
to satisfy our primeval lusts.

This is the anatomy of my world,
a beating heart, a throbbing mind,
a passion fueled by senseless acts,
an anger dowsed by loving hands,
my reason stayed by sharing thus
all the stuff that haunts me.
There is no stopping mankind's folly
that scoops us up, slaps us down
in ways we have no voice against,
no way of making madness cease
as headlong on chaos comes,
sweeps us over madness's cliff.
I close my eyes, try to cope,
come to terms with selfish views
driven by a privileged few.
We see clearly they are wrong,
but life is structured in a way,
we cannot rely on our Gods.
Thus each day travels on,
leaves behind a bit of us.
Which part that is its hard to say,
we shed our woes, our memories,
until a birthday card or note
becomes the sum of our decay.
This is life, we can't escape it,
it is not what we were told
when we were young, in our bloom,
with all our hopes and expectations -
no one prepared us for a time
when all our bones would wither.
What then must an old man do
to grasp at something fresh and new?
How does a pensioner reposition,
find himself with new ideals?
How does he throw off the shackles
binding him to his views?
Escape is in all our minds,
but routine dulls, and destroys
most of the thoughts we possess,
pass through us without a stir -
no finger lifted, step-out made,
inertia is the natural state.
The wearied body sags, and sits,
forgoes the use of brain, and legs,
lounges in the summer heat,
wraps up in the winter bed,
moves not an inch without creaks,
groans and huffs, puffs and more.
This old age world is not for me,
though aches and pains may exist.
I live with all my life-worn scars,
all the honours of my wars with

work and foolish misadventures
that have transpired, let me be.
If I have led a different life
that took me down a different road,
I'm sure it would have turned out fine,
I'd still be me, who I am,
perhaps not whole, for who knows,
the roads we take are often potholed.
While money makes up for time,
time becomes far more rare.
Yet how do we value time,
so the exchange is somehow fair?
We give time, get our goods -
coin, or gold from endless crooks.
That is the feeling of those neglected,
left to rot in their dotage, the folks
that faithfully played the game,
obeyed the rules of their betters;
those swine intent on robbing them
to offer crumbs towards their end.
Ah you say, that is not me!
That is some unlucky, lesser sod.
No its not, its most of us,
caught up in this fool charade,
that what we do is for mankind
when in fact we fuel division.
Let's be frank, what are wars
but idiots bent on being kings.
While thinking that they are saints,
they destroy all that's built,
all that has been achieved,
they bring down around our ears.
Nowhere do they note this better
than in that ancient eastern land -
India where Brahma dwells,
where Vishnu tries to keep the peace
while Shiva waits to unleash hell
if all else fails to quell unrest.
The West will never understand
the endless cycle of this order.
We rush into our endless wars
without a thought for tomorrow.
We point our fingers and our guns,
we bully, cajole, don't ask why.
I am no Hamlet seeking revenge,
racked by indecision I am not.
Do I see the world as barren,
a place where there is no light?
No, I am happy in my skin, while
perhaps less happy in my head.
Alas, are we not all a little giddy,
stirred up by our raging hormones,
influenced by our friends' opinions
when sound advice should be silent,
their wild passions pour on out,
and only add to the confusion.
It is little wonder we wish to run,

perhaps to sleep, or to dream,
not to the extent we do not wake -
such thoughts are for the birds.
Whatever life throws at me,
I must endure the worst.
My worst is but a trifle,
to those fleeing for their lives.
What is a moment of discomfort,
compared to the maimed and dying?
How can I declare I am suffering
when there are millions on the run?

These are our times, our present days
as history replays old scores,
revenge carries with it no honour,
only heartache for all involved,
none get to sit on the sidelines,
war's whirlwind wastes, destroys.
Better then to create, and record
the sins of our leaders, their hordes,
their followers of misguided fashion,
the murmurers of certain propaganda;
for truth is in between the lies,
hidden in a cypher of hypocrisy.
In these times, knowledge is useless,
it has little purpose for those in charge,
knowledge is ignored, replaced with slogans,
evil language that thwarts diplomacy.
We are bombarded with hate and loathing -
God is lost in the bellicose fog.
Yet, still we must survive, get on
with our daily mundane chores,
find ways to feed our children,
devise a living from our resources,
keep our minds from exploding,
keep our heads down, obey the law.
What laws are these? Just laws?
Our loyalty to our country's laws?
Without the need to abide by others,
so we can justify great acts of violence
against those beyond our shores
that we have robbed oft times before?
This was Empire, long gone I thought,
then lo, a new era bubbles forth,
the ashes of the past are stirred,
new patriotic fervours soon awake,
young men, the bravado of their youth,
line-up to save our democracy.
What folly have we not remembered,
the blood-shed, all that's gone before,
the millions who lie in Flanders fields,
the countless in the Second War;
Korea, Vietnam, Iraq, Afghanistan -
when will it stop, death be gone!
As Labour Day comes on us again,
I ask why are brothers thus opposed;
the soldier in the field on duty,

the politicians ratcheting the rhetoric,
making their black tie dinner speeches,
believing they have saved us all?
It is not my world, not my dream,
not the fresh air of the hills,
it is the dullness of government thought,
not the waters of the empty dales,
where life eternal springs anew,
far from the contamination of the few.
For few they are, these Oxford men,
debase, immoral, an elite cabal.
Posing as our moral saviours,
they are hiding out in Babel's tower,
shut off from the endless chaos,
they unleash without remorse.
Their grand ideas, their global schemes
that somehow impoverish us all.
Those less literate read the headlines,
the intellectuals soak up every word,
and in between this wide divide
we all get lost.
Yet still, the roses bud into bloom,
the bluebells shelter in the shade,
the blossom falls to our feet,
the brambles ramble underfoot,
the moss bleaches in the sun,
the summer comes despite the gloom.
The cares we have are all internal,
emotions bubbling from our minds.
Injustice creates the greatest anger,
inherent wrongs will make us boil.
Cry we will at evil deeds,
lash out we shall at evil doers.
These precepts are thoughts eternal,
truths that rule our behaviour,
but only lone souls, not collectives
where influencers sway the crowd,
convince with their warped rhetoric,
the reasons to warp the laws.
How do we cope with such situations,
times where we have no control?
Do we riot? Burn down police stations?
Tear up shops? Loot and rob?
How do we show our disapproval
that is now not worth a jot?
Vote? For whom? For what?
The same old lot with different faces?
I have no answer for you here,
I fail to offer any help -
Revolution is not for old men,
and I am old, my youth spent.

This is the anatomy of my world,
the man who pushes on for seventy,
the white male, English speaking,
the type of human in decline -
I'll gladly crumble into dust,

my race has committed untold wrongs.
For whom does that bell toll?
For us and all that's gone before,
the crimes of which we'll never know.
I sense that they are countless,
the sins of the father stick,
and now those sins are woke.
Should we take on our father's sins?
Hell, yes, we are their flesh and bone,
we cannot whitewash out our blood,
pretend we are not the same,
we are clones, remade again
to repeat the self-same wrongs.
And so our children go to school,
unknowing of what they do not know,
their mothers go about their chores,
doing what they always do,
their father's set out their stalls,
life goes on, each day renewed.
Need we care what else transpires
beyond the patch we inhabit?
Can we not ignore these things
far from us and unimportant?
Our focus on our food and home,
leaves no time for far involvements.
Death stalks us all without exception.
An old man gives out to dementia,
thus today, I mourn my loss -
my father firmly left his body,
passed beyond this known dimension,
that place beyond all comprehension.
I will mourn, try to fathom, how
I could have been a better son?
Dredge the depths of my remorse,
dredge the sins I've inherited -
come to terms will all his flaws,
and all the good I've been left with.
Farewell, father, God bless you now,
pass on to a place of peace,
the torture of this life is over,
you can now rest with grace.
Sleep like you always dreamed,
dream on as we cry for thee.
It is with grief we come to terms,
set out on our pilgrim's trek,
walk the long Camino way,
face our trials each new day,
sleep in simple hostel beds,
rise to greet our fellow sufferers.
To contemplate and mourn,
may be all that is expected -
each mile traveled on the road,
another mile to be accepted -
that loss is a load to bear,
to be unburdened with great care.
What then does a pilgrim learn
when sanctuary is finally reached?

Have all the tears now been shed?
Has all the anger now been spent?
Has the mind been fully cleared
of all the troubles death presents?
Perhaps the lesson is less sharp,
for life is blinding at its most,
the aches and pains of being alive
can numb the troubles of the mind -
cramp can offer up some respite
from the torturous unseen kind.
I think somehow this is true,
fatigue of limb can dull all thought,
a pilgrim walking for ten hours,
a little wine to help his legs,
seeks to flop in a bunk,
sleep, to lay his mind to rest.
What happy days, what great joy
to kneel before St James's church,
to have trekked three hundred miles,
or less, or more, however far
to finally reach your pilgrim's end,
to know you've done your penance.
So then, my father gone, I must
come to terms with my loss,
find a way to make my penance,
shed my tears, dismiss my anger,
walk my own Camino way, ask
my questions, find my answers.
I might as well kick off my shoes,
put up my feet, remember when,
a beer in hand, a joint the other,
was the way I could forget,
that life was not a human rat race,
but something meant to be enjoyed.
It is worth reflecting, that youth,
that time of inexperience and blunder,
gave happy days of 'fuck it!',
an overthrow of controlling older folk
trying to mould my existence,
in a way I unceremoniously rejected.

And now here I am – old,
wondering where it all went wrong.
What may have been, only if?
If only I had listened more intently,
or taken all my given opportunities,
joined the rat race, and got on.
Alas that was, and is not me.
I see no racetrack before me,
no predefined white stripped road
leading me on to nirvana -
that happy place of happy people
who have fulfilled their destiny.
The illusion, the misty perfect life,
the ideal that centuries never change.
Marriage, house, children, retirement,
the middle road explained to Crusoe,

the safe unimaginative contentment
he rejected to leave him shipwrecked.
I have monitored my own shipwreck,
the constant need, the desire for rescue
that never comes as the middle road,
that place of safety I abandoned
to be replaced with endless storms,
followed by lulls, calm, and deep peace.
Is this what I recommend? How life
should be lived by you all? -
No, not at all!, it would be folly
to leave the middle of the road,
cross the white line to the verge,
then beyond into the unknown.
There are dangers – poverty, madness,
crime, murder, and dangerous strangers,
car-wrecked folk, down-trodden wasters,
con-men, prostitutes and their agents;
corruption that knows no borders
on how to break your morals.

There lies the rub, our moral nature,
the depth of our spiritual education,
that upper part of our inner being,
that streak of decency, compassion,
the part that cares for right and wrong
as taught to us as children.
Without a moral compass, that pathway,
that middle road heading to heaven
has a white line that's wonky, broken,
that can veer off in a curve to the verge,
and over, disappearing into the morass
of loss, despair, 'til white is black.
I wouldn't wish that on anyone,
well, not anyone who has a good heart;
for many are ill-suited to wandering
and unable to find their own path.
Better then they take the middle road,
than test their moral fortitude.
At my age, it is too late to re-trek,
return the way that I have passed.
But I have re-found the middle path,
I am back on the white line road -
and on this ancient worn way, I have
re-encountered many friends of old.
Yet still, I am tempted to regress,
return to that wicked, lawless verge,
disappear into the sodden morass,
lose myself in all that mess,
expose myself to the perverse,
and believe I am being progressive.
What delusion wraps the selfish,
those individuals escaping from themselves,
the malcontents full of imperfections,
always attempting to find solutions,
solutions to their own inner flaws
that somehow can never be resolved.

And what of location, where we live?
How we live to get through our days?
The cooking that we do, the eating out,
when we are too tired to labour?
What are the daily chores we do,
the cleaning, and the rubbish recycled?
I am not proud of my humble abode,
two rooms with a kitchen attached,
a spare room for my impoverished friends
who are more nomadic than myself;
those friends who want more from life
who possess nothing but their names.
I can applaud such reckless living -
for they are alive, not dead inside;
they seek out that alternative pathway
that we know they will never find -
they travel with faith and great hope,
with no care to arrive.
A beer to their lips, a sip of wine,
this makes their world go round.
There is always talk of children,
that somehow they have not had -
and though they live for romance,
love never stays beyond the last dance.
What kind of living is this charade?
Are my friends fools, or lost?
No, I say, they are God's people,
kind in their ways, and in their hearts -
they have a love that is not returned
by lesser mortals intent on harm.
Let such friends inherit the Earth
as they surely do with their modesty,
their get-rich-schemes come to nought
as they do not believe they can be rich -
richness is a notion far removed
from those folk who live for profit.
In every age there are great potentates,
individuals who rise out of the muck,
ascend to such heights, that looking up
they make many others dizzy with envy -
they attract many imitating disciples
who replicate by trying to be like them.
Not for me, my friends are angels
compared to the avarice that abounds,
permeates every aspect of our culture,
makes decent honest people bent,
corrupts the young at an early age,
bends morals to the will of the state.
I am not adverse to bending the light,
Einstein proved that nothing was straight,
but how much bend can we make
before we break the stretching line -
infinity at both ends, yes ….
but not until broken beyond repair.
This can be a very lonely world.
My charity is not universal -

I can walk by beggars in the street,
look them in the eye, say hello,
but I do not extend a hand
to lift them from their poverty.
What is wrong with how I am made?
Why can I not help the most needy?
I will lend to a friend without repayment,
but to a stranger my purse is shut.
Is not the beggar sunken in despair
worth helping all the more?
Dickens is silent on this matter,
his foundlings, the boys of the rich,
underwent the greatest deprivation
in order to emerge as a super breed -
the blood of a distant relative, always
made the foundling crave for cream.
Not so for the stories still untold,
the slavery that inequality brings,
the attitude that the poor cannot cook,
they reason they must be given food,
excused as too lazy to feed themselves;
how absurd such statements look.
This is how revolutions begin, first
the hunger, then nowhere warm to sleep.
It is little wonder that mobs collect,
ransack stores, break into houses
when they are living on the edge
with not a thing to lose but their souls.

For this purpose has all learning been
a selfish journey to a pointless end?
A hedonistic sojourn to please myself,
my bouts of altruism but a thin disguise
for my failure to change this world
not made in the fashion I desire?
God, where am I in all this?
This void of human chaos and turmoil,
this Earth hell-bent on being destroyed
for some vague advantage I cannot see?
Some advantage I cannot condone
so our descendants can survive on Mars?
What folly permits such stupidity?
What reasoning dictates such policy?
We spend our Saturdays watching football,
our Sundays, Mondays, watching football,
until we are numb of all feeling -
until we are zombies with no freedom.
This is how we use our leisure,
vent our tribal affiliations through sport,
pick sides, curse the opposition,
take every little skirmish as a war.
For men believe their tribe is special,
worth the fight, worth dying for.
This is how nations come to clash,
take up arms, kill each other,
not because of right or wrong,
not because of greed or want,

but something more akin to loyalty
to their tribe, their clan, and lords.
What store they put in their faith
that they are the chosen ones -
that God is wholly on their side
as they maim, destroy, wipe out
any opposition to their tribe,
blind to all other ways of life.
This is democracy, devised by barons,
it is feudalism by another name,
the gatekeepers of Oxford, Cambridge,
educate the lackeys to do their bidding;
thus the sons and daughters of the poor
are corrupted to the barons' system.
This system of leaning ingrains inequality,
for the barons cannot function without serfs,
and serfs we are to our jobs,
and serfs we are to our houses,
and serfs we are to taxation
until the day we die.
It is no wonder we search for an exit,
try to get off the white lined road,
attempt to find a better end-game
than the one we are currently on
as we zigzag and dodge convention
with our own internal monologue.

This is the anatomy of my universe,
retreating to my shed to make manly
things, not to slave, but to resist,
to contemplate life and to wrestle
with the complexities of my universe -
the world I have created in my head.
Existing solely in my inner temple,
my scrolls, the summation of my thoughts,
my tabernacle unseen by others,
the laws by which I live my life,
at odds at time with convention,
at other times, falling into line.
Then, when something wrong is right,
when enough people buy the lie,
when for some the only way to succeed
is to lie all the way to the top -
woe betide the liar when found out,
descent is swift, the fall immense.
And so master criminals run countries
from the greatest nations to the small,
liars abound at every government level,
as lying is how politics is done -
the vassals of the robber barons
trying themselves to be barons in turn.
As I drag my paintbrush in contemplation,
I look up and gaze at the sun,
nothing matters, they'll soon be gone,
the politicians and their baron gods,
dictating all their daily dodges
while the sands of time run on.

What part play I in this rot,
all this shameful grab for wealth?
What time can I give to this desire
to live my life like a lord?
I'm little more than a beggar
writing this for no reward.

Happy thus to speak my mind,
on no man's time am I being paid.
I don't expect to be well read,
but I'd like my friends to understand
that all the things I do or say,
there's some thought to my rants.
For in old age, you are forgotten,
rarely seen at fine events,
rarely asked to come to dinner,
rarely visited by old friends;
for they too are kept in hiding
by illness, children, and long regrets.
What an age this is, Covid years
laying low the very best -
destroying joy in every way,
preventing us from shrugging off
a decade of festering waste of
xenophobia and financial chaos.
Will the good times soon return?
I cannot see how this can be,
the West has made its wicked bed
and now must lie with its partners;
I dream the bear will not wake
and set on us Armageddon.
Still we stumble on oblivious
to the events that may unfold.
No one can fully know the future,
but history shows what's gone before.
How the past once more returns
to haunt us, make us abhor war.
Not yet, the call for peace is called,
no whispers in our listening ears;
the silence is like the ocean's roar,
a constant static, nothing more,
no single voice to say aloud
what I feel my heart craves for.
Peace, to sleep, perhaps to dream,
to have my final years in quiet,
an old man's hope in a time
when others are for causing strife -
I'll say my prayers, keep right from
wrong, cherish time before its gone.

Thus is the anatomy of my universe,
in part of course, not the whole,
for who can set out in words
the wide expanse of their mind?
For when I go out into the world,
my mind is mine.

BLOOD CLOTS ON THE LUNGS
[20.50, 20th May 2022, Wexham Park]

Lying in a hospital bed,
oxygen tube up my nose,
my hand stayed by a finger clip,
my breathing shallow
as my blood clots thin.
I am no way near death,
but I am nearer than
I've ever been before.

NURSE KRISHNA
[22.26, 21st May 2022, Wexham Park]

Krishna pushed down on my tubes,
red, yellow, green and white,
checked my data every hour,
watched o'er me throughout the night,
turned the lights down on my sleep,
returned at dawn with my pills,
helped to save me from myself -
Oh Hari Krishna, nurse of mine.

OVERWHELMED BY LOVE
[23.15, 25th May 2022, Iver Grove]

Rarely have I been brought so low
in life, to discover my mortality;
but now that it has occurred,
I can rejoice at the care and kindness
given to me so generously by
those who know we are vulnerable
to illness and near death scenarios.

With love I have been overwhelmed
by those who surround me,
those folk who know me best,
those who care for me most,
those who I can rely on -
that small troupe of friends,
in number more than I knew.

To this loyal band, I thank you,
for showing me I am not alone.
You have restored my flagging faith
that life had gone to the dogs.
Not so! I am now reassured
that all is well with people
and that it is I who is flawed.

MY FINAL ABODE
[22.38, 4th June 2022, Ardbrecknish, Argyll]

Back in the land of my birth
with the mountains and lochs,
with the green and the blue,

with its wide expanse of freedom,
free from the London muck,
from the Southern money grubbing,
dragging me down to the Devil
while God lives in the hills.

If you are in the know,
then you will know my feeling,
my longing for clean air,
my desire for wide space,
my foregoing of the rat race
to find my own place -
where I can grow old
and rest without fear.

Where are the swifts and swallows,
the martins and the small buntings,
the wildlife that abounds, missing,
not found in old London,
where no park can replace
the diversity of nature
found on the wild hillsides
of the land that I love.

When will I break free,
realise that I have traded
a life of mid-wealth
for the price of my health.
While the wilderness calls me,
to be where I come from,
I'm a foolish old man
to ignore such advice.

And there rests my quandary,
the old ways and my ways
always tugging on me
to make up my mind -
making me restless
to give up on success,
to reject all I've built
in return for long life.

I live by my choices,
make my many decisions,
foolishly or selfishly,
peddle my code -
while the mountains and lochs,
wait for my homecoming
that I cannot guarantee
will be my final abode.

THE THINGS WE SEEK
[22.13, 12th June 2022, Arbrecknish, Argyll]

Those things we seek are eternal,
love, friendship and respect -
there cannot be a lesser goal,

nor wealth beyond such aspects;
for human nature so triple bound
demands we find this for ourselves.

NOTHING LEFT TO GIVE
[22.39, 12th June 2022, Ardbrecknish, Argyll]

When there is nothing left to give,
emptiness fills the void of being,
day to day in some shadowed life,
between the memories and the hours
that pass without paused respite.

From drudgery to the banal,
the minutes tick with the tide,
fast running the seconds slide
into the abyss of lost time
without a record of their passing.

Doomed to repeating ad infinitum,
the sum of errors made before -
there is no escape from the certainty,
that there seems to be no purpose,
none at all - to give any more.

AS THE GROWN-UPS PARTY
[23.33, 15th June 2022, Ardbrecknish, Argyll]

And so the days go by,
the actors deliver their lines,
the clouds drench the mountains,
the day never becomes night,
the laughter rings out loudly,
the swallows dart to their nests,
the loch shivers in the mist,
the children all sleep soundly,
as the grown-ups party.

THOSE WHO DEPART
[02.01, 18th June 2022, Ardbrecknish, Argyll]

As friends depart, new ones arrive,
this is life, how it works.
No-one is here to take our hand
to guide us to the promised land.
We are travelling on alone,
or think we are to the end -
as we are watched from afar
by those who have departed.

WHEN YOUTH WAS ON US
[20.19, 26th June 2022, Ardbrecknish, Argyll]

What happened to the Monday poker nights?
The chilly and the Texan beer?
The guys fro Austin with their talk,
the gals from Anchorage, their walks,

the sun coming up on their love,
the days when youth was on us.

Those days rest in crop-farm grass,
gone into the distant world,
the rain descends like mountain mist,
jungle drenched the wildlife hides,
no sun to warm their sodden nests,
unlike when youth was on us.

YOUR DRAMA
[23.47, 6th July 2022, Iver Grove]

Your drama is not my drama,
but I wish it was -
then we would see eye to eye
that all that divides us
is actually what unites us,
and the drama would go away
to be replaced by the love
that we know we have.

THE WOMEN ALL LEFT
[20.05, 8th July 2020, Iver Grove]

The women all left, there is bliss,
silence in the house, quietness,
space to dream and float,
to rest and listen to the sounds
beyond the open window, the summer
heat stifling the distant muffle
of cars and cackling rooks.

MY ALTERNATIVE TO KILLING
[23.45, 10th July 2022, North Wraxall, Wilts]

I am not of this generation,
all that I create is worthless,
it has no value to my peers.
There is no doubt that some is good,
but does not sell, give return.

I know that I am an artist,
I make my art for myself,
to give purpose to my life,
otherwise I might go out and
kill, or blow my brains out.

TODAY WAS PERFECT ENOUGH
[00.08, 11th July 2022, North Wraxall, Wilts]

Summer can heal all ills -
the wild abandon of nature,
proof that eternity extends
beyond all human folly -
the heat of the midday sun,
the shade from the afternoon warmth,

the shadows of lingering evening,
the moon in the deep blue dusk -
tomorrow may bring new troubles,
but today was perfect enough.

IF I SAY TOO MUCH
[22.29, 11th July 2022, Iver Grove]

If I say too much to you,
I will recall my depravity, my sins,
expose too much of my mind,
cloud your vision of my nature,
turn you from a lover to a hater
of all that is me, who I am.

THE MAN WITH KNOWLEDGE
[23.29, 11th July 2022, Iver Grove]

Perhaps it is better to have nothing to say
than going on about the weather;
too much prattle, not enough thought,
too much nonsense, not enough wisdom;
the man with the gab can be interesting,
but the man with knowledge a treasure.

THE LITTLE PINK COTTAGE
[19.25, 13th July, Withindale, Longmelford, Suffolk]

The silence is high in the trees,
sparrows hopping on the garden swing,
white umbrellas on the lawn,
cocktail in a dark stemmed glass -
the candelabra under an awning,
spread before the little pink house.

California culture in staid village England,
poetry blasting out from white speakers,
scooter parked on the driveway,
cat licking eagerly on its paws -
marijuana billowing in the evening air
as the hostess serves up her art.

FORTY DEGREES
[21.00, 17th July 2022, Iver Grove]

This heat, this record heat,
baking our skin, burning our grass.
Is it what they say it is?
Global warming? Perhaps it is so,
the proof that we are selfish,
that we are incapable of change.

We are stuck in our ways,
unwilling to compromise, give in
to the notion we are stupid,
incapable of reading the tea leaves -
that many will perish elsewhere,

and here, because of our conceit.

AS OUR PLANET SLOWLY BURNS
[19th July, Bilbao, Spain]

Love the Earth, or save ourselves,
is each the same, or different worlds?
The collective whole is the goal, or
is individual survival more important?
I know not which is right,
the socialist in me for the former,
or the capitalist cad all for survival
at any cost to the world.

And thus our little planet suffers,
human selfishness, personal greed.
The poor lament their stricken state,
the rich lament that the poor exist.
So none know what is right,
though each has their own view,
helplessly we all plod along
as our planet slowly burns.

LIFE IS A CHORE
[14.28, 20th July 2022, Santander, Cantabria, Spain]

God on my left shoulder,
beer in my right hand -
surviving somehow.
Oh life is a chore!

THE MIND IS A TANGLE
[14.28, 21st July 2022, Oviedo, Asturias, Spain]

The mind is a tangle of thought waves,
rippling with torment, never calm,
wave after wave on a surf board,
the ride is rough, brutally hellish,
yet somehow it comes to an end;
the storm abates, the sun comes out,
a coffee or beer numbs the pain -
joy returns to make the day okay.

LEON
[20.57, 21st July 2022, Leon, Castille, Spain]

The light played on the Roman wall
as evening fell on old Leon,
the chatter rose into the night
as young and old strolled the streets.

Arm in arm the lovers drifted
with quivered lips and hungry eyes,
those beyond such tender love
watched wisely as they passed on by.

THE PILGRIM'S DORMITORY
[14.53, 26th July 2022, Santiago D'Compostela, Galicia, Spain]

They sleep like children in their bunks,
the pilgrims tired and worn,
no sound from their lifeless forms
resting in their hostel dorm.

Bunked in fours, some in eight,
their boots lie scattered on the floor,
backpacks propped against the walls,
drying clothes, draped on the doors.

These modern pilgrims in their shorts,
sporty gear and logo'd caps,
on the march across the world,
trudging on come what comes.

Sleep they now in their beds,
is God somewhere in their prayers?
The window open to the night,
stars shining light on their dreams.

THE SUN
[17.28, 26th July 2022, Santiago, Galicia]

All that free energy,
burns as well as warms,
desert life is no life,
we crave it in winter,
curse it when it scorches -
that blazing orb of fire
we cannot blot out,
nor wish to hide.

OUR MODERN MAGAZINES
[20.29, 26th July 2022, Santiago, Galicia]

Our modern magazines are on the web,
pictures of 'me' and 'me's' friends,
Hello magazine without the cost,
free to look at, free to toss into
the bonfire of vanity tosh -
to be reminded many years hence
that what we post, outlives our death.

HOME TO UNFINISHED THINGS
[00.24, 2nd Aug 2022, Iver Grove]

Home to work on unfinished things,
home to my small rented abode,
home to recall everything wrong
with all the years that have passed.

Is there comfort in homely things,
or something sad, that this is all -
the summation of a life's work,

a few soft comforts despite the slog.

Is this the burden of age -
a looking back with some regrets,
wishing that time had dealt
a better hand than the one I played.

Home then to unfinished things,
home again, to get on with life,
home to discover I have traveled
and arrived without a glitch.

FOREBODING
[23.44, 3rd Aug 2022, Iver Grove]

It is to move on in life,
always there is a sense of loss,
foreboding that things will worsen,
go from bad to downright rotten.

THE SUN BEATS DOWN ON US
[22.25, 10th Aug 2022, Iver Grove]

The sun beats down on us,
shows no mercy,
boils our blood, dries our sweat,
until we are almost dead.

This is our daily life,
we run from the sun,
migrate north in survival,
run the perils of traffickers.

We cross seas in tempest,
to be detained in camps,
to be returned to our desert,
too thirsty to escape.

NO GRAND PLAN
[00.29, 12th Aug 2022, Iver Grove]

The heat soaked my bones.
Benin a distant mystery,
elephants always in my thoughts,
bad politics bringing misery,
the cold months to come,
business as usual someplace,
love just over the horizon,
never far away.

NO WAY TO BE
[00.23 18th Aug 2022, Iver Grove]

The battles rage on in the East,
now the heatwave has passed,
autumn is on its way -
that cold Russian winter wind

will bite us all, make us freeze,
for we have not found peace,
found no way to talk.

There is no resolution, just war,
only more artillery and bombings.
It is no way to live,
it is no way to be -
when will we ever learn
that war brings on death,
leaves us nothing at all.

TIME TO TURN OUT THE LIGHT
[23.18, 22nd Aug 2022, Iver Grove]

Have I any more to say to myself?
Any more images to drag from my past?
Any more emotion I have not vented?
Any more bullshit to get out?

Is there anything left to put down,
to drag from my tired soul?
Any glimmer of wondrous fact?
Any information worth some note?

No, I reckon I am burnt out,
ready for the scrapheap of life.
I've nothing more to say on anything.
It is time to turn out the light.

DREAM OF ESCAPE
[23.35, 24th Aug 2022, Iver Grove]

Oh to escape to some unknown place,
up in the mountains in southern lands,
somewhere olives drop from the trees,
where vines hang over the eaves,
where morning comes with a gentle breeze,
and sunset lingers forever.

AND SO SUMMER ENDS
[00.49, 1st Sept 2022, Iver Grove]

And so summer ends, autumn comes
as it always does without fail.
There is sadness and some regrets
for time lost while making hay.

The changes have been too few,
with plans not fully thought out,
going into autumn without a vision
of how the winter will pan out.

THE RAIN HAS FINALLY COME
[22.45, 1st Sept 2022, Iver Grove]

The rain has finally come

825

to end the drought, the burnt
soil, the scorched grass, ochre
coloured, the severed leaves
lying thick on the dry wasteland
of this summer's pastures -
the meadows parched, the fish
in the ponds left thrashing
on the dust cracked earth.

WHETHER TO COMMIT THE CRIME
[00.43, 3rd Sept 2022, Iver Grove]

I sat in the bar with my pint,
debating whether to commit the crime,
white collar worker paperwork scam
that could lead to doing time.

I wrestled with my dire state,
penniless and hopelessly facing debt.
I tried to pretend fraud was fine,
it harmed no-one but the state.

I pondered the enormity of my situation,
the desire to escape, get ahead,
I imagined my future, my other life
if I corrected some figures creatively.

I slowly drained my ultimate pint,
put on my coat, made for the door,
left the pub in a sober mood,
determined to change my life for good.

As I staggered homeward quite drunk,
a little voice told me to stop,
to consider all that I would lose
if I syphoned off what I proposed.

No, I was foolish, silly at most,
to even consider committing fraud,
so I went home, lay on my bed,
woke up innocent with no regrets.

THE THUNDER ROARS
[01.04, 5th Sept 2022, Iver Grove]

The thunder roars. Clear sounding,
echoing as the rain falls heavy
outside my open window,
the roller blind sucked out
as the lightning flashes.
There will be flooding
on the empty roads.

THE QUEEN IS DEAD
[16.12, 9th Sept 2022, Rottendean, Sussex]

The Queen is dead, now we have the King.

Life will change, Empire finally gone.
We can now give up all glory,
adjust to our post imperial past,
stop throwing punches about
like a boxer past his prime.

We have done our allotted rounds,
lets quit before we are on the ropes.
The Queen was the link to Commonwealth,
the nations we dictated to before.
Its over. Let's not prolong the pain.
Elizabeth is dead. King Charles reigns.

THE CHINESE DELEGATION
[01.00, 17th Sep 2020, Iver Grove]

They have banned the Chinese delegation
from attending the funeral of the Queen;
fifteen thousand million people
snubbed by our haughty politicians.
How blind they are to mourning,
how petty in their motivations
to act like petty potentates
while guarded by tin soldiers.

THIS IS HOW IT IS
[01.07, 28th Sept 2022, Iver Grove]

Empty. This is how it is.
How days pass, mornings come,
nothing seems to stick.
Women come and flee,
friends stay for a bit,
cousins die, memories fade.

MY SILENT FILM FLICKERS ON
[01.01, 6th Oct 2022, Iver Grove]

The road ends, the day goes,
my silent film flickers on -
pictures of lost summer fun,
raindrops wiped away like tears,
apes swinging on a rope,
cricket but a distant dream,
time passing like my ship
on its voyage to Zanzibar.

I'M RUNNING OUT OF WORDS
[10.20, 8th Oct 2022, Iver Grove]

I'm running out of words, my energy is spent -
nothing new to speak of, nothing new to trumpet.
I'm a worker tired by labour, my routine is numbing,
I see no quick escape but that of slumber.

I AM DONE
[00.05, 12ᵗʰ Oct 2020, Iver Grove]

I am done, can do no more,
I have reached the cliff edge
of my stock and trade.
This is the end, my final poem
to complete my work.
I cannot predict how long
I will live beyond these words.

The poet in me is dying -
I can no longer rage against the light,
I am seeking peace,
my anger is spent,
I am discarding my pen.
I wish you a sweet adieu,
farewell friends, farewell,
with tears I say goodbye.

Printed in Great Britain
by Amazon

24453153R00463